An Introduction to Contemporary Work Psychology

An Introduction to Contemporary Work Psychology

Edited by

Maria C. W. Peeters, Jan de Jonge
and Toon W. Taris

WILEY Blackwell

This edition first published 2014
© 2014 John Wiley & Sons, Ltd

Registered Office
John Wiley & Sons, Ltd, The Atrium, Southern Gate, Chichester, West Sussex, PO19 8SQ, UK

Editorial Offices
350 Main Street, Malden, MA 02148-5020, USA
9600 Garsington Road, Oxford, OX4 2DQ, UK
The Atrium, Southern Gate, Chichester, West Sussex, PO19 8SQ, UK

For details of our global editorial offices, for customer services, and for information about how to apply for permission to reuse the copyright material in this book please see our website at www.wiley.com/wiley-blackwell.

The right of Maria C. W. Peeters, Jan de Jonge and Toon W. Taris to be identified as the authors of the editorial material in this work has been asserted in accordance with the UK Copyright, Designs and Patents Act 1988.

All rights reserved. No part of this publication may be reproduced, stored in a retrieval system, or transmitted, in any form or by any means, electronic, mechanical, photocopying, recording or otherwise, except as permitted by the UK Copyright, Designs and Patents Act 1988, without the prior permission of the publisher.

Wiley also publishes its books in a variety of electronic formats. Some content that appears in print may not be available in electronic books.

Designations used by companies to distinguish their products are often claimed as trademarks. All brand names and product names used in this book are trade names, service marks, trademarks or registered trademarks of their respective owners. The publisher is not associated with any product or vendor mentioned in this book.

Limit of Liability/Disclaimer of Warranty: While the publisher and author(s) have used their best efforts in preparing this book, they make no representations or warranties with respect to the accuracy or completeness of the contents of this book and specifically disclaim any implied warranties of merchantability or fitness for a particular purpose. It is sold on the understanding that the publisher is not engaged in rendering professional services and neither the publisher nor the author shall be liable for damages arising herefrom. If professional advice or other expert assistance is required, the services of a competent professional should be sought.

Library of Congress Cataloging-in-Publication Data

An introduction to contemporary work psychology / edited by Maria Peeters, Jan de Jonge and Toon Taris.
    pages cm
  Includes bibliographical references and index.
  ISBN 978-1-119-94552-9 (cloth) – ISBN 978-1-119-94553-6 (pbk.)   1. Work–Psychological aspects.
I. Peeters, Maria, editor of compilation.   II. De Jonge, Jan, editor of compilation.   III. Taris, Toon, editor of compilation.
  BF481.I5798 2014
  158.7–dc23
                                2013025412

A catalogue record for this book is available from the British Library.

Cover image: Toy figures on computer circuit board, close-up. © PhotoAlto sas / Alamy
Cover design by Simon Levy Associates

Set in 10.5/12.5pt Galliard by SPi Publisher Services, Pondicherry, India
Printed in Malaysia by Ho Printing (M) Sdn Bhd

1   2014

Contents

About the Editors	vii
About the Contributors	viii

Part A Introduction — 1

1 Introduction: People at Work — 3
   Maria C. W. Peeters, Toon W. Taris and Jan de Jonge

2 Research Methods in Work Psychology — 31
   E. Kevin Kelloway and Arla Day

Part B Theoretical Perspectives on Work — 61

3 The Models that Made Job Design — 63
   Kevin Daniels, Pascale M. Le Blanc and Matthew Davis

4 Current Theoretical Perspectives in Work Psychology — 89
   Jan de Jonge, Evangelia Demerouti and Christian Dormann

Part C Demands — 115

5 Quantitative Job Demands — 117
   Marc van Veldhoven

6 Qualitative Demands at Work — 144
   Dieter Zapf, Norbert K. Semmer and Sheena Johnson

Part D Context — 169

7 Job Control and Social Aspects of Work — 171
   Norbert K. Semmer and Terry A. Beehr

8	Recovery from Demanding Work Hours *Sabine A. E. Geurts, Debby G. J. Beckers and Philip Tucker*	196
9	The Design and Use of Work Technologies *Patrick Waterson*	220

Part E The Worker — 243

10	Individual Characteristics and Work-related Outcomes *Beatrice van der Heijden, Karen van Dam, Despoina Xanthopoulou and Annet H. de Lange*	243
11	Work–Family Interaction *Ulla Kinnunen, Johanna Rantanen, Saija Mauno and Maria C. W. Peeters*	267

Part F Outcomes — 291

12	Burnout, Boredom and Engagement in the Workplace *Wilmar B. Schaufeli and Marisa Salanova*	293
13	Job Satisfaction, Motivation and Performance *Nathan A. Bowling*	321
14	Safety at Work *Nik Chmiel and Toon W. Taris*	342
15	Sickness Absence and Sickness Presence *Rita Claes*	367

Part G Interventions — 391

16	Managing Psychosocial Risks in the Workplace: Prevention and Intervention *Silvia Pignata, Caroline Biron and Maureen F. Dollard*	393
17	Job Crafting *Evangelia Demerouti and Arnold B. Bakker*	414
18	Teams at Work *Amanda L. Thayer, Ramón Rico, Eduardo Salas and Shannon L. Marlow*	434
19	Positive Interventions: From Prevention to Amplification *Carolyn M. Youssef-Morgan and Dale A. Sundermann*	458

Index — 481

About the Editors

Maria C. W. Peeters is Associate Professor of Work and Organizational Psychology at Utrecht University, The Netherlands, and a licensed occupational health psychologist. Her research interests include job stress, work motivation, job performance, work-home interaction and ageing at work. She has published many book chapters as well as articles on these topics in today's leading scientific journals.

Jan de Jonge is Professor of Work and Organizational Psychology at Eindhoven University of Technology, The Netherlands, and Adjunct Professor in the School of Psychology, Social Work and Social Policy at the University of South Australia. He is a licensed work and organizational psychologist as well as a licensed occupational health psychologist. His research interests include the optimization of performance at work and at sports, and he has published extensively with over 100 articles, books and chapters. Until recently, he served as the Editor of the *Journal of Occupational and Organizational Psychology*.

Toon W. Taris is Professor of Work and Organizational Psychology at Utrecht University, The Netherlands. He is currently Scientific Editor of *Work & Stress* and serves on the boards of several other international journals. He has published hundreds of articles and chapters on topics such as occupational health, stress, engagement, workaholism and authenticity at work, as well as on longitudinal research methods and non-response in journals such as *Journal of Applied Psychology, Journal of Organizational Behavior, Journal of Vocational Behavior* and *Journal of Occupational Health Psychology*.

About the Contributors

Arnold B. Bakker, Professor of Work and Organizational Psychology, Department of Work and Organizational Psychology, Institute of Psychology, Erasmus University Rotterdam, Woudestein, T12-47, P.O. Box 1738, 3000 DR Rotterdam, The Netherlands.

Debby G. J. Beckers, Assistant Professor of Work and Organizational Psychology, Radboud University Nijmegen, Behavioural Science Institute, P.O. Box 9104, 6500 HE Nijmegen, The Netherlands.

Terry A. Beehr, Professor of Psychology and Director of the Ph.D. Program in Industrial/Organizational Psychology, Central Michigan University, Department of Psychology, 101 Sloan Hall, Mount Pleasant, Michigan 48858, USA.

Caroline Biron, Assistant Professor of Occupational Health and Safety, Department of Management, Faculty of Administrative Sciences, Laval University, G1V 0A6, Canada.

Nathan A. Bowling, Professor of Industrial and Organizational Psychology, Wright State University, Department of Psychology, 303 C Fawcett Hall, 3640 Colonel Glenn Highway, Dayton, Ohio 45435-0001, USA.

Nik Chmiel, Professor of Occupational Psychology, University of Chichester, Department of Psychology & Counselling, Bishop Otter Campus, College Lane, Chichester, West Sussex, PO19 6PE, UK.

Rita Claes, Professor of Organizational Psychology, Ghent University, Department of Personnel Management, Work and Organizational Psychology, 2 Henri Dunantlaan, 9000 Ghent, Belgium.

Kevin Daniels, Professor of Organizational Behaviour, Norwich Business School, University of East Anglia, NR4 7TJ, UK.

Matthew Davis, Lecturer in Socio-Technical Systems, Socio-Technical Centre, Leeds University Business School, Leeds, LS2 9JT, UK.

Arla Day, Canada Research Chair, Department of Psychology, Saint Mary's University, 923 Robie Street, Halifax, Nova Scotia, Canada, B3H 3C3.

Jan de Jonge, Professor of Work and Organizational Psychology, Eindhoven University of Technology, Department of Industrial Engineering and Innovation Sciences, Human Performance Management Group, P.O. Box 513, 5600 MB Eindhoven, The Netherlands. Also affiliated with the School of Psychology, Social Work and Social Policy, University of South Australia.

Annet H. de Lange, Associate Professor of Work and Organizational Psychology, Radboud University Nijmegen, Behavioural Science Institute, P.O. Box 9104, 6500 HE Nijmegen, The Netherlands, and Professor of Human Resource Management (Lector), Department of Human Resource Management, University of Applied Sciences Arnhem and Nijmegen, P.O. Box 5171, 6802 ED Arnhem, The Netherlands.

Evangelia Demerouti, Professor of Work and Organizational Psychology, Eindhoven University of Technology, Department of Industrial Engineering and Innovation Sciences, Human Performance Management Group, P.O. Box 513, 5600 MB Eindhoven, The Netherlands.

Maureen F. Dollard, Professor, Centre for Applied Psychological Research, University of South Australia, Magill Campus CA1-05, Adelaide, Australia.

Christian Dormann, Professor of Business Education and Management Training, Johannes Gutenberg University Mainz, Department of Business Education and Management Training, Jakob Welder-Weg 9, D-55099 Mainz, Germany.

Sabine A. E. Geurts, Professor of Work and Organizational Psychology, Radboud University Nijmegen, Behavioural Science Institute, P.O. Box 9104, 6500 HE Nijmegen, The Netherlands.

Sheena Johnson, Occupational Psychologist, Senior Lecturer of Organisational Psychology, Manchester Business School, University of Manchester, Booth Street East, Manchester, M15 6PB, UK.

E. Kevin Kelloway, Canada Research Chair, Department of Psychology, Saint Mary's University, 923 Robie Street, Halifax, Nova Scotia, Canada, B3H 3C3.

Ulla Kinnunen, Professor of Work and Organizational Psychology, University of Tampere, School of Social Sciences and Humanities, 33014 University of Tampere, Finland.

Pascale M. Le Blanc, Associate Professor of Organizational Behavior, Eindhoven University of Technology, Department of Industrial Engineering and Innovation Sciences, Human Performance Management Group, P.O. Box 513, 5600 MB Eindhoven, The Netherlands.

Shannon L. Marlow, Research Associate Industrial and Organizational Psychology, University of Central Florida, Institute for Simulation and Training, Department of Human Systems Integration Research, 3100 Technology Parkway, Orlando, FL 32826, USA.

Saija Mauno, Professor of Work and Organizational Psychology (part-time), University of Tampere, School of Social Sciences and Humanities, 33014 University of Tampere, Finland, and Academy Researcher Fellow (part-time), University of Jyväskylä, Department of Psychology, P.O. Box 35, 40014, Jyväskylä, Finland.

Maria C. W. Peeters, Associate Professor of Work and Organizational Psychology, Utrecht University, Department of Work and Organizational Psychology, P.O. Box 80.140, 3508 TC Utrecht, The Netherlands.

Silvia Pignata, Senior Lecturer, School of Engineering, University of South Australia, G.P.O. Box 2471, Adelaide, South Australia 5001, Australia.

Johanna Rantanen, Post Doctoral Researcher, University of Jyväskylä, Department of Psychology, P.O. Box 35, 40014, Jyväskylä, Finland.

Ramón Rico, Associate Professor, Universidad Autónoma de Madrid, Department of Social Psychology and Methodology, C/ Ivan Pavlov, 6, Office #7, 28049 Madrid, Spain.

Marisa Salanova, Professor of Positive Organizational Psychology, Jaume I University, Department of Social Psychology, Avda. Sos Baynat, s/n. 12017 Castellón, Spain.

Eduardo Salas, Trustee Chair and Pegasus Professor of Psychology, University of Central Florida, Department of Psychology and Institute for Simulation and Training, 3100 Technology Parkway, Orlando, FL, 32826, USA.

Wilmar B. Schaufeli, Professor of Work and Organizational Psychology, Utrecht University, Department of Work and Organizational Psychology, P.O. Box 80.140, 3508 TC Utrecht, The Netherlands.

Norbert K. Semmer, Professor for the Psychology of Work and Organizations, University of Bern, Department of Psychology Unitobler, Muesmattstr. 45, 3012 Bern, Switzerland.

Dale A. Sundermann, Co-Founder The Skilz Group, 7018 South 167th Street, Omaha Nebraska, USA.

Toon W. Taris, Professor of Work and Organizational Psychology, Utrecht University, Department of Work and Organizational Psychology, P.O. Box 80.140, 3508 TC Utrecht, The Netherlands.

Amanda L. Thayer, I/O Psychology Doctoral Student and Graduate Research Associate, University of Central Florida, Department of Psychology and Institute for Simulation and Training, 3100 Technology Parkway, Orlando, FL, 32826, USA.

Philip Tucker, Associate Professor, Department of Psychology, Swansea University, Swansea SA2 8PP, UK.

Karen van Dam, Professor of Work and Organizational Psychology, Open University, Faculty of Psychology, P.O. Box 2960, 6401 DL Heerlen, The Netherlands.

Beatrice van der Heijden, Professor of Strategic Human Resource Management, Radboud University Nijmegen, Institute for Management Research, P.O. Box 9108, 6500 HK Nijmegen, The Netherlands. Also affiliated with the Open University and the University of Twente, The Netherlands.

Marc van Veldhoven, Professor of Work, Health and Well-Being, Department of Human Resource Studies, School of Social and Behavioral Sciences, Tilburg University, P.O. Box 90153, 5000 LE Tilburg, The Netherlands.

Patrick Waterson, Senior Lecturer, Co-Director of the Human Factors and Complex Systems Research Group at Loughborough Design School, Loughborough University, LE11 3TU, UK.

Despoina Xanthopoulou, Lecturer in Social-Organizational Psychology, Aristotle University of Thessaloniki, School of Psychology, GR-54124, Thessaloniki, Greece.

Carolyn M. Youssef-Morgan, Redding Chair of Business, Bellevue University, College of Business, 1000 Galvin Road South, Bellevue, Nebraska 68005, USA.

Dieter Zapf, Professor for Work and Organizational Psychology, Goethe University Frankfurt, Institute of Psychology, PEG, Grüneburgplatz 1, D-60323, Frankfurt am Main, Germany.

Part A

Introduction

1

Introduction
People at Work

MARIA C. W. PEETERS, TOON W. TARIS
AND JAN DE JONGE

Chapter Objectives

After studying this chapter, you should be able to:

- describe the key elements of work;
- explain what work psychology is about and what is meant by *contemporary* work psychology;
- specify some main features of the world's labour force;
- understand the selection bias in contemporary work psychology;
- understand what working means to workers;
- summarize the history of work psychology;
- explain five important changes in the world of work;
- explain the crucial role of task analysis in contemporary work psychology;
- understand the general outline and structure of the current book.

For as long as mankind has existed, people have worked. Needless to say the nature of work has changed tremendously: our ancestors were mostly hunters and collectors, nowadays people work with data, 'goods' or other people, or provide services. What has not changed is that we still spend a substantial part of our lives *working*. It is therefore not surprising that some people's work is about understanding the nature and conditions of the work of others in an attempt to predict and improve it. These are work psychologists, teachers, trainers and practitioners in work psychology and those who study the phenomenon of work and worker behaviour: the researchers. This book is aimed at everyone who would like to learn more about work psychology. The primary intended readership consists of advanced (second and third year) BA students as well as MA students in work and organizational psychology programmes. However, this textbook will also be useful for advanced students in related fields, including ergonomics and human factors, (applied) social psychology, clinical psychology, (psycho-)social medicine, occupational health, epidemiology, health sciences, industrial engineering, business administration and management science. Finally, researchers who would like to familiarize themselves quickly with state-of-the-art issues in the area of work psychology will also be interested in this volume.

This chapter starts with a brief introduction to what work involves and what work psychology aims to achieve. Next, we consider the world's labour force and discuss what having work means for individuals. After describing the history of the field of work psychology, we describe some important changes that the world of work has witnessed over the last decennia. Finally, we explain the crucial role of task analysis in contemporary work psychology and the chapter ends by explaining the general outline and structure of the book.

1.1 What We Talk About When We Talk About Work Psychology

This book is about *work*. According to the Merriam-Webster dictionary (2013), in everyday life the term 'work' refers to an 'activity in which one exerts strength or faculties to do or perform something; sustained physical or mental effort to overcome obstacles and achieve an objective or result; the labour, task, or duty that is one's accustomed means of livelihood; a specific task, duty, function, or assignment often being a part or phase of some larger activity'. That is, work is about performing activities to achieve a particular objective, and these activities are conducted to obtain some form of income. More formally, work can be defined as *a set of coordinated and goal-directed activities that are conducted in exchange for something else*, usually (but not necessarily and often not exclusively) some form of monetary reward. Three key elements of this definition are as follows:

1. Work consists of a set of *goal-directed* activities, that is, actions at work are intended to bring about a particular previously specified result. After all, the goal of work is to produce a good or to deliver a particular service (Frese & Zapf, 1994).
2. Work consists of a set of *coordinated* activities. To achieve the intended goal, workers do not act randomly. Rather, successful task accomplishment often requires that workers execute a series of interrelated activities following particular work routines, procedures and guidelines, and often using tools and machinery especially devised to bring about the intended goal. Even the

simplest jobs require incumbents to coordinate their activities. Without coordination, the intended goal will be difficult to achieve, if it is achieved at all.
3. The activities involved in working require some degree of physical, emotional and/or mental effort, and this effort is usually compensated in some way. That is, work is conducted *in exchange for something else*. Few of us would go to work without getting anything in return. Rather, for many people working is a necessary evil: it is easy to think of more attractive, interesting and enjoyable activities, but working is often simply essential for earning a living.

This book is also about *psychology*. Psychology refers to people's behaviour, motivations, thoughts and emotions related to a particular topic. Work psychology thus relates to these concepts in the context of work (Arnold, 2005). As the goal of work is to produce something (goods, services or knowledge), one central aim of work psychology is to facilitate obtaining that goal: how can we use the knowledge and insights of psychology to help workers achieve their work goals in an optimal manner? Or, from an organizational point of view, how can we help organizations achieving their goals?

Note that work psychologists are not only interested in pushing workers' performance to (and perhaps even beyond) their upper limit. On the contrary, at present many work psychologists are primarily interested in maximizing worker health and well-being (this used to be different in the early days of work psychology, see Section 1.3). This interest partly follows from the idea that happy, satisfied workers are presumed to be productive workers (see Chapter 13 for a discussion). In this view, maximizing well-being is the same as maximizing work performance. Additionally, work psychologists are often genuinely interested in workers' health and well-being. After all, as psychologists their task is to improve people's lives. For example, the American Psychological Association (American Psychological Association, 2013), the largest professional organization of psychologists, says in its mission statement that it '… seeks to advance the creation, communication and application of psychological knowledge to *benefit society* and *improve people's lives*' (authors' italics). Similarly, the British Psychological Society (2013) states that it is 'responsible for the development, promotion and application of psychology for *the public good*' (authors' italics). Similar statements can be found on the web sites of other professional organizations for psychologists. Clearly, work psychologists are not solely there for the benefit of organizations or employers, but surely also for the benefit of workers. This is not to say that a focus on employee health and well-being may not also be beneficial for organizations. It is by now well accepted that work can have adverse effects on employee health and well-being (e.g. consider the potential effects of working with harmful and even carcinogenous substances, or of being chronically bullied by your supervisor and co-workers). Since many organizations frequently face difficulties in finding suitably trained personnel, it is important to them that their current staff remain healthy and motivated. Moreover, the costs of replacing sick employees are high, which also underlines the need for organizations to make sure that the workability of their current staff remains high. Stated differently, *contemporary* work psychology aims to promote what might be called *sustainable performance*, maximizing work performance as well as worker health and well-being.

This book is about *work psychology*, that is, the way workers' behaviours, motivations, thoughts, emotions, health and well-being relate to each other, and about ways to influence these concepts. As we have defined work in terms of the specific *activities* that are conducted by workers, work psychology is *not* about the context in which these activities are conducted (e.g. the organization, the work team, leadership) – that is the realm of *organizational psychology*, not work psychology. Similarly, work psychology is *not* about the characteristics of the person conducting a particular work task (e.g. gender, age, ethnicity, level of education, experience, personality) or selecting or hiring new staff – that is the domain of *personnel psychology*. Work psychology is about the tasks that are carried out at work, that is, the specific activities that are conducted to achieve a particular goal. Of course, these activities are accomplished by workers having specific characteristics within a particular context, and in this sense work psychology is inevitably and often strongly related to the other strands of what is often called 'work and organizational', 'personnel' or 'industrial' psychology. We therefore pay brief attention to some of these subjects in this book. In the present introduction we define work psychology in a considerably narrower sense, namely, in terms of the *psychological study of work activities*. For introductions to other subfields of work and organizational psychology we refer to standard texts in these areas, such as Cartwright and Cooper (2008), Doyle (2003) and Jex and Britt (2008).

Replay

- Work can be defined as a set of coordinated and goal-directed activities that are conducted in exchange for something else, usually (but not necessarily and often not exclusively) some form of monetary reward.
- Work psychology refers to people's behaviour, motivations, thoughts and emotions in the context of work.
- Work psychologists aim to simultaneously maximize work performance and worker health and well-being. In that sense they aim to promote sustainable performance.
- Work psychology focuses on the specific activities conducted to achieve work goals. It does not (or at least not primarily) focus on the work context or on worker characteristics; these are the domains of other subfields of what is known as work and organizational psychology (i.e. organizational and personnel psychology, respectively).

1.2 Who Do We Mean When We Talk About *Workers*?

We now have an impression about what we conceive as *work* and what contemporary *work psychology* is about. Next, we turn to the *workers*. There is probably no group in the world that is as heterogeneous and diverse as the world's workforce. This makes it hard to describe this group. For instance, just think about the differences between an elderly woman working in the rice fields in Indonesia and a young urban professional working in Wall Street, New York and you will understand the enormous diversity within the world's workforce.

The world's workforce

In order to have an impression of who we are talking about in the remainder of this book we will present some general figures about the world's workforce. First, however, what do we mean by the workforce of the world? The world labour force comprises people aged 15 and older who meet the International Labour Organization (ILO) definition of the economically active population: all people who supply labour for the production of goods and services during a specified period. It includes both the employed and the unemployed (World Bank, 2013). While national practices vary, in general the labour force includes the armed forces, the unemployed and first-time job-seekers, but excludes homemakers and other unpaid caregivers and workers in the informal sector.

To understand the number of people that are really at work we have to consider unemployment rates. Unemployment rates refer to the share of the labour force that is without work but available for and seeking employment (World Bank, 2013). In 2011 the average unemployment rate in the world was around 6%. In comparison, in the United States the unemployment rate in 2011 was 9%. The average unemployment rate in the 27 EU Member States (EU27) increased from 7% in 2008 to nearly 11% in 2012 (Eurostat, 2012). Taken together, out of a world population of slightly more than 7 billion people, 3 billion are employed and 205 million are unemployed (International Labour Office, 2012).

When considering international labour statistics a distinction is generally made between three different work sectors: (i) agriculture, including forestry, hunting and fishing, (ii) industry, including manufacturing, mining and construction, and (iii) services, including transportation, communication, public utilities, trade, finance, public administration, private household services and miscellaneous other services. Figures from 2007 show that 36.1% of the total labour force was working in agriculture, 21.5% in industry and 42.4% in services (World Bank, 2013). Note that these statistics have been subject to tremendous change during the last decennia and that they differ substantially between countries and regions. For instance, in 1980 agriculture accounted for only 3.4% of employment in the United States, Germany, Canada and the United Kingdom, and that share fell to 1.6% by 2011. Although over the 1999–2008 period the share of agricultural shows generally a declining trend, it remained high in Sub-Saharan Africa, only diminishing from 62.4% to 59%, in South-East Asia and the Pacific, where it declined from 49.3% to 44.3% and in Latin America, where it declined from 21.5% to 16.3%. Employment in industry also declined as a share of total employment in many countries. At the same time, services accounted for a very large share of employment in many Western developed countries. In 2011, about 8 in 10 workers in the United States, Canada, the United Kingdom and France were employed in services and about 7 in 10 workers in Germany, Japan and South Korea.

Selection bias in contemporary work psychology

Does contemporary work psychology really focus on the work of *all* employed workers around the world? Unfortunately the answer to this question is still an undisputed 'no'. One of the major drawbacks of contemporary work psychology is its narrow scope. Work psychological research is predominantly conducted in Western-oriented economies (e.g. the United States, Europe, Japan and Australia). Countries in Africa, South America and South-East Asia (especially the developing countries) are largely neglected. In addition, even within the countries where work psychology is flourishing, there is an inclination to focus on white-collar, professional and middle to highly educated employees working in large organizations. Although historically work psychology is committed to blue-collar workers in large industries with poor working conditions, it is nowadays more common to focus on middle and highly educated workers: these groups are easier to gain access to, response rates are higher and researchers are spared the difficulties of translating instruments and establishing their cultural equivalence. As a result, with some exceptions, there is comparatively little research on the lower segment of the labour market and on ethnic/racial minorities.

The consequences of the choice to focus mainly on specific groups in specific parts of the world may be serious. It limits our ability to generalize findings and hampers the development of adequate theory by ignoring important issues that may be especially pertinent for vulnerable workers in less developed regions of the world. Last but not least, because we have serious restricted ranges in our critical variables we may not appreciate the full impact that work has on the lives of workers around the world and their families. Thus, instead of targeting our research arrows predominantly on the 'happy few of contemporary work psychology', it is critical to extend the next generation of work psychological research to understudied groups of workers and their families in all parts of the world.

Replay

- Around the world 3 billion people are at work (out of a total population of slightly more than 7 billion).
- The global unemployment rate was about 6% in 2011; this figure differs widely across countries.
- The number of people working in the service sector is growing fast.
- Worldwide, the agricultural sector is still the second largest source of employment after services.
- There is an inclination in work psychology to focus predominantly on high-status workers and ethnic majorities in well-developed parts of the world.

1.3 The Meaning of Working

In the preceding sections we argued that work psychologists should aim to simultaneously maximize work performance and worker health and well-being (i.e. strive towards promoting sustainable work performance). However, in spite of these efforts, workers do not always (or 'normally', or even 'frequently') enjoy their work. Popular culture (songs, movies, books, TV series) provides many examples of jobs that are not particularly satisfying, suggesting that the sole reason for working is the fact that it yields the money needed to subsist.

> ### Work Psychology in Action: Popular views on working
>
> One way of understanding of what working means to people (i.e. how they think about work) is to look at *cultural artefacts* relating to work and employment, such as popular songs, movies, books and paintings. The idea behind examining such artefacts is that they reflect real cultural and societal values and attitudes (e.g. DeWall, Pond, Campbell, & Twenge, 2011). What do these artefacts say about work and working?
>
> Whereas most popular music is about love, sex or encourages people to party, a small number of songs actually refer to experiences at work. One interesting example is *Sixteen Tons*, a country song penned by Merle Travis about the dark days of industrial capitalism that reached number one in the 1955 US Billboard charts. In this song, a coal miner warns Saint Peter not to call him to heaven, since however hard he works, he will never have earned enough to pay his debts at the company store (in mining towns the local store was owned by the mining company, and miners often had no choice other than to spend their wage at this store, paying the (high) prices asked for by the mining company). The miner therefore owes his soul to the company and not to God. A more recent example is presented by Dolly Parton's 1980 number one hit song *Nine to Five*, in which the *persona* complains about being underpaid and about bosses taking the credit for others' ideas. In *Factory* (1978), Bruce Springsteen contrasts the fact that working yields the income needed to subsist with the fact that work can take away workers' health and well-being. Indeed, pop singers often have little good to say about work. However, whereas work can be bad, boring and even debilitating (e.g. see NBC's long-running comedy *The Office*, in which many characters mainly spend their time trying to *look* busy), it can also be a source of inspiration and even friendship (as in CBS's sitcom *The Big Bang Theory*, in which the characters' jobs at the California Institute of Technology and similar high-tech research organizations constitute an important part of the personal and professional identities of most of the main characters – all technology geeks, and proud of it).
>
> This short and admittedly ad hoc inventory of some of the artefacts of popular culture shows that work may have both positive and negative features: work provides boredom and challenge, success and failure, and friends and foes.

Research on what working *means* to people has found that people do not just work for money, but that work serves many other functions as well. One way of examining the functions of working is to compare the effects of having a job to those of *not* having a job, especially being unemployed. In a sense, the history of mankind can be construed as a continuous and ongoing pursuit to make working life easier, that is, to reduce the effort needed to subsist. For example, the introduction of new technologies (ranging from the wheel in the distant past to the industrial revolution of the eighteenth century and the rise of information and communication technology (ICT) during the 1980s) all made it easier to accomplish the work tasks of the day – or even made these superfluous, promising to free time and energy to be invested in other, more pleasurable, activities (cf. Basalla, 1988). From the perspective of the individual worker, an important driver of the acceptance of these innovations was the desire to spend less time on work.

What would a world without work look like? Would people be happier without having to work? In many Western societies, unemployed workers receive an unemployment benefit that allows them to subsist (although often only barely) without having to work. Research comparing the quality of life of unemployed and employed people shows that the latter are usually considerably happier than the former. For example, levels of suicide, mortality, long-term illness, anxiety, depression and risky behaviours (drinking and smoking) tend to be higher among unemployed than employed people, whereas for the first group lower levels of life satisfaction and general health have been found (e.g. Paul & Moser, 2009; Wanberg, 2012). The relation between unemployment and health runs both ways: whereas lack of health increases the chances of becoming unemployed, unemployment also contributes to the emergence of health problems.

Apparently, having a job contributes positively to people's health and well-being. But *why* would this be the case? Obviously, being without a job often negatively impacts on one's income, meaning that it is difficult to spend money on goods and activities that go beyond the bare necessities for survival. However, research into unemployment has generated several theoretical perspectives on the reasons why being unemployed yields these negative consequences. The most influential of these is Marie Jahoda's (1982) *Relative Deprivation Model*. Born in Vienna in 1907, Jahoda examined the impact of unemployment on the 478 families living in the small community of Marienthal (now in Germany) during the Great Depression of the 1920s. At the time, the only factory in town was heavily hit by the depression, and Jahoda and her colleagues showed that the often devastating psychological consequences of unemployment went beyond the obvious hardships of financial deprivation. Based on these observations, Jahoda concluded that apart from providing an income, having employment also provides five classes of social benefits: time structure, opportunities for social contact, sharing of a common purpose, social identity or status, and regular activity. Without work, people are deprived of all five benefits, accounting for many of the adverse consequences of unemployment for health and well-being. Of course, this does not imply that having a job is necessarily fun; rather one might say that being unemployed – especially in the dire circumstances of the 1920s – is worse. In this sense, the insights presented in this section can be summarized by paraphrasing Matt Groening's (1987) famous dictum: 'work is hell – but it beats unemployment'.

Replay

- Examining the artefacts of popular culture may provide some insights into what working 'means' to people, that is, what they think of it and what function it has in their lives.
- Popular culture frequently depicts work and working life as something that is unpleasant and may have adverse consequences for health and well-being.
- Contrary to this popular view, research strongly suggests that having a job contributes positively to health and well-being, at least when compared to having no job (i.e. being unemployed).
- According to Marie Jahoda's influential relative deprivation theory, the main drivers for these positive consequences of having employment are the fact that working provides people with time structure, opportunities for social contact, sharing of a common purpose, social identity or status, and regular activity.

1.4 The Roots of Work Psychology

As indicated above, contemporary work psychology is concerned with promoting sustainable performance, that is, stimulating high work performance as well as maintaining (and even enhancing) worker health and well-being (e.g. Frese & Zapf, 1994). Historically, these two foci of work psychology have not always been emphasized equally strongly by researchers and practitioners in the area of work and work performance. Indeed, when researchers and practitioners started to study work and organizations systematically in the middle of the nineteenth century, the emphasis was on the best way of organizing work and the work organization (with an eye to maximizing productivity and profit, leading to what has come to be known as industrial capitalism), and on the socio-political implications of this (e.g. consider the criticism of industrial capitalism by scholars such as Karl Marx and Friedrich Engels).

Systematic thinking about the organization of work

However, far before this era, scholars had already considered how particular tasks should be conducted. For example, Ancient Greek medical knowledge is documented in what is known as the *Hippocratic collection*, a collection of about 60 books written by various authors during the fifth to third centuries BC. The Hippocratic collection provided Greek doctors with detailed guidelines on how particular types of complaints were to be treated, and is basically a collection of routines and guidelines prescribing how the tasks of a medical doctor should be accomplished. As an example, here is how doctors were expected to start their examinations:

> First of all the doctor should look at the patient's face. The following are bad signs – sharp nose, hollow eyes, dry skin, strange colour of face such as green, black or leaden. If the face is like this, the doctor must ask the patient if he has lost sleep, or had diarrhoea, or not eaten. (Lloyd, 1982)

Another early example of systematic thinking is seen in the Roman army, which was organized according to simple and clear rules. Positions in this organization were relatively well-defined in that it was clear what tasks were required of these positions and how these should be conducted. This applied especially to the operation of the army during times of war. The Roman army used several military manuals describing how the various parts of the army could operate in specific situations. For example, based on earlier sources, the Roman writer Vegetius compiled his *De Re Militari* (*On military matters*) around 390 AD, in which he discussed the organization, equipment and drill of the Roman legions, the strategies to be followed, the maintenance of supply lines and logistics, and leadership. Vegetius proposes that Roman soldiers should learn to use their swords as follows:

> [Roman soldiers were] taught not to cut but to thrust with their swords ... A stroke with the edges, though made with ever so much force, seldom kills, as the vital parts of the body are defended both by the bones and armor. On the contrary, a stab, though it penetrates but two inches, is generally fatal. Besides in the attitude of striking, it is impossible to avoid exposing the right arm and side; but on the other hand, the body is covered while a thrust is given, and the adversary receives the point before he sees the sword. (Vegetius, 390 AD)

Interestingly, Vegetius also understood that psychological processes could affect the execution of soldiers' tasks. For instance, he argues that a defeated enemy should always be offered an easy escape route, since in a situation 'where no hopes remain, fear itself will arm an enemy and despair inspires courage. When men find they must inevitably perish, they willingly resolve to die with their comrades and with their arms in their hands'. However, if offered an escape, they would 'think of nothing but how to save themselves by flight', for convenience throwing away their weaponry, meaning that they could be slaughtered easily during the flight. Elsewhere he addresses issues such as the recruitment and selection of soldiers, their socialization, how motivation could be fostered, and the relationship between leadership and performance.

As these examples illustrate, early work on how particular tasks should be conducted largely rested on common sense, moral axioms, tradition, long-standing practices and laymen's psychological insights. A more *scientific* (i.e. systematic, evidence-based) approach to examining work and its effects and antecedents only emerged much later, after the middle ages had ended.

The birth of occupational medicine

The scientific study of work, worker health and well-being, and work performance can be traced back to the 1500s, when Georg Bauer (otherwise known as Agricola) published *De Re Metallica* (*On metal matters*), an influential book on the art and science of mining. Being the town physician in Chemnitz, Saxony (at the time an important mining area in Central Europe), Agricola not only discussed the technical details of mine operation, but also paid attention to miners and their typical diseases: 'It remains for me to speak about the ailments and accidents of miners, and of the methods by which they can guard against these'. He recommended wearing personal protective clothing (e.g. elbow-high leather gloves for work with aggressive minerals, and a veil worn before the face to protect from dusts, since 'The dust which is stirred and beaten up by digging penetrates into the windpipes and lungs and produces difficulty in breathing, and the disease which the Greeks call asthma. If the dust has corrosive qualities, it eats away the lungs, and implants consumption in the body.' Furthermore, Agricola stated that mines should be operated in a 5-day work week with three shifts of 8 hours each per day, and recommended that miners should not work two shifts per day because of the increased risk of occupational injury (Weber, 2002). Agricola's work was later followed up by Bernardino Ramazzini (1633–1714), an Italian physician and university professor who wrote a seminal book on the typical diseases encountered by workers in 52 occupations. These works can be considered the starting point for the discipline now known as occupational medicine (Gochfeld, 2005).

Work psychology, 1850–1930

The industrial revolution of the 1750–1850s marked a transition towards new manufacturing processes, in that production processes were increasingly mechanized (using novel technology such as water power, steam power and machine tools) and industrialized (i.e. production processes changed from artisanal, piece-by-piece production to mass production). These changes reformed the economic system into that of industrial capitalism, transforming the social and physical landscape in the process. Large mills and factories were built, and canals, roads and railways were constructed to transport materials to the factories and their products to the stores selling them. Working people found increased opportunities for employment in the new mills and factories, leading to increased urbanization. However, the working conditions in the mills and factories were harsh, working days were long and pay was low.

From a work-psychological perspective, the nature of the tasks conducted in this new era was different from the pre-industrial (or agrarian) time preceding it. The emergence of the industrial economy meant that young workers entering the labour market could seek out, occupy and identify with jobs that were completely different from the jobs that their fathers and mothers could choose from. However, this also implied that many young people struggled to find a career that suited their interests, talents and accomplishments (Porfeli, 2009). Moreover, the tasks in the factories were characterized by a high level of division of labour and were usually simple, repetitive and boring, requiring few skills. The important issues in this era therefore became how can workers be motivated to work hard and how can they be made more productive?

The then-young science of *psychotechnics* or *applied psychology* promised to provide answers to these issues. Its founders (psychologists such as the Germany-born Hugo Münsterberg and William Stern, who both obtained professorships in the United States early in the twentieth century) attempted to apply psychological insights, obtained through empirical research and rigid measurement, to the work environment. Both Münsterberg and Stern worked in the field of vocational psychology – the branch of personnel psychology that focuses on the link between workers' characteristics and job requirements, assuming that worker well-being and productivity are optimal when there is a good match between the job and the worker.

Scientific management
Productivity could also be optimized by not focusing on the match between the worker and the task, but rather by concentrating on the task itself, especially by simplifying it to such a degree that any worker would be able to do it. This idea was worked out in great detail by the American engineer Frederick Taylor (1856–1915), the founder of the *scientific management approach* (or Taylorism). As one of the first management consultants, he sought to maximize industrial efficiency and his ideas were highly influential until at least the 1950s. His ideas were also controversial because they rested on two basic assumptions, namely, workers are both *lazy* and *stupid*. As regards laziness, Taylor (1911) stated that:

> ... instead of using every effort to turn out the largest possible amount of work, in a majority of the cases [a worker] deliberately plans to do as little as he safely can – to turn out far less work than he is well able to do ... Underworking, that is, deliberately working slowly so as to avoid doing a full day's work ... is almost universal in industrial establishments ... the writer asserts without fear of contradiction that this constitutes the greatest evil with which the working-people of both England and America are now afflicted.

As regards stupidity, Taylor writes that 'one of the very first requirements for a man who is fit to handle pig iron as a regular occupation is that he shall be so stupid and so phlegmatic that he more nearly resembles in his mental make-up the ox than any other type'. Taylor proposed to counter the stupidity issue by:

1. *simplifying tasks* using scientific methods: tasks requiring complicated actions were broken down into considerably smaller and simpler subtasks;
2. *examining the best way to conduct these tasks*: it was assumed that for each task there is *one best way* to accomplish this task and that any other approach is suboptimal and should therefore be discouraged;
3. *training* workers in the 'one best way' to conduct their simplified task so that even relatively unskilled (or dumb) workers could be trained to perform the task fast and efficiently, resulting in higher productivity;
4. *separating the planning of tasks from their execution*: during the execution of their tasks workers should not think about how they should conduct the tasks, but instead this should be decided for them by their supervisors;
5. *selecting workers* for particular tasks: if a major requirement for a man who is fit to handle pig iron is that he is as stupid as an ox (cf. Taylor, 1911), then there are also workers that are too intelligent for this particular task. Similarly, some tasks would involve great strength, other tasks require high levels of precision, and so forth, meaning that not all workers were equally well-suited for all tasks.

The laziness issue was addressed by introducing high levels of control and supervision, as well as by introducing pay-for-performance systems – you work harder, you get paid more; you work slower, you get fired. Taylorism may be construed as being the start of contemporary work science, with standardization and efficiency as its core concepts.

> ### Work Psychology in Action: Discovering the one best way
>
> A basic assumption of scientific management is that there is one best way for each task to be conducted. However, how can this one best way be discovered? Taylor proposed to analyse tasks thoroughly and systematically ('scientifically'). For instance, he often selected the employee most successful in his or her task, studied the way this person worked and then trained the other employees to use these work methods. Later on Taylor used the possibilities offered by modern technology – photography and movies – in order to reduce process times.
>
> The possibilities of these new media were fully explored by the US couple Frank and Lillian Gilbreth, who conducted so-called *time and motion studies* in the 1910s and 1920s. The Gilbreths developed a method based on the analysis of work motions that consisted of filming the details of a worker's activities while recording the time needed for these activities. In this way they could see how the work had been done, showing where improvement was possible (e.g. which motions were superfluous and could be skipped). In doing this, the Gilbreths sought to make processes more efficient by optimizing the *motions* involved, rather than by reducing *process times*, as Taylor had done. After Frank's death in 1924, Lillian Gilbreth continued working in this area and eventually became the first female engineering professor at Purdue University, where she was granted a full professorship in 1940. Dividing her time between industrial psychology, industrial engineering and home economics, she was one of the first work/industrial psychologists as well as a pioneer of the discipline of *human factors* or *ergonomics*. Basically, this discipline involves the study of designing equipment, tools and machines that fit the human body and its cognitive abilities ('cognitive ergonomics').

Work psychology, 1930–present

Perhaps not surprisingly, scientific management became quickly popular among the management of the large factories of the early twentieth century, whereas (equally unsurprisingly) workers and worker unions detested this system. The introduction of Tayloristic principles at work often resulted in repetitive, boring and physically demanding jobs, as the management of these organizations sought to maximize productivity and profit, irrespective of the cost to the workers involved. The heyday of Taylorism was over by the middle of the 1930s. Employers realised that redesigning jobs in line with the principles of scientific management affected worker morale negatively and tended to stimulate conflicts between managers and workers, resulting in the strengthening of the position of labour unions and recurring strikes (e.g. Ingham, 1966). All this neutralized part of the benefits of the productivity gains achieved by the introduction of scientific management, and it was superseded by the *human relations movement*.

The human relations movement
Rather than fitting the worker to the job (as scientific management had attempted), the adage of the human relations movement was to fit the job to the worker, paying special attention to the human side of working. It originated from the series of experiments conducted from 1924 to 1933 by Harvard-based researchers such as Elton Mayo and Fritz Roethlisberger at the Hawthorne plant of Western Electric/AT&T. At the time, some 40,000 people worked at the plant, producing telephones, cables, transmission equipment and switching equipment. Western Electric had adopted the principles of scientific management in the early 1900s, and in the 1920s the company had become aware of its drawbacks for employee well-being and motivation. To promote worker commitment and to discourage worker turnover and unionization, the company's managers began to focus on the well-being of the workers. Western Electric introduced pensions, sick pay and stock purchase plans, and there was a range of educational and recreational programmes for its employees.

It is against this background that Western Electric became increasingly interested in research on the antecedents of worker productivity, motivation and satisfaction, and it undertook a series of behavioural experiments to examine the effects of contextual factors (such as lighting, rest periods and wage incentives) on worker productivity. These studies provided little, if any, evidence for the systematic effects of the factors of interest (later re-analysis of the original data showed that productivity did not even increase; see Kompier (2006) for a discussion). However, during the course of the experiments Mayo and Roethlisberger became convinced that the intimate atmosphere of the experiments led the participants to develop strong friendships across time, and the fact that they were a *team* was the main driver of the increased productivity witnessed by the researchers: 'the most important finding of all was unquestionably in the general area of teamwork and cooperation' (Mayo, 1945, p. 82). Although the evidence for this claim is weak at best, the Hawthorne studies helped develop ground-breaking ideas on social relations at work, motivation, satisfaction, resistance to change, group norms, worker participation and leadership that even today inspire much research on the effects of job characteristics on work performance (Sonnenfeld, 1985).

Contemporary work psychology
Work psychology as it is today builds on the notions discussed in this section. It aims to improve productivity by optimizing the organization of work, work methods and job characteristics, but at the same time strives towards

maximization of worker health and well-being. It is interdisciplinary, in that it builds on, contributes to and blends ideas and findings developed in disciplines such as occupational medicine, ergonomics, organizational sociology, social psychology and personality psychology. However, at its core is always a focus on work as a set of coordinated activities that are conducted by people – each with their own capacities, needs and talents. Added to this, it is assuming that sustainable work performance can only be achieved if task requirements, worker characteristics and worker health and well-being are all taken into account.

Replay

- Scholars have long thought systematically about the best way of conducting work tasks. For example, the Roman army used military manuals that showed how soldiers should conduct their tasks, and medical doctors in Ancient Greece worked according to the routines and guidelines documented in the books of the Hippocratic collection.
- In the early 1500s, the first truly scientific texts on the association between work and health appeared. Agricola documented the impact of working in mines on the health and well-being of miners; later on, Ramazzini extended this work to include no less than 52 occupations. These books constituted the starting point for the discipline now known as occupational medicine.
- The industrial revolution marked a transition to new manufacturing processes. These also affected the shape of employment of the masses, changing it from artisanal piece-for-piece production to mass production.
- A major issue in work concerned the productivity of the workers. Psychotechnics, as introduced in Germany at the end of the nineteenth century, applied psychological insights to working life, focusing on optimizing the match between worker and vocation. Scientific management, as introduced and popularized by Frederick Taylor, focused on the simplification and optimization of tasks and increased work motivation by introducing strict supervision and pay-for-performance systems.
- After 1930, the popularity of Taylor's ideas waned, to be replaced by the insights of the human relations movement. Based on experiments conducted in General Electric's Hawthorne plant, this school of thought focused particularly on the social context in which the work tasks were conducted.
- Contemporary work psychology merges ideas from all these (and other) disciplines in an attempt to promote sustainable performance: high productivity combined with much attention for worker health and well-being.

1.5 The Times, They are A-changin'

As we have seen in the preceding section, systematic thinking about work and the organization of work already dates back to the Ancient Greeks and Romans. However, in Chapter 3 you will learn that most job design theories have been developed in the mid-twentieth century when workers were still predominantly working in large-scale manufacturing plants. After that time, things kept on changing. There is general agreement that the world of work has changed considerably over recent decades. The levels at which transformations take place range from the macro level of economies and demography to the meso level of organizations and the micro levels of tasks. Many of these changes arise from a combination of technological advances and economic trends which themselves often go hand in hand to some extent. 'It is no exaggeration to say that modern technology is changing the way we live and work. The information revolution will transform everything it touches – and it will touch everything' (Cascio, 2003, p. 406).

The changing nature of work

Probably one of the most important changes in the world of work has to do with the *nature of work*. Since the mid-1970s the developed economies have witnessed a vast increase in service sector working and a simultaneous decline in the number of employees working in manufacturing. This transition implies that a larger proportion of workers is involved in less physically strenuous jobs with less exposure to physical health risks. Related to this, heavy manufacturing jobs have been made easier with the help of new technologies that have made jobs less labour-intensive. Working in service jobs is also not without risks as it brings about new types of job demands. Typically, service work requires some degree of emotion labour (see Chapters 6 and 7), in which employees have to adhere to rules regarding the expression of emotions (Hochschild, 1983). Service organizations depend on their customers. This usually implies that service employees have to interact with customers in a positive way, for example by being friendly and showing positive emotions. In this sense 'service with a smile' becomes a job requirement.

Another rapidly growing segment of the workforce is that of the 'knowledge worker', a highly educated employee who applies theoretical and analytical knowledge to developing new products and services. Knowledge workers include those working in the areas of product development, consultancy and information systems. The existence of 'knowledge workers' is not new: it was described by Peter Drucker in his 1959 book *The Landmarks of Tomorrow*. Drucker (1999) states that 'The most valuable assets of a 20th-century company were its production equipment. The most valuable asset of a 21st-century institution, whether business or non-business, will be its knowledge workers and their productivity' (p. 135). Knowledge work is typically characterized by a high degree of cognitive load, a term which is used in cognitive psychology to illustrate the load or effort related to the executive control of the working memory. In knowledge work the level of information processing is high in order to produce intellectual performances.

The changing workforce

Along with the change in the nature of work, the composition of the workforce itself is also very different to the era when work design first became of psychological interest. About 50 years ago the demographic features of most work organizations were fairly homogeneous (William & O'Reilly, 1998). Many employees shared a similar ethnic background, were male and worked for the same employer throughout their working lives. Nowadays managers are confronted with a workforce that is more diverse in terms of gender, age, ethnicity, organizational tenure, educational background and so on. Such demographic changes have a major impact on creating new territories for research and practice in work psychology. Work psychology has much to offer in managing differences between individuals and/or groups at work. However, as it becomes more and more clear that work group diversity may have positive as well as negative effects we have to look more deeply into issues of how we can overcome prejudices and biases, and how we can make diversity work (van Knippenberg & Schippers, 2007).

The changing flexibility of working

Rapid developments in information technology are having major implications for the way in which work is conducted. More and more organizations have started to redesign their approach to work. Central to this new approach is the fact that employees have high work flexibility. Such a flexible work design, also referred to as 'new ways of working' (NWW), is characterized by (i) flexibility in the timing of work, that is, employees have more autonomy in deciding when they work, (ii) flexibility in the place of work, for example employees can work from home, at the office and/or during commuting time (e.g. on the train), and (iii) the facilitation of *new media technologies*, such as smartphones and videoconferencing (Baarne, Houtkamp, & Knotter, 2010). Thus, NWW offer the employee various options for communication with co-workers, supervisors and clients, including phone calls, email, online messaging and (online) virtual meetings. NWW also enable employees in different locations and on different schedules to work together as 'virtual teams' (Duarte & Tennant-Snyder, 2000). Teams located in different countries can even exploit time zone differences to provide 24/7 working. However, whereas the organizational benefits of NWW have been emphasized in previous studies (Sánchez, Pérez, De Luis Carnicer, & Vela Jiménez, 2007), little is known yet about how NWW influence employees and their families. Recently, Demerouti and colleagues (2013) considered the opportunities and pitfalls of NWW, and it seems that NWW have the potential to contribute to work–life balance, as long as they are used in a considerate and moderate way. In other words, NWW can be beneficial for employees and their families if boundaries to separate work and family life are created.

The changing organization

Organizations themselves, whether service, manufacturing or other, have also undergone dramatic changes. They are no longer the rather static and inflexible enterprises of earlier times. Some used to say that the only constant factor that characterizes organizations is 'change'. Two major trends are mainly responsible for the ongoing changes in organizations: (i) globalization, or commerce without borders, which, along with the interdependence of business operations in different locations (Cascio, 2003), changes the markets and environments in which organizations have to operate, thereby creating a global economy with both opportunities and threats, and (ii) ICT, which is redefining how, where and when work is performed. Organizations have responded to these developments with managerial innovations and new organizational forms such as network organizations, strategic alliances and virtual corporations. Fortunately, most organizations seem to undertake the kinds of organizational changes needed to survive and prosper in today's environment (Cummings & Worley, 2009).

The changing psychological contract

Finally, the relationships that employees have with their organizations are also subject to change. Whereas once it was considered normal for employees to spend their entire working career with one or two companies, changed notions of careers prescribe now that employees are expected to move between organizations much more often. Education and training throughout a career have become more common, increasing the potential for employees to continuously develop and improve their own competencies, which improves their employability. As a consequence of all this, the psychological contract – what employees and employers want and expect from each other – has changed dramatically in recent years. Characteristics such as stability, permanent employment, predictability and mutual respect are out. Instead the new features of self-regulation, flexibility and employability are required. More and more, the old psychological contract is paving the way for idiosyncratic deals ('i-deals'), where individual employees negotiate with an employer to adapt work arrangements to better meet their personal needs (Rousseau, 2005).

In conclusion, this brief and necessarily incomplete account shows that the world of work today is very different from the time in which the major work design theories were developed. Altogether, these changes have led to what may be called in developed countries the *intensification of work*. Intensification refers to increasing work hours and work pressure, the need for lifelong learning and the ability and willingness to continuously change the type of work one does (Arnold, 2005). These developments call for some reorientation and new perspectives on job demands. The restricted range of job characteristics and outcomes addressed by traditional theories might become insufficient to capture the salient aspects of modern work. New demands such as illegitimate tasks (Semmer, Tschan, Meier, Facchin, & Jacobshagen, 2010), demands arising from temporal and spatial flexibility (Kattenbach, Demerouti, & Nachreiner, 2010) and demands arising from accelerated change (Obschonka, Silbereisen, & Wasilewski, 2012) might represent promising approaches for future research. In Chapters 5 and 6 you will learn more about job demands.

Replay

- The nature of work has changed from mainly manufacturing work to predominantly service and knowledge work.

- The workforce has become more diverse in terms of gender, age, ethnicity, organizational tenure and educational background.
- New ways of working are characterized by (i) flexibility in the timing of work, (ii) flexibility in the place of work and (iii) the facilitation of information technologies.
- Because of globalization and the increasing use of ICT organizations must continuously adapt to new realities.
- The psychological contract – what employees and employers want and expect from each other – has been changed from an emphasis on stability and permanent employment to a desire for flexibility and employability.

1.6 The Crucial Role of Task Analysis in Contemporary Work Psychology

As discussed earlier, the changing nature of work is associated with new types of demands at work, such as mental and emotional demands. The key question, however, is how can these demands be described and analysed? Such a description and analysis of demands at work has a prominent position within work psychology, and is important for both theory and practice. *Task analysis* is the common name given to any process that identifies and examines the (demanding) tasks that must be performed by employees. Task analysis is a fundamental approach which assists in achieving higher performance and safety standards (cf. Kirwan & Ainsworth, 1992).

Task analysis within work psychology

Task analysis is used in different disciplines, such as ergonomics, design studies, engineering, operations and psychology, to describe, analyse and evaluate human–human and human–machine interactions in systems (Kirwan & Ainsworth, 1992). In general, it can be defined as the study of what an employee (or team) is required to do, in terms of actions and/or processes, to achieve a system goal. The idea is that task analysis provides the user with a 'blueprint' of human involvement in a system, or, to put it another way, to give a detailed picture of that system from a human perspective. This makes it easier to describe how activities fit together and to evaluate the design implications. The resulting information can be used for many purposes, such as tool or equipment (re)design, personnel selection and training, allocation of jobs to 'families' of similar functions, task (re)design, job organization and performance assessment.

Within the context of work psychology, task analysis can be considered a methodology in which data will be collected, ranked and evaluated to say something about the nature of the task, that is, its *psychologically relevant* characteristics (van Ouwerkerk, Meijman, & Mulder, 1994). The aim of work-psychological task analysis is to lead to a more efficient and effective integration of the human factor into system designs and operations via task (re)design in order to optimize human performance and safety.

Task-analysis methods and techniques

Task analysis within work psychology covers a range of *methods* and *techniques* used by work psychologists. Generally, a task-analysis method is based on a theoretical model that indicates which task characteristics will be analysed. An example of a method is Hackman and Oldham's (1975) job characteristics approach (see Chapter 3). In the literature, all methods can be categorized using four different approaches (cf. Fleishman & Quaintance, 1984):

1. *Behaviour description approach*. In this approach the focus is on the actual behaviours employees display in executing the task, such as mopping the floor or reading instruments.
2. *Behaviour requirements approach*. This approach focuses on the actual behaviour employees *should* display to perform the task in a successful way, for example showing dedication and concentration.
3. *Ability requirements approach*. In this approach, tasks are analysed in terms of employees' abilities, knowledge, skills and personal characteristics. These are usually needed to perform a task properly.
4. *Task characteristics approach*. The focus of this approach is to analyse the objective characteristics of a task, independent from the behaviour that is actually displayed (behaviour description) or that should be displayed (behaviour requirements) or the abilities needed (ability requirements).

In addition, there are many task-analysis techniques available that deal with the description and analysis of tasks. Techniques are instruments or protocols with which data can be collected and described in a systematic way. Task-analysis techniques can be divided into at least three broad categories (van Ouwerkerk et al., 1994): (i) data-collection techniques, (ii) task-representation techniques and (iii) task-simulation techniques (see also Kirwan & Ainsworth, 1992). Data-collection techniques consist of interviews, survey questionnaires, observations, and organizational documents and records. These techniques are common in work psychology, for instance to measure quantitative demanding tasks, as discussed in Chapter 5. Task-representation techniques use graphic descriptions such as flow charts and hierarchical networks. The underlying idea is that formal graphical representations of tasks are easier to understand and more concise than textual descriptions. Finally, task-simulation techniques make use of computer modelling and computer-aided design programmes. There are two main types: (i) those which try to simulate the dynamic aspects of tasks in work environment simulation models ('mock-ups') and (ii) those which are used for ergonomically laying out work environments ('workspace designs').

Benefits of task analysis

Task analysis within work psychology can be applied in a wide range of organizations. It is a popular, well-structured and useful approach to describe, analyse and evaluate particular tasks to improve performance and safety by means of task (re)design. Many organizations have made use of task-analysis methods and techniques, and have benefitted from such usage. The interested reader could consult Kirwan and Ainsworth (1992) for 10 successful case studies.

Replay

- Work-psychological task analysis can be considered a methodology in which data will be collected, ranked and evaluated to say something about the nature of the (demanding) task. It is a popular, well-structured and useful approach to describe, analyse and evaluate particular tasks to improve performance and safety by means of task (re)design.
- Task-analysis methods can be categorized using four different approaches: the behaviour description approach, the behaviour requirements approach, the ability requirements approach and the task characteristics approach.
- Task-analysis techniques can be divided in at least three broad categories: data-collection techniques, task-representation techniques and task-simulation techniques.

1.7 The Organization of the Book

This book is organized around seven parts, which are discussed below. At the end of this section we will describe how this book can best be used.

Overview of the book

Now we have explained the background of people at work, we will introduce the general outline and structure of the book. A central assumption in this textbook is that working constitutes a series of usually conscious and goal-directed acts in order to produce a particular good or service. Thus, *worker behaviour* is at the core of work psychology, and work psychology is concerned with the psychological aspects of that behaviour, in terms of both its antecedents and its outcomes. A second important assumption in the present book is that, while working admittedly requires effort expenditure and may result in psychological and/or physiological costs on the side of the worker, working may also result in positive outcomes for both the organization and the worker. Traditionally, work psychology has tended to emphasize the fact that specific constellations of job characteristics could result in adverse consequences for workers (such as high levels of stress, fatigue and sickness absence). More modern approaches acknowledge that work offers incumbents many desirable features. At present, the idea that the consequences of working are not negative by definition certainly enriches current theorizing and research in the area of work psychology. This volume will therefore systematically emphasize not only the negative, but also the positive aspects of working.

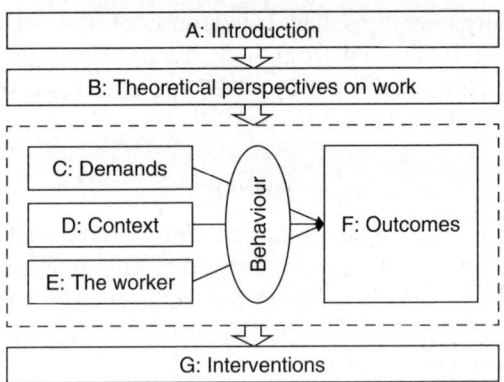

Figure 1.1 General outline of the volume.

The book consists of seven interrelated parts (A–G). Figure 1.1 presents the general outline of the volume graphically. Part A is the *introduction*. It includes two chapters. The current chapter (Chapter 1) presents a general introduction to work psychology. Chapter 2 provides a discussion of research designs and research methods that are typically applied in this area of psychology, including experimental, quasi-experimental, survey methods, cross-sectional and longitudinal designs (including diary research). The basic principles of classical test theory are also explained and the two major characteristics of measurement in work psychology are highlighted: reliability and validity.

Part B consists of two chapters that discuss major *theoretical perspectives* on the relations between job characteristics and work outcomes. Chapter 3 describes the five most significant approaches to job design that have laid the foundation for contemporary work psychology. These models are the Job Characteristics Model (Hackman & Oldham, 1975), the Demand–Control–Support Model (Karasek & Theorell, 1990), the Vitamin Model (Warr, 1987), the Effort–Reward Imbalance Model (Siegrist, 1996) and Contemporary Socio-Technical Systems Thinking (Cherns, 1987; Clegg, 2000). Strengths, weaknesses and empirical evidence for these models are addressed. Many of these models propose a specific and limited set of job characteristics that are presumed to lead to a relatively well-specified set of work outcomes (i.e. they are rather specific and 'closed' models). The second chapter in this part (Chapter 4) presents two current work psychological models that are rapidly developing, that is, Demerouti, Bakker, Nachreiner and Schaufeli's (2001) Job Demand–Resources Model and de Jonge and Dormann's (2003) Demand-Induced Strain Compensation Model. These two models both impose fewer restrictions on the work-related factors that may be included in them or on the outcomes studied (i.e. they are more generic and open, contrary to most approaches discussed in Chapter 3).

Part C (Demands) and Part D (Context) build further on the information discussed in Part B. As mentioned above, Part B discussed several theoretical models for the relations among various job characteristics on the one hand and work outcomes on the other. Parts C and D extend this information with an in-depth focus on specific types of job characteristics and their relations to particular outcomes. Based on the idea that work entails goal-directed behaviour and that these goals usually describe what has to be achieved in a job (i.e. what one's task actually involves), Part C focuses on various types of *job demands*. Basically, a rough distinction can be made of the degree to which the tasks require much effort – either quantitatively (i.e. how much work has to be done during a particular time period) or qualitatively (referring to the difficulty of the task to be done) – versus the content of one's tasks (i.e. is the task physically, emotionally and/or cognitively demanding). Based on these distinctions, Part C includes two chapters, addressing quantitative (Chapter 5) versus qualitative job demands (Chapter 6).

Part D addresses the characteristics of the *context* in which workers must achieve their goals. Contrary to the subject matter discussed in Part C, the material presented here does not refer to *what* has to be achieved, how hard one must work or how difficult the task is, but rather to characteristics of the *situation* in which the work goals have to be reached. This situation has dimensions that are specifically linked to the psychosocial characteristics of the job and the opportunities to recover during and after work. Chapter 7 addresses the *characteristics of the task*. The discussions in Chapters 3 and 4 have shown that a wide array of job characteristics may affect worker performance and well-being. However, two sets of characteristics stand out as being especially important: job control and the social context in which the tasks are done (including social stressors, social support and bullying). As regards *opportunities for recovery*, Chapter 8 builds on Meijman and Mulder's (1998) effort–recovery theory and McEwen's (1998) allostatic load theory to discuss the impact of demanding work hours (i.e. prolonged and abnormal work hours) on recovery, and its potential effect on health and well-being. This chapter also deals with the recovery-promoting potential of worktime control (e.g. flextime) and with modern work practices such as self-scheduling and boundaryless work. Finally, issues such as breaks and holidays, all of which have recovery-promoting potential, are discussed. The final chapter in this part (Chapter 9) discusses the nature and consequences of the growth of new types of technology in work organizations. The chapter reviews theories which seek to explain the impact of technology on individuals and the conduct of their work. The chapter also uses a number of examples of technology which are prevalent within the twenty-first century and are likely to grow in importance, including the design and use of health information technologies (HIT), mobile working and technology-supported virtual team working.

Part E includes two chapters that focus on the *characteristics of the worker* and his/her home environment, insofar as these characteristics are relevant for workers' functioning at work. This part starts from the assumption that work behaviour is not just a function of job demands (Part C) and the characteristics of the work context (Part D), but also depends to some degree on the person conducting the task. Many individual characteristics that could affect workers' functioning at work (e.g. personality factors) traditionally fall within the remit of personnel psychology and therefore are not discussed here. However, several of these characteristics are becoming increasingly important in the area of work psychology, meaning that attention for such characteristics in a textbook on work psychology is warranted. The first chapter in this part (Chapter 10) addresses the role of employee characteristics in the light of work-related outcomes such as motivation, well-being, sustainable employability and job performance. Both objective and subjective employee characteristics are considered. Objective characteristics refer to demographics (such as age, gender and ethnicity) and lifestyle risk factors. Subjective employee characteristics concern 'trait-like' characteristics such as workers' core self-evaluations. 'State-like' characteristics such as psychological capital (a construct encompassing the constructs of hope, self-efficacy, optimism and resilience) and 'states' are also being considered as subjective characteristics of employees. Chapter 11 discusses positive and negative work-to-home and home-to-work interactions, showing that the work–home interface may affect worker motivation and performance, and could moderate and/or mediate the associations between work demands (Part B) on the one hand and work outcomes (Part F) on the other.

Part F is concerned with the *outcomes* of work behaviour. On the one hand, this cluster of outcomes includes instances of individual-level outcomes such as burnout, work engagement and boredom. On the other hand, this part discusses organizationally relevant behaviour, such as motivation, work performance, mistakes and accidents at work, and sickness absence. The first chapter in this part (Chapter 12) deals with burnout, boredom and engagement. These concepts can be placed in a two-dimensional model consisting of an activation dimension and a pleasure dimension. These indicators of work-related well-being have often been related to work performance, and are considered to result from the job characteristics discussed in parts C and D. Regarding the organizationally relevant outcomes, Chapter 13 deals with issues as satisfaction, motivation and performance. As workers may not always be motivated to 'do the right thing', this chapter also addresses counterproductive work behaviour. The chapter ends with a discussion of the possibility that the strength of the satisfaction–performance relationship depends on several factors, such as reward contingency, job complexity and job demands.

Chapter 14 addresses what might be called 'unintended' counterproductive work behaviour: slips, mistakes and accidents at work. This chapter also discusses models for the link between job characteristics, errors and mistakes, and safety at work, and the concept of safety culture. Finally, Chapter 15 deals with work-related sickness absence as well as sickness presence and discusses its prevalence and costs. The chapter introduces contemporary models that consider sickness absence vis-à-vis sickness presence and presents an integrative, multilevel framework for research on and management of work attendance and sickness.

The final part of this volume (Part G) addresses the issues of prevention and *intervention* in the context of work psychology. The introductory chapter to this part (Chapter 16) discusses the basic concepts and approaches relevant to managing psychosocial risks in the workplace. The basic three-phase model for interventions (development, implementation and evaluation of results) is explained and the principles of participatory action research (PAR), that is, how employees, line managers and directors can participate in the development and implementation of interventions, are explained. Finally, the psychosocial safety climate, which can be considered as the 'cause of the causes' of work stress is outlined. The remaining chapters in this part address various interventions. Chapter 17 introduces job crafting as a new form of job redesign. The conceptualization and the predictors and outcomes of job crafting are explained, and the link between job crafting and the implementation of organizational change and innovation is elaborated. Chapter 18 discusses the issues of teams at work, explaining how teams develop, what effective teams are and how team interventions work in organizations. The key processes teams engage in and how they impact performance are discussed. Finally, Chapter 19 deals with the issue of 'positive' interventions, that is, whereas traditional work-psychological interventions usually target stressed or burned-out workers, positive interventions aim to 'amplify' the well-being and productivity of employees who are functioning well. Building on recent insights from positive psychology, this chapter discusses the principles of such positive interventions and presents some examples thereof, showing that interventions may also have positive effects on the functioning of healthy workers.

How to use this book

Each chapter is guided by sections that accommodate learning. These parts are as follows:

- *Chapter objectives*: These are listed at the start of each chapter, and highlight the knowledge and skills students should have acquired after studying the chapter. This section starts with the following statement: '*After studying this chapter, you should be able to: …*'.
- *Replays*: These are situated at regular intervals throughout the text, providing a brief review of the main concepts and topics covered in the preceding section.
- *Work psychology in action*: These boxes encompass real-life and practical examples throughout the text that illustrate cases or case studies in which theoretical concepts are translated and/or applied into practice.
- *Discussion points*: These encourage critical cognitive reflection on the main topics and issues covered in each chapter. They are presented at the end of the main text of the chapter. Discussion points stimulate the students to contemplate critically the themes that are addressed in the chapter.
- *Learning by doing points*: These encourage practical reflection on the main topics and issues covered in each chapter. These points are presented after the discussion points and provide practical assignments or applications.
- *Further reading*: Annotated further reading encourages students to read more widely around the subject and provides a shortlist of literature recommendations.

Discussion Points

1. In Section 1.1 work was defined as 'a set of coordinated and goal-directed activities that are conducted in exchange for something else – usually some form of monetary reward'. Consider the case of someone who has won a large amount of money in a lottery. It frequently occurs that such people continue to go to work, in spite of the fact that they do not *need* to work for their subsistence. Are these people still 'working' in the sense of the definition above? Does work still have the same meaning to these people as before they won the lottery, or is their job now better classified as a form of leisure activity? Similar questions may be raised concerning the nature of volunteer work: is this a form of 'working' according to the definition given above, and in what sense does volunteer work differ from paid work?
2. In response to discussion point 1 above, you may have argued that volunteer work is just another form of working. If so, discuss whether and how the

principles of scientific management would apply to volunteer work. Can the work performance of volunteers be improved using Tayloristic principles? Similarly, would the ideas of the human relations movement help in improving the performance of volunteers? The answers to these questions should help you in determining whether and in which respects 'volunteer work' is comparable to regular, paid work.
3. Suppose you have to assess job characteristics without subjective perceptions of workers (see also Chapter 5). Which task-analysis approach would you prefer as a basis for your examination? Explain why.

Learning by Doing

1. The time-and-motion studies conducted by Frank and Lillian Gilbreth aimed to reduce the steps needed to conduct a particular task. In this way they could improve the efficiency of workers and reduce the effort needed to perform their tasks. The principles behind this approach can also be applied to other contexts in which people conduct particular tasks. Consider the task of preparing a meal, eating it and cleaning up afterwards, with sub-tasks such as (i) take ingredients from the refrigerator, (ii) cook the meal, (iii) put the dishes on the table, (iv) dispose of the waste (empty packages), (v) clean the dishes in the dishwasher and (vi) put the clean dishes in a cupboard. Assume that all these activities are done within your own (large) kitchen. What would the layout of your kitchen look like if you organized your activities according to the principles of Lillian Gilbreth? Where would you put the refrigerator, cupboard, dishwasher, etc. if you wanted to minimize the effort needed to prepare your meal, eat it and clean up afterwards?
2. Modern work is increasingly characterized by flexible work designs such as new ways of working. Think of somebody you know who is currently working under such conditions. Ask this person what he or she considers to be the advantages and disadvantages of this kind of work design. Next, think about the ways in which human resource managers can support employees who face difficulties working in such a context.
3. Pick three models from Chapters 3 and 4, and write down the task-analysis method and technique that fit these models best.

Further Reading

Cascio, W. F. (2003). Changes in workers, work, and organizations. In W. C. Bormann, D. R. Ilgen, & R. J. Klimoski (Eds.), *Handbook of psychology, Vol. 12: Industrial and organizational psychology* (pp. 401–422). Hoboken, NJ: John Wiley & Sons.

International Labour Office (2012). *Global employment trends: Preventing a deeper jobs crisis.* Geneva: International Labour Organization.

Kirwan, B., & Ainsworth, L. K. (1992). *A Guide to task analysis.* London: Taylor & Francis.

References

American Psychological Association (2013). *About APA*. Retrieved January 21, 2013, from http://www.apa.org/about/index.aspx.

Arnold, J. (2005). *Work psychology: Understanding human behaviour in the workplace* (4th ed.). Harlow: Pearson.

Baarne, R., Houtkamp, P., & Knotter, M. (2010). *Het nieuwe werken ontrafeld* [*Unravelling new ways of working*]. Assen, The Netherlands: Koninklijke Van Gorcum/Stichting Management Studies.

Basalla, G. (1988). *The evolution of technology*. Cambridge: Cambridge University Press.

British Psychological Society (2013). *What we do*. Retrieved January 21, 2013, from http://www.bps.org.uk/.

Cartwright, S., & Cooper, C. L. (Eds. 2008). *The Oxford handbook of personnel psychology*. Oxford: Oxford University Press.

Cascio, W. F. (2003). Changes in workers, work, and organizations. In W. C. Bormann, D. R. Ilgen, & R. J. Klimoski (Eds.), *Handbook of psychology, Vol. 12: Industrial and organizational psychology* (pp. 401–422). Hoboken, NJ: John Wiley & Sons.

Cummings, T. G., & Worley, C. G. (2009). *Organization development and change*. Mason, OH: South-Western Cengage Learning.

Cherns, A. (1987). Principles of sociotechnical design revisited. *Human Relations, 40*, 153–161.

Clegg, C. W. (2000). Sociotechnical principles for system design. *Applied Ergonomics, 31*, 463–477.

de Jonge, J., & Dormann, C. (2003). The DISC Model: Demand-induced strain compensation mechanisms in job stress. In M. F. Dollard, H. R. Winefield, & A. H. Winefield (Eds.), *Occupational stress in the service professions* (pp. 43–74). London: Taylor & Francis.

Demerouti, E., Bakker, A. B., Nachreiner, F., & Schaufeli, W. B. (2001). The job demands–resources model of burnout. *Journal of Applied Psychology, 86*, 499–512.

Demerouti, E., Derks, D., ten Brummelhuis, L. L., & Bakker, A. B. (2013). New ways of working: Impact on working conditions, work-family balance, and well-being. In C. Korunka, & P. Hoonakker (Eds.), *ICT and Quality of Working Life*. Amsterdam, New York: Springer.

DeWall, C. N., Pond, R. S., Campbell, W. K., & Twenge, J. M. (2011). Tuning in to psychological change: Linguistic markers of psychological traits and emotions over time in popular U.S. song lyrics. *Psychology of Aesthetics, Creativity, and the Arts, 5*, 200–207.

Doyle, C. E. (2003). *Work and organizational psychology: An introduction with attitude*. Hove: Psychology Press.

Drucker, P. F. (1999). *Management challenges for the 21st century*. Oxford: Butterworth-Heinemann.

Duarte, D., & Tennant Snyder, N. (2000). *Mastering virtual teams: Strategies, tools, and techniques that succeed*. San Francisco, CA: Jossey-Bass Publishers.

Eurostat (2012). Unemployment statistics. Retrieved January 25, 2013, from http://epp.eurostat.ec.europa.eu/statistics_explained/index.php/Unemployment_statistics (accessed June 23, 2013).

Fleishman, E. A., & Quaintance, M. K. (1984). *Taxonomies of human performance: The description of human tasks*. New York: Academic Press.

Frese, M., & Zapf, D. (1994). Action as the core of work psychology: A German approach. In H. C. Triandis, M. D. Dunnette, & L. M. Hough (Eds.), *Handbook of industrial and organizational psychology* (*Vol. 4*, pp. 271–340). Palo Alto, CA: Consulting Psychologists Press.

Gochfeld, M. (2005). Chronologic history of occupational medicine. *Journal of Occupational and Environmental Medicine, 47*, 96–114.

Groening, M. (1987). *Work is hell*. New York: Pantheon Books.

Hackman, J. R., & Oldham, G. R. (1975). Development of the job diagnostic survey. *Journal of Applied Psychology, 60*, 159–170.

Hochschild, A. R. (1983). *The managed heart: Commercialization of human feelings*. Berkeley: University of California Press.

Ingham, J. N. (1966). A strike in the progressive era: McKees rocks, 1909. *The Pennsylvania Magazine of History and Biography, 90*, 353–377.

International Labour Office (2012). *Global employment trends: Preventing a deeper jobs crisis*. Geneva: International Labour Organization.

Jahoda, M. (1982). *Employment and unemployment: A social-psychological analysis*. London: Cambridge University Press.

Jex, S. M., & Britt, T. W. (2008). *Organizational psychology: A scientist-practitioner approach*. Hoboken, NJ: John Wiley & Sons.

Karasek, R. A., & Theorell, T. (1990). *Healthy work: Stress, productivity and the reconstruction of working life*. New York: Basic Books.

Kattenbach, R., Demerouti, E., & Nachreiner, F. (2010). Flexible working times: Effects on employees' exhaustion, work-nonwork conflict and job performance. *Career Development International*, 15, 279–295.

Kirwan, B., & Ainsworth, L. K. (1992). *A guide to task analysis*. London: Taylor & Francis.

Kompier, M. A. J. (2006). The Hawthorne effect is a myth, but what keeps the story going? *Scandinavian Journal of Work, Environment & Health*, 32, 402–412.

Lloyd, G. E. R. (1982). *Hippocratic writings*. New York: Viking. Cited in R. B. Gundermann (2005), The medical community's changing vision of the patient: The importance of radiology. *Radiology*, 234, 339–342.

Mayo, E. (1945). *The social problems of an industrial civilization*. Boston: Harvard University.

McEwen, B. S. (1998). Stress, adaptation, and disease: Allostasis and allostatic load. *Annals of the New York Academy of Sciences*, 840, 33–44.

Merriam-Webster (2013). *Work*. Retrieved January 21, 2013, from http://www.merriam-webster.com/dictionary/work.

Meijman, T. F., & Mulder, G. (1998). Psychological aspects of workload. In P. J. D. Drenth, Hk. Thierry, & Ch. J. de Wolff (Eds.), *Handbook of work and organizational psychology* (2nd ed., pp. 5–33). Hove: Psychology Press/Erlbaum.

Obschonka, M., Silbereisen, R. K., & Wasilewski, J. (2012). Constellations of new demands concerning careers and jobs: Results from a two-country study on social and economic change. *Journal of Vocational Behavior*, 80, 211–223.

Paul, K. I., & Moser, K. (2009). Unemployment impairs mental health: Meta-analyses. *Journal of Vocational Behavior*, 74, 264–282.

Porfeli, E. J. (2009). Hugo Münsterberg and the origins of vocational guidance. *The Career Development Quarterly*, 57, 225–236.

Rousseau, D. M. (2005). *I-deals: Idiosyncratic deals employees bargain for themselves*. New York: M. E. Sharpe.

Sánchez, A. M., Pérez, M., De Luis Carnicer, P., & Vela Jiménez, M. J. (2007). Teleworking and workplace flexibility: A study of impact on firm performance. *Personnel Review*, 36, 42–64.

Semmer, N. K., Tschan, F., Meier, L. L., Facchin, S., & Jacobshagen, N. (2010). Illegitimate tasks and counterproductive work behavior. *Applied Psychology*, 59, 70–96.

Siegrist, J. (1996). Adverse health effects of high-effort/low-reward conditions. *Journal of Occupational Health Psychology*, 1, 27–41.

Sonnenfeld, J. A. (1985). Shedding light on the Hawthorne studies. *Journal of Organizational Behavior*, 6, 111–130.

Taylor, F. W. (1911). *The principles of scientific management*. Retrieved February 28, 2013, from http://www.marxists.org/reference/subject/economics/taylor/principles/index.htm.

van Knippenberg, D., & Schippers, M. C. (2007). Work group diversity. *Annual Review of Psychology*, 58, 515–541.

van Ouwerkerk, R. J., Meijman, T. F., & Mulder, G. (1994). *Arbeidspsychologische taakanalyse [Work-psychological task analysis]*. Utrecht: Lemma.

Vegetius (390 AD). *De re militari*. Retrieved February 28, 2013, from http://www.digitalattic.org/home/war/vegetius (accessed June 23, 2013).

Wanberg, C. R. (2012) The individual experience of unemployment. *Annual Review of Psychology*, 63, 369–396.

Warr, P. B. (1987). *Work, unemployment, and mental health*. Oxford: Oxford University Press.

Weber, L. W. (2002). Georgius Agricola (1494–1555): Scholar, physician, scientist, entrepreneur, diplomat. *Toxicological Science*, 69, 292–294.

Williams, K. Y., & O'Reilly, C. A. (1998). Demography and diversity in organizations: A review of 40 years of research. *Research in Organizational Behavior*, 20, 77–140.

World Bank (2013). Working for a world free of poverty. Retrieved February 28, 2013, from http://data.worldbank.org/indicator/SL.TLF.TOTL.IN.

2
Research Methods in Work Psychology

E. KEVIN KELLOWAY AND ARLA DAY

> ### Chapter Objectives
>
> After studying this chapter, you should be able to:
>
> - recognize the importance and necessity of establishing the reliability and validity of measures used in organizational research;
> - explain the three central dilemmas confronting researchers in selecting an appropriate research design;
> - describe and identify the strengths and limitations of the major research designs used in organizational research;
> - evaluate the basic characteristics of an empirical study in a balanced and well-informed manner.

The happy–productive worker thesis has been one of the most intensely researched questions in work psychology (Locke, 1976; also see Chapter 13). Essentially, the suggestion was that individuals who are happy with their jobs are more productive. This notion was very popular in the early days of work psychology, from the 1950s until about the mid-1970s. However, by the time Locke wrote his review of the job satisfaction literature in 1976, researchers had largely rejected the hypothesis, concluding that the relationship between job satisfaction and job performance is statistically negligible (Iaffaldano & Muchinsky, 1985). Our

An Introduction to Contemporary Work Psychology, First Edition.
Edited by Maria C. W. Peeters, Jan de Jonge and Toon W. Taris.
© 2014 John Wiley & Sons, Ltd. Published 2014 by John Wiley & Sons, Ltd.

understanding of the relationship continues to evolve (research now suggests that there is a relationship between satisfaction and performance; Judge, Thoreson, Bono, & Patton, 2001), and the happy–productive thesis continues to intrigue researchers (Taris & Schreurs, 2009; Zelenski, Murphy, & Jenkins, 2008).

Imagine you are part of our research group, and we want to do a study to test the happy–productive worker relationship. How would we go about conducting such a test? As a first step, you would need to formulate a hypothesis. A *hypothesis* is a testable prediction about the world. In this case, the hypothesis or prediction is that job satisfaction and job performance are positively related (i.e. people who are more satisfied perform better). Although this statement is a prediction, it is not yet testable. Job satisfaction and job performance are *abstract constructs*, that is, we cannot 'see' job satisfaction or performance. We therefore need to determine how these constructs will be measured. We first would use *operational definitions*, which define an abstract construct in *specific, observable, measurable* and *behavioural* terms. Operational definitions can be very specific to the study in which they are used, and they may differ among studies. In the first section of this chapter, we will review how researchers go about making decisions around how to measure the constructs in which they are interested.

Once we have decided how to measure happiness and productivity, we need to consider how we would go about conducting a research study of the happy–productive worker hypothesis. To do this we need to consider a wide variety of issues, ranging from who should participate in our study (e.g. employees in one local organization, employees across Canada, employees from North America or employees across the world) to what we conclude (e.g. if we find an association between the two variables does that mean that happiness causes productivity or does being productive make you happy or perhaps neither conclusion is correct?). These are questions of *research design* to which we turn our attention in the latter half of this chapter.

Replay

- A *hypothesis* is a testable prediction about the world.
- *Hypothetical constructs* are used to label the concepts (such as job satisfaction) that we cannot directly observe in order to organize and classify observations in a meaningful way.
- *Operational definitions* define an abstract construct in *specific, observable, measurable* and *behavioural* terms.

2.1 Measurement

Although this definition is not accepted by everyone, Stevens (1946) defined measurement as 'the assignment of numerals to objects or events according to rules' (p. 670). The rules ensure that the relationships among the numbers convey some information about the relationships among the aspects being measured. As shown in Table 2.1, there are four levels of measurement arranged in ascending order according to how much information they convey about the objects or events being measured: 1, nominal; 2, ordinal; 3, interval; 4, ratio (Stevens, 1946).

Table 2.1 Scaling definition and examples.

Scale	Meaningful order?	Equal distance?	Fixed origin?	Examples
Nominal	No	No	No	Assigning numbers to organizational departments: 1=engineering 2=research and development 3=marketing and sales 4=human resources
Ordinal	Yes	No	No	Assigning numbers to ranked employees in terms of performance: 1=Zara (top salesperson) 2=Heinrich (second-highest salesperson) 3=Miko (third-highest salesperson)
Interval	Yes	Yes	No	Having supervisors rate their sales performance
Ratio	Yes	Yes	Yes	Calculating the value of product sold: Zara's annual sales=$500,000 Heinrich's annual sales=$300,000 Miko's annual sales=$250,000

The *nominal* level of measurement simply uses numbers as labels or names. For example, we could assign numbers to differentiate among employees working in different departments within our company), that is, we could label the engineering department '1', the research and development department '2', marketing and sales '3' and human resources '4'. The numbers differentiate these different departments, but they are not meaningful and they do not allow for any other inference: the numbers (1, 2, 3, 4) tell us that the employees are from different departments, but because we are using the numbers solely as labels, the numbers do not represent any particular 'order' or 'size' of these differences. For example, we cannot say that someone who has received a 4 for their department (human resources) is twice as good as an employee who received a 2 for their department (research and development). It simply means that they work in different departments. We can therefore use *any* four numbers to represent these four different departments (e.g. 1, 2, 3, 4 or 100, 200, 300, 400, etc.) and we can put the departments in any order (e.g. 1=marketing and sales, 2=human resources, 3=engineering and 4=research and development).

The *ordinal* level of measurement not only conveys information about similarity/difference, but also information about rank order. For example, we could ask supervisors to rank their employees in terms of their sales performance. If Zara is ranked 1, we know that she is the top salesperson in the company, so she is not only different from the other employees, but she also is doing better than the others. More specifically, we know that she is doing better than Heinrich, who is ranked second-best salesperson in the company, who is doing better than Miko, who is ranked third. Although we can order employees in this way, the ranks do not convey information about how far apart the employees are, nor can we assume that the differences among the ranks are equal. Thus, Zara may exceed Heinrich by $200,000 in sales, whereas Heinrich may only exceed Miko by $50,000. If we have information only on rank order, we only know that Zara did better than Heinrich, who did better than Miko, but we do not know the magnitude of these differences.

The *interval* level of measurement incorporates this notion of magnitude of differences. More precisely, interval scales have the property of equal intervals so that the difference between a score of 1 and a score of 2 is exactly the same as the difference between a score of 3 and a score of 4. Most measures in work psychology have, or are *assumed* to have, an interval level of measurement. For example, when we measure job satisfaction using a five-point scale, we assume that the distance between 4=satisfied and 5=very satisfied is the same as the distance between 1=very dissatisfied and 2=dissatisfied.

Finally, the *ratio* level of measurement not only has equal intervals among the scores, but also has a true zero. A true zero is when a score of 0 means the absence of the quantity being measured (e.g. height, weight). If we go back to our salesperson performance example, we may be able create a ratio scale to rate sales performance. If we quantify performance in terms of the amount of product sold, we can directly compare the employees' performance because sales performance (in terms of dollars) has a true zero point of $0.00. If Zara has annual total sales of $500,000, and Miko has annual total sales of $250,000, we can say that Zara's sales are double the sales of Miko.

Replay

- Constructs can be measured at different *measurement levels*, and these levels vary in terms of their meaning and the sort of information they convey.
- Table 2.1 summarizes the key characteristics of these measurement levels and provides some illustrative examples.

2.2 Classical Test Theory

To return to our initial satisfaction and performance example, let us suppose that we will be measuring performance on a ratio scale (e.g. the number of widgets produced or total sales) and job satisfaction on an interval measurement. Having made these initial decisions about measuring variables, our concern for measurement is by no means finished. Now we can ask how well each of our measures reflects its intended construct. More specifically, we are going to be concerned with the *reliability* and *validity* of our measures. These issues are the domain of what is usually referred to as *classical test theory* (CTT).

Reliability

Whenever we measure any construct at work, it is important for us to have confidence that the test is reliably measured, that is, there has to be some consistency in the score. Imagine a situation in which we tried to measure your personality, but we got a different score every time we measured it. We do not expect personality to change, so we would expect to get the same (or at least similar) scores each time we measure it. If we get too much variability, the measure of personality is said to be unreliable.

The foundation of measurement in (work) psychology for the past 80 years has been CTT. Although there are many formulations of this theory (Kline, 2005), each version has the following basic assumption at its core:

$$X = T + e$$

This equation says that the *observed score* (i.e. X=the actual test score) is equal to the *true score* (i.e. T=the real score) plus some *error component* (i.e. e=aspects of the test score that have nothing to do with one's true score). This fundamental assumption of CTT tells us that our measures of the constructs are not necessarily *perfect* representations of the constructs we are intending to measure: there is error associated with each measurement. For example, if we have decided to measure productivity as the number of widgets produced by a factory worker in an hour, our measure might be subject to a number of sources of variation. It might matter, for example, which hour in the day we measure productivity: our hypothetical worker might produce fewer units in the afternoon following a heavy lunch or may slow down as the day progresses and s/he grows tired. Even worse, these sources of error might be unique to the individual, with some workers being slower in the morning and others starting out quickly but then slowing down.

A host of factors other than job satisfaction might also affect productivity. If, for example, a worker is ill but has come to work anyway (i.e. presenteeism, see Chapter 15), his/her productivity might be impaired. Or perhaps s/he has had a fight with their spouse that morning and is distracted, resulting in decreased productivity. Other individuals may become even more productive in such circumstances as they attempt to 'bury themselves' in their work.

All of these factors – the time of day, the mental and physical state of the employee, individual differences in work patterns – are sources of error. Each of them detracts from the quality of our measurement. When we speak of the *reliability* of our measures, we are talking about the extent to which measurement reflects the 'true' score and is free of these random errors, such that the items consistently measure the same attribute or construct. Essentially, we are asking whether all of the items measure the same thing, and whether the scale measures the same thing over time. We can therefore define reliability in terms of the proportion of true score variance contained in our observed scores (Nunnally & Bernstein, 1994), that is, reliability refers to the stability or dependability of a measure (Kerlinger, 1986) or to the consistency of a measure when a testing procedure is repeated on a population of individuals or groups (American Educational Research Association, American Psychological Association, & National Council on Measurement in Education, 1999).

There is a variety of ways to estimate the reliability of a measure, and each of these methods reflects slightly different perspectives of reliability: (i) test–retest reliability, (ii) alternative forms reliability, (iii) inter-rater reliability and (iv) internal reliability. Table 2.2 presents an overview of these methods.

Table 2.2 Five ways to estimate reliability.

Approach	Assesses...
Test–retest reliability	the degree to which the same test measures the same thing on two different occasions (i.e. the extent to which the test is *consistent*)
Alternative forms reliability	the extent to which two different, but equal, forms of a test measure the same thing (i.e. the extent to which the tests are *equivalent*)
Split-half reliability	the degree to which two halves of the same test measure the same thing (i.e. the extent to which the tests are equivalent)
Inter-rater reliability	the consistency of the observations across different raters (i.e. the extent to which ratings are *similar*)
Internal consistency	the degree to which all of the items in a test are measuring the same thing and are equivalent, typically measured using *Cronbach's alpha*

Test–retest reliability
The simplest form of reliability may have already occurred to you. If we are concerned that a worker's productivity in a single hour might be affected by something else, then we could take more measurements. Perhaps we might measure productivity in the morning as well as in the afternoon. These multiple testing sessions would be an example of *test–retest reliability*, in which identical procedures are used to measure the same construct or variable on two different occasions. The underlying assumption of this approach is that the error components of the score will cancel each other out (because error is assumed to be random), and thus the association between the two time periods is a reflection of the true score variance in the measure. This reliability coefficient is known as the *coefficient of stability* (i.e. the extent to which the scores on the test stabilize over time).

Alternative forms reliability
Another form of reliability used in many areas of psychology is *alternative forms reliability*, in which two different, but equal, forms of the test are developed and compared with each other. It is advantageous to develop alternative ways of measuring behaviour, particularly when measures are reactive (i.e. when people know they are being measured and this knowledge might affect their behaviour). For example, an organization may use a cognitive ability test as part of its selection procedure. It may want to use multiple versions of the same ability test that are

designed to measure the same content, using similar (but not exactly the same) questions at the same level of difficulty. The overall content is similar (in that is measures cognitive ability), but the individual items may differ. Having multiple versions of the selection test may decrease an applicant's ability to cheat using another test, and it may allow an applicant to be tested more than once (without compromising the content of the test). Having two or more forms of the same test is valuable, but it is imperative that the test is comparable in terms of content and difficulty. We can calculate alternative forms reliability by assessing the relationship between scores on two comparable forms of our cognitive ability measure. A high correlation between the two versions would indicate high equivalence of the two forms (i.e. the two forms are equivalent to each other in terms of content).

Inter-rater reliability
Another form of reliability is to calculate the *inter-rater reliability* of a measure in terms of the consistency of the observations across different raters (i.e. the researchers who are measuring the behaviours; Crocker & Algina, 1986). Particularly for behavioural constructs such as productivity, the number of items produced might contain two sources of random error. First, as previously discussed, the worker might be subject to a variety of external influences. The researcher or rater – the person counting the number of widgets produced – is subject to similar errors. Counting is boring and the researcher's attention may stray, s/he may be thinking of other things. In this situation we commonly have two people making observations. The extent to which these two observers (or raters) agree on the behaviour is the inter-rater reliability of the measure.

Internal reliability
An obvious difficulty with both test–retest and alternative forms reliabilities is that they require us to make two sets of measures, which may not be practical in many situations. For example, most companies would not want to repeatedly survey employees in order to assess employee morale or job satisfaction. One solution to this problem is to consider each question on a survey as a test and assess the overall test's *internal reliability*. If we have a 20-item measure of job satisfaction (see Chapter 13), each item can be considered to be a measure of job satisfaction, and we can simply look at how the items relate to one another to determine whether or not the overall test is reliable. If, for example, a worker indicates being very satisfied with his/her job but dissatisfied with his/her tasks then these inconsistent responses might suggest that our measure is unreliable.

We can assess the internal reliability in different ways. If we had 20 items in our measure, we would have a very large number of item pairs to consider. Researchers might choose to split the test into two parts and correlate the two scores. This procedure is known as a *split-half reliability*. Of course, there are a large number of ways to split the test into two. One might, for example, divide the test into the first 10 questions and the last 10 questions, or one might compare the answers to all the even-numbered items to those of all the odd-numbered items.

If we calculated all possible split-halves (i.e. calculated all of the correlations between all possible pairs of items) and then averaged these correlations together, we would obtain a measure of the internal consistency of the tests, that is, the degree to which all of the questions in the set are measuring the same construct. These estimates are called *alpha* coefficients or *Cronbach's alpha* (Cronbach, 1951), and are known as the coefficient of precision (Crocker & Algina, 1986).

Cronbach's alpha ranges from 0 (no reliability) to 1 (complete reliability), and it is by far the most commonly used measure of reliability in work psychology. Because it is based on every item and only requires one administration of one measure at one point in time, it is both comprehensive and easy to calculate. In general, researchers frequently express the view that the scale has acceptable reliability if alpha is equal to or greater than 0.70 (Cortina, 1993). However, Cortina (1993) also goes on to note that unthinking application of this standard is problematic. We must remember that alpha is a function of both the inter-correlations of items and the number of items, so a very long scale could demonstrate an 'acceptable' alpha of 0.70, even if the inter-correlations of items were very low (Schmitt, 1996). Conversely, a scale that has only three items may demonstrate a 'poor' alpha of 0.65 even if the items are quite homogenous. We must therefore take the length of the scale into consideration, and examining the inter-item correlations is always encouraged to ensure that there are no items that demonstrate low correlations with other items. Schmitt (1996) also reminded researchers that alpha is not a measure of the unidimensionality of measure, that is, a measure could have a high reliability, but could still contain multiple subscales. It is therefore important to examine both the inter-item correlations and the factor structure (see below) when examining the internal reliability of a scale. Alpha is typically calculated for continuous items, but Kuder and Richardson (1937) proposed alternative formulae – known as the KR20 and KR21 – that are appropriate for dichotomously scored items (e.g. 0 versus 1).

Replay

- *Reliability* refers to the extent to which measurement reflects the 'true' score and is free of random errors, such that the items consistently measure the same attribute or construct.
- Table 2.2 presents a summary of various approaches to establishing the reliability of a measure.

Validity

As we have previously defined it, reliability is the consistency of test scores. If we have high reliability, then we are reasonably assured that the items on the test are all measuring the same thing. However, we do not yet know exactly *what* that 'thing' is, that is, what construct is being measured by the test or measure? The question of whether or not the test is measuring what we think it is measuring is a question of *validity*.

It is important and necessary to demonstrate that a measure is reliable: Without reliability, we cannot determine validity. But simply having a reliable scale doesn't mean that the scale also is valid: reliability is a *necessary*, but *not sufficient*, condition for validity. It is also necessary to show that the measure captures the essence of the characteristic or attribute being measured. More generally, *validity* refers to the extent to which a measure actually assesses what it claims to assess (i.e. the degree to which the inferences made about a measure are legitimate; Cronbach, 1971).

Before using any set of measurements, it is essential to demonstrate that the measurements lead to valid inferences about the characteristic or construct under study. Although there are a variety of strategies for assessing the validity of any given measure, ultimately they are all trying to establish the same thing – whether or not the test is actually measuring what we think it is measuring (American Educational Research Association et al., 1999; Binning & Barrett, 1989). There are essentially two types of validation strategies: (i) validation strategies based on the content of the test and (ii) validation strategies based on the relationship between a test and other variables.

Test content strategies
Using *content validation strategies* involves logical and empirical analyses of how well the contents of the test represent the intended construct. For example, if you administered a test of aviation knowledge to a group of military personnel who had just completed pilot training, you would expect all the questions on the test to deal with the course content (i.e. weather, radio communications, airport indicator codes and aerodynamics) and not include questions on extraneous information, such as financial management. One method that is often used to assess or develop content validity in a test is to have experts review and evaluate the items. The researcher creates a set of potential items that are then reviewed by experts. The experts may be provided with a formal definition of the construct and asked to indicate which of the items represents the intended construct. Only those items that elicit a high level of agreement or endorsement by the experts are included in the final measure.

Variable relationships strategies
Another way to establish the validity of a measure is by assessing how scores on the measure relate to other variables. For example, if we create a new measure of job satisfaction, we might have a group of individuals complete both our measure and a pre-existing, well-established measure, such as the job satisfaction scale (Spector, 1997). If our new scale truly measures job satisfaction, then scores on both should be highly correlated. Correlating a scale with other measures of the same construct is typically referred to as a *construct validation strategy*.

Of course, often there are no comparable scales that measure the construct we want to assess. Indeed, sometimes we are developing scales simply because nobody else has developed the measure that we need. In this case, we can also compare our measure with existing scales of important outcomes (or criteria) to determine whether or not we are measuring the right thing. For example, if we are developing a measure of job satisfaction, we know that job satisfaction is related to turnover intent (Tett & Meyer, 1993) and to health (Faragher, Cass, & Cooper, 2005). If our new measure really measures job satisfaction, then it should be correlated with both turnover intent and health. This strategy is known as criterion-referenced validation strategy. If we gather the outcome measures at the same time as our satisfaction measure, it is known as *concurrent validation*. Alternatively, if we measure job satisfaction now, and then measure health and turnover intentions in the future (e.g. in 6 months), this is known as *predictive validation*.

Of course, simply correlating our measure with one outcome provides only very limited evidence for the validity of our scale. Cronbach and Meehl (1955) articulated the notion of a nomological network, which is widely used in work psychology to establish the validity of new measures. A nomological network is a series of propositions about how constructs are related and how measures are related to the constructs. It is a chain of inferences that must be satisfied in order to validate a measure. For example, we can construct a nomological network around job satisfaction. We would expect it to be positively related to certain variables (e.g. job engagement) and may be predicted by certain job and work factors (e.g. having a supportive boss or having control over one's work). Additionally, we can create hypotheses about how our construct may be related to certain groups. We might believe, for example, that managers would be more satisfied with their jobs than front-line production workers.

Replay

- *Validity* is the extent to which a test is measuring what it claims to measure.
- *Content validation strategies* are based on either logical or empirical analyses of how well the contents of the test represent the intended construct.
- *Construct validation strategies* involve different methods of assessing the extent to which the measure is related to other measures of the same construct, similar constructs or other theoretically relevant constructs.
- *Criterion-related validation strategies (concurrent and predictive validation)* involve assessing how scores on the measure relate to outcomes, such as job performance and employee well-being.
- A nomological network involves a series of propositions about how constructs are interrelated.

Problems in establishing validity

There are at least three basic problems we face in attempting to show that our measures are valid: (i) construct deficiency, (ii) construct contamination (see Figure 2.1) and (iii) common method variance. *Construct deficiency* occurs when our measure does not measure the entirety of the intended construct. For example, if you were writing a test on the contents of this book, but all the questions were based on this chapter on research methods, the test would demonstrate construct deficiency. Scores on such a test would not be a valid measure of your knowledge of work psychology.

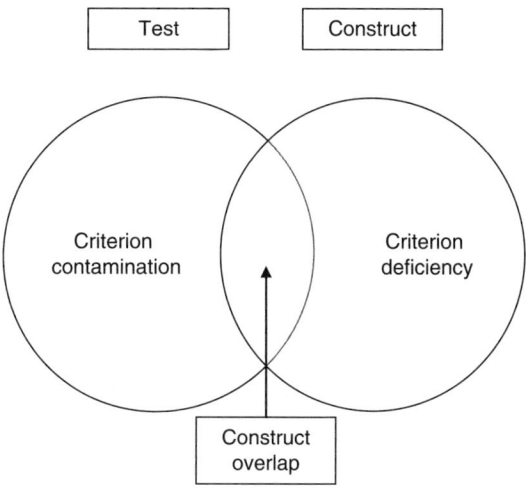

Figure 2.1 Criterion contamination and criterion deficiency.

Construct contamination is when we measure something other than the intended construct. An interesting study by Brief, Houston and Roberson (1995) illustrates this notion of construct contamination in measures. They conducted a survey of employee morale containing a measure of job satisfaction. Employees were asked to come in groups to a specific room in the building to complete the survey. The researchers also arranged that some employees received cookies and others did not. They found that employees who received cookies reported higher levels of job satisfaction than employees who did not get cookies. These results suggest that the measure of job satisfaction was actually measuring something else (e.g. positive affect or positive mood), not strictly job satisfaction.

Perhaps the most troubling form of construct contamination in work psychology is the issue of common method variance (CMV). CMV occurs when relationships can be explained, in part, by *how* the data were collected rather than true relationships among constructs (Campbell & Fiske, 1959). It is a particular concern in work psychology research because many of the variables we study in work psychology are measured through self-report measures. For example, measures of job satisfaction, stress, perceptions of leaders and reports of employee motivation all are typically collected using a survey or some form of self-report measure. It is possible that other factors, such as mood, personality traits (such as negative affectivity) or other construct-irrelevant factors are being measured in addition to the constructs we intend to measure. For example, compared to pessimists, optimists may tend to rate satisfaction as high, stress as being low and their leaders as being capable and trustworthy, *regardless* of the actual, 'true' levels of all of these variables. The measured relationships among these concepts become inflated because optimism is related to all three of these variables.

The extent to which CMV is a serious issue in work psychology research is debatable. Some researchers argue that the potential for CMV virtually invalidates the use of self-report measures and many scientific journals are increasingly reluctant to accept papers wherein the data are collected solely through self-report.

> ### Work Psychology in Action: Modern psychometric theory
>
> Classical test theory (CTT) focuses on the use of 'tests' (i.e. collections of items) to estimate the true score of individuals. In contrast, modern psychometric theory (more commonly called *item response theory*, IRT) focuses on individual items to derive an estimate of the true score. Specifically, IRT uses the known properties of items to estimate an individual's true score on a given test.
>
> Although simpler models are often used, a common IRT model uses three parameters to estimate the individual's probability of getting a given item 'correct'. The *item difficulty parameter* reflects how hard the item is. For example, on a vocabulary test an item that asked you to define 'antidisestablishmentarianism' tends to be more difficult than an item that asks you to define the word 'flower'. The second parameter is the *item discrimination parameter*, which reflects the extent to which an item differentiates between individuals who are 'high' and 'low' on a given trait. Finally, IRT models may use a third parameter, the *guessing parameter*, which reflects the extent to which an item can be guessed. On a multiple-choice test in which every item has four response options, random guessing should result in 25% correct answers.
>
> IRT uses these parameters to estimate individual ability. One of the most useful applications of IRT has been the development of tailored testing or computer-adaptive testing. Using computers to administer the test, test-takers are given an initial item. Given their response (i.e. correct or incorrect), the program calculates an estimate of the individual's ability and the second item is chosen based on this initial estimate (i.e. if they get the answer correct, the second item will be more difficult; if they get it wrong, the second item will be easier). The answer to the second question is used to refine the ability estimate and determines the difficulty of the third item, and this process is continued to the end of the test. Adaptive testing is efficient in that an accurate measure of ability can be made with fewer questions than would be typically used in traditional tests. For those interested in this approach, Kline (2005) presents a more elaborate discussion of classical versus modern psychometric theory.

Other researchers argue that the potential effects of CMV are vastly overstated and that there is little evidence for its effects (Spector, 1987, 2006). At this point, the best strategy may be to follow the recommendations of Podsakoff, MacKenzie, Lee and Podsakoff (2003), who outline methodological and statistical approaches to testing for or minimizing the effects of CMV (see also Lance, Dawson, Birkelbach, & Hoffman, 2010).

The third problem in validating a scale using a nomological network (i.e. in terms of relationships among variables) is that validation of the scale and validation of the theory are inextricably linked. For example, you may hypothesise that your scale measuring X should be related to Y, and conduct a study testing this relationship as evidence for the validity of your scale using a measure of Y that has previously been shown to possess high validity. If you fail to find a relationship between X and Y, there are three possible explanations: (i) your measure of X is not really a measure of X, (ii) the hypothesis that X should be related to Y is wrong or (iii) both your measure is invalid and the theory is wrong! The challenge in doing validity studies is that we cannot disentangle these three explanations. There is no easy solution to this dilemma: The best that researchers can do is to design high-quality studies based on solid theory, using a strong research design to minimize alternative explanations.

Replay

- *Construct deficiency* occurs when the measure does not measure the entirety of the intended construct.
- *Construct contamination* occurs when the test measures something else other than the intended construct.
- Common method variance (CMV) occurs when relationships can be explained, in part, by *how* the data were collected rather than true relationships among constructs (Campbell & Fiske, 1959). It is a particular concern in work psychology research because many of the variables we study in work psychology are measured through self-report measures.

2.3 Research Design

Now that we have established reliable and valid measures of job satisfaction and performance, let us return to the original question. How would you test the hypothesis that happy workers are productive workers? Several options are readily apparent. One option may involve surveying employees at a given company to obtain job satisfaction scores and then consulting company records to obtain measures of performance. Another option may be to bring students into the laboratory and have them do a task on which we can obtain a measure of performance under satisfying (e.g. good pay, considerate supervision, pleasant environment) and dissatisfying (e.g. poor pay, abusive supervision, unpleasant environment) conditions. Finally, a third option involves a cross-national study where we collect nationwide measures of job satisfaction and correlate them with an index of national productivity such as gross domestic product.

Each of these options will generate an answer to the question of whether or not job satisfaction is related to productivity. Each of the answers generated will have both strengths and weaknesses. For example, the first option (i.e. a survey) is based on 'real' data in an organization and therefore, maximizes the realism of the situation. The laboratory option allows us to be more precise and control multiple variables affecting satisfaction, whereas the cross-national options help ensure that the results represent the entire population. Your job as the researcher is to use theory and past research to help you decide which factors are most important when designing the study to examine your research question.

Research design requirements

McGrath (1981) identified three key requirements of research design that we want to achieve when conducting our research: precision, existential realism and generalizability. Precision involves control over the variables in the study and other aspects of the study setting. Existential realism is the extent to which the design uses 'real' tasks (e.g. actual team performance in an organization) rather than artificial tasks (e.g. a fake team created in a laboratory situation solely for the purpose of the study). Related to the realism of the study is generalizability, or the extent to which the results from the study can be generalized to the population.

McGrath (1981) argued that these three features (precision, existential realism and generalizability) pose a three-horned dilemma for researchers. This dilemma means that, in any given research project, we can maximize one of the three criteria, but we always do so at the expense of the other two. Somewhat tongue in cheek, McGrath concludes that it is not possible to do 'good' research, that is, it is not possible for a researcher to design a study that simultaneously maximizes all three of the criteria. A somewhat more reasoned approach would suggest that each research design has strengths and weaknesses, and researchers should choose the design that best suits their purpose.

Designs that maximize precision

The precision of research design refers to the degree to which a researcher has control over the variables in the study and other aspects of the study setting. Three typical designs that aim to maximize precision are the laboratory experiment, the field experiment and the quasi-experiment.

Laboratory experiments
In many ways a laboratory experiment is often thought of as the gold standard for researchers. Laboratory experiments maximize precision and control over variables and allow researchers to isolate causal mechanisms among the variables under investigation. Classically, we think of three conditions for causality. In order for A to cause B, (i) A and B must covary, (ii) A must precede B in time and (iii) these conditions must hold, controlling for all other variables (Shadish, Cook, & Campbell, 2002). Laboratory experiments achieve these three conditions through random assignment to conditions and manipulation of variables. Thus, in an experiment researchers create at least two conditions or groups: one group receives the treatment and the other does not. The only difference between the conditions is the variable under investigation, referred to as the independent

variable. Random assignment means that every individual has an equal probability of being assigned to each condition. For two groups, one might flip a coin to determine to which group an individual is assigned. Because the study is conducted in a laboratory, the researcher can control all extraneous variables that might affect the outcome of the study.

In giving the researcher this amount of control over the environment, laboratory experiments sacrifice both existential realism and generalizability. Laboratory studies often use artificial tasks and are unable to duplicate all the conditions of a real workplace, thereby sacrificing existential realism. Some of the phenomena experienced in the workplace may not be easily replicated in a laboratory setting for several reasons, such as lack of feasibility (e.g. examining the effects of chronic long-term fatigue on well-being) or ethical reasons (e.g. creating injuries or having an abusive or aggressive colleague). At the same time, the generalizability of laboratory studies – particularly those studies that use student participants as opposed to real workers – is frequently called into question. Indeed, many academic journals that publish research in work psychology refuse to publish data from laboratory studies that use student participants. This concern may be overstated in that many findings derived from laboratory investigations do appear to generalize to organizations (Locke, 1986; Mitchell, 2012). Moreover, laboratory studies in work psychology appear more likely to generalize than do laboratory studies in other areas of psychology (Mitchell, 2012). Nonetheless, true laboratory experiments are not commonly used in work psychology as a result of these concerns.

Field experiments
The basic logic of the experiment does not, however, require a laboratory study. One could conduct a true experiment in which participants are randomly assigned to conditions and variables are manipulated in organizations using real employees as participants. Such field experiments are often held up as the example of an ideal study in work psychology. Because they are based on the same principles as laboratory experiments, such designs allow for causal inference and allow the researcher a great deal of precision and control, although perhaps not as much as in a laboratory experiment. Often, researchers find that they do not have the control that they would have had in a laboratory experiment simply because the study is occurring in a real organization where other events (e.g. layoffs, reorganizations) may influence study results.

Moreover, because the studies occur in work and organizations, existential realism is enhanced. On the other hand, because employees are in their actual work environment, the demands of their jobs or other considerations at work may result in them dropping out of the study before it is completed. Thus, although field experiments have become very popular methods of research in work psychology, subject attrition remains one of the biggest concerns for this type of design (Shadish, 2002).

Field experiments are real experiments that occur in work and organizations. They therefore enhance both precision and existential realism, but the generalizability of such experiments may be questionable. Typically, the logistic requirements of conducting a field experiment mean that researchers only conduct such studies within certain companies. As you might gather, the organization must be 'research friendly' in order to allow researchers to implement random assignment and experimental control. One might legitimately suspect that such organizations may differ in some fundamental ways from other organizations and that the results obtained from a field experiment might not replicate or generalize to another organization.

> ### Work Psychology in Action: Evaluating a workplace incivility programme
>
> Workplace incivility is a growing problem in organizations. Although much is known about the prevalence, nature and consequences of uncivil behaviour in organizations, until recently little was known about what to do about this problem. Leiter, Laschinger, Day and Gilin (2011) reported on an intervention called CREW: civility, respect and engagement at work.
>
> To evaluate the CREW programme, the authors used a quasi-experimental design. Employees in 41 existing hospital units participated in the study and completed questionnaires before and after the intervention. Although 41 units participated, the intervention was conducted in only eight units. Leiter and colleagues (2011) reported that the eight treatment units reported improvements in civility, respect, cynicism, job satisfaction, trust in management and absence that were larger than any changes observed in the non-treatment units.
>
> The design of the study is considered to be quasi-experimental because it incorporates an intervention, but it uses intact groups (i.e. the work units) rather than randomly assigning participants to conditions.

Quasi-experiments
Similar to laboratory or field experiments, a quasi-experiment involves manipulation of a variable (such as leadership training). Also similar to field experiments, quasi-experiments in work psychology typically take place within a real organization, thereby enhancing the realism of the design. The principal difference between field and quasi-experimental designs is that the researcher is not able to assign participants to conditions in quasi-experiments. Rather, quasi-experiments are often conducted with intact groups. One might, for example, implement a new training programme in one area of the organization but not in another and then compare the two groups to see if the new training was effective. The inability to form groups using random assignment, however, makes the quasi-experiment vulnerable to a number of threats (Cook, Campbell, & Peraccio, 1990) to what is often called the *internal validity* of the study. Internal validity is the ability to draw a causal inference from a given design.

Field experiments and quasi-experiments move us toward optimizing two criteria. They offer some degree of existential realism because they frequently take place in actual organizations rather than in laboratories. Although these studies occur in more realistic settings, they may also require participating in activities (e.g. training, group discussions) that are not normally part of the workplace. They also offer us some degree of precision and control, although it is not possible to exert the same control in a field study as one does in a laboratory. Field experiments and quasi-experiments, like true laboratory experiments, may not be generalizable as they are typically implemented within one organization.

Replay

- The three key features of research design are precision, existential realism and generalizability.
- These three features present a three-horned dilemma for researchers: in any given research project, one of the three criteria can be maximized, but only at the expense of the other two.
- *Precision* refers to the degree to which the variables and the research setting are under the control of a researcher. For example, precision will be high in randomized experiments that are conducted in a laboratory setting because in these types of studies virtually all aspects of the study are under the control of the researcher.
- In *laboratory experiments* researchers use random assignment to conditions and manipulate the independent variables in order to maximize precision and control over variables and allow researchers to isolate causal mechanisms among the variables under investigation.
- *Field experiments* are similar to laboratory experiments in that participants are randomly assigned to conditions and variables are manipulated. However, they are conducted in organizations and work sites using real employees as participants. They may have as much control as laboratory experiments because other events (e.g. layoffs, reorganizations) may influence the study results.
- *Quasi-experiments* are similar to both laboratory and field experiments in that they involve the manipulation of a variable. Also, similar to field experiments, they typically take place within a real organization. However, instead of assigning participants to conditions, quasi-experiments are often conducted with intact, pre-existing groups.

Designs that maximize generalizability

The generalizability of research design refers to the extent to which the results from the study can be generalized to the population. A typical design that aims to maximize generalizability is the (longitudinal) survey design.

Surveys
Generalizability is enhanced when one carefully collects data from a sample of individuals that is explicitly designed to provide precise estimates of the population parameters. In work psychology, such studies are typically conducted as surveys that use probability sampling. Probability sampling requires that each member of the population has some known and non-zero probability of being

sampled. For example, if we want to generalize our results to all employees of a given company, we would start with a complete list of all employees (i.e. the population). We would then determine which employees would receive our survey by some form of probability sampling.

The simplest probability sampling strategy that can be used is probably *random sampling*. In random sampling each member of the population has an equal and independent probability of being selected into the sample. Typically a random number table, or its digital equivalent, is used to form a random sample. Although easy to implement, random sampling has some disadvantages. Most importantly, random sampling may fail to capture groups that are in the population, especially if the groups are relatively small. For example, in a survey of hospital employees, the population might consist of 1,900 female employees and only 100 male employees. Constructing a simple random sample of 200 employees might well result in a final sample in which male employees are seriously under-represented. In such a situation, researchers will often construct a stratified random sample. In *stratified sampling*, the population is divided into strata or groups and researchers randomly sample from within each group to ensure that the sample represents the population in terms of group make-up. For the example given above, we might divide the population into female employees ($n=1,900$) and male employees ($n=100$). Female employees represent 95% of the sample, with male employees representing the remaining 5%. To construct a sample of 200 employees we would want to ensure that 95% of the sample ($n=190$) was female with the remaining 5% ($n=10$) male.

Surveys that use probability sampling are useful in work psychology because they allow us to determine the prevalence of the phenomenon in which we are interested. For example, one might wish to know how many people in a given population experience workplace violence or workplace aggression (see Schat, Frone, & Kelloway, 2006). Probability sampling would be appropriate in this situation. However, questions of prevalence or incidence are comparatively rare in work psychology prevalence: typically, researchers are more interested in the relationship among variables than they are in the absolute prevalence of a given experience. As a result, the use of probability samples in work psychology is comparatively rare.

In contrast, surveys that are based on non-probability samples comprise the single most widely used design in work psychology research. Non-probability samples are those in which some members of the population have no chance of being in the sample. For example, when we survey all the employees of one firm, this is a non-probability sample of the national workforce. Members of the population who do not work for our target company have no chance of being in the sample. Note that the determination of whether the survey is based on probability or non-probability sampling is based on two considerations: (i) how the sample was selected and (ii) the population to which you wish to generalize. Thus, a stratified random sample of hospital employees is a probability sample for that organization, but a non-probability sample if one wishes to generalize to all healthcare employees, including those working for other healthcare organizations.

Much research in work psychology uses a *non-probability* or *convenience sample*. The researchers typically get permission to survey the employees of one organization. We refer to this as a convenience sample because the organization may not be selected according to the goals of the research. Rather, the organization is selected purely because it is agreeable to participating in the research.

Surveys are designed to generate generalizable results and no matter how carefully the researcher constructs a sample, there are always individuals who, for whatever reason, chose not to respond to an invitation to participate in the survey. Researchers are understandably concerned with response rates – the percentage of invited individuals who actually respond to a survey. A low response rate can invalidate the most carefully defined sampling strategy. As a result, researchers often implement strategies designed to increase response rate. Researchers might, for example, send multiple reminders to potential respondents reminding them to complete and return the survey. Researchers also frequently offer incentives for participating in the survey (e.g. a small payment or entry into a lottery for a prize).

Baruch and Holtom (2008) found that response rates for individuals in organizational research averaged around 50%. However, there was a large range to their estimate and response rates of 20% or 30% in organizational research are certainly not uncommon. Although researchers still debate the minimum acceptable response rate, there is widespread agreement that one should try to get the maximum number of responses in any given study. Researchers often try to encourage individuals to respond by using incentives and reminders. Baruch and Holtom found that incentives and reminders were unrelated to response rates. Nonetheless, both strategies are widely used in work psychology research.

The general concern with low response rates is the introduction of *non-response bias*. Non-response bias occurs when people who choose to not participate in a survey differ from those who choose to participate in some relevant fashion. Thus, in a study of work–family conflict, it is possible that only parents of small children choose to participate whereas single people without children do not. The resulting sample may represent only a subset (employees with children) of the intended population (all employees).

The extent to which a low response rate is a problem for survey research is partially a function of the type of sampling strategy used. As previously mentioned, a low response rate can invalidate a probability-based sampling scheme and, as a result, the sample results may not be at all representative of the population. It is unclear whether or not a low response rate has any effect on the generalizability of non-probability based samples. If we choose to use a convenience sample that does not necessarily represent a population in any meaningful sense, the response rate may not be critical so even with a 100% response rate, the sample is still unrepresentative of the population.

Aside from sampling issues, at least two issues are raised as concerns with surveys in work psychology. First, as discussed in the section on measurement, surveys often rely on self-report measures and therefore may be influenced by CMV. Second, researchers who use surveys are quick to acknowledge that a survey design often does not allow for causal inference. This limitation follows from the use of a cross-sectional design in which survey data are collected at one time period (snapshot approach). As you will recall, causality requires covariation (i.e. correlation), temporal order and control for *all* possible confounding variables. A cross-sectional survey allows us to establish covariation (i.e. that A is correlated with B), but it does not allow us to establish the remaining two conditions for causality (although strong theory can help us hypothesise the order of relationships and controls).

A longitudinal survey, however, in which data are collected at different points in time, may allow us to establish the temporal ordering of variables (e.g. does A come before B). Establishing temporal order simply means that the predictor must occur before the outcome. In the case of specific events this is fairly straightforward. For example, if we want to determine whether a salary increase reduces absenteeism, it is easy to determine when the salary increase occurred and to compare absenteeism before and after the increase. In the case of psychological variables (e.g. job satisfaction, motivation; see Chapter 13), establishing temporal order is a little more difficult because the time of measurement does not necessarily coincide with the time of occurrence. For example, if employees' job satisfaction is *measured* today that does not mean that job satisfaction was *caused* today; it could very well be due to events that occurred in the past. Indeed, there are some data suggesting substantial stability in job satisfaction over years (Staw & Ross, 1985).

Perhaps the most commonly used longitudinal research design in organizational research is the two-wave panel design in which a group of employees (i.e. the panel) answer a survey comprising the same measures at each of two time periods (Kelloway & Francis, 2012). By controlling for the stability of measures across time, researchers are able to determine which variable precedes a change in the other.

Although the two-wave panel design continues to be used in work psychology research, it is increasingly recognized that it is beneficial for longitudinal research to have at least three waves of data collection (Rogosa, 1995). Including at least three waves of data collection allows researchers to understand how variables change over time and leads to better causal inference (Kelloway & Francis, 2012; Ployhart & Vandenberg, 2010). Despite these advantages, two-wave panel designs continue to be a useful and popular approach in work psychology.

In their review, Ployhart and Vandenberg (2010) suggested that longitudinal research can be used in two ways in organizational research. Descriptive longitudinal research is focused on 'how a phenomenon changes over time' (p. 99). Thus, we might ask how the individual experience of stress or individual levels of motivation change from day to day (or even within the day). On the other hand, 'explanatory longitudinal research seeks to identify the cause of the change process by the use of one or more substantive predictor variables' (Ployhart & Vandenberg, 2010, p. 99), that is, the purpose of explanatory research is to predict the changes in a variable over time.

Well-conducted surveys offer the researcher generalizability at the expense of both precision and existential realism. Although the use of longitudinal survey designs can enhance precision (although not to the same level as in an experiment), existential realism remains a problem for survey research. Respondents are doing something 'artificial' (i.e. completing an often lengthy questionnaire) and are often asked to recall events or moods over a long period of time. For example, we might ask survey respondents to think about how satisfied they have been with their job over the last six months. It is not clear that we can give an accurate answer to such a question, particularly if job satisfaction varies from day to day, or within days.

Replay

- *Generalizability* is related to the realism of the study, and it refers the extent to which the results from the study can be generalized to the population.
- Generalizability is enhanced when one carefully collects data from a sample of individuals that is explicitly designed to provide precise estimates of the population parameters. In work psychology, such studies are typically conducted as *surveys* that use probability sampling. Probability sampling requires that each member of the population has some known and non-zero probability of being sampled. For example, if we want to generalize our results to all employees of a given company, we would start with a complete list of all employees (i.e. the population). We would then determine which employees would receive our survey by some form of probability sampling.
- There are different types of probability sampling strategies. The simplest form is *random sampling*, in which each member of the population has an equal and independent chance of being selected, but this may under-represent some groups. In *stratified sampling*, the population is divided into groups (for example based on age, gender or ethnicity) and researchers randomly sample from within each group to ensure that the sample represents the population in terms of group make-up.
- *Non-probability* or *convenience samples* are samples in which some members of the population have no chance of being selected. For example, if we survey employees from an international company, but only sample from workplaces in one country, the sample is a non-probability sample of the entire company.
- *Longitudinal surveys* involve collecting data at different points in time, which may help us to establish the temporal order of variables (i.e. the predictor occurs before the outcome).
- Researchers still debate the minimum acceptable *response rate*, but there is widespread agreement that one should try to maximize the number of responses. *Non-response bias* is a concern of low response rates, and it occurs when people who choose not to participate in a survey differ from those who choose to participate in some relevant fashion.

Designs that maximize existential realism

Throughout this chapter we have focused on quantitative research methodologies in which issues of measurement, reliability, validity and the ability to test predictions are paramount concerns. However, there is also a broad domain of qualitative research in which a common aim is to develop thick, rich descriptions of a given situation in order to understand what it is really like to be in that situation. For example, to learn what it was like to become a police officer, John Van Maanen actually joined the police force and went through training (Van Maanen, Dabbs, & Faulkner, 1982). In this chapter we will consider four ways of maximizing existential realism. Three are qualitative approaches (the interview, focus groups and observation methods) and one (experience sampling) is a quantitative approach to the same issue.

As one might expect, interviews simply involve asking people questions about their experience. Interviews can range from very structured – with every question predetermined and asked of every interviewee – to very unstructured (with questions that might change for each participant). In his widely cited work on the long interview, McCracken (1988) advocated starting with a few 'grand tour' questions (i.e. broad open-ended questions) and then following up on promising avenues of enquiry with each participant. Thus, in a workplace setting, one might begin with a broad question such as 'Tell me what it is like to work here' with subsequent questions designed to draw out particular themes or follow up on points made in the initial response.

> ### Work Psychology in Action: Organizational restructuring
>
> In times of economic uncertainty, it is common for organizations to restructure, resulting in layoffs and downsizing. Not surprisingly, there is a large research literature on the effects of being a 'victim' of such layoffs. There is also a large literature on the 'survivors' of layoffs. However, Wright and Barling (1998) noted that little is known about the 'executioners' of layoffs and set out to describe what it was like to be a manager who had to implement layoffs.
>
> To do so, they conducted semi-structured interviews with 10 senior managers who had been responsible for layoffs. They recruited participants from an executive training centre and purposively constructed a sample comprising representatives from both public and private sector firms. They tried to include both male and female informants, and each informant had to have personally told people that they were to be let go. Wright and Barling conducted semi-structured long interviews with informants and found that they reported increased professional demands, role overload and a search for meaning as well as an increased sense of social isolation at work. These results shed the first light on what it is like to be responsible for layoffs in organizations.

A common experience in conducting interviews is that the researcher becomes overwhelmed with the amount of text that results. Even with a small number of interviewees (e.g. 10), it is quite possible to generate several hundred pages of transcribed interview material that then has to be coded and analysed. Although there are no concrete guidelines as to how many interviews to conduct in a given project, it is generally recommended that interviewers use purposive sampling (i.e. interview people with different perspectives on an issue). For example, if you are conducting a workplace study, you would want to interview people at different levels in the organizational hierarchy (e.g. workers, supervisors, managers), with different levels of organizational tenure, and both male and female workers. The intent is not to generate a statistical representation of the population but rather to capture different perspectives on the problem of interest. Interview researchers also frequently continue to collect data until they have reached saturation point, that is, they continue to collect data until additional interviews are not contributing new themes or insights into the situation.

In some sense, *focus groups* can be thought of as a group interview. Focus groups typically involve six to ten participants who are asked to discuss issues of interest. They are most useful when researchers want to collect a variety of perspectives on an issue or when it is thought that the group interaction may result in additional insights. In a given project, researchers might conduct multiple focus groups, with participants in each group sharing some common characteristics. For example, focus groups might be conducted with supervisors, executives and several groups of employees to understand the operations of a given company. By sampling across different organizational levels (executives, supervisors, employees), a more complete picture of company operations can be captured.

Observational studies also aim to provide rich descriptions of the environment. Unlike interviews or focus groups, data collection does not rely on asking people about their experiences but instead relies on direct observation of an environment. For example, if you wanted to know what it was like to work in a given factory, you could simply go to the factory and observe how employees interact and go about their duties. Such observations often result in reactivity, whereby the presence of the observer changes the behaviour. Alternative techniques of observation might involve using video recording or photographs as less intrusive means of observing an environment. Participant observation is a particularly powerful form of observation in which the researcher becomes both a participant and an observer. For example, one might learn what it is like to work in a factory by getting a job there. Typically you would not reveal yourself to be an observer (i.e. you would present yourself as a regular employee), thereby minimizing problems of reactivity.

Of course, quantitative techniques can also be used to maximize realism. The experience sampling methodology, for example, is designed to collect data on everyday experiences and events. As Bolger, Davis and Rafaeli (2003) phrased it, the use of this type of methodology is designed to capture 'life as it is lived' (p. 579). Experience sampling is a method of data collection in which participants are assessed at repeated moments over the course of time while functioning in their natural settings. Experience sampling studies typically ask individuals to complete measures (either surveys or physiological measures) multiple times. For example, respondents might be contacted multiple times in a day, or once a day for a week, or once a week for a month. In essence, experience sampling becomes a short-term longitudinal study. Although most research on the subjective experience of work has relied on single-time, self-report measures that are vulnerable to such methodological problems as memory biases (Scollon, Kim-Prieto, & Diener, 2003; Smyth & Stone, 2003), experience sampling offers the potential to overcome these difficulties. It has distinct advantages over laboratory assessments, global surveys or observer ratings.

Advances in technology have facilitated the use of experience sampling studies. As noted below, Fullagar and Kelloway (2009) used personal digital assistants

(PDAs) to collect data and other studies have used pagers or even mobile phones to conduct experience sampling studies. Although useful, these devices also require additional planning on the part of the researcher to ensure that they are compatible with the survey format and that participants know how to use them. On the other hand, a growing number of people now carry smartphones, which makes the use of internet-based surveys increasingly convenient.

> ### Work Psychology in Action: Examining flow in a diary design
>
> A core construct in positive psychology (see also Chapter 19) is the notion of 'flow' – the experience of being totally involved in a task. Flow has been most frequently studied in voluntary activities but is also frequently reported at work. Fullagar and Kelloway (2009) used an experience sampling approach to study the experience of flow among architecture students doing their laboratory or practical experience.
>
> Fullagar and Kelloway (2009) gave 40 students hand-held personal digital assistants (PDAs, in this case Palm Pilots) that they were required to carry during the study period. The PDAs were programmed to beep at two random times during each of three specified laboratory periods. When the PDA beeped, students were asked to complete the task in which they were engaged and then to complete a short survey administered on the PDA. This procedure was repeated throughout the semester until each individual had completed 25 surveys.
>
> Although Fullagar and Kelloway used these data to examine the connection among work conditions, flow and well-being, the study also illustrates important characteristics of experience sampling. Although only 40 individuals participated, the study comprised 1,000 data points (25 per participant). The small number of participants raises questions about generalizability, but the large number of observations allows for a detailed understanding of the phenomenon of flow.

Secondary research

Although it does not fit neatly into McGrath's (1981) framework, it should be noted that organizational researchers often rely on secondary data in their investigations. Secondary data are data that are collected by others, often for different purposes. For example, many organizations regularly conduct employee attitude surveys and rather than administering a new survey a researcher may be able to access and use the data that have already been collected. Organizations also keep detailed records on absenteeism, performance and other variables that might be useful for research purposes and these data can be accessed from the records rather than by collecting new data.

There are some obvious advantages to using secondary (collected by others) rather than primary (collected by the researchers) data. Secondary data are often readily available and cheaper to obtain than primary data. However, there are also limitations to the use of secondary data. Perhaps most importantly, secondary data may not be focused specifically on the researchers' questions or may not measure a construct in the way that a researcher would desire.

Meta-analysis is also a common use of secondary data (Hunter, Schmidt, & Jackson, 1982). In many areas of enquiry there is a long history of research. For example, over 30 years ago Locke (1976) noted that there were already over 5,000 studies dealing with job satisfaction. Many of these studies have dealt with the association between job satisfaction and job performance (see Chapter 13). Rather than conducting yet another study on this issue, it is possible to combine the results of all of these studies. This approach results in a stronger conclusion about the relationship than would data from any single study.

Meta-analyses and other uses of secondary data are increasingly common in organizational research. Like primary data, such studies are subject to the same constraints noted by Locke (1976). Thus, using data from organizational records enhances existential realism and meta-analysis tends to enhance generalizability. At the same time, such techniques do not resolve the dilemmas noted by McGrath (1981) – the use of secondary data is not a cure-all but it can be a valuable technique for organizational researchers.

Replay

- *Existential realism* is the extent to which the design uses real tasks, such as real team performance on a job, or artificial tasks, such as fake team performance on a task in a laboratory situation.
- *Focus groups* can be viewed as a type of group interview typically involving six to ten participants who are asked to discuss issues of interest. They are most useful when researchers want to collect a variety of perspectives on an issue or when it is thought that the group interaction may result in additional insights.
- *Observational studies* typically rely on direct observation of an environment, although the presence of the observer may change the behaviour of those being observed (i.e. reactivity). Alternatively, other techniques of observation may be less intrusive (e.g. video recording).
- *Experience sampling studies* typically involve repeatedly assessing participants (through surveys or physiological measures) in their natural settings.
- *Secondary data* may offer both advantages and limitations for organizational researchers.

2.4 Conclusions

In this chapter we have discussed several major aspects of doing research in work psychology. In the first half of this chapter we addressed the importance of first identifying, defining and operationalizing the constructs in work psychology research. We highlighted two major characteristics of measures in work psychology: (i) reliability (the extent to which the same thing is consistently measured) and (ii) validity (the extent to which we are measuring what we intended to measure). Reliability is a *necessary*, but *not sufficient*, condition for validity. Scales that are not reliable cannot, by definition, be valid. However, reliability in and of itself does not guarantee that the scale is valid. It is important to remember that there are different types of reliability: assessing stability over time, equivalence of two measures or two halves of the same measure, and the internal consistency of the items. However, although there are different methods of establishing the validity of a scale, validity always defined as measuring what we intend to measure. It is important to gather multiple evidences of the validity of a scale to ensure that it truly measures what it claims to measure. Reliable and valid measurement is the basis for all research in work psychology.

In the second part of this chapter, we have addressed research methods and designs. All methods of research in work psychology offer some significant advantages as well as some significant disadvantages. Laboratory experiments maximize precision but may not be generalizable or realistic. Experience sampling studies maximize existential realism but may not be generalizable. Surveys may be generalizable but lack precision and existential realism. McGrath (1981) describes this situation as a three-horned dilemma in which a researcher always has to sacrifice one goal in order to achieve another. There does not appear to be an easy resolution to this dilemma in the confines of a single study. However, by using different designs to examine the same question, we may obtain better answers to our questions and a more informed development of research in work psychology.

Discussion Points

1. What type of study would you use to examine the relationship between job satisfaction and performance? Why?
2. You are recommending a research design to a CEO who is interested in assessing the effectiveness of their new workplace health intervention programme. What issues are you going to discuss with her?
3. You have just developed a new measure of work motivation. What would you do to establish the reliability and validity of your new measure?
4. If McGrath (1981) is correct, then every research design has strengths and weaknesses, and it is not possible to conduct one 'perfect' study. That being the case, what should researchers do?
5. A colleague is proposing to conduct qualitative interviews with 10 participants to understand the causes of stress in the workplace. What are the strengths and weaknesses of this approach?

Learning by Doing

1. Although researchers put a great deal of effort into designing rigorous studies for publication in an academic journal, managers are more likely to read about the results in a newspaper or popular magazine. Find an example of research results reported in the popular media then find the original research

article in the academic literature. Is the study accurately described (in terms of its design, findings, limitations and conclusions) in the popular media?
2. The concept of a nomological network was introduced in the chapter as a means of establishing validity. Find an example of a nomological network in the research literature.
3. One of the most interesting concepts to be introduced in positive psychology is the notion of positivity (see Chapter 19). Dr Barbara Frederickson (2009) claims that individuals should experience three times as many positive as negative emotions in order to thrive and be healthy. She calls this the positivity ratio.
   a. To see how scales are constructed, go to www.positivityratio.com/single.php and complete Dr Frederickson's measure. Can you see which items contribute to the positive and negative scores?
   b. Check your reliability. After recording your scores, fill out the measure again the next day. Have your scores changed or are you consistent?

Further Reading

Crocker, L., & Algina, J. (1986). *Introduction to classical and modern test theory.* Fort Worth, TX: Holt, Rinehart, & Winston.

Hinkin, T. R. (1998). A brief tutorial on the development of measures for use in survey questionnaires. *Organizational Research Methods, 1,* 104–121.

Hunter, J., Schmidt, F., & Jackson, G. (1982). *Meta-Analysis: Cumulating research findings across studies.* Thousand Oaks, CA: Sage Publications.

Podsakoff, P. M., & Organ, D. W. (1986). Self-reports in organizational research: Problems and prospects. *Journal of Management, 12,* 531–544.

Podsakoff, P. M., MacKenzie, S. B., Lee, J. Y., & Podsakoff, N. P. (2003). Common method biases in behavioral research: A critical review of the literature and recommended remedies. *Journal of Applied Psychology, 88,* 879–903.

Schmitt, N. (1996). Uses and abuses of coefficient alpha. *Psychological Assessment, 8,* 350–353.

Shadish, W. R. (2002). Revisiting field experimentation: Field notes for the future. *Psychological Methods, 7,* 3–18.

Shadish, W. R., Cook, T. D., & Campbell, D. T. (2002). *Experimental and quasi-experimental designs for generalized causal inference.* Boston, MA: Houghton Mifflin.

References

American Educational Research Association, American Psychological Association, & National Council on Measurement in Education. (1999). *Standards for educational and psychological testing.* Washington, DC: American Educational Research Association.

Baruch, Y., & Holtom, B. C. (2008). Survey response rate levels and trends in organizational research. *Human Relations, 61,* 1139–1160.

Binning, J. F., & Barrett, G. V. (1989). Validity of personnel decisions: A conceptual analysis of the inferential and evidential bases. *Journal of Applied Psychology, 74,* 478–494.

Bolger, N., Davis, A., & Rafaeli, E. (2003). Diary methods: Capturing life as it is lived. *Annual Review of Psychology, 54,* 579–616.

Brief, A. P., Butcher, A. H., & Roberson, L. (1995). Cookies, disposition, and job attitudes: The effect of positive mood-inducing events and negative affectivity on job satisfaction in a field experiment. *Organizational Behavior and Human Decision Processes, 62,* 55–62.

Campbell, D. T., & Fiske, D. W. (1959). Convergent and discriminant validation by the multitrait–multimethod matrix. *Psychological Bulletin, 56*, 81–105.

Cook, T. D., Campbell, D. T., & Peraccio, L. (1990). Quasi-experimentation. In M. D. Dunnette, & L. M. Hough (Eds.), *Handbook of industrial and organizational psychology* (Vol. 1, 2nd ed., pp. 491–576), Palo Alto, CA: Consulting Psychologists Press.

Cortina, J. M. (1993). What is coefficient alpha? An examination of theory and applications. *Journal of Applied Psychology, 78*, 98–104.

Crocker, L., & Algina, J. (1986). *Introduction to classical and modern test theory*. Fort Worth, TX: Holt, Rinehart, & Winston.

Cronbach, L. J. (1951). Coefficient alpha and the internal structure of tests. *Psychometrika, 16*, 297–334.

Cronbach, L. J., & Meehl, P. E. (1955). Construct validity in psychological tests. *Psychological Bulletin, 52*, 281–302.

Cronbach, L. J. (1971). Test validation. In R. L. Thorndike (Ed.), *Educational measurement* (2nd ed., pp. 443–507). Washington, DC: American Council on Education.

Faragher, E. B., Cass, M., & Cooper, C. L. (2005). The relationship between job satisfaction and health: A meta-analysis. *Occupational and Environmental Medicine, 62*, 105–112.

Frederickson, B. (2009). *Positivity*. New York: Crown.

Fullagar, C., & Kelloway, E. K. (2009). 'Flow' at work: An experience sampling approach. *Journal of Occupational and Organizational Psychology, 82*, 595–615.

Hunter, J., Schmidt, F., & Jackson, G. (1982). *Meta-Analysis: Cumulating research findings across studies*. Thousand Oaks, CA: Sage Publications.

Iaffaldano, M. T., & Muchinsky, P. M. (1985). Job satisfaction and job performance: A meta-analysis. *Psychological Bulletin, 97*, 251–273.

Judge, T. A., Thoresen, C. J., Bono, J. E., & Patton, G. K. (2001). The job satisfaction–job performance relationship: A qualitative and quantitative review. *Psychological Bulletin, 127*, 376–407.

Kelloway, E. K., & Francis, L. (2012). Longitudinal research methods. In M. Wang, R. Sinclair, & L. Tetrick (Eds.), *Research methods in occupational health psychology* (pp. 374–394). New York: Elsevier.

Kerlinger, F. N. (1986). *Foundations of behavioral research* (3rd ed.). New York: Holt, Rinehart, & Winston.

Kline, T. J. (2005). *Psychological testing: A practical approach to design and evaluation*. Thousand Oaks, CA: Sage Publications.

Kuder, G. F., & Richardson, M. W. (1937). The theory of the estimation of test reliability. *Psychometrika, 2*, 151–160.

Lance, C. E., Dawson, B., Birkelbach, D., & Hoffman, B. J. (2010). Method effects, measurement error, and substantive conclusions. *Organizational Research Methods, 13*, 435–455.

Leiter, M., Laschinger, H. S., Day A., & Gilin, D. (2011). The impact of civility interventions on employee social behavior, distress, and attitudes. *Journal of Applied Psychology, 96*, 1258–1274.

Locke, E. A. (1976). The nature and causes of job satisfaction. In M. D. Dunnette (Ed.), *Handbook of industrial and organizational psychology* (pp. 1297–1349). Chicago, IL: Rand McNally.

Locke, E. A. (1986). *Generalizing from laboratory to field settings: Research findings from industrial-organizational psychology, organizational behavior, and human resource management*. Lexington, MA: Lexington Books.

McCracken, G. (1988). *The long interview*. Thousand Oaks, CA: Sage Publications.

McGrath, J. E. (1981). Dilemmatics: The study of research choices and dilemmas. *American Behavioral Scientist, 25*, 179–202.

Mitchell, G. (2012). Truth or triviality: The external validity of research in the psychological laboratory. *Perspectives on Psychological Science, 7*, 109–117.

Ployhart, R. E., & Vandenberg, R. K. (2010). Longitudinal research: The theory, design, and analysis of change. *Journal of Management, 36*, 94–120.

Podsakoff, P. M., MacKenzie, S. B., Lee, J.-Y., & Podsakoff, N. P. (2003). Common method biases in behavioral research: A critical review of the literature and recommended remedies. *Journal of Applied Psychology, 88*, 879–903.

Rogosa, D. R. (1995). Myths and methods: "Myths about longitudinal research," plus supplemental questions. In J. M. Gottman (Ed.), *The analysis of change* (pp. 3–65). Hillsdale, NJ: Lawrence Erlbaum Associates.

Schat, A. C. H., Frone, M. R., & Kelloway, E. K. (2006). Prevalence of workplace aggression in the U.S. workforce: Findings from a national study.

In E. K. Kelloway, J. Barling, & J. Hurrell (Eds.), *Handbook of workplace violence* (pp. 47–89). Thousand Oaks, CA: Sage Publications.

Schmitt, M. (1996) Individual differences in sensitivity to befallen injustice (SBI). *Personality and Individual Differences, 21*, 3–20.

Scollon, C. N., Kim-Prieto, C., & Diener, E. (2003). Experience sampling: Promises and pitfalls, strengths and weaknesses. *Journal of Happiness Studies, 4*, 5–34.

Shadish, W. R. (2002). Revisiting field experimentation: Field notes for the future. *Psychological Methods, 7*, 3–18.

Shadish, W. R., Cook, T. D., & Campbell, D. T. (2002). *Experimental and quasi-experimental designs for generalized causal inference*. Boston, MA: Houghton Mifflin.

Smyth, J. M., & Stone, A. A. (2003). Ecological Momentary Assessment research in behavioral medicine. *Journal of Happiness Studies, 4*, 35–52.

Spector, P. E. (1987). Method variance as an artifact in self-reported affect and perceptions at work: Myth or significant problem? *Journal of Applied Psychology, 72*, 438–443.

Spector, P. E. (1997). *Job satisfaction: Application, assessment, causes, and consequences*. Thousand Oaks, CA: Sage Publications.

Spector, P. E. (2006). Method variance in organizational research: Truth or urban legend? *Organizational Research Methods, 9*, 221–232.

Staw, B. M., & Ross, J. (1985). Stability in the midst of change: A dispositional approach to job attitudes. *Journal of Applied Psychology, 70*, 469–480.

Stevens, S. S. (1946, June 7). On the theory of scales of measurement. *Science, 103*, 677–680.

Taris, T. W., & Schreurs, P. J. G. (2009). Well-being and organizational performance: An organizational-level test of the happy-productive worker hypothesis. *Work & Stress, 23*, 120–136.

Tett, R. P., & Meyer, J. P. (1993). Job satisfaction, organizational commitment, turnover intention, and turnover: Path analyses based on meta-analytic findings. *Personnel Psychology, 46*, 259–293.

Wright, B., & Barling, J. (1998). The executioner's song: Listening to downsizers reflect on their experience. *Canadian Journal of Administrative Science, 15*, 339–355.

Van Maanen, J., Dabbs, J. M., & Faulkner, R. R. (1982). *Varieties of qualitative research*. Thousand Oaks, CA: Sage Publications.

Zelenski, J. M., Murphy, S. A., & Jenkins, D. A. (2008). The happy-productive worker thesis revisited. *Journal of Happiness Studies, 9*, 521–537.

Part B
Theoretical Perspectives on Work

3

The Models that Made Job Design

Kevin Daniels, Pascale M. Le Blanc
and Matthew Davis

> **Chapter Objectives**
>
> After studying this chapter, you should be able to:
>
> - describe the *features* of well-designed work as described in classic models of job design;
> - understand the *key processes*, as described in classic models of job design, through which well-designed work contributes to employee health and performance;
> - describe some of the *research evidence* that supports classic models of job design;
> - appreciate how classic models of job design can be *applied in practice*;
> - understand the *limitations* of classic models of job design.

It is the purpose of this chapter to describe and evaluate five of the most significant approaches to job design that have laid the foundation for contemporary work psychology: the Job Characteristics Model (JCM; Hackman & Oldham, 1976, Section 3.2), the Demand–Control–Support Model (DCSM; Karasek & Theorell, 1990, Section 3.3), the Vitamin Model (VM; Warr, 1987, Section 3.4), the Effort–Reward Imbalance Model (ERI Model; Siegrist, 1996; Peter & Siegrist, 1997, Section 3.5), and contemporary Socio-Technical Systems Thinking (STST; see Cherns, 1987;

Clegg, 2000, Section 3.6). As we will see in this chapter, these models have not only stimulated the psychological science of job design, but have influenced how national governments monitor and regulate the workplace in order to provide psychologically healthy work. Because of the great influence of these models on research, management practice and policy, these models are the modern classics of job design that made the psychology of job design that we know today.

3.1 Background of Job Design

Job design is concerned with the activities of workers, and relates to the duties and tasks required to perform their work, and how those tasks and duties are structured and scheduled (Morgeson & Humphrey, 2008; Parker & Ohly, 2008). Job design has a long history of political regulation, for example medieval Europe had a six-day working week, with a day of rest enforced by the Christian Church.

The publication of Adam Smith's *Wealth of Nations* (1776/1904) marked a significant shift in how job design was construed (Leahey, 1987). Smith was concerned with efficient production and argued that tasks should be divided into their smallest possible components and that workers should perform one task only. This division of labour exerted huge influence on the Industrial Revolution, which started in England in the eighteenth century and spread throughout the Western world in the nineteenth century. The division of labour became the basis of scientific management, introduced by the American management thinker Frederick Taylor (1911) in the early twentieth century. Scientific management was based on a simple – and flawed – view of human motivation: workers were rewarded on the basis of how many times they completed simplified tasks.

One of the best-known critics of the division of labour is Karl Marx (1971a, 1971b). Writing in the nineteenth century, Marx argued that the division of labour was a process through which owners/managers could extract the maximum amount of 'surplus value' from workers. In order to make a profit, owners/managers require industrial processes that produce goods cheaper than their price, which, Marx argued, entails paying workers less for their labour than the value of their labour in the production process. Moreover, because unskilled labour can be provided by anyone, the division of labour pushes down the price of labour, as only the possession of rare skills can attract a premium in the labour market.

Psychological thinking on job design, rather than economic or political thinking, became profoundly influenced by the landmark Hawthorne studies at the Western Electric Company in the United States (see Mayo, 1933). These studies indicated the importance of motivational and social factors in the workplace, and suggested that workers needed cognitively and socially enriched work environments to be productive. This marked a shift in thinking from notions of division of labour and scientific management. Over the next three decades, writers such as Trist and Bamforth (1951), Likert (1961) and Herzberg (1966) argued for the importance of job design that allowed for worker participation in decisions, use of skills, delegated authority to workers and production processes that preserved social relationships in the workplace. Of outstanding significance in themselves, the contributions of Trist and Bamforth, Likert, Herzberg and others provided the platform for models of job design based on psychological processes. These models based on psychological processes have exerted, and still exert, a huge influence on how practicing work psychologists, managers and industrial policy makers think about job design. Unlike scientific management, which is based on trying to achieve efficiency through a simple system of performance-related pay, the modern classics we describe in this chapter are linked by a concern with making jobs somehow more involving, satisfying and/or health promoting (i.e. making good jobs) and enhancing job performance through improving the quality of working life. Like many of the models in this book, these modern classics were developed by researchers based predominantly in Western developed economies and predominantly researching work in those countries.

> **Work Psychology in Action: The Hawthorne studies**
>
> A series of studies was conducted at the Hawthorne plant of the Western Electric Company in the United States. Initially the research team was concerned with the physical conditions of work. The researchers evaluated changes to working conditions, including changes to lighting and rest breaks. The researchers also conducted many interviews with workers about their working conditions, management and other factors. As the research progressed, the importance of human and social factors became evident – factors such as supportive supervision, informal group relations and power. Although we cannot be certain of the validity of the specific conclusions drawn from the Hawthorne studies, the studies provided the basis for thinking about how psychological and social factors can be changed to improve the experience of work.

3.2 The Job Characteristics Model

The first modern classic of job design was Hackman and Oldham's (1975, 1976) Job Characteristics Model (JCM). This model was developed against a backdrop in the 1960s and 1970s of stable employment and mass manufacture in developed economies. The JCM is concerned with developing jobs that are motivating, satisfying and performed well. This model concentrates on five key features or characteristics of work:

- *Skill variety (SV)*: Jobs with more skill variety require workers to use a range of skills. For example, a carpenter who designs and produces his own furniture using a range of tools and carpentry techniques has more skill variety than a warehouse worker who simply has to load boxes onto lorries.
- *Task identity (TI)*: Jobs with task identity allow the worker to produce or deliver an identifiable, complete outcome. For example, a call-centre operator who deals with customers from the start of their enquiry until the enquiry is answered has more task identity than a call-centre operator who is the first

point of contact with the customer but acts as a filter, passing the customer on to another operative to deal with the rest of the call.
- *Task significance (TS)*: More significant jobs have an impact on other people, both inside and outside the organization. For example, jobs related to medical care or the provision of education have more task significance than jobs in retail outlets.
- *Autonomy (AU)*: Jobs with more autonomy allow the worker to make decisions concerning how to perform tasks, when and where to perform tasks, and even how success in performing work tasks is evaluated. For example, architects and construction engineers will usually have a great deal of autonomy in the overall design of a building, the materials to use in a building, how different elements of a building fit together and the sequence in which the elements are to be put together. In contrast, construction workers have less autonomy, as they are constrained by the design and project management schedules decided by architects and construction engineers.
- *Feedback from the job (FB)*: Jobs that provide feedback give an indication of how well the worker is performing. For example, a computer programmer who compiles her own code gets feedback from the job when the program compiles or fails to compile. In contrast, a journalist gets lower feedback direct from the job and the feedback does not occur close to task completion. For the journalist, performance is gauged by how well the editor and readers react to the journalist's story.

Hackman and Oldham consider that these five job characteristics produce three critical psychological states: *experienced meaningfulness of work, experienced responsibility for the outcomes of work* and *knowledge of the results of work activities*. Skill variety, task identity and task significance influence the experienced meaningfulness of work because the work is experienced as challenging, and meaningful units of work can be seen to have a beneficial impact on others. Autonomy influences the experienced responsibility for the outcomes of work because the worker is responsible for the decisions and activities that make up the work. Feedback influences knowledge of the results of work because workers can see how well they are performing their work.

In turn, the critical psychological states make work more satisfying and because the work is satisfying, workers gain an intrinsic motivation to perform the work well to experience more satisfaction. It is the motivating potential of the work that influences workers to work more effectively, turn up for work rather than going absent and to stay with the organization rather than looking for work with other organizations (i.e. low staff turnover). Hackman and Oldham (1976) state that the motivating potential of a job can be given by the following equation:

$$\text{motivating potential score} = \frac{(\text{SV} + \text{TI} + \text{TS})}{3} \times \text{AU} \times \text{FB}$$

Figure 3.1 summarizes the JCM and also shows a key difference between people that Hackman and Oldham argue is important for determining how much

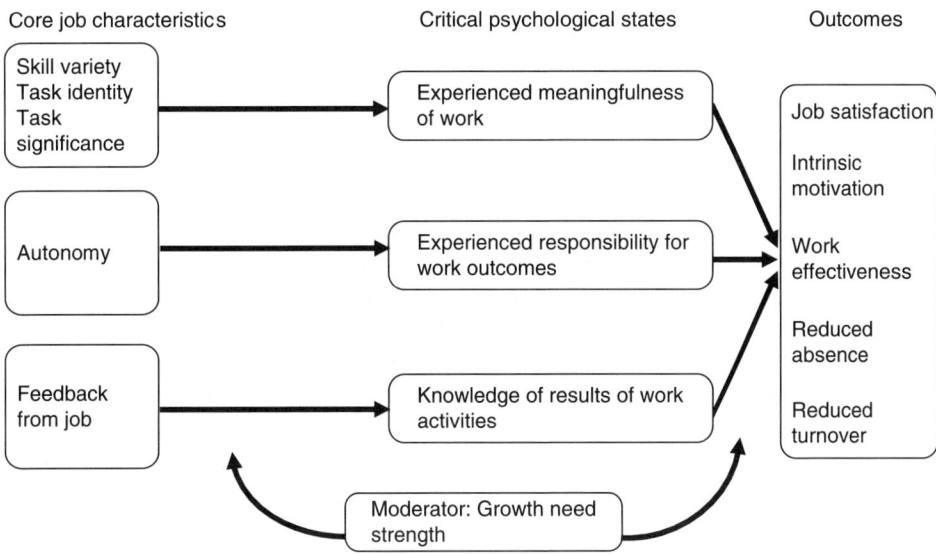

Figure 3.1 The Job Characteristics Model. Reprinted from "Motivation Through the Design of Work: Test of a Theory," by J. R. Hackman and G. R. Oldham (1976), in *Organizational Behavior and Human Performance, 16*(2), 250–279, 1976, with permission from Elsevier.

each job characteristic will contribute to enhanced motivation, satisfaction and work performance. This individual difference is known as *growth need strength* and is the extent to which people have a need to develop and grow psychologically (e.g. through developing new skills). Hackman and Oldham predict everyone will benefit from improvements in the five job characteristics in the JCM, but that people with high growth need strength will benefit more.

Evaluation of the JCM

In general, research on the JCM has been supportive of the core principles, that is, research has shown that the five core job characteristics in the JCM are related to factors such as job satisfaction and intrinsic motivation, although the research is less clear on whether the critical psychological states actually translate the key job characteristics into the outcomes (Parker & Ohly, 2008). Indeed, as other models of job design and chapters in this book indicate, it is not just the motivating potential of job characteristics that can lead to motivation, job satisfaction and performance. For example, it might be that some job characteristics allow workers to solve problems, be more creative, implement minor innovations in how work is performed and develop their own skills through self-directed learning so that they are better able to perform work. The JCM also has some other problems. Some of these are generic to the classic job design models covered in this chapter and will be covered later. More specific to the JCM, the model only examines a narrow range of job characteristics, ignores the social elements of work and concentrates on the positive features of work (see e.g. Morgeson & Humphrey, 2008).

Work Psychology in Action: The Job Characteristics Model

One of the key practical benefits of the JCM is that practitioners are able to compute a *motivating potential score* (MPS) for jobs and then discern ways in which to improve the MPS for any given job. To do this practitioners need to make accurate assessments of skill variety, task identity, task significance, autonomy and feedback. In 1975, Hackman and Oldham presented an instrument to help practitioners do this. This instrument is known as the job diagnostic survey (JDS). The JDS allows practitioners to assess the five job characteristics and a few ancillary dimensions (e.g. feedback from others), the three critical psychological states, satisfaction with work and motivation. The survey requires workers to answer a series of questions about their jobs by rating the extent to which each job characteristic is present in their job on a seven-point scale. An example question is 'Does the job require a number of complex or high-level skills?'. Several questions tap into different facets of each of the job characteristics. A score for each job characteristic is created by summing the answers provided. When practitioners have an assessment of each job, they can then proceed to redesign the job to increase those job characteristics that are deficient.

For example, a secretarial job might be characterized by scores on the JDS of 4.0 for skill variety, 4.7 for task identity, 5.3 for task significance, 4.5 for autonomy and 4.6 for feedback from the job. Substituting these figures into the equation above, we get:

$$\text{motivating potential score} = \frac{(4.0 + 4.7 + 5.3)}{3} \times 4.5 \times 4.6$$
$$= 4.67 \times 4.5 \times 4.6$$
$$= 96.6$$

This figure of 96.6 is below the figure of 106 reported as the average for clerical work in Oldham, Hackman and Stepina's study of norms of the JDS (1978).

A look at the detail of the equation indicates that skill variety, with a score of 4.0, is the area that might most easily be increased, as skill variety is the lowest score. Task significance is highest, so may need the least improvement and may be harder to increase as it is already relatively high compared to the other job features. However, because of the weighting system (skill variety is divided by three), the MPS might be best increased by increasing autonomy or feedback as the influence of these job features is not divided by three to calculate the MPS.

> A secretary's autonomy may be increased in many ways. Perhaps the secretary could be given more latitude in scheduling of his/her daily and weekly tasks. Perhaps the secretary might be allowed to decide how certain tasks are done, such as how databases are compiled, rather than having to follow pre-set procedures. Feedback might be increased by scheduling regular meetings with those to whom the secretary provides clerical and administrative support.
>
> Some time after changes have been made, practitioners can re-administer the JDS to check whether the job redesign had the intended effects on workers' job characteristics and motivation.

Replay

The JCM is a model of work motivation. It indicates that jobs have five core job characteristics that influence how motivating a job is for people: skill variety, task identity, task significance, autonomy and feedback from the job. The JCM suggests that jobs that are high on all of these job characteristics have a greater motivating potential and provide workers with greater job satisfaction. Because of the motivating potential of such jobs, the JCM suggests workers will work better, be absent less and be less inclined to look for jobs with other organizations. Finally, the JCM predicts everyone will benefit from improvements in the five job characteristics, but that people with high growth need strength will benefit more.

3.3 The Demand–Control–Support Model

One highly influential model that addresses some of the negative as well as positive features of work and the social elements of work is Karasek and Theorell's (1990) Demand–Control–Support Model (DCSM). In contrast to the JCM's primary focus on motivation, the DCSM is primarily concerned with health, but it does have something to say about work performance. Like the JCM, the DCSM was initially developed in the 1970s in the context of relatively stable employment in developed economies. However, the DCSM's focus on demands and health seemed relevant to increased competition from Japanese manufacturers, other economic problems in the West and increasing requirements for flexibility in working practices that emerged in the 1970s and grew through the 1980s.

Originally the model had just two components, job demands and decision latitude (Karasek, 1979; see Figure 3.2). Job demands have many components, but are primarily related to expending psychological effort (see Chapter 1 for a general definition of job demands), for example time pressure and difficult work. Decision latitude is a combination of skill use and job control. Job control is defined broadly in the same way as autonomy is in the JCM – job control and autonomy are effectively interchangeable labels for the same concept. Skill use and job control often occur together in the same jobs. The two dimensions of job

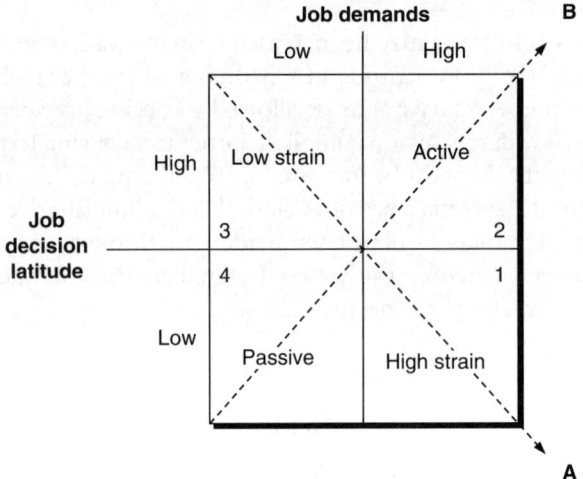

Figure 3.2 The Demand–Control Model. Reprinted from "Job Demands, Job Decision Latitude, and Mental Strain: Implications for Job Redesign," by R. A. Karasek (1979), in *Administrative Science Quarterly, 24*(2), 285–308, by permission of the publisher. Published by SAGE Publications, on behalf of Johnson Graduate School of Management, Cornell University. Copyright © 1979 Johnson Graduate School of Management, Cornell University.

demands and decision latitude combine to produce four major classes of jobs that are defined by whether the job is high or low on the characteristics of job demands and decision latitude.

Jobs that are low on job demands and low on decision latitude are called *passive* jobs. A watchman is a good example.

Jobs that are high on job demands but low on decision latitude are called *high-strain* jobs. A call-centre operator is a good example.

Jobs that are low on job demands but high on decision latitude are called *low-strain* jobs. A wildlife photographer is a good example.

Jobs that are high on job demands and high on decision latitude are called *active* jobs. A physician is a good example.

Over the years, the model has evolved to concentrate on job control rather than the broader concept of decision latitude. The model has also evolved to include workplace social support, as depicted in Figure 3.3 (Johnson & Hall, 1988). Workplace social support is characterized by helpful interactions with supervisors and co-workers. Of particular interest are jobs that are labelled *iso-strain* jobs – these are jobs that are low on support and job control but high on job demands. Iso-strain jobs are jobs considered to be particularly harmful to health. Bowles and Dodds (2002), for example, consider psychiatric nurses working on acute wards to be particularly at risk of iso-strain jobs because the chaotic environments of acute care wards mean workload is always high, job control is limited as medical staff typically have most power and the busy environment limits opportunities for structured support and development.

Like the JCM, the DCSM has an assessment instrument, in the form of a questionnaire completed by workers. This instrument allows practitioners to assess the

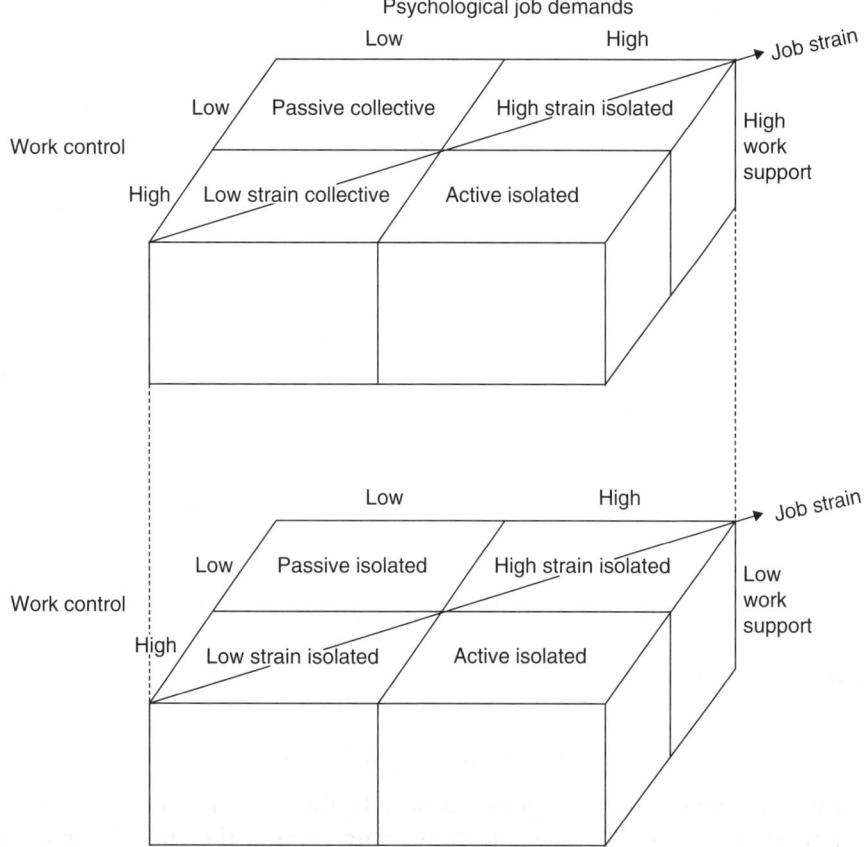

Figure 3.3 The Demand–Control–Support Model. Reprinted from "Job Strain, Work Place Social Support, and Cardiovascular Disease: A Cross-Sectional Study of a Random Sample of the Swedish Working Population," by J. V. Johnson and E. M. Hall (1988), in *American Journal of Public Health, 78*(10), 1336–1342, by permission of the Sheridan Press on behalf of the American Public Health Association.

key characteristics from the model as well as other characteristics. This is called the Job Content Questionnaire (JCQ; Karasek et al., 1998) and it can be used in a similar way to the JDS to determine appropriate job re-design interventions and assess whether those interventions had their intended consequences.

In the DCSM, the three key job characteristics of job demands, job control and workplace social support work in combination to create healthy (and productive) work. The DCSM has two key hypotheses: the *strain hypothesis* and the *active learning hypothesis*.

The strain hypothesis

The strain hypothesis indicates that job control and social support can offset the detrimental effects of job demands on health. Job demands can be detrimental to health because they place both a psychological and physiological load on the individual – a stress response. The stress response activates psychological and physiological resources to deal with the stress. First, mental effort is directed towards dealing with the source of stress. Second, physiological systems are geared towards making a physical response to the source of stress, so blood pressure and heart rate increase, for example. Provided people can cope with job demands, then the stress response will not be prolonged and workers will recover the mental and physical energy lost during it. However, if workers cannot cope with the job demands then workers will not recover their mental and physical energy, and the stress response will be prolonged. In the DCSM, the psychological and physiological detrimental effects of job demands lead to psychological and physical health problems such as depression and heart disease.

However, in the DCSM, job control and social support can offset the harmful impact of job demands by allowing workers to cope with them. For example, workers with control over their work schedules can take breaks after particularly demanding episodes at work to recover from the demands (see Chapter 8 for the important role of recovery) rather than having to wait for a normal break period to come round. Similarly, workers may receive emotional support from others, in the form of direct help with job demands or friendly interactions with co-workers, that restores a good mood after an emotionally demanding episode at work.

In the strain hypothesis, job control and social support *buffer* the adverse impact of job demands on psychological and physical health. Put another way, without job control and social support to facilitate coping, job demands have an adverse impact on health.

The active learning hypothesis

The active learning hypothesis goes one step further than the strain hypothesis. Because job control and social support facilitate coping, they may facilitate one particular form of coping related to better productivity. Karasek and Theorell (1990) call this active coping and it essentially refers to coping directed at solving problems caused by high job demands. In the active learning hypothesis, solving problems leads to workers learning how to solve problems faster and more effectively, to build skill levels and so to become more productive. Moreover, as learning and skills accumulate, workers become more confident, leading to improvements in mood and further inhibiting the effects of job demands on health, that is, learning impedes strain. Conversely, strain can impede learning if workers are unable to cope with demands, and skills and confidence deteriorate.

Evaluation of the DCSM

There have been extensive reviews of the vast research literature on the DCSM (e.g. de Lange, Taris, Kompier, Houtman, & Bongers, 2003; Häusser, Mojzisch, Niesel, & Schulz-Hardt, 2010). These reviews indicate that job control, social support and low job demands are associated with the best psychological and physical health. Evidence from the smaller set of studies of the active learning hypothesis indicates that job control is reliably linked to learning outcomes, although the evidence is less clear concerning whether job demands have a negative or positive impact on learning outcomes (Taris & Kompier, 2004). Furthermore, these reviews indicate that there tends to be little support for the notion that job control and social support can offset the adverse consequences of high levels of job demands. This has important practical consequences. If job control and social support can offset the adverse effects of job demands, then healthy work can be optimized merely by increasing levels of job control and social support. Levels of job demands need not be changed. However, the research data indicate that in order to create healthy work, jobs should be redesigned to minimize job demands as well as increase job control and social support. However, reducing levels of job demands too far could lead to under-stimulation, boredom (see Chapter 12) and reduced motivation. Moreover, it is clear that reducing job demands too much would be impractical, as workers do need to attain a certain level of performance in their work for the job to be economically viable. In practical terms, it is perhaps better to say that healthy work is characterized by moderate levels of job demands, high job control and high social support.

There are at least two reasons why research, in general, has failed to demonstrate that job control and social support can help workers cope with high levels of job demands. One reason is that job control, social support and job demands are concepts that may be too broad to be of any theoretical or practical value in deciding how best to optimize work design for health. A focus on more specific types of demands, control and support is needed (see Chapter 4). A second reason is that the DCSM has traditionally been tested by assessing how much job control and social support workers have in their jobs rather than examining what it is that workers actually do in response to job demands. Yet the DCSM proposes that it is workers' coping – enabled by job control and social support – that offsets the harmful effects of job demands. Recent research that has examined how workers use job control and social support to cope with job demands indicates that workers who actually use job control and social support to solve problems benefit from enhanced mood, learning and, in some cases, enhanced creativity and innovation (Daniels, 2011, 2012).

Replay

The DCSM indicates that a combination of negative and positive features of jobs – specifically job demands, job control and workplace social support – predicts healthy work. Although the DCSM suggests that high levels of job control and workplace social support can offset the adverse impact of job demands on health, the majority of the research evidence indicates that healthy work is characterized by low job demands, high job control and high social support, although practically, moderate rather than low levels of job demands are perhaps more desirable.

3.4 The Vitamin Model

Motivated by mass unemployment in the 1980s, the British psychologist Peter Warr decided to study what makes employment psychologically healthy. Based on his findings, he developed his Vitamin Model (VM), which indicates that some job characteristics can be harmful if present at levels that are too high or too low

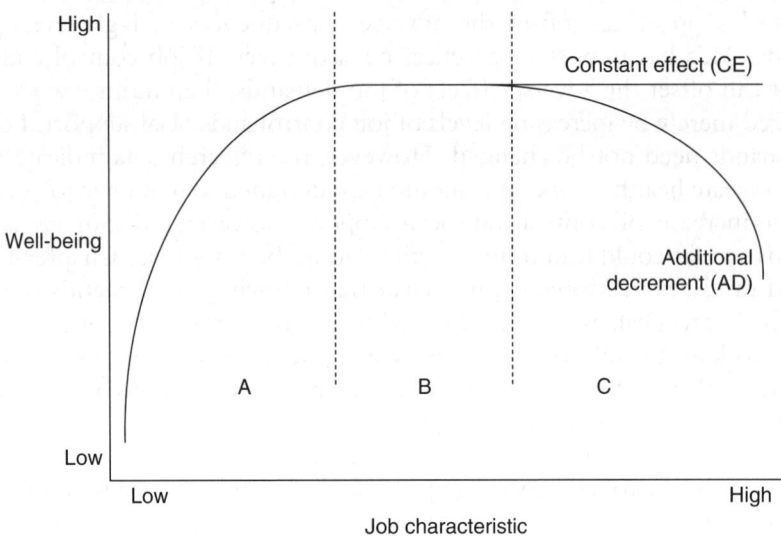

Figure 3.4 The Vitamin Model. Republished with permission of Lawrence Erlbaum Associates, from *Work, Happiness and Unhappiness* by P. Warr (2007); permission conveyed through Copyright Clearance Center, Inc.

(Warr, 1987, 2007). Thus, the VM focuses on job-related mental health and psychological well-being. Like the JCM and DCSM, the central idea underlying the VM is that mental health is affected by job characteristics that are features of the psychosocial work environment. Warr suggested that certain job characteristics have effects on mental health and psychological well-being in a way that is analogous to the effects that vitamins are supposed to have on our physical health. Following this line of reasoning, de Jonge and Schaufeli (1998) refer to these job characteristics as 'psychological work vitamins'.

In the VM, mental health is conceptualized in terms of *job-related* affective well-being along three dimensions (Warr, 1994). Affective well-being refers to whether we tend to experience more pleasant emotional (affective) states or more negative emotional (affective) states. In order to measure job-related affective well-being, Warr (1994) proposed three dimensions: displeasure-to-pleasure, anxiety-to-comfort and depression-to-enthusiasm. Job-related affective well-being has most commonly been studied by measures of job satisfaction and job-related anxiety or tension, and by measures of occupational burnout and depression accordingly.

Generally, as Figure 3.4 shows, the absence of certain job characteristics impairs psychological well-being, whereas their presence initially has a beneficial effect on affective well-being (segment A). Beyond a certain required level, vitamin intake no longer has any positive effects: a plateau has been reached and the level of affective well-being remains constant (segment B). The next segment (C) shows that further increase in job characteristics may either produce a 'constant effect' (CE) or be harmful and impair mental health ('additional decrement', AD). According to Warr (1987, 1994), which of the two effects will occur depends on the particular job characteristic.

Table 3.1 The 12 job characteristics of the Vitamin Model.

CE job characteristics	AD job characteristics
Availability of money (e.g. salary, income level)	Opportunity for control (e.g. job autonomy/control)
Physical security (e.g. absence of danger)	Opportunity for skill use (e.g. applying expertise)
Valued social position (e.g. status in society)	Externally generated goals (i.e. demands)
Supportive supervision (e.g. concern for employee welfare)	Variety (e.g. variety in tasks performed)
Career outlook (e.g. secure employment, promotion opportunity)	Environmental clarity (e.g. clarity of role requirements)
Equity (e.g. absence of unfair discrimination)	Opportunity for interpersonal contact (e.g. quantity of interaction)

CE, constant effect; AD, additional decrement.

Warr (1987, 1994) identified nine job characteristics that may act as determinants of job-related mental health (see Table 3.1). In 2007, Warr added three more job characteristics (supportive supervision, career outlook and equity), bringing the total number of job characteristics in the VM to 12. Note that Warr refers to job demands as externally generated goals – goals that others in an organization or customers assign to workers to attain. Warr assumes that six of these job characteristics (opportunities for control and variety) have curvilinear effects (inverted U-shaped). The lack of such features or an excess of such features will affect mental health negatively. These are additional decrement job characteristics. The remaining six job characteristics (physical security, availability of money, valued social position, supportive supervision, career outlook and equity) are supposed to follow a *monotonic* pattern: the higher the availability of such a job characteristic, the higher the level of mental health will tend to be. These are the constant effect job characteristics. Warr (1998) noted, however, that it is improbable that the latter associations are purely linear. For instance, it seems plausible that an increase in income will have greater benefits at low income levels than at extremely high income levels.

Essentially, the VM is situation-centred in that it focuses on the association between job characteristics and mental health. However, there are undoubtedly differences between people in the nature of these associations (Warr, 1994, 2007), that is, personal characteristics can alter the strength of the relation between job characteristics and mental health. Three categories of individual characteristics are viewed as possible moderators of the effects of job characteristics on mental health: *values* (e.g. preferences and motives), *abilities* (like intellectual and psychomotor skills) and *baseline mental health* (e.g. low self-esteem, disposition to excessive worrying). Moderating effects are expected especially in the case of a so-called 'matching' individual characteristic (Warr, 1994). Individual characteristics that correspond to particular job characteristics will cause a stronger effect of job characteristics than those that lack this matching property. For example, people with high levels of skills might be thought to benefit most from the opportunity to use skills in their work.

Evaluation of the VM

Like the DCSM, the VM incorporates negative (e.g. excessive demands) and positive (e.g. social support) features of work. Whereas the JCM focuses on improving work through enhancing positive job characteristics and the DCSM indicates that adverse job characteristics (i.e. demands) can be offset by positive job features (e.g. job control), the VM concentrates on optimizing each job characteristic in the model. The VM is also a far more comprehensive model of job design than either the JCM or the DCSM, as it includes a wider range of job characteristics.

Warr (2007) reviewed studies that have examined associations between the 12 job characteristics and different aspects of well-being. The evidence indicates that there are positive associations between the constant effect job characteristics and well-being. However, the VM supposes that well-being will tend to plateau once a certain threshold is reached for the constant effect job characteristics. Warr has noted that in general these threshold effects in the VM have rarely been examined and no definitive conclusions can be drawn. For the additional decrement job characteristics of opportunity for job control and opportunity for skill use, most of the evidence indicates that both seem to behave more like constant effect job characteristics, that is, most of the evidence does indicate that the more opportunity for job control and opportunity for skill use there is the better. At best, the evidence for proposed curvilinear effects is equivocal or limited. For externally generated goals (demands), there is more support for the notion that levels of demands that are too low and levels of demands that are too high are both harmful to well-being. However, studies have tended to examine either underload or overload separately, and it is rarer to find studies that have examined the full continuum of demands.

Replay

The VM is a model of job characteristics and mental health. Job characteristics are seen as 'psychological vitamins' that provide nutrients for mental health. The VM has the following principal aspects:

- Job characteristics are grouped into 12 categories that relate linearly or curvilinearly to mental health outcomes according to the type of 'vitamin' they represent: constant effect or additional decrement. Affective well-being is the core aspect of job-related mental health and consists of three dimensions: displeasure-to-pleasure, anxiety-to-comfort and depression-to-enthusiasm.
- Personal factors and situational factors interact to predict mental health, particularly in case of a match between both types.

3.5 The Effort–Reward Imbalance Model

The Effort–Reward Imbalance (ERI) Model of Siegrist and colleagues (e.g. Siegrist, 1996; Peter & Siegrist, 1997) has a more sociological focus, yet has still been influential in how psychologists think of the relation between work and the experience of work. The model attempts to tie together sociological factors concerned with labour markets and employment, psychological factors concerned with differences between individuals and biological factors concerned with health. Like the DCSM and the VM, the ERI Model is therefore very much focused on stress and health, in particular (the onset of) cardiovascular-related outcomes. Like the DCSM and the VM, the ERI Model was developed in the 1980s and 1990s against a backdrop of concern regarding the effects of employment and unemployment on health.

In the ERI Model, as depicted in Figure 3.5, the work role is crucial to the fulfilment of individual, self-regulatory needs (i.e. self-esteem, self-efficacy and self-integration) and links these to the societal structure of opportunities and rewards. Based on the principle of (social) reciprocity, the employee invests efforts and expects proportionate rewards in return. At particular risk are people who expend high effort at work who receive low reward from work, that is, people who do not have their effort reciprocated in the form of adequate rewards. High effort spent at work in combination with low reward obtained in turn may cause a state of emotional and physiological distress, which in turn increases the risk of physical as well as mental diseases (van Vegchel, de Jonge, Bosma, & Schaufeli, 2005).

According to Peter, Geißler and Siegrist (1998), rewards are distributed to employees in three different ways: *money* (i.e. adequate salary), *esteem* (e.g. respect and support) and *security/career opportunities* (e.g. promotion prospects, job security). Effort is evaluated as two components: extrinsic effort or *job demands*

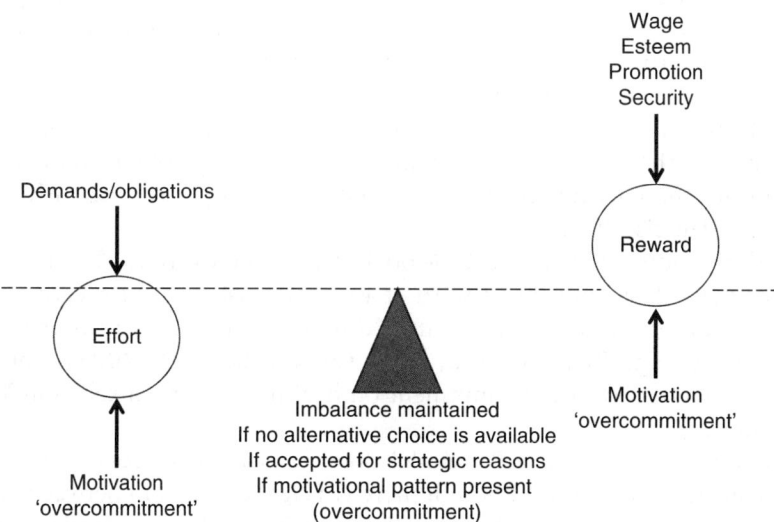

Figure 3.5 The Effort–Reward Imbalance Model (adapted from Siegrist, 2012 and printed with the permission of J. Siegrist).

(like time pressure, responsibility and physical demands) and intrinsic effort or *overcommitment*. Overcommitment reflects ambition in combination with a need for approval and esteem. Highly overcommitted employees underestimate challenging situations and overestimate their own capability, and consequently they tend to invest (too) much effort. Thus, a mismatch between high extrinsic effort (i.e. demands and obligations from work) or intrinsic effort (i.e. overcommitment) and low rewards may lead to adverse effects on health. In addition, although their excessive efforts often are not met by adequate rewards, overcommitted people tend to maintain their level of involvement. As this will be exhausting in the long run, overcommitment is also thought to have a direct effect on health (van Vegchel et al., 2005).

Evaluation of the ERI Model

The ERI Model focuses on factors concerned with work – rewards – that would not be considered as conforming to traditional definitions of job characteristics (see Morgeson & Humphrey, 2008; Parker & Ohly, 2008). Certainly some aspects of rewards, more related to intrinsic motivation, such as greater opportunity to exercise control or use skills, are directly related to definitions of job characteristics focused on the organization of work tasks. However, remuneration and career opportunities are not pure job characteristics as such. Even so, in integrated human resource management systems there should be close relations between the work that people do, the manner in which people are expected to perform their work, how they are paid and the career development they may expect.

Unlike the JCM, DCSM and VM, the ERI Model incorporates elements of job characteristics and personal behavioural patterns (i.e. overcommitment) as directly involved in the development of ill-health. Critically, by incorporating overcommitment, the ERI Model indicates that what workers do at work can affect their health rather than the job characteristics they are exposed to. The notion of worker agency in shaping the experience of work is something that is picked up in later chapters in this book, although many researchers would also point out that workers are capable of proactive actions to enhance their health rather than acting solely to make health worse, as the ERI Model suggests (e.g. Daniels, 2011).

Empirical studies with the ERI Model clearly demonstrate that the combination of high effort and low reward at work is a risk factor for cardiovascular health, depressive symptoms, burnout, sickness absence and turnover intention (for reviews see e.g., Kivimäki et al., 2006; van Vegchel et al., 2005). The results regarding the effect of overcommitment on health are more mixed (van Vegchel et al., 2005).

There are issues that the ERI Model does not clearly address (see also Kasl, 1996; Siegrist, 1996). First, although there is a clear distinction between extrinsic and intrinsic efforts in the ERI Model, there is no clear distinction between extrinsic and intrinsic rewards. Second, one might question the extent to which the overcommitment construct is a stable trait and to what extent it is related to the work environment. For instance, will some employees experience more stress because of their character or do some job characteristics evoke overcommitment? Third, although the model encompasses a broad social context, little attention has been paid so far to the relation between work and family life as an environmental factor of possible relevance (work–home interference, see Chapter 11, and effort–reward imbalance in aspects of life other than work).

Finally, a last comment concerns the dynamic nature of the ERI Model. It is possible that health and effort–reward imbalances are reciprocally related. On the one hand, it might be expected that people who develop signs of ill-health because of a perceived imbalance may act to protect their health by restoring a sense of balance by altering the level of effort they put into their work. In other words, people might be expected to attempt to regulate the imbalance of effort and rewards. On the other hand, in a longitudinal study of Japanese male blue-collar workers, Shimazu and de Jonge (2009) found that effort–reward imbalance predicted subsequent psychological ill-health and physical symptoms, but also that psychological ill-health predicted future effort–reward imbalance. Clearly, the nature and processes underpinning the dynamic relations between effort–reward imbalance and health need further investigation.

Replay

The ERI Model gives prominent positions to work and differences between individuals in how work-related ill-health develops. The model is based on the principle of (social) reciprocity. The level of effort expended at work needs to be proportionate to the level of rewards gained from work. Of particular risk are people who expend high effort at work who receive low reward from work. Rewards are distributed in three ways: money, esteem and security/career opportunities. Effort has two major components: extrinsic effort or job demands (like time pressure, responsibility and physical demands) and intrinsic effort or overcommitment. Overcommitted people tend to become ill because they maintain their level of involvement even if they are not rewarded.

3.6 Contemporary Socio-Technical Systems Thinking

An alternative to the formal models of job design described in this chapter is Socio-Technical Systems Thinking (STST). This approach to job design grew out of the influential work of Trist and Bamforth (1951) into the introduction of large-scale machinery in the UK coal industry. The organization of work around new machinery disrupted the previous social structures and work methods of the coal mining teams, resulting in productivity problems. Trist and Bamforth identified aspects of the old style of working as being particularly effective, notably the use of small groups of workers who self-organized, self-supervised, collectively completed the whole work-cycle, were multi-skilled and carried out multiple tasks. This understanding regarding the organization of work teams laid the foundations for contemporary STST.

STST can be described as a way of thinking about the design of work and provides an organizing framework to approach problems, rather than a hard and fast theory or model. At its heart, STST suggests that systems work at their best when social and technical aspects are *jointly optimized*. The STST approach requires the whole organization, including the individual workers, the technology, work processes, physical work environment and so on, to be considered as a single system (Cherns, 1987). This way of thinking suggests that when social aspects of work, such as job and work design, are designed to fit with the tools and technologies, and *vice versa*, the whole system is more efficient.

A number of principles have been developed to provide a framework for the design of work and technologies (see Cherns, 1987; Clegg, 2000). A few general principles have most frequently been used to guide the design of modern work groups:

Control of variance at source: This design principle recommends that workers be given the control, opportunity and training to respond to problems as they occur. It is similar to the notion of autonomy or decision latitude in the JCM and DCSM. The premise, especially where technologies or machinery are concerned, is that if individual workers are allowed to respond to problems as and when they happen, they can be resolved more quickly and efficiently. This is exemplified by the increase in manufacturing productivity experienced when shop-floor workers are able to fix routine machine problems as they occur, rather than waiting for specialist engineers (Wall, Jackson, & Davids, 1992).

End-user engagement: This principle has increased in prominence and extends the notion of employee autonomy. STST suggests that system design, including the design of jobs, should be led and informed by the users themselves. The idea is that employees are able to provide context and knowledge about how things work that managers or external designers may not know. Involving employees in design decisions can also improve the acceptance of changes to working practices or conditions (Clegg, 2000).

Minimal specification: This principle recommends that job roles and tasks, and the allocation of tasks to individuals do not have to be overly specified and prescribed. In other words, roles and ways of working should not be so rule bound or set in stone that they stop workers from innovating and finding ways of adapting to the changeable work environment. For example, it acknowledges that individuals often do far more and work in more creative ways than managers and designers can envisage. The difficulty facing designers in specifying all of the in-role behaviours required to perform a job well are obvious when employees work to rule and work-places grind to a halt.

Support congruence: This suggests that the social structures within an organization need to reflect and reinforce the behaviours that job design is seeking to promote. For example, if a company wants to promote team working or project-based working, then the pay and rewards should reflect group rather than individual effectiveness. Likewise, if employees are expected to act on their own initiative (i.e. control variance at source), then bonuses or rewards should reflect this additional responsibility.

Multi-skilled or multi-functional: This principle is similar to task variety in the JCM. It recommends that work roles and teams provide enlarged roles, with multiple tasks, allowing skills to be passed along organically. In essence, this allows more redundancy in the system (more people are skilled in a particular task) and enriches the individual's work experience.

Self-management: This principle is implicit in STST, with the recommendation that in return for workers being given the skills, expertise and equipment to perform tasks, they should also be made responsible for the work they perform. Essentially this involves workers self-managing themselves and taking responsibility for the completion and quality of tasks they are charged with.

STST is, in essence, a toolkit or framework – a set of suggestions about how to go about designing systems. Not all the principles apply to every situation and it is up to the designer or manager to decide what is appropriate for a particular organization, system or problem. It is this flexibility in specification that is one of STST's great strengths.

Evaluation of socio-technical systems thinking

STST has influenced how researchers and managers think about job design and in particular the interaction of workers and technology. Its contribution is best illustrated by the popularity of semi-autonomous work groups (SAWGs) in the workplace (Wall, Kemp, Jackson, & Clegg, 1986). The philosophical nature of the theory has meant that it continues to be used to consider how to optimize workers' job roles to adapt to the changing nature of modern workplaces, for example new manufacturing technologies, new forms of information technology, innovative work-space and flexible work environments (Davis, Leach, & Clegg, 2011).

Although the broad nature of STST is a strength, as it allows it to be applied to many differing situations, it is also a weakness. STST has been criticized for being under-specified (Parker, Wall, & Cordery, 2001). In other words, although there are numerous principles, they are too broad to allow researchers to examine specific predictions from STST and hence evaluate the model comprehensively. There needs to be greater explanation as to expected effects and outcomes. There has been good research evidence supporting STST in general, in particular the use of SAWGs and providing workers with the opportunity to resolve problems at source, with some studies finding benefits for productivity, motivation and well-being (Grant, Fried, & Juillerat, 2011). However, much of the research examining the approach has been collected from the manufacturing sector and there is a need for further evaluations from knowledge and service sectors. Finally, a great deal of the focus of STST in job design has been on team and work groups, with little consideration or specific guidance regarding individual roles (Clegg & Spencer, 2007).

> ### Work Psychology in Action: Socio-Technical Systems Thinking
>
> The most successful application of STST in job design has been the popular introduction of semi-autonomous work groups (SAWGs). SAWGs typically involve the creation of self-managing work groups that are able to set and organize their own work (within boundaries). A classic example of this is the implementation of SAWG within two Volvo automobile production plants in Sweden in the 1970s and 1980s (Walker, Stanton, Salmon, & Jenkins, 2008). The factories were organized around group production, with a move away from workers carrying out single, monotonous tasks. In the Uddevalla plant, for example, the production line disappeared completely, instead workers were organized into small SAGWs and between the members of the SAWG they built entire automobiles. Workers rotated group leadership roles and distributed tasks amongst themselves, allowing individuals to vary tasks and responsibilities if they wished. These work practices were claimed to provide Volvo with greater flexibility (in labour and production) and increased quality and production levels comparable to other Western auto plants. The SAWG practices were also credited with providing workers with tangible job enrichment (Sandberg, 2007). In later years both plants were closed in favour of larger, more efficient facilities, but many of the SAWG principles still influence contemporary practice at Volvo.

Replay

STST is a set of principles and a framework based on the understanding that systems work most effectively when social and technical aspects are designed to fit together. Control of variance at source (autonomy), end-user engagement, minimal specification, support congruence, multi-skilling and self-management are at its heart. The approach has led to the widespread use of SAWGs. The intention of STST is to design jobs that provide an enhanced work experience for employees, jobs that also support efficient processes and high-quality work outputs.

> ### Work Psychology in Action: Applying the JCM, DCSM, VM and ERI Model to policy for healthy work
>
> The JCM, DCSM, VM, ERI Model and to a lesser extent STST share some common ground, that is, all of the models share the idea that certain generic features of work can be changed to improve health at work and so reduce absence from work. This idea has formed the basis for at least two attempts

by national governments to influence how jobs are designed in workplaces. Specifically, both the Dutch and UK governments introduced guidance on factors such as appropriate levels of job demands, job control and social interactions at work, and accompanied that guidance with recommendations for how to assess appropriate levels of job characteristics. These attempts by the Dutch and UK governments represent some of the most sophisticated and wide-ranging applications of job design principles underpinned by the research evidence on job design and health.

For example, the UK government's Health and Safety Executive issued an Indicator Tool – a questionnaire to be completed by workers based on the principles in instruments such as the JDS and JCQ – and an Excel spreadsheet for scoring it. The Indicator Tool assesses seven job features: demands, control, support from managers, support from co-workers, relationships at work, clarity concerning roles at work and consultation during change. Ratings are made on scales ranging from 1 (poor) to 5 (good). Depending on how jobs are rated by workers, jobs could be red lighted (immediate action required), amber lighted (action required), blue lighted (low priority for action but jobs could be improved) or green lighted (very low priority for action).

Table 3.2 shows an example of the output from the Indicator Tool based on the ratings of a job.

In the example, the job scores very well on colleagues' support and relationships at work (green light), has good but improvable ratings for job control and managers' support (blue light), needs to improve on the level of consultation regarding change (amber light) and urgently needs to reduce demands and improve role clarity (red light). The Indicator Tool also suggests interim targets to be achieved on the job features and longer-term aspirations. In order to check on the findings from the Indicator Tool and develop action plans for improving jobs, the UK management standards approach encourages managers to conduct focus groups with workers, thus involving workers in the process of improving their work (cf. STST).

Table 3.2 Example output from the UK Health and Safety Executive's Indicator Tool.

	Your results	Suggested interim target	Suggested longer-term target
Demands	1.75	2.98	3.29
Control	3.67	3.72	3.72
Managers' support	3.60	3.65	3.65
Peer support	4.00	4.00	4.00
Relationships	4.50	4.50	4.50
Role	3.60	4.07	4.31
Change	3.00	3.04	3.24

> In schools in the English county of Oxfordshire, the use of the management standards process and involvement of teachers in generating solutions led to a number of solutions tailored to specific problems in schools:
>
> 1. One school introduced a soccer-style yellow and red card system for bad behaviour to support staff. If students were rude to support staff, students were issued with cards and the class teacher would decide on a consequence for the students for getting the card.
> 2. Another school encouraged teachers to leave school at a particular time and not take work home, thus helping teachers in the school think about how to use their time in school more effectively.
> 3. A school rescheduled non-essential meetings so they did not clash with periods of particularly heavily work-load, specifically the examination period. (Health and Safety Executive, 2012)
>
> It is the case that more recent developments in job design research have indicated other ways in which governments may issue guidance on job design (Daniels, 2011) and the extent is unknown to which Dutch and UK efforts were primarily responsible for reductions in work-related absence in these countries (Daniels, Karanika-Murray, Mellor, & van Veldhoven, 2012). However, the Dutch and UK efforts do indicate that it is possible for governments to develop policy, guidance and instruments for practical use on the basis of the modern classics of job design.

3.7 Conclusions

The modern classics of job design have been highly influential on research and in practice. The Work Psychology in Action box indicates one particularly influential practical outcome of these models.

In spite of generating a large volume of research and having a demonstrable practical impact on management practice and how policy makers attempt to influence management thinking on job design, the modern classics of job design highlight areas in which job design and work psychology can be developed. The generic issues raised by the models form the basis for some of the developments outlined in subsequent chapters and form the basis of key discussion points from this chapter.

Discussion Points

1. Approaches to job design models such as the JCM, DCSM, VM, ERI Model and STST tend to focus on changing the nature of work and downplay the importance of ancillary interventions. For example, the JCM, DCSM, VM and STST

all indicate the importance of job autonomy and skill use, yet without adequate training in decision-making, problem-solving and other relevant skills, improving opportunities to exercise control and use skills may be counter-productive.

2. The JCM, DCSM, VM and ERI Model might be read as encouraging management-led, top-down, permanent changes to psychosocial features of work to enhance well-being and performance. Even STST, with its core principles of end user engagement and minimum specification, places great emphasis on managers initiating changes to system design.
3. Approaches to job design models such as the JCM, DCSM, VM, ERI Model and STST tend generally to concentrate on static changes to job design. Although the DCSM and STST both indicate that workers may seek to improve their work conditions if there is sufficient autonomy, even these models ignore hourly or daily variations in the extent to which workers – collectively and individually – and managers actively alter job characteristics to lead to temporary or semi-permanent changes in work.
4. The modern classics are still relatively untested in new organizational forms (e.g. project-based organizations, distributed working teleworking arrangements, flexible working practices) and were developed when organizations were much more likely to have clear lines of reporting and bounded job descriptions, and when disruptive change was a rare occurrence. The more dynamic and fluid nature of many emerging organizational forms may challenge some of the core assumptions of the modern classics.

Learning Points

1. One of the key practical benefits of the JCM is that practitioners are able to compute a *motivating potential score* (MPS) for jobs using the following formula (defined in the chapter):

$$\text{motivating potential score} = \frac{(\text{SV} + \text{TI} + \text{TS})}{3} \times \text{AU} \times \text{FB}$$

Practitioners can then discern ways in which to improve the MPS for any given job. Given values of 2.5 for skill variety, 3.5 for task identity, 3.0 for task significance, 1.5 for job autonomy and 3.0 for feedback, compute the MPS for laboratory staff. Given you desire laboratory staff on average to have an MPS of 128, is the computed value high or low? Which job characteristic in particular is contributing to a low or high MPS?

2. Ask a family member or friend (and one who knows very little about work psychology) how they would react if their manager informed them their job would require them to make more decisions on their own and to use a wider range of skills. Ask them what they would expect from their manager and organization in return for using more skills and taking more decisions. Ask them how they expect the transition to be managed. Which of the modern classics best reflects the answers to the questions?

3. Imagine you work for a small software company with clients around the globe. You are a virtual worker: your manager is based in New York, other members of your team are scattered across several continents and time zones. The company you work for is German, but English in the common language. You are based in a small rural town, 150 kilometres from Sydney, Australia. Taking each of the job features listed in the JCM, DCSM and VM, do you think your job would be high or low on these features? What factors would make your job high or low on these factors? Are there any characteristics of your job that are not covered by the features listed in the JCM, DCSM and VM?
4. Imagine you remain in the job listed under point 3. You perform your job well and get promoted to manage your own virtual, multilingual, multicultural, geographically dispersed team of software engineers. You decide to improve the design of your team's work using socio-technical system principles. In this circumstance, what factors would you need to consider in order to ensure end-user engagement and participation in job redesign? Dealing with distance and dispersion are not the only issues – think about cross-cultural differences in preferences for different forms of job design.

Acknowledgements

We would like to thank Carolyn Axtell, Institute of Work Psychology, University of Sheffield, and Phil Almond, de Montfort University, for their feedback on the content and structure of this chapter.

Further Reading

Allvin, M., Aronsson, G., Hagström, Johansson, G., & Lundberg, U. (2011). *Work without boundaries: Psychological perspectives on the new working life*. Chichester: John Wiley & Sons.

Daniels, K. (2011). Stress and well-being are still issues and something still needs to be done: Or why agency and interpretation are important for policy and practice. In G. P. Hodgkinson, & J. K. Ford (Eds.), *International review of industrial and organizational psychology* (Vol. 26, pp. 1–46). New York: John Wiley & Sons.

Morgeson, F. P., & Humphrey, S. E. (2008). Job and team design: Toward a more integrative conceptualization of work design. *Research in Personnel and Human Resources Management, 27*, 39–91.

Parker, S. K., & Ohly, S. (2008). Designing motivating work. In R. Kanfer, G. Chen, & R. Pritchard (Eds.), *Work motivation: Past, present and future* (pp. 233–384). New York: Routledge.

References

Bowles, N., & Dodds, P. (2002). The use of refocusing in acute psychiatric care. *Nursing Times, 98(22)*, 44.

Cherns, A. (1987). Principles of sociotechnical design revisited. *Human Relations, 40*, 153–161.

Clegg, C. W. (2000). Sociotechnical principles for system design. *Applied Ergonomics, 31*, 463–477.

Clegg, C. W., & Spencer, C. (2007). A circular and dynamic model of the process of job design. *Journal of Occupational and Organizational Psychology, 80*, 321–339.

Daniels, K. (2011). Stress and well-being are still issues and something still needs to be done: Or why agency and interpretation are important for policy and practice. In G. P. Hodgkinson, & J. K. Ford (Eds.), *International review of industrial and organizational psychology* (Vol. 25, pp. 1–46). Chichester: John Wiley & Sons.

Daniels, K., (2012). Jobs and problem-solving. In A. B. Bakker, & K. Daniels, (Eds.), *A Day in the Life of A Happy Worker*. London: Psychology Press.

Daniels, K., Karanika-Murray, M., Mellor, N., & van Veldhoven, M. (2012). Moving policy and practice forward: Beyond prescriptions for job characteristics. In C. Biron, M. Karanika-Murray, & C. L. Cooper (Eds.), *Improving organizational interventions for stress and well-being: Addressing process and context* (pp. 313–332). London: Routledge.

Davis, M. C., Leach, D. J., & Clegg, C. W. (2011). The physical environment of the office: Contemporary and emerging issues. In G. P. Hodgkinson, & J. K. Ford (Eds.), *International review of industrial and organizational psychology* (Vol. 26, pp. 193–235). Chichester: John Wiley & Sons.

de Jonge, J., & Schaufeli, W. B. (1998). Job characteristics and employee well-being: A test of Warr's Vitamin Model in health care workers using structural equation modeling. *Journal of Organizational Behavior, 19*, 387–407.

de Lange, A. H., Taris, T. W., Kompier, M. A. J., Houtman, I. L. D., & Bongers, P. M. (2003). 'The very best of the millennium': Longitudinal research and the demand-control-(support) model. *Journal of Occupational Health Psychology, 8*, 282–305.

Grant, A. M., Fried, Y., & Juillerat, T. (2011). Work matters: Job design in classic and contemporary perspectives. In S. Zedeck (Ed.), *APA handbook of industrial and organizational psychology, Vol. 1: Building and developing the organization* (pp. 417–453). Washington, DC, US: American Psychological Association.

Hackman, J. R., & Oldham, G. R. (1975). Development of the job diagnostic survey. *Journal of Applied Psychology, 60*, 159–170.

Hackman, J. R., & Oldham, G. R. (1976). Motivation through the design of work: Test of a theory. *Organizational Behavior and Human Performance, 16*, 250–279.

Häusser, J. A., Mojzisch, A., Niesel, M., & Schulz-Hardt, S. (2010). Ten years on: A review of recent research on the Job Demand-Control (-Support) model and psychological well-being. *Work & Stress, 24*, 1–35.

Health & Safety Executive (2012). http://www.hse.gov.uk/stress/casestudies/oxfordshirecounty-council.htm. Accessed September 28, 2012.

Herzberg, F. (1966). *Work and the nature of man*. Cleveland, OH: World Publishing.

Johnson, J. V., & Hall, E. M. (1988). Job strain, work place support, and cardiovascular disease: A cross-sectional study of a random sample of the Swedish population. *American Journal of Public Health, 78*, 1336–1342.

Karasek, R. A. (1979). Job demands, job decision latitude, and mental strain: Implications for job redesign. *Administrative Science Quarterly, 24*, 285–307.

Karasek, R. A., & Theorell, T. (1990). *Healthy work: Stress, productivity and the reconstruction of working life*. New York: Basic Books.

Karasek, R., Brisson, C., Kawakami, N., Houtman, I., Bongers, P., & Amick, B. (1998). The Job Content Questionnaire (JCQ): An instrument for internationally comparative assessments of psychosocial job characteristics. *Journal of Occupational Health Psychology, 3*, 322–355.

Kasl, S. V. (1996). The influence of the work environment on cardiovascular health: A historical, conceptual, and methodological perspective. *Journal of Occupational Health Psychology, 1*, 42–56.

Kivimäki, M., Virtanen, M., Elovaino, M., Kouvonen, A., Vaananen, A., & Vahtera, J. (2006). Work stress in the etiology of coronary heart disease: A meta-analysis. *Scandinavian Journal of Work Environment & Health, 32*, 431–442.

Leahey, T. H. (1987). *A history of psychology: Main currents in psychological thought*. London: Prentice Hall.

Likert R. (1961). *New patterns of management*. New York: McGraw-Hill.

Marx, K. (1971a). The sociology of capitalism. In K. Thompson, & J. Tunstall (Eds.), *Sociological perspectives*. Harmondsworth, Middlesex: Penguin.

Marx, K. (1971b). Alienated labour. In K. Thompson, & J. Tunstall (Eds.), *Sociological perspectives*. Harmondsworth: Penguin.

Mayo, E. (1933). *The human problems of an industrial civilization*. New York: MacMillan.

Morgeson, F. P., & Humphrey, S. E. (2008). Job and team design: Toward a more integrative conceptualization of work design. *Research in Personnel and Human Resources Management, 27*, 39–91.

Oldham, G. R., Hackman, J. R., & Stepina, L. P. (1978). *Norms for the job diagnostic survey* (No. TR-16). Yale University, New Haven, CT, School of Organization and Management.

Parker, S. K., & Ohly, S. (2008). Designing motivating work. In R. Kanfer, G. Chen, & R. Pritchard (Eds.), *Work motivation: Past, present and future* (pp. 233–384). New York: Routledge.

Parker, S. K., Wall, T. D., & Cordery, J. L. (2001). Future work design research and practice: Towards an elaborated model of work design. *Journal of Occupational and Organizational Psychology, 74*, 413–440.

Peter, R., Geißler, H., & Siegrist, J. (1998) Associations of effort–reward imbalance at work and reported symptoms in different groups of male and female public transport workers. *Stress Medicine, 14*, 175–182.

Peter, R., & Siegrist, J. (1997). Chronic work stress, sickness absence, and hypertension in middle managers: General or specific sociological explanations? *Social Science & Medicine, 45*, 1111–1120.

Sandberg, Å. (2007). *Enriching production: Perspectives on Volvo's Uddevalla plant as an alternative to lean production.* Retrieved from http://freyssenet.com/files/Enriching%20Production%20-complete%20book_0.pdf.

Shimazu, A., & de Jonge, J. (2009). Reciprocal relations between effort–reward imbalance at work and adverse health: A three-wave panel study. *Social Science & Medicine, 68*, 60–68.

Siegrist, J. (1996). Adverse health effects of high-effort/low-reward conditions. *Journal of Occupational Health Psychology, 1*, 27–41.

Siegrist, J. (2012). *Effort–reward imbalance at work – theory, measurement and evidence.* Düsseldorf: Department of Medical Sociology, University of Düsseldorf.

Smith, A. (1776/1904). *An inquiry into the nature and causes of the wealth of nations.* London: Dent & Sons.

Taris, T., & Kompier, M. (2004). Job characteristics and learning behavior: Review and psychological mechanisms. *Research in Occupational Stress and Well-being, 4*, 127–166.

Taylor, F. W. (1911). *Principles of scientific management.* New York: Harper.

Trist, E. L., & Bamforth, K. W. (1951). Some social and psychological consequences of the long wall method of coal getting. *Human Relations, 4*, 3–38.

van Vegchel, N., de Jonge, J., Bosma, H., & Schaufeli, W. B. (2005). Reviewing the Effort–Reward Imbalance model: Drawing up the balance of 45 empirical studies. *Social Science & Medicine, 60*, 1117–1131.

Walker, G. H., Stanton, N. A., Salmon, P. M., & Jenkins, D. P. (2008). A review of sociotechnical systems theory: A classic concept for new command and control paradigms. *Theoretical Issues in Ergonomics Science, 9(6)*, 479–499.

Wall, T. D., Jackson, P. R., & Davids, K. (1992). Operator work design and robotics system performance: A serendipitous field study. *Journal of Applied Psychology, 77*, 353–362.

Wall, T. D., Kemp, N. J., Jackson, P. R., & Clegg, C. W. (1986). Outcomes of autonomous workgroups: A long-term field experiment. *Academy of Management Journal, 29*, 280–304.

Warr, P. B. (1987). *Work, unemployment and mental health.* Oxford: Clarendon Press.

Warr, P. (1994). A conceptual framework for the study of mental health. *Work & Stress, 8*, 84–97.

Warr, P. (1998). Age, work, and mental health. In K. W. Schaie, & C. Schooler (Eds.), *The impact of work on older adults* (pp. 252–303). New York: Springer.

Warr, P. (2007). *Work, happiness and unhappiness.* Mahwah: Lawrence Erlbaum Associates.

4
Current Theoretical Perspectives in Work Psychology

JAN DE JONGE, EVANGELIA DEMEROUTI AND CHRISTIAN DORMANN

> **Chapter Objectives**
>
> After studying this chapter, you should be able to:
>
> - describe the general development of theoretical models (i.e. meta-theory);
> - describe the key characteristics of a theoretical model in general;
> - discuss the Job Demands–Resources Model, its key processes, its strengths and limitations, and the evidence supporting it;
> - discuss the Demand-Induced Strain Compensation Model, its key processes, its strengths and limitations, and the evidence supporting it;
> - discuss the models' practical implications for job (re)design.

In the light of the conceptual, methodological and practical limitations of the classic models depicted in Chapter 3, and more recent insights in the area of job stress and work motivation, in this chapter we will describe two theoretical approaches that have evolved rapidly in the last decade. These approaches are the Job Demands–Resources Model (JD–R Model; Demerouti, Bakker, Nachreiner, & Schaufeli, 2001) and the Demand-Induced Strain Compensation (DISC) Model (de Jonge & Dormann, 2003). We will focus on these two models because they both provide extensions to and refinements of classic models in such a way that they give more detailed descriptions of working conditions and better tailored ways to improve these conditions, such that positive outcomes for employees and organizations can be enhanced and negative outcomes can be diminished. First, to understand theory development in work psychology, we will start with several meta-theoretical issues and criteria that are being proposed for the development and evaluation of theoretical models in general. Next, we will introduce the two above-mentioned models (i.e. their background, initial development, progress and current description) and present their empirical evidence and practical implications for job (re)design. We will end this chapter with several conclusions and suggestions for further reading.

4.1 Meta-theoretical Issues regarding Theoretical Model Development and Evaluation

The foundation of professional knowledge in any scientific area is *theory*. Theory provides a more systematic and complete picture for real practice than day-to-day knowledge. To understand theory development in work psychology we should discuss the philosophical origin of theories, so-called *meta-theory* (see Walker & Avant, 1995). The highest level of meta-theory is the *meta-paradigm* (see Figure 4.1). Its focus is on broad and paradigmatic issues related to theory in general, such as the purpose and kind of theory needed in a field, proposing and criticizing sources and methods of theory development, and proposing criteria most suitable for evaluating theories. Meta-paradigmatic examples in psychology are general psychological phenomena such as behaviour, mental processes and consciousness.

The second level of theory development is that of *grand theories*. Grand theories are highly abstract and are proposed to give a broad perspective on a research area like psychology. Examples of grand theories in psychology are the psychodynamic approach, the behavioural approach and the cognitive approach.

The third level of theory development is reflected by *middle-range theories*. These theories encompass a set of propositions about concepts and their interrelations in order to describe, explain and predict these concepts and their relations. Theories at

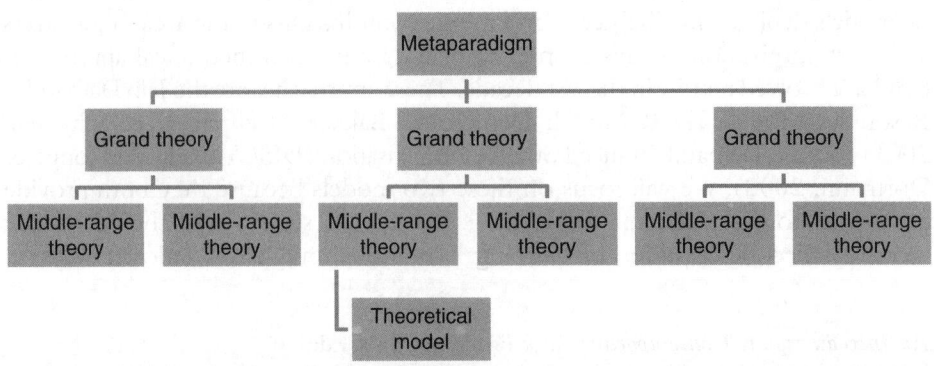

Figure 4.1 Levels of theory development in general.

this level usually contain a limited number of key concepts as well as a limited number of hypotheses, and hence are more limited in scope than grand theories. In other words, middle-range theories share some of the conceptual economy of grand theories, but provide the specificity needed for usefulness in psychological research and practice. Examples of middle-range theories in psychology are Piaget's theory of cognitive development, the theory of operant conditioning of human behaviour and Lazarus' transactional stress and coping theory (see also Chapter 6).

We now arrive at the stage of a *theoretical model* and will explain some basic characteristics of theoretical models as well as their purposes. In general, theoretical knowledge can be condensed into models. Theoretical models may serve different purposes, but generally they are both explanatory and predictive in nature, and are constructed from existing theories as well as empirical findings. Theoretical models typically emerge from middle-range theories. This implies that a theoretical model (i) is relatively small in its scope, (ii) contains a limited number of concepts or variables, (iii) reflects a limited number of relations via hypotheses and, most importantly, (iv) can be tested empirically (Walker & Avant, 1995). These characteristics imply that a theoretical model has heuristic value for today's practice.

Why is it necessary to develop and test theoretical models in work psychology? One could imagine that it is not an easy task for a scientist to find characteristics that are both relevant for the numerous different jobs and also have predictable effects on employee outcomes. The theoretical models presented in this chapter are able to reduce the complexity of almost every job into relevant characteristics that are predictive of health and motivational outcomes. This is not only helpful for research purposes (i.e. models can be tested empirically to (dis-)confirm assumptions about reality), but also for today's practice as theoretical models help practitioners to recognize those job characteristics that need to be redesigned to maximize favourable and minimize unfavourable outcomes.

Replay

Meta-theory is the philosophical origin of theories and consists of several levels with increasing specificity, that is, meta-paradigm, grand theories and middle-range theories (Walker & Avant, 1995). Theoretical models emerge from middle-range theories. A theoretical model is relatively small in its scope, contains a limited number of concepts and associations, and can be tested empirically. Theoretical models are helpful for both research and practical purposes as they help to recognize those job characteristics that need to be redesigned to optimize health and motivational outcomes.

4.2 The Job Demands–Resources Model

The JD–R Model is a theoretical model introduced by Demerouti et al. in 2001. These researchers tried to understand the key antecedents of burnout, drawing on a meta-analysis by Lee and Ashforth (1996). In their seminal paper, Demerouti and colleagues identified 21 so-called *job demands* and *job resources* as potential causes of burnout. In addition, they drew on a broad conceptualization of burnout, which is reflected in the Oldenburg Burnout Inventory (OLBI) and differentiates between exhaustion and disengagement from work as core dimensions of burnout that can occur in virtually every job. Almost immediately after its launch, the JD–R Model gained tremendous popularity, with many empirical studies applying it to various occupational groups. In line with the DCSM and the ERI Model described in Chapter 3, the JD–R Model assumes that employee adverse health and poor motivation result from the interplay between (high) job demands and (low) job resources. However, unlike those two models, the JD–R Model does not restrict itself to *a single* job demand and *a single* job resource. The model assumes that *any* job demand and *any* job resource may affect employee health and motivation, as long as these demands and resources are a salient or relevant aspect of a particular job. As we will explain later in this chapter, the application of the JD–R Model in specific jobs usually starts with an inventarization of the salient demands and resources for those jobs (i.e. through interviews with job holders and/or supervisors). Thus, the scope of the JD–R Model is much broader than that of the two other models because it potentially includes *all* salient demands and resources that can prevail in a particular job. The JD–R Model is therefore more flexible and can be tailored to a much wider variety of work settings. The broader scope of the model as well as its simplicity appeals to researchers, just as its flexibility is attractive to practitioners (Schaufeli & Taris, in press).

Key assumptions of the JD–R Model

At the heart of the JD–R Model lies the premise that every occupation may have its own specific risk factors associated with job stress. These factors can be classified in two general categories (i.e. job demands and job resources), constituting an overarching model that may be applied to various occupational settings, irrespective of the particular job demands and job resources involved (Bakker & Demerouti, 2007). Job demands refer within the JD–R Model to those physical, psychological, social or organizational aspects of the job that require sustained physical and/or psychological (cognitive and emotional) effort or skills and are therefore associated with certain physiological and/or psychological costs (see also Chapters 5 and 6). Examples are a high work pressure, an unfavourable physical environment and emotionally demanding interactions with clients. Although job demands are not necessarily negative in nature, they may turn into so-called *job stressors* when meeting those demands requires too much effort.

Job resources refer within the JD–R Model to those physical, psychological, social or organizational aspects of the job that are (i) functional in achieving work goals, (ii) reducing job demands and the associated physiological and psychological costs or (iii) stimulating personal growth, learning and development. Hence, job resources are not only necessary to deal with job demands, but they also are important in their own right. This agrees with Hackman and Oldham's (1980) Job Characteristics Model (see Chapter 3), which emphasizes the motivational potential of job resources at the task level, including autonomy, feedback and task

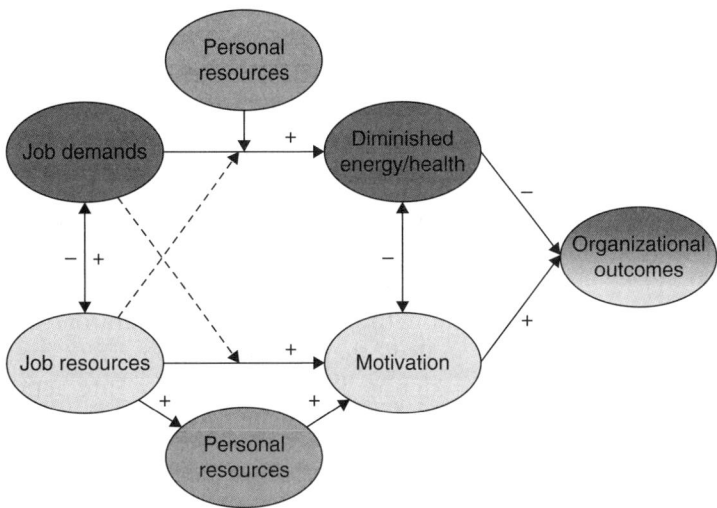

Figure 4.2 The JD–R Model.

significance. On a more general level, this agrees also with Hobfoll's (2002) Conservation of Resources (COR) theory, which states that the prime human motivation is directed towards the maintenance and accumulation of resources. Accordingly, resources are valued in their own right or because they are means to the achievement or protection of other valued resources. Resources may be located at the level of the organization at large (e.g. pay, career opportunities, job security), the interpersonal and social relations (e.g. supervisor and co-worker support, team climate), the organization of work (e.g. role clarity, participation in decision making) and at the level of the task (e.g. skill variety, task identity, task significance, autonomy, performance feedback).

Finally, although too-high demands and lack of resources could both be experienced as negative, there are substantial differences in reasons and consequences of these negative experiences. Too-high demands could be experienced as negative because they consume energy with impaired health as a potential outcome. Lack of resources could also be experienced as negative because their facilitating role is absent, which leads to reduced motivation.

A second premise of the JD–R Model is that two different underlying psychological processes play a role in the development of health and motivation (see Figure 4.2). In the first process, the so-called *energetic* or *health impairment* process, chronic job demands (e.g. work overload, emotional demands) exhaust employees' mental and physical resources and may therefore lead to the depletion of energy (i.e. a state of exhaustion, which represents the prime indicator of burnout) and to health problems. Such a gradual draining of resources occurs because employees want to maintain their performance at work. When individuals are confronted with high job demands or environmental stressors (e.g. noise, heat, workload, time pressure), they use performance-protection strategies (Hockey, 1993). Performance protection is achieved through the

> **Box 4.1 Mediation and moderation**
>
> Mediation and moderation are key parts of what has been called 'process analysis'. There is interest in these topics to try to understand the (causal) mechanisms through which the initial variable X via another variable M affects the outcome variable Y.
>
> In a *mediation model*, the effect of X on Y is transmitted by M, and X may still affect Y. For example, high job demands (X) lead to exhaustion (M), which in turn lead to sickness absence (Y). Complete or *full mediation* occurs when the effect of X on Y is completely transmitted via M. Here, X has a direct effect on M and M has a direct effect on Y (X→M→Y). Consequently, there is *no* direct effect of X on Y. In contrast, *partial mediation* occurs when the effect of X on Y is transmitted both directly (X→Y) and indirectly via M (X→M→Y). This means that X influences Y directly and indirectly via M.
>
> In a *moderation model*, variable M moderates the relation between X and Y if the effect of X on Y is different for each level of M. In other words, their relation depends on the level of the moderator M. This is also called an interaction effect (frequently denoted as X*M→Y). Interactions can buffer or strengthen relations between X and Y. For instance, the effects of job demands (X) on ill-health (Y) are weaker when employees have control in their work (buffering effect of M). Alternatively, the effects of job demands (X) on work motivation (Y) are stronger when employees have support from their supervisor (strengthening effect of M).

mobilization of sympathetic activation (e.g. cardiovascular reactivity) and increased subjective effort (i.e. self-reports on having to mobilize many resources). Use of these strategies prevents overt decrements in primary task performance. Hockey (1993) called these attempts of people to sustain their performance standards 'resistance to degradation'. However, these strategies are not always effective. According to Hockey, several patterns of indirect degradation may be identified, such as risky choices and high subjective fatigue, and it is these patterns that ultimately lead to diminished job performance. The long-term effect of these strategies may be a draining of an individual's energy resources, but also deterioration of performance on specific task dimensions, such as task quality. Energy depletion and health problems are therefore assumed to (partly) mediate the relation between job demands and organizational outcomes (see also Box 4.1).

The second process is *motivational* in nature. It is assumed that job resources have motivational potential and lead to high work engagement, low cynicism and consequently to good job performance (see Chapter 3). Within the JD–R Model, by definition, job resources may play an intrinsic motivational role because they foster employee growth, learning and development. They also help to achieve work goals. Specifically, job resources fulfil basic human needs, such as a need for autonomy, competence or relatedness. For instance, proper feedback fosters learning, thereby increasing job competence, whereas job discretion and social support satisfy the need for autonomy and the need for affiliation, respectively. Another example is that supportive colleagues and proper feedback from one's superior increases the likelihood of being successful in achieving one's work goals. To summarize, the presence of job resources leads to engagement, whereas their absence evokes a cynical attitude towards work. In turn, this affective-motivational state fosters positive organizational outcomes, such as organizational commitment and job performance. Thus, motivation and engagement are assumed to (partly) mediate the relation between job resources and organizational outcomes.

Job demands and resources initiate different processes, but they also have joint effects (reflected by the dotted lines in Figure 4.2). The third proposition put forward by the JD–R Model is that job resources can buffer the impact of job demands in predicting employee health and motivation. Typically, the buffer or interaction hypothesis explains interactions between job demands and job resources by proposing that the relation between job demands and adverse health will be weaker for those enjoying a high degree of job resources (see also Box 4.1). The buffer hypothesis is consistent with Kahn and Byosiere (1992), who argue that the buffering or interaction effect could occur between any pair of variables in the stressor-strain sequence. They claim that properties of the work situation, as well as characteristics of the individual, can buffer the effects of a demand. The buffering effect of resources can take two basic forms. First, they can reduce the perception of demands as stressful. For instance, debriefing meetings at the end of a shift can generate social support that helps nurses to experience patient interactions as less demanding. Second, resources can reduce the reactions of individuals to demands and related consequences. Workload, for example, might not be detrimental for employees when they get sufficient recognition of the hard work (Kahn & Byosiere, 1992).

Which job demands and job resources play a role in a certain organization or job function depends on the specific job characteristics that prevail. In support of this suggestion, several studies have shown that job resources like social support, autonomy, performance feedback and opportunities for development can mitigate the impact of job demands (such as work pressure, emotional demands) on job-related strain, including burnout (e.g. Bakker, Demerouti, & Euwema, 2005; Xanthopoulou, Bakker, Demerouti, & Schaufeli, 2007). Employees who have sufficient levels of job resources available can cope better with their daily job demands. This proposition is similar to the proposition of the DCSM that job control and workplace social support can buffer the detrimental effects of job demands or to the proposition of the ERI Model that occupational rewards can buffer the detrimental effects of efforts at work. Thus, the JD–R Model states that different types of job demands and job resources may interact in predicting both health and motivation.

The fourth proposition of the JD–R Model is that job resources particularly influence motivation or work engagement when job demands are *high*. This represents the so-called *coping hypothesis* (Bakker, Hakanen, Demerouti, & Xanthopoulou, 2007). Coping can be defined as 'constantly changing cognitive and behavioural efforts to manage specific demands that are appraised as taxing' (cf. Cummings, Greene, & Karraker, 1991, p. 92). This hypothesis suggests that job resources become most salient under highly demanding conditions. In that case, employees will be more likely to use job resources as a coping mechanism.

> ## Work Psychology in Action: Application of the JD–R Model to analyse jobs
>
> The JD–R Model can be used as a tool to uncover the factors that may be responsible for impaired health and reduced motivation among employees. In close collaboration with human resources managers and consultants, the model has now been applied in more than 200 different organizations in The Netherlands (Bakker & Demerouti, 2007). Because every occupation may have its own unique constellation of job characteristics, a two-stage procedure is followed to analyse jobs according to the JD–R Model.
>
> The first, *qualitative* phase of the research includes explorative interviews with job incumbents from different layers of an organization (e.g. representatives from management, staff and shop floor). The interviews include open questions about their jobs. This phase is valuable because it generates knowledge about expected and unexpected, organization-specific, job demands and job resources that will be overlooked by highly standardized approaches such as survey questionnaires. For example, it is conceivable that employees of a production company are exposed to high physical job demands, whereas employees of a financial institution are not exposed to such demands at all. In addition, in certain companies, employees are confronted with mergers, which may cause job insecurity and role ambiguity. Such organization-specific job demands and resources can be traced in this exploratory phase.
>
> In the second, *quantitative* phase of the research, a tailor-made survey questionnaire consisting of salient job demands and resources is distributed and filled out by all employees. This enables a quantitative analysis of the job demands and job resources that have been identified in the qualitative phase, and play a potential role in the development of ill-health and motivation, and consequently organizational outcomes such as job performance. The quantitative analysis usually focuses on differences between departments and job positions. Subsequent subgroup analyses can provide indications for workplace interventions, since they highlight the strengths and weaknesses of departments and job positions.

The JD–R Model was initially developed as a work-psychological model, focusing on job demands and job resources only. An important extension and fifth proposition of the model is the inclusion of personal resources in the model. *Personal resources* are aspects of the self that are generally linked to resiliency and refer to individuals' sense of their ability to control and impact their environment successfully (Hobfoll, Johnson, Ennis, & Jackson, 2003). Examples of personal resources that have been studied within the JD–R Model are self-efficacy, optimism and organizational-based self-esteem (Xanthopoulou, Bakker, Heuven, Demerouti, & Schaufeli, 2008; see also Chapter 10). The reason for this is that the higher an individual's personal resources, the more positive the person's self-regard and the more goal self-concordance is expected to be experienced (Judge, Bono, Erez, & Locke, 2005). Individuals with goal self-concordance are intrinsically motivated to pursue their goals and as a result trigger higher performance and satisfaction. As depicted in Figure 4.2, personal resources might have two functions in the JD–R Model: (i) to buffer the impact of job demands on health or energy-related outcomes (vertical line in Figure 4.2) and (ii) to mediate the relation between job resources and motivational outcomes.

Evidence for the JD–R Model

The JD–R Model has been tested in many countries and cultures (e.g. see overviews in Bakker & Demerouti, 2007; Crawford, LePine, & Rich, 2010; Demerouti & Bakker, 2011). At a general level, and in line with the assumptions of the model, most empirical studies provide evidence that irrespective of cultural background and the unique occupation, the working conditions (i.e. job demands and job resources) evoke two distinct processes, namely (i) the energetic/health impairment process that links job demands with burnout and (ii) the motivational enhancement process that links job resources with engagement. Accordingly, job demands are related to job strain (including lack of energy and development of health problems) and job resources are related to motivation (including engagement and commitment). Also, several job resources such as autonomy, feedback and social support buffered the impact of job demands on employee health/well-being (burnout and to a lesser extent engagement). In addition, although some studies failed to confirm the moderating role of personal resources (such as self-efficacy, organizational-based self-esteem and optimism) in predicting health outcomes (e.g. Xanthopoulou et al., 2007), other studies confirmed the suggested effect. For instance, self-efficacy was found to buffer the relation between emotional job demands and emotional dissonance, and the relation between emotional dissonance and work engagement (Heuven, Bakker, Schaufeli, & Huisman, 2006). In addition, personal resources were found to partially mediate the relation between job resources and work engagement, suggesting that job resources foster the development of personal resources. A longitudinal study by Xanthopoulou, Bakker, Demerouti and Schaufeli (2009a) suggests that job resources predict personal resources and motivational outcomes like work engagement, and that personal resources and work engagement, in turn, predict job resources. In light of these findings, the JD–R Model suggests that personal resources might have a complex role in transforming the work environment into positive or negative outcomes.

> **Work Psychology in Action: An empirical test of the JD–R Model**
>
> Xanthopoulou, Bakker, Demerouti and Schaufeli (2009b) investigated how daily fluctuations in job resources are consecutively related to personal resources, work engagement and financial returns. Participants indicated how much job resources they experienced during the working day, and this was positively associated with their level of engagement afterwards. For participants with high levels of personal resources, this effect was even stronger than for others. In addition, day-level supervisory coaching was positively related to day-level work engagement, which, in turn, predicted daily financial returns. It is remarkable that financial returns were mainly influenced by situational factors and work engagement, but not by personal resources such as self-efficacy and optimism. The results of this study stressed the importance of taking daily fluctuations in work characteristics and work engagement into account when examining momentary performance indicators. Practically, this paper first suggested that work-related interventions particularly focusing on supervisory coaching might create engaged and productive employees. Second, work redesign strategies that aim at job enrichment could also activate employees' personal resources. Finally, organizations should rely not only on general, enduring work redesign, but also on daily reinforcements of job resources.

Evaluation of the JD–R Model

We noticed that research findings largely support the JD–R Model's assumptions. Evaluation of the model shows that it has two clear benefits. First, it has opened the field for considering a broad range of demands, resources and outcomes. As such, it is a general, heuristic and flexible model that comes closer to a middle-range theory than a pure theoretical model. A second benefit of the JD–R Model is that it has shown that two different underlying psychological processes can at the same time play a substantial role in the development of health *and* motivation. This opens up the possibility of simultaneously investigating both negative and positive effects of work. The motivational process is in line with current ideas of positive psychology in the workplace (see Chapter 19).

However, there are also a few limitations (for an overview, see Schaufeli & Taris, in press). First and foremost, the model's openness and flexibility could be also its Achilles' heel, as this comes at the cost of specificity and the quality of its predictions. It may cause ambiguity as to whether a specific characteristic represents a demand or a resource or whether an outcome is health-related or motivational in nature. For instance, does a high level of responsibility for the outcomes of one's work represent a job demand or a job resource? Is life satisfaction a motivational or a health-related outcome? Perhaps the answer to these questions largely depends on the work context (e.g. a particular constellation of different demands and resources) or the worker's own experience. Although the JD–R Model is parsimonious there are some issues that could be misinterpreted. One issue is the role of job demands and job resources. As already indicated, they are responsible for different processes and are associated with different consequences. Take, for instance, a receptionist who needs to work irregular hours. Shiftwork represents a job demand with substantial effects on health (particularly sleep problems). When the receptionist does not need to work on shifts, his/her job is not more resourceful. In other words, the absence or reduction of demands is not equal to the presence or enhancement of resources, and largely depends on the work context and the receptionist's own experience.

Second, the model lacks specificity in explaining *why* certain job demands or resources exert their effects and on which target variable (i.e. health or motivational outcomes) they do so. Some of the job characteristics are also difficult to categorize in the presumed effects on either health or motivational outcomes, such as predictability of workload or cognitive demands. This implies that, apart from the two existing psychological processes, additional explanatory theoretical frameworks are necessary to argue why specific demands interact with specific resources to influence specific outcome variables.

Replay

We discussed the development of the JD–R Model and its key processes. This theoretical model assumes that every occupation has its own unique job demands and resources. These demands and resources are important because they evoke two relatively independent psychological processes, i.e. (i) the energetic or health impairment process and (ii) the motivational process. Although there is strong empirical evidence for both processes, there are still several important issues that have to be considered when evaluating the model's status. Furthermore, the relevance of personal resources in these processes has been justified particularly for their role in the motivational process. The most distinctive features of the JD–R Model, which explain its popularity, are its generality and flexibility. However, the model's openness and flexibility come at the cost of specificity of predictions.

4.3 The Demand-Induced Strain Compensation Model

In 2003, de Jonge and Dormann published a theoretical model that particularly focuses on the issue of 'match' between job demands, job resources and job-related outcomes. This model, the so-called Demand-Induced Strain Compensation (DISC) Model, tries to unify principles that are common to more classic models, and claims to be a more comprehensive theoretical model of job stress and work motivation than other models. The model elaborates on the idea that measures of job characteristics need to be *specific* and *targeted* rather than broad and general in order to find the proposed stress-buffering effects of job resources.

Within the area of job design and work stress, research has predominantly attempted to establish broad parameters of job design that are universally applicable (e.g. Demerouti et al., 2001; Karasek & Theorell, 1990; Siegrist, 1996). For example, according to Karasek and Theorell's DCSM (see Chapter 3), stressful work is characterized by high job demands, low job control and low workplace social support, or, according to the JD–R Model, any job demand and any job resource may affect employee health and motivation, as long as these demands and resources are a salient aspect of a particular job. Such universal approaches to job design have been very successful thus far, in terms of influence on both research and practice. One particular line of enquiry concerns *interactions* (see Box 4.1) between job characteristics that are meant to enhance health or well-being (often known as job resources, particularly job control and social support) and those that are meant to be detrimental to health or well-being (often known as job demands). The idea behind proposing such interactions is that broad job characteristics like job control or social support (see Chapter 7) enable people to cope better with stressful work conditions, so that job control and social support buffer the detrimental effects of job demands. This is both practically and theoretically important. Job demands, such as high work pace or problem-solving demands might be harmful to health and well-being, but they may be beneficial to productivity or innovation. Moreover, jobs that are inherently risky, such as those on offshore oil platforms, may bring with them psychological effects such as worry. If it can be demonstrated that some job characteristics can eliminate the harmful effects of other job characteristics that may be impossible or undesirable to eliminate out of a job, then there is a basis for redesigning these jobs in such a way that they can at least diminish their negative effects. From a practical viewpoint, because job demands can often not be reduced or optimally designed, the idea of increasing job resources instead of combatting job strain is appealing. However, the main concern of organizations should always be to reduce or redesign harmful job demands.

Reviews of the extensive research base in this area indicate, however, that the main effects of demands and resources rather than the interaction effects dominate the empirical evidence (see de Lange, Taris, Kompier, Houtman, & Bongers, 2003; van der Doef & Maes, 1999). In the social support literature, it has long been argued that the stress-buffering effects of social support are most likely to be found if the kind of social support investigated is *specific* and *targeted* towards the kind of demand that is considered (Cohen & Wills, 1985; Viswesvaran, Sanchez, & Fisher, 1999). The idea that measures of job characteristics need to be more specific and targeted, and the practical imperative of finding ways to attenuate the harmful effects of job demands have opened avenues in relation to 'match'.

Matching hypothesis

De Jonge and Dormann (2003, 2006) argued that the probability of finding stress-buffering effects of job resources is largely affected by the conceptualization and operationalization of job demands and job resources. In other words, the *specificity* with which job demands and job resources are measured, and the extent to which specific types of job resources correspond to or match specific types of job demands could determine the extent to which the stress-buffering effects of job resources can be observed. The idea that the stress-buffering effects of job resources are largely dependent on the match between specific types of job demands and job resources finds expression in the *matching hypothesis* (Cohen & McKay, 1984). According to the matching hypothesis, the stress-buffering effects of job resources are most likely to occur if specific types of job resources are matched to specific types of job demands, that is, when the job resources measured are those that are most relevant for the job demands a worker is faced with. For instance, a nurse who has to lift heavy patients will probably benefit more from a bed-lift than from a colleague who offers her a shoulder to cry on. However, although this may seem logical, in many empirical studies such specific combinations of job demands and job resources are not presented as an *a priori* hypothesis. Instead, studies usually measure job demands and job resources at a global level, and include them in a non-systematic way. As a result, most job resources are probably useful to deal with certain job demands, but probably no job resource is useful to deal with *any* job demand, and, therefore, probably no job resource is likely to operate as a general stress buffer.

Two questions regarding the issue of 'match' remain in this context. First, what does 'match' within the framework of the DISC Model exactly mean? Match is conceptualized in terms of complementary fit. In other words, when job demands and job resources match, resources are not similar to demands, but complementary. For instance, physical job resources provide the physical energy that is needed to deal with physical job demands. Second, how is this matching principle exactly working? Matching processes could be explained by using self-regulation theory transferred to work (see Pomaki & Maes, 2002). Self-regulation theory at work proposes that employees in general apply functional self-regulation strategies whose function it is to cope with states of psychological imbalance induced by high job demands. Transferred to the DISC Model, it is assumed that employees show functional self-regulatory behaviour in combating specific job demands. More specifically, workers who face a specific type of job demands are generally inclined to use functional matching job resources to deal with these demanding aspects at work. For instance, when emotional problems with customers arise (e.g. insolent customers), emotional self-regulation strategies will be applied by engaging emotional resources, such as emotionally supportive colleagues. However, if these supportive colleagues are unavailable, other job resources can be useful to some extent, such as information provided by a supervisor about how to handle a troublesome customer. The DISC Model proposes that job demands are first dealt with by turning to easily available and matching job resources. If these resources are not available or depleted, employees may apply less-matching or non-matching job resources instead, which may help to cope with extant demands. According to the DISC Model, however, they are less effective. In this approach, the focus of interest is on relations between specific job demands on the one hand and 'matching', 'less-matching' and 'non-matching' job resources on the other. We will elaborate on this issue in the next section. To conclude, rather than the universal statement of many job stress models that *any* sort of variables can interact, the

DISC Model goes further in stating that the chances of finding such interactions increase when there is a better match between variables of interest.

Key principles of the DISC Model

The DISC Model is particularly premised on two key principles, namely *multidimensionality of constructs* and the *triple-match principle* (de Jonge, Dormann, & van den Tooren, 2008). In line with Karasek and Theorell (1990), Siegrist (1996) and Demerouti and colleagues (2001), crucial and initial components of the DISC Model are job demands and job resources. Job demands are defined as work-related tasks that place brief or persistent requirements on workers, and that require physical and/or psychological effort to meet the tasks. Examples of job demands are time pressure, complexity, lifting heavy objects or dealing with aggressive clients. Job resources, on the other hand, are instrumental or psychological means at work that can be employed to deal with job demands. Examples of job resources are job autonomy (i.e. the opportunity to determine the order and method of one's work activities), emotional support from colleagues or technical equipment.

With respect to the multidimensionality principle, the DISC Model distinguishes three specific types of job demands, job resources and job-related outcomes. More specifically, the model proposes that job demands, job resources and job-related outcomes may each contain cognitive, emotional and physical elements. As far as job demands are concerned, three types can be distinguished (see also Chapter 6): (i) cognitive demands that impinge primarily on human information processing, (ii) emotional demands, mainly concerning the effort needed to deal with organizationally desirable emotions during interpersonal transactions, and (iii) physical demands that are primarily associated with the muscular-skeletal system (i.e. sensorimotor and physical aspects of behaviour). Similarly, job resources may have a cognitive-informational component (e.g. colleagues or computer systems providing information), an emotional component (e.g. colleagues providing sympathy, affection and a listening ear) and a physical component (e.g. instrumental help from colleagues or ergonomic aids). Finally, in a similar vein to demands and resources, job-related health, well-being and performance-based outcomes may also comprise cognitive, emotional and physical dimensions. These outcomes can be either negative or positive. For instance, concentration problems and employee creativity represent cognitively laden outcomes, emotional exhaustion and positive affect represent emotionally laden outcomes, and physical health complaints and physical strength can be reasonably assumed to mainly reflect bodily sensations (i.e. physical outcomes). To assess the six types of demands and resources, the so-called DISC questionnaire, labelled DISQ, has been developed. The DISQ is available in several languages in full and short versions, and can be downloaded from www.jandejonge.nl/disq.html.

The second key principle is the *triple-matching* of concepts (i.e. matching demands, resources and outcomes). The triple-match principle (TMP) proposes that the strongest interactive relations between job demands and job resources are observed when demands *and* resources *and* outcomes are based on qualitatively identical dimensions. For instance, emotional support from colleagues is most likely to moderate (i.e. mitigate) the relation between emotional demands (e.g. irate customers) and emotional outcomes (e.g. emotional exhaustion). So, the TMP suggests not only that job demands and job resources should match, but also that both job demands and job resources should successively match job-related outcomes. For instance, insolent customers are more likely to cause emotional disorders than physical complaints, and cognitive job resources are more likely to be helpful to engage creativity than increasing physical fitness. To summarize, the complementary fit of the TMP applies to three different levels: (i) the match between job demands and job resources, (ii) the match between *either* job demands *or* job resources and job-related outcomes, and (iii) the match between job demands *and* job resources *and* job outcomes.

The two key principles of the DISC Model are guided by two further corollaries pertaining to compensation and balance mechanisms (de Jonge et al., 2008). The *compensation* or *stress-buffering* mechanism proposes that the adverse effects of high job demands on worker health and well-being can be counteracted if workers have sufficient job resources to deal with their demanding work tasks. Job resources from the same conceptual domain as job demands are most likely to counteract these negative effects. For instance, it is proposed that employees who are confronted with high physical job demands (e.g. moving heavy objects) are least likely to experience health problems (e.g. low back pain) if they have sufficient physical job resources (e.g. a bed lift) to deal with their physically demanding job. The *balance* or *activation-enhancing* mechanism proposes optimal conditions for employee learning, growth, creativity and performance if there is a balanced mixture of high (but not overwhelming) job demands and high matching job resources. For instance, employees who need to solve complex problems are most likely to experience creativity if they have sufficient cognitive job resources (e.g. instant access to information or authority to decide the work method themselves) in order to deal with their cognitively demanding job.

Finally, it should be noted that the TMP is a so-called probabilistic principle. This means that TMP effects are considered to be more likely in empirical research studies than non-matching effects, but the model does *not* argue that such non-matching effects should not occur at all. As mentioned before, the focus of interest is on associations between specific job demands on the one hand and 'matching', 'less-matching' and even 'non-matching' job resources on the other. Findings other than triple matches are therefore no counterevidence to the DISC Model.

Beyond DISC: Integration of detachment from work

So far, the DISC Model has mainly focused on processes occurring at work. However, it might not only restrict itself to the work situation (and a match between job demands and job resources) and to the related health and well-being outcomes. Experiences and events happening *off the job* may also be related to employee health and well-being. Specifically, research on recovery (see Chapter 8) has shown that recovery experiences during non-work time interact with job demands (Sonnentag, Binnewies, & Mojza, 2010) and job resources (Siltaloppi, Kinnunen, & Feldt, 2009) in the prediction of employee health and well-being. These earlier studies, however, did not systematically test the interaction between job demands, job resources and off-job recovery, and they did not differentiate between the cognitive, emotional and physical aspects of demands, resources and recovery. Thus, the extended DISC Model goes beyond earlier research on recovery by describing specific combinations of job demands and resources on the one hand, and off-job recovery on the other. Gaining knowledge about how job demands, job resources and off-job recovery are related to employee outcomes is highly relevant for both theory and practice.

The extended DISC Model, labelled DISC-R (R for recovery), was introduced by de Jonge and colleagues in 2012 (de Jonge, Spoor, Sonnentag, Dormann, & van den Tooren, 2012b) and focuses on the recovery concept of *detachment from work*. Detachment can, in general, be seen as the most promising strategy as far as job-related recovery is concerned (see Sonnentag & Geurts, 2009). Etzion, Eden and Lapidot (1998) defined detachment from work as an 'individual's sense of being away from the work situation' (p. 579). It is an experience of leaving one's work behind when returning home (i.e. 'switching-off' through off-job recovery). Low detachment from work implies that the functional bodily systems remain in a state of prolonged activation. To recover from high job demands, it is important that employees ideally engage in off-job activities that appeal to other systems or do not engage at all in effort-related activities (see Geurts & Sonnentag, 2006). For instance, a healthcare worker whose job requires high emotional effort would be better off avoiding engagement in off-job activities that put high demands on the same (i.e. emotional) systems. Similarly, a construction worker with a highly demanding physical job would be better off avoiding engagement in activities after work that put high demands on the same (i.e. physical) systems. In this context, Sonnentag and Niessen (2008) proposed that a full degree of off-job recovery is attained when the employee feels that both cognitive and physical as well as emotional systems called on during work have returned to their baseline levels after work. It is therefore assumed that detachment from work should encompass a cognitive, emotional and physical switch-off from work, which is in line with the three DISC dimensions. In agreement with theory about the role of off-job recovery in the job stress process (Geurts & Sonnentag, 2006), the DISC-R Model proposes that detachment from work has an additional, moderating, effect in the relation between job demands, job resources and employee outcomes. Furthermore, in line with earlier DISC and recovery theory, it is assumed that detachment from work that matches particular demands will be most effective (e.g. emotional detachment in relation to emotional demands).

The question remains how detachment from work will function in either unfavourable or favourable work situations. First, in unfavourable work situations when job demands are high and job resources are low, detaching from work (cognitively, emotionally or physically) could have a *positive* effect on an employee's health. These situations are high-strain jobs in Karasek and Theorell's (1990) terms (see Chapter 3), and phases of switching off through off-job recovery seem to be very important for employees facing these situations. Put differently, being busy with job-related thoughts after work drains energy that will impair health. Detachment could indeed support health in high-strain jobs due to the restoration of internal resources. Second, in more favourable work situations, when job demands and job resources are both high (i.e. active jobs in Karasek's terms), the effect of (cognitively) detaching from work on performance-based outcomes such as active learning and creativity is more ambivalent. It is well-known that cognitive job demands are, in principle, useful to ignite active learning and creative behaviour, but there are ramifying conditions that must be met. First, learning and creativity at work are likely to occur when there is at least a slight surplus of available cognitive job resources (see de Jonge & Dormann, 2003). Only when this surplus is available is there room to think about existing problems and to develop new and innovative ways of how to handle the cognitive job demands. The question now is how this interplay between demands and resources is conditioned by cognitive detachment. At first glance, cognitively detaching from work means leaving cognitive job demands and job resources behind, which could mitigate active learning and creativity. In addition, because of a better segmentation of work and non-work roles caused by high levels of cognitive detachment, employees may need more time to return to their working mode. This implies that employees will not be as creative as they could have been when they had spent some time prior to work thinking about work problems. Put differently, in cases of high cognitive job demands and high job resources, detachment from work as a cognitive recovery strategy hampers active learning and creativity. However, it may well function as an effective way to prevent, for instance, concentration problems.

To recapitulate, the DISC-R Model proposes that detachment from work has an additional, moderating, effect in the relation between job demands, job resources and employee outcomes. In addition, it is hypothesized that detachment from work that matches particular demands will be most effective (e.g. emotional detachment to reduce emotional exhaustion that is merely caused by emotional demands). It is further assumed that the positive effect of detachment is only valid in case of high-strain jobs and health-based outcomes: high detachment from work (either cognitive or emotional or physical) represents an important source of off-job recovery, which particularly may foster health. In contrast, in active jobs, and with regard to performance-based outcomes, this positive effect of detachment is not expected. Rather, high cognitive detachment from work might be detrimental for processes of learning and creativity to occur, whereas low cognitive detachment could be particularly beneficial to learning and creative behaviour.

A graphical representation of the DISC-R Model is shown in Figure 4.3. The model consists of three key components (i.e. job demands, job resources and off-job recovery), each consisting of cognitive (indicated by a head), emotional (heart) and physical (hand) dimensions. A balance of the different components will lead to favourable outcomes in terms of employee health, well-being and performance, whereas an imbalance will lead to unfavourable outcomes.

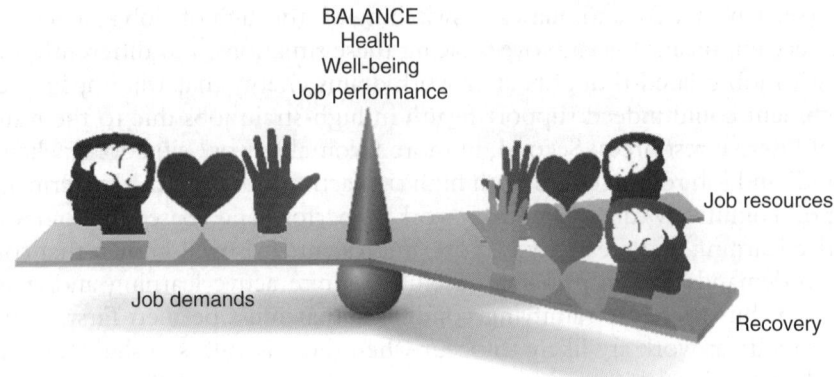

Figure 4.3 The DISC-R Model.

Evidence for the DISC Model

Although the DISC Model is a relatively young model, it has been tested in different kinds of empirical studies in lots of countries. These studies encompass different kinds of research designs, such as cross-sectional and longitudinal surveys, daily diary studies, and psychometric, vignette and laboratory studies (see also Chapter 2). Different kinds of employees were used, although the majority of them were human-services workers such as nursing, retail and teaching staff. Van den Tooren, de Jonge and Dormann (2011) conducted a review study of 29 DISC studies to investigate the empirical evidence for the key assumption of the model, that is, the TMP. Results showed that the TMP was supported largely with regard to the stress-buffering effect of (matching) job resources (i.e. the model's compensation mechanism). Specifically, there were 32 out of 108 tested triple-match interactions (29.6%), 36 out of 327 tested less-matching interactions (11.0%) and 6 out of 76 tested non-matching interactions (7.9%). Note that the last percentage comes close to what can be expected by chance combined with publication bias (i.e. the tendency to publish studies supporting the hypotheses more often than studies showing null or negative findings). The general outcome of this review suggested that matching job resources are more functional resources than less-matching and non-matching job resources to deal with specific types of job demands, at least as far as the stress-buffering effects of those job resources are concerned. This review did not lend strong support with respect to the so-called activation-enhancing effect of (matching) job resources (i.e. the model's balance mechanism), although more recent DISC studies are in favour of this effect (for overviews see van de Ven, 2011; Niks, de Jonge, Gevers, & Houtman, 2013).

Furthermore, the extended version of the model, the DISC-R Model, was investigated in a study by de Jonge and colleagues (2012b) among nearly 400 Dutch human services employees from three organizations. They indeed found moderating effects of matching job resources as well as matching off-job recovery (i.e. detachment from work) on the relation between corresponding job demands and employee outcomes. More specifically, results showed that cognitive detachment from work had negative effects on learning and creativity, whereas emotional and physical detachment from work had positive effects on employees health, and even on creativity. The effects of cognitive detachment on creativity were also found in a daily diary study by Spoor, de Jonge and Hamers (2010).

> **Work Psychology in Action: The diagnostic profile of the DISC-R Model**
>
> One of the key practical benefits of the extended DISC Model, or DISC-R, is that practitioners can compute a *diagnostic profile* for all kinds of jobs, and then discern ways in which to improve job resources or off-job recovery for any given job. This requires practitioners to use employees' scores on the DISC questionnaire (DISQ) as input, based on their assessments of the three types of job demands, job resources and off-job recovery. A short version of the DISQ requires employees to answer 28 questions about their jobs by rating the extent to which each job characteristic is present in their job on a five-point scale (from 1 = never to 5 = always). Specifically, they have to indicate what the work would be like for them, and how things are now rather than how things may be in the future. Example questions for each component are 'I will need to display high levels of concentration and precision at work' (cognitive demand), 'I will have the opportunity to determine my own work method' (cognitive resource) and 'I put all thoughts of work aside' (cognitive detachment). Several questions (three or four) tap into different factors of each job characteristic. A total score for each job characteristic is created by summing the answers provided. When practitioners have a diagnostic profile of each job as depicted in Figure 4.4, they can proceed to
>
>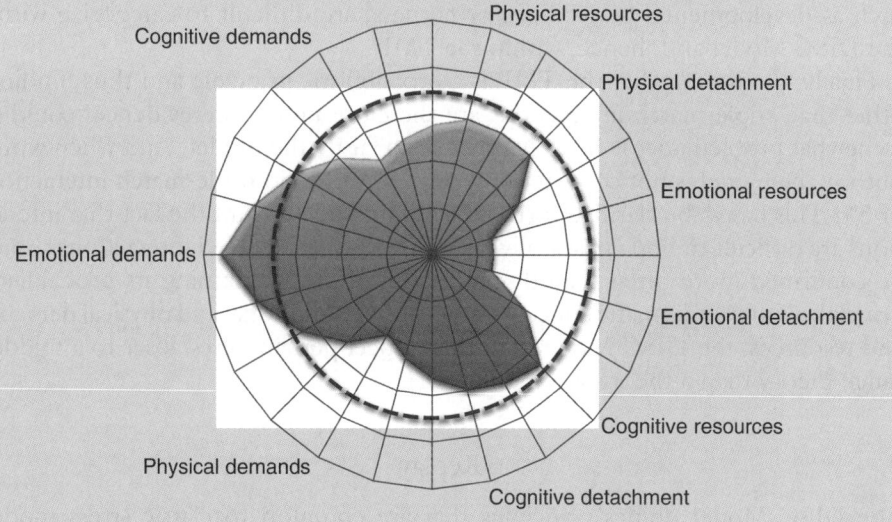
>
> **Figure 4.4** DISQ-R diagnostic profile.

> redesign the job to increase those job resources or off-job recovery that is deficient (i.e. significantly lower than their matching job demands). The dotted circle in the figure denotes a threshold of relatively high scores. In this case, it appears that particularly emotional resources and emotional detachment from work are deficient compared to the huge amount of emotional demands. These two components could be the starting point for workplace interventions or employee training. Finally, it should be noted that this tool has been profoundly tested in practice (de Jonge, Spoor, Hamers, & Bergman, 2012a; Niks et al., 2013).

Evaluation of the DISC Model

In general, research on the DISC Model has been supportive of the stress-buffering part of the TMP. Past research is less clear about its activation-enhancing effect, although a few more recent studies are in favour of it.

Furthermore, similar to the JD–R Model, the conceptual and empirical difference between job demands and job resources is not as clear as it may seem at first glance. Different kinds of job demands and job resources usually constitute separate factors in successive factor analyses. This is probably because, in general, job demands are valued negatively and job resources are valued positively. Consequently, it might be that relations with outcome variables depend on the precise nature of either job demands or job resources.

Although the JD–R Model has been criticized for being overly open and flexible, the DISC Model can be criticized for the opposite, namely its restrictive nature to focus on the match of only three types of demands and resources. Some job demands, such as reorganization and role conflict, and specific job resources, such as developmental possibilities or fairness, are difficult to categorize within the DISC Model and, hence, within the TMP.

Finally, the notion that the TMP is a probabilistic principle and thus 'findings other than triple-match interactions are therefore no counterevidence' could be somewhat problematic. Is it really possible to falsify the model? And when would one say the model is not confirmed: at only 10% of valid triple-match interactions or 5%? This has to be clarified further by taking into account the fact that interactions are difficult to find empirically and also that the expected interactions should be confirmed more often than disconfirmed. So, by combining its probabilistic principle with paradigmatic concepts of cognitive, emotional and physical demands and resources, the DISC Model is in this respect perhaps also closer to a middle-range theory than a theoretical model.

Replay

The DISC Model unifies principles that are common to classic stress models and claims to be a more comprehensive theoretical model of job stress and work motivation. We have discussed its development and key processes. Based on the multi-dimensionality of job demands and job resources, the model assumes triple-matching of concepts (i.e. matching demands *and* resources *and* outcomes). The TMP proposes that the strongest interactive relations between job demands and job resources are observed when demands, resources and outcomes are based on qualitatively identical dimensions. In line with theorizing about the role of off-job recovery in the job stress process, the extended DISC-R Model proposes that detachment from work has an additional moderating effect in the relation between job demands, job resources and outcomes. Furthermore, it is assumed that detachment from work that matches particular demands will be most effective. In general, there is mounting empirical evidence for the triple-match stress-buffering mechanism of the model. The support for the activation-enhancing mechanism is promising, although still in its infancy. Furthermore, several issues have to be considered when evaluating the model's current status. The most distinctive features of the model are its specificity (i.e. multi-dimensionality of all concepts) and the matching hypothesis. However, the model's specificity and probabilistic character come at the cost of generalizability and confirmation of assumptions.

4.4 Conclusions

We started this chapter with several meta-theoretical issues and criteria that are being proposed for the development and evaluation of theoretical models. We then introduced two recent theoretical models, the JD–R Model and the DISC-R Model. Specifically, we described their background, development, progress, current shape and empirical evidence.

During the time both models were introduced into the literature, the basic tenets of these models were not as new as they are frequently perceived post hoc. Indeed, many scholars in the field already had a broad understanding of job stress as a result of high job demands and a lack of job resources. Also, researchers were aware of the fact that ill-health and lack of motivation are not the same, as well as the fact that job demands and resources should somehow fit to each other. And in those days, studies were already being published that built on such ideas. However, at the turn of the century, common thinking on such issues was more on an abstract and broad theoretical level. It was, however, not condensed into single theoretical models.

The JD–R Model and the DISC-R Model share some common ground: they share the idea that two key job characteristics (i.e. job demands and resources) can be changed via relatively independent psychological processes to improve employee health and to enhance work motivation and work engagement. Further, where the JD–R Model is trying to make progress in the direction of the moderating role of personal resources, the DISC Model is trying to extend itself in the direction of the moderating role of off-job recovery (i.e. detachment from work). Both avenues seem to be promising and offer ample opportunities for research and practice.

Practically, how can both models be used to improve employee health and motivational outcomes? First, both models stress the important role of *job resources* to deal with demands at work. In addition, the JD–R Model mentions the important role of *personal resources* and the DISC-R Model the important role of *detachment from work*. Second, they consider both negative and positive outcomes via corresponding health impairment and motivational processes. This is attractive for both occupational health professionals and human resource professionals. Third, whereas the flexibility and openness of the JD–R Model is attractive for tailor-made investigations in different occupational groups and different organizations, the specificity of the DISC-R Model paves the way for tailored work-oriented interventions in today's practice. Finally and more generally, both models help researchers and practitioners to get a thorough idea of work-related risk factors by means of a systematic and theory-driven analysis, to improve employee health, work motivation, work engagement and job performance.

Discussion Points

1. What arguments can be made to classify the JD–R Model or the DISC-R Model as middle-range theories or as theoretical models?
2. Suppose you have to examine employees' health and well-being in several supermarkets. What job stress model would you prefer as a basis for your examination? Explain why, taking both theoretical and practical arguments into account.
3. Compare the JD–R Model with the DCSM and the ERI Model from Chapter 3. What are the key differences?
4. The DISC Model is trying to extend itself in the direction of the moderating role of off-job recovery (i.e. detachment from work). Could you come up with other extensions of the DISC Model?

Learning by Doing

1. Try to reflect on your study or, if applicable, on the job that you currently hold. Make a list of the tasks that you perform daily. On the basis of these tasks, make a list of at least three demands that you are faced with. Next, we hope that you are lucky enough to enjoy the presence of some factors that help you to deal with these demands. Name at least three resources that are relevant for your work or your study. Do these resources help you in dealing with your demands? What can you conclude about your level of energy (or exhaustion) and motivation? Is this in line with your own feelings?
2. Conduct at least two semi-structured interviews (see Chapter 2) with people from different professions (e.g. a construction worker, nurse, police officer, taxi-driver). Prepare a number of questions that allow you to address the relevant concepts dealt with in the present chapter (e.g. What do you find

most demanding in your job? What are the most important resources in your job? How do you feel when coming home from work? Do you find your job motivating and, if so, why? Are you feeling burned out? How do you detach from work?). Make a theoretical interpretation of the responses and align them with the figures shown in this chapter. Think about what you could do to help these employees if you were in a supervisory position. Come back to your interviewees and discuss your solutions with them. Give them the chance to improve your suggestions.
3. The JD–R Model stresses the role of personal resources such as self-efficacy and optimism. Read the studies of Heuven and colleagues (2006) or Xanthopoulou and associates (2009a) and explain their findings that personal resources appear to be more important for the motivational process than for the health impairment process.
4. Imagine a sales department of an insurance company in which employees face high cognitive job demands, low cognitive resources and high cognitive detachment from work. On the basis of the assumptions of the DISC-R Model predict employees' scores on creative behaviour. What would you advise the manager of the department to do?

Further Reading

de Jonge, J., & Dormann, C. (2006). Stressors, resources, and strain at work: A longitudinal test of the Triple-Match Principle. *Journal of Applied Psychology, 91*, 1359–1374.

Demerouti, E., Bakker, A. B., Nachreiner, F., & Schaufeli, W. B. (2001). The job demands–resources model of burnout. *Journal of Applied Psychology, 86*, 499–512.

Demerouti, E., & Bakker, A. B. (2011). The Job Demands–Resources model: Challenges for future research. *SA Journal of Industrial Psychology, 37*, 974–983.

van den Tooren, M., de Jonge, J., & Dormann, C. (2011). The Demand-Induced Strain Compensation Model: Background, key principles, theoretical underpinnings, and extended empirical evidence. In A. Caetano, S. A. Silva, & M. J. Chambel (Eds.), *New challenges for a healthy workplace in human services* (pp. 13–59). (Series: Organizational Psychology and Health Care, edited by J. M. Peiro, & W. B. Schaufeli). Mering: Rainer Hampp Verlag.

References

Bakker, A. B., & Demerouti, E. (2007). The job demands–resources model: State of the art. *Journal of Managerial Psychology, 22*, 309–328.

Bakker, A. B., Demerouti, E., & Euwema, M. C. (2005). Job resources buffer the impact of job demands on burnout. *Journal of Occupational Health Psychology, 10*, 170–180.

Bakker, A. B., Hakanen, J. J., Demerouti, E., & Xanthopoulou, D. (2007). Job resources boost work engagement, particularly when job demands are high. *Journal of Educational Psychology, 99*, 274–284.

Cohen, S., & McKay, G. (1984). Social support, stress and the buffering hypothesis: A theoretical analysis. In A. Baum, S. E. Taylor, & J. E. Singer (Eds.), *Handbook of psychology and health* (pp. 253–267). Hillsdale, NJ: Lawrence Erlbaum Associates.

Cohen, S., & Wills, T. A. (1985). Stress, social support, and the moderating hypothesis. *Psychological Bulletin, 98*, 310–357.

Crawford, E. R., LePine, J. A., & Rich, B. L. (2010). Linking job demands and resources to employee engagement and burnout: A theoretical extension and meta-analytic test. *Journal of Applied Psychology, 95*, 834–848.

Cummings, E. M., Greene, A. L., & Karraker, K. H. (1991). *Life-span developmental psychology: Perspectives on stress and coping*. Hillsdale, NJ: Lawrence Erlbaum Associates.

de Jonge, J., & Dormann, C. (2003). The DISC Model: Demand-Induced Strain Compensation mechanisms in job stress. In M. F. Dollard, H. R. Winefield, & A. H. Winefield (Eds.), *Occupational stress in the service professions* (pp. 43–74). London: Taylor & Francis.

de Jonge, J., & Dormann, C. (2006). Stressors, resources, and strain at work: A longitudinal test of the Triple-Match Principle. *Journal of Applied Psychology, 91*, 1359–1374.

de Jonge, J., Dormann, C., & van den Tooren, M. (2008). The Demand-Induced Strain Compensation Model: Renewed theoretical considerations and empirical evidence. In K. Näswall, J. Hellgren, & M. Sverke (Eds.), *The individual in the changing working life* (pp. 67–87). Cambridge: Cambridge University Press.

de Jonge, J., Spoor, E., Hamers, J., & Bergman, M. (2012a). DISCovery: een interventiemethodiek op basis van digitale zelfanalyse [*DISCovery:* an intervention method based on digital self-analysis]. In J. de Jonge, M. Peeters, S. Sjollema, & H. de Zeeuw (Eds.), *Scherp in werk: 5 routes naar optimale inzetbaarheid* (pp. 101–129). Assen: Koninklijke van Gorcum BV.

de Jonge, J., Spoor, E., Sonnentag, S., Dormann, C., & van den Tooren, M. (2012b). 'Take a break?!': Off-job recovery, job demands and job resources as predictors of health, active learning, and creativity. *European Journal of Work and Organizational Psychology, 21*, 321–348.

de Lange, A. H., Taris, T. W., Kompier, M. A. J., Houtman, I. L. D., & Bongers, P. M. (2003). 'The *very* best of the millennium': Longitudinal research and the Demand-Control-(Support) model. *Journal of Occupational Health Psychology, 8*, 282–305.

Demerouti, E., & Bakker, A. B. (2011). The Job Demands–Resources model: Challenges for future research. *SA Journal of Industrial Psychology, 37*, 1–9.

Demerouti, E., Bakker, A. B., Nachreiner, F., & Schaufeli, W. B. (2001). The Job Demands–Resources model of burnout. *Journal of Applied Psychology, 86*, 499–512.

Etzion, D., Eden, D., & Lapidot, Y. (1998). Relief from job stressors and burnout: Reserve service as a respite. *Journal of Applied Psychology, 83*, 577–585.

Geurts, S. A. E., & Sonnentag, S. (2006). Recovery as an explanatory mechanism in the relation between acute stress reactions and chronic health impairment. *Scandinavian Journal of Work, Environment & Health, 32*, 482–492.

Hackman, J. R., & Oldham, G. R. (1980). *Work redesign*. Reading, MA: Addison-Wesley.

Heuven, E., Bakker, A. B., Schaufeli, W. B., & Huisman, N. (2006). The role of self-efficacy in performing emotion work. *Journal of Vocational Behavior, 69*, 222–235.

Hobfoll, S. E. (2002). Social and psychological resources and adaptation. *Review of General Psychology, 6*, 307–324.

Hobfoll, S. E., Johnson, R. J., Ennis, N., & Jackson, A. P. (2003). Resource loss, resource gain, and emotional outcomes among inner city women. *Journal of Personality and Social Psychology, 84*, 632–643.

Hockey, G. R. J. (1993). Cognitive-energetical control mechanisms in the management of work demands and psychological health. In A. Baddely, & L. Weiskrantz (Eds.), *Attention: Selection, awareness, and control* (pp. 328–345). Oxford: Clarendon Press.

Judge, T. A., Bono, J. E., Erez, A., & Locke, E. A. (2005). Core self-evaluations and job and life satisfaction: The role of self-concordance and goal attainment. *Journal of Applied Psychology, 90*, 257–268.

Kahn, R. L., & Byosiere, P. (1992). Stress in organizations. In M. D. Dunnete, & L. M. Hough (Eds.), *Handbook of industrial and organizational psychology* (Vol. 3, 2nd ed., pp. 537–650). Palo Alto, CA: Consulting Psychologists Press.

Karasek, R. A., & Theorell, T. (1990). *Healthy work: Stress, productivity and the reconstruction of working life*. New York: Basic Books.

Lee, R. T., & Ashforth, B. E. (1996). A meta-analytic examination of the correlates of the three dimensions of job burnout. *Journal of Applied Psychology, 81*, 123–133.

Niks, I. M. W., de Jonge, J., Gevers, J. M. P., & Houtman, I. L. D. (2013). Design of the DISCovery project: Tailored work-oriented interventions to improve employee health, well-being, and performance-related outcomes in hospital care. *BMC Health Services Research, 13*, 66.

Pomaki, G., & Maes, S. (2002). Predicting quality of work life: From work conditions to self-regulation. In E. Gullone, & R. A. Cummins (Eds.), *The universality of subjective well-being indicators* (pp. 151–173). Dordrecht: Kluwer Academic.

Schaufeli, W. B., & Taris, T. W. (in press). A critical review of the Job Demands–Resources Model: Implications for improving work and health. In G. Bauer, & O. Hammig (Eds.), *Bridging occupational, organizational and public health: A transdisciplinary approach*. Dordrecht: Springer.

Siegrist, J. (1996). Adverse health effects of high effort–low reward conditions. *Journal of Occupational Health Psychology, 1*, 27–41.

Siltaloppi, M., Kinnunen, U., & Feldt, T. (2009). Recovery experiences as moderators between psychological work characteristics and occupational well-being. *Work & Stress, 23*, 330–348.

Sonnentag, S., Binnewies, C., & Mojza, E. J. (2010). Staying well and engaged when demands are high: The role of psychological detachment. *Journal of Applied Psychology, 95*, 965–976.

Sonnentag, S., & Geurts, S. (2009). Methodological issues in recovery research. In S. Sonnentag, P. L. Perrewe, & D. C. Ganster (Eds.), *Current perspectives on job stress recovery* (pp. 1–36). Bingley: Emerald Group Publishing.

Sonnentag, S., & Niessen, C. (2008). Staying vigorous until work is over: The role of trait vigour, day-specific work experiences and recovery. *Journal of Occupational and Organizational Psychology, 81*, 435–458.

Spoor, E., de Jonge, J., & Hamers, J. P. H. (2010). Nu even niet…! Of toch wel…? Een dagboekstudie naar detachment en creativiteit [Not right now…! Or just right now…? A daily-survey study on detachment and creativity]. *Gedrag & Organisatie, 23*, 296–315.

van de Ven, B. (2011). *Psychosocial well-being of employees in the technology sector: The interplay of job demands and job resources*. Doctoral dissertation. Ghent University, Ghent.

van den Tooren, M., de Jonge, J., & Dormann, C. (2011). The Demand-Induced Strain Compensation Model: Background, key principles, theoretical underpinnings, and extended empirical evidence. In A. Caetano, S. A. Silva, & M. J. Chambel (Eds.), *New challenges for a healthy workplace in human services* (pp. 13–59). (Series: Organizational Psychology and Health Care, edited by J. M. Peiro & W. B. Schaufeli). Mering: Rainer Hampp Verlag.

van der Doef, M., & Maes, S. (1999). The job demand–control(–support) model and psychological well-being: A review of 20 years of empirical research. *Work & Stress, 13*, 87–114.

Viswesvaran, C., Sanchez, J. I., & Fisher, J. (1999). The role of social support in the process of work stress: A meta-analysis. *Journal of Vocational Behavior, 54*, 314–334.

Walker, L. O., & Avant, K. C. (1995). *Strategies for theory construction in nursing* (2nd ed.). Englewood Cliffs, NJ: Prentice Hall.

Xanthopoulou, D., Bakker, A. B., Demerouti, E., & Schaufeli, W. B. (2007). The role of personal resources in the job demands–resources model. *International Journal of Stress Management, 14*, 121–141.

Xanthopoulou, D., Bakker, A. B., Heuven, E., Demerouti, E., & Schaufeli, W. B. (2008). Working in the sky: A diary study on work engagement among flight attendants. *Journal of Occupational Health Psychology, 13*, 345–356.

Xanthopoulou, D., Bakker, A. B., Demerouti, E., & Schaufeli, W. B. (2009a). Reciprocal relationships between job resources, personal resources, and work engagement. *Journal of Vocational Behavior, 74*, 235–244.

Xanthopoulou, D., Bakker, A. B., Demerouti, E., & Schaufeli, W. B. (2009b). Work engagement and financial returns: A diary study on the role of job and personal resources. *Journal of Occupational and Organizational Psychology, 82*, 183–200.

Part C
Demands

5
Quantitative Job Demands

Marc van Veldhoven

> **Chapter Objectives**
>
> After studying this chapter, you should be able to:
>
> - give a *definition* of quantitative job demands;
> - describe *antecedents* and *consequences* of quantitative job demands;
> - discuss objective and subjective approaches of *measuring* quantitative job demands, and how these two approaches *relate* to each other;
> - mention several *practical applications* that relate to quantitative job demands.

5.1 Introduction

The amount and pace of work is an important concern for well-being and performance at work. Indeed, work pressure seems to increase worldwide (Schnall, Dobson, & Rosskam, 2009). Results from the European Working Conditions Survey, which was performed five times between 1990 and 2010 with five-year intervals, illustrate this trend. The percentage of workers reporting working at high speed for 25% of the time or more increased from 47% to 59% over this period (Paoli, 1992; Parent-Thirion et al., 2012).

An Introduction to Contemporary Work Psychology, First Edition.
Edited by Maria C. W. Peeters, Jan de Jonge and Toon W. Taris.
© 2014 John Wiley & Sons, Ltd. Published 2014 by John Wiley & Sons, Ltd.

> ### Work Psychology in Action: Observing Thomas at work and at play
>
> Thomas is a 25-year-old employee working in one of the branches of a major accountancy firm. His job mainly consists of assisting a team of local accountants with entering and checking financial data. His job is performed behind a computer and when observed in his workplace, you see him performing a rapid series of mouse movements on a complicated screen layout during most of the day.
>
> Lately, the firm has been under a lot of pressure to increase quality as well as productivity. For Thomas this results in ever greater numbers of financial records to process. He complains about the work pressure and signals repeatedly to his boss that the amount of work is more than he can perform in a reliable way. Small mistakes start creeping into his work.
>
> Thomas leaves the office after a particularly busy day muttering about feeling stressed, but when you meet him in the corridor next morning he states that he has had a wonderful evening and feels relaxed. When asked about what he did last evening, he explains that he has been playing this great new computer game until after midnight. If you had observed Thomas sitting behind his game computer, you would have seen him performing another rapid series of mouse movements on a complicated screen layout for most of the evening.

Although the amount and speed of work is an important societal issue, it is not a phenomenon that is easy to grasp. This is illustrated by the example in the Work Psychology in Action box. The same kind of task and workload that can be stressful in one context can be relaxing in another. Apparently, context and other work-related factors such as the amount of control over and variety in the task are important in determining how people experience job demands and how this perception affects their well-being, health and performance. This is exactly the point that has been made in the previous two chapters: job demands have taken a central place in the theoretical models presented, and it is the way in which these job demands combine and interact with other factors that determines whether there is risk or not, as explained, for example, in the Demand–Control–Support Model and the Job Demands–Resources Model. What constitutes pressure and a stressful experience in one context may be experienced as a challenge and a pleasurable experience in another (see Chapters 3 and 4).

Quantitative and qualitative job demands

In dealing with job demands, it is important to discriminate between quantitative and qualitative demands (French, Caplan, & van Harrison, 1982; Karasek & Theorell, 1990). Quantitative demands relate to the amount and pace of work, whereas qualitative demands pertain to the type of skills and/or effort needed in order to perform work tasks, for instance cognitive, emotional or physical skills and/or effort. For example, the complexity of the design of a new building can be huge, challenging the mental capacities and skills of architects (i.e. cognitive demands). This challenge is rather different from the heavy loads lifted and moved by workers in the logistics department of an industrial company (i.e. physical demands). Also quite different are the job demands of hospital nurses, who provide care to people who are seriously ill or dying (i.e. emotional demands). In each of these three examples, the qualitative side of job demands is about the difficulty level or complexity of the job (Bowling & Kirkendall, 2012), in contrast to the quantitative side of job demands. The present chapter focuses on quantitative job demands, while the next chapter deals with qualitative job demands.

The chapter has three sections. In the first section a definition is given of quantitative job demands, and their antecedents and consequences are discussed. The second section deals with the issue of objective and/or subjective measurement of job demands. Finally, in the third section some practical applications with regard to quantitative demands are introduced. The chapter ends with conclusions and points for discussion and learning.

5.2 Defining Quantitative Job Demands

There is a whole range of words that people use in common language to describe quantitative job demands, such as long working hours, working overtime, amount of work, work pressure, work speed and workload. Each of these terms carries different associations and has different nuances. These will be discussed here briefly before this chapter's working definition is given.

Long working hours and working overtime

It is rather obvious that if quantitative work demands are high, this will lead to work tasks requiring more time than scheduled or contracted. Consequently, one would expect long working hours and/or working overtime, as well as an associated high level of job strain, to occur (see also Chapter 8). Contrary to such expectations, however, research has shown that the association between overtime, job demands and job strain is not particularly strong (Beckers, 2008). This is probably because there is a category of workers for whom long working hours and working overtime is not stressful. A study by van der Hulst, van Veldhoven and Beckers (2006) showed that this is true for employees in so-called passive jobs, as defined in the Demand–Control–Support Model (Karasek & Theorell, 1990) (see Chapter 3). An example of a passive job is a receptionist at a relatively quiet entrance desk. Her main tasks are to help visitors find their contact persons and to take occasional phone calls. Because of the opening hours of the office she occasionally works paid overtime. As the overtime work is not intensive and pays well (double the hourly pay) she actually likes overtime.

It is probably better to think of long working hours and working overtime as possible indicators of high quantitative job demands, but not as defining characteristics.

Work speed, amount of work, work intensity and workload

Given any fixed amount of time available to do a job, the amount of effort invested is strongly dependent on the amount of work to be completed and the speed with which this work has to be performed. Rather than using two terms to refer to these dual aspects of speed and amount of work, often a single term is used: work intensity or workload. High work intensity or high workload both indicate a high work amount and/or work performed at high speed. Work intensity or workload has shown to be related to work effort in a systematic way, in both laboratory and field studies (Zijlstra, 1993).

Work pressure and work overload

The terms mentioned above all relate to more or less observable elements that produce quantitative job demands. These observable elements are associated with time, speed and amount of work. However, often people use terms that include more than just observable elements. They add a more evaluative judgement to the way they talk about the level of quantitative job demands. Common words used in this context are 'work pressure' and 'work overload'. These words carry connotations of different degrees of job demands rising above acceptable levels, with work pressure indicating milder levels of job demands above normal, and work overload indicating more severe levels of job demands above normal.

Karasek (1979) argued that both work pressure and work overload contain an element of failing job control. Most workers do not like pressure or overload, and will attempt to prevent this from happening by exercising job control. When workers report overload and pressure, their job control is probably low. Based on this, Karasek (1979) advocated against using constructs and measures of pressure and overload in work psychological research, as they essentially prohibit separate assessment of job demands and job control. As explained in Chapter 3, separate assessment of demands and control is essential according to the Demand–Control–Support Model.

Working definition of quantitative job demands

Given that different terms and connotations of quantitative job demands are common, attempts have been made to standardize terminology, at least among researchers and professionals in the area of work psychology and work (re)design (see also Chapters 1, 3 and 18). The most important attempt was made by the International Organization for Standardization (ISO), inspired by the way in which concepts and measures are usually standardized in the field of ergonomics. After years of discussions by expert groups, ISO guideline number 10075 appeared in 1991. It contains general principles, definitions and terminology in relation to mental workload (Nachreiner, 1999). More than 20 years later it can be concluded that the guideline has not become a common language standard in research on work psychology. The terms discussed above are still interchangeably used in today's research and practice.

To overcome the lack of a commonly accepted definition of quantitative job demands, the following working definition is adopted in this chapter:

> Quantitative job demands constitute those elements of the work environment that concern the amount and speed of work to be performed, and require physical and/or psychological effort.

This working definition is rather neutral in its implications. Several of the words mentioned earlier in this chapter to denote quantitative job demands have a decidedly negative connotation. A more neutral terminology and definition is preferred because this opens up the possibility of positive effects of demands, too. This concurs with current research emphasizing that a certain amount of quantitative job demands is necessary to challenge workers, to let them learn and thrive (Bakker, van Veldhoven, & Xanthopoulou, 2010), and to keep them alert, motivated and free from boredom (Loukidou, Loan-Clarke, & Daniels, 2009). This will be explained in more detail later on.

As a final note, this working definition focuses on how the job and its context impact on the worker or, in other words, on the externally generated side of quantitative job demands. The internally generated side of job demands, derived from the worker him/herself, such as ambition level, is beyond the scope of this chapter. Interested readers are referred to Warr (2008) and Edwards, Caplan and van Harrison (1998) for more information.

After defining quantitative job demands, the next step is to discuss antecedents and consequences.

Replay

Words that are commonly used to refer to high quantitative job demands, such as long working hours, working overtime, work pressure, work overload, amount of work, work speed, work intensity and workload are reviewed. Although long working hours and overtime are intuitively indicative for high quantitative job demands, this has not been clearly established in research. In some jobs long working hours and overtime are accompanied by low quantitative job demands. Work pressure and work overload carry an implicit element of failing control and are negative in their connotation. Given the former, a working definition is preferred that is both less ambiguous and more neutral. Quantitative job demands are therefore defined as those elements of the work environment that concern the amount and speed of work to be performed and require physical and/or psychological effort. The terms 'workload' and 'work intensity' can be used as synonyms.

5.3 Antecedents of Quantitative Job Demands

Theories in work psychology often start with the key characteristics of work and continue with a detailed description of the mechanisms leading to employee well-being, health and performance. However, work psychology does not operate in a vacuum: job characteristics are shaped and are transformed by factors in organizations and societies over time. It is therefore important to pay attention to the context of work in this chapter.

The context of work

At the turn of the twenty-first century, a renowned group of work psychologists set out to take stock of the state of the field (Parker, Wall, & Cordery, 2001). They distinguished between two important groups of factors in the context of work: external and internal organizational factors. External organizational factors impinge on the organization from the outside environment. They influence the level of quantitative demands mostly through the choices made by the organization in how to deal with its environment. Internal organizational factors are characteristics of the organization itself that impact on the level of quantitative demands in a job. Below, external organizational factors are elaborated first, followed by internal organizational factors.

External organizational factors
A first external factor that influences quantitative job demands relates to *uncertainty in the environment* of the organization. Competition between firms, whether global, national or regional, is translated into flexibility and/or productivity norms that have consequences for the level of job demands of employees.

A second external factor concerns the *legal and political institutions* determining the leeway of organizations in dealing with employees. Such institutional mechanisms function as a kind of buffer against, or amplifier of, initiatives by organizations that want to increase the demands placed on employees. Such institutional factors are related to wider cultural backgrounds. Across the globe, large cultural differences exist with regard to the importance of work (work values) and the number of working hours per week (working time) considered acceptable. Such cultural differences influence exposure levels to high quantitative job demands as well as employees' expectations associated with such demands (Karasek et al., 1998).

Third, the *labour market* is an external factor determining quantitative job demands. Shortages in the market with regard to knowledge, skills and abilities (KSAs) that are crucial to organizational functioning and business advantage influence job demands for workers. For example, a shortage of technically skilled workers may result in staff shortages in certain machine-related areas of industry in western Europe. Talented young people refrain from taking the technological education necessary to prepare for such jobs because they consider it a relatively difficult and labour-intensive type of study. Furthermore, they perceive that this qualification ultimately brings them a job that may contain certain inconveniences (such as shift work, heavy work and/or dirty work) compared to other technological jobs, for instance in information and communication technology.

Finally, *technological innovations* have facilitated new ways of organizing work that make it easier to work anytime and anyplace. From the perspective of job demands, this has reduced barriers against work carrying over to private life, possibly enhancing the experience of work–family conflict (Bailey & Kurland, 2002; see also Chapter 11).

Internal organizational factors
The external factors mentioned above determine the leeway of organizations in how they shape the jobs of workers. However, the way organizations handle this leeway is quite different from one organization to another. At this point, internal organizational factors come into play.

A first and important internal factor is *management style*, which is often intertwined with organizational culture and the climate concerning performance. Management may to some extent be interested in employee well-being as opposed to employee productivity. Such managerial priorities tend to translate into the level of job demands experienced by workers (Quinn & Rohrbaugh, 1983; Peccei, van de Voorde, & van Veldhoven, 2013). In extreme cases, a management style could be called exploitative or even abusive (Tepper, 2000, 2007) if an unreasonable amount of work is assigned to employees.

Second, a whole series of *managerial practices and innovations* has been initiated by organizations over recent decades to increase performance levels (Holman, Wall, Clegg, Sparrow, & Howard, 2003). It is beyond the scope of this chapter to elaborate such practices and innovations in detail, but a couple of salient examples can be mentioned. For instance, just-in-time management is about producing goods and services at exactly the time they are required for the next step in the production chain or for the customer. For employees this may imply tighter deadlines and/or additional effort to complete tasks in time. Second, lean manufacturing is targeted at making products with as few employee resources left unused as possible. For employees this may result in operating a machine with fewer workers than before.

Finally, the way the organization deals with people management is a crucial third internal factor that impacts on quantitative job demand levels. This area is generally referred to as *human resource management (HRM)*. Certain practices in HRM are known to be particularly important in shaping job demands. One example is the type of pay and reward scheme implemented. When worker pay is based on a piece rate (when workers are paid according to the number of products they make), this creates an incentive for speeding work up. Similar effects are achieved by introducing a low-level standard wage, supplemented by a performance-based bonus. When the standard wage is so low as to make workers dependent on the bonus, an incentive is created for speeding work up or for increasing the amount of dedicated time and effort (Gerhart & Rynes, 2003). Other HRM practices that impact on quantitative job demands are training and development as well as recruitment and selection (better qualified employees can cope better with job demands) and performance appraisal and feedback (any problems in coping with job demands might be signalled and discussed by employees during performance appraisal and feedback).

All in all, there are many contextual factors that might play a role in shaping the quantitative job demands that employees are facing. However, empirical research on the antecedents of quantitative job demands is particularly rare. Wiezer, Smulders and Nelemans (2005) investigated the contribution of a complex and instable environment, increasing organizational flexibility, understaffing, organizational renewal and change, as well as unattractive working conditions leading to labour market shortages. Key informants of more than 3,000 companies participated in the study. All of the factors investigated, except for understaffing, appeared to be important predictors of a high level of quantitative job demands as experienced by workers in organizations. Unattractive working conditions, especially physically heavy labour, appeared to be the most important factor predicting high quantitative job demands.

High-performance work systems and work intensification

All of the external and internal factors discussed above provide opportunities for organizational decision making that impact on quantitative job demands. However, several authors have pointed out that the combination of all these factors has stimulated the emergence of so-called high-performance work systems (HPWSs; Appelbaum, Bailey, Berg, & Kalleberg, 2000). Such systems have organizations implementing a series of organizational and HRM practices that stimulate abilities in, motivation of and opportunities for employees in such a way that they are likely to increase their work effort. High levels of employee involvement in decision making, accompanied by investments in employee skills and changes in performance-related incentives are among the key practices here (Boxall & Purcell, 2011).

HPWSs are expected to lead to work intensification for employees (Schnall, Dobson, & Rosskam, 2009). Some research evidence is available to back up this claim. Landsbergis, Cahill and Schnall (1999), for example, reviewed the health effects of lean production and related techniques. For the automobile industry they found indications that lean production is causing work intensification. For other sectors they stated that evidence is inconclusive. Van de Voorde, Paauwe and van Veldhoven (2012) reviewed the literature on high-performance HRM, well-being and organizational performance. High-performance HRM appears to benefit the organization more consistently than the employee. Studies tend to find that better organizational performance is often accompanied by better employee well-being (in terms of happiness, engagement, satisfaction and commitment; see also Chapters 12 and 13). Nevertheless, there are also studies showing that work is becoming more intensive at the same time, with higher levels of employee effort and job strain and poorer worker health as a result.

Replay

The 'intensity' of work is influenced by a range of factors in the work context, some of which are external and others internal to the organization. External factors mentioned were uncertainty in the organization's environment, legal and political institutions, the labour market, and technological innovations. Internal organizational factors concerned management style, managerial practices and innovations, as well as HRM. The way in which these external and internal factors are combined into the work system as practiced in an organization determines the level of demands in a job. For so-called high-performance work systems it has been argued that these might be accompanied by increased quantitative job demands.

5.4 Consequences of Quantitative Job Demands

The level of quantitative job demands is important for job performance and for employee well-being and health. It is common to distinguish between short-term and long-term effects when reviewing the consequences of job demands (Meijman, 1989). Sometimes the words acute (short-term) and chronic (long-term) are used to refer to the same distinction (Tattersall, 2000).

Short-term effects of quantitative job demands

In the controlled environment of a laboratory it is quite easy to manipulate the amount of work required in a task and the speed required to complete it. One can keep track of performance and error levels on a continuous basis. Such research has been performed since the late nineteenth century and it points towards an inverted, U-shaped relation between the level of activation generated by the demands in the task and the quality of the performance by the worker or test subject. This is known as the Yerkes–Dodson law (Yerkes & Dodson, 1908).

This means, in practical terms, that there is an optimal level of activation, hence an optimal level of job demands. Below that optimal level, demands and the associated activation are (too) low: the person has difficulty staying concentrated on the task and needs to become more activated. On the other side of the inverted U-curve, above the optimal level, are those people who are (too) highly activated in relation to the level of job demands. Their main problem is to manage their tension levels so as to be able to perform the task well (Gaillard, 2003).

Meijman (1989) outlined how fatigue and other short-term load effects result from work execution during the working day. Fatigue is the normal consequence of the effort invested in work. In healthy workers, fatigue responds to rest, and adequate rest returns fatigue to baseline levels (see also Chapter 8).

It is important to call specific attention here to tasks where employees are under-stimulated or satiated. This may happen in monotonous tasks, for example the monitoring of a highly standardized production process. In such a job, workers need to act only when things go wrong, which is – if everything is well-organized – not very often. In such a context, symptoms such as reduced vigilance, low concentration or boredom are found (see Chapter 12). These workers look fatigued when actually they are not. ISO 10075 calls these symptoms 'fatigue-like' *states* (Nachreiner, 1999). When a new stimulus is offered, these fatigue-like states disappear almost immediately. This is in contrast with fatigue itself: fatigue symptoms do not disappear by offering a new stimulus. As mentioned before, fatigue only responds to relaxation and rest (see Chapter 8).

Another issue that is important in relation to the short-term effects of quantitative job demands is the interference between different task elements. The quality of task performance may be limited not only because of fatigue, but also due to other ongoing tasks that need the employee's attention and/or action. Generally, employees' cognitive and behavioural resources are limited, and hence it is important to design jobs, workplaces and human–machine systems that allow employees control over the allocation of these resources to ongoing tasks (Tattersall, 2000; see also Chapter 3).

A final category of short-term effects of quantitative job demands is motivational in nature. Bowling and Kirkendall (2012) reviewed the literature on how quantitative job demands relate to employee's attitudes and related behaviour. On the whole, they reported that findings on such relations are rather mixed. At first sight, it seems easy to predict that high quantitative job demands lead to negative attitudes (e.g. low satisfaction, involvement and commitment) and negative behaviour (e.g. low task performance, low organizational citizenship behaviour, high counterproductive work behaviour, high turnover and high absenteeism; see also Chapters 13 and 15). However, there is also a mounting body of research indicating that a (moderately) high level of job demands will challenge workers and trigger learning and skill development (Karasek & Theorell, 1990; Bakker et al., 2010; see also Chapter 3). Given these two lines of reasoning, it is not entirely surprising that research so far has produced limited and inconsistent findings on the link between quantitative job demands and worker attitudes and related work behaviours.

Long-term effects of quantitative job demands

What happens when quantitative job demands are chronically high? There is a substantial body of evidence pointing to the possible long-term harmful consequences for employee health and well-being. Sustained activation over longer periods of time in combination with insufficient recovery (Eriksen, Olff, Murison, & Ursin, 1999; see Chapter 8) leads to the accumulation of fatigue-based symptoms, and this will ultimately lead to negative outcomes for performance, well-being and health. The crucial part in the sustained activation argument is to show that increased job demands lead to physical reactions that might negatively affect health and well-being in the long run. A field experiment reported in Meijman (1989) provides exactly such evidence (see Work Psychology in Action box).

> ### Work Psychology in Action: A field experiment among driving examiners
>
> Meijman (1989) reported a study among 27 driving examiners. Figure 5.1 contains the results of this study.
> Urine samples were taken across the day on one free day and on three working days. Adrenalin breakdown products were measured, indicating the

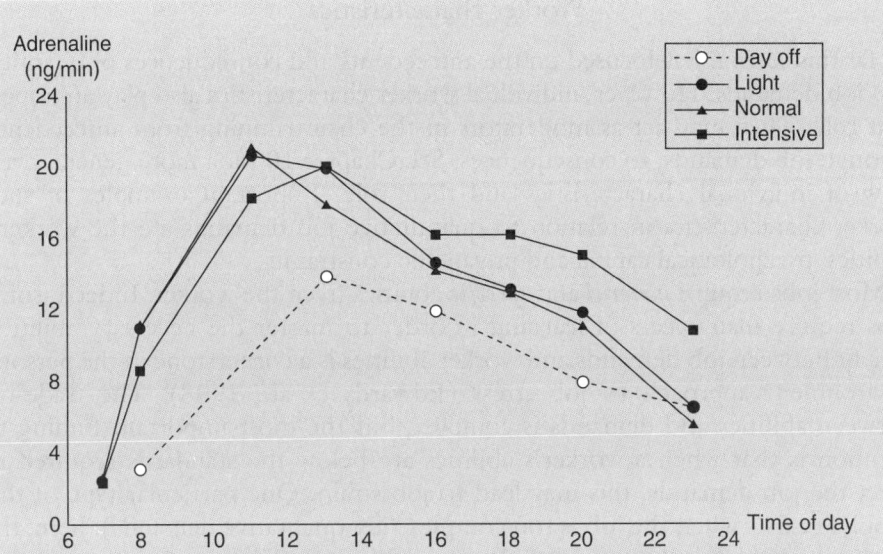

Figure 5.1 Excretion rate of adrenaline during working days (light, 5-minute breaks; normal, 2-minute breaks; intensive, no breaks) and a day off for 27 driving instructors (Meijman & Mulder, 1998, Figure 2.6).

level of activation of the body. The dotted line, which represents a day off, illustrates how activation rises slowly between 8 am and 1 pm. In the afternoon, activation wears down till bedtime (11 pm). On each of the three working days, the morning pattern is similar: a sharper increase and earlier peak (at 12 am) for each of the three conditions.

The three days differ in work intensity. The driving examiners complete seven (light), eight (normal) or nine (intensive) exams a day. During a light day, there are 5-minute breaks between the exams, and there is time for a longer lunch break. During a normal day breaks are down to 2 minutes and the lunch break is shorter. During a nine-exam day, there is no opportunity for breaks or lunch.

After 11 am, activation starts to decline. The decline is slower for the intensive day. At 11 pm on an intensive day, the driving examiners are still as alert as when they are at their peak on a free day.

This demonstrates that during work-intensive days the body is experiencing more strain and there is a phenomenon of carry-over from the activation during task performance to the hours and free time after work. If such carry-over or after-effects of strain are repeated over a longer period of time, the heightened level of activation will begin to affect other bodily systems, like sleep, the cardiovascular system and the immune system (Eriksen et al., 1999).

Worker characteristics

So far this section has focused on the antecedents and consequences of quantitative job demands. However, individual worker characteristics also play an important role. They may act as moderators in the chain running from antecedents, through job demands, to consequences. See Chapter 10 for a more general overview of individual characteristics and their role. Important examples of such worker characteristics in relation to quantitative job demands are the workers' abilities, psychological capital and private life constraints.

Most jobs require *general* and *specific* abilities from the worker. Indeed, some jobs require many years of learning in order to master the necessary abilities. The fit between job demands and worker abilities is a cornerstone in the person–environment approach to job stress (Edwards et al., 1998). The trade-off between abilities and demands is complex, but the most important finding to mention is that when a worker's abilities are below the standards required to meet the job demands, this may lead to job strain. One particular type of this problem exists when the job is too complex (i.e. qualitative demands): here, the worker probably needs more time than available according to existing standards, resulting in high quantitative demands in turn. In this case, an interaction between quantitative and qualitative aspects of job demands occurs.

Psychological capital (see Chapters 10 and 19) refers to personal resources of efficacy, optimism, hope and resilience that are at the disposal of a worker (Luthans, Avolio, Avey, & Norman, 2007). Some people lack the psychological capital to effectively deal with quantitative job demands. The unpredictability of quantitative demands and the associated negative thoughts and feelings may require psychological capital to persist with task performance.

Private life circumstances (such as care responsibilities for young children or disabled and/or elderly people, or living with or without a partner) may act as constraints in dealing with quantitative job demands. This was studied in a line of research on work–home interference (Frone, 2002; see Chapter 11). One particular type of such interference relates to private life problems carrying over to the job setting. For instance, when parents have a child who develops health problems, this may influence their functioning at work. Carry-over from private to working life could limit a worker's capacity to handle quantitative job demands.

Replay

The consequences of quantitative job demands can be categorized into short term and long term. In the short term, there is an optimal level of quantitative demands for any given task. When job demands are below the optimal level, the worker needs to become more activated to maintain performance. When job demands are above the optimal level, the worker needs to manage tension levels so as to maintain performance.

In the short term, quantitative job demands require action and effort, and therefore result in fatigue. Fatigue responds to rest. When job demands are low, workers may give the impression of being fatigued, while actually they are not: they are in a fatigue-like state that responds to new stimulation rather than to rest.

In the long term, when effort and activation induced by quantitative job demands remain high over a prolonged period of time and recovery is insufficient, worker health, well-being and performance may be impaired.

Individual worker characteristics may act as moderators in the chain leading from antecedents, through job demands to consequences. Several examples of important individual worker characteristics have been given: general and specific abilities, psychological capital and private life circumstances.

5.5 Measuring Quantitative Job Demands: Objective and Subjective Approaches

In trying to establish the amount of quantitative job demands in a job, an important issue is how to actually measure this work characteristic. There has been considerable academic debate about this topic (Frese & Zapf, 1988). On the one hand, there are academics who prefer 'objective measures' or even experimental manipulations of the speed and amount of work required. In other words, they prefer to quantify the number of clients served, the number of sales made, the number of buttons pressed, the number of pages read and so on. In this objective measurement approach, quantitative job demands are measured independently from the workers involved. The focus is on their external exposure to job demands.

On the other hand, there are academics who insist that subjective perceptions and experiences of workers are of key importance. Not everyone serving many clients or performing a large number of tasks within a certain time span experiences high work intensity or a high workload. So why bother if the worker does not seem to have a problem? In this 'subjective measurement' approach, quantitative job demands are measured through the lens of the workers involved. Alternatively, other raters (e.g. supervisors, colleagues, HRM professionals, trained experts) are asked to give their opinion on the level of job demands that is affecting workers. The focus in the subjective approach is on how workers (might) perceive and evaluate their job demands. Let us consider both approaches in more detail.

Objective approach of measurement

In the objective approach the core idea – as is emphasized in the Work Psychology in Action box – is to develop measures of the amount and speed of work that are completely independent from any personal standards on behalf of the workers that perform the tasks.

In the example, the number of people served per time unit and the number of specific transactions made per time unit are examples of objective measures of quantitative job demands.

When objective measures are used in practice, it is hard to eliminate the personal element completely. The problem does not lie in the measures themselves, but the personal element enters whenever objective measures are used in decisions. This

> **Work Psychology in Action: A visit to the town hall**
>
> Next time you are at the council offices on local council business, take a seat and observe how the working day of the employees there unfolds. There may be a queue of people in front of a ticket dispenser. Each person takes a ticket when entering and is seated while waiting for his/her number to show up above a line of transaction desks.
>
> When you take a ticket, you are now part of the task list waiting in the departmental buffer for assignment to one of the employees. Employees may be able to choose from this buffer. If you have indicated the purpose of your visit at the ticket dispenser, the employees may be involved in self-selecting which citizen to serve with what question. This gives them some control over their task variety during the working day.
>
> When your number shows up on one of the signposts above your designated desk you go there, get served and then leave. This is how it continues all day long during opening hours. How can the objective demands of the employees working here be described?
>
> For a start, the number of people served per given time unit (hour/day/week) could be counted or the number of specific issues dealt with could be specified. The average time that a specific type of transaction takes could be calculated. This may vary from one service employee to the next.
>
> You may think that this would give you a clear measure of the objective job demands that these workers are faced with, but what about these complications: there are many unclassified actions that need to be arranged, which could involve a lot of work or very little. How can these additional activities be accounted for in your demands assessment? To make things worse employees do not spend the entire working day behind the service desk. They spend part of the day in a back office to provide some variation in the job. Here they do things such as filing records or forwarding messages to other departments or external institutions. How do these additional activities compare to the main task of service-desk work, which is face-to-face with people? How will you combine such additional activities with the face-to-face activities to assess the overall level of demands? Finally, some tasks are not performed by a single employee, but by small groups of employees (such as discussing non-standard issues and queries), bringing a collective or relational element to the job demands. How can this be included in your assessment of individual job demands levels?

is because questions as to whether objective levels of quantitative demands are adequate, normal, too low or too high require some reference to how the average or ideal typical worker would react to such circumstances (Frese & Zapf, 1988). As a consequence, specification of average or ideal typical worker characteristics is necessary before the implications of objective measures of quantitative job demands can be evaluated for any group of workers exposed. In addition, specification of how an individual person deviates from the average or ideal typical worker is necessary before the implications of objective quantitative job demands can be evaluated for any specific worker.

As also becomes clear in the council offices example, it is not at all straightforward to describe the objective work amount and speed in detail completely and concisely for the employees in this particular department. Of course, there may be other departments where it is easier to define objective demands, but there are most certainly also other departments where it is even more difficult than in the example. There invariably are complicating tasks and circumstances. As a result, the formal objective tasks that translate into the objective demands on employees' action and effort are actually vague and implicit in many jobs, rather than standardized and explicit (Meijman & Mulder, 1998).

One other thing the council offices example illustrates is that, when one observes a worker in another job, for instance a teacher or a machine operator, it is impossible to use the same indicators for objective demands as in the example for council officers. Any exact list of objective job demands is strongly context dependent. It has proven to be impossible to develop clear, practical, as well as comprehensive systems for describing quantitative job demands objectively that can be used across all possible jobs.

Notwithstanding these limitations, an objective approach to measuring quantitative job demands can be extremely useful for answering practical questions in specific jobs and settings, as illustrated in the Work Psychology in Action box on p. 132.

A specific setting where quantitative job demands can be objectively measured, monitored and even controlled is the laboratory experiment (see also Chapter 2). In most regular jobs and contexts, neither objective measures nor laboratory-controlled conditions are possible or practical for assessing job demand levels. In practice, it has therefore become common to simply ask job incumbents how they feel about their quantitative job demands, or to ask external raters, such as supervisors, colleagues, HRM professionals or trained experts to evaluate the level of job demands in a group of workers. In other words, subjective measures have to be used.

Subjective approach to measurement

In the subjective approach to measurement the focus is on how workers themselves or other raters perceive and evaluate the level of quantitative demands in a job. Self-rated measures of quantitative job demands (employee interviews but especially employee surveys) are used much more often in practice than other-rated measures (expert ratings, supervisor ratings, etc.). Below, employee surveys are discussed at some length and then other-rated measures are briefly introduced. This section ends with a comparison of self-ratings and other ratings.

> ### Work Psychology in Action: How many operators do we need?
>
> If there is one thing that is plentiful in The Netherlands, it is water (i.e. sea, rivers, channels, lakes, creeks, ditches). Boats use this water intensively for both commercial transport and recreation. This means that this rather small country is full of bridges and locks that need human operators.
>
> The Ministry of Infrastructure and Environment, always looking for ways to cut public spending, initiated a study that investigated whether the number of people required to operate these bridges and locks could be reduced. In the high season (summer) it was expected that a full complement of operators was necessary, whereas in the low season (winter) cuts would appear feasible, for instance by sharing a more limited number of operators across a series of bridges and locks in a specific area.
>
> An applied ergonomic research and consultancy business was invited to do a study that involved measuring the number of times the bridges and locks were operated and the time needed to do so (in relation to the number of boats waiting) across the year. Once the number of movements and the time involved were charted, a proposal was prepared for how to staff the sites during different parts of the year. This objective analysis of quantitative job demands was also used by the Ministry of Infrastructure and Environment to develop policy on whether and how to implement systems that operate multiple sites in a specific area from one new control room, and how many human operators would be needed in such a scenario.

There are two ways to ask the incumbents of a particular job about the level of job demands they experience with a survey. One is to ask them to describe their quantitative demands in terms of time, amount and speed using a frequency measure. The other option is to ask them for an evaluation of their work speed and work amount (usually an evaluation in terms of satisfaction is used). It is commonly advised to use the former method (Dewe, 1991) as this is expected to stay closer to an assessment of external job demands exposure. The latter (evaluation) method is expected to foster overlap between separate measures of different job characteristics: asking an employee about satisfaction with workload, pay satisfaction, satisfaction about the relationship with colleagues, etc. will give an idea of the general satisfaction level of an employee rather than an assessment of the environmental factors separately. This kind of response tendency may be good for measuring general employee attitudes, but not for measuring exposure to working conditions, such as quantitative job demands. Also, satisfaction-oriented measures may boost the problem of common method variance (see also Chapter 2).

An example of a scale measuring the amount and speed of work through frequency-oriented items is presented in the Work Psychology in Action box.

Work Psychology in Action: How high are my quantitative job demands?

In 1994, van Veldhoven and Meijman constructed a scale for measuring work speed and quantity. It is part of a larger questionnaire for measuring psychosocial job conditions and job stress with the acronym VBBA (in Dutch) or QEEW (in English). The scale consists of 11 items. Respondents are asked to rate their quantitative job demands by means of a frequency scale: always (3), often (2), sometimes (1), never (0). This means that all respondents ultimately score between 0 (11 times 'never') and 33 (11 times 'always') when all the items in the scale are added together. The scale was constructed in such a way that it produces orderly item steps from 0 to 33 that can be used to characterize a person's level of work speed and quantity. Below are the item steps and the percentage of respondents (N = 324 from the scale construction study) that are at a certain level of work speed and quantity.

Step	Item content	Percentage passed
33	Always problems with work speed	0.3
32	Always problems with work pressure	0.9
31	Would always want to work more slowly	2.2
30	Often problems with work speed	2.5
29	Often has to hurry	3.1
28	Often behind schedule	3.2
27	Always needs to work extra hard	5.0
26	Always has to work very fast	5.9
25	Often problems with work pressure	6.2
24	Always time pressure	7.2
23	Always too much work	8.4
22	Would often want to work more slowly	10.4
21	Never work at ease*	12.9
20	Often behind schedule	13.0
19	Often needs to work extra hard	22.4
18	Often needs to hurry	25.6
17	Often too much work	34.3
16	Often time pressure	34.4
15	Often has to work very fast	35.8
14	Sometimes problems with work speed	37.8
13	Sometimes problems with work pressure	54.2
12	Sometimes wants to work more slowly	63.9
11	Sometimes works at ease*	68.4
10	Sometimes behind schedule	69.2
09	Never too little work*	73.1
08	Sometimes time pressure	86.0
07	Sometimes needs to work extra hard	87.3
06	Sometimes too much work	91.5

(*continued*)

Step	Item content	Percentage passed
05	Sometimes has to hurry	95.0
04	Sometimes too little work*	97.2
03	Often works at ease*	97.9
02	Sometimes needs to work very fast	98.7
01	Often too little work*	100
0		100

*This item is reverse scored.

One could interpret this as a 33-item yes/no multiple-choice knowledge exam: the more difficult the question, the fewer students know the correct answer to this item. The most difficult question is 'Do you always have problems with your work speed?'. If this were an exam, only 0.3% of students would correctly answer this question. It has been shown for this test that any worker 'passing' this most difficult item is likely to have also passed all the other items, much as one would expect a student who passes the most difficult question to also have correctly answered all the other, easier, questions. At the other end of the scale, it can be seen that an actual score of 0 was never observed. The lowest score was 1, corresponding with the item 'Do you often have too little work?'.

When using this as an indicator for the complete workforce, the above information can be used to say that in 1994, 3% of the workforce often fell behind in their work. Similarly, 25% of the workforce often needed to hurry with work. Also, 54% of people sometimes had problems with work pressure. Only 2% of the workforce said, however, that they could often work at ease, which means 98% of the respondents 'passed' this level of work-intensity item.

Interestingly, all these percentages (98%, 54%, 25%, 3%) measure exactly the same level of quantitative job demands at the workforce level. The differences in the percentages are caused by the different choice of words in the questions, and indeed it is the purpose of scale construction to find a range of items that does exactly this.

Whatever self-report approach is chosen, each approach involves the personal standards of the worker in how quantitative job demands are measured. As a consequence, these personal standards – based on the cognitive and emotional processing by individual employees – are reflected in the measurements. Research has shown that within a given group of people doing a job, differences occur in their appraisal of the level of exposure to environmental job demands.

For some academics this is also an important and substantial reason to prefer subjective measures: the workers reporting high levels of subjective demand levels are more likely to develop symptoms of fatigue, burnout, performing badly, making errors and causing accidents (see also Chapters 12 and 14). Subjective measures are therefore one step closer to health and safety outcomes, and it is these outcomes that ultimately give legitimacy to measuring the levels of job demands in first place.

Where do the subjective twists to the perceptions and experiences of common exposure come from? Spector (1992) provided a list of reasons why people's perceptions and experiences of job demands could be different from one group member to the next, even when their exposure to 'objective demands' is the same. Laboratory studies suggest that the cues that workers get about their performance levels influence their task perceptions. Variation in the salience and feedback quality of such *performance cues* might influence perceptions of the amount of (remaining) job demands. Also, people are susceptive to the *social information* they get from their immediate colleagues, supervisor and clients about their demand levels. Furthermore, the way people perceive their environment is influenced by individual differences in how they perceive the world. *Personality characteristics* like negative affectivity or locus of control have been shown to affect how people perceive external stimuli. Finally, the *attitude* and *mood* during job performance may play a role in the assessment of a specific work characteristic, such as job demands. The most important thing to remember from this list of factors is that subjective evaluations by means of an employee survey are always more than just an indicator of external (objective) exposure. They are also indicative of the employee doing the rating.

At this stage, it is important to mention that some circularity may be entering the argument here when relating high job demands to job stress using subjective measures. It is likely that high demands foster job stress, but a reverse argument can also be true, for instance that workers experiencing high job stress are likely to rate new demands higher than workers who are not stressed because they estimate the effort involved in dealing with these new demands as more problematic. Scholars with a more epidemiologic background have warned against the use of subjective measures for demands as well as work stress because correlations found between the two might be trivial and non-informative because of common method variance (Kasl, 1978). See Chapter 2 for a more profound discussion on this topic.

Apart from the personal factors mentioned above that lead to variance in job demand ratings from workers sharing similar exposure levels, there may also be certain differences within groups as to the true exposure level per person. Literature on *idiosyncratic deals* or I-deals (Rousseau, 2005), for example, suggests that some employees may be able to strike special bargains as to the content and timing of their work, which could influence the level of their job demands. For example, suppose a boss agrees to a request by an employee to start late (1 pm) and end late (9 pm) for reasons of synchronization with private life. If 9 am to 1 pm is always the busiest part of the day, such an individual agreement (I-deal) granted by the supervisor has the net effect of lowering the personal exposure to high job demands of this employee.

Now that self-rated measures have been discussed, let us also pay some attention to subjective measures by using others as raters. In the literature, several systems for other-based work analysis have been developed, especially in Germany. Trained experts and supervisors are the most common instances of such others doing the rating, but HRM professionals and colleagues are sometimes also involved. Other-based systems of work analysis are typically labour intensive and require substantial training and practice before they can be reliably applied (Zapf, 1989). This is partially caused by the fact that a specific, abstract terminology typically needs to be adopted in order to be able to analyse work in detail. Rating, evaluating and reporting a single job (job demands inclusive) according to such a method might take a well-trained rater up to one day or more, making this measurement approach laborious and expensive.

Furthermore, Zapf (1989) provided a list of biases that play a role in other-ratings of quantitative job demands: the observation time frame may be too short or not representative to provide a reliable and valid assessment (this may not apply to colleagues and supervisors, but it certainly does to external experts and HRM professionals): the presence of the rater may change the work situation and may prohibit a reliable and valid assessment, the rater may be strongly influenced by first impressions and no longer observe in an open manner afterwards (a so-called 'halo effect'), the rater may have personal reasons and vested interests (such as when an expert is paid by the employer or when a supervisor rates his/her own department) which urge towards biased ratings. In conclusion, other-ratings of quantitative job demands face similar problems to self-ratings when it comes to biases entering the rating.

A final problem of other ratings that needs to be mentioned is that in as far as emotional and cognitive processes are involved in quantitative job demands it may be difficult for others to actually observe such processes. In order to complete their assessment, external raters are therefore likely to ask questions of some of the job incumbents, bringing a self-rating element into the assessment.

Linking self-ratings with other ratings

The literature on factors influencing self-ratings and other ratings of job demands would lead one to expect that the correspondence between self-rated and other-rated job demands is not necessarily very strong. The question is if this is really true. Across existing studies (Algera, 1981; Zapf, 1989; Meijman & van Ouwerkerk, 1999) it has appeared that the association between self-ratings and other ratings of job demands is indeed weak to moderate (correlations from 0.23 to 0.35).

Replay

In this section we discussed objective and subjective measurement approaches. In the objective measurement approach, quantitative job demands are measured as external situational exposure, independently from the workers involved. In the subjective measurement approach, quantitative job demands are measured as perceptions and evaluations, either by the workers themselves or by other raters (supervisors, colleagues, HRM professionals, trained experts).

Objective measures are difficult to translate into decisions without referring to some average or ideal typical worker, again bringing a personal element into the equation. Furthermore, it has proven to be impossible to measure job demands in comparable units of actions or tasks across jobs, therefore in practice subjective measures are more commonly found. These are self-rated by employees or other-rated. The biases entering self- and other ratings have been discussed. Self- and other ratings are only weakly to moderately related as a result.

It is best to consider both objective and subjective approaches to measuring quantitative job demands as valuable: each contribute a unique kind of information. Which method to choose largely depends on the kind of practical problem and/or research question.

5.6 Practical Applications

Now that conceptual and measurement issues have been discussed, this chapter concludes with a short overview of practical applications. These can take two main routes: (i) focus on the person or (ii) focus on work and its organizational context.

Focus on the person

Focus on the person means fitting the person to his or her job. In general, this is about selection, training and performance management.

Selection, training and performance management of workers
The person-environment fit approach (Edwards, Caplan, & van Harrison, 1998) to job stress was mentioned earlier in this chapter. In this approach, a crucial factor counteracting job demands are the worker's abilities. Thus, some key applications of the issues presented in this chapter can be found in the areas of HRM that are related to the abilities and capacities of employees. Selection and recruitment, training and development, as well as performance management are examples of HRM practices that are important here. Taking good care of HRM contributes to preventing well-being and performance problems in employees that may arise from a mismatch of demands and abilities. The interested reader is referred to Noe, Hollenbeck, Gerhart and Wright (2003). It is important to mention that training and performance management are probably the practices that are most under the control of organizations. Selection and recruitment are very important, but organizations are – as mentioned earlier – dependent on the availability of skilled workers and professionals on the labour market. When qualified personnel are not available or too expensive, organizations may be forced to hire employees that are underqualified. The low abilities of these workers may then be the root cause of the performance problems of organizations as well as of workers' complaints of high workload and job strain.

Focus on work

Focus on work and its organizational context implies fitting the job to the person. Generally, this is about job and workplace (re)design, but it can also be about improving psychosocial working conditions in the general workforce.

Job and workplace (re)design in critical jobs
The issues discussed in this chapter play a large role in the (re)design of jobs and workplaces, especially jobs and workplaces that relate to critical tasks for organizations and/or society as a whole. At a societal level, examples of such jobs are air traffic control, emergency medical care or nuclear electricity plant control. In a more commercial setting, one could think of dealing rooms in large financial institutions and logistics control centres in the postal industry. Job and workplace (re)design relates to the field of ergonomics (Kroemer & Grandjean, 1997). The reader is referred to Chapter 9 for a more profound discussion about this area of knowledge and research.

The common theme in all critical settings is that performance loss and/or failure to achieve optimum activation levels in individual workers may result in serious societal and organizational consequences (Wagenaar, Hudson, & Reason, 1990), therefore, apart from designing the best possible technological devices and workplaces, additional measures could be taken to optimize performance and minimize error. Gaillard (2003) provides a useful list of such measures that will be discussed here.

First, a task that is high on job demands should be performed in a situation that has few other working conditions that may detract from performance, such as extreme noise or low/high temperatures. The job should have an adequate level of variety, control and feedback. Where possible, buffers should be designed into the workflow to protect workers from situations where too many tasks need to be handled simultaneously. Second, the job and workplace should be designed in such a way that workers are enabled to use different strategies of work execution depending on the job demands. Examples are the possibility for workers to slow down work execution depending on fatigue levels or to focus on core tasks while letting other task elements pile up (temporarily). Third, it is important to avoid effort levels that are extremely high in critical jobs. Fourth, computer technology can monitor performance accuracy and/or generate diverging stimuli to keep operators awake during monotonous tasks.

Improving psychosocial working conditions in the general workforce
Although only critical jobs were considered in the former paragraph, high quantitative job demands can be a risk to well-being, health and safety in any job. What is being done to prevent workers in everyday jobs from experiencing negative consequences due to high job demands? The answer to this question varies greatly between countries and organizations. Good examples of prevention and intervention programmes are presented in Kompier and Cooper (1999) as well as in Biron, Karanika-Murray and Cooper (2012; see also Chapter 16).

Many countries have implemented specific legal working conditions that pertain to quantitative job demands. It is not possible to review this important development here, but for purposes of illustration the so-called 'management standards for work-related stress' approach as adopted in the United Kingdom is briefly introduced. Based on the European working conditions framework, the UK government has developed a series of six standards for good management of work-related stress. The first standard concerns quantitative job demands. Organizations can compare their own stress-relevant working conditions (including job demand levels) with the conditions suggested in the standards and take appropriate action (Mackay, Cousins, Kelly, Lee, & McCaig, 2004). An indicator tool (based on a survey) has been developed and reference scores are available against which any workplace can benchmark itself (Edwards, Webster, van Laar, & Easton, 2008). Professional guidance is available in several forms (written materials, web-based, expert assistance) for any project aiming to apply the standards to a UK workplace. The management standards have now been in place for several years and it is safe to say that they have stimulated many UK employers to act on high quantitative job demands in their workplaces.

Replay

Practical applications concentrate either on the person or on the work and its organizational context. On the person side, the workers' abilities are important. Adequate selection, training and performance management can ensure that workers have the adequate knowledge, skills and abilities to deal with quantitative job demands. On the work side, the setting of critical jobs was differentiated from the general workforce. (Re)designing adequate jobs and workplaces is most evident in jobs that are critical to organizations and society. Ergonomics is the academic discipline specifically studying such (re)design issues. Quantitative job demands have also become a major employment and working conditions issue for which regulations exist through working conditions laws in many countries. In addition, at the country level all kinds of initiatives can be found that try to promote the prevention of work-related stress, and attention to quantitative job demands plays an important part here.

5.7 Conclusions

In this chapter quantitative job demands were defined, their antecedents and consequences introduced, and their objective and subjective measurement options discussed (pros and cons). Finally, several key practical areas for application of such knowledge were indicated.

A working definition was adopted that defines quantitative job demands as 'those elements of the work environment that concern the amount and speed of work to be performed, and require physical and/or psychological effort'.

The amount and speed, or 'intensity', of work are influenced by a wide range of factors in the work context. External factors mentioned were uncertainty in the organizations' environment, legal and political institutions, the labour market and technological innovations. Internal organizational factors concerned management style, managerial practices and innovations, and HRM.

The consequences of quantitative job demands can be categorized into short-term and long-term consequences. In the short term, there is an optimal level of quantitative demands for any given task. Also, quantitative job demands require action and effort, and therefore result in fatigue. Fatigue responds to rest. In the long term, when effort and activation induced by quantitative job demands remain high over a prolonged period of time and recovery is insufficient, worker health, well-being and performance may be impaired (see also Chapters 12 and 13).

Individual worker characteristics such as general and specific abilities, psychological capital and private life circumstances play a role in modifying the impact of antecedents on job demands, and of job demands on consequences.

An overview of objective and subjective measurement approaches revealed that there is no ideal method for measuring quantitative job demands. Rather, each method has its advantages and disadvantages. Objective measurement approaches deliver information that is independent from personal standards. However, personal standards do come into the picture when one wants to interpret objective measures. Furthermore, objective measures are context-specific and cannot be used across all possible jobs in the workforce. Subjective measurement approaches (both self- and other rated) are influenced by several sources of bias. Self-ratings and other ratings of quantitative job demands are only weakly to moderately related. It is best to consider both objective and subjective approaches to measuring quantitative job demands as valuable: each contributes a unique kind of information. Which method to choose largely depends on the kind of practical problem and/or research question at hand.

Knowledge on quantitative job demands is used in practical applications towards (re)designing jobs and workplaces. This is especially evident in jobs that are critical to organizations and society. In addition, job demands have become a major employment and working conditions issue for which regulations and laws exist in many countries. Finally, HRM pays much attention to achieving appropriate individual worker knowledge, skills and abilities as these are necessary for dealing with the quantitative demands in a job.

At the beginning of this chapter it was stated that the amount and speed of work is not a phenomenon that is easy to grasp. Why is that? First, quantitative job demands appear to be a double-edged sword: the challenge that is inherent in high job demands can help people thrive at work, but it can also cause problems when workers are challenged too much, especially when this 'too much' lasts for too long. Second, any initiative directed at preventing adverse health, well-being and safety outcomes resulting from high quantitative job demands needs to consider both the objective environmental exposure as well as the worker's individual subjective evaluation. This is likely to be complicated in practice. Reducing objective exposure may eliminate risks for most people, but self-rated subjective measures may be necessary for those vulnerable workers who run a high risk even under conditions that are acceptable for most workers, and for those workers who are under-challenged in the same setting.

Discussion Points

1. The antecedents of quantitative job demands concern factors both in the organizational environment (market, technology, etc.) and within the organization (management style, HRM practices, etc.). Choose a specific job that you know about in some detail. Discuss how these antecedents together play a role in shaping the quantitative demands in this job.

2. Self-ratings and other ratings of quantitative job demands are only weakly to moderately related. This is probably because job demands only partially lend themselves to external observation. Discuss which aspects of quantitative job demands you think are more conducive to external observation and which aspects are less easily observed.

Learning Points

1. Ask someone you know (family, friend or neighbour) who has a job in a large company or institution about the current amount and speed of work in their job. Next, ask this person to describe the factors causing this amount and speed of work. Stop when you have identified several factors lying outside the organization/institution as well as several factors inside the organization/institution. For the latter, do these apply to all people in this organization/institution or only to this particular workplace, this particular job, this particular person?
2. Together with some other students, visit several pubs and/or restaurants and observe the barkeepers and/or waiters. Don't visit these workplaces as a group, but use a timetable in which you specify when one of you visits a particular place and for how long. Which of these workplaces has the highest work amount and speed? Do all the group members have the same assessment? What causes possible overlaps or differences in your judgements?

Further Reading

Bowling, N., & Kirkendall, C. (2012). Workload: a review of causes, consequences and potential interventions. In J. Houdmont, S. Leka, & R. Sinclair (Eds.), *Contemporary occupational health psychology: Global perspectives on research and practice, Volume 2* (Vol. 2, pp. 221–238). Chichester: John Wiley & Sons.

Parker, S. K., Wall, T. D., & Cordery, J. L. (2001). Future work design research and practice: Towards an elaborated model of work design. *Journal of Occupational and Organizational Psychology, 74*, 413–440.

Peccei, R., van de Voorde, K., & van Veldhoven, M. (2013). HRM, performance and well-being. In D. Guest, J. Paauwe, & P. Wright (Eds), *Managing people and performance* (pp. 15–46). Chichester: John Wiley & Sons.

Schnall, P. L., Dobson, M., & Rosskam, E. (2009). *Unhealthy work: Causes, consequences, cures.* Amityville, NY: Baywood Publishing.

References

Algera, J. E. (1981). *Kenmerken van werk [Characteristics of work]*. Lisse: Swets & Zeitlinger.

Appelbaum, E., Bailey, T., Berg, P., & Kalleberg, A. (2000). *Manufacturing advantage: Why high performance work systems pay off.* New York: Cornell University Press.

Bailey, D., & Kurland, N. (2002). A review of telework research: Findings, new directions, and lessons for the study of modern work. *Journal of Organizational Behavior, 23*, 383–400.

Bakker, A., van Veldhoven, M., & Xanthopoulou, D. (2010). Beyond the Demand–Control Model:

Thriving on high job demands and resources. *Journal of Personnel Psychology*, 9, 3–16.

Beckers, D. G. J. (2008). *Overtime work and well-being: Opening up the black box.* PhD Dissertation. Nijmegen: Radboud University Nijmegen.

Biron, C., Karanika-Murray, M., & Cooper, C. L. (Eds.) (2012). *Organizational stress and well-being interventions: Addressing process and context.* London: Routledge.

Bowling, N., & Kirkendall, C. (2012). Workload: A review of causes, consequences and potential interventions. In J. Houdmont, S. Leka, & R. Sinclair (Eds.), *Contemporary occupational health psychology: Global perspectives on research and practice* (Vol. 2, pp. 221–238). Chichester: John Wiley & Sons.

Boxall, P., & Purcell, J. (2011). *Strategy and human resource management.* Basingstoke: Palgrave Macmillan.

Dewe, P. (1991). Measuring work stressors: The role of frequency, duration, and demand. *Work & Stress*, 5, 77–91.

Edwards, J., Caplan, R., & van Harrison, R. (1998). Person–environment fit theory: Conceptual foundations, empirical evidence, and directions for future research. In C. L. Cooper (Ed.), *Theories of organizational stress* (pp. 28–67). Oxford: Oxford University Press.

Edwards, J. A., Webster, S., van Laar, D., & Easton, S. (2008). Psychometric analysis of the UK Health and Safety Executive's Management Standards work-related Stress Indicator Tool. *Work & Stress*, 22, 96–107.

Eriksen, H. R., Olff, M., Murison, T, & Urson, H. (1999). The time dimension in stress response: Relevance for survival and health. *Psychiatry Research*, 85, 39–50.

French, J. R. P. Jr., Caplan, R. D., & van Harrison, R. (1982). *The mechanisms of job stress and strain.* New York: John Wiley & Sons.

Frese, M., & Zapf, D. (1988). Methodological issues in the study of work stress: Objective vs. subjective measurement of work stress and the question of longitudinal studies. In C. L. Cooper, & R. Payne (Eds.), *Causes, coping and consequences of stress at work* (pp. 375–410). Chichester: John Wiley & Sons.

Frone, M. R. (2002). Work–family balance. In J. Quick, & L. Tetrick (Eds.), *Handbook of occupational health psychology* (pp. 143–162). Washington, DC: American Psychological Association.

Gaillard, A. (2003). *Stress, productiviteit en gezondheid [Stress, productivity and health].* Amsterdam: Uitgeverij Nieuwezijds.

Gerhart, B., & Rynes, S. (2003) *Compensation: Theory, evidence, and strategic implications.* Thousand Oaks, CA: Sage Publications.

Holman, D., Wall, T. D., Clegg, Ch. W., Sparrow, P., & Howard, A. (2003). *The new workplace: A guide to the human impact of modern working practices.* Chichester: John Wiley & Sons.

Karasek, R. A. (1979). Job demands, job decision latitude, and mental strain: implications for job redesign. *Administrative Science Quarterly*, 24, 285–308.

Karasek, R., Brisson, Ch., Kawakami, N., Houtman, I., Bongers, P., & Amick, B. (1998). The Job Content Questionnaire (JCQ): An instrument for internationally comparative assessments of psychosocial job characteristics. *Journal of Occupational Health Psychology*, 3, 322–355.

Karasek, R., & Theorell, T. (1990). *Healthy work: Stress, productivity and the reconstruction of working life.* New York: Basic Books.

Kasl, S. (1978). Epidemiological contributions to the study of work stress. In C. L. Cooper, & R. Payne (Eds.), *Stress at work* (pp. 3–48). New York: John Wiley & Sons.

Kompier, M. A. J., & Cooper, C. L. (Eds.) (1999). *Preventing stress, improving productivity: European case studies in the workplace.* London: Routledge.

Kroemer, K., & Grandjean, E. (1997). *Fitting the task to the human: A textbook of occupational ergonomics.* Philadelphia: Taylor & Francis.

Landsbergis, P. A., Cahill, J., & Schnall, P. (1999). The impact of lean production and related new systems of work organization on worker health. *Journal of Occupational Health Psychology*, 4, 103–130.

Loukidou, L., Loan-Clarke, J., & Daniels, K. (2009). Boredom in the workplace: More than monotonous tasks. *International Journal of Management Reviews*, 11, 381–405.

Luthans, F., Avolio, B., Avey, J. B., & Norman, S. M. (2007). Positive psychological capital: Measurement and relationship with performance and satisfaction. *Personnel Psychology*, 60, 541–572.

Mackay, D., Cousins, R., Kelly, P., Lee, S., & McCaig, R. (2004). Management standards and work-related stress in the UK: Policy background and science. *Work & Stress*, 18, 91–112.

Meijman, T. F. (1989). Belasting en herstel: een begrippenkader voor arbeids-psychologisch onderzoek van werkbelasting [*Effort and recuperation: a conceptual framework for psychological research of workload*]. In T. F. Meijman (Ed.), *Mentale belasting en werkstress: een arbeidspsychologische benadering* [*Mental workload and job stress: a work psychological approach*] (pp. 5–20). Assen/Maastricht: van Gorcum.

Meijman, T. F., & Mulder, G. (1998). Psychological aspects of workload. In P. J. D. Drenth, H. K. Thierry, & Ch. J. de Wolff (Eds.), *Handbook of work and organizational psychology* (2nd ed., pp. 5–33). Hove: Psychology Press.

Meijman, T. F., & van Ouwerkerk, R. (1999). Zien anderen ook wat wij van ons werk vinden? Over de samenhang van observaties met zelfbeoordelingen van psychosociale taakkenmerken [*Do others see what we think of our work? About the relationship between expert ratings and self-reports of psychosocial job characteristics*]. *Gedrag en Organisatie, 12*, 384–396.

Nachreiner, F. (1999). International standards on mental work-load: The ISO 10,075 series. *Industrial Health, 37*, 125–133.

Noe, R., Hollenbeck, J., Gerhart, B., & Wright, P. (2003). *Human resource management: Gaining a competitive advantage*. New York: McGraw-Hill/Irwin.

Paoli, P. (1992). *First European survey on the work environment*. Dublin: European Foundation for the Improvement of Living and Working Conditions.

Parent-Thirion, A., Vermeylen, G., van Houten, G., Lyly-Yrjänäinen, M., Biletta, I., Cabrita, J., & Niedhammer, I. (2012). *Fifth European working conditions survey*. Dublin: European Foundation for the Improvement of Living and Working Conditions.

Parker, S. K., Wall, T. D., & Cordery, J. L. (2001). Future work design research and practice: Towards an elaborated model of work design. *Journal of Occupational and Organizational Psychology, 74*, 413–440.

Peccei, R., van de Voorde, K., & van Veldhoven, M. (2013). HRM, performance and well-being. In D. Guest, J. Paauwe, & P. Wright (Eds.), *Managing people and performance* (pp. 15–46). Chichester: Wiley.

Quinn, R., & Rohrbaugh, J. (1983). A spatial model of effectiveness criteria: Towards a competing values approach to organizational analysis. *Management Science, 29*, 363–377.

Rousseau, D. (2005). *I-deals: Idiosyncratic deals employees bargain for themselves*. New York: M. E. Sharpe.

Schnall, P. L., Dobson, M., & Rosskam, E. (2009). *Unhealthy work: Causes, consequences, cures*. Amityville, NY: Baywood Publishing.

Spector, P. E. (1992). A consideration of the validity and meaning of self-report measures of job conditions. *International Review of Industrial and Organizational Psychology, 7*, 123–151.

Tattersall, A. (2000). Workload and task allocation. In N. Chmiel (Ed.), *Introduction to work and organizational psychology* (pp. 181–205). Oxford: Blackwell.

Tepper, B. J. (2000). Consequences of abusive supervision. *Academy of Management Journal, 43*, 178–190.

Tepper, B. J. (2007). Abusive supervision in work organizations: Review, synthesis, and research agenda. *Journal of Management, 33*, 261–289.

van der Hulst, M., van Veldhoven, M., & Beckers, D. (2006). Overtime and need for recovery in relation to job demands and job control. *Journal of Occupational Health, 48*, 11–19.

van de Voorde, K., Paauwe, J., & van Veldhoven, M. (2012). Employee well-being and the HRM-organizational performance relationship: A review of quantitative studies. *International Journal of Management Reviews, 14*, 391–407.

van Veldhoven, M., & Meijman, T. (1994). *Het meten van psychosociale arbeidsbelasting met een vragenlijst: de vragenlijst beleving en beoordeling van de arbeid (VBBA)* [*Measuring psychosocial job demands with a survey: the questionnaire on the experience and evaluation of work (QEEW)*]. Amsterdam: Nederlands Instituut voor Arbeidsomstandigheden.

Wagenaar, W. A., Hudson, P. T. W., & Reason, J. T. (1990). Cognitive failures and accidents. *Applied Cognitive Psychology, 4*, 273–294.

Warr, P. (2008). *Work, happiness, and unhappiness*. Mahwah, NJ: Lawrence Erlbaum Associates.

Wiezer, N., Smulders, P., & Nelemans, R. (2005). De invloed van organisatiekenmerken op werkdruk in organisaties [*How organizational characteristics influence work pressure in organizations*]. *Tijdschrift voor Arbeidsvraagstukken, 21*, 228–244.

Yerkes, R. M., & Dodson, J. D. (1908). The relation of strength of stimulus to rapidity of habit-formation. *Journal of Comparative Neurology and Psychology, 18*, 459–482.

Zapf, D. (1989). *Selbst- und Fremdbeobachtung in der psychologische Arbeitsanalyse*. Göttingen: Hogrefe.

Zijlstra, F. (1993). *Efficiency in work behaviour: A design approach for modern tools*. PhD Dissertation. Delft University.

6

Qualitative Demands at Work

DIETER ZAPF, NORBERT K. SEMMER
AND SHEENA JOHNSON

Chapter Objectives

After studying this chapter, you should be able to:

- understand qualitative demands at work and how these can affect employees;
- use action regulation theory as a framework for understanding how demands at work affect workers;
- appreciate the different types of stressful demands we might face at work (e.g. regulation problems, physical demands, cognitive demands, role stress and emotional demands);
- differentiate between challenge and hindrance demands;
- describe the research that contributes to our understanding of qualitative demands at work.

In this chapter, we focus on the *qualitative* rather than the *quantitative* aspects of demands (the latter are discussed in Chapter 5), but it should be noted that quantity can turn into quality. Feeling overwhelmed because of demands that are too high has distinct consequences in terms of arousing negative affect, and so does feeling bored because of demands that are too low. We therefore will not be able to completely separate the two; we can only try to focus on the qualitative aspect.

An Introduction to Contemporary Work Psychology, First Edition.
Edited by Maria C. W. Peeters, Jan de Jonge and Toon W. Taris.
© 2014 John Wiley & Sons, Ltd. Published 2014 by John Wiley & Sons, Ltd.

A special focus will be on stressors, that is, demands that enhance the risk of people experiencing stress (Semmer, McGrath, & Beehr, 2005). Note that we talk about a risk. Stressors do not inevitably induce stress in everyone under all circumstances, just as a potentially lethal virus does not kill everyone infected with it. Because demands often become stressful, many authors actually refer to stressful demands when they talk about demands (see also Chapter 7).

In this chapter, we will first present a general framework concerning the nature of demands (Section 6.1) and the way in which people deal with demands through a discussion of action regulation theory (Section 6.2). In Section 6.3, we briefly talk about physical demands and subsequently about cognitive demands (Section 6.4). We then consider regulation problems (Section 6.5) before moving on to discuss emotional demands (i.e. emotional labour or emotion work) in Section 6.6. Next, we conclude with some thoughts about the quantity and quality of demands, and how it is probably the combination of demands that influences how we react to demands (Section 6.7). We end this chapter with concluding remarks in Section 6.8.

6.1 The Nature of Demands

By definition, work puts demands on those who work. As already mentioned in Chapter 1, work is a goal- and effort-related activity that typically requires people to reach specific goals (e.g. producing a certain part, fixing a broken machine, improving the state of a patient or performing a piece of music). The actions one carries out to reach these goals are typically specified at least to some degree. Furthermore, goals usually have to be reached within a given time frame. All these characteristics imply that work puts demands on people. These demands may relate to external, visible activities (e.g. driving a bus to a given destination) and to dealing with external influences, such as noise and heat; these represent *physical* demands. But demands also relate to internal processes. One has to interpret what one is supposed to do (a process that is often not as easy as it may look at first sight), remember (or develop) strategies for dealing with task requirements, keep important information in mind that needs to be considered (e.g. possible allergies of a patient) and make decisions about the most efficient way of dealing with a problem or about the strategy that carries the least risk in the case of risky decisions; these are *cognitive* demands. Furthermore, work (as any other activity) is associated with emotions. Some things are pleasant to do, some are aversive, some arouse interest and some are boring. In addition, other people may arouse emotions, for instance (un)co-operative colleagues, (un)supportive supervisors or (un)friendly customers. In many cases, a worker has to deal with these emotions, so work also implies *emotional* demands. Finally, we can talk of *motivational* demands, that is, demands that require motivating oneself in moments in which there is not enough motivational potential (see Chapters 3 and 12) in the situation (e.g. boring activities) or in the person (e.g. being tired). All these distinctions are analytical distinctions. In reality, many different demands occur together: every physical activity implies cognitive demands. Cognitions, in turn, are often tied to emotions ('hot cognitions') and so on.

The term 'demands' is used in many different ways in work psychology. It can be used as a neutral term, implying simply that internal human resources (physical strength, attention, emotion regulation, etc.) are being used. Such demands have a quantitative dimension (see Chapter 5). At a moderate level, internal resources are sufficient for meeting demands and there is enough recovery between demanding situations. By being used in this way, resources are being maintained and developed, as when riding a bike strengthens muscles and circulation. At too high a level, internal resources are not enough and we either fail to reach our goal or 'overuse' our resources, which may result in damage to our health if the overload is too high and/or goes on for too long. Finally, demands that are too low imply that internal human resources are not being used enough, and this 'underuse' may lead to resources wasting away (cf. Matthews, Davies, Westerman, & Stammers, 2000).

Demands may refer to a narrow or a broad set of competences, implying work that offers little versus much variety, requires few versus many different skills, etc. In addition, however, the qualitative aspects of demands are characterized by the rich emotional experiences attached to them, such as anger, despair or anxiety versus joy, pride and relief. The former typically characterizes the domain of stress (Lazarus, 1999; Semmer, McGrath, & Beehr, 2005). Note, however, that some authors use the term 'stress' in a neutral way, characterizing the 'result of any demand upon the body' (Selye, 1993, p. 7), reserving the term 'distress' to a negative emotional experience. Conversely, the term 'demand' is sometimes used in a more negative way, for instance in the Job Demand-Control Model, where Karasek (1979) characterizes job demands as including 'work load demands, conflicts or other stressors' (p. 287).

Recently, a distinction has been made between so-called *challenge demands* and *hindrance demands* (Crawford, LePine, & Rich, 2010; originally called challenge–hindrance stressors; LePine, Podsakoff, & LePine, 2005; Podsakoff, LePine, & LePine, 2007). This concept builds on Lazarus' (1999) stress appraisal theory and assumes that a potentially stressful situation contains threatening elements, but may also contain challenging aspects: There may be worry about the potential negative consequences, but if the situation can be mastered, the consequences will be very attractive. Accordingly, these authors introduced a distinction between challenge demands and hindrance demands.

Both challenge and hindrance demands can be seen as stressors, and are thus expected to be associated with stress symptoms (e.g. irritation, frustration). However, challenge demands are also viewed as potentially rewarding work experiences that may create opportunity for personal growth (Crawford et al., 2010). Examples include workload and time pressure. Hindrance demands, on the other hand, refer to job demands viewed as obstacles to personal growth or demands that interfere with or hinder one's ability to achieve valued goals (see the section on regulation problems). Hindrance demands are assumed to have negative outcomes such as psychological strain, including emotional exhaustion or psychosomatic symptoms, but also dissatisfaction, absenteeism, turnover and counterproductive behaviour. Challenge demands may also lead to psychological strain, but may at the same time lead to positive consequences such as job satisfaction, feelings of personal accomplishment and high performance.

Uncertainty, role ambiguity and role conflict, as well as work constraints (obstacles), have been found to have the characteristics of hindrance demands, whereas time pressure and concentration demands, which belong to the over-taxing regulation category, are challenge demands (cf. Widmer, Semmer, Kälin, Jacobshagen, & Meier, 2012; Zapf, Seifert, Schmutte, Mertini, & Holtz, 2001). High physical demands often are hindrance demands, although there is little research available here. A professional lifeguard may be exposed to high physical demands that are more like challenge demands, and sometimes people may take pride in their capacity to deal with adverse circumstances, such as working in a very cold environment (Meara, 1974). Finally, emotional demands show the effects of hindrance demands (Hülsheger & Schewe, 2011), whereas sensitivity requirements in interacting with customers or clients show the effects of challenge demands. More specifically, they show negative effects such as emotional exhaustion but also positive effects such as personal accomplishment (Zapf et al., 2001).

Note that the positive and negative effects of challenge demands occur simultaneously, therefore one cannot say that challenge demands are 'good', as in Selye's (1993) eustress concept, and do not represent a problem. Rather, challenge demands are a double-edged sword; indeed, the rewards associated with successful mastery of challenge demands (e.g. good results leading to pride, appreciation and status) may well induce people to ignore the negative aspects, thus being (and feeling) successful but heading towards burnout or a heart attack in the long run (cf. Widmer et al., 2012).

Replay

- Work puts demands on people. These demands may relate to external, visible activities and to dealing with external influences (i.e. physical demands). Demands also relate to internal processes, reflected by cognitive and emotional demands.
- Both challenge and hindrance demands can be considered stressors that can cause stress-symptoms.
- Challenge demands can also be seen as rewarding and providing opportunities.
- The rewarding aspects of challenge demands may induce people to accept stressful conditions that represent a risk for their health in the long run.

6.2 A General Framework for Dealing with Demands: Action Regulation Theory

Dealing with any type of demand requires cognitive activity. A worker needs to perceive what happens and interpret the situation in terms of available possibilities and necessities for action, etc. All this occurs in relation to goals, from very general goals (e.g. maintaining a good reputation, helping one's company survive) to rather specific ones (e.g. satisfying the current customer, producing a certain number of goods by the end of the day). In the latter case, a specific action is directly guided by a specific goal. Through these cognitive activities we 'regulate' our actions. It follows that we cannot understand work activity just by observing what someone does; rather, his or her actions are regulated by internal activities. These internal activities are based on our models of the world, which therefore often are termed 'mental models'. Miller, Galanter and Pribram (1960), who had a strong influence on this type of theory, used the term 'image'. Hacker (2003), who developed action regulation theory in Germany, used the term 'operative image', where 'operative' implies that the mental model is not an abstract concept but closely tied to concrete action. On the basis of such mental models, people develop 'plans' (Miller et al., 1960) or 'action programs' (Hacker, 2003) for carrying out specific actions. The mental representation of the goal(s), and of ways to reach them, serves as a standard for monitoring and interpreting feedback so the action can be adjusted if the feedback signals that things are not going as anticipated. The repeated cycles of monitoring (testing) and acting (operating) have become well known under the name of TOTE units (test–operate–test–exit), proposed by Miller et al. (1960).

The sequential aspect

An action process has to go through several stages (Frese & Zapf, 1994). First, one must have a goal. Second, one has to monitor the environment with regard to the possibilities for pursuing the goal, also called the orientation phase (Hacker, 2003). Third, one must develop an action plan or several options for such a plan. Fourth, one has to decide on a particular plan from available plans. Finally, one must execute the plan and monitor plan implementation so that feedback is obtained in terms of process (are things unfolding as they should?) and result (is the final product as it should be?). The chosen plan may be changed during execution as a consequence of this feedback.

A few more explanations are necessary for the order of the stages. First, the order is not absolutely fixed. For instance, an employee may have a plan of execution ready and waiting for an opportunity to execute it, which requires orientation as a prerequisite to activating the goal. Second, in the context of work goals are usually given by the organization, although they differ in specificity and may leave room for specifying details oneself (cf. the discussion of control in Chapter 7). Third, goals have a cognitive and a motivational aspect. Cognitively, they are the anticipation of future results and thus constitute the standard against which one can judge progress and result. At the same time, once one has decided to implement a goal, this goal also develops motivational qualities and reaching it becomes a source of satisfaction and joy (see goal setting theory; Locke & Latham, 2012). Fourth, motivation often is not enough. Rather, in many cases a specific intention has to be formed and a decision has to be taken to start the action, representing an act of volition, which in everyday terms often is referred to as willpower (Achtziger & Gollwitzer, 2008).

It should be noted that the demands for regulating one's own motivation and volition are growing to the extent that restrictions on people's work behaviour are reduced. Whereas work at an assembly line is regulated externally, people who have much control over what they do, how they do it, when they do it and where they do it face not only cognitive demands in terms of planning and scheduling, but also motivational and volitional demands in terms of not postponing things (procrastinating; Steel, 2007), keeping going in when difficulties arise, etc. (Boekaerts, Maes, & Karoly, 2005). Students know these problems well, as the decision to start working on a term paper early on requires volitional efforts; if these are not successful, one often ends up starting late and experiencing stress.

The hierarchical aspect

Humans are able to act in a very flexible manner and even rather simple and repetitive acts are never exactly the same: we adjust our steps to the conditions of the ground (e.g. to avoid stumbling over an object lying on the ground), we adjust our way of talking on the basis of feedback by our dialogue partner, etc. Such flexibility is only possible if elements of our actions are not simply stored in memory in a fixed sequence and activated when we act. Rather, we must be able to adjust elements activated from memory or to generate elements flexibly as they are needed. Such complicated and flexible processes are hard to imagine unless one assumes a hierarchy. Higher-order elements (e.g. call a customer) trigger more elementary acts (e.g. find out her number, press buttons on the phone) *as they are needed*. Thus, one can imagine actions as a hierarchy of functional units (such as the TOTE units mentioned above). This is illustrated in Figure 6.1, which shows a higher-order functional unit (left) and the same unit together with lower-order units (right).

There is yet another aspect to this way of conceptualizing actions in terms of hierarchies: the idea of psychological automatization or routinization. A large part of our everyday behaviour is more or less automatic. Under normal circumstances, we do not have to think about how to use a pen or a screwdriver, experienced workers do not have to think about the meaning of a gauge turning red because water pressure is too low and experienced physicians may see a bone fracture on

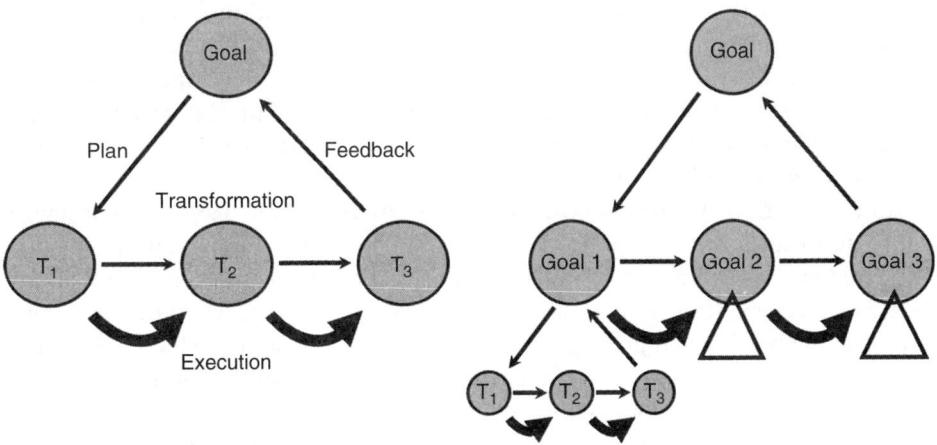

Figure 6.1 The functional unit (after Volpert, 1982; Bamberg, Mohr, & Busch, 2012).

an X-ray without having to go through an extended diagnostic process (Bargh & Chartrand, 1999). These phenomena have become natural to most of us and we only realize to what extent daily (work) activities are routinized when confronted with the need to re-learn them (e.g. after a stroke).

These processes of routinization have far-reaching consequences because they imply a qualitative difference in the way we regulate our actions. The more we have routinized a certain type of action, the fewer cognitive resources are required to execute it and thus identical external demands imply different loads for individuals, depending on their experience (see Work Psychology in Action box).

> **Work Psychology in Action: Automatization and driving**
>
> The more processes are automatized, the fewer cognitive resources they need and the more we can focus on other things. For example, an experienced driver does not focus on driving in the same way a novice driver needs to. Automatization means cognitive capacity is 'freed up' for other activities. Thus, highly automatized processes (i) are fast, (ii) allow us to do other things in parallel (multitasking, for instance talking to a passenger while driving), (iii) do not require much attention and thus cognitive capacity, (iv) often happen outside conscious perception and (v) are not easily changed once they have been triggered.
>
> At the other extreme are what are called 'controlled processes' (Shiffrin & Schneider, 1984). When things are new to us (as in the first driving experience), we have to fully invest our cognitive resources and then (i) things are slow, (ii) we cannot do anything in parallel but have to (iii) fully focus on them, (iv) we are fully aware of what we are doing and (v) can change the course of action rather easily.

It is obvious that the process of increasing automatization frees our working memory and thus helps us not to spend too much effort on the details of what we are doing, at least as long as things go as usual. A well-developed hierarchical regulation of our activities therefore makes us very efficient and very flexible, as we can make use of routines as we need them and revert to a conscious mode of control when difficulties arise.

Automatization also has its costs, however (Frese & Zapf, 1994). For instance, if one has routinized a response to certain situation, the same response may be triggered by a situation that is similar to this situation. If the response is not appropriate to that new (but similar) situation, errors can result, as when one automatically hits the break when getting into difficulty on an icy street (which would have been appropriate if the street were dry, but aggravates problems on ice).

One can think of a continuum from controlled to automatic processes, but many theorists have postulated that there are specific qualitative distinctions between different levels of regulation (see Matthews, Davies, Westerman, & Stammers, 2000). Thus, Hacker (2003, 2005) distinguishes (i) an automatic mode, which is basically unconscious, (ii) a knowledge-based mode, which is partly conscious, and (iii) an 'intellectual' mode, which implies problem solving and is conscious (see Rasmussen, 1983, for a similar distinction, although with different terminology). The reason why it makes sense to distinguish different levels is that the 'middle' level refers to specific features that characterize 'routine actions'. As we gain experience, we increasingly combine single elements (e.g. using the clutch, taking the foot off the accelerator, moving the gear shift into neutral and from there into the next gear) into single units (shifting gears). Such units are known as 'chunks' in cognitive psychology. These units form patterns (or schemas), which are triggered by specific stimuli and then executed with some conscious control but not very high demands on cognitive capacity (as long as things go as usual).

The action regulation theory is a framework that focuses on describing *ideal processes*. It has a number of implications, for instance in terms of a better understanding and prevention of errors, or in terms of suggestions for effective training methods (Frese & Zapf, 1994). Task design as well as training processes should take account of action regulation principles. Three aspects are distinguished: (i) the regulation requirements of a task, (ii) the resources for regulation and (iii) regulation problems. The latter will be addressed in Section 6.5.

Regulation requirements

From an action-oriented perspective, the most important aspect is completeness of actions: since an optimal action goes through the sequence from goal definition to feedback we described above, tasks should be designed in such a way that they make such a sequence possible. Tasks that prescribe every part of the required actions in detail (such as Tayloristic job design, see Chapter 1) do not allow for individual goal setting, planning and use of feedback. They are regarded as sequentially incomplete as they miss some of these stages (Frese & Zapf, 1994; Hacker, 2005). Similarly, tasks should be hierarchically complete by requiring problem-solving activities (upper level) as well as routinized parts (middle and lower level). Sequential and hierarchical completeness are related. For instance, in a 'classic' assembly line production, goals are given in detail (including, for instance, speed), feedback is left to quality control and the same movements are repeated over and over, so that cognitive regulation is restricted to the lowest level.

Such a view results in a call for task design that converges with many theories of job design (e.g. Hackman & Oldham, 1980; see Chapter 3). Specifically, the involvement of higher levels of action regulation implies a minimum of *complexity* and *variety*, otherwise regulation requirements are too low. Furthermore, in order to set goals and to plan, a certain amount of regulation possibilities is called for, resulting in control (or autonomy) at work. As job control is treated in Chapter 7, we will not go into detail here. It should be emphasized, however, that tasks that show these characteristics tend to be associated with more job satisfaction and work motivation, and with less job strain (Humphrey, Nahrgang, & Morgeson, 2007).

*Regulatory resources r*efer to aspects of the work situation that make action regulation easier. The most important one is job control, which is discussed in Chapter 7.

Replay

- We use cognitive activities to regulate our actions towards goals; we develop mental models and, based on these mental models, we follow plans or action programmes to attain goals.
- An action process has a *sequential* (goes through several stages) and a *hierarchical* (one goal can incorporate a number of sub-goals) aspect.
- Automatization or routinization helps us to complete tasks more quickly and to use less cognitive capacity, but may also induce routine errors.

6.3 Physical Demands

The term 'physical demands' is an umbrella term for any kind of *environmental demand*, such as physical, chemical or biological factors, that impacts on workers, but also refers to aspects such as dealing with heavy weights (physical load), working in unusual body positions and carrying out unusual movements. Physical demands are not at the core of work psychology, but fall into the domain of occupational medicine or ergonomics. The focus of this chapter is more on psychological than physical demands therefore we only talk briefly about physical demands in this section. However, we cannot ignore physical demands completely because there are psychological aspects to them. Thus, being exposed to physical demands may be experienced as aversive and constitute a stressor. Being bothered by loud noise, disgusting odours or aching body positions would be examples, as would concerns about hurting oneself (e.g. medical personnel dealing with contaminated blood) or suffering damage from chemicals one has to deal with. Furthermore, environmental factors may have indirect effects that are stressful. They require attention, and if the working memory capacity that is drawn on is not available for the task at hand it may be experienced as an interruption and hinder performance, in which case the environmental demand creates regulation problems (Baethge & Rigotti, 2013; Zijlstra, Roe, Leonora, & Krediet, 1999). Sustaining aversive situations due to such demands may have similar psychological costs as psychological demands. Physical demands (environmental demands and physical load) were, for example, related to psychosomatic complaints in the studies by Semmer, Zapf and Greif (1996) as well as Demerouti, Bakker, Nachreiner and Schaufeli (2001).

The following physical demands can be differentiated:

Environmental demands
- physical (e.g. noise, high or low temperature, vibration, radiation)
- chemical (e.g. asbestos, smoke, poisonous gases)
- biological (e.g. bacteria, viruses, fungi)

Heavy loads
- lifting loads
- carrying loads

Unusual or tiring body positions and movements
- standing
- repetitive movements

By requiring attention and evoking emotional responses, environmental demands also imply psychological demands.

Replay

- The term 'physical demands' is an umbrella term for any kind of environmental demand that impacts on workers, but also refers to aspects such as dealing with heavy weights (physical load), working in unusual body positions and carrying out unusual movements.

> **Work Psychology in Action: Physical demands**
>
> A representative interview study of the European Union carried out in 2010 (Eurofound, 2012) shows that a substantial part of the European working population is exposed to high physical demands, with especially high percentages for standing, repetitive hand or arm movements and tiring or painful positions. Some of these demands are gender specific. Men are more often exposed to vibrations, noise, smoke, dust and vapours, heavy loads and high and low temperatures, whereas women are more often exposed to lifting or moving people.

6.4 Cognitive Demands

Cognitive demands refer to information processing. We have to perceive information, deal with it (e.g. combine different pieces of information) and use it for making decisions. In doing so, we have to deal with current information, which is processed in working memory, and we combine this current information with knowledge stored in long-term memory (Baddeley, 2012; see the section on operative images). Working memory has limited capacity. Early models of working memory assumed that any cognitive demand 'consumes' this capacity in the same way (single capacity models), implying that any additional demand may interfere with ongoing processes if the capacity limit is reached. Newer models usually assume that different demands consume different resources, so that, for instance, a visual demand (monitoring the road when driving) is disturbed more by a similar demand (*looking* at the GPS) than by a different demand (*listening* to directions given by the system). In addition, there is a 'central executive' that manages the allocation of cognitive resources. Taxing the capacity of working memory is one of the most important sources of human error, caused by an information overload that is difficult to manage, and/or by reduced capacity due to fatigue. In both cases, people tend to revert to strategies that reduce cognitive demands by simplification. Examples are (over-)using routine strategies (which imply lower cognitive demands; see section on automatization) or neglecting information that seems secondary (e.g. checking the success of an action, systematically monitoring the environment); this change in strategies often results in acceptable performance yet increases the risk of error and makes more vulnerable to additional demands (Hockey, 2002). High demands imply high arousal, which tends to narrow our attentional focus (tunnel vision). Fatigue implies low arousal, which tends to lead to less focusing and less systematic information processing. Maintaining attention for long periods of time implies severe cognitive load. Particularly under conditions of low stimulation (e.g. driving on a straight highway at night, monitoring a not very crowded airspace by radar), vigilance can only be maintained for about 30 minutes (Matthews, Davies, Westerman, & Stammers, 2000). High cognitive demands quickly result in fatigue, which can best be prevented by short but frequent breaks (Tucker, Folkard, & Macdonald, 2003). Because time is so important for the effects of cognitive demands, the focus in work and organizational psychology is often on '*sustained* mental effort' (Peeters, Montgomery, Bakker, & Schaufeli, 2005, p. 45; italics added).

In a broader sense, one can conceive cognitive demands also in terms of the difficulty of decisions that have to be made, in terms of demands for developing new ideas and in terms of the knowledge that is required for carrying out one's tasks. In moderate amounts, these demands constitute resources (and therefore are associated with well-being and satisfaction), whereas in too high, or too low, amounts, they are stressful and lead to overload or boredom.

Qualitative and quantitative overload and underload

One of the first attempts to differentiate between quantitative and qualitative job demands was Frankenhaeuser and Gardell's (1976) differentiation between qualitative and quantitative overload and underload at work on the basis of the person–environment fit approach. Quantitative overload means that you have too much to do, which usually goes along with time pressure. This was dealt with in Chapter 5. Qualitative overload involves complex tasks that are too difficult to carry out. Qualitative overload taxes or exceeds a person's skills to deal with one's work tasks. Qualitative underload implies that carrying out work tasks does not require substantial requirements of conscious thinking and planning, which leads to boredom or the experience of monotony, that is, a person has too few opportunities to use his/her working skills, offering little opportunity for success. Quantitative underload means that there is too little to do, which is usually associated with boredom, but can also cause more serious aversive states (psychological saturation; Richter & Hacker, 1998).

The role stress concept

One widely used concept of demands at work is that of role demands or role stress (Beehr & Glazer, 2005). The concept of role stress is based on the idea that members of an organization often take on one or more roles in it. For example, you could be a customer service representative and a supervisor and a mentor to new trainees, all as part of your day-to-day job. Each of these roles is tied to a set of goals that you would need to work towards in order to complete your work successfully, and often the actions needed to reach these goals are specified at least to some degree. Role theory and action regulation theory converge in this respect, although action regulation theory specifies the regulatory processes involved in much more detail. Put differently, a role implies role *expectations*: what an employee is expected to do in order to complete a particular job. These expectations can differ depending on which role or task you are working on at a given time. Sometimes the goals may be complementary, for instance an employee can focus on meeting customer needs (thus fulfilling his/her goals as a customer service representative) and provide advice to his/her mentee on how (s)he could deal with customers (thus fulfilling his/her role as a mentor). Sometimes goals can be in conflict with each other, for example having to discipline your team in your role as a supervisor, which may conflict with being supportive to your mentee. This example shows possible role conflict, which is one form of role stress. Kahn, Wolfe, Quinn, Snoek and Rosenthal (1964) first highlighted the importance of these three role demands in the experience of stress at work and detailed how they can lead to higher job strain. They can be defined as follows:

- *Role conflict*: job demands that compete or conflict with each other;
- *Role ambiguity*: job demands that are unclear;
- *Role overload*: job demands that exceed an employee's ability to complete work successfully. This concept originally was part of the role conflict construct and was introduced as a separate construct later. Overload is part of just about any stress concept. It is a quantitative rather than a qualitative concept, and it differs qualitatively from role conflict and role ambiguity in that it can be regarded as a 'challenge demand'. For that very reason, it will not be treated here.

A *role conflict* arises if there are different contradicting expectations of one or more persons. A supervisor who gives inconsistent instructions may create an *intra-sender* conflict. Two supervisors giving conflicting instructions create *inter-sender* conflict. Finally, if there are different roles that partly contradict (e.g. employee role versus parent role), a *role–role* conflict develops. Role conflicts also appear when employees are required to do things they do not really want to do, for instance because they find it ethically not correct or because they believe that certain requirements are not part of the job. This can result in a *person–role* conflict (the concept of illegitimate demands described in Chapter 7 can be seen as a type of person–role conflict). Role conflict is, for example, high when call centre agents are required to solve 80% of all customer problems within one call but at the same time are expected to complete each call within 5 minutes.

Role ambiguity occurs when it is unclear what is actually expected to fulfil the work role. It arises when employees are unsure with regard to expectations from supervisors and co-workers as well as the scope and responsibilities of their job. Role ambiguity may be especially high when starting a new job or when changes happen (e.g. a change in the work structure, a new supervisor or new colleagues).

Meta-analyses (Lee & Ashforth, 1996; Tubré & Collins, 2000) reported moderate to medium associations between role demands and various measures of psychological strain. In addition, meta-analyses by Gilboa, Shirom, Fried and Cooper (2008) and by Örtqvist and Wincent (2006) showed associations with low job performance. Furthermore, role demands have been linked to reduced job satisfaction (Örtqvist & Wincent, 2006; Beehr & Glazer, 2005). As mentioned above, a common element of both role conflict and role ambiguity is that they both create uncertainty. Thus, when a secretary working for two supervisors receives a demand to finish a report on Friday late afternoon from each of the two supervisors, these conflicting demands imply uncertainty for the secretary as to which demand should be given priority. Similarly, when one is not sure exactly what supervisors expect, uncertainty results. Uncertainty can be regarded as a central element of many stress experiences (Beehr, 2000). Some authors therefore have combined role conflict and role ambiguity to yield a measure of role uncertainty, and they have shown that role uncertainty is, indeed, related to well-being (Semmer et al., 1996; Widmer et al., 2012) and to physiological stress reactivity (Wirtz, Ehlert, Kottwitz, La Marca, & Semmer, 2013).

Replay

- Employees often take on more than one role in an organization.
- Each role has role expectations which include what a worker is expected to do to complete their job successfully.
- Role conflict can occur if an employee has job demands that compete or conflict with each other.
- Having unclear job demands can lead to role ambiguity.
- Role conflict and role ambiguity share the element of uncertainty.
- An employee can be overloaded if there are too many demands placed on him or her.

6.5 Regulation Problems

Stress concepts converge in regarding a threat to goal attainment as a central element of stress (Lazarus, 1999). Since work implies goal-directed action, it is useful to ask in what way demands can make it difficult to reach goals. In the framework of action regulation theory, this implies disturbing action regulation, thus creating regulation problems. One can distinguish between (i) regulation obstacles, (ii) regulation uncertainty and (iii) demands that overtax regulation capacities (Frese & Zapf, 1994).

Regulation obstacles (or work obstacles) are events or conditions that are directly related to the task at hand and make it harder or even impossible to pursue a goal and to regulate an action (Greiner, Ragland, Krause, Syme, & Fisher, 1997, Leitner & Resch, 2005). Although goals, plans, execution and feedback processing are well-known, (unnecessary) circumstances in the situation make task execution difficult. Extra effort has to be spent to reach work goals, for instance, because necessary information is missing or outdated, tools do not really work or controls are hard to reach (poor work organization). Regulation obstacles have a negative influence on an otherwise intact action. They can be conceptualized as 'daily hassles' (Lazarus, 1999) in the workplace. The concept of regulation obstacles comes close to Peters and O'Connor's (1988) concept of work obstacles, Semmer, Zapf and Dunckel's (1995) concept of work organization problems and Spector and Jex's (1998) organizational constraints scale. Several studies have shown that among various stressful aspects ascertained, this kind of work obstacles is one of the best predictors of psychosomatic complaints (Greiner et al., 1997; Leitner & Resch, 2005; Semmer, 1984) and of burnout (Zapf et al., 2001). Another subcategory refers to *interruptions* that are produced by unpredictable outside events. Interruptions can be due to other people (colleagues, supervisors) or to technical (machine breakdown) and organizational problems (lack of supplies). Interruptions often induce negative emotions (Zijlstra et al., 1999).

At the core of regulation obstacles is that they are not core task characteristics but are often seen as *potentially avoidable* conditions that make work unnecessarily effortful. Demands falling into this category are therefore strongly correlated with irritation (Zapf, 1993) or frustration (Spector & Jex, 1998; see also Chapter 7).

Regulation uncertainty means that one does not know how to achieve a certain goal, which kinds of plans are useful and what feedback is to be trusted (Semmer, 1984). This can be so because a task is too complex, resulting in qualitative overload (Frankenhaeuser & Gardell, 1976). Another issue is uncertainty because of insufficient, unclear or delayed feedback. For example, process control operators who never know whether or not their decisions really produce the chemical correctly until much later have to live with this stressor even when they are performing optimally. Also, the concepts of role ambiguity and role conflict (see previous section) fall into this category, as uncertainty of which goal to pursue and which plan to carry out is the common core of role ambiguity and role conflict (Frese & Zapf, 1994), which predicts reactions to acute stress (Wirtz et al., 2013) and burnout (Zapf et al., 2001).

A special case of uncertainty arises when the environment requires constant checking for potential dangers. This threat avoidant vigilance is typical, for instance, when driving a bus in heavy traffic, and is associated with an increased risk of developing cardiovascular disease (Landsbergis, Schnall, & Dobson, 2009).

Overtaxing regulation refers to taxing the person's capabilities by the speed and intensity of regulation or by information overload of short-term working memory during action execution (concentration demands). Too much information has to be kept and processed in the working memory at the same time (Zapf, 1993). Overtaxing reflects quantitative demands and is therefore only mentioned briefly here (see Chapter 5).

Replay

- Demands at work can make it difficult to reach goals. Within action regulation theory, this implies disturbing action regulation and thus creating regulation problems.
- Regulation or work obstacles (such as missing information or broken tools) are events related to a task that can make attainment of a goal hard or even impossible.
- Regulation uncertainty occurs when it is not known how to achieve a goal, for instance because of insufficient information, delayed feedback or contradictory instructions.
- Overtaxing regulation occurs when a worker's capabilities can be overwhelmed because of too much regulation.

6.6 Emotional Demands (Emotional Labour or Emotion Work)

Service organizations largely depend on their customers, therefore they need to be customer oriented. This usually means that service employees have to interact with customers in a positive way, for instance by being friendly and showing positive emotions. In this sense a friendly smile becomes a job requirement. It is assumed that organizations have either explicit or implicit so-called *display rules* (Ashforth & Humphrey, 1993), which prescribe what kind of emotions have to be shown in a service interaction. Most often, emotion labour or emotion work means showing positive emotions. Flight attendants, for example, have to be friendly and cheerful (see box), but there are also other emotions required. Nurses have to show sympathy emotions (Zapf et al., 2001) and debt collectors are required to display negative emotions (Sutton, 1991). Emotion work also may imply retaining a neutral appearance, thus *not* expressing emotions (usually negative ones). Thus, the core of emotion work is the required expression of appropriate emotions during face-to-face or voice-to-voice interactions (Hochschild, 1983). This is an important job demand for many employees in the service industry.

The problem is that nobody would expect that service employees always feel the emotions they have to display to a customer. Rather, they may sometimes be bored and they may encounter situations eliciting undesired negative emotions such as anger, fear or disappointment. Emotion work as part of the job, however, implies the display of organizationally desired emotions even when employees do not feel the required emotion. This means employees have to work at showing the right emotion to the customer even if they are feeling something different (for example being annoyed with a demanding customer but still being polite to him/her). Emotion work can therefore be defined as psychological processes necessary to regulate organizationally desired emotions as part of one's job (Rafaeli & Sutton, 1987; Zapf, 2002).

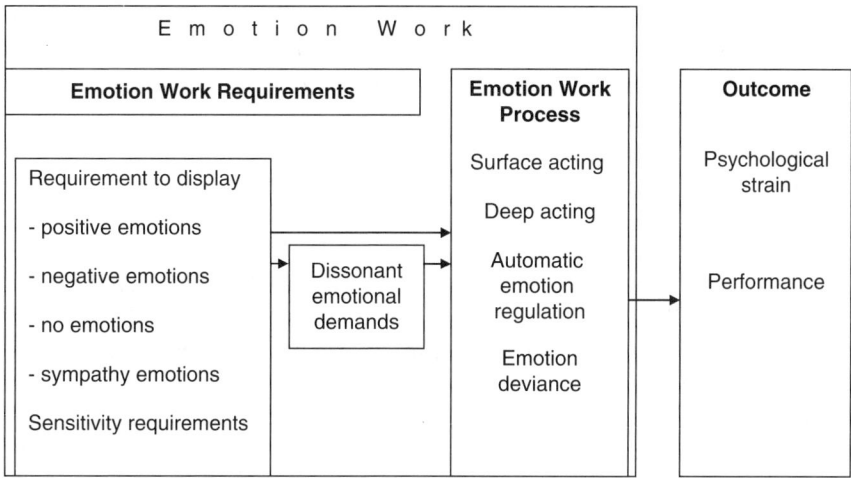

Figure 6.2 The process of emotion work.

Box 6.1   Emotion work

A young businessman said to a flight attendant: 'Why aren't you smiling?' She put her tray back on the food cart, looked him in the eye, and said: 'I'll tell you what. You smile first, then I'll smile.' The businessman smiled at her. 'Good,' she replied. 'Now freeze, and hold that for fifteen hours.' Then she walked away. (Hochschild, 1983, p. 127)

Research into emotion work shows that it consists of two key aspects: (i) the emotional work requirements and (ii) the emotion work process (see Figure 6.2; Grandey, 2000; Zapf, Isic, Fischbach, & Dormann, 2003). The remainder of this section will describe these elements of emotion work in more detail.

Emotion work requirements

Research into emotion work requirements focuses on how frequently emotions have to be displayed in a particular job, and the different types of emotions that are required (e.g. Brotheridge & Lee, 2002; Schaubroeck & Jones, 2000). In addition to the requirement to show (or not show) emotions, one can also distinguish jobs with regards to sensitivity requirements: knowing how other people feel. Employees who deal with others, especially with vulnerable people (e.g. patients or trauma victims) need to be able to detect emotions, even if they are not explicitly expressed (Zapf, Vogt, Seifert, Mertini, & Holz, 1999).

So is it stressful to display organizationally desired emotions? The requirement to display negative emotions usually goes along with negative effects such as emotional exhaustion (e.g. Zapf et al., 2001). The requirement to display positive emotions sometimes has negative effects, sometimes no effects and in some cases positive effects. Associations found are typically not very high (e.g. Brotheridge & Grandey, 2002; Zapf et al., 1999). It seems that simply having to display emotions does not cause undue stress at work; there must be additional factors involved. The central feature seems to be *dissonant emotional demands*, that is, having to show emotions one does not feel (or suppress emotions one does feel).

Dissonant emotional demands
Empirical studies show that it is not the requirement to display an emotion as such which is stressful. Rather, it is stressful if an emotion has to be shown that will likely not be felt in a particular situation. In such situations people often are required to express emotions they don't feel. Such dissonant emotional demands often lead to the experience of emotional dissonance (Holman, Martínez-Iñigo, & Totterdell, 2009) and are strongly related to key aspects of burnout (emotional exhaustion, depersonalization), psychological strain and psychosomatic complaints (Hülsheger & Schewe, 2011). Dissonant emotional demands are typically assessed by asking how frequently one has to hide or suppress negative emotions (e.g. Brotheridge & Lee, 2003; Schaubroeck & Jones, 2000) or whether one is required to show an emotion that is actually not felt (Zapf et al., 1999). The next section looks at the different ways to regulate one's emotions.

The emotion work process

What are people doing when they do emotion work? They usually regulate their emotions to bring them in line with the emotions that are required by the organization. This is the emotion work process. There are different ways of dealing with these requirements, namely surface acting and deep acting (Hochschild, 1983), automatic emotion regulation (Zapf, 2002), and emotion deviance (Rafaeli & Sutton, 1987).

Surface acting is when employees try to manage the display of emotions that appear on the surface. They bring them in line with the organizationally expected emotions while the inner feelings remain unchanged. Surface acting implies a state of emotional dissonance between inner feelings and outer expression, which persists during the interaction. An example of surface acting is smiling at a customer even when you would rather be shouting at him or her!

Deep acting is where individuals not only focus on their outside behaviour but also try to influence what they feel. Such deep acting may, for instance, occur when we tell ourselves that a customer who is behaving inappropriately behaves in this way not to offend us but because he or she is stressed, due, say, to an illness of his or her child. Our anger might then disappear and give way to sympathy; the emotional dissonance is resolved. This mechanism corresponds to a reappraisal strategy (Lazarus, 1999; Mikolajczak, Tran, Brotheridge, & Gross, 2009).

Automatic emotion regulation is where the required emotions correspond to emotions that are automatically elicited by the situation. In a diary study by Tschan, Rochat and Zapf (2005) this was by far the most frequently applied strategy. An example of this is a nurse feeling care and sympathy for a patient who is in pain, even without having to actively engage in a deep-acting strategy.

Finally, *emotion deviation* occurs if employees do not show the expected emotions. This could be because they refuse to act in accordance with organizational rules or because they do not have enough resources for regulating their emotions, for instance because they are emotionally exhausted or burned out. This is unhealthy for the employee and can have negative consequences for the organization and customers.

> **Work Psychology in Action: Emotion work and health**
>
> In experiments by Hopp, Rohrmann, Zapf and Hodapp (2010) and Rohrmann, Bechtholdt, Hopp, Meixner, Dinand and Zapf (2011) participants took over the role of service employees and had to deal with a complaining customer. The display rule for the experimental groups was to be friendly, no matter what happened. The control groups were asked to always show their true emotions. They were told that showing true emotions will be the better strategy in the long run. The experimental group that had to suppress their negative emotions (primarily anger about the customer) showed a higher increase in heart rate (Rohrmann et al., 2011) and blood pressure (Hopp et al., 2010). In the experiments the situations (and thus the elicited negative emotions) were held constant, therefore is was thought that the emotion regulation efforts of the experimental groups were responsible for the higher changes in heart rate and blood pressure.

Outcomes of emotion work

Looking at the relations between emotion work variables and psychological strain, job satisfaction and job performance, reveals that the requirement to display negative emotions and dissonant emotional demands shares the properties of hindrance demands. Negative emotions and dissonant emotional demands are positively related to psychological strain and negatively related to job satisfaction and performance (e.g. Hülsheger & Schewe, 2011; Zapf et al., 2001).

In contrast, the requirement to display positive emotions or sympathy and sensitivity requirements shares the properties of challenge demands. They often show a positive association with psychological strain but they also frequently show a positive association with job satisfaction and performance. This is so when automatic emotion regulation or deep acting can be used, so that the employee actually feels the required emotion. Working with people and showing and perceiving emotions is not negative per se. Rather, emotion work can be a source of stress but it can also be a source for feelings of personal accomplishment and satisfaction with one's job (Hülsheger & Schewe, 2011; Zapf et al., 2001).

Replay

- Many jobs have emotional demands and display rules that employees must adhere to in order to successfully complete their work.
- Emotion work requirements differ within and across jobs, for example showing *positive* or *negative* emotions to customers.
- Dissonant emotional demands imply that employees have to show an emotion they do not actually feel.
- People can deal with such situations by *surface acting* (regulating the emotion *display*), *deep acting* (regulating one's *emotions*), *automatic regulation* (the situation automatically triggers the emotion) or *emotional deviance* (showing the felt but undesired emotion).
- Negative emotions, dissonant emotional demands and surface acting are linked to poor health, low job satisfaction and reduced performance.

6.7 Constellations of Demands and Resources

Looking at specific demands is important, but they are only a part of the work situation. In the end, it is *constellations* that are decisive. Among the factors that determine constellations are combinations of demands (e.g. physical demands plus cognitive and emotional demands), but also constellations of demands and resources, at work (e.g. control and social support; see Chapters 3, 4 and 7), in private life (e.g. social support from one's family and friends; see Chapter 11) and in the individual (e.g. self-efficacy, locus of control; Meier, Semmer, Elfering, & Jacobshagen, 2008; see also Chapters 7 and 10).

Constellations of different demands, and of demands and resources, may produce effects in different ways:

- They may add up, so that an additional demand simply produces more stress.
- They may compensate each other, as when high demands are compensated by high control.

Both adding up and compensation represents an additive effect, as each of the influencing factors adds to (or subtracts from) an effect, independent of the other:

- One demand (or resource) may change the effect of the other, as when high demands have an effect on well-being/health only if control is low; statistically speaking, this represents an interaction (or moderation) effect (see Chapter 4).

We do not understand such constellations very well yet. For instance, the interaction postulated in the Job Demand–Control Model of Karasek (1979) is sometimes found, but sometimes only additive effects are found (see also

Chapters 3, 4 and 7). Some studies look at combinations of resources in general (e.g. job control, social support) in dealing with demands in general, whereas some find that the type of resources has to be specifically matched to the type of demands (de Jonge & Dormann, 2006; see Chapter 4). This is not to say that nothing is known. We do know, for instance, that combinations of different demands, and combinations of high demands and low resources do have clear effects. This has been demonstrated, for instance, by the impressive results concerning the effort–reward imbalance model, which show that demands that are not compensated by rewards in terms of financial rewards, support and appreciation, and job prospects (job security; promotion possibilities) imply a risk for health and well-being (Siegrist, 2002; see Chapter 3), or by the findings by Chandola, Brunner and Marmot (2006) that people who are exposed to high demands, low control and low social support over several years have a higher risk of developing the so-called metabolic syndrome. Furthermore, the social meaning of demands, in terms of legitimacy and fairness, plays an important role (see Chapter 7), but we do need more research in order to improve our understanding of the processes involved.

6.8 Conclusions

Demands at work are important not only in terms of quantity (too low/adequate/too high) but also in terms of quality. Qualitative demands have in common the assumption of person–environment fit. Demands at work must fit human needs. The best way to achieve fit is a mix of different demands that avoids not only too low and too high demands, but also too great a dominance of specific demands. With regard to physical demands, sitting all day without having the possibility of occasionally walking around is worse than occasional walking around and moving arms and legs. Similarly, as humans are social beings, it is natural to communicate with others and to sense and express emotions. Therefore emotional demands are not negative per se. It is the expression of emotions one does not feel that is stressful. Problem-solving requirements (i.e. cognitive demands) that correspond with the person's cognitive skills are better than routine work without such requirements. A variety of tasks is better than doing the same task all day.

Such considerations are compatible with many theoretical models in work psychology (see Chapters 3 and 4), but the action regulation theory seems particularly suited to provide a unifying framework for many of these aspects. Most notably, this framework emphasizes meeting human needs of understanding (making sense, predictability), competence (self-efficacy, mastery, accomplishment) or control (over-processing, outcomes and the environment) by actions that are complete hierarchically as well as sequentially, and it emphasizes the stressful nature of work obstacles that make attaining work goals unnecessarily difficult. Optimizing qualitative demands at work increases the chances for employees being satisfied and healthy, and it increases productivity (Harter, Schmidt, Asplund, Killham, & Agrawal, 2010).

Discussion Points

1. Can action regulation theory always adequately explain our behaviour at work? Explain why or why not.
2. What should an organization consider if it is preparing to change job content so an employee works on multiple projects rather than devoting their time to one task? Is this likely to be a positive or negative change for the employee?
3. Should organizations be responsible for preparing employees to cope with the emotional demands of work?
4. Do all people react to work pressures in the same way? Can work pressures be seen as challenge demands to one person and yet hindrance demands to another? What influences these reactions?

Learning by Doing

1. Consider a work (or study) task you have recently completed in terms of action regulation theory. What was your goal? What stages can you identify that helped you work towards this goal? Are these stages sequential, hierarchical or both?
2. Imagine you are discussing a recent failed project with a local company. What regulation obstacles would you suggest could have contributed to this failure?
3. Find a friend or family member who has a demanding yet rewarding job. Ask them about their work pressures and consider whether these are challenge or hindrance demands.
4. Think about a time when you have received good and bad customer service. Consider how this was related to emotions at work, for example did the employee show you emotions you shouldn't have seen or did they not show emotional sensitivity to how you were feeling?

Further Reading

Beehr, T. A., & Glazer, S. (2005). Organizational role stress. In J. Barling, E. K. Kelloway, & M. R. Frone (Eds.). *Handbook of work stress* (pp. 7–34). Thousand Oaks, CA: Sage Publications.

Frese, M., & Zapf, D. (1994). Action as the core of work psychology; A German approach. In H. C. Triandis, M. D. Dunnette, & L. M. Hough (Eds.), *Handbook of industrial and organizational psychology* (Vol. 4, pp. 271–340). Palo Alto, CA: Consulting Psychologists Press.

Matthews, G., Davies, D. R., Westerman, S. J., & Stammers, R. B. (2000). *Human performance: Cognition, stress and individual differences.* Hove: Psychology Press.

Widmer, P. S., Semmer, N. K., Kälin, W., Jacobshagen, N., & Meier L. L. (2012). The ambivalence of challenge stressors: Time pressure associated with both negative and positive well-being. *Journal of Vocational Behavior, 80,* 422–433.

Zapf, D. (2002). Emotion work and psychological well-being: A review of the literature and some conceptual considerations. *Human Resource Management Review, 12,* 1–32.

References

Achtziger, A., & Gollwitzer, P. M. (2008). Motivation and volition in the course of action. In J. Heckhausen, & H. Heckhausen (Eds.), *Motivation and action* (pp. 272–295). New York: Cambridge University Press.

Ashforth, B. E., & Humphrey, R. H. (1993) Emotional labor in service roles: The influence of identity. *Academy of Management Review, 18,* 88–115.

Baddeley, A. (2012). Working memory: Theories, models, and controversies. *Annual Review of Psychology, 63,* 1–29.

Baethge, A., & Rigotti, T. (2013). Interruptions to workflow: Their relationship with irritation and satisfaction with performance, and the mediating roles of time pressure and mental demands. *Work & Stress, 27,* 43–63.

Bamberg, E., Mohr, G., & Busch, C. B. (2012). *Arbeitspsychologie* [Work psychology]. Göttingen: Hogrefe.

Bargh, J. A., & Chartrand, T. (1999). The unbearable automaticity of being. *American Psychologist, 54,* 462–479.

Beehr, T. A. (2000). An organizational psychology meta-model of occupational stress. In C. L. Cooper (Ed.), *Theories of organizational stress* (pp. 6–27). Oxford: Oxford University Press.

Beehr, T. A., & Glazer, S. (2005). Organizational role stress. In J. Barling, E. K. Kelloway, & M. R. Frone (Eds.). *Handbook of work stress* (pp. 7–34). Thousand Oaks, CA: Sage Publications.

Boekaerts, M., Maes, S., & Karoly, P. (Eds.). (2005). Self-regulation across domains of applied psychology: Is there an emerging consensus? *Applied Psychology: An International Review, 54,* 149–154.

Brotheridge, C. M., & Lee, R. T. (2002). Testing a conservation of resources model of the dynamics of emotional labor. *Journal of Occupational Health Psychology, 7,* 57–67.

Brotheridge, C. M., & Lee, R. T. (2003). Development and validation of the emotional labour scale. *Journal of Occupational and Organizational Psychology, 76,* 365–379.

Brotheridge, C. M., & Grandey, A. A. (2002). Emotional labor and burnout: Comparing two perspectives of people work. *Journal of Vocational Behavior, 60,* 17–39.

Chandola, T., Brunner, E., & Marmot, M. (2006). Chronic stress at work and the metabolic syndrome: Prospective Study. *British Medical Journal, 332,* 521–525.

Crawford, E. R., LePine, J. A., & Rich, B. L. (2010). Linking job demands and resources to employee engagement and burnout: A theoretical extension and meta-analytic test. *Journal of Applied Psychology, 95,* 834–848.

de Jonge, J., & Dormann, C. (2006). Stressors, resources, and strain at work: A longitudinal test of the triple-match principle. *Journal of Applied Psychology, 91,* 1359–1374.

Demerouti, E., Bakker, A. B., Nachreiner, F., & Schaufeli, W. B. (2001). The job demands–resources model of burnout. *Journal of Applied Psychology, 86,* 499–512.

Eurofound (2012). *Fifth European Working Conditions Survey: Overview report.* Dublin: Publications Office of the European Union.

Frankenhaeuser, D. M., & Gardell, D. B. (1976). Underload and overload in working life: Outline of a multidisciplinary approach. *Journal of Human Stress, 2,* 35–46.

Frese, M., & Zapf, D. (1994). Action as the core of work psychology: A German approach. In H. C. Triandis, M. D. Dunnette, & L. M. Hough (Eds.), *Handbook of industrial and organizational psychology* (Vol. 4, pp. 271–340). Palo Alto, CA: Consulting Psychologists Press.

Gilboa, S., Shirom, A., Fried, Y., & Cooper, C. L. (2008). A meta-analysis of work demand stressors and job performance: Examining main and moderating effects. *Personnel Psychology, 61,* 227–271.

Grandey, A. A. (2000). Emotion regulation in the workplace: A new way to conceptualize emotional labor. *Journal of Occupational Health Psychology, 5,* 95–110.

Greiner, B. A., Ragland, D. R., Krause, N., Syme, S. L., & Fisher, J. M. (1997). Objective measurement of occupational stress factors – An example with San Francisco urban transit operators. *Journal of Occupational Health Psychology, 2,* 325–342.

Hacker, W. (2003). Action regulation theory: A practical tool for the design of modern work processes? *European Journal of Work and Organizational Psychology, 12,* 105–130.

Hacker, W. (2005). *Allgemeine Arbeitspsychologie. Psychische Regulation von Wissens-, Denk- und körperlicher Arbeit* [*General work psychology. Psychological regulation of knowledge-related, cognitive and physical work*]. Bern: Huber.

Hackman, J. R., & Oldham, G. R. (1980). *Work redesign*. Reading, MA: Addison-Wesley.

Harter, J. K., Schmidt, F. L., Asplund, J. W., Killham, E. A., & Agrawal, S. (2010). Causal impact of employee work perceptions on the bottom line of organizations. *Perspectives on Psychological Science, 5*, 378–389.

Hochschild, A. R. (1983). *The managed heart: Commercialization of human feelings*. Berkeley: University of California Press.

Hockey, R. (2002). Human performance in the working environment. In P. Warr (Ed.), *Psychology at work* (5th ed., pp. 26–50). London: Penguin.

Holman, D., Martínez-Iñigo, D., & Totterdell, P. (2009). Emotional labor, well-being, and performance. In S. Cartwright, & C. L. Cooper (Eds.), *The Oxford handbook of organizational well-being* (pp. 331–355). New York: Oxford University Press.

Hopp, H., Rohrmann, S., Zapf, D., & Hodapp, V. (2010). Psychophysiological effects of emotional dissonance in a face-to-face service interaction. *Anxiety, Stress, & Coping, 23*, 399–414.

Hülsheger, U. R., & Schewe, A. F. (2011). On the costs and benefits of emotional labor: A meta-analysis of three decades of research. *Journal of Occupational Health Psychology, 16*, 361–389.

Humphrey, S. E., Nahrgang, J. D., & Morgeson, F. P. (2007). Integrating motivational, social, and contextual work design features: A meta-analytic summary and theoretical extension of the work design literature. *Journal of Applied Psychology, 92*, 1322–1356.

Kahn, R. L., Wolfe, D. M., Quinn, R. P., Snoek, J. D., & Rosenthal, R. A. (1964). *Organizational stress: Studies in role conflict and role ambiguity*. New York: John Wiley & Sons.

Karasek, R. A. (1979). Job demands, job decision latitude, and mental strain: Implications for job redesign. *Administrative Science Quarterly, 24*, 285–308.

Landsbergis, P. A., Schnall, P. L., & Dobson, M. (2009). The workplace and cardiovascular disease. In P. L. Schnall, M. Dobson, & E. Rosskam (Eds.), *Unhealthy work: Causes, consequences, cures* (pp. 89–111). Amityville, NY: Baywood Publishing.

Lazarus, R. (1999). *Stress and emotion: A new synthesis*. New York: Springer.

Lee, R. T., & Ashforth, B. E., (1996). A meta-analytic examination of the correlates of the three dimensions of job burnout. *Journal of Applied Psychology, 81*, 123–133.

Leitner, K., & Resch, M. G. (2005). Do the effects of job stressors on health persist over time? A longitudinal study with observational stressor measures. *Journal of Occupational Health Psychology, 10*, 18–30.

LePine, J. A., Podsakoff, N. P., & LePine, M. A. (2005). A meta-analytic test of the challenge stressor – hindrance stressor framework: An explanation for inconsistent relationships among stressors and performance. *Academy of Management Journal, 48*, 764–775.

Locke, E. A., & Latham, G. P. (Eds.) (2012). *New developments in goal setting and task performance*. New York: Routledge.

Matthews, G., Davies, D. R., Westerman, S. J., & Stammers, R. B. (2000). *Human performance: Cognition, stress and individual differences*. Hove: Psychology Press.

Meara, H. (1974). Honor in dirty work. *Sociology of Work and Occupations, 1*, 259–283.

Meier, L. L., Semmer, N. K., Elfering, A., & Jacobshagen, N. (2008). The double meaning of control: Three-way interactions between internal resources, job control, and stressors at work. *Journal of Occupational Health Psychology, 13*, 244–258.

Mikolajczak, M., Tran, V., Brotheridge, C. M., & Gross, J. J. (2009). Using an emotion regulation framework to predict the outcomes of emotional labor. In C. E. J. Härtel, N. M. Ashkanasy, & W. J. Zerbe (Eds.), *Emotions in groups, organizations and cultures (Research on Emotion in Organizations*, Vol. 5, pp. 245–273*)*. Bingley: Emerald Group Publishing.

Miller, G. A., Galanter, E., & Pribram, K. H. (1960). *Plans and the structure of behavior*. New York: Holt, Rinehart & Winston.

Örtqvist, D., & Wincent, J. (2006). Prominent consequences of role stress: A meta-analytic review. *International Journal of Stress Management, 13*, 399–422.

Peeters, M. C. W., Montgomery, A. J., Bakker, A. B., & Schaufeli, W. B. (2005). Balancing work and home: How job and home demands are related to burnout. *International Journal of Stress Management, 12*, 43–61.

Peters, L. H., & O'Connor, E. J. (1988). Measuring work obstacles: Procedures, issues, and implications. In F. D. Schoorman, & B. Schneider (Eds.), *Facilitating work effectiveness* (pp. 105–123). Lexington, MA: Lexington Books.

Podsakoff, N. P., LePine, J. A., & LePine, M. A. (2007). Differential challenge stressor-hindrance stressor relationships with job attitudes, turnover intentions, turnover, and withdrawal behavior: A meta-analysis. *Journal of Applied Psychology, 92*, 438–454.

Rafaeli, A., & Sutton, R. I. (1987). Expression of emotion as part of the work role. *Academy of Management Review, 12*, 23–37.

Rasmussen, J. (1983). Skills, rules, and knowledge: Signals, signs, and symbols, and other distinctions in human performance models. *IEEE Transactions on Systems, Man, and Cybernetics, 13*, 257–266.

Richter, P., & Hacker, W. (1998). *Belastung und Beanspruchung: Streß, Ermüdung und Burnout im Arbeitsleben [Stress and strain: Stress reactions, fatigue, and burnout in working life]*. Heidelberg, Germany: Asanger.

Rohrmann, S., Bechtholdt, M. N., Hopp, H., Meixner, N., Dinand, D., & Zapf, D. (2011). Psychophysiological effects of emotion suppression and the moderating role of trait anger in a call center-scenario. *Anxiety Stress & Coping, 24*, 421–438.

Schaubroeck, J., & Jones, J. R. (2000). Antecedents of workplace emotional labor dimensions and moderators of their effects on physical symptoms. *Journal of Organizational Behavior, 21*, 163–183.

Selye, H. (1993). History of the stress concept. In L. Goldberger, & S. Brenitz (Eds.), *Handbook of stress: Theoretical and clinical aspects* (2nd ed., pp. 7–17). New York: The Free Press.

Semmer, N. K. (1984). *Stressbezogene Tätigkeitsanalyse [Stress-oriented job analysis]*. Weinheim and Basel: Beltz.

Semmer, N. K., McGrath, J. E., & Beehr, T. A. (2005). Conceptual issues in research on stress and health. In C. L. Cooper (Ed.), *Handbook of stress medicine and health* (pp. 1–43). Boca Raton: CRC Press.

Semmer, N. K., Zapf, D., & Dunckel, H. (1995). Assessing stress at work: A framework and an instrument. In O. Svane, & C. Johansen (Eds.), *Work and health – Scientific basis of progress in the working environment* (pp. 105–113). Luxembourg: Office for Official Publications of the European Communities.

Semmer, N., Zapf, D., & Greif, S. (1996). 'Shared job strain': A new approach for assessing the validity of job stress measurements. *Journal of Occupational and Organizational Psychology, 69*, 293–310.

Shiffrin, R. M., & Schneider, W. (1984). Automatic and controlled processing revisited. *Psychological Review, 91*, 269–276.

Siegrist, J. (2002). Effort–reward imbalance at work and health. *Research in Occupational Stress and Well-being, 2*, 261–291.

Spector, P. E., & Jex, S. M. (1998). Development of four self-report measures of job stressors and strain: Interpersonal Conflict at Work Scale, Organizational Constraints Scale, Quantitative Workload Inventory, and Physical Symptoms Inventory. *Journal of Occupational Health Psychology, 3*, 356–367.

Steel, P. (2007). The nature of procrastination: A meta-analytic and theoretical review of quintessential self-regulatory failure. *Psychological Bulletin, 133*, 65–94.

Sutton, R. I. (1991). Maintaining norms about expressed emotions: The case of bill collectors. *Administrative Science Quarterly, 36*, 245–268.

Tschan, F., Rochat, S., & Zapf, D. (2005). It's not only clients: Studying emotion work with clients and co-workers with an event-sampling approach. *Journal of Occupational and Organizational Psychology, 78*, 195–220.

Tubré, T. C., & Collins, J. M. (2000). Jackson and Schuler (1985) revisited: A meta-analysis of the relationships between role ambiguity, role conflict and job performance. *Journal of Management, 26*, 155–169.

Tucker, P., Folkard, S., & Macdonald, I. (2003). Rest breaks and accident risk. *The Lancet, 361*, 680.

Volpert, W. (1982). The model of the hierarchical-sequential organization of action. In W. Hacker, W. Volpert, & M. Cranach (Eds.), *Cognitive and motivational aspects of action* (pp. 35–51). Berlin: Deutscher Verlag der Wissenschaften.

Widmer, P. S., Semmer, N. K., Kälin, W., Jacobshagen, N., & Meier, L. L. (2012). The ambivalence of challenge stressors: Time pressure associated with both negative and positive well-being. *Journal of Vocational Behavior, 80*, 422–433.

Wirtz, P. H., Ehlert, U., Kottwitz, M., La Marca, R., Grebner, S., & Semmer, N. K. (2013). Occupational role stress is associated with higher cortisol reactivity to acute stress. *Journal of Occupational Health Psychology, 18*, 121–131.

Zapf, D. (1993). Stress-oriented job analysis of computerized office work. *The European Work and Organizational Psychologist, 3*, 85–100.

Zapf, D. (2002). Emotion work and psychological well-being: A review of the literature and some conceptual considerations. *Human Resource Management Review, 12*, 1–32.

Zapf, D., Isic, A., Fischbach, A., & Dormann, C. (2003). Emotionsarbeit in Dienstleistungsberufen: Das Konzept und seine Implikationen für die Personal- und Organisationsentwicklung [*Emotion work in service occupations: The concept and its implications for personnel and organisatinal development*]. In K. C. Hamborg, & H. Holling (Eds.). *Innovative Personal- und Organisationsentwicklung* (pp. 266–288). Göttingen: Hogrefe.

Zapf, D., Seifert, C., Schmutte, B., Mertini, H., & Holz, M. (2001). Emotion work and job stressors and their effects on burnout. *Psychology and Health, 16*, 527–545.

Zapf, D., Vogt, C., Seifert, C., Mertini, H., & Isic, A. (1999). Emotion work as a source of stress: The concept and development of an instrument. *European Journal of Work and Organizational Psychology, 8*, 371–400.

Zijlstra, F. R. H., Roe, R. A., Leonora, A. B., & Krediet, I. (1999). Temporal factors in mental work: Effects of interrupted activities. *Journal of Occupational and Organizational Psychology, 72*, 163–185.

Part D

Context

7

Job Control and Social Aspects of Work

Norbert K. Semmer and Terry A. Beehr

> ### Chapter Objectives
>
> After studying this chapter, you should be able to:
>
> - understand the basic mechanisms through which job control can have a positive influence on well-being and performance;
> - distinguish *job control* from *control beliefs* and describe possible consequences of a mismatch between the two;
> - describe threats to successful implementation of control-enhancing change projects;
> - describe the nature of social stressors and their effects on employees;
> - describe the two basic forms of functional social support;
> - understand under what circumstances social support may have negative effects; and
> - describe why control, social support and task design must be understood in terms of their social meaning.

Workers have needs other than money that can be fulfilled in their jobs, and two of these are the needs for a *sense of control* and for *social contact*. Overall, both job control and social interactions have the potential to result in favourable outcomes for both the worker and the organization. They are important in reducing threats to employees' well-being (e.g. Karasek & Theorell, 1990) because they are resources employees can use to combat the effects of occupational stress (Hobfoll, 2001) and in enhancing organizational learning (Phipps, Malley, & Ashcroft, 2012). Employees' control over important aspects of their jobs has long been considered a factor in their pride, motivation and satisfaction. Their social interactions in the workplace can be a source of both pleasure and pain, just as they are outside of work. However, social aspects go beyond direct social interaction: as for any aspect of conditions at work, they can have a social meaning as well. This chapter deals first with issues of job control and then with social aspects of work, which refer to (i) social stressors, (ii) social support and (iii) the social meaning of conditions at work.

7.1 Job Control

Arguably, job control is one of the most important aspects of working life (Semmer, 1990; Spector, 1998). There are many concepts that have job control as their core, including autonomy, job decision latitude, decision authority, participation and empowerment. The essence of job control is the degree to which employees have a say about activities and the conditions under which they work so that they correspond most closely to their needs and goals. In this chapter we use the term *job control* to represent this central characteristic that these terms have in common. Control can be used globally or it can refer specifically to *what* we do, *how* we do it, *when* we do it, etc.

In the context of job control, one important historical development is *Taylorism* or *scientific management* (see Chapter 1). Tayloristic work design emphasizes breaking tasks into pieces that are as small as possible, prescribing exactly what to do when and how, thus reducing skill, planning and thinking, and control over one's activities as much as possible (cf. Humphrey, Nahrgang, & Morgeson, 2007; Parker & Wall, 1998). Taylorism not only met with resistance, but also sparked research that increasingly demonstrated the negative impact of job simplification on employee attitudes, motivation and behaviour (cf. Parker & Wall, 1998). As a result, it inspired movements such as the socio-technical approach to job design (see Chapter 3) and related developments in Europe and the United States (cf. Clegg, 2000). Their emphasis on autonomy at the group level is shared by similar concepts on the individual level (cf. Humphrey et al., 2007).

Jobs with some degree of control usually result in feelings of satisfaction with the job. However, there are other reasons why control is important (Semmer, 1990; Spector, 1998). It can allow employees to change an undesired job situation (e.g. do a certain task at times where they feel more ready for it). Employees tend to be motivated by having control, and to be motivated by jobs that offer possibilities for control (Parker & Wall, 1998; see also Chapters 3 and 4). They also may show more persistence in dealing with difficult situations. Control over the job situation helps employees to feel more responsible for their work. This leads to intrinsic motivation to perform well because their performance is a reflection of their own abilities and self-worth, therefore performing well makes them feel good.

Functions of job control

The motivational aspect of job control has been emphasized for a long time in job design theory, research and applications (see Humphrey, Nahrgang, & Morgeson, 2007; Parker & Wall, 1998; cf. Chapter 13). There are good reasons to assume that people have a general need for control or autonomy in their lives (Gagné, 2003; Sheldon & Hilpert, 2012). Although this need probably varies from one person to another, most people feel better about their lives and themselves if they believe they have at least some control over important parts of their lives.

In addition, job control is of special importance in the realm of *stress* at work. Language about occupational stress varies, but the word *stressor* refers to a characteristic of the worker's environment that is likely to be appraised as stressful (i.e. harmful or threatening) or as challenging, which implies motivating and harmful aspects simultaneously; see Chapter 6. Many stressors are demands from other people (i.e. social stressors) or from the job itself (i.e. job stressors), for example when too much work is demanded from a worker or when the demands for performance on the job might have an ambiguous or conflicting character. Many social stressors are not demands, however. Instead they are simply ill-treatment of one person by another in the workplace, such as psychological or even physical harassment or abuse.

If stressors are very strong or last for a long time, they can cause stress symptoms in terms of psychological and physical health (labelled *strains*). Many theories of occupational stress include job control as an important variable. The most obvious are probably the Job Demand–Control Model (Karasek & Theorell, 1990) and the Job Demands–Resources Model (Bakker & Demerouti, 2006; see Chapters 3 and 4). Spector (1998) also puts control at the centre of his model of stress at work, emphasizing its impact on perceiving and interpreting stressors as well as on reacting to them. Control is a resource that may help (i) preventing stressors in the first place, (ii) alleviating the impact of job stressors (a buffering or moderating effect) and (iii) fostering feelings of self-efficacy in employees, implying a direct effect on psychological health.

There is also a *cognitive or learning aspect* of control. It offers possibilities to explore things and to experiment. By doing so, and using the feedback from these efforts, employees can acquire new knowledge and skills, and develop better strategies for reacting to problems, etc. Such cognitive processes, which refer to a deeper understanding of one's tasks, are emphasized in action regulation theory (see also Chapter 6), which focuses on the way people integrate information to decide about actions and to execute them in order to reach their goals (Hacker, 2003; cf. Frese & Zapf, 1994). Employees can react quickly to problems when they have more control over their work (and information to make decisions) (Wall, Corbett, Clegg, Jackson, & Martin, 1990). Thus, in addition to motivating employees and to alleviating stress, job control can help employees to learn and make more informed choices.

So far, we have emphasized the role of control in job design. However, employees differ in their tendency to *perceive* control over their lives, that is, in their control beliefs. In other words, the job itself can give employees more or less control, but in addition some people simply believe they have more control, similar to a personality trait. Therefore, when one asks employees how much control they have in their jobs, their answers are likely to be influenced both by the actual nature of their work and by their own personal characteristics (cf. Spector, 2006). Two personal characteristics stand out with regard to control: locus of control (LoC) and self-efficacy (cf. Judge & Bono, 2001). LoC refers to the tendency to perceive the world as being responsive to one's actions (internal LoC) versus being dependent on forces that cannot be controlled (external LoC). Self-efficacy refers to the belief that one is able to carry out a given action successfully. These two concepts combine in a chain of judgments that are extremely important for motivation. For example, when confronted with a problem, one may ask: 'Can this be influenced by a specific action?'; this question refers to LoC. If the answer is 'Yes', a second question arises: 'Am *I* able to carry out that action?', and this question refers to self-efficacy. Note that the LoC-related question resembles the instrumentality component and the self-efficacy-related question resembles the expectancy component of expectancy-value theories of motivation (cf. Kanfer, 2005) and is therefore closely linked to employees' motivation. Both LoC and self-efficacy are also part of an overarching concept of core self-evaluations (Judge & Bono, 2001), which is a factor in positive psychological health (see Chapter 10). In addition to being components of motivation, therefore, such control-related beliefs can positively influence the perception of, and the reaction to, stressful events (cf. Semmer & Meier, 2009).

Replay

- Control is part of the characteristics of an employee's job, known by terms such as work or job control, job autonomy, empowerment, job decision latitude, participative management and decision authority.
- Job control exists to the degree that employees have a say in or can influence their own work activities and conditions in a way that is consistent with their higher-order needs (e.g. for esteem and a sense of self-worth). Job control is important for employees because:
  - it can motivate them to take charge of their work and do the job well;
  - it can help to reduce strains that are due to job stressors;
  - it can satisfy a human higher-order need to have control over one's life, resulting in need satisfaction, happiness and a sense of esteem; and
  - it can put people in situations where they learn new things about their work and become more competent.
- Control *beliefs* represent a trait-like characteristic of the person, known by terms such as internal locus of control and efficacy beliefs.

Research findings: General trends

The importance of job control and control beliefs (LoC and self-efficacy, as noted earlier) has now been confirmed in a large amount of research, and one can conclude that control is an overall positive feature of work design (Spector,

1998). It is positively related to employees' motivation and performance as well as to job satisfaction, commitment and (less) emotional distress and (fewer) physical symptoms (Humphrey, Nahrgang, & Morgeson, 2007). However, these associations are usually based on employees' self-reports, which may result in an overestimation of associations with other variables that also are measured by self-reports (see Chapter 2 for a discussion). However, a recent meta-analysis (Humphrey et al., 2007) found a positive relationship between job control and non-self-report performance measures. Also, longitudinal studies have shown that low job control is associated with a higher risk for cardiovascular disease, both for self-reports and for objective ratings of control (Bosma, Stansfeld, & Marmot, 1998). A diary study by Berset, Semmer, Elfering, Amstad and Jacobshagen (2009) showed that for employees who had Saturdays and Sundays off work, more perceived job control was associated with a reduction in salivary cortisol (a stress indicator) from workdays to Sunday. This suggests better recovery from work stressors for employees with higher levels of job control (see also Chapter 8).

Many studies investigating the Job Demand–Control Model of job stress (Karasek & Theorell, 1990) found effects of job control on psychological well-being (Häusser, Mojzisch, Niesel, & Schulz-Hard, 2010), although the evidence is somewhat weaker for longitudinal than for cross-sectional studies (de Lange, Taris, Kompier, Houtman, & Bongers, 2003; Häusser et al., 2010). On the other hand, the association of low job control and cardiovascular disease is also quite well established, although more consistently for men than for women (Marmot, Bosma, Hemingway, Brunner, & Stansfeld, 1997). However, the reviews and studies cited also show that support for control buffering the effects of demands (the interactive effect postulated by the Job Demand–Control Model described in Chapter 3) is rather weak (Häusser et al., 2010).

Also, research on cognitive aspects concerning learning and performance is supportive of a beneficial effect of job control (cf. Humphrey, Nahrgang, & Morgeson, 2007). In a study of Dutch school teachers, for example, difficult situations such as unruly students hindered the teachers' new learning, but having control in their jobs did the opposite: it motivated them to learn how to deal with the students better. In addition to helping with job stress, therefore, job control also is likely to be beneficial for developing better performance strategies (Taris, Kompier, de Lange, Schaufeli, & Schreurs, 2003).

Finally, research on the positive effects of control-related beliefs (personal characteristics) also shows positive effects (cf. Judge & Bono, 2001; Semmer & Meier, 2009). It should be noted, however, that some people prefer less control than others (i.e. less 'need' for control or even control rejection; Frese, 1992). However, preferring low control does not seem to protect against the impact of stressors, but rather is associated with a number of indicators of poor well-being (e.g. depressive tendencies, psychosomatic complaints). It seems that one cannot simply change one's preferences in order to accommodate low levels of job control without some personal cost (Semmer & Meier, 2009).

Research findings: Boundary conditions and caveats

Whereas control is typically beneficial, it also can be too high, forcing people to constantly make decisions. This is likely to result in more rather than less stress (Warr, 2007). Furthermore, there are indications that job control helps most when it relates to the specific conditions that may cause problems, thus time control may not help dealing with difficult customers, whereas control over who one interacts with might well help (Häusser et al., 2010; cf. de Jonge & Dormann, 2006; see also Chapter 4). Also, we tend to avoid control if our decisions are associated with a risk of failure and high failure costs (cf. Semmer, 1990; Humphrey, Nahrgang, & Morgeson, 2007) because failing at things under our control is an indicator that we are incompetent, but failure at things not under our control can be seen as no fault of our own. Furthermore, there are indications that the interaction between job control and demands postulated by the Demand–Control–Support Model (Karasek & Theorell, 1990) may hold only for employees who also have personal resources to efficiently use their control options. Two examples of such personal resources are LoC and self-efficacy (described earlier in this chapter; Meier, Semmer, Elfering, & Jacobshagen, 2008; Schaubroeck, Jones, & Xie, 2001). For employees with external LoC or low self-efficacy, job control may actually increase their stress (in terms of hindrance stress) because they do not believe they can effectively deal with the options provided by high job control.

Interventions for improving job control

Given the beneficial effects of control in general, it is not surprising that increasing job control frequently is among the goals for work-related interventions (cf. Biron, Karanika-Murray, & Cooper, 2012; Mackay, Cousins,

---

Work Psychology in Action: Increasing job control

The upper-level management of a manufacturing company hires an outside consultant with the general charge of improving worker effectiveness and product quality. The consultant organizes group meetings of workers to *participate in decision-making* about how to become more effective. These groups decide that there is inefficiency in correcting product quality errors because the errors are not 'caught' until the product reaches the end of the assembly line and is checked by the quality control person. After further discussions among management, workers, industrial engineers and quality control personnel, it is decided (i) to train production workers in relevant quality control skills and (ii) to *empower* them with the *control* to temporarily slow the line down if they catch an error, long enough to fix it or, if necessary, to remove it so that workers further down the line do not continue to work on the faulty item. Here, the process of the change led by the consultant includes worker control (they have influence on what changes to make) and the change in the job itself includes increased job control (workers are given the power to use their own judgment and take action if necessary) (cf. Leach, Wall, & Jackson, 2003; Semmer, 2006).

Kelly, Lee, & McCaig, 2004; Semmer, 2006). Indeed, interventions that include increasing job control often do report positive outcomes on well-being (e.g. Orth-Gomer, Eriksson, Moser, Theorell, & Fredlund, 1994; cf. Bambra, Egan, Thomas, Petticrew, & Whitehead, 2007) or performance (e.g. Cohen & Ledford, 1994).

Nevertheless, for several reasons clear conclusions on the effects of these control-oriented interventions are not easily drawn (cf. Biron, Karanika-Murray, & Cooper, 2012; Semmer, 2006). First, many studies are methodologically rather weak. Experimental methods in which some employees are randomly chosen to have their job control increased and the others are not are the strongest methods for being sure control causes good effects in the workplace. However, this is hard to do in organizations (see Chapter 2). Second, results are inconsistent because some studies do not show effects and some even show negative effects of job control (cf. Semmer, 2006). Third, many interventions include not only job control but also other job variables, which makes it difficult to attribute changes specifically to control. Fourth, effects are often obtained for some employee reactions but not for others, and there is not much consistency across studies with regard to which effects are obtained. Table 7.1 provides a selective overview of the reasons for this state of affairs.

Table 7.1 Seven reasons why control interventions may have inconsistent results.

Insufficient participation	Participation is not a quick and easy thing. It needs time, thorough preparation (including an analysis of problems and needs), patience, comprehensive information and skilful moderation.
Lack of management support	Management, including top management, has to demonstrate support for the change process – not only initially but throughout the whole process, including (unavoidable) setbacks. When key supporters leave, a project often is endangered.
Resistance	Often, some people resist changes; they may fear to lose privileges (granting more control to certain employees may reduce control for others, such as supervisors and specialists). Also, changes often have to be implemented while business as usual is going on. It therefore involves additional effort.
Over-enthusiasm and resignation	Sometimes there is an enthusiastic start, followed by resignation when progress is not as anticipated. It is important not to make unrealistic promises, and to ensure some short-term changes (even if small) while patiently working for changes that need more time.
Side effects	Sometimes unanticipated side effects occur, as when a team runs into conflict because there is no supervisor anymore and they are not trained in conflict management.
Spotty success	Control has more positive effects for specific jobs or with specific employees than for others.
Co-occurring changes	Autonomy is sometimes accompanied by other changes in the job, such as an increased workload or company downsizing, which can counteract some of its positive effects.

Replay

- Even though people differ in how much control they would like to have, most employees want some amount of control in their work. In fact, the workplace normally has rules that take some control from the workers (e.g. one must arrive at work at a certain time and accomplish specific activities during a certain time period).
- Because of this, jobs providing more control are often appreciated by employees. Overall, research suggests that control is usually positive for employees' well-being and/or job performance.
- At the same time, the exceptions show that there are many boundary conditions, both structural and personal, that have to be taken into account. Complete job control cannot usually be given to the employees, and not every employee wants the same amount of control.

7.2 Social Aspects of Work

Just as employees have the need to control parts of their own work life, they also have social needs. Their employer is typically an organization composed of a social structure, that is, there are other people whose roles have various types and degrees of interdependence with their own. These other people can have an impact on the employee even if they are merely present and do not interact directly with him or her. However, they usually do interact and fortunately these interactions are usually friendly and helpful. Occasionally, however, people in the workplace can interact in harmful ways.

Other people can be a direct source of stress or stress-relief for an employee. As noted in Chapters 5 and 6, demands (which often derive from the wishes or needs of supervisors, colleagues, customers, clients, etc.) can be stressful but people can also be stressful to each other in more direct ways. People can treat each other well (e.g. with care and respect) or badly (e.g. harshly and punitively). The former can help to relieve our strains and can be considered social support, and the latter tend to make our strains worse and can be considered social stressors, regardless of whether they are demanding anything of us or not. We will first discuss the negative side (social stressors) and then the positive side (social support). Finally, we will emphasize a point that is sometimes overlooked: not only social behaviour in the narrow sense but working conditions in general have a social meaning, and their effects often cannot be understood unless this social meaning is taken into account.

Social stressors at work

Social stressors imply some kind of interpersonal tension. They go under different names, such as bullying, mobbing, harassment, violence, aggression, interpersonal conflict, social undermining, abusive supervision and (supervisory) petty tyranny.

Table 7.2 Types of harassment.

Abusive supervision	Sustained verbal and non-verbal hostile behaviour by the supervisor, but excluding physical contact.
Aggression	Verbal or non-verbal behaviour intended to cause harm to or establish dominance over an employee, by anyone in the workplace. If it involves physical aggression, it becomes violence.
Interpersonal conflict	Arguing or other disagreeable behaviour toward an employee, usually not physical, by anyone in the workplace.
Social undermining	Behaviours by anyone in the workplace that intentionally make it more difficult for an employee to accomplish work, ruins their reputation or makes it more difficult to have good relationships with others at work.
Supervisory petty tyranny	The supervisor uses his or her power to oppress and degrade subordinate employees, often arbitrarily and for self-aggrandisement.
Bullying	Repeated mistreatment of an employee by anyone in the workplace, verbal and non-verbal, including hindering an employee's work. Mobbing is often used in the same way; it has to be directed against a specific person (or group of persons) over an extended period of time, and it often involves supervisors.

Note: All behaviours cited in this box may be involved in bullying/mobbing.

As noted earlier, they are not demands in the sense of requests of demands for the employee to behave differently. Instead they are general ill-treatment of the employee. Each of these social stressors has different characteristics (see Table 7.2), but they all are forms of interpersonal harassment and they can be stressors for an employee (Bowling & Beehr, 2006). They are often labelled as hindrance stressors and sometimes as hindrance demands (see Chapter 6).

Historical notes about social stressors in the workplace
Workplace stress seems obviously important to many of us today. Historically, however, stress was first of interest to biologically oriented researchers like Cannon (1932) and Selye (1956), who tended to focus on the endocrine and nervous systems of animals (see also Chapter 8). The topic increasingly drew interest after Kahn and colleagues introduced their concept of role stress, involving ambiguous demands, conflicting demands or overloading (Kahn & Byosiere, 1992; cf. Beehr & Glazer, 2005), and after reviews of the topic appeared in the 1970s (e.g. Beehr & Newman, 1978). Reflecting social expectations that are ambiguous (role ambiguity), conflicting (role conflict) or overloading (role overload), role stressors can be regarded as social stressors. At the same time, however, they imply demands, and the emphasis in stress research has been on the demand aspect (which is why role stress is treated in a chapter that deals with demands in this book, see Chapter 6). Somewhat slowly, the stressfulness of social interactions at work also became recognized as another

category of work-related stressors, a category that is different from demands, and publications began to appear in the late 1980s (cf. Dormann & Zapf, 2002; Spector, Dwyer, & Jex, 1988). As noted above, employees can be subject to many forms of harassment in the workplace, and these are stressors. More recently, research on justice/fairness has been more strongly aligned with research on stress and well-being, as lack of fairness/justice can be regarded as a stressor (Cohen-Charash & Spector, 2001; Greenberg, 2010). Also, emotion work (also called emotional labour) has received some attention (Grandey, 2000; Zapf & Holz, 2006). Like the demands of role stressors, emotion work represents a social stressor in that it involves difficult interactions with others (mostly customers), but it also implies demands (i.e. regulating one's emotions), which is why it is discussed in Chapter 6.

Research findings regarding social stressors
Now that there has been quite a bit of research on social stressors (the various forms of harassment at work), we can conclude that they are indeed likely to cause employee strains (Bowling & Beehr, 2006). Employees experiencing harassment from people such as supervisors and co-workers (Bruk-Lee & Spector, 2006) or even customers (Dormann & Zapf, 2004) can suffer from the experience. Because social stressors often involve disagreement, the reader may wonder if conflict may not have a positive effect at times, for instance by stimulating creativity and innovation and by avoiding decision making without considering different viewpoints. Such effects may occur, but only under rather special circumstances (de Dreu, 2008). Specifically, they require an atmosphere that is characterized by trust and by 'psychological safety', that is, the feeling that one can speak up and voice disagreement and concern without fear of being put on the spot (Edmondson, 1999).

A final remark concerns the role of individual differences. Employees (or supervisors, clients) who are high in hostility (a personality trait) are likely to interpret ambiguous behaviour of others in a negative way. In other words, they might experience malicious intentions when actually none exists. For example, a co-worker who forgot to pass on information is seen as trying to undermine one's work. In addition, an individual's characteristic (e.g. being different, such as being overweight; Sliter, Sliter, Withrow, & Jex, 2012) can increase the likelihood of being a target of harassment, and a person's own behaviour may contribute to *creating* social stressors, for instance if one accuses a co-worker of undermining one's work, thus provoking a negative reaction (cf. Spector, Zapf, Chen, & Frese, 2000). Some personality characteristics, most importantly negative affectivity (i.e. the tendency to experience negative emotions), are likely to augment both the perception of harassment and the display of behaviour that provokes harassment, for example, lacking tact in dealing with others (Bowling & Beehr, 2006). Apparently some people are more likely to be subject to social stressors than others.

Social support at work

People around us at work can provoke stress, but they can help to relieve some of our problems as well. Interpersonal relationships have such strong effects on us that the Greek philosopher Aristotle called humans the 'social' animal.

Most of us like to have others 'support' us, but what does that mean? Sometimes we talk about support as meaning that others agree with us on important issues and on decisions we are making. In this way, they support our views and actions. Social support might mean that others will literally support us materially, even financially. They might loan us a car to get to work when our own car breaks down, for example. In general, social support is the existence of other people who care about us and who help us when we need it. Social support exists when we are actually receiving that support (received support), but is also considered to exist when we simply realize that it is available if we need it (perceived support). Both its receipt and its availability make us feel supported.

Occasionally social support is a term used simply to mean that we are not isolated – we are embedded within a social structure. Employees are nearly always in a social structure, their employing organization, which implies 'structural support', but they do not always *feel* supported by the organization or the people in it (which is called functional support). Functional social support means that other people do (or are likely to do) things that will provide a useful function for employees, and functional support is usually the kind that people care most about (cf. Beehr, 1995).

Historical notes about social support in the workplace
Some professions, notably counselling, have historically engaged in practices resembling social support, that is, a counsellor often shows caring and sympathy and offers suggestions to people who are having difficulties. Thus, providing social support to troubled people is accepted as a treatment for stress-related issues outside the workplace, and it makes sense that non-professionally provided support to employees would also be useful. Sometimes non-professional help has special advantages; these are best exemplified by support groups, which typically consist of people having similar problems. People who have experienced similar problems often can empathize with and help each other better than people who are different from each other, and so their support meets more acceptance than support by people who do not share similar experiences. Examples might be a support group of people who have had traumatic experiences (e.g. war veterans or victims/witnesses of a bank robbery).

Counselling especially, and support groups to a lesser extent, has been around for a long time. Regarding *workplace* social support specifically, however, the history is shorter. Some forms of social support were considered important in the workplace long before occupational stress became a well-recognized problem (Beehr, 1995). For example, the leadership style of leader consideration resembles supervisor support, and it is a likely cause of subordinate's job satisfaction and performance (Judge, Piccolo, & Ilies, 2004). Similarly, group cohesiveness, which contains elements of social support from peers, has also long been known to affect employee well-being and behaviours (e.g. Beehr, 1995). The idea that social support can alleviate harmful effects of occupational stress is relatively new.

Functional social support for workers
The most common examples of functional support are other people providing emotional sympathy, tangible help, useful information and appraisal of and feedback

about our work. These are usually considered helpful and/or comforting. In practice, these forms of functional support come in two main categories: emotional support and instrumental support (cf. Beehr, 1995).

Emotional support. People can recognize, have empathy for, and sympathise with an employee's emotions. When an employee feels positive emotions (e.g. loves the work, and values the supervisor and co-workers), it can be easy for others to join in and to share these positive feelings – after all, it feels good to do that. A more difficult situation to support occurs, however, when an employee is feeling bad. Emotions can be contagious, and empathizing with a co-worker's negative emotions might make the empathizer feel worse too. Nevertheless, social support can be a significant resource to help employees when they are having trouble. Other people can show emotional support by listening to the employee talking about how he or she feels and showing understanding and sympathy for those feelings, as well as respect and esteem for the distressed person. By sharing and talking about a problem, the employee will often feel better. From the stressed employee's viewpoint, the idea is expressed by the idiom that 'a trouble shared is a trouble halved'.

Instrumental support. While emotional support of employees comprises social interactions that sympathize with the employees' emotions, instrumental social support is more problem-solving in nature. It includes interactions that are instrumental in helping the employee solve a problem or improve what he or she is already doing. The two types of support are linked in several ways, but one obvious link is that, if an employee has a problem causing his or her negative emotions, helping to solve the problem should also help to improve the emotions. Instrumental support takes many forms, but it can include giving information that helps to solve a problem, for example information like 'the instruction manual for this machine says to operate it this way, but the machine has been adjusted to work better if you operate it a little differently'. Instrumental support can also entail actually helping to do a task, such as cleaning up the employee's worksite at the end of a shift for him or her so they can leave work right away in order to pick up their children without paying extra to day-care services for being late.

Which type of social support is most helpful?
The question of which type of support is most helpful has been hotly debated (Semmer et al., 2008). Many authors agree that the emotional aspect is most important. Others argue that the type of support that should be given also depends on the situation. More specifically, when something can be done about the situation, instrumental support should be given (as it may help to alleviate the problem). However, if the situation is uncontrollable, emotional support would yield the best match as it signals empathy, understanding, esteem and caring, even if nothing can be done about the current situation. Both perspectives can be combined, as instrumental support may also carry emotional meaning.

> ### Work Psychology in Action: The meaning of social support is caring
>
> Karl's job at the Eterli Chemical Corporation is to test the quality of samples of large batches of chemical products that are sold to other companies, which will make final consumer products from them. His work is usually quite routine, so he acquires samples and tests them at regularly scheduled times. He now has received an unexpected deadline, however, which was changed from 7 days to 1 day, and it may not be possible to draw the samples, run all the tests and make corrections to the batch in time to meet the new deadline. He is pretty sure that it cannot be done unless he stays at work for a few hours past his normal quitting time. When he was hired, he was told he would not have to do that (and he is not paid extra for working overtime). Furthermore, his daughter is playing a game with her soccer team tonight, and he promised her he would come to the game. Nicole is one of his co-workers.
>
> NICOLE TO KARL: 'You look like something is bothering you.'
> KARL: 'The boss just told me I have to have this batch done by tomorrow, and it's probably going to take a few hours' overtime to do it!'
>
> NICOLE (EXPRESSING SYMPATHY, I.E. EMOTIONAL SUPPORT): 'That doesn't seem fair – I'm sorry they did that to you.'
> KARL: 'Yes, and it means I will have to miss Chelsea's soccer match tonight – it's a big game and I promised her I would be there.'
>
> NICOLE (OFFERING INSTRUMENTAL SUPPORT): 'Well, I really don't have any other obligations this afternoon – let me help you and see if we can get the work done more quickly.'
>
> KARL (ACKNOWLEDGING THE EMOTIONAL MEANING OF INSTRUMENTAL SUPPORT): 'Nicole, that's really nice of you to care enough to help out – thank you!'

Sources of social support
Social support for employees can come from many different sources or people, including co-workers, supervisors and people outside the workplace such as family and friends (Beehr, 1995). Co-workers might be experiencing the same difficulties and would easily understand a stressful or problematic work situation. This would make it easy for them to sympathize with other employees and be willing to help them. They can be instrumentally helpful because they are often in a position to understand the employee's problems and can do something tangible to help out, like assisting in the work when an employee is not feeling well.

Just like co-workers, supervisors can offer sympathy or emotional support as well as instrumental support. Providing information (e.g. feedback and appraisal about the subordinate's work and value), sometimes even practical support, to help their subordinates complete their tasks is actually part of many supervisors' jobs. In addition, they can allow the subordinates some 'slack' or assign someone else to help when subordinates are overwhelmed with too much work at times of heavy workloads. The specific ways in which supervisors can offer such instrumental support vary widely depending on nature of the job and the organization, but supervisors usually have some leeway to help their subordinates.

Although family and friends are not present in the workplace, they can still offer social support to the employee outside the workplace. Problems at work often keep us occupied after we leave the workplace, and spill over into private life (see Chapter 11). Close friends and family members usually care about us enough to listen, sympathize and offer suggestions, thus lending social support outside the workplace. It is unlikely that family and friends will be able to offer instrumental support to the employees to help them get the job done in the way that co-workers and supervisors can, but in special circumstances they can offer such tangible help. They especially can be helpful in problems occurring at the interface of work and family life, for example. They might be able to pick up the children from day care so that the employee can work overtime to complete some tasks, or they can babysit while the employee works on a weekend. It can be very helpful for the employee to have this 'extra' time to overcome certain problems like heavy workloads.

Mechanisms: how does social support affect employees?
As with other resources, social support can be helpful in several ways. It can prevent people from getting into stressful situations (e.g. when someone's help makes it possible to meet a deadline), it also can alleviate reactions to stressful experiences (knowing that someone is ready to help can make the employee less tense) or it can make people feel good even in the absence of stress because knowing that others care satisfies the need to belong and to be accepted by others. As Figure 7.1 shows, the first of these mechanisms would imply a negative correlation between social support and stressors, the second one would imply a moderating effect of support (i.e. the association between stressors and strain should be weaker when support is present) and the third would imply a direct effect of support on well-being (statistically speaking, a main effect). All three effects have been supported (Beehr, 1995). Often, social support can be considered a form of coping with stress: seeking social support may be a coping strategy and knowing that support is available may make people more persistent in coping attempts (Beehr, 1995).

Negative effects of social support
It is clear that social support is helpful when employees think support will be *available* if they need it ('When things get difficult, I can count on ...'). When social support is actually *received*, however, there is occasionally a positive

association with strain, that is, people who have experienced support are *worse* off than those who have not. Partly, such an association is likely to be due to the fact that employees receive support when they are stressed, and then social support may become a proxy for stressful conditions. In addition, however, the effects of receiving support depend on how support is given; social support should be given skilfully, otherwise it will backfire. Thus, it is important to make sure that support is wanted, otherwise it might be resented (Beehr, Bowling, & Bennet, 2010). However, even support that is accepted may have negative side effects. Thus, relieving someone who has a health problem (e.g. back pain) from job duties that might cause pain may actually become overprotective and reinforce inactivity, which may even aggravate the health problem (Fordyce, 1988). Also, if a conversation with supporters focuses exclusively on the negative and stressful aspects of the situation, these negative aspects (and the corresponding emotions) might be reinforced rather than alleviated (Beehr, 1995). Furthermore, receiving social support may produce a feeling of a 'social debt', that is, feeling obliged to reciprocate; many employees dislike the idea of being in somebody's debt in that way (Buunk, de Jonge, Ybema & de Wolff, 1998).

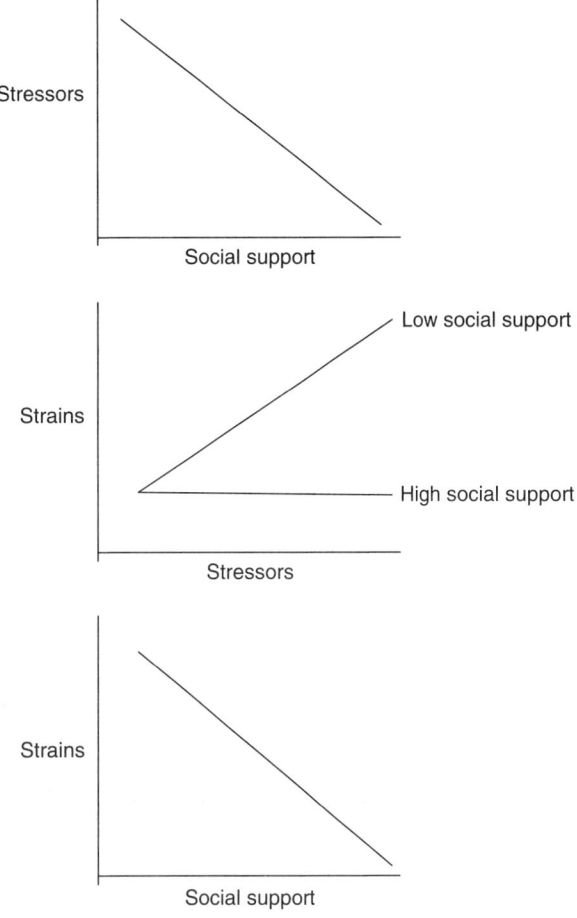

Figure 7.1 Three effects of social support.

Another problem is presented by the tendency of supporters to expect specific behaviours that they regard as adequate coping, and to withdraw their support or even blame the recipients if these do not follow their suggestions. Finally, receiving support carries a risk for one's self-esteem: needing support may be interpreted as being inferior by lacking competence, motivation or resilience (Beehr et al., 2010; Deelstra, Peeters, Schaufeli, Stroebe, Zijlstra, & van Doornen, 2003).

Support recipients and providers
Not only providers of help have to be careful – so do recipients (see Winnubst, Buunk, & Marcelissen, 1988). Giving social support over extended periods of time becomes a burden and can create stress, which is why support may be activated during an acute crisis but then wear off. Recipients therefore have to be careful not to over use support. Finally, receiving support partly depends on the characteristics of the receiver. Socially competent employees may be better able to

mobilize support. In contrast, employees who show strong signs of distress and keep complaining are less attractive to others and may alienate others, who then provide less support.

Appreciation
As discussed above, an important function of social support is that it signals acceptance and appreciation in difficult situations. However, feeling appreciated is important not only in stressful situations but also in a more general sense. Hardly anyone would contest this statement, and appreciation is mentioned as an important element of many interpersonal concepts. For instance, appreciation is part of good leadership (the consideration aspect; Judge, Piccolo, & Ilies, 2004), and it is one of the reward components in Siegrist's (e.g. 2002) model of effort–reward imbalance (and arguably the most important one; van Vegchel, de Jonge, Bakker, & Schaufeli, 2002; see Chapter 3). In our view, the importance of managers appreciating their employees and of employees appreciating their fellow employees can hardly be overestimated (Stocker, Jacobshagen, Semmer, & Annen, 2010). It is more surprising that there is not much systematic research on appreciation as a phenomenon in its own right.

Replay

- For most employees, there are other people nearby as they go about their work. People can be both helpful and harmful to others, and this is true in the workplace as well as elsewhere in life.
- Social stressors at work consist of ill-treatment of other people and result in interpersonal tension. They can cause strain – physical and emotional problems for employees.
- Individual differences among employees are partly responsible for determining who will become targets of social stressors, but the differences among people also mean that some employees are likely to be able to deal with the stressors more effectively than others.
- Social support is a very important and powerful phenomenon, and it can be offered either as instrumental help or emotional sympathy. It is usually helpful in reducing an employee's strains.
- At the same time, support must be provided skilfully and used carefully if negative side effects are to be avoided. In addition, the importance of showing appreciation for others at work (and outside work) can hardly be overestimated and deserves more attention in research and practice.

The social meaning of conditions at work

Humans actively seek meaning in the things they do and the things that happen to them. Not finding meaning can be stressful, but finding meaning is associated with better well-being (Humphrey, Nahrgang, & Morgeson, 2007). Meaning is not a physical property of things, but it depends on interpretative processes. The same events may have quite different effects on employees, depending on these interpretations. We will discuss three topics: (i) the meaning of control, (ii) the meaning of social support and (iii) the meaning of conditions at work in general.

The meaning of control: trust and confidence in workers' abilities
If employees' jobs give them control, they are likely to conclude that the organization (or its representatives, such as managers and supervisors) trusts them and has confidence in their abilities (Clegg & Spencer, 2007). Management would not let workers take charge of their own jobs unless they believed the workers were both (i) capable of making good judgments and (ii) trustworthy (would faithfully try to do a good job for the employer). On the other hand, if management closely supervises employees (gives explicit directions, watches closely to see that directions are followed and withholds rewards if a good job is not done), employees can conclude that management either does not trust them or does not have confidence that they are capable of doing good work if left on their own. Thus the meaning of control is social because workers get the meaning from how supervisors treat them. Furthermore, these social meanings of how the job is designed affect the actions of the employees. When employees do not feel valued (i.e. that they have valuable skills and can be trusted), they are less likely to be intrinsically motivated by pride in their work and are less likely to care about or take responsibility for helping the employer.

However, under specific circumstances the very same fact of granting job control or not may have another meaning. For example, when even minor deviations from standard procedures can have serious consequences (e.g. flying an airplane), most people will probably feel that it is reasonable to prescribe exactly how something should be done. In these cases, low control will likely be attributed to a legitimate reason and therefore be much more acceptable than when it is attributed to the personal preference of a supervisor or due to mistrust of the subordinate (Semmer, 2000). Conversely, when employees feel that supervisors have a laissez-faire style of leadership and avoid being bothered with problems and difficult decisions, they might interpret job control not as a sign of trust but as lack of caring and concern. Thus the same acts (granting control or controlling tightly) can have different meanings under different circumstances, and it is their perceived meaning that influences how employees will react.

The meaning of social support: caring and esteem
We noted earlier that social support can be instrumental (helping to solve a problem) or emotional (showing sympathy), but the same act of helping someone can be both. For instance, in one study (Semmer et al., 2008), a participant told how someone bought groceries for her when she was ill. When asked why this was helpful, her answer did not have instrumental meaning (e.g. 'I had something to eat in the house'), but was more emotional, showing that it mattered that the person cared about her ('He invested two hours of his time for me') Such an emotional meaning was cited as important in many situations involving instrumentally supportive actions. Thus even instrumental support can have an emotional meaning to the person receiving it.

That the emotional meaning is important even for instrumental support suggests that instrumental support that does *not* carry a message of caring and esteem might not feel supportive or, worse, might even be detrimental. Such 'dysfunctional support' is actually associated with *lower* well-being (Beehr, Bowling, & Bennett, 2010).

> **Work Psychology in Action: How can you support someone and yet hurt him or her at the same time?**
>
> Giving instrumental support may be hurtful if it is combined with a message that implies a lack of esteem, as these examples show:
>
> - *Blaming the recipient of help.* 'I told you this would not work!' is exactly not what we want to hear when we have manoeuvred ourselves into a difficult situation. And if our neighbour gives us a ride to the airport because we don't have enough gasoline in our car, it can be frustrating to be lectured about the necessity to always have enough gasoline in one's car on the way to the airport.
> - *Emphasizing one's helpful role.* When we are being helped, we don't like the helper emphasizing how much we need him or her to solve the problem ('Without me you would be in real trouble now'), as such an attitude emphasizes our weakness or lack of competence.
> - *Suggesting solutions prematurely.* If we have a problem that has troubled us for some time, it may happen that someone tells us after only a few minutes how we should solve it. These suggestions belittle our problem – after all, why are we troubled by it if it could be solved so easily?
>
> Semmer and colleagues have devised a questionnaire asking for this type of messages associated with instrumental help. Their results show that having this type of 'dysfunctional' support is actually associated with more stress symptoms (cf. Semmer, 2011).

Beyond control and support: the social meaning of tasks and working conditions

Being granted job control can have different meanings, and the same is true for social support. However, the issue of social meaning goes even further. It involves the tasks one is assigned and the conditions under which one works. For instance, Semmer (2000) reports interviews with nurses responding to a hypothetical but realistic scenario. They were asked if it was stressful for them to have a patient who was seriously ill and who kept calling them to do all kinds of things (e.g. opening the window, bringing tea, helping them to the toilet, etc.) even in rather hectic and difficult situations. Often, the nurses replied 'That's not very stressful, that's part of the job!' However, when asked about the same behaviour of the patient after he or she had improved and could do many of these things by him- or herself, the reaction to the same type of requests was very different. Many nurses felt treated like a maid, and they exclaimed 'We are not a hotel!'

The very same tasks, therefore, may carry a different meaning when they are a legitimate part of one's professional role (and, thus, one's professional identity) than when they are not. Tasks that are considered unnecessary (e.g. having to produce documents that no one ever reads) or unreasonable (i.e. outside the core activities of one's profession, such as non-nursing activities) are considered illegitimate and thus inappropriate (Kottwitz et al., 2013; Semmer, Jacobshagen, Meier, & Elfering, 2007) and, in a broader sense, unfair (Cohen-Charash & Spector, 2001). Note that the (lack of) legitimacy does not reside in the task itself; the very same things may be perfectly normal under different circumstances. It is the social meaning of the activity that determines the degrees to which it is considered illegitimate. Not only tasks can be illegitimate, so can stressors, even physical stressors, as when the fact that an air-conditioning unit that does not work is not being fixed is interpreted as lack of care by management.

The value of focusing on social meaning
Social interactions have a social meaning, but so do circumstances at work, including physical properties. How is such meaning inferred? Inferring social meaning is an interpretative process that can evolve differently for different employees. For instance, an employee high in hostility may be more likely to attribute lack of control to bad organizational intent than an employee low in hostility. Meaning is also partly determined by a given culture. There are local/organizational cultures in which members of a team talk to each other and determine whether the poor quality of their computers is due to a lack of concern by management or the difficult economic situation of the company. And there are many other layers of culture, such as professional cultures (the nursing community may achieve some consensus regarding which activities are a legitimate part of the nursing profession and which are considered non-nursing activities), cultures of regions, countries, religious communities, etc. Interpretations can become 'givens' in a culture (e.g. everybody 'knows' it is wrong for a nurse to disobey a doctor's orders even the nurse is better informed about a situation). This implies that they become part of the objective social reality to which individuals are exposed, and the same fact may have different meaning in different cultures (e.g. accepting support may be seen as a sign of weakness in 'macho' cultures, low autonomy may be considered more acceptable in strongly hierarchical cultures). Knowing the objective facts is likely to explain employees' reactions to them only partially. Knowing the cultural meaning of these facts may help to understand their reactions more profoundly and can help to avoid hurting someone by inadvertently communicating lack of esteem and caring. Perceptions of justice/fairness play an especially important role in meaning issues (Cohen-Charash & Spector, 2001; Greenberg, 2010).

Replay
- Acts such as helping someone out, giving someone job control and assigning a certain task have a social meaning. They can be interpreted in terms of caring and esteem but also as a sign of indifference, neglect or even malicious intent.
- The social meaning of conditions at work depends on individual interpretations, but also on interpretations that are established in a given cultural environment.
- Knowing the potential social meaning of one's actions (e.g. helping someone out without communicating care and esteem) may help supervisors to avoid inadvertently sending social messages that may hurt employees.

7.3 Conclusions

Economics are not the only thing people get from working. Job characteristics such as the amount of control an employee has in the job and the social support offered by people in the workplace are also important in determining their well-being and their job performance. People have basic needs both to control their immediate environment and for positive social contact.

Many jobs have been designed in a way that limits the employee's control to an unnecessary extent. Because of this some worker goodwill and motivation are lost, but interventions can increase their job control and thereby regain these positive reactions. Some people believe they generally have more control over their lives than others. However, giving workers more job control can be a message that the employer has trust and confidence in them, and they can become more motivated to perform because of this understanding. Of course, it is always possible that a few job elements must be more tightly determined by the employer (e.g. in dangerous jobs), but historically many jobs have unnecessarily exaggerated control of the workers rather than control by the workers.

Having meaningful and pleasant social contact is another basic human need, and because most workers have others around them there is usually an opportunity to partake in such contact. Unfortunately, other people can also be sources of stress if they are overly critical, unsympathetic or harassing. These stressors can result in poor adjustment and health of an employee who is the target of these acts. Other people can also be very helpful to their fellow employees, and socially supportive actions are common. Social support can serve two functions for the recipient of the support. It can be either instrumental (offering tangible help to get the job done) or emotional (sympathizing with an employee's emotional reactions to the job). Even instrumentally supportive actions of co-workers can convey the meaning of emotional caring for the employee receiving it, and they can backfire if they don't.

Job control and social support are two of the most important characteristics of the work environment (see also Chapters 3 and 4). Part of the reason for their importance is that they convey meaning to the employee – a meaning of caring and respect. It is not only the simple facts of granting control to employees or of lending help to them that matters. Because actions and circumstances at work have social meanings, supervisors are well-advised to take this social meaning into account in order to avoid misunderstandings.

Discussion Points

1. If having control can be interpreted in so many different ways, depends so much on individual and cultural processes of interpretation, and can even have detrimental consequences does it make sense to advocate increasing job control as a way of improving employee health and performance?
2. If giving social support requires so many considerations of the person and the circumstances involved, and of the style it is given, can we ever expect supervisors to have the time and the skills needed to figure out how to deliver social support so that it is helpful?
3. We have emphasized the importance of appreciation in this chapter. What does that imply for the development and the handling of interpersonal conflict?
4. If people think they should not have to carry out a certain task (even though they are well able to do it), isn't that a sign of a lack of flexibility?

Learning by Doing

You could ask the following questions with regard to a job you have (or had), or you can ask friends or relatives about them.

1. Note for a few days whenever you think 'How nice (or how convenient) that I can decide that myself' or 'Why can't I decide that myself?' or 'Why do I have to decide about that?'
2. Think about an event where you felt really well supported and about an event where someone tried to support you (i.e. had good intentions) but did not give you the feeling that you were well supported. Try to describe what made the difference.
3. Think about something at work that made you think 'I should not have to do this; this should be done by someone else!' Why did you feel that way?

Further Reading

Daniels, K., & de Jonge, J. (2010). Match making and match breaking: The nature of match within and around job design. *Journal of Occupational and Organizational Psychology, 83*, 1–16.

Häusser, J. A., Mojzisch, A., Niesel, M., & Schulz-Hardt, S. (2010). Ten years on: A review of recent research on the Job Demand-Control (-Support) model and psychological well-being. *Work & Stress, 24*, 1–35.

Luchman, J. N., & González-Morales, M. G. (2013). Demands, control, and support: A meta-analytic review of work characteristics interrelationships. *Journal of Occupational Health Psychology, 18*, 37–52.

References

Bakker, A. B., & Demerouti, E. (2006). The Job Demands–Resources Model: State of the art. *Journal of Managerial Psychology, 22*, 309–328.

Bambra, C., Egan, M., Thomas, S., Petticrew, M., & Whitehead, M. (2007). The psychosocial and health effects of workplace reorganization: 2. A systematic review of task restructuring interventions. *Journal of Epidemiology and Community Health, 61*, 1028–1037.

Beehr, T. A. (1995). *Psychological stress in the workplace*. London: Routledge.

Beehr, T. A., Bowling, N. A., & Bennett, M. M. (2010). Occupational stress and failures of social support: When helping hurts. *Journal of Occupational Health Psychology, 15*, 45–59.

Beehr, T. A., & Glazer, S. (2005). Organizational role stress. In J. Barling, E. K. Kelloway, & M. R. Frone (Eds.), *Handbook of work stress* (pp. 7–33). Thousand Oaks, CA: Sage Publications.

Beehr, T. A., & Newman, J. E. (1978). Job stress, employee health, and organizational effectiveness: A facet analysis, model, and literature review. *Personnel Psychology, 31*, 665–699.

Berset, M., Semmer, N. K., Elfering, A., Amstad, F. T., & Jacobshagen, N. (2009). Work characteristics as predictors of physiological recovery on weekends. *Scandinavian Journal of Work, Environment & Health, 35*, 188–192.

Biron, C., Karanika-Murray, M., & Cooper, C. L. (Eds.) (2012). *Improving organizational interventions for stress and well-being: Addressing process and context*. London: Routledge.

Bosma, H., Stansfeld, S. A. & Marmot, M. G. (1998). Job control, personal characteristics, and heart disease. *Journal of Occupational Health Psychology, 4*, 402–409.

Bowling, N. A., & Beehr, T. A. (2006). Workplace harassment from the victim's perspective: A theoretical model and meta-analysis. *Journal of Applied Psychology, 91*, 998–1012.

Bruk-Lee, V., & Spector, P. E. (2006). The social stressors-counterproductive work behaviors link: Are conflicts with supervisors and coworkers the same? *Journal of Occupational Health Psychology, 11*, 145–156.

Buunk, B. P., de Jonge, J., Ybema, J. F., & de Wolff, Ch. J. (1998). Psychosocial aspects of occupational stress. In P. J. D. Drenth, H. K. Thierry, & Ch. J. de Wolff (Eds.), *Handbook of work and organizational psychology: Work psychology* (2nd ed., pp. 145–182). Hove: Psychology Press.

Cannon, W. B. (1932). *The wisdom of the body*. New York: Norton.

Clegg, C. W. (2000). Sociotechnical principles for system design. *Applied Ergonomics, 31*, 463–477.

Clegg, C. W., & Spencer, C. (2007). A circular and dynamic model of the process of job design. *Journal of Occupational and Organizational Psychology, 80*, 321–339.

Cohen, S. G., & Ledford, G. E. (1994). The effectiveness of self-managing teams: A quasi-experiment. *Human Relations, 47*, 13–43.

Cohen-Charash, Y., & Spector, P. E. (2001). The role of justice in organizations: A meta-analysis. *Organizational Behavior and Human Decision Processes, 86*, 278–321.

de Dreu, C. K. W. (2008). The virtue and vice of workplace conflict: Food for (pessimistic) thought. *Journal of Organizational Behavior, 29*, 5–18.

de Jonge, J., & Dormann, C. (2006). Stressors, resources and strain at work: A longitudinal test of the triple-match principle. *Journal of Applied Psychology, 91*, 1359–1374.

de Lange, A. H., Taris, T. W., Kompier, M. A. J., Houtman, I. L. D., & Bongers, P. M. (2003). 'The very best of the millennium': Longitudinal research and the demand–control–(support) model. *Journal of Occupational Health Psychology, 8*, 282–305.

Deelstra, J. A., Peeters, M. C. W., Schaufeli, W. B., Stroebe, W., Zijlstra, F. R. H., & van Doornen, L. P. (2003). Receiving social support at work: When help is not welcome. *Journal of Applied Psychology, 88*, 324–331.

Dormann, C., & Zapf, D. (2002). Social stressors at work, irritation, and depressive symptoms: Accounting for unmeasured third variables in a multi-wave study. *Journal of Occupational and Organizational Psychology, 75*, 33–58.

Dormann, C., & Zapf, D. (2004). Customer-related social stressors and burnout. *Journal of Occupational Health Psychology, 9*, 61–82.

Edmondson, A. (1999). Psychological safety and learning behavior in work teams. *Administrative Science Quarterly, 44*, 350–383.

Fordyce, W. E. (1988). Pain and suffering: A reappraisal. *American Psychologist, 43*, 276–283.

Frese, M. (1992). A plea for realistic pessimism: On objective reality, coping with stress, and psychological dysfunction. In L. Montada, S.-H. Filipp, & M. J. Lerner (Eds.), *Life crises and experiences of loss in adulthood* (pp. 81–94). Hillsdale, NJ: Lawrence Erlbaum Associates.

Frese, M., & Zapf, D. (1994). Action as the core of work psychology; A German approach. In H. C. Triandis, M. D. Dunnette, & L. M. Hough (Eds.), *Handbook of industrial and organizational psychology* (Vol. 4, pp. 271–340). Palo Alto, CA: Consulting Psychologists Press.

Gagné, M. (2003). The role of autonomy support and autonomy orientation in prosocial behaviour engagement. *Motivation and Emotion, 27*, 199–223.

Grandey, A. A. (2000). Emotion regulation in the workplace: A new way to conceptualize emotional labor. *Journal of Occupational Health Psychology, 5*, 95–110.

Greenberg, J. (2010). Organizational injustice as an occupational health risk. *The Academy of Management Annals, 4*, 205–243.

Hacker, W. (2003). Action regulation theory: A practical tool for the design of modern work processes? *European Journal of Work and Organizational Psychology, 12*, 105–130.

Häusser, J. A., Mojzisch, A., Niesel, M., & Schulz-Hard, S. (2010). Ten years on: A review of recent research on the Job Demand–Control(–Support) model and psychological well-being. *Work & Stress, 24*, 1–35.

Hobfoll, S. E. (2001). The influence of culture, community, and the nested-self in the stress process: Advancing conservation of resources theory. *Applied Psychology: An International Review, 50*, 337–421.

Humphrey, S. E., Nahrgang, J. D., & Morgeson, F. P. (2007). Integrating motivational, social, and contextual work design features: A meta-analytic summary and theoretical extension of the work design literature. *Journal of Applied Psychology, 92*, 1332–1356.

Judge, T. A., & Bono, J. E. (2001). Relationship of core self evaluation traits – self-esteem, generalized self-efficacy, locus of control, and emotional stability with job satisfaction and job performance: A meta-analysis. *Journal of Applied Psychology, 86*, 80–92.

Judge, T. A., Piccolo, R. F., & Ilies, R. (2004). The forgotten ones? The validity of consideration and initiating structure in leadership research. *Journal of Applied Psychology, 89*, 36–51.

Kahn, R. L., & Byosiere, P. (1992). Stress in organizations. In M. D. Dunnette, & L. M. Hough (Eds.), *Handbook of industrial and organizational psychology* (Vol. 3, 2nd ed., pp. 571–650). Palo Alto, CA: Consulting Psychologists Press.

Kanfer, R. (2005). Motivation and performance. In N. Nicholson, P. Audia, & M. Pillutla (Eds.), *Blackwell encyclopedic dictionary of organizational behavior* (2nd ed., pp. 233–241). Malden, MA: Blackwell.

Karasek, R. A., & Theorell, T. (1990). *Healthy work: Stress, productivity and the reconstruction of working life*. New York: Basic Books.

Kottwitz, M. U., Meier, L. L., Jacobshagen, N., Kälin, W., Elfering, A., Hennig, J., & Semmer, N. K. (2013). Illegitimate tasks associated with higher cortisol levels among male employees when subjective health is relatively low: An intra-individual analysis. *Scandinavian Journal of Work, Environment and Health*. Advance online publication.

Leach, D. J., Wall, T. D., & Jackson, P. R. (2003). The effect of empowerment on job knowledge: An empirical test involving operators of complex technology. *Journal of Occupational and Organizational Psychology, 76*, 27–52.

Mackay, C. J., Cousins, R., Kelly, P. J., Lee, S., & McCaig, R. H. (2004). 'Management standards' and work-related stress in the UK: Policy background and science. *Work & Stress, 18*, 91–112.

Marmot, M. G., Bosma, H., Hemingway, H., Brunner, E., & Stansfeld, S. (1997). Contribution of job control and other risk factors to social variations in coronary heart disease incidence. *Lancet, 350*, 235–239.

Meier, L. L., Semmer, N. K., Elfering, A., & Jacobshagen, N. (2008). The double meaning of control: Three-way interactions between internal resources, job control, and stressors at work. *Journal of Occupational Health Psychology, 13*, 244–258.

Orth-Gomer, K., Eriksson, I., Moser, V., Theorell, T., & Fredlund, P. (1994). Lipid lowering through work stress reduction. *International Journal of Behavioral Medicine, 1*, 204–214.

Parker, S., & Wall, T. (1998). *Job and work design: Organizing work to promote well-being and effectiveness*. London: Sage Publications.

Phipps, D. L., Malley, C., & Ashcroft, D. M.(2012). Job characteristics and safety climate: The role of effort–reward and demand–control–support models. *Journal of Occupational Health Psychology, 17*, 279–289.

Schaubroeck, J., Jones, J. R., & Xie, J. L. (2001). Individual differences in utilizing control to cope with job demands: Effects on susceptibility to infectious disease. *Journal of Applied Psychology, 86*, 265–278.

Selye, H. (1956). *The stress of life*. New York: McGraw-Hill.

Semmer, N. K. (1990). Stress und Kontrollverlust [*Losing control and stress*]. In F. Frei, & I. Udris (Eds.), *Das Bild der Arbeit* (pp. 190–207). Bern: Huber.

Semmer, N. K. (2000). Control at work: Issues of specificity, generality, and legitimacy. In W. J. Perrig, & A. Grob (Eds.), *Control of human behavior, mental processes, and consciousness* (pp. 555–574). Mahwah, NJ: Lawrence Erlbaum Associates.

Semmer, N. K. (2006). Job stress interventions and the organization of work. *Scandinavian Journal of Work, Environment and Health, 32*, 515–527.

Semmer, N. K. (2011). *Occupational health psychology: The 'Stress-as-Offense-to-Self' perspective*. Invited presentation at the 26th Annual Conference of the Society of Industrial and Organizational Psychology, Chicago, IL.

Semmer, N. K., Elfering, A., Jacobshagen, N., Perrot, T., Beehr, T. A., & Boos, N. (2008). The emotional meaning of instrumental social support. *International Journal of Stress Management, 15*, 235–251.

Semmer, N. K., Jacobshagen, N., Meier, L. L., & Elfering, A. (2007). Occupational stress research: The 'Stress-as-Offense-to-Self' perspective. In J. Houdmont, & S. McIntyre (Eds.), *Occupational health psychology: European perspectives on research, education and practice* (Vol. 2, pp. 43–60). Castelo da Maia, Portugal: ISMAI Publishing.

Semmer, N. K., & Meier, L. L. (2009). Individual differences, work stress, & health. In C. L. Cooper, J. Campbell Quick, & M. J. Schabracq (Eds.), *International handbook of work and health psychology* (3rd ed., pp. 99–121). Chichester: John Wiley & Sons.

Sheldon, K. M., & Hilpert, J. C. (2012). A balanced measure of psychological needs (BMPN) scale: An alternative domain general measure of need satisfaction. *Motivation and Emotion, 36*, 439–451.

Siegrist, J. (2002). Effort-reward imbalance at work and health. *Research in Occupational Stress and Well-being, 2*, 261–291.

Sliter, K. A., Sliter, M. T., Withrow, S. A., & Jex, S. M. (2012). Employee adiposity and incivility: Establishing a link and identifying demographic moderators and negative consequences. *Journal of Occupational Health Psychology, 17*, 409–424.

Spector, P. E. (1998). A control model of the job stress process. In C. L. Cooper (Ed.), *Theories of organizational stress* (pp. 153–169). London: Oxford University Press.

Spector, P. E. (2006). Method variance in organizational research: Truth or urban legend? *Organizational Research Methods, 9*, 221–232.

Spector, P. E., Dwyer, D. J., & Jex, S. M. (1988). Relation of job stressors to affective, health, and performance outcomes: A comparison of multiple data sources. *Journal of Applied Psychology, 73*, 11–19.

Spector, P. E., Zapf, D., Chen, P. Y., & Frese, M. (2000). Why negative affectivity should not be controlled in job stress research: Don't throw out the baby with the bath water. *Journal of Organizational Behavior, 21*, 79–95.

Stocker, D., Jacobshagen, N., Semmer, N. K., & Annen, H. (2010). Appreciation at work in the Swiss Armed Forces. *Swiss Journal of Psychology, 69*, 117–124.

Taris, T. W., Kompier, M. A. J., de Lange, A. H., Schaufeli, W. B., & Schreurs, P. J. G. (2003). Learning new behaviour patterns: A longitudinal test of Karasek's active learning hypothesis among Dutch teachers. *Work & Stress, 17*, 1–20.

van Vegchel, N., de Jonge, J., Bakker, A. B., & Schaufeli, W. B. (2002). Testing global and specific indicators of rewards in the Effort–Reward Imbalance model: Does it make any difference?

European Journal of Work and Organizational Psychology, 11, 403–421.

Wall, T. D., Corbett, J. M., Clegg, C. W., Jackson, P. R., & Martin, R. (1990). Advanced manufacturing technology and work design: Towards a theoretical framework. *Journal of Organizational Behavior, 11*, 201–219.

Warr, P. (2007). *Work, happiness, and unhappiness.* Mahwah, NJ: Lawrence Erlbaum Associates.

Winnubst, J. A. M., Buunk, B. P., & Marcelissen, F. H. G. (1988). Social support and stress. In S. Fisher, & J. Reason (Eds.), *Handbook of life stress, cognition and health* (pp. 511–528). Chichester: John Wiley & Sons.

Zapf, D., & Holz, M. (2006). On the positive and negative effects of emotion work in organizations. *European Journal of Work and Organizational Psychology, 15*, 1–28.

8

Recovery from Demanding Work Hours

SABINE A. E. GEURTS, DEBBY G. J. BECKERS
AND PHILIP TUCKER

> **Chapter Objectives**
>
> After studying this chapter, you should be able to:
>
> - understand why recovery from work is crucial to preserve employee health in the long run;
> - explain why effort–recovery theory and allostatic load theory form suitable frameworks for understanding the role of recovery from work;
> - understand under what circumstances prolonged work hours have adverse health effects;
> - describe why abnormal work hours can constitute a health risk;
> - explain why both internal and external recovery are important;
> - describe how work-time control can promote recovery.

8.1 Introduction

Research on the relation between work and stress has a long history. Selye (1938), a Hungarian endocrinologist, first accidently discovered physiological stress while studying the impact of sex hormones among rodents. During World War II, psychiatrists became interested in stress as a mental phenomenon (i.e. war stress or combat stress). It took until the 1960s before psychologists paid attention to

An Introduction to Contemporary Work Psychology, First Edition.
Edited by Maria C. W. Peeters, Jan de Jonge and Toon W. Taris.
© 2014 John Wiley & Sons, Ltd. Published 2014 by John Wiley & Sons, Ltd.

stress in daily life, for instance at the work place (Kahn, Wolfe, Quinn, Snoek, & Rosenthal, 1964). Since then, scientific attention on the relation between work, stress and health has grown in both Europe and the United States. From the 1970s, numerous studies addressed the linkages between work, stress and health in various populations and in various work settings.

This intensive focus on work, stress and health is in contrast with the limited attention that has been paid to recovery from work and stress. During the 1980s, Dutch researchers were among the first to emphasize the important role of recovery from work and stress in preserving health. In particular, the effort–recovery theory of Meijman and Mulder (1998) has inspired many researchers in the field of work and stress. Research based on this theory has shown that recovery from work effort and stress plays an important role in the protection of health (Geurts & Sonnentag, 2006).

We start this chapter by explaining why recovery from work is a crucial mechanism in the work–stress–health relation. Next, we will focus on demanding work hours as environmental stressors and risk factors for insufficient recovery. Hereby, we will discuss prolonged work hours (i.e. long work hours and overtime work) and abnormal work hours (e.g. shift work, weekend work) as two manifestations of demanding work hours. In addition, we will discuss empirical evidence of their association with adverse health and well-being. After that, we will discuss the recovery-promoting potential of work-time control (e.g. flextime) and of related modern work practices (e.g. self-scheduling and boundaryless work). We will end this chapter with some conclusions and discussion points.

8.2 The Concepts of Stress and Recovery

To better understand the concept of recovery, one should first have some understanding of stress, and in particular of the role of stress physiology in the association between work and health. Stress can be defined as a psycho-physiological, subjective state, characterized by the combination of high arousal and displeasure (Kristensen, Kornitzer, & Alfredsson, 1998). Stress is manifested in three types of responses (Sutherland & Cooper, 1990): psychological (e.g. irritability), physiological/bodily (e.g. sweating) and behavioural (e.g. restless behaviour). Stress is generally evoked in situations where individuals are confronted with threatening environmental demands (e.g. job stressors). In their cognitive activation theory of stress (CATS), Ursin and Eriksen (2004) consider a general stress response as a non-specific alarm response of the body that does not fade out as long as the individual does not perceive possibilities (e.g. job resources) to effectively deal with threatening job demands or stressors (i.e. coping).

Let us take a closer look into the role of the bodily alarm response to stressful (work) situations. As illustrated in Figure 8.1, we can distinguish two bodily stress systems, namely the sympathetic–adrenal–medullary (SAM) system and the hypothalamic–pituitary–adrenal (HPA) system.

In essence, a stress response is initiated by the perception of a stressor. Via the SAM system, the brain stimulates the adrenal glands to release catecholamines (adrenalin

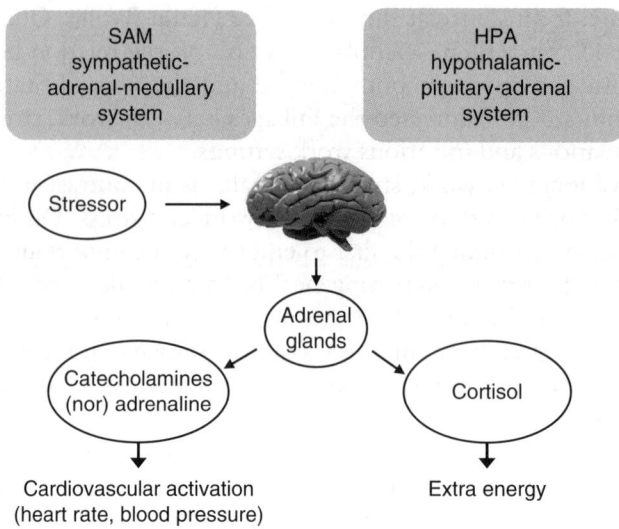

Figure 8.1 Two bodily stress systems.

and noradrenalin). These hormones are responsible for direct cardiovascular activation: through an instant acceleration of heart rate and a rise in blood pressure, the brain and muscles are immediately provided with energy. Via the HPA system, the brain also produces a hormone that stimulates the adrenal glands to release cortisol, often referred to as the stress hormone. The production of cortisol causes the mobilization of *extra* energy. In general, the SAM system facilitates the expenditure of mental and physical effort irrespective of the stressfulness of the situation. The HPA system, on the other hand, is more likely to be activated in more extreme and stressful circumstances, promoting the release of extra energy to deal with the stressor.

A key issue in research is to identify the mechanisms by which environmental stressors and stress responses lead to adverse long-term health effects. In principle, stress reactions have an adaptive function to effectively deal with the threatening situation, and are normally short-lived and reversible. It was long thought on the basis of animal research that stress reactivity was the most important predictor of ill-health (Linden, Earle, Gerin, & Christenfeld, 1997). According to the reactivity hypothesis, health problems result from very intense physiological reactions that occur *during* exposure to a stressor. However, there is emerging evidence that it is not stress reactivity that is most predictive of ill-health, but rather how long it takes before one has recovered after exposure to the stressful situation (Brosschot, Gerin, & Thayer, 2006). Stress recovery can be described as a process whereby psychophysiological systems that were activated during stress exposure return to and stabilize at baseline level *after* the stressful situation has ended (Geurts & Sonnentag, 2006). This definition indicates that recovery is a process that develops over time and that manifests in both psychological (e.g. affect) and (neuro)physiological indices of recovery (e.g. blood pressure and adrenaline; Sonnentag & Geurts, 2009). Relevant theories of effort and recovery further illuminate *how* incomplete recovery from work effort and work stress impairs health.

8.3 Theories of Effort and Recovery

The effort–recovery theory (Meijman & Mulder, 1998) explicitly emphasizes the key role of complete day-to-day recovery in the relation between work effort and health. This theory is depicted in Figure 8.2. Its core assumption is that working has benefits (in terms of productivity) but also has short-term costs or load effects (e.g. fatigue, stress or negative effect, see Box 1 in Figure 8.2). To ameliorate these load effects, individuals require a period of recovery during which the psycho-physiological systems that have been activated during work can return to baseline levels. If recovery from work effort and work stress is completed, an individual will start the next working day in a recuperated condition. However, in case of insufficient recovery from work effort and work stress (Box 2, Figure 8.2), individuals will start the next working day in a suboptimal condition (Box 3, Figure 8.2), which necessitates the expenditure of additional (compensatory) work effort (Box 4, Figure 8.2) to maintain adequate job performance. This additional work effort will make an even higher demand on the recovery process, which can initiate a negative process of accumulation of load effects (Box 5, Figure 8.2), resulting in health problems.

Whereas the effort–recovery theory (Meijman & Mulder, 1998) emphasizes the importance of sufficient day-to-day recovery from work effort and work stress, McEwen's allostatic load theory (1998) complements this theory by explaining how accumulation of load effects (Box 5, Figure 8.2) may, in the long run, result in chronic and serious health problems (Box 6, Figure 8.2). McEwen refers to

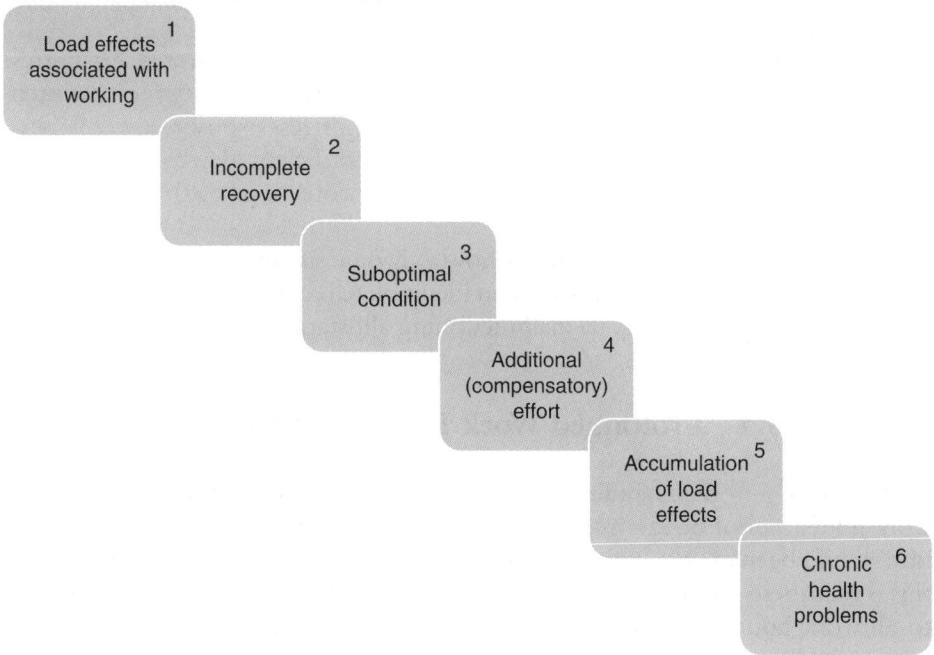

Figure 8.2 A depiction of effort–recovery theory.

'allostatic systems' (including not only the SAM and the HPA systems, but also the related immune system) that are crucial for maintaining bodily homeostasis and for dealing effectively with environmental challenges, such as job stressors. In a chronic situation of repeated or prolonged exposure to job stressors and insufficient recovery, the initially protective allostatic systems may start to malfunction: they may fail to shut-off (overactivity) or fail to respond adequately (inactivity). An imaginable example is the immune system: it may start to dysfunction by either being not attentive enough, enabling infectious agents to enter the body, or by being overactive, causing allergic or autoimmune diseases. McEwen (1998) used the term 'allostatic load' to describe such harmful and long-lasting effects of malfunctioning allostatic systems.

Both the effort–recovery theory (Meijman & Mulder, 1998) and the allostatic load theory (McEwen, 1998) represent a suitable framework for understanding how environmental stressors (e.g. demanding work hours) can put a high demand on the day-to-day recovery process and can impair health in the long run. In the next sections we will take a closer look at how two manifestations of demanding work hours (prolonged work hours and abnormal work hours) impact the recovery process.

Replay

- Stress responses are manifested on three levels: psychological, physiological and behavioural.
- Two bodily systems are involved in stress responses. The SAM system involves the release of catecholamines responsible for direct cardiovascular activation. The HPA system involves the production of cortisol responsible for the release of extra energy to deal with stressors.
- Stress recovery (i.e. how long it takes before one has recovered *after* stress exposure) is a better predictor of ill-health than stress reactivity (i.e. the intensity of physiological reactions that occur *during* stress exposure).
- The effort–recovery theory postulates that sufficient day-to-day recovery from work effort and work stress is crucial for protecting health and maintaining job performance.
- The allostatic load theory clarifies how a chronic situation of repeated or prolonged exposure to job stressors and incomplete recovery can result in chronic and serious diseases due to malfunctioning allostatic systems (allostatic load).

8.4 Prolonged Work Hours and Recovery

Within a chapter on demanding work hours and recovery, the topic of prolonged work hours cannot be ignored. When defining prolonged work hours, a distinction should be made between long work hours and overtime work. The reason for this is that these concepts are intertwined, but not identical. *Overtime work* refers to all work hours that an employee works on top of his/her contractual work hours (Beckers, 2008). In accordance with the European Foundation for the Improvement of Living and Working Conditions (EFILW) and the International

Labour Office (ILO), *long work hours* are defined as 'work hours that are equal to or exceed 48 hours a week'. Comparing these definitions leads to the conclusion that long work hours by definition imply a certain number of overtime hours, but the reverse is not necessarily true. Employees with a part-time contract can also work overtime (e.g. working 24 contractual work hours and 10 overtime hours), but this overtime does not automatically result in long work hours.

With regard to long work hours, the threshold of 48 hours accords with common international working-time regulations, such as the European Working Time Directive (EWTD; European Parliament, 2003). The purpose of working-time regulations is to ensure that workers are protected from extremely long work periods and are entitled to rest breaks and holidays as a means for recovery. Around the world, close to 80% of countries have legislative provisions on maximum weekly or monthly work hours (including overtime), but the specific thresholds vary considerably (International Labour Office, 2011). About 41% of countries have established a 48 hours threshold for weekly work hours (e.g. the EU member states), whereas 37% of countries allow work weeks of over 49 hours (even up to 60 or 72 hours a week). Especially in Asia, the United States, Latin America and the Middle East, a relatively high percentage of countries and/or states either include high legal work-time limits (60+ hours a week) or no limits at all, and thus no legal protection (International Labour Office, 2011; National Conference of State Legislatures, 2012).

Prevalence of prolonged work hours

Various institutes (e.g. the EFILW and the ILO) regularly publish figures on the international prevalence of long work hours. The ILO recently estimated that approximately 22% of the world's workforce (i.e. about 614 million workers) works more than 48 hours a week (Lee, McCann, & Messenger, 2007). Figures 8.3 and 8.4 are drawn from the recent ILO-report *Working time in the twenty-first century* (2011) and show the percentage of workers with long work hours in so-called developed countries (Figure 8.3), as well as in developing and transition countries (Figure 8.4).

Figure 8.3 shows that long work hours decreased in the developed countries during the last decade, yet several developed countries still have a high prevalence of long work hours: within Asian developed countries (e.g. Singapore, Japan and Korea) approximately 25–35% of employees work 48+ hours a week. The west-European countries and the United States have 7–17% working long hours. It must be noted, however, that large differences exist within the United States and within Europe. For instance, Figure 8.4 shows that in Turkey almost 50% of workers work at least 48 hours a week.

Taking a closer look at Figure 8.4, we can see that many developing and transition countries show relatively high percentages of workers with long work hours. International reports show that in many developing and transition countries long work hours are prevalent among both men and women (e.g. within Ethiopia, Jordan, Nigeria, Peru, Philippines, Saudi Arabia, Thailand and Turkey), whereas in most developed countries long work hours are mainly a male phenomenon

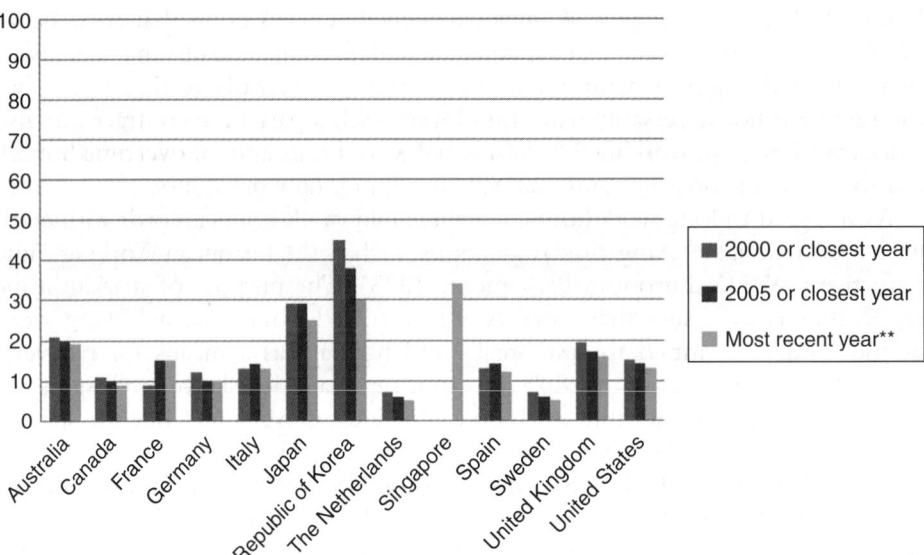

Figure 8.3 Developed countries: Percentage of workers with long work hours (derived from the ILO-report *Working time in the twenty-first century* [Copyright © International Labour Organization, 2011; Source: Eurostat, National Statistical Offices, OECD]).

Notes: When possible, working more than 48 hours per week was considered long work hours. Due to availability of data, for the Republic of Korea the cut-off used is 53 hours, for Australia, Canada, Singapore, and the United States 49 hours. For the same reason, information for the United States is derived from employed workers only.
**2010 or 2009. The global economic crisis might have had an impact on these data.

(Japan, Korea and Singapore are notable exceptions to this rule; International Labour Office, 2011).

These international figures on long work hours provide a useful indication of the prevalence of long work hours worldwide. However, they represent an underestimation of all overtime work being undertaken, as part-timers with overtime work and full-timers with moderately long work hours (resulting in less than 48 work hours a week) are not represented in Figures 8.3 and 8.4.

Risks of prolonged work hours for recovery and health

Overtime work and long work hours are generally believed to have adverse health effects. Two hypothetical mechanisms are suggested that may explain these adverse effects.

The first is the *lack of recovery* mechanism. Overtime work and long work hours hamper recovery in several ways. First, the prolongation of work is directly at the expense of time left for off-job recovery. Second, prolonged working implies that an incessant demand is being made on the same (cognitive, emotional and/or physical) 'resources' that were already taxed during official working time. This constitutes the risk of resource depletion, which puts an even

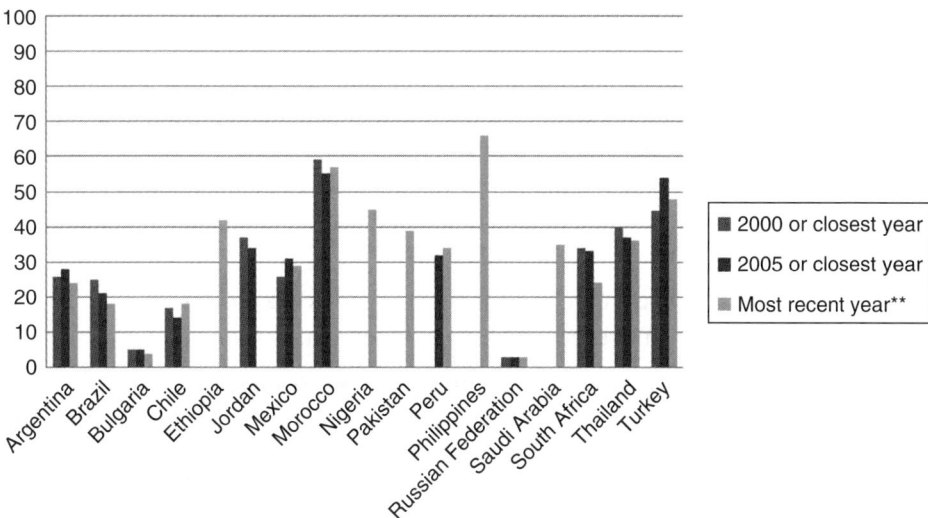

Figure 8.4 Developing and transition countries: Percentage of workers with long work hours (derived from the ILO-report *Working time in the twenty-first century* [Copyright © International Labour Organization, 2011; Source: Eurostat, National Statistical Offices, OECD]).

Notes: When possible, working more than 48 hours per week was considered long work hours. Due to availability of data, for Saudi Arabia the cut-off used is 54 hours, for the Russian Federation 51, for Jordan 50, for Chile 49 (in 2010: 50), for Mexico 49 (in 2000), for Thailand and Turkey 49, for Morocco and Nigeria 47, for the Philippines 40.
**Where possible, data for the years 2010 or 2009 have been used. Due to availability of data, for Brazil, Morocco, Peru, and the Russian Federation 2008 have been used. The global economic crisis might have had an impact on the 2009/2010 data.

higher demand on the recovery process. Third, overtime and long work hours may interfere with demands and responsibilities in one's private life (i.e. negative work–home interference; see Chapter 11) and, as such, may create new stressors (e.g. time-based conflicts, quarrels with family members) which further induce stress and hamper the recovery process (Geurts & Demerouti, 2003). The lack of recovery mechanism is supported by empirical studies that found associations of long work hours with fatigue, difficulty relaxing at home, negative affect, low sleep quality and subjectively reported ill-health (e.g. Rau & Triemer, 2004; van der Hulst, 2003).

The second potential mechanism that can explain the adverse health effects of prolonged work hours is the *behavioural lifestyle* mechanism. Overtime work and long work hours may adversely alter employees' lifestyle behaviours as a result of energy and time depletion. After a long work day or week, employees may have neither the time nor energy left to engage in healthy behaviours (e.g. healthy cooking, spending time on exercise and sports). They may also be more easily drawn to *unhealthy* behaviours (e.g. fast-food meals, inactive behaviour patterns, delayed bedtime, alcohol consumption and late-night snacking) that may be experienced as rewarding after a hard day's work. Some evidence has been found for an association between overtime work and a lower prevalence of healthy behaviours (i.e. less physical exercise and less healthy food intake; Lallukka et al., 2008; Taris et al., 2011). Mixed or only weak evidence has been found for an association with unhealthy behaviours (e.g. alcohol consumption, smoking; van der Hulst, 2003; Taris et al., 2011).

We should note here that the lack of recovery mechanism and the behavioural lifestyle mechanism are not contradictory or mutually exclusive, but may operate simultaneously.

Empirical evidence on prolonged work hours and recovery-related outcomes

Over the past five decades, more than 200 scientific studies have examined the association of overtime work and long work hours with recovery-related outcomes, such as health and well-being. In this chapter, we will limit our description to a general summary of the most important and robust findings.

Overviewing the multitude of studies, it becomes clear that the effects of prolonged work hours seem to depend on their quantity and quality. Regarding the *quantity* of prolonged work hours, empirical research has shown in particular that chronic excessively long work hours and extreme overtime (i.e. working equal to or more than 55 or 60 hours a week) have adverse health effects. For instance, 70% of studies that were conducted within one decade (1996–2007) found evidence that extreme overtime work is a serious risk factor for ill-health (Beckers, 2008). In line with this, Spurgeon and colleagues concluded that 'it is difficult to escape the conclusion that schedules of this nature are detrimental to health and well-being' (Spurgeon, Harrington, & Cooper, 1997, p. 374). Dahlgren and colleagues showed that even short-term exposure to excessive overtime had implications for health and well-being (Dahlgren, Kecklund, & Åkerstedt, 2006; see also the Work Psychology In Action box).

No such straightforward conclusions can be drawn about the adverse health effects of less extreme overtime work. Some studies have found moderate overtime (less than 10 hours a week) or moderately long work hours (approximately 48–50 hours a week) to be related to impaired health, whereas others did not find proof of adverse effects of moderate overtime (Spurgeon et al., 1997; van der Hulst, 2003; Beckers et al., 2004).

These inconsistent findings can be understood when taking into account the *quality* of overtime: it can be expected that the effects of moderately long work hours and moderate overtime depend on the circumstances under which one works overtime (i.e. the quality of overtime work). These circumstances can relate to the physical work environment (e.g. temperature, ergonomics), the psychosocial work environment (e.g. the availability of job resources such as job autonomy, social support and task variety) and also the nature of overtime (e.g. mandatory versus voluntary overtime and whether overtime hours are rewarded or not).

Recent empirical studies have indeed confirmed that the quality of overtime work is an important moderator in the relation between overtime work and health. For instance, it was shown that moderate overtime hours and moderately long work hours were only associated with fatigue and health problems within high-strain work environments (including high demands, low autonomy and/or low social support), as opposed to low-strain or active work environments (van der Hulst, van Veldhoven, & Beckers, 2006; Tucker & Rutherford, 2005; see also Chapter 3). Moreover, mandatory overtime has been related to low job satisfaction and high work–home interference, and employees with mandatory, unrewarded overtime work were found to be at risk of occupational burnout (Beckers et al., 2008; van der Hulst & Geurts, 2001).

These studies show that moderate overtime is related to poor health in case of adverse overtime working conditions. In addition, several studies have also shown that in situations of favourable overtime working conditions (e.g. voluntary overtime work), moderate overtime work was related to positive indicators of well-being, such as high work motivation, job satisfaction, work pleasure and work engagement (cf. Beckers, 2008, for an overview).

In summary, it can be concluded that excessively long work hours are detrimental for health in the long run and should therefore be avoided. The scientific evidence on which this conclusion is based supports the existence of worldwide working-time regulations that legally restrict the maximum number of weekly work hours and prohibit excessive overtime. In the case of moderately long work hours and moderate overtime work, the quality of the circumstances under which one works prolonged hours (i.e. the physical and psychosocial work environment and the nature of overtime) is an important factor determining the (adverse) health effects of those prolonged work hours.

Replay

- Overtime work can be defined as all work hours that an employee works on top of his/her contractual work hours. Long work hours can be characterized as work hours that are equal to or exceed 48 work hours a week.
- Working-time regulations specify the maximum weekly number of work hours that employees are legally allowed to work.
- The lack of recovery mechanism implies that prolonged work hours hamper recovery by inducing (i) prolonged effort and reduced recovery time, (ii) resource depletion (prolonged taxing of the same resources) and (iii) work–home conflict and related stress.
- The behavioural lifestyle mechanism suggests that prolonged work hours may adversely alter employees' lifestyle behaviours (e.g. less time/energy for engaging in sports or healthy cooking).
- Regarding the *quantity* of prolonged work hours, research has shown that excessively long work hours and extreme overtime are serious risk factors for long-term health problems.
- The effects of moderately long work hours and moderate overtime depend on the circumstances under which one works prolonged hours, i.e. the *quality* of overtime work.

> **Work Psychology in Action: The effects of short-term exposure to excessive overtime**
>
> Dahlgren and colleagues (2006) examined whether short-term exposure to excessive overtime had implications for physiological and psychological indicators of well-being. In an experimental field study, 16 white-collar workers undertook one work week with normal work hours (i.e. 8 hours a day, 40 hours a week) and one week of overtime with 4 extra daily hours of regular work tasks (i.e. 12 work hours a day, 60 hours a week). The two work weeks differed only in terms of work hours, and there were no additional manipulations of workload or stress. During every day of both work weeks, the participants wore so-called *actigraphs* (watches that register sleep quantity) during the night, rated sleepiness throughout the day and rated how exhausted they felt. Cortisol samples (from saliva) were collected on Mondays and Thursdays. The results of this study showed that, compared to the normal work week, the overtime work week was associated with higher levels of exhaustion and higher levels of sleepiness at the end of it. Moreover, total sleep time was shorter in the overtime week. Cortisol showed a circadian variation but did not differ significantly between both work weeks. This study shows that one week of excessive overtime work with a moderate workload does adversely affect psychological indicators of well-being, but not physiological stress markers. Nevertheless, as sleep, sleepiness and exhaustion were negatively affected after just one week, unfavourable physiological changes could become a problem after longer periods of excessive overtime.

8.5 Abnormal Work Hours and Recovery

Recovery will not only be crucially affected by the amount of time a person spends working but also the way in which that working time is arranged (i.e. their working time arrangements). This issue becomes especially important when the working time arrangements diverge from what may be considered normal work hours, and even more so when they conflict with the normal human activity–rest cycle.

Defining abnormal work hours

While there is no universally accepted definition of abnormal work hours, the concept is commonly defined in terms of working outside normal or standard hours. Of course, normal work hours are themselves hard to define precisely, not least because they vary between and within countries and cultures. Within Europe, normal or standard work hours may be regarded as working between 07.00–08.00 (7–8 am) and 17.00–18.00 (5–6 pm), from Monday to Friday. However, some countries in Europe and elsewhere may have different work patterns. For example, many workers in warmer climates take a siesta during the afternoon. Moreover, the days of the week that are designated as weekends vary from region to region around the world.

Prevalence of abnormal work hours

According to the results of the 3rd European Survey on Working Conditions only 24% of the working population (27% of employed and 8% of self-employed workers) were engaged in so-called 'normal' or 'standard' day work (Costa et al., 2004). This means that the vast majority of workers are engaged in abnormal work hours, including shift and night work, weekend work, compressed work weeks, extended work hours, split shifts, on-call work, etc. The 5th European Survey on Working Conditions (European Agency for Safety and Health at Work, 2012) found that in 2010 17% of the total working population were involved in shift work, which includes night work, with large differences among countries (from 4% in Turkey to 38% in Montenegro). In 2004, almost 15% of full-time salaried workers in the United States usually worked on alternating shifts, including nights. In the United States, men were more likely than women to work such shifts (17% and 12%, respectively), blacks or African Americans were more likely than whites, Hispanics or Latinos, or Asians, and shift work decreased progressively with age (US Bureau of Labor Statistics, 2005).

Risks of abnormal work hours for recovery and health

One of the primary causes of health problems among those working abnormal hours is the disruption of the normal *human activity–rest cycle*. Human beings have evolved a natural tendency to be awake and active during daylight and consequently to be at rest and asleep at night. This behaviour is determined by the regular oscillation of bodily functions (circadian rhythms). For example, core body temperature decreases during the night when people are asleep, down to a minimum of 35.5–36.0°Celcius in the early hours of the morning, and increases during the waking day to reach a maximum of about 37.0–37.3°Celcius at around 17.00 (5 pm). This *circadian rhythmicity* is controlled by an internal mechanism (the body clock), located in the suprachiasmatic nuclei area of the brain (in the hypothalamus), and is influenced by environmental factors such as work, activity, sleep, meals and, in particular, light exposure.

Night work forces individuals to change their normal sleep/wake cycle. It requires them to attempt to adjust to their nocturnal activity by a progressive alteration in the timing of their circadian rhythms. This adjustment may be more or less complete, depending on the number of successive night shifts that are worked. However, circadian rhythms very seldom show a complete adaptation to a nocturnal routine. That is to say, it is rare that individuals achieve a level of adjustment that allows them to remain fully alert during the night and to sleep as well during the day as they normally would do at night. Indeed, even in those who only ever work night shifts (permanent night workers), the vast majority show insufficient adjustment of their body clocks for it to be of any real benefit (Folkard, 2008). The general lack of circadian adjustment is due both to the continuous swapping between day and night shifts (rotation) that occurs in most shift systems, and to the fact that most individuals try to maintain a normal, day-oriented, social and family life during their free time and on rest days.

These disturbances of normal circadian rhythms may have negative effects on health and well-being. Recovery between shifts is often incomplete due in large part to the impact that circadian disruption has on sleep duration and quality. This, together with the disturbance of other biological rhythms and the stress associated with disrupted family and social life, eventually results in the manifestation of a wide range of complaints and illnesses.

Empirical evidence on abnormal work hours and recovery-related outcomes

There is considerable literature on the impact of abnormal work schedules (particularly those involving night work) on *physical* health and a rather smaller one on the effects on *psychological* health. In many cases, the precise aetiology of the complaints remains unclear. However, it seems likely that impaired recovery will play a role, alongside the effects of disturbed biological rhythms and, in some cases, the disruption of life outside work.

Abnormal work schedules may differ from one another with respect to a fairly wide range of work schedule features. These features will jointly influence the extent of the potential impact on the disturbance of sleep, the biological rhythms (body clock) and life outside work (family and social life). The most important features of work schedules in these respects are those that determine how much fatigue is accumulated, both over an individual shift and over successive shifts, and how much opportunity is provided for recovery. These features include the frequency of breaks, duration of breaks, start times of shifts, duration of shifts, start times of off-duty periods following shifts, duration of off-duty periods following shifts, number of successive shifts of a given type, sequencing of spans of successive shifts, number of successive work days, start time of a period of rest days, number of successive rest days, and the frequency and duration of longer periods of rest days such as annual leave.

Schedules that involve working only one to three consecutive shifts of the same type (e.g. nights) before changing to another (e.g. days) are known as very rapidly rotating shift systems. These tend to promote better sleep between shifts and less fatigue during the shift compared to more slowly rotating ones (Sallinen & Kecklund, 2010). This is thought to be because, like the majority of people who work permanent nights (see above), workers on a more slowly rotating shift system will rarely achieve sufficient adjustment to derive any benefit from it. Instead, they are likely to experience a substantial degree of circadian disruption, such that their circadian rhythms remain in a state that is neither fully diurnal nor nocturnal, and hence suffer disturbed sleep between shifts.

In a rotating shift system, the change from one type of shift to another entails altering the timing of the sleep and most other aspects of daily routine (e.g. meal times, free-time activities and so on). When a worker changes from morning shifts (e.g. working from 06.00 (6 am) to 14.00 (2 pm)) to afternoon shifts (e.g. working from 14.00 (2 pm) to 22.00 (10 pm)) they will probably go to bed and wake later in the day following the change. Conversely, changing from afternoon shifts to morning shifts will probably mean going to bed and wake up earlier, following the change. The majority of people tend to find it easier to delay sleep onset and waking than to advance the timing of their sleep. This is thought to reflect on the natural tendency of the body clock to cycle with a period of slightly longer than 24 hours. Thus from a circadian perspective, forward rotating shift systems (morning → afternoon → night shifts), which involve delaying the timing of one's rhythms, have been argued to be preferable to backward rotating ones (night → afternoon → morning shifts), which involve advancing the timing of circadian rhythms. However, in practice the evidence regarding the effects of direction of rotation on sleep, fatigue and health is equivocal (Sallinen & Kecklund, 2010; see also the Work Psychology In Action box).

Abnormal work schedules are often a source of psychological and emotional distress (Bara & Arber, 2009). The extent of these effects partly depends upon the way in which the schedule is designed (see above), as this will determine how much recovery opportunity is afforded to the shiftworker, as well as the degree of time-based work/non-work conflict (see Chapter 11) that is experienced. With respect to physical health, a number of epidemiological studies have yielded data suggesting an association between shiftwork and cardiovascular diseases (CVD). More specifically, it has been shown that there is (i) a higher level of cardiovascular risk factors, angina pectoris and hypertension among shiftworkers, (ii) more ill-health related to cardiocirculatory and coronary artery diseases with increasing age and shiftwork experience, and (iii) an increased likelihood of heart attack in occupations with a high proportion of shiftworkers (Knutsson, 2003). The higher rates of CVD among shiftworkers has been linked to their increased susceptibility to metabolic disorders (e.g. metabolic syndrome, diabetes, obesity), which in turn may be linked to chronic sleep deprivation as well as other aspects of circadian disruption (Lowden, Moreno, Holmback, Lennernas, & Tucker, 2010). Other possible mediators of the relation between shiftwork and CVD include the stress that accompanies social isolation and an unfavourable distribution of health behaviours, for instance smoking, poor diet, alcohol and lack of exercise (Bøggild & Knutsson, 1999). Sleep disruption and/or impaired recovery, along with the disturbance of other circadian rhythms, is also thought to play a role in the development of certain other health disorders that tend to be more common among shiftworkers, such as cancer (Stevens et al., 2011), gastro-intestinal problems such as duodenal ulcers (Pietroiusti et al., 2006), maternity problems in women (Mahoney, 2010) and musculo-skeletal disorders (Caruso & Waters, 2008).

Replay

- A significant proportion of the workforce in the industrialized world works abnormal or non-standard work hours, that is, working in the evening, at night and/or at weekends.

- Abnormal work hours can disrupt the naturally evolved human activity–rest cycle, that is, being awake during the day and sleeping at night.
- Circadian rhythmicity is controlled by the body clock, which is influenced by environmental factors such as activity, sleep, meals and especially light.
- Disturbances of normal circadian rhythms may have negative effects on sleep, health and life outside work.
- Work schedule features such as the number of consecutive shifts and the direction of rotation will determine how much fatigue is accumulated, how much opportunity there is for recovery and consequently whether abnormal work hours result in ill-health.

> **Work Psychology in Action: Redesigning a work schedule to mitigate the negative effects of shift work**
>
> Viitasalo, Kusosma, Laitinen, & Härmä (2008) describe a change in shift system that took place within the maintenance unit of an airline company in Finland. The order of the shifts in the old schedule was EEE–MMM–NNN–– (E = evening shift, M = morning shift, N = night shift, – = day off). This shift system was backwards rotating. One of the new shift systems rotated very rapidly forward, in the order MEN–. (The other new system allowed the workers some individual flexibility and control over their work hours). The employer and the representatives of the employees wanted the workers to be able to select their new shift systems and so it was not possible to randomize the allocation of participants into study groups. The 40 participants who changed to the rapidly forward rotating system reported less daytime sleepiness following the change, while the 22 participants who remained in the old shift system reported a slight increase. Thus, while it was evident that the introduction of a more rapidly forward rotating shift system had been beneficial, it remained unclear whether it was the speed or the direction of rotation that was primarily responsible for the improvement.

8.6 Recovery During and After Work Hours

The potential risks of prolonged and abnormal work hours make clear that it is important for workers to recover sufficiently from their work effort and demanding work hours. We can distinguish between two types of recovery from work and work stress. Recovery may occur during work hours, often referred to as *internal recovery*, as well as after work hours, called *external recovery* (Geurts & Sonnentag, 2006).

The notion of recovery during work hours may initially seem a bit strange, as the workplace is not the most obvious recovery setting. However, internal recovery is very important in order to prevent a high need for recovery at the end of the working day. Internal recovery may above all be promoted by appropriate job design. Healthy job design prevents accumulation of load effects during the working day by allowing workers to (i) manipulate their job demands, for instance, by conducting tasks at a lower pace, (ii) change to a lower level of information processing, for instance by conducting tasks on a more routine basis, (iii) switch from complex to easier tasks and (iv) ask for help from colleagues or supervisors. Thus, a well-designed job provides job control, job variety and job support that allow workers to create spontaneous breaks between tasks (mini-breaks) and to adjust their work strategy to their current need for recovery (see also Chapter 3).

In addition, a proper work–rest schedule is important. Relatively little research in work psychology has focused on within-day work breaks (coffee or lunch breaks) as an important tool for recovery. The most frequently studied aspects of work breaks are their frequency, timing and length (Tucker, 2003). For instance, regarding the length of breaks, researchers in the field of ergonomics have explored the role of micro-breaks as a means to lighten musculoskeletal discomfort. Micro-breaks are very short breaks (from a few seconds up to one minute) as a means to micro recovery. According to Dembe (1999), a lack of micro-breaks may at least partly explain the increasing rates of repetitive strain injuries among office workers. In general, a combination of very short as well as somewhat longer work breaks during the work day seem to be effective means of managing fatigue and enhancing performance, well-being and safety (Trougakos & Hideg, 2009; Tucker, 2003).

When during a demanding work day internal recovery opportunities have been insufficient and intensive load reactions have developed, it is important that workers recover sufficiently during free time. External recovery may occur in various temporal and situational settings (Sonnentag & Geurts, 2009). In this chapter we distinguish among three recovery settings. A first and most prevalent recovery setting is the daily recurring free period between two consecutive work days, mostly free evenings. A second recovery setting is the weekly recurring free period between work weeks, mostly free weekends. A third and less prevalent recovery setting is vacation (most workers take a vacation several times a year). However, vacation may be an especially powerful weapon against work stress and its health consequences because it involves a relatively long and uninterrupted period of rest, often spent away from daily hassles in the work and home situation.

Vacation may contribute to recovery from work through two mechanisms: a passive one and an active one. The *passive mechanism* reflects a direct release from daily exposure to job demands and stressors. De Bloom and colleagues showed that employees recovered substantially from work during various types of vacation (de Bloom, Geurts, & Kompier, 2010, 2013): employee health and well-being (measured by recovery indicators such as fatigue, mood, tension, health and vigour) were significantly higher during short vacations (4–5 days), moderately long vacations (9 days) and long summer vacations (on average 22 days), as compared to during work periods before and after vacation. The results also showed, however, that these positive vacation effects on health and well-being were generally short-lived: they faded out within the first week after resuming work, irrespective of the type and duration of the holiday.

The *active mechanism* through which vacation may facilitate recovery covers the engagement in valued, pleasant and self-chosen non-work activities (e.g. hobbies, sports and fulfilling family activities). Being able to freely pursue one's own interests will help workers to resume their work with 'refilled batteries' (Eden, 2001). De Bloom and colleagues found that the recovery-potential of *vacation activities* depends on the vacation setting and on one's preferences and control. For instance, engagement in passive activities contributed to recovery during a long summer vacation (de Bloom, Geurts, & Kompier, 2013), but did not during a winter sports vacation (de Bloom et al., 2011). In the latter setting, vacationers were forced to be passive due to negative incidents, whereas in the summer vacation being passive was a free choice that was associated with feelings of relaxation and a sense of being physically and mentally away from work (also referred to as psychological detachment; see also Chapter 4).

De Bloom and colleagues showed that particularly positive *vacation experiences* contributed to recovery during vacation, such as pleasure derived from vacation activities, relaxation and control over how to spend one's vacation time (de Bloom, Geurts, & Kompier, 2013; de Bloom et al., 2011). These findings are in line with research findings on recovery during free weekends: workers experience more positive feelings during free weekends than during work periods because they have more control over how to spend their time (i.e. time control; Ryan, Bernstein, & Brown, 2010). Having control over how one spends one's time may be important not only during non-work time (vacations, weekends, free evenings), but also during work time. In the next section, we will take a look at the recovery potential of work-time control and at modern work-time control practices (i.e. self-scheduling and boundaryless work).

8.7 Work-time Control and Recovery

Employee work-time control (WTC) refers to employees' abilities to control the duration, position and distribution of work time. In other words, WTC refers to autonomy regarding work time (Härmä, 2006). The most well-known sub-dimensions of WTC are flexibility regarding the starting and ending times of the work day, control over when to take a break, day off or vacation, control over the distribution of work hours over the work week (work schedule), and control over whether and when to work overtime (Nijp, Beckers, Geurts, Tucker, & Kompier, 2012). WTC enables workers to adjust their working times to meet obligations in private life and, accordingly, has the potential to be an excellent buffer against work–home interference (see Chapter 11). Moreover, WTC has recovery potential as it allows workers to adjust their working times to their current need for recovery. In this respect, WTC may facilitate recovery during the work day (internal recovery) as well as recovery between work periods (external recovery). A recent review of empirical literature confirms that WTC is a promising tool for maintaining health and well-being by promoting positive effort–recovery balance and work/non-work balance (Nijp et al., 2012).

Two modern WTC practices are currently gaining popularity within organizations: self-scheduling and boundaryless work. Self-scheduling (also known as self-rostering) is mostly applied in shiftwork settings. The employer starts by defining the number of workers needed for separate time units. Employees can then sign up for specific time units, thereby taking into account their personal preferences, working time regulations and the minimum number of work hours they have to work according to their contract. Ideally, self-scheduling systems result in preferred rosters for all individual employees. However, when several employees prefer to work the same hours or when unpopular hours remain vacant, preferred rosters need to be adjusted. Other potentially unfavourable side effects of self-scheduling are that well-established teams are split up by individualized rostering, employees may choose rosters that are financially attractive but are sub-optimal from a recovery perspective (e.g. many nightshifts) and predictability of work hours is reduced as work hours are not established a year ahead but are scheduled monthly (which may induce problems with combining work and family life rather than resolving them).

Boundaryless work has recently become fashionable in office settings. It includes a combination of extensive WTC and spatial flexibility. Employees can thus decide for themselves when and where to work (Beckers, Kompier, Kecklund, & Härmä, 2012). Anecdotal stories from practice show that boundaryless work is often accompanied by a stronger focus on performance management as compared to more traditional work organizations. It is not yet clear to what extent boundaryless work is accompanied by positive outcomes (e.g. a better work/non-work balance, more job autonomy) and/or negative outcomes (e.g. a worse work/non-work balance, higher work pressure, more overtime work). Future research is needed to establish the effects of these modern work practices.

Replay

- Two types of recovery are important: recovery during work hours (internal recovery) and recovery after work hours (external recovery).
- External recovery may occur in various temporal and situational settings: free evenings, free weekends and vacations.
- Vacation is a potentially powerful external recovery opportunity that may contribute to recovery from work through a passive or an active mechanism.
- The passive recovery mechanism implies recovery through the direct release from exposure to job demands. The active recovery mechanism refers to recovery by engaging in valued, pleasant, self-chosen non-work activities.
- Work-time control (WTC) refers to the extent to which employees can decide for themselves when to work. WTC can have advantages for work–life balance and well-being (recovery).
- Self-scheduling is a modern WTC practice that is assumed to provide shift-workers with high(er) WTC. Employers define the number of workers needed for separate time units and employees can sign up for specific time units based on their personal preferences.

- Boundaryless work is a modern WTC practice in office settings. It includes a combination of high WTC and spatial flexibility (employees can self-decide when and where to work), and is often accompanied by an emphasis on performance management.

8.8 Conclusions

Sufficient recovery from demanding and stressful work is crucial for protecting health and maintaining adequate performance. While effort–recovery theory emphasizes the importance of sufficient day-to-day recovery from stressful job demands, allostatic load theory explains how a chronic situation of repeated or prolonged exposure to job stressors and insufficient recovery may result in harmful and long-lasting health effects. Demanding work hours, such as prolonged work hours and abnormal work hours, are environmental stressors that put a high demand on the recovery process.

Overtime work and long work hours are well-known types of prolonged work hours. Close to 80% of countries worldwide have legislative provisions on maximum weekly or monthly work hours, although the specific thresholds vary considerably. Accordingly, the prevalence of long work hours varies greatly between countries. Prolonged work hours challenge the recovery process because of the extended effort expenditure at the cost of potential recovery time, and the potential adverse effect on employees' lifestyle behaviours (e.g. less healthy meals) as a result of energy and time depletion. Chronic excessively long work hours and extreme overtime work are serious risk factors for adverse health and should therefore be avoided. The effects of moderately long work hours and moderate overtime depend upon the circumstances: moderate overtime is related to poor health in case of adverse overtime working conditions (e.g. mandatory, unrewarded overtime) and to positive well-being in case of favourable overtime working conditions (e.g. voluntary overtime work).

A significant proportion of the workforce in the industrialized world is engaged in abnormal work hours (e.g. shift work), with considerable variation between countries. Abnormal work hours are potentially highly disruptive of recovery, particularly when the working-time arrangements conflict with the normal human activity–rest cycle (e.g. when working at night). Humans have evolved physiological mechanisms (circadian rhythms) that promote being active during the day and sleeping at night. Night workers have to work in opposition to their natural circadian rhythms, attempting to adjust these rhythms to a nocturnal routine. However, the majority are unsuccessful, failing to sleep well during the day and/or having problems maintaining alertness throughout the night. Impaired recovery is thought to be partly responsible for the health problems that are more prevalent among those working abnormal hours, alongside the effects of disturbed biological rhythms and the disruption of life outside work. The amount of recovery opportunity afforded by a work schedule, and hence the impact that it has on employees' health, will depend upon the way the work hours are arranged (e.g. the timing and sequence of shifts) and the distribution of rest opportunities between and within shifts. Work–rest cycles should be designed to minimize the development of negative load effects and the disruption of sleep and circadian rhythms.

The potential risks of prolonged and abnormal work hours make clear that it is important for workers to recover sufficiently from these environmental stressors. Recovery may occur during work hours (internal recovery) as well as during free time (external recovery). Internal recovery will be promoted by well-designed jobs (e.g. sufficient job autonomy, task variety and social support; see also Chapters 3 and 4) and adequate internal recovery opportunities (i.e. work breaks). External recovery takes place during off-job time (e.g. free evenings, free weekends and vacation) through a passive mechanism (direct release from exposure to job stressors) and an active mechanism (engagement in valued, pleasant and self-chosen activities).

WTC, which refers to employee autonomy regarding work time, can be an especially important tool for employees to preserve sufficient internal and external recovery and to uphold a favourable work–life balance. Self-scheduling (shift workers indicate their preferred rosters) and boundaryless work (office workers are provided with high work-time flexibility and spatial flexibility) are two modern WTC practices. Both practices are expected to have a positive impact on recovery and work–life balance as they enable employees to align their working times with their current need for recovery and with their family responsibilities.

Discussion Points

1. Do you think it would make a difference for employee health and well-being whether a worker has 40 contractual hours and 5 overtime hours or whether he or she has 20 contractual hours and 25 overtime hours? Notice that the total workload in both situations is 45 hours.
2. What do you think should be preferred and why: permanent night work or a rotating shift system?
3. Why should we keep going on vacation if research shows that positive vacation effects fade out immediately after resuming work?
4. Do you think that boundaryless work is primarily advantageous for employees or are there potential disadvantages for employees as well?

Learning by Doing

1. At certain times you might have to expend a great deal of effort on working for exams or assignments and maybe doing a job on the side.
   a. How do you notice that you have reached your limits or that your resources are depleted?
   b. Explain what happens psychologically and physiologically when you continue to expend effort beyond your limits.
   c. What helps you to replenish your resources?
2. On some weekends it can be difficult to decide for yourself how to spend your time due to, for instance, domestic and/or social obligations. On other

weekends you can mostly decide for yourself how to spend your time. Register your level of health and well-being (e.g. by recovery indicators such as fatigue, mood, tension, health and vigour) across both types of weekends at the beginning of the weekend (Friday evening) and at the end of the weekend (Sunday evening). What can you say about the recovery potential of each weekend? Try to explain your answer.

3. Interview an individual (e.g. family member, neighbour) across a holiday period: four days before (pre-vacation), directly after (post-vacation 1) and four days after the holiday (post-vacation 2). At each time point register the respondents' level of health and well-being (e.g. using the recovery indicators mentioned earlier). At post-vacation 1 also ask the respondent what type of holiday activities he/she was engaged in, what pleasure he/she derived from these activities and whether the holiday activities matched his/her individual preference (i.e. the level of control over holiday activities). Compare the three time points:
   a. Is there a difference in health and well-being indicators between pre-vacation and post-vacation 1? What does this result mean?
   b. Does post-vacation 2 differ from pre-vacation and from post-vacation 1? What do these results mean?
   c. Would an extra measurement point during the holiday have been informative and why?
4. Find an individual (e.g. family member, neighbour, friend) who works at a company that has implemented boundaryless work. Ask him/her the following questions:
   a. Do you experience much freedom and flexibility in work hours and work location?
   b. Do you work a lot of overtime hours?
   c. Are you satisfied with the opportunities for functional and social contacts with colleagues and supervisor(s)?
   d. Do you experience negative side effects of boundaryless work?
   e. Are these negative side effects mainly related to work-time flexibility, spatial flexibility or to other elements of boundaryless work?
   f. If you had a choice, would you prefer a fixed work-time schedule and fixed location, or would you prefer temporal and spatial flexibility? Why?

Further Reading

Arendt, J. (2010). Shift work: coping with the biological clock. *Occupational Medicine, 60*, 10–20.

Beckers, D. G. J., Kompier, M. A. J., Kecklund, G., & Härmä, M. (2012). Worktime control: theoretical conceptualization, current empirical knowledge, and research agenda. *Scandinavian Journal of Work, Environment & Health, 38*, 291–297.

Burke, R. J., & Cooper, C. L. (2008). *The long work hours culture: causes, consequences and choices.* Bingly: Emerald Group Publishing.

Geurts, S. A. E., & Sonnentag, S. (2006). Recovery as an explanatory mechanism in the relation between acute stress reactions and chronic health impairment. *Scandinavian Journal of Work, Environment & Health, 23*, 482–492.

Härmä, M. (2006). Workhours in relation to work stress, recovery and health. *Scandinavian Journal of Work, Environment & Health*, 32, 502–514.

Sallinen, M., & Kecklund, G. (2010). Shift work, sleep, and sleepiness – differences between shift schedules and systems. *Scandinavian Journal of Work, Environment & Health*, 36, 121–133.

References

Bara, A. C., & Arber, S. (2009). Working shifts and mental health – findings from the British Household Panel Survey (1995–2005). *Scandinavian Journal of Work, Environment & Health*, 35, 361–367.

Beckers, D. G. J. (2008). *Overtime work and well-being: Opening up the black box*. PhD Dissertation. Nijmegen. Radboud University Nijmegen.

Beckers, D. G. J., Kompier, M. A. J., Kecklund, G., & Härmä, M. (2012). Worktime control: theoretical conceptualization, current empirical knowledge, and research agenda. *Scandinavian Journal of Work, Environment & Health*, 38, 291–297.

Beckers, D. G. J., van der Linden, D., Smulders, P. G. W., Kompier, M. A. J., Taris, T. W., & Geurts, S. A. E. (2008). Voluntary or involuntary? Control over overtime and rewards for overtime in relation to fatigue and work-satisfaction? *Work & Stress*, 22, 33–50.

Beckers, D. G. J., van der Linden, D., Smulders, P. G. W., Kompier, M. A. J., van Veldhoven, M. J. P. M., & van Yperen, N. W. (2004). Working overtime hours: relations with fatigue, work motivation, and the quality of work. *Journal of Occupational and Environmental Medicine*, 46, 1282–1289.

Bøggild, H., & Knutsson, A. (1999). Shift work, risk factors and cardiovascular disease. *Scandinavian Journal of Work, Environment & Health*, 25, 85–99.

Brosschot, J. F., Gerin, W., & Thayer, J. F. (2006). The perseverative cognition hypothesis: A review of worry, prolonged stress-related physiological activation, and health. *Journal of Psychosomatic Research*, 60, 113–124.

Caruso, C., & Waters, T. (2008). A review of work schedule issues and musculoskeletal disorders with an emphasis on the healthcare sector. *Industrial Health*, 46, 523–534.

Costa, G., Åkerstedt, T., Nachreiner, F., Baltieri, F., Carvalhais, J., Folkard, S., et al. (2004). Flexible working hours, health, and well-being in Europe: Some considerations from a SALTSA project. *Chronobiology International*, 21, 831–844.

Dahlgren, A., Kecklund, G., & Åkerstedt, T. (2006). Overtime work and its effects on sleep, sleepiness, cortisol and blood pressure in an experimental field study. *Scandinavian Journal of Work Environment & Health*, 32, 318–327.

de Bloom, J., Geurts, S. A. E., & Kompier, M. A. J. (2010). Vacation from work as prototypical recovery opportunity. *Gedrag & Organisatie*, 23, 333–349.

de Bloom, J., Geurts, S. A. E., Sonnentag, S., Taris, T., de Weerth, C., & Kompier, M. A. J. (2011). How does a vacation from work affect employee health and well-being? *Psychology & Health*, 26, 1606–1622.

de Bloom, J., Geurts, S. A. E., & Kompier, M. A. J. (2013). Vacation (after-)effects on employee health and well-being, and the role of vacation activities, experiences and sleep. *Journal of Happiness Studies*, 14, 613–633.

Dembe, A. (1999). The changing nature of office work: effects on repetitive strain injuries. *Occupational Medicine: State of the Art Reviews Philadelphia*, 14, 1–12.

Eden, D. (2001). Vacations and other respites: studying stress on and off the job. In C. Cooper, & I. T. Robertson (Eds.), *Well-being in organizations* (pp. 305–330). Chichester: John Wiley & Sons.

European Agency for Safety and Health at Work (2012). *Fifth European Working Conditions Survey*, from www.eurofound.europa.eu.

European Parliament (2003). Directive 2003/88/EC of the European Parliament and of the Council of 4 November 2003 concerning certain aspects of the organization of working time. *Official Journal L 299*, 18/11/2003, 9–19.

Folkard, S. (2008). Do permanent night workers show circadian adjustment? A review based on the endogenous melatonin rhythm. *Chronobiology International*, 25, 215–224.

Geurts, S. A. E., & Demerouti, E. (2003). Work/nonwork interface: A review of theories and findings. In M. Schabracq, J. Winnubst, & C. L. Cooper (Eds.), *Handbook of work and health psychology* (pp. 279–312). Chichester: John Wiley & Sons.

Geurts, S. A. E., & Sonnentag, S. (2006). Recovery as an explanatory mechanism in the relation between acute stress reactions and chronic health impairment. *Scandinavian Journal of Work, Environment & Health, 32*, 482–492.

International Labour Office (2011). Working time in the twenty-first century. Geneva: International Labour Organization.

Härmä, M. (2006). Workhours in relation to work stress, recovery and health. *Scandinavian Journal of Work, Environment & Health, 32*, 502–514.

Kahn, R. L., Wolfe, D. M., Quinn, R. P., Snoek, J. D., & Rosenthal, R. A. (1964). *Organizational stress: Studies in role conflict and ambiguity.* New York: John Wiley & Sons.

Knutsson, A. (2003). Health disorders of shift workers. *Occupational Medicine, 53*, 103–108.

Kristensen, T. S., Kornitzer, M., & Alfredsson, L. (1998). *Social factors, work, stress and cardiovascular disease prevention in the European Union.* Brussels: The European Heart Network.

Lallukka, T., Lahelma, E., Rahkonen, O., Roos, E., Laaksonen, E., Martikainen, P., Head, J., Brunner, E., Mosdol, A., Marmot, M., Sekine, M., Nasermoaddeli, A., & Kagamimori, S. (2008). Associations of job strain and working overtime with adverse health behaviors and obesity: Evidence form the Whitehall II Study, Helsinki Health Study, and the Japanese civil servants study. *Social Science and Medicine, 66*, 1681–1698.

Lee, S., McCann, D., & Messenger, J. C. (2007). Working time around the world: Trends in working hours, laws and policies in a global comparative perspective. Geneva: International Labour Office/ New York: Routledge.

Linden, W. L. E. T., Earle, T. L., Gerin, W., & Christenfeld, N. J. F. (1997). Physiological stress reactivity and recovery: Conceptual siblings separated at birth? *Journal of Psychosomatic Research, 42*, 117–135.

Lowden, A., Moreno, C., Holmback, U., Lennernas, M., & Tucker, P. (2010). Eating and shift work – effects on habits, metabolism and performance. *Scandinavian Journal of Work, Environment & Health, 36*, 150–162.

Mahoney, M. M. (2010). Shift work, jet lag, and female reproduction. *International Journal of Endocrinology*, doi: 10.1155/2010/813764.

McEwen, B. S. (1998). Stress, adaptation, and disease: Allostasis and allostatic load. *Annals of the New York Academy of Sciences, 840*, 33–44.

Meijman, T. F., & Mulder, G. (1998). Psychological aspects of workload. In P. J. D. Drenth, H. Thierry, & Ch. J. de Wolff (Eds.), *Handbook of work and organizational psychology* (2nd ed., pp. 5–33). Hove: Psychology Press/Erlbaum.

National Conference of State Legislatures (2012). http://www.ncsl.org/issues-research/labor/state-laws-on-work-hours-amp-overtime.aspx.

Nijp, H. H., Beckers, D. G. J., Geurts, S. A. E., Tucker, P., & Kompier, M. A. J. (2012). Systematic review on the association between employee work-time control and work-nonwork balance, health and well-being, and job-related outcomes. *Scandinavian Journal of Work, Environment & Health, 38*, 299–313.

Pietroiusti, A., Forlini, A., Magrini, A., Galante, A., Coppeta, L., Gemma, G., Romeo, E., & Bergamaschi, A. (2006). Shift work increases the frequency of duodenal ulcer in H pylori infected workers. *Occupational and Environmental Medicine, 63*, 773–775.

Rau, R., & Triemer, A. (2004). Overtime in relation to blood pressure and mood during work, leisure, and night time. *Social Indicators Research, 67*, 51–73.

Ryan, R. M., Bernstein, J. H., & Brown, K. W. (2010). Weekends, work, and well-being: psychological need satisfactions and day of the week effects on mood, vitality, and physical symptoms. *Journal of Social and Clinical Psychology, 29*, 95–122.

Sallinen, M., & Kecklund, G. (2010). Shift work, sleep and sleepiness – differences between shift schedules and systems. *Scandinavian Journal of Work, Environment & Health, 36*, 121–133.

Selye, H. (1938). Adaptation Energy. *Nature, 141*, 926–926.

Sonnentag, S., & Geurts, S. A. E. (2009). Methodological issues in recovery. In S. Sonnentag, P. Perrewe, & D. Ganster (Eds.), *Current perspectives on job-stress recovery: Research in occupational stress and well being* (Vol. 7, pp. 1–36). Bingley: JAI Press.

Spurgeon, A., Harrington, J. M., & Cooper, C. L. (1997). Health and safety problems associated with long working hours: A review of the current position. *Occupational and Environmental Medicine, 54*, 367–375.

Stevens, R. G., Hansen, J., Costa, G., Haus, E., Kauppinen, T., Aronson, K., Castano-Vinyals, G., Davis, S., Frings-Dresen, M., Fritschi, L., Kogevinus, M., Kogi, K., Lie, J., Lowden, A., Peplonska, B., Pesch, B., Pukkala, E., Schernhammer, E., Travis, R., Vermeulen, R., Zheng, T., Cogliano, V., & Straif, K. (2011). Considerations of circadian impact for defining 'shift work' in cancer studies: IARC Working Group Report. *Occupational and Environmental Medicine, 68*, 154–162.

Sutherland, V. J., & Cooper, C. L. (1990). *Understanding stress: A psychological perspective for health professionals.* London: Chapman and Hall.

Taris, T. W., Ybema, J. F., Beckers, D. G. J., Verheijden, M. W., Geurts, S. A. E., & Kompier, M. A. J. (2011). Investigating the associations among overtime work, health behaviors, and health: A longitudinal study among full-time employees. *International Journal of Behavioral Medicine, 18*, 352–360.

Trougakos, J. P., & Hideg, I. (2009). Momentary work recovery: The role of within-day work breaks. In S. Sonnentag, P. Perrewe, & D. Ganster (Eds.), *Current perspectives on job-stress recovery: Research in occupational stress and well being* (Vol. 7, pp. 37–84). Bingley: JAI Press.

Tucker, P. (2003). The impact of rest breaks upon accident risk, fatigue and performance: A review. *Work & Stress, 17*, 123–137.

Tucker, P., & Rutherford, C. (2005). Moderator of the relationship between long work hours and health. *Journal of Occupational Health Psychology, 10*, 465–476.

Ursin, H., & Eriksen, H. (2004). The cognitive activation theory of stress. *Psychoneuroendocrinology, 29*, 567–592.

US Bureau of Labor Statistics (2005). *Occupational outlook handbook.* From www.bls.org.

van der Hulst, M. (2003). Long workhours and health [review]. *Scandinavian Journal of Work, Environment & Health, 29*, 171–188.

van der Hulst, M., & Geurts, S. A. E. (2001). Associations between overtime and psychological health in high and low reward jobs. *Work & Stress, 15*, 227–240.

van der Hulst, M., van Veldhoven, M., & Beckers, D. (2006). Overtime and need for recovery in relation to job demands and job control. *Journal of Occupational Health, 48*, 11–19.

Viitsalo, K., Kusosma, E., Laitinen, J., & Härmä, M. (2008). Effects of shift rotation and the flexibility of a shift system on daytime alertness and cardiovascular risk factors. *Scandinavian Journal of Work, Environment & Health, 34*, 198–205.

9

The Design and Use of Work Technologies

PATRICK WATERSON

> **Chapter Objectives**
>
> After studying this chapter, you should be able to:
>
> - understand the context within which work technologies operate and some of the problems associated with their implementation and adoption by end users;
> - describe some of the recent developments within the field of work psychology and the study of work technologies;
> - describe some of the types of approaches which have been applied to the study of work technologies (e.g. human–computer interaction and work and organizational psychology);
> - understand two of the most common theoretical approaches used to analyse the impact of technology on work (socio-technical systems theory and adaptive structuration theory);
> - appreciate how these theoretical approaches are applied in practice;
> - understand some of the limitations of the theories, as well as new developments and future issues within the field of work psychology as it applies to technology.

An Introduction to Contemporary Work Psychology, First Edition.
Edited by Maria C. W. Peeters, Jan de Jonge and Toon W. Taris.
© 2014 John Wiley & Sons, Ltd. Published 2014 by John Wiley & Sons, Ltd.

9.1 Introduction

The aim of this chapter is to introduce some of the developments that have occurred over the last decade or so as regards the design and use of technology within the workplace. In order to illustrate the ways in which work psychologists have studied these technologies, the chapter reviews the types of disciplines which have been used to study work technologies (e.g. human factors and ergonomics) alongside a set of approaches and theories that seek to explain the impact of technology on individuals and the conduct of their work. In particular, we focus on popular approaches such as human–computer interaction (HCI) and work and organizational psychology. A separate section describes research on two of the most popular theories applied to work technologies, namely socio-technical systems theory and adaptive structuration theory (see also Chapter 3). Approaches and theories of these kinds have been applied to a wide variety of technologies and working environments (e.g. manufacturing, healthcare and global teamworking) and have proved to be useful in explaining some of the factors that determine the likelihood that the implementation of technology in the workplace will succeed or fail. The chapter also uses a number of examples of technology that are prevalent within the twenty-first century and are likely to grow in importance, including the design and use of health information technologies (HIT), mobile working and technology-supported virtual teamworking.

9.2 Work Technologies: A Context for their Use and Design

Despite the growth of new types of technology and claims that it has the potential to revolutionize how we work, the available evidence suggests a very mixed picture of success combined with widespread failure. Many new technologies prove to be difficult, if not impossible, to use, and in some cases have contributed to disasters and subsequent loss of life (see also Chapter 14). The past few years have seen a number of prominent disasters that have been brought to the attention of the wider public through newspapers and television. These include the failure of systems designed to schedule ambulance call-outs, advanced technology used to fly aircraft automatically and more recently the abandonment of plans for the UK National Programme for Information Technology (NPfIT) programme to implement electronic record systems within the UK National Health Service (Eason, 2007; Waterson, Glenn, & Eason, 2012). Table 9.1 shows a timeline that illustrates how what began as enthusiasm for the programme eventually ended with abandonment. Figure 9.1 summarizes some of the unexpected outcomes for users that come about as a result of poorly designed technologies. In the worst cases these outcomes can include a failure to use the technology and its eventual rejection. In other cases, the system may be used but a set of workarounds have to be put in place (e.g. devising alternative ways of using the technology in order to carry out a task; Ash, Berg, & Coiera, 2004).

Alongside these headline-grabbing disasters there is also a growing body of systematic evidence that technology consistently fails to realize many of the benefits that are claimed for it. Landauer (1995), for example, reviewed economic

Table 9.1 National Programme for Information Technology (NPfIT) timeline (1998–2012).

	Timeline
Date	Key development
1998	NHS Executive commits to detailed health care records
2002	NPfIT starts
2004	British Telecom offered broadband contract
2006	Withdrawal of major contractors (Accenture)
2008	Major contractor (Fujitsu) terminated
2009	NHS CfH reorganized; NPfIT Director resigns
2010	March deadline for delivery of Lorenzo system missed; Coalition Government (May)
2011	August 'Not fit for purpose' (Government MPA) October 'focus now on connecting up good local practice' (Managing Director, NHS Informatics)
2012	September 'The government announced today that the NPfIT would be dismantled' (UK Department of Health)

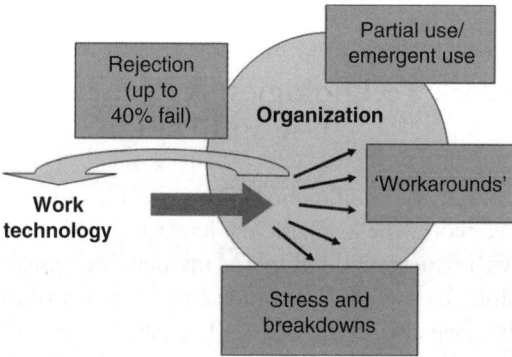

Figure 9.1 Outcomes from implementing work technologies. Source: Waterson (2013).

data relating to the impact of information technology (IT) within the United States over a 15-year period and found that productivity decline in the USA broadly coincided with the large-scale deployment and investment of US companies in IT. Strassman (1990) similarly found no consistent relation between the level of computer spending by US firms and the amount of money they earned after the costs of buying and implementing the technology were taken into account. Surveys of managers and IT experts within the UK have revealed a similar picture. Clegg et al. (1996), for example, found that 80–90% of investments in new technology within the UK fail to meet all of their objectives. A key message of this chapter is that technology in all its forms is very much a double-edged sword – it has the potential to enhance, as well as diminish, the lives of its users (Norman, 1998). A major challenge for those involved in the study of work technology is to demonstrate how disasters and poor performance can be avoided.

9.3 The Changing Nature of Work Technologies

To a large extent research by work psychologists and other researchers on new technology is a constantly moving target (Grudin, 2012). One of the main reasons for this is the exponential growth in IT and computing power over the course of the twentieth century. Moore's law, for example, describes a long-term trend in the history of computing hardware and states that the number of transistors that can be placed inexpensively on an integrated circuit doubles approximately every two years. Some indication of the speed at which change takes place within the study of work technology can be seen by comparing the contents of book chapters covering the area over the last few decades. In the 1970s the focus was on manufacturing systems and shopfloor production tasks. Typical concerns were the impact of automation on the skills of workers, the relationship between working hours and fatigue, and training (Singleton, 1974). In the 1980s attention shifted to new technologies such as the use of microcomputers in the workplace. The context for these studies was still within manufacturing, but now concentrated specifically on job design issues such as worker control of tasks and job characteristics (Wall, 1987; see also Chapter 3). By the 1990s and the early part of the new millennium, research on work technologies had expanded in coverage and included a wider variety of computer-based technologies in a variety of settings, including offices, the home and a variety of other work-based environments. Waterson (2000), for example, describes a set of case studies covering early forms of electronic books and applications designed to support communication and collaboration within groups.

Table 9.2 provides a brief summary of some of the main changes over the last 50 or so years as they relate to the study of computer-based work technologies.

Forecasting the future

Predictions of how work technologies will evolve in the future are always difficult and often turn out to be wrong. Nevertheless, some of the trends described later (e.g. mobile and virtual working) are more likely to increase than fade away. One consequence of these developments will be a greater need to examine issues such as work–life balance as the boundary between work and non-work becomes more and more blurred (see Chapter 11). An additional consequence is the potential for information overload and the stress/strain this places on individuals as a result of an 'always on', 24/7 society. A recent report, for example, found that one in three people felt overwhelmed by new communications technologies such as texting, email and social networking (Mieczakowski, Goldhaber, & Clarkson, 2011). In addition, issues such as digital divides between those who can use the technologies and those who can't or don't choose to use them are likely to become more prominent (Harper, Rodden, Rogers, & Sellen, 2008). Finally, demographic changes such as the increased life expectancy of individuals are likely to place an even greater emphasis on the design of HITs that can monitor and support the care of older people in contexts such as the home (Barlow, Bayer, & Oliviera, 2011). All of these concerns are likely to place even more emphasis and

Table 9.2 The expansion of work technologies since the 1950s.

Work technologies	Growth period	Main users	User issues
Purpose-built research machines	1950s	Mathematicians, engineers and other scientists	Reliability; users must learn programming; one computer for many users
Mainframe computers	1960s and 1970s	Data processing professionals	Users mainly managers and specialists; one computer per user
Minicomputers	1970s	Engineers and other non-computer professionals	Users still do much of the programming; usability starts to be recognized as an issue
Microcomputers	1980s	Almost everyone	Usability viewed as an issue
Laptops, notebooks, electronic mail systems	1990s	Almost everyone	Usability; several computers per user
Internet-based appliances, mobile technologies, ubiquitous technologies	2000+	Everyone (with some exceptions)	Privacy; security and confidentiality of data; thousands of computers per user
	2012+	Everyone	Information overload; strains placed on work-life balance; increasing 'blurring' of boundaries between home and work life; concerns about the digital divide between young and older users

importance on the need for closer attention by work psychologists and experts from related disciplines to the design and use of new technologies.

9.4 Work Technologies: A Systems Approach

A wide variety of disciplines share an interest in the design and use of work-related technologies. These disciplines include human factors and ergonomics, work psychology and sociology of work. In what follows, it is important to bear in mind that they are by no means exclusive of one another. In any one study a number of the approaches may be applied, along with different methods spanning a range from questionnaire-based studies through to extended periods of participant-based observation. Table 9.3 sets out the main areas on which some of the disciplines focus in their study of work technologies, alongside details of the methods they use and example studies.

> ### Work Psychology in Action: Mobile working and work–life balance
>
> A recent report by Carolyn Axtell (2011) summarizes studies that have examined the relation between mobile working and well-being. Mobile working takes a number of forms, including working on trains or in cafes and other public spaces away from the office. The report describes how mobile working can have positive and negative outcomes for individuals. Mobile technologies such as smartphones and laptops allow workers to make better use of so-called 'dead time', such as the daily commute to work or waiting for a flight at an airport. Mobile work can also help relieve the pressure of being restricted to a particular work schedule (e.g. working 9 am to 5 pm every day) and allow workers to have greater flexibility and control over their working arrangements.
>
> Mobile workers also report a number of negative consequences of working outside traditional office settings. These include working excessive hours, experiencing higher levels of stress and getting less sleep due to worrying about work (see also Chapter 8).
>
> One of the conclusions from Axtell's work is that mobile working doesn't necessarily have to be associated with negative outcomes. A number of individual and organizational strategies can be put in place to avoid disruptions to work–life balance, for example. These include developing the ability to detach from work and setting strict work–home boundaries. Organizations can also help by providing more support for employees in the form of training for mobile working arrangements and reducing the expectation that working hours need to be extended.

The study of technology also cuts across a number of levels of analysis, including cognitive, organizational and social issues, and to some extent the separation of the disciplines has come about through historical accident rather than by design. What unites these disciplines is a concern with applying a *systems approach* to the study of work technologies. In the past few years this has been given greater prominence, and researchers and practitioners have begun to recognize the importance of viewing the study of technology from a systems-based perspective (Hendricks, 1997). The systems approach has a number of advantages in terms of understanding the demands technology can place on the individual and the impact it can have upon social factors involved in work, as well as the influence it may have on organizational concerns (e.g. power relationships and overall organizational structure). It also has the advantage that it facilitates an interdisciplinary perspective on work technologies that unites some of the disciplines listed in Table 9.3. Figure 9.2 shows an example of a systems model for HITs drawn from human factors and ergonomics (Carayon et al., 2006).

Table 9.3 Examples of the aims, methods and types of studies used by different disciplines in studying work technology.

Discipline	Primary focus	Methods used	Example studies
Human factors and ergonomics	Understanding the physical and psychological impact associated with the implementation, adoption and use of work technologies	Surveys, checklists, task analysis, interviews and observation	Use of technology in complex work systems such as railways networks (Wilson, Farrington-Darby, Cox, Bye, & Hockey, 2007); hospitals (Waterson, 2014)
Work psychology	Psychological consequences of implementation, adoption and use of work technologies (often focused on specific issues such as job design, skills and knowledge of users)	Surveys, interviews and observation	Impact of new technology on teamworking and job design (Wall, 1987); teleworking and its impact on home life (Daniels, Lamond, & Standen, 2001)
Sociology of work	Understanding the impact of work technologies within the wider context of society, as well as more specifically on teams and individuals	Surveys, interviews, ethnographic methods of participant observation (e.g. ethnography, using video and photography)	London Underground control rooms (Heath and Luff, 1992); use of technology in ship navigation (Hutchins, 1995a)

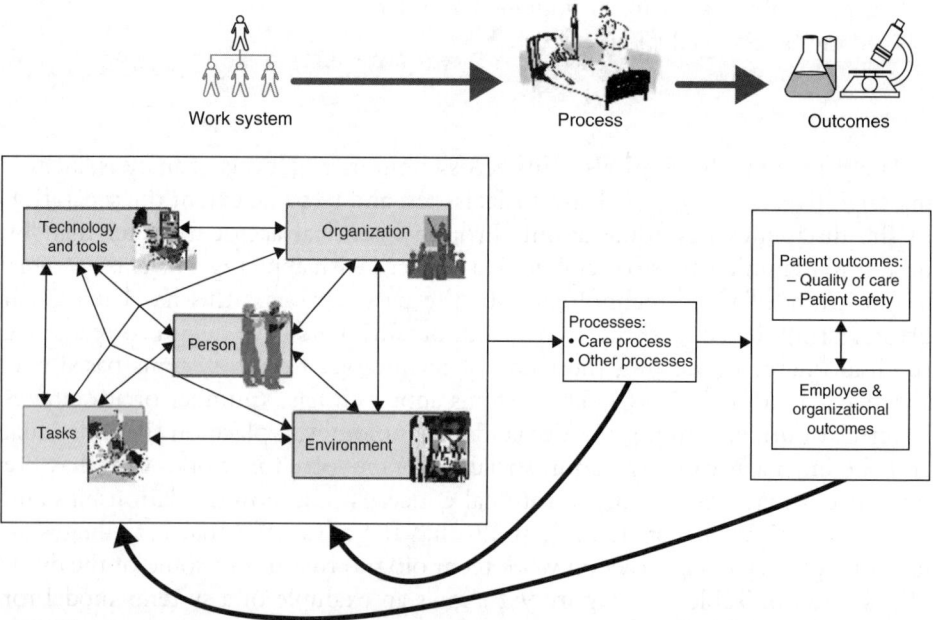

Figure 9.2 The systems engineering initiative for patient safety (SEIPS) model.
Source: Carayon et al. (2006).

Table 9.4 Different types of interfaces with technology.

Technology interface	Example issues
Human technology	Physical characteristics of the user
	Display design
	Usability and user satisfaction
	Job and workspace design
	Workload
	Health and safety
Team (group) technology	Job and team design
	Leadership and team responsibilities
	Allocation of tasks and functions within teams
Organization technology	Communication and coordination
	Knowledge sharing
	Participation in design
	Organizational culture
	Management of change

The model aims to demonstrate the types of dynamic inter-relationships which exist within healthcare as they apply to patient safety. The model also is intended to underline the role of individual, organizational, task-based and technological factors, and the part they play in 'shaping' how care processes are delivered, alongside determining outcomes for patients such as quality of care and safety.

A second advantage is that a systems perspective allows the researcher to examine the different types of *interfaces* that should be addressed when considering the impact of a new technology (Hendricks, 1997; Table 9.4). Interfaces can be described as the gap between an individual user or a group of users and the task(s) they are trying to carry out. In this particular situation, interfaces include the human–machine interface (e.g. the study of human and physical characteristics and their application to design), the team (group) interface (e.g. how the new technology fits within existing team working arrangements) and the organization–technology interface (e.g. the study of the effect technology can bring to organizational processes, such as communication and the way work is carried out in general). Finally, viewing the study of technology within a systems-based framework, it is important to bear in mind that the design and use of technology passes through a number of generic phases, ranging from initial requirements gathering (i.e. finding out what capabilities the new technology should provide) through to stages of design and deployment in the workplace and later redesign (i.e. where the technology is modified in the light of user feedback and other aspects of its use).

9.5 Studying Work Technologies: Two Approaches

There are two approaches which seek to explain the impact of technology on individuals and the conduct of their work: (i) human–computer interaction and (ii) work and organizational psychology.

Human–computer interaction

One of the best-established ways of examining the relation between individuals and technology is to focus on the nature of the interface separating users and the technology they are using. This is called *human–computer interaction* (HCI). A particular focus of the HCI is on cognitive models of the user and attempts to formalize the types of knowledge that an individual needs to make use of when operating a machine or system (e.g. a word processor or a graphics package). Cognitive models such as task-action grammar (TAG; Payne & Green, 1986) can be used to predict whether one interface will take longer to learn than another. Similarly, the goals, operators, methods and selection rules (GOMS; Card, Moran, & Newell, 1983) model has been successfully used in deciding on alternative interfaces for applications such as work stations for telephone operators (Gray, John, & Atwood, 1993). More recent models have tended to be built within larger cognitive architectures which attempt to simulate aspects of human skill acquisition (e.g. Newell, 1990; Anderson, 1993). In addition, many cognitive models have been built to accommodate user interaction with the external environment and representations such as displays and other interfaces (e.g. Payne, 1991; Zhang, 1997). Howes (1995) provide good reviews of the developments that took place in cognitive models during the 1990s.

A central concern of HCI is *usability*. Nielson (1993) draws a distinction between formative and summative evaluation of the usability of a system, the latter taking place after most of the design of the system has been completed, while formative evaluation takes place while design is ongoing and aims to contribute towards it. A number of methods spanning both qualitative (e.g. user questionnaires, interviews and focus groups) and quantitative (e.g. laboratory-based experiments) approaches have been used to carry out usability testing of an interface or overall system. Some of these methods have been designed to be used to produce fast evaluation results (e.g. heuristic evaluation), whereas others are designed to provide conceptual support to designers (May & Barnard, 1995) or integration with the system development process (Lim & Long, 1994).

More recently, approaches such as distributed cognition and ethnography have been used to contribute to the assessment of wider concerns, such as organizational usability and the overall coordination of work and its relationship to technology. Distributed cognition emphasizes the distributed nature of cognitive phenomena across individuals, technology and internal and external representations in terms of a common language of 'representational states' and 'media'. In so doing, it dissolves the traditional divisions between the inside/outside boundary of the individual and the culture/cognition distinction that anthropologists and cognitive psychologists have historically created. Instead, it focuses on the interactions between the distributed structures of the phenomenon that is under scrutiny (Rogers, 1997). One of the most common ways in which distributed cognition is studied is by using ethnographic methods. These involve periods of intensive participant observation of work contexts, often involving the use of video and photography. Discussion of these two approaches is taken up in the next section, as they are sometimes seen as providing a bridge between HCI and organizational psychology (Anderson, Heath, Luff, & Moran, 1993).

Work and organizational psychology

Organizational approaches, as one might expect, typically address issues relating to work technology at a higher level of granularity as compared to the other approaches described in this section. The questions that are addressed from an organizational point of view involve a consideration of the social context in which technology is being placed, changes to working practices, job teams and arrangements for team working, as well as issues relating to changes to the distribution of power and responsibilities of users which may come about as a result of the technology. A consideration of organizational issues may well extend beyond the normal bounds of system development and often involves an in-depth understanding of how users incorporate a new system into their work once it has been implemented (Henderson, 1991; Jones, 1995).

The growth of computer-supported cooperative work (CSCW) systems during the past few years has to some extent led to the development of approaches that cut across cognitive, social and organizational levels of analysis. Hutchins (1995a), for example, utilized ethnography in order to provide a better understanding of how teams coordinate work among themselves and the artefacts which make up their work environment. Hutchins (1995b) presents an analysis of the distribution of cognitive tasks in an airline cockpit (i.e. the distributed cognition approach). The analysis shows that airline pilots make use of a number of external cues and aids in the cockpit, including non-verbal cues (e.g. environmental sounds) as well as modifications to designs that are improvised (e.g. empty coffee cups placed on levers signalling they are not currently for use; Norman, 1998).

One of the main strengths of the distributed cognition approach is that it can be used to identify issues that are either taken for granted or not identified by traditional analyses of usability and organizational design. The distributed cognition approach and ethnographic analyses have provided a number of important insights into environments as diverse as ambulance call-out scheduling (McCarthy, Healey, Wright, & Harrison, 1998) and the work of software developers (Heath & Luff, 1992; Button & Sharrock, 1994). In addition, the approach has been instrumental in underlining the importance of the idea that technology has an active role to play in changing the cognitive requirements of tasks (e.g. Hollnagel & Woods, 1983).

Replay

The study of work technologies is a multidisciplinary endeavour involving people with a range of backgrounds, including work psychology, the sociology of work, human factors and ergonomics. These people typically adopt a systems-based perspective on the design and use of work technologies. The most important aspect of this is that a range of concerns covering individual, team and organizational levels of analysis are addressed. The systems approach is related to one of the most well-known theories of work technologies, namely socio-technical systems theory.

> ### Work Psychology in Action: An ethnographic study of London Underground control rooms
>
> Heath and Luff (1992) describe an ethnographic study of control rooms within the Bakerloo Line, part of the London Underground network. The study focused on two key members of staff within the control rooms, the controller and the divisional information assistant, and highlighted the importance of these two individuals maintaining a good understanding of the other's activities, whilst also specializing in their own roles. For the information assistant, the key responsibility was communicating with staff and passengers at stations, while for the controller it was managing the day-to-day running of the line (e.g. scheduling trains, making sure trains are running on time and dealing with delays). The study demonstrated that ethnographic study comprising detailed analysis of video data and recordings of the work of London Underground personnel could help to optimize the design of new workstations and other information systems. In particular, Heath and Luff pointed to the importance of the ability to 'overhear' the work of various roles on the control room and to coordinate their actions in the light of this information. Conventional system design (e.g. based exclusively on the analysis of work tasks) might have missed this detail. One outcome might have been new workstations and workspaces that did not support coordinated, collaborative working arrangements (e.g. workstations in different parts of the control room). Ethnographic work of this kind provides insights into the requirements of new systems and is often used in parallel with other types of data collection (e.g. interviews, focus groups, user surveys). More recent work by Luff and Heath (2000) presents an analysis of a Docklands Light Railway control room.

9.6 Work Technologies: Theories

This section describes research on two of the most popular theories applied to work technologies: socio-technical systems theory and adaptive structuration theory. Theories of these kinds have been applied to a wide variety of technologies and working environments (e.g. manufacturing, healthcare and global teamworking) and have proved to be useful in explaining some of the factors that determine the likelihood that the implementation of technology in the workplace will succeed or fail.

Socio-technical systems theory

The socio-technical systems theory (STST) of work has a long history, dating back to some of the earliest studies of the use of technology within work settings (e.g. Trist & Bamforth, 1951; Emery, 1959). The theory has a number of distinctive features, the most important of which is the recognition that organizations should consider the joint optimization and parallel design of both social and technical systems when designing new technology (see also Chapter 3). The principle of joint optimization came about as a result of the widespread recognition that great effort is placed on the technical aspects of the systems, often to the detriment of human and organizational concerns. Such a bias leads to what has been termed a technology-led approach to systems design, and continues to be one of the most prevalent strategies adopted by companies when introducing new technology to the workplace (Blackler & Brown, 1986; Doherty & King, 1998). Aside from joint optimization, the STST provides a number of other principles or guidelines that are designed to be used when introducing technology (Cherns, 1976, 1987; Clegg, 2000). These include:

- Methods of working should be minimally specified (i.e. not overly prescribed, with some decision-making freedom left to the worker).
- Variances in the work processes (e.g. production breakdowns, changes in product) should be handled at source (i.e. as near as possible to location of breakdown or change-over).
- Those who need resources should have access to and authority over them.
- Roles should be multifunctional and multiskilled.
- Redesign should be continuous, not 'once and for all' change.

Application of the STST typically involves using a number of methods, including the use of interviews with those likely to be affected by new technology, questionnaires to evaluate the impact of the technology on psychological aspects of job design (e.g. satisfaction, opportunity for skill usage), and consultation of company documentation and records in order to assess the objectives of the implementation. In addition, techniques such as *variance analysis* (Davis & Wacker, 1987) and *soft systems analysis* (Checkland, 1981) are sometimes used to assess likely areas that may prove problematic when introducing technology (e.g. areas which require high levels of skill and knowledge use in the event of breakdowns) and to plan for the introduction of technology by considering specific scenarios of use.

Replay

STST proposes that a balance needs to be struck between aspects of the technical design of systems and the work (social) system in which the technology will be used. Technical and social elements of design should be carried out in parallel in order to ensure worker satisfaction and productivity. One of the ways in which STST works is by using a set of guiding principles that cover issues related to job and teams design, as well as the process of carrying out change within work settings.

> ### Work Psychology in Action: New technology on the shopfloor
>
> Buchanan and Boddy (1983) describe an example of a case study which used the STST to evaluate the impact of a new computer system on the work of biscuit-making operators. They found that different types of application of the new computer technology had very different effects on the work of operators within the company. The system which controlled dough-mixing tasks largely replaced the craft-based skills of doughmen and led to simplified jobs that were less satisfying than those done before the introduction of the system. By contrast, the part of the system that controlled weighing tasks largely complemented the work of other operators and led to more interesting and rewarding jobs.
>
> Buchanan and Boddy found that the differential impact of the new technology could largely be explained by the objectives of managers, and the way in which the new system was planned and introduced. In the case of mixing tasks, the system largely removed a number of tasks that were viewed as being important in terms of control and decision-making responsibilities among doughmen. These tasks were automated, and managers failed to consider the impact such automation would have on the quality of life and overall job satisfaction of operators. On the other hand, the new weighing system retained a number of key tasks for operators and removed some tasks that were viewed as being repetitive or tedious to complete. For example, the new weighing system allowed operators to control weighing tasks more effectively and gain rapid feedback on their performance, leading to a more interesting and challenging job as a result.
>
> Overall, the case study demonstrated that the implementation of new technology needs to be sensitive to the views of those involved in the change and that the design of the technology should complement, rather than conflict with, existing skills and knowledge levels. Buchanan and Boddy's study also demonstrates once again that technology can be a 'double-edged sword'.

Adaptive structuration theory

Adaptive structuration theory (AST) is often used to understand change processes that occur when information systems are implemented and adopted. This is achieved by examining two vantage points in parallel: (i) the types of structures that are provided by information systems (e.g. the functionality of the technology) and (ii) the structures that emerge in human action as a result of people interacting with the new technology. AST is based on structuration theory, which was originally developed by the sociologist Anthony Giddens (1984). Structuration theory proposes that a complete understanding of social interaction requires incorporating explanations of both the structure of relationships and the dynamics or processes of relationships. The processes both take place in social structures and shape those structures over time. The heart of AST is the role of advanced information technology and its appropriation by members of the organization as they work together. The theory describes how a technology's inherent structural characteristics shape interaction patterns without determining the interaction in a definitive way. How people choose to adopt or appropriate the technology helps to shape their decision processes. Patterns of social structure emerge in the group over time and are influenced by use of the new technology. DeSanctis and Poole (1994) also suggest that analysis based on AST can identify certain patterns as more likely to be associated with organizational effectiveness than others.

> ### Work Psychology in Action: Technology-supported virtual teams
>
> Maznevski and Chudoba (2000) report a longitudinal study of a large US manufacturing company which made use of virtual team working to coordinate working arrangements across the USA and Europe. Over a period of 21 months the study examined communication patterns between members of three virtual teams and how these changed over time. The work of the teams involved a mixture of face-to-face interaction as well as the use of communication technologies such as video conferencing, teleconferencing, email and telephone. In order to categorize how communication patterns evolved over time, Maznevski and Chodoba (2000) used a coding framework for their interviews and observations based on AST. The framework included codes covering four main aspects of the work of the virtual teams: (i) the structural elements which shaped the work of the teams (e.g. task characteristics such as the degree of interdependence requires by a task across team members), (ii) technology appropriation (e.g. how the teams used communication technologies and which they chose to convey a specific message), (iii) decision-making processes (e.g. idea construction, problem solving) and (iv) decision outcomes (e.g. how teams rated the quality of decision-making and the extent to which they enjoyed working together).
>
> One of the most interesting findings from the study was that the most effective virtual teams established regular patterns of interaction which repeated over time. These temporal patterns typically involved an initial co-located, face-to-face team meeting with attempts by team members to resolve problems and build relationships. This co-ordination meeting served like a 'heartbeat' which revitalised the relationships between team members and improved other aspects of team processes. Regular meetings of this kind helped to ensure that when the teams where working across distance and using technologies such as video conferencing, their work was cohesive and collaborative. One of the implications from the study is that virtual teams need to punctuate remote working with face-to-face meetings in order to ensure that the teamwork remains effective and productive.

Replay

AST attempts to understand the nature of how structural properties of work technologies and the context in which they are used (e.g. the functionality provided by the technology, hierarchical structures in the organization) combine with longitudinal patterns of technology use and adoption by end users in order to determine the degree to which the technology succeeds in supporting work activities.

Combining STST and AST

Waterson, Glenn and Eason (2012) describe a case study that combined elements of STST and AST in order to understand the preparations which were being made for the introduction of paperless working within a large UK hospital. The study took place in an outpatients department and focused on how the current system for patient records worked, the expectations of staff and the likely outcomes of introducing technology in the form of an electronic patient record (EPR) system. The study used a combined STST and AST model (Figure 9.3) as a template to code interviews with staff within the outpatients department. The STST part of the model examined how work tasks were likely to be impacted by the new technology, as well as how the structure and roles of the department were likely to change as a result of the new EPR system. The elements of the model which drew on AST were included as they placed emphasis on the dynamic way in which user attitudes towards the new technology were likely to be shaped not only by the features offered by the new EPR, but also by the support provided to them in the form of training, guidance and general advice (labelled 'appropriation support/scaffold' in Figure 9.3) by the hospital management.

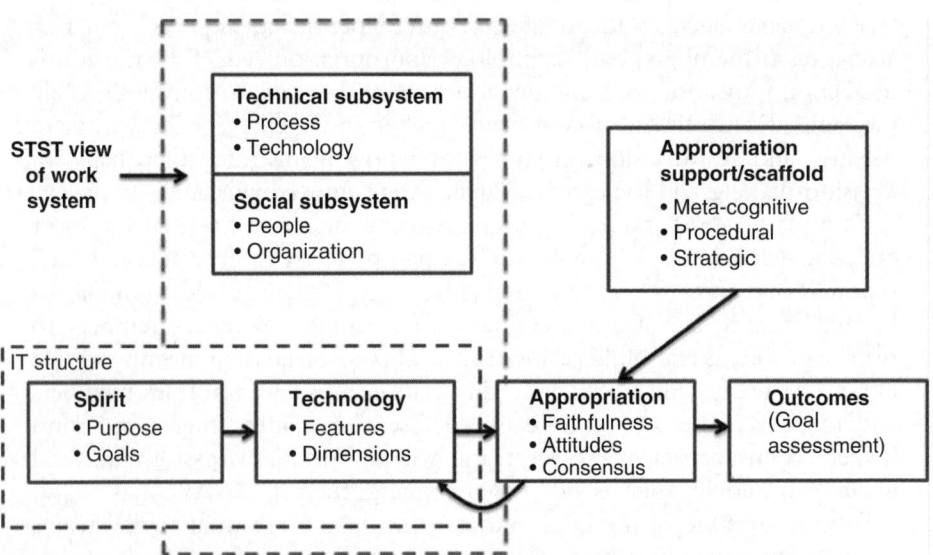

Figure 9.3 Combined model with elements drawn from sociotechnical and structuration theory. Source: Waterson, Glenn and Eason (2012).

The study found that one of the main influences on attitudes towards the type of EPR that should exist within the department was prompted by negative reactions to the way in which previous IT systems had been managed and attempted to be introduced in the past. A strong commitment to end-user involvement in the design of the new EPR system also shaped attitudes towards future expectations of the adoption of new EPRs within the department. In combination, these attitudes served as a 'scaffold' which influenced their 'mental model' of how the new EPR system might work. In addition, part of this appropriation scaffold involved a high degree of scepticism that a rapid change to paperless working was likely to be possible.

9.7 Conclusions

One of the consistent themes in this chapter is that the appropriate design of technology has the potential to transform our working lives and make it more satisfying and productive. At the same time, technology has a dark side; it can also serve to make work harder, less satisfying for individuals and as a result less efficient and productive. The main lesson from research on work technologies is that regardless of our disciplinary background (work psychology, HCI and so on) or preference for specific theories, focused study of the likely impact of the technology on work practices, alongside carefully evaluated post implementation is essential in order to ensure that the technologies ultimately prove successful for individuals and the organization they work within. In many respects, this might not seem a surprising conclusion, but the high number of failure rates for large-scale systems, as well as many examples of poorly designed systems, demonstrates that the message still needs to be repeated and communicated to system designers and those responsible for commissioning new technological systems. In many respects, we still need to learn from the past. It is nearly 20 years since Thomas Laudauer (1995) wrote his study on the impact of work technology on individual and organizational productivity. The key message in that study and this chapter is that careful attention to the user of the technology and their work system needs to be at the heart of any change management initiative that involves technology.

Work Psychology in Action: LEO: Learning from the past

The science writer Georgina Ferry describes in her book *A Computer Called LEO* (2003) the history of the development of the first large-scale office information system (the Lyons Electronic Office (LEO) system). LEO was designed and implemented during the 1950s and 1960s within the British food and catering company J. Lyons and Co., and continues to be in operation today. One of the key factors that distinguishes the development of LEO from many other systems developed during the last half-century is the attention paid to managers within the company to the need to consider the technological and organizational implications of using LEO to replace tasks that had previously been carried out manually (e.g. accounting and operation planning tasks). Although they didn't know it at the time, the engineers developing LEO were following many of the principles of user-centred design set out 25–30 years later (Gould & Lewis, 1985), namely:

- an early focus on users and their tasks;
- the need for empirical measurement of the impact of the new technology on users and their work;
- the need for iterative design that follows a cycle of design, testing and measurement, and redesign.

Discussion Points

1. Despite a long tradition of research, little attention is paid to the design of new technologies and the impact these may have on individuals and the work systems. Technology is often badly designed and failure rates continue to be high.
2. User-centred design, although more common now compared to 20 years ago, is still the exception rather than the norm. Convincing designers and employers of the value of adopting an early focus on users and the value of user participation in design still remains a challenge.
3. Some theories of work technology remain under-specified and are aimed at a primarily academic audience. There is a need to make these more comprehensible and in a form where they can be used by non-specialists to guide design activity.
4. The use of work technologies tends to evolve over time and sometimes the characteristics of usage patterns are difficult to predict. Many theories of work technology (e.g. STST) still assume a static model, rather than a dynamic approach to understanding patterns of technology use.

Learning by Doing

1. The next time you go to the doctor or visit someone in hospital, think of the healthcare-related information (e.g. some of it covering your address and date of birth, some of it relating to your medical history) that might be related to either you or the person you are visiting. How much of it is stored in electronic form (e.g. databases) and how much of it is paper based (e.g. documents in files)? How do you think that information 'flows' around the various parts of the healthcare system (e.g. local doctors' surgeries,

hospitals)? Ask the doctor, nurse or other healthcare staff about their views and see if they can fill in any missing information.
2. Imagine a busy manager tells you his company is considering invested in a large-scale IT system (e.g. a new financial system or IT that helps to schedule production processes). What advice would you give to the manager to help with the implementation and to encourage users to make the most of the system?
3. As learning point 2 above, but this time consider how theories such as socio-technical systems and adaptive structuration theory might help you to carry out a study of the implementation and adoption patterns over time.

Further Reading

The following references may help the reader to gain an understanding of some of the issues raised in this chapter. Some of the references are books aimed at the general public (e.g. Ferry, Norman), but they also provide an accessible introduction to many of the issues mentioned in this chapter. These should be read alongside examples of reviews of specific areas (e.g. HCI, Winograd; socio-technical systems, Waterson, Eason).

Eason, K. D. (2002). People and computers: Emerging work practice in the information age. In P. B. Warr (Ed.), *Psychology at work* (5th ed., pp. 77–99). Harmondsworth: London.

Ferry, G. (2003). *A computer called LEO*. London: Harper Perennial.

Grudin, J. (2012). A moving target: The evolution of HCI. In J. A. Jacko (Ed.), *Human-Computer Interaction Handbook* (3rd ed.). London: Taylor & Francis.

Landauer, T. K. (1995). *The trouble with computers*. Cambridge, MA: MIT Press.

Norman, D. A. (1988). *The psychology of everyday things*. New York: Doubleday.

Waterson, P. E. (2005). Sociotechnical design of work systems. In J. R. Wilson, & N. Corlett (Eds.), *Evaluation of human work* (3rd ed., pp. 769–792). London: Taylor & Francis.

Winograd, T. (Ed.) (1996), Bringing software to design. Oxford: Addison-Wesley, ACM Press.

References

Anderson, J. R. (1993). *Rules of the mind*. Hillsdale, NJ: Lawrence Erlbaum Associates.

Anderson, R., Heath, C., Luff, P., & Moran, T. P. (1993). The cognitive and the social in human–computer interaction. *International Journal of Man–Machine Studies, 38*, 999–1016.

Ash J. S., Berg M., & Coiera E. (2004). Some unintended consequences of information technology in health care: The nature of patient care information system-related errors. *Journal of the American Medical Information Association, 11*, 104–112.

Axtell, C. (2011). *The well-being of the mobile workforce*. iPass Inc. Available at: http://mobile-workforce-project.ipass.com/reports/well-being-report (last accessed April 8, 2012).

Barlow, J., Bayer, S., & Oliviera, T. C. (2011). Remote care: Health at home. In R. Harper (Ed.), *The connected home: The future of domestic life* (pp. 269–280). London: Springer.

Blackler, F., & Brown, C. (1986). Alternative models to guide the design and introduction of new technologies into work organisations. *Journal of Occupational Psychology, 41*, 211–221.

Buchanan, D. A., & Boddy, D. (1983). Advance technology and the quality of working life: the effects of computerized controls on biscuit-making operators. *Journal of Occupational Psychology, 56*, 109–119.

Button, G., & Sharrock, W. (1994). Occasioned practices in the work of software engineers. In

M. Jirotka, & J. Goguen (Eds.), *Requirements engineering: Social and technical issues* (pp. 217–240). London: Academic Press.

Carayon, P., Hundt, A. S., Karsh, B. T., Gurses, A. P., Alvarado, C. J., Smith, M., & Brennan, P. F. (2006). Work system design for patient safety: The SEIPS model. *Quality and Safety in Health Care, 15 (Suppl. I)*, 50–58.

Card, S. K., Moran, T. P., & Newell, A. (1983). *The psychology of human–computer interaction*. Hillsdale, NJ: Lawrence Erlbaum Associates.

Checkland, P. B. (1981). *Systems thinking, systems practice*. Chichester: John Wiley & Sons.

Cherns, A. B. (1976). The principles of sociotechnical design. *Human Relations, 29*, 783–792.

Cherns, A. B. (1987). Principles of sociotechnical design revisited. *Human Relations, 40*, 153–162.

Clegg, C. W. (2000). Sociotechnical principles for system design. *Applied Ergonomics, 31*, 463–477.

Clegg, C. W., Axtell, C., Damodaran, L., Farbery, B., Hull, R. Lloyd-Jones, R., Nicholls, J., Sell, R., & Tomlinson, C. (1996). Information technology: A study of performance and the role of human and organisational factors. *Ergonomics, 40*, 851–871.

Daniels, K., Lamond, D., & Standen, P. (2001). Teleworking: Frameworks for organizational Research. *Journal of Management Studies, 38*, 1151–1185.

Davis, L. E., & Wacker, G. L. (1987). Job design. In G. Salvendy (Ed.), *Handbook of human factors* (pp. 431–452). New York: John Wiley & Sons.

DeSanctis, G., & Poole, M. S. (1994). Capturing the complexity in advanced technology use: Adaptive structuration theory. *Organization Science, 5*, 121–147.

Doherty, N., & King, M. (1998). The consideration of organisational issues during the systems development process. *Behaviour and Information Technology, 17*, 41–51.

Eason, K. D. (2007). Local sociotechnical system development in the NHS National Programme for Information Technology. *Journal of Information Technology, 22*, 257–264.

Emery, F. E. (1959). Characteristics of sociotechnical systems. Reprinted in L. E. Davis, & J. C. Taylor (Eds.), *Design of jobs* (1972, pp. 177–198). Harmondsworth: Penguin.

Ferry, G. (2003). *A computer called LEO*. London: Harper Perennial.

Giddens, A. (1984). *The constitution of society*. Berkeley: University of California Press.

Gould, J. D., & Lewis, C. H. (1985). Designing for usability: Key principles and what designers think. *Communications of the ACM, 28*, 300–311.

Gray, W. D., John, B. E., & Atwood, M. E.(1993). Project Ernestine: validating a GOMS analysis for predicting and explaining real-world task performance. *Human–Computer Interaction, 8*, 237–309.

Grudin, J. (2012). A moving target: The evolution of HCI. In J. A. Jacko (Ed.), *Human–computer interaction handbook* (3rd ed.). London: Taylor & Francis.

Harper, R., Rodden, T., Rogers, Y., & Sellen, A. (Eds.) (2008). *Being human: Human–computer interaction in the year 2020*. Microsoft Research. http://research.microsoft.com/en-us/um/cambridge/projects/hci2020/download.html (last accessed March 27, 2012).

Heath, C., & Luff, P. (1992). Collaboration and control: Crisis management and multimedia technology in London Underground line control rooms. *Computer-Supported Cooperative Work, 1*, 69–94.

Henderson, A. (1991). A developmental perspective on interface, design and theory. In J. M. Carroll (Ed.), *Designing interaction* (pp. 254–268). Cambridge: Cambridge University Press.

Hendricks, H. (1997). Organizational design and macroergonomics. In G. Salvendy (Ed.), *Handbook of human factors and ergonomics* (pp. 594–636). London: John Wiley & Sons.

Hollnagel, E., & Woods, D. D. (1983). Cognitive systems engineering: new wine in new bottles. *International Journal of Human Computer Studies, 18*, 538–600.

Howes, A. (1995). An introduction to cognitive modelling in human-computer interaction. In A. F. Monk, & G. N. Gilbert (Eds.), *Perspectives on HCI: Diverse approaches* (pp. 97–119). London: Academic Press.

Hutchins, E. (1995a). *Cognition in the wild*. Cambridge, MA: MIT Press.

Hutchins, E. (1995b). How a cockpit remembers its speeds. *Cognitive Science, 19*, 126–289.

Jones, M. (1995). Organizational analysis and HCI. In A. F. Monk, & G. N. Gilbert (Eds.), *Perspectives on HCI: Diverse approaches* (pp. 249–269). London: Academic Press.

Landauer, T. K. (1995), *The trouble with computers*. Cambridge, MA: MIT Press.

Lim, K. Y., & Long, J. (1994). *The MUSE method for usability engineering*. Cambridge: Cambridge University Press.

Luff, P., & Heath, C. (2000) The collaborative production of computer commands in command and control. *International Journal of Human–Computer Studies*, 52, 669–699.

May, J., & Barnard, P. (1995), The case for supportive evaluation during design. *Interacting with Computers*, 7, 115–143.

Maznevski, M. L., & Chudoba, K. M. (2000). Bridging space over time: Global virtual team dynamics and effectiveness. *Organization Science*, 11, 473–492.

McCarthy, J. C., Healey, P. G. T., Wright, P. C., & Harrison, M. D. (1998). Accountability of work activity in high-consequence work systems: human error in context. *International Journal of Human Computer Studies*, 47, 735–766.

Mieczakowski, A., Goldhaber, T., & Clarkson, J. (2011). *Culture, communication and change: Report on an investigation of the use and impact of modern media and technology in our lives*. http://www-edc.eng.cam.ac.uk/~akm51/PD_Final_Reports/long_report_23.06.11.pdf (last accessed March 27, 2012).

Newell, A. (1990). *Unified theories of cognition*. Cambridge, MA: Harvard University Press.

Nielson, J. (1993). *Usability engineering*. Boston: Academic Press Professional.

Norman, D. A. (1998). *The design of everyday things*. New York: Basic Books.

Payne, S. J. (1991). Display-based action at the user interface. *International Journal of Man–Machine Studies*, 35, 275–289.

Payne, S., & Green, T. R. G. (1986). Task-action grammars: A model of the mental representation of task languages. *Human–Computer Interaction*, 2, 93–133.

Rogers, T. (1997). *A brief introduction to distributed cognition*. Unpublished manuscript available at: http://www.id-book.com/downloads/chapter%208%20dcog-brief-intro.pdf (last accessed October 13, 2012).

Strassman, P. A. (1990). *The business value of computers: An executive's guide*. New Canaan, CT: Information Economics Press.

Singleton, W. T. (1974). *Man-machine systems*. Harmondsworth: Penguin.

Trist, E. L, & Bamforth, K. W. (1951). Some social and psychological consequences of the long-wall method for coal-getting. *Human Relations*, 4, 3–38.

Wall, T. D. (1987). New technology and job design. In P. B. Warr (Ed.), *Psychology at work* (3rd ed., pp. 270–290). Harmondsworth: Penguin.

Waterson, P. E. (2000). The design and use of work technology. In N. Chmiel (Ed.), *An Introduction to work and organisational psychology* (pp. 231–254). Oxford: Blackwell.

Waterson, P. E. (2013). Health information technology and sociotechnical systems: A progress report on recent developments within the English NHS. *Applied Ergonomics*, DOI: 10.1016/j.apergo.2013.07.004.

Waterson, P. E. (2014). Sociotechnical design of work systems. In J. R. Wilson, & S. Sharples (Eds.), *Evaluation of human work* (4th ed.). London: Taylor & Francis.

Waterson, P. E., Glenn, Y., & Eason, K. (2012). Preparing the ground for the 'Paperless Hospital': A case study of medical records management in a UK Outpatient Services department. *International Journal of Medical Informatics*, 81, 114–129.

Wilson, J. R., Farrington-Darby, T., Cox, G., Bye, R., & Hockey, G. R. J. (2007). The railways as a socio-technical system: Human factors at the heart of successful rail engineering. *Proceedings of Institute of Mechanical Engineers*, 22, Part F: Tail and Rapid Transit, 101–115.

Zhang, J. (1997). The nature of external representations in problem solving. *Cognitive Science*, 21, 179–217.

Part E

The Worker

10
Individual Characteristics and Work-related Outcomes

BEATRICE VAN DER HEIJDEN, KAREN VAN DAM,
DESPOINA XANTHOPOULOU AND ANNET H. DE LANGE

> **Chapter Objectives**
>
> After studying this chapter, you should be able to:
>
> - distinguish between objective and subjective employee characteristics;
> - understand the diversity and complexity of ageing in the workplace;
> - understand gender differences with regard to work-related outcomes;
> - understand possible effects of ethnicity;
> - understand possible effects of lifestyle risk factors;
> - distinguish among three categories of subjective employee characteristics, based on their levels of changeability (i.e. trait-like characteristics, state-like characteristics and states);
> - understand how these categories of subjective employee characteristics relate to work-related outcomes.

10.1 Introduction

In this chapter we discuss the role of individual employee characteristics in the light of work-related outcomes such as motivation, well-being, sustainable employability and job performance. Current developments in the field of work psychology suggest that work behaviour is not just a function of the characteristics

An Introduction to Contemporary Work Psychology, First Edition.
Edited by Maria C. W. Peeters, Jan de Jonge and Toon W. Taris.
© 2014 John Wiley & Sons, Ltd. Published 2014 by John Wiley & Sons, Ltd.

of a job (such as job demands and job resources) and the context that workers are facing, but that it also depends, to some degree, on the person conducting the task. Today, the labour market undergoes radical changes in terms of the demographic, cultural and ethnical mixture of the working population. As a result, the management of work organizations must deal with the increasing diversity of their human capital. The increasing variety in individual (psychosocial and personal) characteristics of employees offers a rich source of opportunities, yet also implies possible threats. An in-depth understanding of the impact of key individual characteristics of employees on work-related outcomes allows us to better explain and predict those outcomes. In this chapter, we distinguish between objective and subjective employee characteristics. Objective characteristics refer to demographics (such as age, gender and ethnicity) and lifestyle risk factors, while subjective characteristics concern characteristics that are experienced introspectively and that are manifested through certain behaviours.

With respect to objective employee characteristics, this chapter first focuses on the influence of age on work-related outcomes. Given recent demographic developments (more specifically, the ageing and dejuvenization of the working population), organizations are facing far-reaching changes in the composition of the workforce. Moreover, as ageing workers face many psychological, organizational and social changes across their individual lifespan, this chapter takes a long-term developmental perspective on an individual's work and career (cf. de Lange et al., 2006). Next, we discuss current research on the effects of gender, ethnicity and lifestyle risk factors (e.g. smoking, alcohol use, poor diet and exercising) on work-related outcomes.

With respect to subjective employee characteristics, we follow Luthans, Avolio, Avey and Norman (2007) and recognize three categories of subjective characteristics based on their level of changeability. The first category concerns the 'trait-like' characteristics that are relatively stable and difficult to change. We focus in particular on workers' core self-evaluations, since these are associated with important positive outcomes, such as worker motivation, goal attainment and job performance (Judge & Bono, 2001). The second category concerns the so-called 'state-like' characteristics that are relatively changeable and malleable. These may range from more negative (e.g. being bad-tempered) to more positive (e.g. self-efficacy and resilience) characteristics. In this chapter, we focus exclusively on positive state-like characteristics (i.e. personal resources) because of the vast amount of empirical knowledge that has been built around these qualities. The significance of these state-like characteristics is that they are developable and open to change, and may therefore be positively influenced through organizational interventions. Finally, we discuss the role of 'states' that refer to those employee characteristics that vary significantly within the same person over short periods of time and across situations. A focus on states, over and above a focus on trait- and state-like characteristics, is important because it shows how specific individual characteristics that vary from one day or moment to another can explain fluctuations in workers' motivation and performance (Xanthopoulou, Bakker, & Ilies, 2012). Table 10.1 presents an overview of the worker characteristics that are addressed in this chapter.

Table 10.1 Workers' key individual characteristics.

Objective characteristics	Subjective characteristics
Age	Trait-like characteristics (core self-evaluations: self-esteem, generalized self-efficacy, emotional stability and locus of control)
Gender	State-like characteristics (personal resources: specific self-efficacy, optimism, hope, control, resilience and learning orientation)
Ethnicity	States (emotions, cognitive appraisals and personal resources)
Lifestyle factors	

10.2 Objective Individual Characteristics and Work-related Outcomes

In this section we discuss several demographic factors (age, gender and ethnicity), as well as lifestyle risk factors of employees and how these relate to work-related outcomes. A better understanding of the influence of these factors is necessary when dealing with the challenges of a diverse workforce and it provides us with tools to respond to current labour market demands.

Age and work-related outcomes

Due to the ageing and dejuvenization of the global workforce, companies must increasingly rely on the contribution of older workers. More specifically, economic realities blur the institutionalized retirement age of 65, and the traditional safety net of funded, age-prescribed retirement is currently withdrawn worldwide (van der Heijden, de Lange, Demerouti, & van der Heijde, 2009). As a result, many workers born between 1945 and 1960 will not be able to retire at or even prior to the age of 65. This scenario presents critical challenges for managers and emphasizes the importance of the work behaviour of ageing workers as a key factor for survival in the fierce and competitive global market.

Ng and Feldman (2010), in their exemplary meta-analysis on the relation between employee age and job attitudes, concluded that the relationships between chronological age and favourable attitudes (and/or less unfavourable attitudes) toward work tasks, colleagues, supervisors and organizations are generally significant and weak-to-moderate in magnitude. Specifically, although they found age to be unrelated to core task performance, creativity and performance in training programmes, age appeared to be strongly associated with organizational citizenship behaviour (OCB) (positively), safety performance (positively), general counterproductive work behaviour (negatively), workplace aggression (negatively), on-the-job substance use (negatively) and tardiness (negatively).

Although employee age is an important factor to take into account in explaining and predicting work-related outcomes, researchers agree that ageing is not simply an effect of time (here expressed as calendar age), as time does not directly measure the experienced changes (Arking, 1998). Several reviews of earlier organizational behaviour research suggest that calendar age in itself is relatively less interesting as compared to underlying age-related processes, such as the decreasing physical reserves of workers as they age (Kanfer & Ackerman, 2004). As such, age or ageing can be better portrayed as a multidimensional process that is not easily captured within one single definition. Rather, it refers to many changes in biological, psychological and social or even societal functioning across time (de Lange et al., 2006).

Five different approaches to the ageing of workers have been distinguished: (i) chronological, (ii) performance-based or functional, (iii) psychosocial or subjective, (iv) organizational and (v) lifespan (Sterns & Doverspike, 1989). These different approaches may affect worker behaviour through different processes.

First, the *chronological* approach is based on a worker's chronological or calendar age. The term 'older worker' may refer to workers from ages 40 to 75, depending on the purpose of the organization as well as the specific needs of the worker (Stein & Rocco, 2001). Although the cut-off point between young and older workers is not fixed, the age of 50 years is often used as a threshold to refer to older versus younger workers.

Second, the *performance-based or functional approach* recognizes, more than the chronological approach, individual variation in abilities and functioning at all ages, and argues that the measurement of age should be based on objective functional measures (such as one's physical health status or cognitive ability, physical capacity and objective performance). These functional capabilities can provide a better explanation for possible intra- and inter-group diversity compared to calendar age (van der Heijden, Schalk, & van Veldhoven, 2008).

Third, the *psychosocial or subjective approach* to age is based on social or self-perceptions of the 'older worker'. Important indicators for this age type are (i) how old the worker feels, looks, and acts, (ii) with which age cohort the worker identifies and (iii) how old the worker desires to be. This psychosocial perception of age might be affected by the age of other employees in the organization, but also by age attitudes, beliefs or norms that exist within an occupation, company or society. Moreover, some persistent stereotypes about older workers may exist regarding older workers' flexibility, creativity, adaptability to technology, motivation for learning or training and their well-being, which might result in negative differential treatment (Posthuma & Campion, 2009). For instance, older workers sometimes receive fewer opportunities for development since their managers reason that the required investments in this development might not pay off (Boerlijst, van der Heijden, & van Assen, 1993). It should be noted, however, that perceptions of older workers' ages might also have positive outcomes, for example when the worker is perceived as more experienced or wise (Baltes & Finkelstein, 2011).

Fourth, the *organizational approach* to age assumes that age and tenure are related, and that effects of ageing are often confounded by effects of tenure, and vice versa. Tenure relates to the time employees have spent in their jobs (job tenure) or a specific organization (organizational tenure). The ageing of workers in their jobs and organizations is an important topic in the literature on seniority and on employees' sustainable employment. Organizational age may also refer to the career stage of an employee, to skills obsolescence (i.e. the degree to which employees lack the up-to-date knowledge and skills necessary to maintain effective performance in their current or future work roles; Kaufman, 1974) and to age norms within the company (i.e. the age is viewed as typical for a given role or status by the modal group of members of a social system). In this context, Lawrence (1996) showed that managers who were regarded as younger than their typical age group were more likely to receive positive performance ratings, and that age norms influenced work behaviour.

Finally, *the lifespan approach* to age is based on elements of all the aforementioned approaches, but additionally emphasizes the complex behavioural changes at any point in the life cycle. This more elaborate approach uses variables like family status or economic constraints, but also interactions between the indicators of all aforementioned approaches to age. Obviously, it is important to take all five approaches into account in order to establish the impact of age on work outcomes, and to be able to increase awareness of possible underlying causal factors that might play a role in these processes.

Replay

- Age is not just a demographic characteristic. Rather, work psychologists study age as a multidimensional construct.
- There are five different approaches to conceptualize employees' ages: (i) chronological, (ii) performance-based or functional, (iii) psychosocial or subjective, (iv) organizational and (v) lifespan.
- These different approaches are complementary and explain how age may affect work-related outcomes through different processes.

Gender and work-related outcomes

The role of gender has been investigated systematically to better understand social phenomena in the workplace. Where gender previously was only included as a control variable, recent studies have tried to increase our insight into the role of gender in itself. Specifically, issues like the specific sources of stress for professional women, different career orientations of females, the effects of gender for managerial promotion and advancement, and the influence of gender on performance ratings are exemplary for the gender perspective in research on work-related outcomes (see Mayerhofer, Meyer, & Steyrer, 2007).

Traditional gender roles imply that work is more important for men, whereas home and family issues are more important for women (Gutek, Searle, & Klepa, 1991). Given the prevalence of traditional views on gender, women often face different and more unfavourable working conditions than men, including pay inequity, with women receiving less pay than men when performing similar tasks (Blau & Kahn, 2007). Women also experience fewer task-related developmental assignments and promotion opportunities during their careers than men (Ohlott, Ruderman, & McCauley, 1994).

These differences in work-related experiences suggest that women are more vulnerable to job strain and burnout. However, a recent meta-analysis of Purvanova and Muros (2010) has challenged this commonly held belief. Their results showed that although women appear to be somewhat more exhausted than men, men are more cynical about their jobs than women. In a similar vein and despite data showing that women's jobs are often less attractive than men's jobs, women seem to be more satisfied with their work (Clark, 1997). Moreover, the psychological processes that explain the spillover of work demands to the home situation (i.e. work–home interference; see Chapter 11) appear to be similar for men and women (Bakker, Demerouti, & Dollard, 2008).

A final issue relates to job performance and productivity: Do men and women perform differently? The findings are mixed. Whereas previous studies suggested that men outperform women, the recent meta-analysis of Roth, Purvis and Bobko (2012) showed that women, on average, received slightly better performance evaluations (e.g. in the form of supervisor ratings and output) than men. Furthermore, and despite the fact that performance ratings were better for women, ratings on promotion potential were found to favour men. These results are in line with earlier findings showing that women have less access to higher-level jobs through promotion or the commonly held assumption of managers that women face higher levels of work–life conflict and, as such, are restrained to lower level positions within the organization.

Ethnicity and work-related outcomes

The importance of ethnicity in research aimed at predicting work-related outcomes is widely recognized. Throughout history and across the world, specific ethnic groups have been marginalized by being denied active participation in working life. Social marginality refers to a condition of being deprived of full participation in a society's key institutions, including work, and can occur primarily because of individuals' memberships of specific social identity groups, such as women, ethnic groups, the aged and so forth (Prasad, D'Abate, & Prasad, 2007). In the past 100 years, people have become increasingly aware of this phenomenon, and the issue of discrimination has motivated researchers to understand better the possible effects of membership of an ethnic minority group on work-related outcomes.

Specifically, ethnic membership significantly predicts job performance evaluations, ratings of managers' promotion potential or career success, actual career outcomes, income and the composition of work units (Mayerhofer et al., 2007), with members of ethnic minority groups being at a disadvantage. A possible explanation for this disadvantage in work-related opportunities for ethnic minorities can be found in Byrne's (1971) similarity-attraction theory that states that people will be evaluated more positively with increasing similarity to the rater, or the more similar the rater believes people to be to himself or herself.

At this point, it can be concluded that next to age and gender, ethnicity in the workplace does matter. It is therefore important for managers in organizations to strive for a better understanding of the challenges and opportunities that are inherent to the increasing diversity of the labour market.

Lifestyle risk factors and work-related outcomes

Lifestyle risk factors are also important in the light of work-related outcomes. Lifestyle risk factors relate to unhealthy lifestyle choices that should be modified in order to prevent disability, absenteeism and turnover, and to enhance workers' employability. Research on lifestyle factors has focused predominantly on behavioural risk factors, such as tobacco use, alcohol misuse, poor diet and physical inactivity that relate negatively to positive functioning at work (operationalized as a composite measure of cognitive, emotional and physical functioning) (Peel, McClure, & Bartlett, 2005).

Since most lifestyle risk factors develop at earlier ages and their impact accumulates over time, lifestyle interventions should take a population-based, life-course perspective. To be most effective, interventions aimed at addressing smoking, alcohol misuse, inadequate exercise and poor nutrition should target all age groups in the workplace. Lifestyle risk factors are a highly delicate topic to deal with because they comprise employees' private life sphere. Yet, not only employees themselves but also management in work organizations should take responsibility for workers' well-being and employability by focusing on the prevention of lifestyle risk factors, and facilitate and stimulate healthy behaviour.

In the light of work-related outcomes, it is of utmost importance that management in organizations has a better understanding of the possible effects of lifestyle risk factors across the lifespan, and that they put increased effort into developing and implementing interventions that are in line with nationwide health policies.

Replay

- Studies suggest that women experience more unfavourable working conditions than men.
- Despite facing unfavourable working conditions, women are not more burned out than men, they experience higher levels of job satisfaction and they get more favourable performance evaluations.
- However, men are still considered more suitable for promotion because of the dominance of traditional views on gender.
- Members of minority groups are often discriminated against when it comes to performance evaluations and career opportunities.
- Lifestyle risk factors, such as tobacco use, alcohol misuse, poor diet and physical inactivity, have a negative effect on workers' health and employability.

Now that we have more insight into the effects of objective individual characteristics, let us continue with discussing the possible impact of subjective individual characteristics.

10.3 Subjective Individual Characteristics and Work-related Outcomes

In presenting an overview of the most important subjective worker characteristics, we will discuss these in the context of their degree of stability or change/malleability. Our categorization of three types of individual characteristics is based on the theoretical assumptions underlying the historical development in research evolving from the traditional trait approach to the more contemporary state or situational approach.

From traits to states: A historical overview

A trait is an individual disposition that is relatively stable over the course of a lifespan, is difficult to change and drives human behaviour (Pervin, 1993). Intelligence, talents and personality characteristics are typical examples of traits. Throughout a large part of the twentieth century, the trait approach was dominant among work psychologists. During the past decades, however, researchers have started to question the predictive validity of the trait approach because of inconsistent findings between traits, well-being and behaviour across different situations at work (Nezlek, 2007).

Criticism regarding the predictive validity of the trait approach gave rise to the so-called state or situational approach, which recognizes that some subjective individual characteristics exhibit significant variation within the same person, from one situation to another, in response to specific characteristics of the environment. Affect is a typical example of a state, in that emotions may vary from one moment to the other depending on external stimuli. For example, consider Grace. She works as a secretary in a large multinational company in London. Although she is generally an emotionally stable person, sometimes she 'loses it'. Grace may become extremely frustrated every time her old computer is stuck, but the next moment she may be extremely helpful and considerate toward a colleague who is asking for help to finalize a certain task. In other words, she is likely to exhibit affective spins (from positive to negative emotions, and vice versa) depending on the specific situations that arise at work.

As the example of Grace illustrates, the trait and the state approaches are not mutually exclusive; rather, they complement each other. As George (1991) noted, traits may have an impact on states or related behaviours, yet states are those individual characteristics that initiate the psychological processes explaining day-to-day well-being and behaviour. This is because states are in close proximity to the individual's actual experiences and his or her consequent behaviours. It is therefore important to think in terms of both the trait approach (i.e. how one employee differs from another) and the state approach (i.e. how the characteristics of the same employee may vary over short periods of time) when attempting to explain the role of individual characteristics on workers' functioning at work.

Following Luthans and colleagues (2007), we distinguish three categories of subjective personal characteristics of employees depending upon their level of malleability: trait-like characteristics, state-like characteristics and states. These three categories should be conceived along the same continuum, where trait-like characteristics are placed at the stability end, states are placed at the change/malleability end and state-like characteristics are placed in the middle of the continuum. Note that we do not focus on 'hard-core' traits like intelligence or other inheritable characteristics that are non-changeable.

Two issues are important when considering subjective individual characteristics. The first issue is that certain subjective personal characteristics may be strictly located at only one point of the continuum. For instance, conscientiousness is by definition categorized as a trait-like characteristic, while positive and negative emotions can only be categorized as states. The second issue encompasses that the very same characteristic (e.g. self-efficacy) may be defined as a trait-like characteristic (if one is interested in generalized self-efficacy), as a state-like characteristic (if one is interested in domain-specific or work-related self-efficacy) or as a state (if one is interested in momentary levels of self-efficacy with respect to the specific situation under study; see Allen & Potkay, 1981). This choice depends on the level of specificity that one is interested in. In what follows, we discuss how specific characteristics within each of the three distinguished categories relate to work-related well-being and performance.

Replay

- Individual characteristics can be distinguished based on the level of within-person malleability that they exhibit.
- Trait-like characteristics are relatively stable across domains and situations, state-like characteristics vary from one life domain to another, while states exhibit significant within-person fluctuations from one moment to another, as an immediate response to the characteristics of the environment.

Trait-like individual characteristics and work-related outcomes

The first category of subjective employee characteristics comprises the so-called 'trait-like' characteristics that are relatively stable and difficult to change. In this chapter, we focus on core self-evaluations (CSEs). CSEs represent the fundamental appraisals that individuals make about their self-worth, competence and capabilities, thus reflecting a baseline appraisal that is implicit in all other beliefs and evaluations (Judge et al., 1997). The concept of CSEs is conceptualized as a higher-order construct composed of four broad and evaluative traits (self-esteem, generalized self-efficacy, emotional stability and locus of control) that are inter-related and share similar relations with various work-related outcomes (Chang, Ferris, Johnson, Rosen, & Tan, 2012).

> **Work Psychology in Action: Nature and nurture with regard to job satisfaction**
>
> Job satisfaction is generally defined as the affective evaluation of one's job. As such, one would expect that job satisfaction is solely a function of different aspects of the job, such as satisfaction about the salary, the content of the job and the learning possibilities, and that this evaluation varies with these aspects. However, that is not always true. Research has shown that an employee's job satisfaction tends to be rather stable even when the employee changes employers or occupations (Staw, Bell, & Clausen, 1986).
>
> Moreover, there is evidence indicating that some individuals might be genetically predisposed to a certain level of job satisfaction. For example, Arvey, Bouchard, Segal and Abraham (1989) collected job satisfaction reports from monozygotic twins (i.e. twins who originate from the same fertilized ovum and are genetically identical) who were reared apart. Their findings demonstrated that genetic factors explained approximately 30% of the variance in job satisfaction scores. Subsequent studies found several dispositions to relate to job satisfaction, such as positive and negative affectivity, emotional stability and core self-evaluations (e.g. Judge, Locke, & Durham, 1997). This effect is partly due to the fact that individuals with positive dispositions hold more positive perceptions of their job attributes, that is, they are more satisfied because they are inclined to see more challenge and intrinsic worth in their jobs.
>
> Does this imply that employers do not need to provide a healthy and challenging work situation? Not at all! As the other chapters in this book indicate, a healthy and stimulating work environment is crucial for employee well-being. After all, there is still another 70% of variance in job satisfaction to be accounted for.

Self-esteem is an overall appraisal of one's self-worth (Rosenberg, 1965). *Generalized self-efficacy* comprises an estimate of one's general perception of ability to deal successfully with demanding situations in a broad array of contexts (Chen, Gully, & Eden, 2001). *Emotional stability* (being the counterpart of neuroticism) is the propensity to feel calm and secure (Eysenck, 1990). Lastly, *locus of control (LoC)* is the belief that desired effects result from one's own behaviour rather than by fate or powerful others (Rotter, 1996; see also Chapter 7).

Empirical research indicates that the concept of CSE is associated with a range of positive outcomes. A meta-analysis by Chang et al. (2012) provides valuable information on these outcomes. First, the findings suggest that CSEs have strong, positive relations with both job and life satisfaction. Moreover, CSEs relate to organizational commitment. Employees who are higher in CSEs report more affective commitment, indicating that they are more attached to their organization. In contrast, employees who are lower on CSEs report more continuous commitment, which might indicate that they are likely to feel trapped and do not perceive alternative employment outside their current organization (Johnson, Chang, & Yang, 2010). In addition, CSEs relate negatively to turnover intention. Together, these findings suggest that individuals scoring high on CSEs are happier with their jobs, more attached to the organization and less likely to leave the organization.

Research further suggests that employees with high CSEs are more motivated (Ferris et al., 2011). The meta-analysis by Chang and colleagues (2012) showed a positive relation between CSEs and goal level, indicating that individuals scoring high on CSEs tend to set goals that are more challenging. Also, CSEs relate positively to goal commitment and intrinsic motivation. Together, these findings indicate that high-CSE employees are inclined to challenge themselves by setting high-level goals, and that they are more likely to be motivated to pursue these goals since they believe that working persistently towards goal achievement will ultimately lead to the desired promotion in the organization.

Moreover, CSEs relate positively to task performance and organizational citizenship behaviours, and show negative relations with counterproductive work behaviours (Chang et al., 2012). These outcomes suggest that high-CSE workers not only fulfil their job duties by meeting job requirements and carrying out their assigned responsibilities, but also contribute to the psychosocial environment by helping co-workers, promoting the organization, and by not harming the organization and its members. CSEs also related positively to salary level, suggesting that high-CSEs is a possible predictor of career advancement.

Next, the meta-analytic findings by Chang et al. (2012) emphasized the importance of CSEs for employees' perceptions of their work situations. CSEs relate positively to perceived job characteristics as well as to perceived fairness and perceived support. Accordingly, it seems that high-CSE employees are more likely to focus on positive aspects of their work environment and are less sensitive to negative aspects of their job. This might explain why they more often report higher job satisfaction, as we mentioned previously.

Finally, CSEs relate to occupational stress. Chang et al. (2012) reported a negative association between CSEs and employees' perception of work stressors (i.e. environmental stimuli that are perceived as threatening and that require coping efforts from the side of the employees) and strains (i.e. employees' maladaptive responses to stressors). This implies that a low-CSE employee, compared to a high-CSE employee, is more likely to perceive a demanding situation at work as stressful, and is more likely to feel stressed in this situation. This may eventually relate to the occurrence of psychosomatic disorders, such as low back pain, or psychological disorders, such as a burnout.

To conclude, trait-like characteristics such as CSEs help to explain differences in employee well-being and performance. These characteristics allow understanding of why employees react differently to the same working conditions. An employee who is high in CSE is likely to be more motivated and committed than an employee low in CSE. This is important information, particularly when one is interested in explaining why, within the same work environment, one employee is more motivated than the other. Yet, trait-like characteristics are difficult to change since these comprise rather stable characteristics. Thus, a low CSE proves to be more a given than a characteristic that can be enhanced through training and development programmes. Although trait-like characteristics help to explain employees' behaviour and performance, they provide organizations (and individuals) with little opportunities for interventions and modification. These issues can be better addressed by state-like and state characteristics.

State-like individual characteristics and work-related outcomes

The second category of workers' subjective characteristics concerns state-like characteristics that are relatively malleable. As indicated in the introductory section, in this chapter we focus solely on state-like personal resources. State-like personal resources are defined as those positively oriented human strengths that are malleable and contribute to optimal functioning at work (Luthans & Youssef, 2007; see also Chapter 19). They are especially important for high performance in dynamic organizations since they increase workers' adaptation to fast-changing work environments and therefore can provide organizations with a potential source of competitive advantage (van Dam, 2013). Note that state-like personal resources are developable through organizational training and, as a result, may be positively influenced by means of organizational interventions (Luthans, Avey, Avolio, Norman, & Combs, 2006).

Various state-like personal resources have been proposed as being important for work-related outcomes. Six such state-like personal resources (self-efficacy, optimism, hope, control, resilience and learning orientation) will be defined and discussed in the next part of this chapter. These six personal resources have been chosen as they have been extensively studied and are generally recognized as crucial precursors of individuals' well-being and behaviour, both on and off the job. They all comprise factors that are more malleable than trait-like characteristics, but not as malleable as momentary states.

First, *self-efficacy* refers to individuals' perceptions of their ability to behave or perform in a certain manner in order to attain a specific set of goals (Bandura, 2001). Efficacy beliefs determine how individuals respond to specific situations in different areas of everyday life. Those who believe that they are capable of handling a situation at work successfully are more likely to show initiative, will put more effort in the situation and will sustain their behaviour in the face of failure or barriers. In addition to perceptions of one's generalized self-efficacy (that should be seen as a trait-like characteristic), individuals may exhibit different self-efficacy levels in relation to different areas of life, such as sports, health and work, or in relation to specific work tasks, such as teaching young children or repairing computers. State-like self-efficacy is a typical personal resource since it may vary from one life domain (or task) to another. For instance, an academic may show high levels of self-efficacy as concerns her research skills, but low levels of self-efficacy as concerns her teaching skills. Therefore, this academic may be trained to enhance her teaching-related self-efficacy.

Second, *optimism* represents a favourable approach of the world and relates to the expectancy that good things will happen (Scheier & Carver, 1985). Optimistic workers are inclined to attribute positive events to personal and stable causes, such as their abilities, and to attribute negative events to external and unstable causes, such as the weather. Accordingly, they will develop positive outcome expectancies and an approach motivation towards goals.

Third, *hope* has been defined as a state-like personal resource that consists of two interrelated aspects: agency and pathway (Snyder et al., 1991). Agency refers to a sense of successful determination to meeting goals; pathway refers to a sense of being able to identify and pursue the paths to meet these goals successfully. These two components are considered to work in concert. In other words, when people have hope in a certain situation, they will both 'have the will' and 'see the way' to achieve their goals.

Fourth, *control* relates to the belief that one is able to influence a certain situation (Rotter, 1966). When workers think that they can have a considerable impact on their environment, they will display more initiative and feel better after successful performance than when they think they have little control over the situation and believe that external forces largely determine what happens to them.

Fifth, *resilience* refers to the capability to 'bounce back' from negative emotional experiences associated with adversity, uncertainty and threat (Tugate & Fredrickson, 2004). In the past, resilience was considered a trait that only few people possessed. Nowadays, it is recognized as a relatively malleable, state-like characteristic that can be further developed (Masten, 2001). In the context of everyday working life, resilience is assumed to go beyond maintaining oneself and is thought to be related to workers' perceptions of adversities and setbacks as opportunities for development and growth (Luthans & Youssef, 2007).

Learning orientation, being the sixth state-like personal resource, refers to a desire to develop competence through obtaining new skills and mastering new situations and tasks, and the tendency to view tasks and situations as valuable learning experiences and development opportunities (Dweck, 1986). Employees' learning orientations are central to continuous career development, and contribute to initiatives for beneficial change and adaptation to the ever-changing demands at work (Fugate, Kinicki, & Ashforth, 2004). A high learning orientation predisposes workers to view change as a challenge instead of as a threat.

It is noteworthy that Luthans (2002; Luthans & Youssef, 2007) emphasized the relevance of four of these state-like personal resources, self-efficacy, hope, optimism and resilience, and labelled these psychological capital or PsyCap (see also Chapter 19). As Luthans and his colleagues argued, PsyCap denotes a higher-level core construct that represents the communalities among these resources. Research using these PsyCap resources, either as separate predictors or as a combined predictor, indeed showed positive relations to organizational outcomes such as performance, job satisfaction, commitment and work engagement (Luthans, Avolio, Avey, & Norman, 2007; Sweetman & Luthans, 2010).

To conclude, state-like personal resources have three common characteristics: agency, positive outcomes and malleability (van Dam, 2013). First, state-like personal resources help individuals to encounter their environment positively, take initiative and engage in self-regulation (i.e. individual agency; Bandura, 2001), that is, they contribute to both the formation of motivational forces and to the transformation of these forces into behaviour and performance, for instance through goal setting, planning, effort expenditure and perseverance (Gollwitzer, 1996).

Second, state-like personal resources relate to positive outcomes. Extant evidence indicates that individuals who have developed their personal resources report higher well-being, are better capable of handling demanding situations at work and perform better (Luthans et al., 2006). The third and most important characteristic of state-like personal resources that helps to distinguish them from trait-like personal resources is that they are malleable. Specifically, these resources are dynamic constructs that change over time as new information and experience are acquired (cf. Gist & Mitchell, 1992), while empirical evidence indicates that at least to some degree they are subject to development. For instance, Luthans et al. (2006) applied and tested a micro-intervention to develop PsyCap with encouraging outcomes.

> ### Work Psychology in Action: A micro-intervention as a means to increase self-efficacy
>
> How can state-like personal resources, such as self-efficacy and hope, be developed? Albert Bandura (2001), one of the main researchers of self-efficacy, distinguishes four categories of experiences that contribute to the development of individuals' self-efficacy: (i) direct personal experiences with (un)successful behaviour (enactive mastery), (ii) observing others behaving (un)successfully (vicarious experiences), (iii) feedback from others about (un)successful performance (social persuasion) and (iv) physiological and/or psychological arousal (such as energy or anxiety) that makes one feel (in)competent. Based on these theoretical notions, Luthans and colleagues (2006) developed a micro-intervention that addressed several personal resources, including self-efficacy. The micro-intervention consisted of a group session with a facilitator that lasted about one to three hours, depending on the number of participants and exercises that were required. Participants first had to identify a personally valuable goal that they would focus on during the session. Next, they had to specify a concrete end-point that would indicate success, and describe the ways they would use in proactively approaching this end-point. They were also stimulated to describe sub-goals that could be obtained on the way to the end-point. In order to develop participants' self-efficacy, the facilitator allowed participants to experience and model successful behaviour that aimed at reaching these personal goals and sub-goals. The self-efficacy building process was supported by positive feedback from the facilitator and the other participants, and by the positive emotions that were elicited during the exercise. This micro-intervention has been developed and tested among management students, and has been successfully applied to a sample of managers.

It is clear from the above that state-like personal resources, either alone or in combination, may have broad and positive implications for workers' career developments and for organizations. Extant evidence indicates that positive states of mind can lead to a healthy, happy and productive (working) life.

States and work-related outcomes

States concern those individual characteristics that show significant levels of variation within the same person, and may change from one day or moment to another in response to environment changes (Xanthopoulou, Bakker, & Ilies, 2012). This definition emphasizes the dynamic nature of states, which is attributed to their high sensitivity to external stimuli, and through which they exhibit more frequent within-person fluctuations in comparison to state-like characteristics. For instance, consider Henry, a medical doctor. Henry may be happy and proud of himself when interacting with a patient who is recovering fast, but the next moment he may be angry with a patient who refuses to comply with the proposed therapy. In the first work situation, Henry's optimism with regard to the patient's recovery is likely to be enhanced, while in the second situation his optimism is likely to be reduced. The way Henry feels about himself and his capabilities in a certain situation at work may explain whether he feels stressed or motivated, and how well he performs at a specific time.

Recently, researchers have suggested that in order to understand fully the psychological processes that explain employee well-being and performance, it is important to adopt a micro-perspective. Such a perspective allows work-related outcomes to be studied the moment they occur or very close to their occurrence (Beal, Weiss, Barros, & MacDermid, 2005; see also Chapter 2). Employee trait-like or state-like characteristics may explain momentary well-being and performance up to a point, but states are the strongest determinants of how workers will feel and behave at work at each particular moment in time. This is because states on the one hand and attitudes and behaviours on the other hand evolve simultaneously.

Beal and colleagues (2005) proposed such a micro-perspective for studying performance. Accordingly, since performance shows significant within-person fluctuations (i.e. even highly performing workers do not perform equally well every day or moment at work), researchers should put more emphasis on understanding specific performance episodes. Performance episodes are performance units within the daily behaviours at work that 'are naturally segmented, relatively short and thematically organized around work-related goals' (Beal et al., 2005, p. 1055). As such, a worker's ability to perform effectively in each performance episode is influenced by both relatively stable (i.e. trait-like) characteristics and relatively malleable (i.e. state-like) and transient (i.e. state) factors. In this context, the work day of a lawyer could be divided into three performance episodes: (i) meet up with a client, (ii) defend a case at court and (iii) finalise a report. How well this lawyer will perform at court does not only depend on his emotional stability (trait-like characteristic), but also on his case-related self-efficacy (state-like characteristic), as well as on his optimism during the hearing (state).

Work Psychology in Action: Testing teachers' performance across various episodes during the day

How can one apply the micro-perspective proposed by Beal and colleagues (2005) in order to test within-teacher variations in performance across different episodes? The daily performance of primary school teachers could be divided into at least three performance episodes: (i) teaching, (ii) marking papers and (iii) preparing for the next day's class. Beal and colleagues suggested that a teacher may reach different performance levels in each of these three daily episodes. In other words, performance may fluctuate from one episode to the other because of the conditions of the episode and the states of the teacher.

In order to capture empirically and to explain such within-teacher variations in performance, it is important to measure corresponding within-person variations in a teacher's states. To do so, it is necessary to turn from more traditional between-person empirical designs (i.e. cross-sectional studies or longitudinal studies over long periods of time) to study designs that allow dynamic changes to be captured. Diaries and experience sampling methods allow data collection data at the daily level or several times (i.e. episodes) during a day (Ohly, Sonnentag, Niessen, & Zapf, 2010).

It could be hypothesized that the quality of each episode during a teacher's work day is determined by trait-like characteristics (i.e. the teacher's conscientiousness), by state-like characteristics (i.e. the teacher's self-efficacy with regard to teaching), but also by specific individual states (i.e. enjoyment, concentration). After all, how well the teacher will manage to transmit knowledge to students or to prepare for the next day's class depends on his or her level of concentration during each episode or on how much (s)he enjoys each task (Beal et al., 2005).

To test these hypotheses, one could conduct a diary study where one follows a number of teachers for one working week (Monday–Friday). On Monday morning, teachers will be asked to fill out a questionnaire in which their levels of conscientiousness (i.e. trait-like characteristic) and their levels of self-efficacy with regard to their work (i.e. state-like characteristic) will be assessed. Next, these teachers will be asked to fill out a diary (short) questionnaire for five consecutive work days, three times a day, right after the end of each performance episode: as soon as they finish teaching, as soon as they finish marking and as soon as they finish their preparation for the next day. After each episode, teachers will rate: (i) how interesting the task was during the episode, (ii) how much they enjoyed work during this episode, (iii) how concentrated they were and (v) how well they performed during the episode. In this way, it is possible to examine the degree to which variations in the characteristics of the task (i.e. level of interest) relate to the states of the teacher (i.e. enjoyment, concentration) and, consequently, to changes in performance levels across episodes, over and above the teacher's conscientiousness and work-related self-efficacy.

The notion of states is mainly used when referring to affect or emotions. Although affect is defined as an experiential state that may vary within the same person, depending on the situation that the person finds himself or herself in, researchers often have treated affect as a trait, focusing on positive or negative affectivity. Studies that examined affect as a momentary state appeared quite successful in explaining employee well-being and performance. For instance, a diary study among healthcare workers showed that workers who regulated their emotions (i.e. hiding negative emotions or faking positive emotions) were experiencing increased momentary stress and decreased momentary job satisfaction (Bono, Jackson Foldes, Vinson, & Muros, 2007).

It has been suggested that cognitive appraisals may also vary within the same person, from one situation to another. For instance, in their diary study among engineers, Ohly and Fritz (2010) found within-person variation in workers' challenge appraisals. Furthermore, their results showed a positive relation between challenge appraisals on the one hand, and creativity and proactive behaviour on the other.

As explained earlier, a particular individual characteristic may be viewed as a trait-like characteristic, a state-like characteristic or as a state, depending on the level of specificity that one is interested in. Personal resources may be placed at all levels of malleability. With regard to the state facet of personal resources, recent daily diary studies have demonstrated that participants showed significant within-person fluctuations, from one day to another, which, in turn, explained daily worker well-being and performance. For instance, Xanthopoulou, Bakker, Heuven, Demerouti and Schaufeli (2008) conducted a diary study among flight attendants during consecutive flights to three intercontinental destinations. Results showed that self-efficacy beliefs related to the flight varied substantially within the same flight attendant from one flight segment to another. Furthermore, in flights during which attendants were more self-efficacious than usual, they were more engaged in their task and as a result they performed better. In another study, Xanthopoulou, Bakker, Demerouti and Schaufeli (2009) reported daily within-employee fluctuations in job resources (i.e. autonomy, coaching and team climate). Moreover, they found that on days that employees were experiencing more job resources than usual, they reported higher levels of (state) personal resources and, consequently, work engagement. In addition, this study showed that on days that employees were more engaged than usual, the company's financial returns were higher.

Finally, Seo and Ilies (2009) used an internet-based stock investment simulation, where participants engaged in a series of stock trading activities, and showed that in activities wherein self-efficacy was higher than usual, performance was also better. The review of these studies emphasizes the importance of the state approach and implies that momentary beliefs about how adequate workers are at a specific moment at work are important for understanding their well-being, motivation and performance at a specific moment in time.

To conclude, the significance of the study of states, over and above the study of trait-like and state-like characteristics, lies in the fact that states allow dynamic changes in employee psychological conditions and behaviours to be explained. In other words, employee subjective characteristics that are operationalized and conceptualized as states explain what happens when there are variations of these characteristics from a person's baseline. On days, in episodes or in moments when employees feel more efficacious than usual (i.e. above their baseline), they are more likely to perform better. On days, in episodes or in moments when they feel less self-efficacious than usual (i.e. below their baseline), they are less likely to meet high performance standards.

Replay

- Trait-like characteristics allow between-employee differences in work-related well-being and performance to be explained. Core self-evaluations (comprising self-esteem, generalized self-efficacy, emotional stability and locus of control) represent the fundamental appraisals employees make about their self-worth, competence and capabilities, and reflect a baseline appraisal that is implicit in all other beliefs and evaluations employees make.
- State-like characteristics and states allow within-employee differences across different contexts and across different moments, episodes and days, respectively, to be explained.
- Six state-like personal resources were analysed in this chapter: self-efficacy, optimism, hope, control, resilience and learning orientation. Luthans (2002; Luthans, Avolio, Avey, & Norman, 2007) emphasized four of these resources (i.e. self-efficacy, hope, optimism and resilience) and labelled them as psychological capital (PsyCap). PsyCap is a higher-level construct that represents what these four resources have in common.
- States add to the study of trait-like and state-like characteristics because they help to explain dynamic changes in work-related experiences.

10.4 Conclusions

In this chapter we proposed a distinction between objective and subjective characteristics of employees that are equally significant in explaining work-related outcomes, but that are more or less malleable. More specifically, we argued that trait and state approaches to subjective individual characteristics should not be viewed as separate, but rather as complementary approaches in studying the relationship between employees' key individual characteristics and work-related outcomes.

Researchers should therefore first address the conceptualization and operationalization of one's research topic and included concepts. Do they intend to measure objective (e.g. gender) versus subjective employee characteristics? Are they subjective characteristics of a trait-like nature (e.g. emotional stability) or do they address more malleable worker characteristics, that is, state-like ones (e.g. optimism), or even highly dynamic states that may fluctuate from day to day, episode to episode or moment to moment (e.g. self-efficacy beliefs)? To make it even more complex, yet more valuable, given the fact that a particular individual characteristic may be viewed as a trait-like characteristic, a state-like characteristic or as a state, depending on the level of specificity that one is interested in, one may want to include all three types of measures into the study.

The available empirical evidence indeed suggests that the simultaneous examination of both objective worker characteristics and all three categories of subjective worker characteristics (i.e. trait-like, state-like and states) provides a promising framework for a better understanding of well-being and job performance. In this chapter, we have argued that different conceptualizations of age, gender, ethnicity and lifestyle risk factors all do matter in the light of work-related outcomes, therefore management in working organizations should pay serious attention to these while considering the development and implementation of interventions that are aimed to bring about or prevent certain work-related outcomes.

As regards the subjective characteristics, Judge, Fluegge Woolf and Hurst (2009) investigated the role of both trait-like characteristics (extraversion) and states (emotional regulation) on worker affect and well-being (i.e. emotional exhaustion and job satisfaction). The results of their study showed that worker well-being was better explained when the interaction effects of both traits and states were considered. Namely, it was found that emotional regulation had fewer negative effects on well-being for extraverts compared to introverts.

In addition, in this chapter we explained that the same subjective individual characteristic may be defined and measured at different levels of specificity, and that each level of the same variable may relate in a different way to the criterion of interest. For instance, Yeo and Neal (2006) examined both generalized self-efficacy (i.e. trait-like) and task-specific self-efficacy (i.e. state-like) in relation to performance on an air-traffic control task. Their outcomes showed that task-specific self-efficacy related negatively to task performance at the within-person level, while generalized self-efficacy related positively to task performance at the between-person level. Such findings are interesting because they suggest that psychological processes may not be parallel across different (between- and within-person) levels of analysis, thus calling for theory refinement (Xanthopoulou et al., 2012).

To conclude, the present review of studies on subjective worker characteristics suggests that the best framework for studying their role in the light of work and career experiences and behaviours is one that takes into account both between-person differences (i.e. trait-like characteristics) and within-person and situation-dependent fluctuations (i.e. state-like characteristics and states). The outline that has been given in this chapter indicates that state-like characteristics and states, next to traits, seem to be critical in explaining worker well-being and work-related outcomes. Therefore, it is important for organizations to monitor states on a short-term basis in order to find out on which days/episodes/moments and under which circumstances employees feel and function better at work. Additionally, given that personal resources vary significantly within the same person from one day to the other, managers could try to inspire and stimulate employees so that they feel highly competent and self-efficacious on a daily basis. This can be accomplished by sustaining resourceful work environments where employees have, or can create, the means they need to deal with environmental challenges and threats on a daily basis. Obviously, it is important to take age and physical and psychological condition into account as well. Age-related human resources measures that are fine-tuned in close cooperation between workers and their direct supervisor might enhance workers' employability and prevent premature leave from the profession or from the labour market as a whole.

Discussion Points

1. Which age conceptualisations are important to predict differences between younger and older workers? Provide reasons for your answer.
2. Self-efficacy may be viewed as a trait-like characteristic, as a state-like characteristic or as a state. How is this possible? Provide one example from everyday working life for each of these three views.
3. Summarize the main advantages of adopting a micro-perspective approach in explaining sick leave.
4. What counts most in explaining work-related outcomes, objective or subjective worker characteristics? Think of a concrete example when formulating your answer, for instance by focusing on predicting premature leave of employees from the labour market (before their official retirement age).

Learning by Doing

Roger (46 years) is the CEO of a large UK-based financial company. He faces the challenge of having many new vacancies and few new young workers to hire. Moreover, he has a large group of older workers who will retire soon. One of these workers is the extraverted Julia. Julia is aged 55 and has been working for the company for the past ten years in an administrative job. She is eager to take on a new work-related challenge and decides to apply for one of the vacancies, a PR function. Considering her extraverted nature and the fact that she loves working with other people, she considers herself fit to take on the job. However, she wonders whether she will be hired as an older worker in this company with many relatively younger colleagues.

Another challenge that Roger is facing is that employees who generally exhibit high levels of performance are not performing equally well every day. This is particularly the case with employees in the sales department. These employees were selected on the basis of their high levels of core self-evaluations. In addition, the employees themselves are quite confident with regard to their sales performance, since they have been very successful during the previous year. However, lately there have been some complaints from clients who said that there were times that employees were impolite and unfriendly towards them. Roger has asked you, a talented work psychologist from the HR department, to figure out why this is the case. Try to answer the following questions:

1. Should Roger hire the older, extraverted and highly motivated Julia, with relatively little job experience for the PR function, or would he be better to choose another worker?

2. Besides the aforementioned relevant characteristics, the new job requires a high amount of learning orientation. To what extent do you think one can train Julia in order to increase her learning orientation or change the task to induce a certain learning orientation?
3. Ask some family members and friends (who know very little about work psychology) whether they would hire Julia. Ask them why they would or would not like to do so. What have you learned about age-related stereotyping after this exercise?
4. Why do employees who are highly conscientious and self-efficacious vary in their performance over time? What could managers do in order to deal with this and to guarantee high-quality output at the workplace?
5. How do the individual characteristics that are dealt with in this case influence sustainable employment in a financial company?
6. Imagine that you are the CEO of a large company. What factors would you have to consider in order to make sure that workers are happy, healthy and employable, while at the same time striving to reach the organizational objectives?

Further Reading

Chen, G., Gully, S. M., Whiteman, J. A., & Kilcullen, R. N. (2000). Examination of relationships among trait-like individual differences, state-like individual differences, and learning performance. *Journal of Applied Psychology, 85*, 835–847.

Schalk, R., van Veldhoven, M., de Lange, A. H., de Witte, H., Kraus, K., Roßnagel, C., Tordera, N., van der Heijden, B. I. J. M., Zappalà, S. et al. (2010). Moving European research on work and ageing forward: Overview and agenda. *European Journal of Work and Organizational Psychology, 19*, 76–101.

van der Heijden, B. I. J. M., & de Lange, A. H. (2011). Employability across the lifespan: Towards new pathways for age research. In R. Ennals, & R. Salomon (Eds.), *Older workers in a sustainable society* (pp. 19–33). Brussels: Peter Lang.

References

Allen, B. P., & Potkay, C. R. (1981). On the arbitrary distinction between states and traits. *Journal of Personality and Social Psychology, 41*, 916–928.

Arking, R. (1998). *Biology of aging: Observations and principles* (2nd ed.). Sunderland, MA: Sinauer Associates Inc.

Arvey, R. D., Bouchard, T. J., Segal, N. L., & Abraham, L. M. (1989). Job satisfaction: environmental and genetic components. *Journal of Applied Psychology, 74*, 187–192.

Bakker, A. B., Demerouti, E., & Dollard, M. F. (2008). How job demands affect partners' experience of exhaustion: Integrating work–family conflict and crossover theory. *Journal of Applied Psychology, 93*, 901–911.

Baltes, B. B., & Finkelstein, L. M. (2011). Contemporary empirical advancements in the study of aging in the workplace. *Journal of Organizational Behavior, 32*, 151–154.

Bandura, A. (2001). Social cognitive theory: An agentic perspective. *Annual Review of Psychology, 52*, 1–26.

Beal, D. J., Weiss, H. M., Barros, E., & MacDermid, S. M. (2005). An episodic process model of affective influences on performance. *Journal of Applied Psychology, 90*, 1054–1068.

Blau, F. D., & Kahn, L. M. (2007). The gender pay gap: Have women gone as far as they can? *Academy of Management Perspectives, 21*, 7–23.

Boerlijst, J. G., van der Heijden, B. I. J. M., & van Assen, A. (1993). Veertigplussers in de onderneming [*Over-forties in the organization*]. Assen: van Gorcum/Stichting Management Studies.

Bono, J. E., Jackson Foldes, H., Vinson, G., & Muros, J. P. (2007). Workplace emotions: The role of supervisor and leadership. *Journal of Applied Psychology, 92*, 1357–1367.

Byrne, D. (1971). *The attraction paradigm*. New York: Academic Press.

Chang, C. H., Ferris, D. L., Johnson, R. E., Rosen, C. C., & Tan, J. A. (2012). Core self-evaluations: A review and evaluation of the literature. *Journal of Management, 38*, 81–128.

Chen, G., Gully, S. M., & Eden, D. (2001). Validation of a new generalized self-efficacy scale. *Organizational Research Methods, 4*, 62–83.

Clark, A. E. (1997). Job satisfaction and gender: Why are women so happy at work? *Labour Economics, 4*, 341–372.

de Lange, A. H., Taris, T. W., Jansen, P. G. W., Smulders, P., Houtman, I. L. D., & Kompier, M. A. J. (2006). Age as a factor in the relation between work and mental health: Results from the longitudinal TAS survey. *Occupational Health Psychology: European Perspectives on Research, Education and Practice, 1*, 21–45.

Dweck, C. S. (1986). Motivational processes affecting learning. *American Psychologist, 41*, 1040–1048.

Eysenck, M. W. (1990). *Happiness: Facts and myths*. London: Lawrence Erlbaum Associates.

Ferris, D. L., Rosen, C. R., Johnson, R. E., Brown, D. J., Risavy, S. D., & Heller, D. (2011). Approach or avoidance (or both?): Integrating core self-evaluations within an approach/avoidance framework. *Personnel Psychology, 64*, 137–161.

Fugate, M., Kinicki, A. J., & Ashforth, B. E. (2004). Employability: A psycho-social construct, its dimensions, and applications. *Journal of Vocational Behavior, 65*, 14–38.

George, J. M. (1991). State or trait: Effects of positive mood on prosocial behaviors at work. *Journal of Applied Psychology, 76*, 299–307.

Gist, M. E., & Mitchell, T. R. (1992). Self-Efficacy: A theoretical analysis of its determinants and malleability. *Academy of Management Review, 17*, 183–211.

Gollwitzer, P. M. (1996). The volitional benefits of planning. In P. M. Gollwitzer, & J. A. Bargh (Eds.), *The psychology of action: Linking cognition and motivation to behavior* (pp. 287–312). New York: Guildford.

Gutek, B. A., Searle, S., & Klepa, L. (1991). Rational versus gender role explanations for work–family conflict. *Journal of Applied Psychology, 76*, 560–568.

Johnson, R. E., Chang, C. H., & Yang, L. (2010). Commitment and motivation at work: The relevance of employee identity and regulatory focus. *Academy of Management Review, 35*, 226–245.

Judge, T. A., & Bono, J. E. (2001). Relationships of core self-evaluations traits – self-esteem, generalized self-efficacy, locus of control, and emotional stability – with job satisfaction and job performance: A meta-analysis. *Journal of Applied Psychology, 86*, 80–92.

Judge, T. A., Fluegge Woolf, E., & Hurst, C. (2009). Is emotional labor more difficult for some that for others? A multilevel, experience-sampling study. *Personnel Psychology, 62*, 57–88.

Judge, T. A., Locke, E. A., & Durham, C. C. (1997). The dispositional causes of job satisfaction: A core evaluations approach. *Research in Organizational Behavior, 19*, 151–188.

Kanfer, R., & Ackerman, P. L. (2004). Aging, adult development, and work motivation. *Academy of Management Review, 29*, 440–458.

Kaufman, H. G. (1974). *Obsolescence and professional career development*. New York: Amacom.

Lawrence, B. S. (1996). Organizational age norms: Why is it so hard to know when you see one? *Gerontologist, 36*, 209–220.

Luthans, F. (2002). The need for and meaning of positive organizational behavior. *Journal of Organizational Behavior, 23*, 695–706.

Luthans, F., Avey, J. B., Avolio, B. J., Norman, S. M., & Combs, G. M. (2006). Psychological capital development: Toward a micro intervention. *Journal of Organizational Behavior, 27*, 387–393.

Luthans, F., Avolio, B. J., Avey, J. B., & Norman, S. M. (2007). Positive psychological capital: Measurement and relationship with performance and satisfaction. *Personnel Psychology, 60*, 541–572.

Luthans, F., & Youssef, C. M. (2007). Emerging positive organizational behavior. *Journal of Management, 33*, 321–349.

Masten, A. S. (2001). Ordinary magic: Resiliency processes in development. *American Psychologist, 56*, 227–239.

Mayerhofer, W., Meyer, M. & Steyrer, J. (2007). Contextual issues in the study of careers. In H. Gunz, & M. Peiperl (Eds.), *Handbook of career studies* (pp. 215–240). Los Angeles: Sage Publications.

Nezlek, J. (2007). A multilevel framework for understanding relationships among traits, states, situations and behaviours. *European Journal of Personality*, *21*, 789–810.

Ng, T. W. H., & Feldman, D. C. (2010). The relationships of age with job attitudes: A meta-analysis. *Personnel Psychology*, *63*, 677–718.

Ohlott, P. J., Ruderman, M. N., & McCauley, C. D. (1994). Gender differences in managers' developmental job experiences. *Academy of Management Journal*, *37*, 46–67.

Ohly, S., & Fritz, C. (2010). Work characteristics, challenge appraisal, creativity, and proactive behaviour: A multi-level study. *Journal of Organizational Behavior*, *31*, 543–565.

Ohly, S., Sonnentag, S., Niessen, C., & Zapf, D. (2010). Diary studies in organizational research: An introduction and some practical recommendations. *Journal of Personnel Psychology*, *9*, 79–93.

Peel, N. M., McClure, R. J., & Bartlett, H. P. (2005). Behavioral determinants of healthy aging. *American Journal of Preventive Medicine*, *28*, 298–304.

Pervin, L. (1993). *Personality theory and research* (6th ed.) New York: John Wiley & Sons.

Posthuma, R. A., & Campion, M. A. (2009). Age stereotypes in the workplace: Common stereotypes, moderators, and future research directions. *Journal of Management*, *35*, 158–188.

Prasad, P., D'Abate, C., & Prasad, A. (2007). Organizational challenges at the periphery. In H. Gunz, & M. Peiperl (Eds.), *Handbook of career studies* (pp. 169–187). Los Angeles: Sage Publications.

Purvaona, R. K., & Muros, J. P. (2010). Gender differences in burnout: A meta-analysis. *Journal of Vocational Behavior*, *77*, 168–185.

Rosenberg, M. (1965). *Society and the adolescent self-image*. Princeton: Princeton University Press.

Roth, P. L., Purvis, K. L., & Bobko, P. (2012). A meta-analysis of gender group differences for measures of job performance in field studies. *Journal of Management*, *38*, 719–739.

Rotter, J. B. (1966). Generalized expectancies for internal versus external control of reinforcement. *Psychological Monographs: General & Applied*, *80*, 1–28.

Scheier, M. F., & Carver, C. S. (1985). Optimism, coping and health: Assessment and implications of generalized outcome expectancies. *Health Psychology*, *4*, 219–247.

Seo, M., & Ilies, R. (2009). The role of self-efficacy, goal, and affect in dynamic motivational self-regulation. *Organizational Behavior and Human Decision Processes*, *109*, 120–133.

Snyder, C. R., Harris, C., Anderson, J. R., Holleran, S. A., Irving, L. M., Sigmon, S. T. et al. (1991). The will and the ways: Development and validation of an individual-differences measure of hope. *Journal of Personality and Social Psychology*, *60*, 570–585.

Staw, B. M., Bell, N. E., & Clausen, J. A. (1986). The dispositional approach to job attitudes: A lifetime longitudinal test. *Administrative Science Quarterly*, *31*, 56–77.

Stein, D., & Rocco, T. S. (2001). The older worker: Myths and realities. *Eric Clearinghouse on Adult, Career, and Vocational Education*, *18*. Columbus: ERIC Publications.

Sterns, H. L., & Doverspike, D. (1989). Aging and the retraining and learning process in organizations. In I. Goldstein, & R. Katzel (Eds.). *Training and development in work organizations* (pp. 229–332). San Francisco: Jossey-Bass.

Sweetman, D., & Luthans, F. (2010). The power of positive psychology: Psychological capital and work engagement. In A. B. Bakker, & M.P. Leiter (Eds.), *Work engagement: A handbook of essential theory and research* (pp. 54–68). New York: Psychology Press.

Tugate, M. M., & Fredrickson, B. L. (2004). Resilient individuals use positive emotions to bounce back from negative emotional experiences. *Journal of Personality and Social Psychology*, *86*, 320–333.

van Dam, K. (2013). Employee adaptability to change at work: A multidimensional, resource-based framework. In S. Oreg, A. Michel, & R. T. By (Eds.), *The psychology of organizational change: Viewing change from the employee's perspective* (pp. 123–142). Cambridge: Cambridge University Press.

van der Heijden, B. I. J. M., de Lange, A. H., Demerouti, E., & van der Heijde, C. M. (2009). Age effects on the employability-career success relationship. *Journal of Vocational Behavior*, *74*, 156–164.

van der Heijden, B. I. J. M., Schalk, R., & van Veldhoven, M. J. P. M. (2008). Ageing and careers:

European research on long-term career development and early retirement. *The Career Development International, 13*, 85–94.

Xanthopoulou, D., Bakker, A. B., Demerouti, E., & Schaufeli, W. B. (2009). Work engagement and financial returns: A diary study on the role of job and personal resources. *Journal of Occupational and Organizational Psychology, 82*, 183–200.

Xanthopoulou, D., Bakker, A. B., Heuven, E., Demerouti, E., & Schaufeli, W. B. (2008). Working in the sky: A diary study on work engagement among flight attendants. *Journal of Occupational Health Psychology, 13*, 345–356.

Xanthopoulou, D., Bakker, A. B., & Ilies, R. (2012). Everyday working life: Explaining within-person fluctuations in employee well-being. *Human Relations, 65*, 1051–1069.

Yeo, G. B., & Neal, A. (2006). An examination of the dynamic relationship between self-efficacy and performance across levels of analysis and levels of specificity. *Journal of Applied Psychology, 91*, 1088–1101.

11
Work–Family Interaction

ULLA KINNUNEN, JOHANNA RANTANEN,
SAIJA MAUNO AND MARIA C. W. PEETERS

> **Chapter Objectives**
>
> After studying this chapter, you should be able to:
>
> - define and compare the basic constructs used in the area of work–family interaction, and understand the context in which they have been developed;
> - explain the most common theories applied in work–family interaction research and know their limitations;
> - recognize the potential antecedents and outcomes of work–family conflict and work–family enrichment in the domains of both work and family;
> - understand the roles of individual coping strategies and work–family policies and culture in promoting work–family balance in individuals' lives;
> - evaluate the practical value of existing research from the perspectives of employees, employers and organizations.

The issue of how to balance the demands of work and family life receives much attention in today's Western society for a number of reasons. Important examples of such reasons are the increasing participation of women in the workforce, the greater numbers of working single parents and dual-earner families, and increased eldercare responsibilities due to increasing life expectancies.

An Introduction to Contemporary Work Psychology, First Edition.
Edited by Maria C. W. Peeters, Jan de Jonge and Toon W. Taris.
© 2014 John Wiley & Sons, Ltd. Published 2014 by John Wiley & Sons, Ltd.

Working life itself has also witnessed rapid changes during the past two decades. As a result of globalization, the competition between companies has become increasingly heavy. This has put great pressure on organizations and employees to be more flexible and more responsive to changes in working life. Moreover, technological advances have enabled working at almost any time and in any place, therefore the boundaries between work and non-work (such as family, leisure and sleep) are nowadays often blurred. Not being able to separate work from other important parts of life and being accessible all the time reduces the time for rest and recovery (see also Chapter 8). All these changes challenge a healthy balance between work and family.

This chapter aims to explain the issue of the interaction between work and family in individuals' lives, and to understand the context in which research on the links between work and family has developed. Broadly defined, work–family interaction can be seen as comprising the *combined* effects that work and family characteristics *together* exert on work, family and individual level outcomes such as well-being, health or performance (Voydanoff, 2002). We begin this chapter with a theoretical discussion concerning the constructs and theories of work–family interaction, and continue with an empirical review of the antecedents and outcomes related to work–family interaction. Finally, we discuss what can be done to promote a healthy work–family balance from the viewpoint of both individual employees and employers as well as entire organizations.

11.1 Basic Concepts of Work–Family Interaction

Work–family interaction has been studied since the 1930s. The earliest studies were mostly conducted in agrarian environments where work and family were tightly intertwined. Along with the industrial revolution and the growing market economy a counter movement emerged around the 1950s. At that time, there was predominantly a rigid differentiation between work and family roles, as men adopted the breadwinner role outside home and women were homemakers. In the 1970s, when women increasingly entered the workforce, it was claimed that work and family roles interact with each other in the lives of women, but in the lives of men. Thus, at that time it was common to see work–family interaction as a typical women's issue. Nowadays there is to a large extent consensus that work and family life interact in both genders. However, as can be seen in the use of work family-friendly arrangements (e.g. parental leave, flexible working times), even today women seem to be more active than men in combining work and family roles.

Before elaborating on the issue of work–family interaction it is first important to understand what exactly constitutes work and what constitutes family. In the work–family literature, *work* traditionally refers to paid employment as well as self-employment and entrepreneurship, but volunteer work is not included as it may have a different meaning for people. For example, volunteer work may be a very central part of life for a part-time worker, whereas for a full-time worker it may be a way of recovering from one's paid work. *Family* most typically refers to a situation living with a partner and/or children, but it may also include ageing parents or good friends with whom one is living. However, based on the fact that the term 'family' excludes singles, broader terms such as non-work, home and private life have also been suggested. Although these are important neighbour concepts for family, in this chapter the term 'work–family interaction' is used because it is the term most frequently used by scholars in the field.

Basically, work–family interaction can best be described through three aspects: degree, direction and valence.

Degree
The degree of work–family interaction refers to the degree of segmentation versus integration of the work and family domains. In *segmentation*, the work and family domains are seen as relatively non-influential towards each other due to strict physical, temporal, functional and psychological boundaries between them (Edwards & Rothbard, 2000; Frone, 2003). In contrast, in *integration*, work and family domains are tightly intertwined in terms of time, place, people, behaviour, thoughts and emotions, and there is no clear distinction between work and family domains (Frone, 2003). For example, such work arrangements in which one commutes physically from home to work and in which doing job-related tasks at home is rare refer to a high degree of segmentation. Conversely, work arrangements in which completing job-related duties at home is rather a rule than an exception refer to a high degree of integration.

Direction
The direction of the work–family interaction refers to a reciprocal relation between work and family domains: work can affect family life (work-to-family direction) and family can affect working life (family-to-work direction).

Valence
The valence of the work–family interaction refers to the fact that the encounter between work and family can be either negative or positive. The combination of direction and valence implies that there are four kinds of interaction between work and family: (i) negative work-to-family interaction, (ii) negative family-to-work interaction, (iii) positive work-to-family interaction and (iv) positive family-to-work interaction.

Negative work–family interaction

The roots of the concept of negative work–family interaction, which has been widely studied since the 1980s, lie in the role stress theory and in the scarcity approach to multiple roles. *The role stress theory* postulates that if a given set of social roles impose conflicting role expectations and pressures towards a focal person, it can create psychological conflict and role overload (Kahn, Wolfe, Quinn, Snoek, & Rosenthal, 1964). According to the *scarcity approach*, time, energy and commitment are finite and scant individual resources which can easily drain, leading to role strain (Marks, 1977). Based on these ideas many concepts of negative work–family interaction have been presented, such as negative work–family *spillover*, work–family *interference* and work–family *conflict*. Of these, work–family conflict is most widely used, and therefore it is also used in this chapter. It is defined as:

> A form of inter-role conflict in which the role pressures from the work and family domains are mutually incompatible in some respect. That is, participation in the work (family) role is made more difficult by virtue of participation in the family (work) role. (Greenhaus & Beutell, 1985, p. 77)

The mechanisms through which work–family conflict occurs in both directions (that is, from work-to-family as well as from family-to-work) are threefold (Greenhaus & Beutell, 1985). Overlapping schedules and time demands between work and family roles may make it difficult to be present within both roles as expected. This phenomenon is known as *time-based* work–family conflict. Also, work- and family-related stressors and concerns may produce psycho-emotional strain and/or physical fatigue, due to which the demands of the other life domain are difficult to fulfil. This situation is called *strain-based* work–family conflict. In turn, *behaviour-based* work–family conflict refers to different behavioural expectations within work (e.g. being formal and strict) and family (e.g. being loving and tender), and the inability to adjust one's behaviour according to these expectations within each life domain.

Positive work–family interaction

The roots of the concept of positive work–family interaction, which has received increasing attention after the 1990s, lie in the role accumulation theory (Sieber, 1974) and expansion approach (Marks, 1977), according to which having multiple roles is not harmful, but rather beneficial for individuals. Barnett and Hyde (2001) have elaborated this notion as an *expansionist theory of multiple roles* with four principles of work–family interaction. First, having multiple roles is generally beneficial for both men and women, as it has been shown that adding worker roles for women and family roles for men produces better mental, physical and relationship health. Second, Barnett and Hyde (2001) state that the processes which foster positive work–family interaction are numerous (also Sieber, 1974). For example, success or satisfaction in one role buffers stress or failure in another role and the added income of dual-earner couples reduces the financial strain of families. In addition, received social support, opportunities to experience success, expanded frame of reference and increased self-complexity of occupying both work and family roles may all be processes that improve individual well-being. Third, the advantageousness of multiple roles on health depends both on the number of roles and the quality of roles. It has been found that five roles (i.e. different combinations of the roles of spouse, parent, worker, friend, relative and group member) might be an optimal number. More important, however, is the subjective feeling that the roles are satisfying and reasonably manageable (Barnett & Hyde, 2001; Marks, 1977). Finally, contrary to what is often claimed, gender differences in personality as well as in workplace and family behaviour are for the

Table 11.1 The four dimensions of work–family interaction with examples.

Direction	Valence	
	Negative	Positive
Work-to-family	Work-to-family conflict '*I am often late to pick up my children from day care due to my excessive workload and deadlines.*'	Work-to-family enrichment '*My current work is so rewarding that even my spouse often comments on my good mood and effort spent on my family after a work day.*'
Family-to-work	Family-to-work conflict '*I often find it difficult to concentrate on my clients' sorrows due to problems with my spouse.*'	Family-to-work enrichment '*I have applied my skills and experience from raising five kids many times in my work as a student counsellor.*'

most part small. Moreover, even when they exist, these gender differences have been mixed and do not predetermine men and women into highly differentiated, traditional gender roles with regard to work–family interaction.

Unlike the concept of work–family conflict, as yet there is not one established definition of positive work–family interaction. The most often used concept is work–family *enrichment*, which refers to 'the extent to which experiences in one role improve the quality of life in the other role' (Greenhaus & Powell, 2006, p. 73). The most fundamental feature that characterizes the various definitions – including, for example, work–family enhancement, facilitation and enrichment – is the emphasis on bi-directional beneficial effects between work and family domains. Table 11.1 summarizes and gives examples of the four dimensions of work–family interaction.

Replay

Work–family interaction refers to the combined effects of work and family characteristics on work, family and individual outcomes. Although reconciliation of work and family life was at first seen an issue that mostly women needed to solve, today it touches the lives of both men and women. This is due to the increase in dual-earner couples as well as technological advances and global competition that obscure the physical and temporal boundaries between work and family lives. Thus, although in some occupations work and family domains can still be segmented in place, time and thoughts (i.e. a low degree of work–family interaction), nowadays integration is common and work and family domains are seen as both conflicting and enriching each other (i.e. a high degree of work–family interaction). These negative and positive interactions between work and family domains are bi-directional: work can affect family life and family can affect work life (i.e. valence and direction of work–family interaction). The negative work–family conflict perspective is based on the role stress theory and the scarcity approach, whereas the positive work–family enrichment perspective is based on the role accumulation theory and the expansion approach.

11.2 Theoretical Models of Work–Family Interaction

In this section the most important theoretical models that help to further understand the work–family interaction are presented. These models can roughly be classified into two perspectives. In *antecedent–outcome models*, the aim is to illustrate what factors are likely to increase the experiences of negative and positive work–family interaction and what the possible consequences are. In *spillover models*, the emphasis is on explaining how moods, values, skills, resources and behaviours transfer from one life domain to another. Thus, the difference between antecedent–outcome and spillover models is that the former concentrate on explaining the antecedents and outcomes of perceived (in)compatibility between work and family roles, whereas the latter focus on mechanisms that produce similarity between work and family domains, for example how good time management at work transfers into good time management at home or how irritation towards spouse transfers into resentment towards clients.

Antecedent–outcome models

The basic principles of antecedent–outcome models of work–family interaction (e.g. Frone, Yardley, & Markel, 1997; Wayne, Grzywacz, Carlson, & Kacmar, 2007) are presented in Figure 11.1. First, this figure shows that work–family interaction consists of four dimensions: work-to-family conflict (WFC), family-to-work conflict (FWC), work-to-family enrichment (WFE) and family-to-work enrichment (FWE). WFC and FWC tend to coexist, as do WFE and FWE. Moreover, the relation between conflicts (WFC and FWC) and enrichments (WFE and FWE) is negative: more conflict experienced is linked to less enrichment, and vice versa.

Second, these four dimensions are seen as mediators between work and family characteristics on the one hand and work-related, non-work-related (including family) and overall stress and health consequences on the other hand. Specifically, work and family-related demands are assumed to increase the experiences of WFC and FWC, and to decrease the experiences of WFE and FWE. In contrast, work

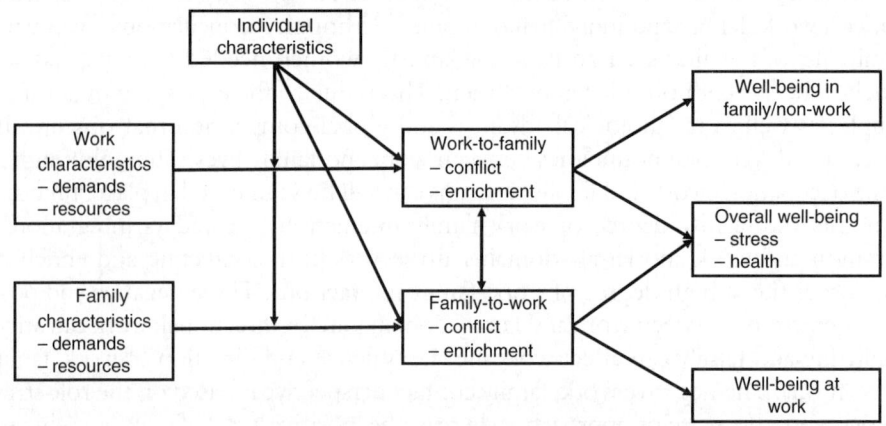

Figure 11.1 Antecedent–outcome model of work–family interaction.

and family-related resources are expected to decrease experiences of WFC and FWC and to increase experiences of WFE and FWE. In turn, WFC and FWC are expected to decrease an individual's well-being within each specific life domain as well as overall in life. In the same vein, WFE and FWE are expected to increase an individual's well-being within the specific life domain and overall in life. The specific antecedents and outcomes of work–family conflict and enrichment are introduced in more detail in Section 11.3.

Third, according to the so-called *domain specificity principle* (Frone, Yardley, & Markel, 1997), work characteristics are primary antecedent factors generating the experiences of WFC and WFE, which in turn give rise to ill-being or well-being in the family domain. Accordingly, family characteristics are primary antecedent factors for FWC and FWE, which in turn give rise to ill-being or well-being mainly in the work domain.

Finally, various individual characteristics (e.g. gender, socioeconomic status, personality traits, coping strategies) are seen as both antecedents of the four dimensions of work–family interaction as well as moderators of the links between work and family characteristics and the four dimensions of work–family interaction. This means that, depending on such individual characteristics, WFC, FWC, WFE and WFE are experienced more or less frequently. For example, individuals high in neuroticism (a tendency to experience greater anxiety, stress and depression) tend to experience more WFC and FWC. Also, overload and time pressure at work may generate less WFC in individuals who have effective ways to cope with demands (e.g. better time management skills) compared to those with less effective coping strategies.

Spillover models

According to spillover models of work–family interaction, both negative and positive experiences are carried over by an individual from work to family and vice versa without a mediating role of work–family conflict or enrichment. These spillover effects, in turn, generate similarity of experiences within these two life domains. What is essential for the existence of spillover between work and family domains is the *positive relation* between a work construct and a distinct, but related, construct in the family domain (Edwards & Rothbard, 2000). For example, if a worker has had an exhausting day at work, he/she is likely to come home in a bad mood. This bad mood may then result in tense interactions at home and produce a poor family climate. Thus, a worker's work-related distress is positively linked to his or her family distress.

Lambert (1990) was among the first to describe processes of spillover. She distinguished between direct and indirect spillover. *Direct spillover* occurs when the objective conditions of one life domain affect directly the outcomes in the other life domain, whereas *indirect spillover* occurs when an individual's subjective reactions to objective conditions mediate the effect of these conditions on the outcomes. For example, low wage may directly cause poverty and strain for a family, but one's dissatisfaction with one's low wage can also indirectly lead to marital dissatisfaction through worries and disagreements with one's spouse about financial issues.

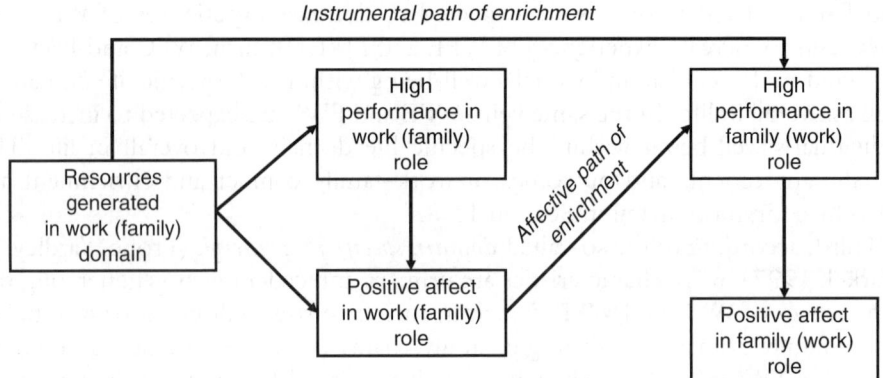

Figure 11.2 Positive spillover of resources, performance and affect from one life domain to another (adapted from Greenhaus & Powell, 2006, p. 79, Figure 1).

Later, finer-grained models of spillover have been presented that describe better the process of how the experiences, skills or emotions actually transfer from one domain to another, producing similarity between work and family domains (cf. Edwards & Rothbard, 2000; Lambert, 1990). In other words, these finer-grained models of spillover consider in more detail the mediating mechanisms between work and family constructs. One example is the *theory of work–family enrichment* by Greenhaus and Powell (2006), which focuses on positive spillover (see Figure 11.2). According to this theory, in the *affective path of enrichment*, different resources, such as skills and perspectives (i.e. ways of perceiving, handling and understanding different situations), as well as flexibility, psychological, physical, social-capital and material resources generated in the work (family) domain enhance first both high performance and positive affect in the *work* (family) role. Positive affect in the work (family) role then enhances high performance in the *family* (work) role, and it is this improved performance that then elicits positive mood and affects in the *family* (work) domain. The resources of the work (family) domain may also enhance the performance in the family (work) role directly, producing positive affect in the family (work) role. This is called an *instrumental path of enrichment*. Hence, this model emphasizes improved performance that is the mediating mechanism explaining positive spillover effects from one domain to another domain.

Replay

Two broad categories of models explaining the interaction between work and family – antecedent–outcome models and spillover models – have been introduced. Models in the first category emphasize the importance of determining the key demands that increase work–family conflict and the key resources that enhance work–family enrichment. This is because reducing work–family conflict and enhancing work–family enrichment is related to well-being of employed individuals both at their work and in their family lives. Spillover models do not contain concepts such as conflict or enrichment. Instead, they use the concept of spillover (i.e. transfer of experiences, moods, skills and behaviours from one life domain to another) to explain the processes through which resources or demands in one domain are linked to individuals' well-being or performance in the other domain.

Work–family balance

Thus far we have discussed the linkage between work and family by explaining and theorizing on four different dimensions of work–family interaction. But how are these two constructs related to *work–family balance* — a term used more frequently in everyday life than work–family conflict and enrichment? Frone (2003) has stated that just the absence of work–family conflict does not imply the presence of work–family balance. Instead, Frone proposes that work–family balance consists of the simultaneous experience of *high* work–family enrichment and *low* work–family conflict. Grzywacz and Carlson (2007) have further discussed the essence of work–family balance and have classified the scientific views on this concept into two approaches: work–family balance can be seen as either (i) an overall, subjective appraisal of one's work–family situation or (ii) comprising several components of the work–family situation that give meaning and define it.

Overall appraisal of work–family balance
An overall appraisal of work–family balance refers to an individual's general assessment concerning the entirety of his or her life situation. For example, work–family balance has been defined as 'satisfaction and good functioning at work and home, with a minimum of role conflict' (Clark, 2000, p. 751), 'equilibrium or maintaining overall sense of harmony in life' (Clarke, Koch, & Hill, 2004, p. 121) and 'global assessment that work and family resources are sufficient to meet work and family demands such that participation is effective in both domains' (Voydanoff, 2005, p. 825).

Components approach to work–family balance
According to the components approach, work–family balance consists of several sub-dimensions instead of one general assessment of one's life situation (Grzywacz & Carlson, 2007). For example, Greenhaus, Collins and Shaw (2003, p. 513) defined work–family balance as 'the extent to which an individual is equally engaged in – and equally satisfied with – his or her work and family role'. According to these authors, the three sub-dimensions of work–family balance are *time balance* referring to equal time devoted to, *involvement balance* referring to equal psychological effort invested in, and *satisfaction balance* referring to equal satisfaction expressed across work and family roles. In each of these dimensions the degree of work–family balance is regarded as a continuum where imbalance in favour of the work role lies at one end, imbalance in favour of the family role lies at the other end and balance lies in the middle, favouring neither work nor family role.

Another example of the components approach is to construe work–family balance as consisting of a distinct combination of work–family conflict and enrichment experiences (Grzywacz, Butler, & Almeida, 2008; Rantanen, 2008; Rantanen, Kinnunen, Mauno, & Tillemann, 2011). This typological approach to work–family

Work–family enrichment	Work–family conflict	
	Low	*High*
High	Beneficial	Active
Low	Passive	Harmful

Figure 11.3 Typological view of work–family balance (adapted from Rantanen, Kinnunen, Mauno, & Tillemann, 2011, p. 33).

balance is illustrated in Figure 11.3. According to this approach, work–family balance has four types: beneficial, harmful, active and passive. In the first two types the experiences of work–family conflict and enrichment are each other's' *opposite*: either enrichment is high and conflict is low (beneficial type) or conflict is high and enrichment is low (harmful type). In the latter two types, the experiences of work–family conflict and enrichment are *equivalent*: both are high (active type) or both are low (passive type). The main differentiating factor between the beneficial and the harmful type is assumed to be psychological functioning and well-being, which is high for the beneficial type and low for the harmful type. This assumption has been confirmed both among professional (Rantanen et al., 2011) and non-professional employees (Grzywacz et al., 2008; Rantanen, 2008). Instead, the active and the passive types are assumed to differ in the extent of effort invested to work and family domains, that is, high effort for the active and low effort for the passive type. This assumption has also been confirmed (Rantanen, 2008).

Replay

At present there is no strong theoretical consensus regarding the definition of work–family balance, in spite of the fact that terms like work–family balance and work–life balance are frequently used in everyday language. Work–family balance can be seen as (i) a single, overall appraisal of one's work–family situation, as (ii) consisting of several dimensions such as time, involvement and satisfaction balance over work and family lives, or as (iii) different combinations of work–family conflict and enrichment experiences. To achieve conceptual clarity about work–family balance, more theoretical work and empirical research is still needed.

11.3 Work–Family Interaction: Antecedents and Outcomes

In this section the antecedents and outcomes of work–family interaction – both conflict and enrichment – are discussed in line with the antecedent–outcome models discussed in Section 11.2. The antecedents are categorized into three broad categories relating to work, family and personality characteristics. The outcomes include work, non-work and stress-related outcomes. We first discuss the antecedents and outcomes of work–family conflict, after which the antecedents and outcomes of work–family enrichment are addressed.

Antecedents of work–family conflict

According to the theories of work–family interaction discussed in Section 11.2, antecedents within the work and family domains should be related to WFC and FWC, respectively. Empirical studies seem to confirm this domain specificity expectation. In a meta-analysis concerning the antecedents of work–family conflict (Michel, Kotrba, Mitchelson, Clark, & Baltes, 2011), the potential antecedents were categorized into five groups: (i) role stressors, (ii) role involvement, (iii) social support, (iv) work/family characteristics and (v) personality characteristics. The main findings are summarized in Table 11.2.

Job role stressors and social support at work were the best predictors of *WFC*. Of the role stressors, having too many tasks to do (i.e. role overload), incompatible role pressures within the work domain (i.e. role conflict) and a large amount of time devoted to work (i.e. work time demands) were linked to higher WFC. Of the forms of social support, organizational support (i.e. employees' belief that their work organization values their contributions and cares about their well-being) in particular, but also supervisor support and co-worker support, was related to lower WFC.

In the family domain, the best predictors of *FWC* were family role stressors. Of these, incompatible role stressors within the family domain (i.e. role conflict) and having too many family tasks (i.e. role overload) were related to higher FWC. However, social support in the family domain, like spousal support, was only weakly related to lower FWC.

In addition to these expected relations, Michel, Clark and Jaramillo's (2011) meta-analysis revealed some unexpected findings: role conflict and role overload appeared to be related to both forms of work–family conflict. Thus, work role conflict and work overload were linked to higher FWC and, correspondingly, family role conflict and family role overload were linked to higher WFC. One key explanation to these unexpected findings suggests that work and family stressors are highly pervasive phenomena that permeate both WFC and FWC.

Table 11.2 Main antecedents of work–family conflict.

Work-to-family conflict	*Family-to-work conflict*
Job role stressors	*Family role stressor*
Role overload (+)	Role overload (+)
Role conflict (+)	Role conflict (+)
Work-time demands (+)	
Social support	
Organizational support (−)	
Personality characteristics	*Personality characteristics*
Neuroticism (+)	Neuroticism (+)
Internal locus of control (−)	Internal locus of control (−)

Besides these domain-specific antecedents, personality characteristics have received some attention. Of these, locus of control and the Big Five personality characteristics (i.e. neuroticism, extraversion, openness to experiences, agreeableness and conscientiousness) received sufficient empirical attention to allow meta-analytic examination (Allen et al., 2012; Michel, Clark, & Jaramillo, 2011). Of these factors, neuroticism seems to be the most crucial. It is moderately related to both higher WFC and higher FWC. Also, internal locus of control – the extent to which an individual feels outcomes are caused by the individual or self, as opposed to external variables such as chance – contributed slightly to both forms of work–family conflict: internal orientation was related to a lower level of WFC and FWC. The other personality characteristics (e.g. conscientiousness) were less important.

In general, the fact that work and family factors are emphasized among the sources of work–family conflict provides a good starting point in preventing work–family conflict because these factors can be improved more easily than the more permanent individual factors (e.g. personality). However, studies have mainly been cross-sectional, which means that the causal direction of the relations between the predictors and work–family conflict has thus far not been established.

> ### Work Psychology in Action: Parents' experiences of stressful situations in work–family interaction
>
> In a Finnish study by Anna Rönkä and her colleagues (2009), parents who had pre-school children were asked to describe the most stressful situations in their lives concerning work–family interaction. Both mothers and fathers reported equally often situations in which lack of time (i.e. hurry, too little time for the family) generally produced challenges. However, mothers experienced family-related stressful situations more often than fathers, and fathers, in turn, reported job-related situations more often. This occurred despite the fact that both mothers and fathers were in paid work. Thus, fathers complained about situations in which workload and unsuitable working times were in a main role, whereas mothers described situations in which dealing with domestic duties and taking care of children were the main focus. All in all, mothers reported more stressful situations than fathers. The differences in the descriptions can be explained by the traditional gender roles: women still have more responsibility for family matters than men, and work still plays a greater role in men's lives. For example, men have longer working hours than women. It is also possible that gender roles make women and men more sensitive to challenges in their traditional role areas.

Replay

The potential antecedents of work–family conflict can be divided into five categories: (i) role stressors, (ii) role involvement, (iii) social support, (iv) work/family characteristics and (v) personality characteristics. Of these, the most important predictors of WFC and FWC belong to role stressors and social support: work role overload and low organizational support best predict WFC, whereas FWC is best predicted by family role conflict and overload. In addition, personality factors such as neuroticism and locus of control also play a role, although seemingly minor.

Outcomes of work–family conflict

Work–family interaction has many important outcomes for individuals, families and work organizations. The traditional assumption in work–family research was for a long time that WFC predominantly has consequences for the family (i.e. receiving) domain, whereas FWC impacts the work domain. This assumption is referred to as the so-called *cross-domain principle*. However, in one of the first reviews on the consequences of WFC (Allen, Herst, Bruck, & Sutton, 2000) it was found that things were not that simple. Allen and colleagues distinguished among three different types of outcomes: (i) work-related outcomes, (ii) non-work-related outcomes and (iii) stress-related outcomes. They found that WFC was related to all types of outcomes. With regard to the work-related consequences, WFC was most strongly related to increased turnover intentions. Among the non-work-related consequences, life dissatisfaction was most strongly related to WFC. Finally, their review revealed that one of the most consistent and strongest findings in the literature was that WFC related to increased burnout and stress symptoms. Apparently, for many employees work–family conflict goes hand in hand with higher risks of stress and burnout.

Meta-analyses (Amstad, Meier, Fasel, Elfering, & Semmer, 2011; Shockley & Singla, 2011) also support the view that the cross-domain principle is not valid. Amstad et al.'s results indicate that both types of conflict (WFC and FWC) showed stronger relations to within-domain (i.e. the originating role) outcomes than to cross-domain (i.e. the receiving role) outcomes (see Figure 11.4). Thus, WFC was more strongly associated with work-related than with family-related outcomes, and FWC was more strongly associated with family-related than with work-related outcomes. These relations can be explained by cognitive attributions regarding the source of conflict. For instance, when an employee feels that the work role

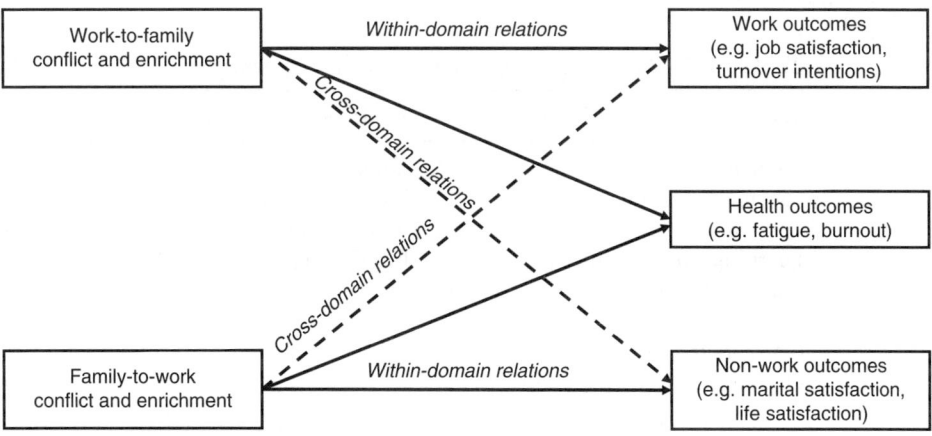

Figure 11.4 Outcomes of work–family conflict and enrichment.

drains his or her resources and leaves less time for family obligations (WFC), he or she is likely to blame the work role and as a consequence feels less satisfied with it.

It has been argued that the cross-domain principle might work best in longitudinal studies, where outcomes are assessed at a later point in time than the experience of work–family conflict. However, in a review that focused on longitudinal studies, Peeters, ten Brummelhuis and van Steenbergen (2013) reported with respect to WFC that consequences can be found in both the originating (work) and the receiving (family) domain, and health consequences are also to be expected. Again, these results do not support the cross-domain principle and are in line with those of Allen, Herst, Bruck and Sutton's (2000) meta-analysis. With regard to the effects of FWC, the results were less clear, but it seems that employees' health is particulary likely to suffer from FWC. So, after a decade of extensive research, the conclusion seems to be that consequences of WFC and FWC can be expected across different life domains and that an individual's health may suffer from high levels of WFC and FWC.

Replay

Research on the consequences of WFC and FWC has received much attention. Early theorists assumed, on the basis of the cross-domain principle, that WFC would primarily have consequences for the family domain and that FWC would result in problems in the work domain. However, later research showed convincingly that WFC and FWC may have consequences across different life domains.

Antecedents of work–family enrichment

As yet there are no meta-analytic studies available on the antecedents of *work-to-family* and *family-to-work enrichment*. In line with the enrichment theories (see Section 11.2) the empirical studies conducted thus far suggest that various resources may play a main role in enrichment experiences. These resources can be divided into three categories: (i) work-related, (ii) family-related and (iii) individual resources. The main findings are summarized in Table 11.3.

Table 11.3 Main antecedents of work–family enrichment.

Work-to-family enrichment	*Family-to-work enrichment*
Job resources	*Family resources*
Job autonomy (+)	Family support (+)
Task variety (+)	Spousal support (+)
Learning opportunities (+)	Relationship satisfaction (+)
Social support (+)	
Supervisor support (+)	
Co-worker-support (+)	
Organizational support (+)	
Personality characteristics	*Personality characteristics*
Extraversion (+)	Extraversion (+)

According to the Job Demands–Resources (JD-R) Model (see Chapter 4), job resources consist of aspects of a job that may help reduce job demands and achieve work goals, and may stimulate personal growth and development (Demerouti, Bakker, Nachreiner, & Schaufeli, 2001). Thus far empirical studies have found that job autonomy, task variety, learning opportunities and various forms of support at work are important job resources contributing to perceptions of high WFE. Longitudinal studies are rare, but Hakanen, Peeters and Perhoniemi (2011) found that job resources (craftsmanship, pride of the profession and direct and long-term results) indeed predicted high WFE across time, for both men and women.

Family-related resources have rarely been examined, but in cross-sectional studies resources such as family and spousal support, as well as relationship satisfaction have been found to be related to high FWE. This suggests that a high level of family-related resources promotes the experience of FWE. However, longitudinal research shows the relations between these concepts to be more complicated. For example, in a longitudinal study by Hakanen et al. (2011) family resources, including social support from one's family/partner/friend, did not predict FWE across time. Instead, FWE predicted higher family resources later on, implying that the relation might be reversed. More research is needed before firm conclusions on these relations can be drawn.

Of the individual resources, personality characteristics have received most attention thus far. Extraversion – a tendency to be sociable, dominant and experience positive emotionality – turned out to have the strongest relation with high positive work–non-work (including family) enrichment, whereas the other Big Five characteristics (except for neuroticism, which was not significantly related to enrichment experiences) related only weakly to high enrichment experiences in both directions (Michel, Clark, & Jaramillo, 2011). It has been argued that extraversion promotes enrichment by building up individual resources in a given domain by eliciting positive emotions that support both the discovery of novel and creative actions and ideas, as well as seeking out constructive solutions and resources to help reduce work–family conflict.

Replay

Current evidence supports the view that various resources at work (e.g. job autonomy) and in the family (e.g. spousal support) facilitate the enrichment process in the domains of work and family. In addition, of the personality characteristics, extraversion in particular seems to be important in promoting the enrichment process.

Outcomes of work–family enrichment

Compared to research on WFC and FWC, a limited number of studies has examined the consequences of WFE and FWE. Fortunately, a meta-analysis by Shockley and Singa (2011) has summarized the results of studies that have examined job and family satisfaction as possible outcomes of WFE and FWE. They found substantial evidence that affective reactions (satisfaction) for WFE occur mostly in the work domain and for FWE in the family domain, rather than the other way around. That is, WFE relates more strongly to job satisfaction than to family satisfaction and FWE relates more strongly to family satisfaction than to job satisfaction (see Figure 11.4). Thus, again, the cross-domain principle was not supported: rather, within-domain relations were stronger.

Because there are no meta-analyses available on other outcomes than satisfaction, we discuss three well-designed single studies in this area. First, van Steenbergen and Ellemers (2009) demonstrated that WFE and FWE predicted an increase in objectively recorded job performance across one year. Moreover, they found that WFE predicted a lower, healthier body mass index (BMI) one year later. This study shows the positive effects of the positive side of the work–family interaction in terms of objective measures like performance and health. Second, Hakanen et al. (2011) found that WFE and work engagement reciprocally influenced each other over time. In addition, they noted that FWE had a longitudinal effect on marital satisfaction. Finally, Carlson and colleagues (2011) found that women's WFE (assessed four months after childbirth, when they had already returned to work) predicted better self-reported physical health eight months after childbirth. In conjunction, these findings suggest that work–family enrichment may have positive effects on performance, well-being and health.

Replay

Research on the consequences of work–family enrichment is rather scarce. However, existing studies show promising results, indicating that positive outcomes can be expected across different life domains for both WFE and FWE. Examples of such outcomes are job and marital satisfaction, work engagement and good health and performance.

11.4 Ways of Dealing with Work and Family Demands

This section discusses how employees and organizations deal with work and family demands. First, individual coping strategies are discussed. Next, the roles of organizations and society in supporting the reconciliation of work and family demands are considered.

Individual coping strategies

Coping strategies refer to 'an individual's cognitive and behavioural efforts to manage specific external and/or internal demands that are appraised as taxing or exceeding the resources of the person' (Lazarus & Folkman, 1984, p. 141). Thus far it has quite consistently been shown that active, *problem-focused coping* aiming to solve the stressful situation is beneficial in reducing both WFC and FWC. This was also confirmed in Byron's (2005) meta-analysis: those with better time-management skills and an active coping style tended to have less WFC as well as less FWC.

In contrast, *emotion-focused coping* (referring to emotional regulation behaviour, e.g. talking to someone, showing one's irritation or anxiety) and *avoidance-focused coping* (e.g. wishful thinking, denying the stressful situation, hoping that time will resolve the problem) have received limited attention in work–family research. However, it has been shown that the use of emotion-focused coping gave rise to higher WFC and the use of avoidance coping to higher FWC and WFC.

Work–family research has recently shifted toward more context-specific or situational coping strategies that are assumed to explain better why some individuals experience more work–family conflict and less work–family enrichment than others. Work–family coping strategies describe what people do/think when they face challenges in combining work and family demands (Mauno, Kinnunen, Rantanen, Feldt, & Rantanen, 2012; Somech & Drach-Zahavy, 2007).

These work–family coping strategies can be divided into two types: strategies that decrease demands and strategies that increase resources (see also Chapter 17). Reducing working hours, giving up some tasks at work/home, prioritizing, restricting social life and lowering one's role expectations (e.g. being 'good enough' at work/home) are examples of demand-decreasing coping strategies. In contrast, seeking work–family support (e.g. by delegating tasks to one's spouse/co-workers, hiring domestic help), trying to find benefits/learn from difficult situations and using proactive/future-oriented coping (e.g. planning one's work week, building a back-up system within the family, proactive negotiations with one's spouse/supervisor) are examples of resource-increasing coping strategies within the work–family context. Thus far the evidence about how beneficial these situational work–family coping strategies are in combining work and family demands is quite limited. However, it seems that resource-increasing coping strategies are beneficial (Mauno, Kinnunen, Rantanen, Feldt, & Rantanen, 2012; Neal & Hammer, 2007).

Work–family policies and culture

Organizations can also support their employees in balancing work and family life. Work–family policies and a supportive work–family culture prevailing in the organization play an important role in this respect. Work–family policies refer to formal support and a supportive work–family culture refers to informal support in assisting employees' work–family integration. Because organizations are always operating as a part of larger socio-political cultures or regimes, the national context plays also an important role.

Formal work–family policies cover leave (e.g. parental leaves, reduced working hours for family reasons) and flexibility arrangements (e.g. flexible working hours, telework), and their availability varies strongly across different welfare regimes. For example, the Nordic countries (including the Scandinavian countries and The Netherlands) have a good package of statutory work–family policies, whereas in more liberal or conservative welfare regimes (such as those in the United Kingdom and the United States) these have a weaker legislative basis.

Informal work–family culture refers to the shared assumptions, beliefs and values regarding the extent to which an organization supports and values the integration of work and family lives (Thompson, Beauvais, & Lyness, 1999).

This kind of culture has been given more emphasis in psychological work–family studies than work–family policies. According to Thompson et al. (1999), work–family culture consists of three specific components: (i) managerial support, that is, whether managers show social support for and sensitivity to employees' family responsibilities, (ii) career consequences, which refer to the perception of negative career development opportunities as a consequence of utilizing work–family benefits or spending time in family-related activities, and (iii) organizational time demands that refer to expectations that employees prioritize working time above family time.

Both supportive work–family policies and supportive work–family culture are beneficial for work–family interaction (for reviews, see Kinnunen, Mauno, Geurts, & Dikkers, 2005; Kossek, Pichler, Bodner, & Hammer, 2011; Mesmer-Magnus & Viswesvaran, 2006). However, studies which have compared the relative importance of work–family policies vis-à-vis culture have indicated that culture has more impact than policies (Allen, 2001; Behson, 2002). If the organizational culture is not family-supportive, work–family policies are useless because a non-supportive culture discourages using these policies. For example, men's infrequent use of family leave has been explained by the prevailing culture: it does not encourage men to utilize the available leave arrangements.

Replay

Both individual coping efforts (like problem solving) and organization-based work–family support (in terms of supportive work–family culture and work–family policies) seem to be beneficial for balancing work and family demands. The specific coping efforts employees use in combining work and family life have thus far received limited attention in work–family research. However, resource-increasing coping efforts (e.g. delegating at home/work) seem to be most promising. Moreover, supportive work–family culture has turned out to be more beneficial than formal work–family-friendly policies. Namely, work–family culture that does not support employees' work–family interaction (e.g. lack of work–family support from managers) may inhibit the use of formal work–family policies, making them useless.

11.5 Conclusions

This chapter aimed to understand the combined effects of work and family roles on work, family and individual outcomes, that is, work–family interaction in individuals' lives. Until recently, the negative conflict perspective has dominated work–family interaction studies, and the positive enrichment perspective did not gain attention until the 2000s. However, nowadays there is consensus that work–family interaction has four dimensions: work-to-family conflict (WFC), work-to-family enrichment (WFE), family-to-work conflict (FWC) and family-to-work enrichment (FWE). Work–family conflict is a form of inter-role conflict in which the role pressures from the work and family domains are mutually incompatible in some respect, whereas work–family enrichment refers to the extent to which experiences in one role improve the quality of life in the other role.

The antecedents of WFC and WFE seem to be mainly work-related. Job role stressors and demands (e.g. role conflict and work overload) relate to WFC and job resources (e.g. job autonomy and social support) relate to WFE. Similarly, the antecedents of FWC and FWE are family-related. Family role stressors and demands (e.g. role conflict and overload) relate to FWC and family resources (e.g. spousal support) to FWE. In addition, personality characteristics, such as neuroticism and extraversion, are also relevant. Neuroticism relates to WFC and extraversion to WFE. Although early research and theories assumed that WFC would primarily have outcomes for the family domain and that FWC would result in problems in the work domain, later research showed convincingly that WFC and FWC may have negative consequences across different life domains, including health. Similarly, the positive consequences of WFE and FWE can be found in both the work and family domains as well as in overall health.

In order to contribute to good psychological well-being and functioning of employed individuals, a key question is how to decrease work–family conflict and to increase work–family enrichment. From the conflict perspective, decreasing job demands (e.g. time pressure and overload) and family demands (e.g. overload) is important. Similarly, increasing job resources (e.g. job autonomy and social support) and family resources (e.g. relationship support and satisfaction) is significant from the enrichment perspective. There are several things that individual employees might do to reduce both types of conflict as well as to increase both types of enrichment. They can seek out and develop appropriate social support networks at work and at home, reduce or reorganize the time devoted to work and family demands, and find ways to reduce or better cope with stressors and demands at work and home. Also, between partners who both work full-time an equal division of domestic duties

Work Psychology in Action: Ways of dealing with the challenges of the sandwiched generation

In a US study entitled *Working couples caring for children and aging parents* (Neal & Hammer, 2007), participants sandwiched between care demands from two generations were asked to evaluate how often they used different coping strategies in response to their many work and family duties. The strategy that both men and women used most was prioritizing ('*I prioritize and do the things that are most* necessary'). Humour was among the strategies most used ('I try and find humour in the situation'). Women also planned how to use their time and energy, concentrated on the positive sides of their situation and gave up their personal time and leisure activities. Men instead tended not to do tasks that could be done by other available persons. Participants also mentioned limiting their social activities as a common coping strategy, but the researchers found that this was not advisable: limiting social activities as well as spending less time with spouse and other family members was related to higher work–family conflict and decreased well-being.

would be beneficial, especially for women, because women spend still more time doing domestic tasks than men. This might also improve relationship satisfaction.

Work–family interaction is not only an individual-level phenomenon: work–family conflict and enrichment both have organizational-level antecedents and outcomes. The organizational initiatives can be discussed under the general label of work–family policies and culture. These initiatives fall into several categories, which include flexible work arrangements, work leave, dependent-care assistance and general resource services. However, a key question is how to improve the degree of informal support of organizations, that is, the work–family culture. In this regard, the role of managers is important. When managers are supportive towards their employees' needs related to life outside work, employees find it easier to reach a healthy work–family balance, which has positive consequences for their health and well-being.

Discussion Points

1. In this chapter, four different types of work–family interaction were distinguished. Give two examples for each type of interaction.
2. Which model describing work–family interaction, introduced in Section 11.2, would be your personal favourite and why? Explain why this model would be especially suitable to apply to everyday practice.
3. What can you say about causality in the antecedent–outcome model? Would it be possible that distress or satisfaction experienced at work or family elicits the experiences of work–family conflict or enrichment?
4. How might individual differences (e.g. personality characteristics, coping strategies) moderate (i.e. strengthen or weaken) the effects of (i) work- and family-related antecedents on work–family conflict and (ii) work–family conflict on outcomes (e.g. well-being at work)? Think about a potential research study to test your ideas.

Learning by Doing

1. Imagine that you work as a work psychologist and that your clients have problems in reaching a balance between their work and family demands. In fact they already suffer from distress and show various stress symptoms. What sort of advice would you give them based on the insights provided in this chapter? Be as concrete as possible.
2. Imagine that you want to convince the management of an organization that this organization should support employees' work–family interaction. What sort of reasoning could you use to convince them? Which counter-arguments do you anticipate from the management?
3. What kinds of organizational interventions would help employees to balance work and family life? On which job-related and/or organization-related aspects should these interventions focus? Can you give recommendations for best practices?

Further Reading

Amstad, F. T., Meier, L. L., Fasel, U., Elfering, J., & Semmer, N. K. (2011). A meta-analysis of work–family conflict and various outcomes with a special emphasis on cross-domain versus matching-domain relations. *Journal of Occupational Health Psychology, 16,* 151–169.

Greenhaus, J. H., & Allen, T. D. (2011). Work–family balance: A review and extension of the literature. In J. C. Quick, & L. E. Tetrick (Eds.), *Handbook of occupational health psychology* (2nd ed., pp. 165–183). Washington, DC: American Psychological Association.

Mauno, S., Kiuru, N., & Kinnunen, U. (2011). Relationships between work–family culture and work attitudes at both the individual and the departmental level. *Work & Stress, 25,* 147–167.

Rantanen, J., Kinnunen, U., Pulkkinen, L., & Kokko, K. (2012). Developmental trajectories of work–family conflict for Finnish workers in midlife. *Journal of Occupational Health Psychology, 17,* 290–303.

ten Brummelhuis, L. L., & Bakker, A. B. (2012). A resource perspective on the work–home interface: The work–home resources model. *American Psychologist, 67,* 545–556.

References

Allen, T. D. (2001). Family-supportive work environment: The role of organizational perceptions. *Journal of Vocational Behavior, 58,* 414–435.

Allen, T. D., Herst, D. E., Bruck, C. S., & Sutton, M. (2000). Consequences associated with work to family conflict: A review and agenda for future research. *Journal of Occupational Health Psychology, 5,* 278–308.

Allen, T. D., Johnson, R. C., Saboe, K. N., Cho, E., Dumani, S., & Evans, S. (2012). Dispositional variables and work–family conflict: A meta-analysis. *Journal of Vocational Behavior, 80,* 17–26.

Amstad, F. T., Meier, L. L., Fasel, U., Elfering, J., & Semmer, N. K. (2011). A meta-analysis of work–family conflict and various outcomes with a special emphasis on cross-domain versus matching-domain relations. *Journal of Occupational Health Psychology, 16,* 151–169.

Barnett, R. C., & Hyde, J. S. (2001). Women, men, work, and family. *American Psychologist, 56,* 781–796.

Behson, S. J. (2002). Which dominates? The relative importance of work–family organizational support and general organizational context on employee outcomes. *Journal of Vocational Behavior, 61,* 53–72.

Byron, K. (2005). A meta-analytic review of work–family conflict and its antecedents. *Journal of Vocational Behavior, 67,* 169–198.

Carlson, D. S., Grzywacz, J. G., Ferguson, M., Hunter, E. M., Clinch, C. R., & Arcury, T. A. (2011). Health and turnover of working mothers after childbirth via the work–family interface: An analysis across time. *Journal of Applied Psychology, 96,* 1045–1054.

Clark, S. C. (2000). Work/family border theory: A new theory of work/family balance. *Human Relations, 53,* 747–770.

Clarke, M. C., Koch, L. C., & Hill, E. J. (2004). The work–family interface: Differentiating balance and fit. *Family & Consumer Sciences Research Journal, 33,* 121–140.

Demerouti, E., Bakker, A. B., Nachreiner, F., & Schaufeli, W. B. (2001). The job demands–resources model of burnout. *Journal of Applied Psychology, 86,* 499–512.

Edwards, J. R., & Rothbard, N. P. (2000). Mechanisms linking work and family: Clarifying the relationship between work and family constructs. *Academy of Management Review, 25,* 178–199.

Frone, M. R. (2003). Work–family balance. In J. C. Quick, & L. E. Tetrick (Eds.), *Handbook of occupational health psychology* (pp. 143–162). Washington, DC: American Psychological Association.

Frone, M. R., Yardley, J. K., & Markel, K. S. (1997). Developing and testing an integrative model of the work–family interface. *Journal of Vocational Behavior, 50*, 145–167.

Greenhaus, J. H., & Beutell, N. J. (1985). Sources and conflict between work and family roles. *Academy of Management Review, 10,* 76–88.

Greenhaus, J. H., Collins, K. M., & Shaw, J. D. (2003). The relation between work–family balance and quality of life. *Journal of Vocational Behavior, 63,* 510–531.

Greenhaus, J. H., & Powell, G. N. (2006). When work and family are allies: A theory of work–family enrichment. *Academy of Management Review, 31,* 72–92.

Grzywacz, J. G., Butler, A. B., & Almeida, D. M. (2008). Work, family, and health: Work–family balance as a protective factor against stresses of daily life. In A. Marcus-Newhall, D. F. Halpern, & S. J. Tan (Eds.), *The changing realities of work and family* (pp. 194–215). Oxford: John Wiley & Sons.

Grzywacz, J. G., & Carlson, D. S. (2007). Conceptualizing work–family balance: Implications for practice and research. *Advances in Developing Human Resources, 9,* 455–471.

Hakanen, J. J., Peeters, M. C. W., & Perhoniemi, R. (2011). Enrichment processes and gain spirals at work and at home: A 3-year cross-lagged panel study. *Journal of Occupational and Organizational Psychology, 84,* 8–30.

Kahn, R. L., Wolfe, D. M., Quinn, R. P., Snoek, J. D., & Rosenthal, R. A. (1964). *Organizational stress: Studies in role conflict and ambiguity.* Oxford: John Wiley & Sons.

Kinnunen, U., Mauno, S., Geurts, S., & Dikkers, J. (2005). Work–family culture in organizations: Theoretical and empirical approaches. In S. Poelmans (Ed.), *Work and family: An international research perspective* (pp. 87–121). Mahwah: Lawrence Erlbaum Associates.

Kossek, E., Pichler, S., Bodner, T., & Hammer, L. (2011). Workplace social support and work–family conflict: A meta-analysis clarifying the influence of general and work–family-specific supervisor and organizational support. *Personnel Psychology, 54,* 289–313.

Lambert, S. J. (1990). Processes linking work and family: A critical review and research agenda. *Human Relations, 43,* 239–257.

Lazarus, R. S., & Folkman, S. (1984). *Stress, appraisal, and coping.* New York: Springer.

Marks, S. R. (1977). Multiple roles and role strain: Some notes on human energy, time and commitment. *American Sociological Review, 42,* 921–936.

Mauno, S., Kinnunen, U., Rantanen, J., Feldt, T., & Rantanen, M. (2012). Relationships of work–family coping strategies with work–family conflict and enrichment: The roles of gender and parenting status. *Family Science, 3,* 109–125.

Mesmer-Magnus, J. R., & Viswesvaran, C. (2006). How family-friendly work environments affect work/family conflict: A meta-analytic examination. *Journal of Labor Research, 27,* 555–574.

Michel, J., Clark, M., & Jaramillo, D. (2011). The role of the Five Factor Model of personality in the perceptions of negative and positive forms of work–nonwork spillover: A meta-analytic review. *Journal of Vocational Behavior, 79,* 191–203.

Michel, J., Kotrba, L., Mitchelson, J., Clark, M., & Baltes, B. (2011). Antecedents of work–family conflict: A meta-analytic review. *Journal of Organizational Behavior, 32,* 689–725.

Neal, M., & Hammer, L. (2007). Work–family coping strategies: What are the effects on work family fit, well-being and work? In M. Neal, & L. Hammer (Eds.), *Working couples caring for children and ageing parents* (pp. 143–155). Mahwah, NJ: Lawrence Erlbaum Associates.

Peeters, M. C. W., ten Brummelhuis, L. L., & van Steenbergen, E. F. (2013). Consequences of combining work and family roles: A closer look at cross-domain versus within-domain relations In J. G. Grzywacz, & E. Demerouti (Eds.), *New frontiers in work and family research.* New York: Routledge.

Rantanen, J. (2008). *Work–family interface and psychological well-being: A personality and longitudinal perspective* (Jyväskylä Studies in Education, Psychology and Social Research, 346). Jyväskylä: University of Jyväskylä.

Rantanen, J., Kinnunen, U., Mauno, S., & Tillemann, K. (2011). Introducing theoretical approaches to work–life balance and testing a new typology among professionals. In S. Kaiser, M. Ringlstetter, D. R. Eikhof, & M. Pina e Cunha (Eds.), *Creating balance? International perspectives on the work–life integration of professionals* (pp. 27–46). Berlin: Springer.

Rönkä, A., Malinen, K., & Lämsä, T. (Eds.) (2009). Perhe-elämän paletti. [*The palette of family life*]. Jyväskylä: PS-kustannus.

Sieber, S. D. (1974). Toward a theory of role accumulation. *American Sociological Review, 39,* 567–578.

Shockley, K. M., & Singla, N. (2011). Reconsidering work–family interactions and satisfaction: A meta-analysis. *Journal of Management*, *37*, 861–886.

Somech, A., & Drach-Zahavy, A. (2007). Strategies for coping with work–family conflict: The distinctive relationships of gender role ideology. *Journal of Occupational Health Psychology*, *12*, 1–19.

Thompson, C. A., Beauvais, L. L., & Lyness, K. S. (1999). When work–family benefits are not enough: The influence of work–family culture on benefit utilization, organizational attachment, and work–family conflict. *Journal of Vocational Behavior*, *54*, 392–415.

van Steenbergen, E. F., & Ellemers, N. (2009). Is managing the work–family interface worthwhile? Benefits for employee health and performance. *Journal of Organizational Behavior*, *30*, 617–642.

Voydanoff, P. (2002). Linkages between the work–family interface and work, family, and individual outcomes: An integrative model. *Journal of Family Issues*, *23*, 138–164.

Voydanoff, P. (2005). Toward a conceptualization of perceived work–family fit and balance: A demands and resources approach. *Journal of Marriage and Family*, *67*, 822–836.

Wayne, J. H., Grzywacz, J. G., Carlson, D. S., & Kacmar, K. M. (2007). Work–family facilitation: A theoretical explanation and model of primary antecedents and consequences. *Human Resource Management Review*, *17*, 63–76.

Part F

Outcomes

12
Burnout, Boredom and Engagement in the Workplace

WILMAR B. SCHAUFELI AND MARISA SALANOVA

> **Chapter Objectives**
>
> After studying this chapter, you should be able to:
>
> - define and *assess* job burnout, boredom at work and work engagement;
> - *differentiate* between 'good' and 'bad' ways of working hard;
> - identify the main *drivers* of engagement as well as the causes of burnout and boredom;
> - identify the major *consequences* of burnout, boredom and engagement;
> - understand the *psychological mechanisms* that are involved in employee affective well-being.

This chapter is about how employees feel at work. In other words, it is concerned with their psychological well-being, which can be either negative or positive. For instance, employees may feel worn out, cynical or bored, or in contrast, they may feel enthused and full of pep. The way employees feel has not only to do with 'who they are' – i.e. their personality – but also with 'where they are' – i.e. in their jobs. In essence, employee well-being results from the interaction between person and (work) environment. It depends on the interplay of person-related factors such as temperament and past experiences, and job-related factors such as job characteristics and interpersonal relations at work. More particularly, this chapter

An Introduction to Contemporary Work Psychology, First Edition.
Edited by Maria C. W. Peeters, Jan de Jonge and Toon W. Taris.
© 2014 John Wiley & Sons, Ltd. Published 2014 by John Wiley & Sons, Ltd.

focuses on job burnout, boredom at work and work engagement. After a brief historical overview (Section 12.1), these three types of employee well-being are described in greater detail (Section 12.2) and a taxonomy is presented that allows a differentiation with workaholism and job satisfaction (Section 12.3). Next, the antecedents, consequences and correlates of burnout, boredom and engagement are discussed (Section 12.4), as well the role of individual differences (Section 12.5). Finally, psychological explanations for burnout, boredom and work engagement are discussed (Section 12.6), and the chapter closes with some overall conclusions (Section 12.7).

12.1 A Brief History

The practical and scientific interest in employee feelings at work developed relatively recently, although the first accounts date back over a century ago. Historically speaking the interest in employee feelings is intertwined with stress, in this context loosely defined as a physical, mental or emotional response to events or demands that cause bodily or mental tension. Strange as it may seem, both World Wars have contributed much to the interest in employee feelings. During World War I (1914–1918), the British government commissioned the Industrial Fatigue Research Board to come up with solutions to tackle the problem of industrial fatigue in ammunition factories, which caused many injuries and fatal accidents. At about the same time army physicians described 'shell shock', an acute stress-reaction that resulted from the extreme demands to which soldiers were exposed in combat situations. During World War II (1940–1945), for the first time quantitative studies of the impact of war on the mental and emotional life of individuals (i.e. soldiers and civilians) were carried out (Stouffer, Suchman, de Vinney, Stra, & Williams, 1949). In the 1940s and 1950s the US Air Force funded a large laboratory research programme about the effects of stress on task performance. This programme was led by Richard Lazarus, who later developed his renowned stress and coping theory (Lazarus & Folkman, 1984). Throughout the 1960s and 1970s the field was dominated by the Institute of Social Research of the University of Michigan, where Kornhauser (1965) carried out a ground-breaking survey on the mental health of automotive workers. In Europe the British Tavistock Institute played a major role with a landmark study in the late 1940s on stress in British coalmines that uncovered the role of social and organizational factors, such as group norms. In the 1970s and 1980s Scandinavian job stress research was highly influential, particularly the work of Karasek and Theorell (1990), who conceived the well-known Demand–Control–Support Model (see Chapter 3).

Initially, no sharp distinction was made between different kinds of mental strain and ill-being, and omnibus measures were used for their assessment. This changed, however, in the late 1970s when *job burnout* appeared on the scene. This notion entered science through the backdoor, so to speak. 'Burnout' is a metaphor that was used by professionals, particularly those working in the human services such as health care, social work, psychotherapy and law enforcement, to describe a state of mental exhaustion. It has been argued that the emergence of burnout is rooted in the social and cultural changes that have taken place since the 1960s, such as the growth and bureaucratization of welfare institutions and the weakening of professional authority, both of which put considerable strain on human services professionals (Schaufeli, Leiter, & Maslach, 2009). In fact, the history of burnout developed along two lines: a practical, interventionist tradition that focused on the assessment, prevention and treatment of burnout, and an academic research tradition that focused on identifying its causes and consequences, and uncovering its psychological underpinnings. Quite remarkably, both traditions developed relatively independently and only occasional overlap, for instance in case of the practical use of validated burnout measures and the scientific evaluation of interventions to prevent or to combat burnout. Meanwhile, 'burnout business' is booming and over 6,600 scientific articles have been published on the subject.

Although *boredom at work* was recognized as a topic worthy of scientific inquiry by the pioneer of applied psychology Hugo Münsterberg back in 1913, it is still investigated only occasionally. Traditionally boredom, which is conceived as a state of low arousal and dissatisfaction due to an unchallenging work situation, is investigated in relation to monotonous and repetitive work, for instance at assembly lines. The first empirical studies on boredom were carried out before and during World War II using a human factors perspective and focused on task performance in a laboratory setting. Boredom in organizations was not studied until the 1960s and 1970s, and currently fewer than 400 scientific studies have appeared.

Since the turn of the century, *work engagement* has emerged as the opposite of burnout, namely a state of mental energy. Like burnout, the notion of engagement was first used in practice in business settings by human resources-professionals and consultants because an organization's mental capital, that is, the cognitive and emotional fortitude and strength of its employees, is nowadays of increasing economic significance. For modern organizations, employees' *mental* fitness rather than their mere physical fitness provides a decisive competitive advantage. From a scientific point of view, the emergence of work engagement has been fostered by the rise of positive psychology, which studies human strength and optimal functioning, since the turn of the century. From 2000 till 2012 over 1,100 scientific publications were published on work or employee engagement (these terms are used interchangeably).

12.2 Defining and Assessing Burnout, Boredom and Engagement

In this section we will describe how the three different indicators of psychological well-being are generally defined and assessed.

Burnout

As mentioned earlier, burnout is a metaphor that is commonly used to describe a state or process of mental exhaustion, similar to the smothering of a fire or the extinguishing of a candle. The Merriam-Webster dictionary defines 'to burn out' as 'to fail, wear out, or become exhausted by making excessive demands on energy, strength, or resources'.

Although various definitions of burnout exist, the most often cited academic definition comes from Maslach, Jackson and Leiter (1986, p. 1): 'Burnout is a syndrome of emotional exhaustion, depersonalization, and reduced personal accomplishment that can occur among individuals who do "people work" of some kind.' So burnout consists of three dimensions in this definition. Emotional exhaustion refers to the depletion or draining of emotional resources caused by interpersonal demands. Depersonalization points to the development of negative, callous and cynical attitudes towards the recipients of one's services. The term 'depersonalization' may cause some confusion since it is used in a completely different sense in psychiatry, namely to denote a person's extreme alienation from self and the world. However, in Maslach and Jackson's definition, depersonalization refers to an impersonal and dehumanized perception of *recipients*, rather than to an impersonal view of *self*. Finally, lack of personal accomplishment is the tendency to evaluate one's work with recipients negatively. Burned-out professionals believe that their objectives are not achieved, which is accompanied by feelings of insufficiency and poor professional self-esteem. For a description of burnout see the story of Peter – a burned-out teacher (Work Psychology in Action box).

Initially, Maslach and Jackson claimed that burnout exclusively occurs among professionals who deal with recipients (e.g. students, pupils, clients, patients or delinquents) face-to-face. Hence, in their view burnout is restricted to the helping professions, at least initially. But in the 1990s the concept of burnout was broadened and defined as a crisis in one's relationship with work *in general* and not necessarily as a crisis in one's relationship with *people* at work (Maslach, Schaufeli, & Leiter, 2001). From that time onwards burnout was also investigated outside the human services. For that purpose, the three original burnout dimensions were redefined: *exhaustion* refers to fatigue irrespective of its cause, *cynicism* reflects an indifferent or distant attitude towards work instead of other people and *lack of professional efficacy* encompasses both social and non-social aspects of occupational accomplishment. In other words, burnout is a multidimensional construct that includes a stress reaction (exhaustion or fatigue), a mental distancing response (depersonalization or cynicism) and a negative belief (lack of accomplishment or efficacy).

Psychologically speaking these three components are related (see also Section 12.6). Exhaustion results from exposure to chronic stressors at work (e.g. work overload, emotional demands, interpersonal conflicts). In an attempt to prevent further energy depletion, employees distance themselves mentally from their work by developing depersonalizing or cynical attitudes. In doing so, their work performance is likely to diminish and as a result they may feel incompetent and inefficacious. This dynamic interplay is illustrated by a study that showed that the depersonalizing and cynical attitudes of Dutch physicians towards their patients negatively affected the doctor–patient relationship (Bakker, Schaufeli, Sixma, Bosveld, & van Dierendonck, 2000). In its turn, this poor and demanding relationship led to higher levels of burnout, including reduced accomplishment. Seen from this perspective, excessive mental distancing is an inadequate strategy to deal

> ### Work Psychology in Action:
> ### Peter – a burned-out teacher
>
> During the past two years, Peter, a 48-year-old teacher, has played a crucial role in the merging of his school with another school. It has been a very hectic and busy time because he was one of the advocates and active agents who promoted the merger. After the merger was concluded Peter felt very disappointed since he was not promoted to the newly created job as department coordinator in the new school. Instead, the job he hoped to receive was offered to a younger colleague who had always been sceptical of the merger. Peter felt hurt, resentful and unfairly treated; in his opinion he had put much more time and effort into reorganizing the school than his younger colleague, yet he was denied the appropriate reward. Soon after this event Peter feels extremely tired and anxious, and it takes an extreme effort for him to take on anything. He is no longer able to perform his job at school and consequently he is on sick leave. Peter sleeps till ten o'clock in the morning and he feels tired all day long. Although he would have enough time now to pursue his hobbies (refurbishing antique furniture and playing bridge), he lacks the energy and doesn't fancy it. Instead, he worries a lot and has problems concentrating (e.g. after reading some lines in the newspaper he has forgotten what he has read previously). Moreover, he suffers from headaches and pain in the neck, and feels depressed and restless. Peter feels particularly uncomfortable in social situations and, as a consequence, he avoids others and becomes more and more isolated. If things do not work out properly or when somebody is unkind, Peter gets upset. He is irritable and easily hurt, which strains his family, especially his two teenage daughters. But perhaps the most frightening of all is that Peter doesn't recognize himself anymore, he feels powerless and totally out of control. He cannot understand what has happened to him.
>
> Source: Based on a real case, reported by Schaap, Schaufeli and Hoogduin (1995).

with emotional strain. Schaufeli and Taris (2005) argued that exhaustion and mental distancing constitute the core of burnout and that rather than being a constituting dimension, professional efficacy should be a consequence of exhaustion and distancing. As far as burnout is concerned, the *inability* to spend effort (because of being exhausted) and the *unwillingness* to spend effort (because of distancing and withdrawal) are two sides of the same coin.

The most widely used instrument to assess burnout is the Maslach Burnout Inventory (MBI; Maslach et al., 1996), which includes three subscales reflecting the three dimensions, i.e. (emotional) exhaustion, depersonalization or cynicism, and reduced accomplishment or efficacy. In fact, three versions of the MBI exist, a general version that can be used in every occupational context and specific versions for human service professionals and educators, respectively. However, other questionnaires also exist that either tap the exhaustion dimension only or include the mental distancing dimension as well (see Maslach, Leiter, & Schaufeli, 2008). Examples of items are 'I feel emotionally drained by my work' (exhaustion), 'I doubt the significance of my work' (cynicism) and 'I can effectively solve the problems that arise in my work' (efficacy; this last item is reversely scored).

Based on a large epidemiological study among around 12,000 Dutch employees, it is estimated that about 16% of the Dutch working population is at risk of burnout and that each year 6% of the Dutch workforce develops serious burnout complaints (Kant, Jansen, van Amelsfoort, Mohren, & Swaen, 2004). From this it is calculated that, on average, burnout symptoms last 2.5 years, which makes it a chronic condition. The highest levels of burnout are found among teachers and those with higher education. Although in general no systematic gender differences are found, occasionally higher levels of burnout are reported for women aged between 35 and 45. Males sometimes exhibit higher levels of cynicism than females, but this is probably caused by sex-role socialization. For instance, boys learn to distance themselves emotionally more than girls ('boys do not cry').

Boredom

Whereas much current psychological research focuses on the causes and consequences of overstimulation at work, including burnout, the problem of under-stimulation (boredom) has largely been neglected. Interestingly, the Merriam-Webster dictionary describes boredom as 'the state of being weary and restless through lack of interest'. First, this suggests that the effects of overstimulation (burnout) and under-stimulation (boredom) seem to overlap to some extent since both are characterized by feeling worn out. Traditionally, two schools of thought exist when it comes to defining boredom. According to the first approach, boredom is associated with conducting monotonous and repetitive tasks (O'Hanlon, 1981). Second, it is suggested that the experience of boredom at work is due to an internal need for high stimulation; the greater this internal need, the more susceptible one would be to feeling bored (Farmer & Sundberg, 1986). Both perspectives define boredom in terms of its antecedents, so these definitions are circular: employees feel bored because they work in boring (monotonous) jobs or because they are boredom-prone by nature. In order to avoid this circularity, Loukidou, Loan-Clake and Daniels (2009, p. 383) define boredom simply as an 'unpleasant and deactivated affect'. However, this description is rather narrow and unspecific because it limits boredom to a mere affect and does not refer to the work context. We therefore propose to follow Mikulas and Vodanovich (1993, p.3) and define boredom at work as an unpleasant state of relatively low arousal and dissatisfaction, which is attributed to an inadequately stimulating work situation. For a description of boredom see the story of Geoff – a bored assistant (Work Psychology in Action box).

> **Work Psychology in Action:
> Geoff – a bored assistant**
>
> 'I've had a few boring jobs in my day, but the most depressing one was my first job out of college. I was bored stiff, and I didn't want to be. It was an exciting job for a then 22-year-old. I had landed a job as an office production assistant, working at the studios of 20th Century Fox. One of my highlights was looking out a window into a parking lot one afternoon and seeing Sean Connery get out of the car. I had arrived, sort of. But while the office needed help, it turned out that they didn't need all that much help. Within a few days, I had organized the filing cabinets, run several errands and helped get the television production office running smoothly. But I was an assistant of an assistant, and after about a week there, it started to become apparent that there was no longer much for me to do. Every day became more and more boring, and I became more and more desperate to look busy. I think it worked too well. When I resorted to polishing the picture frames on the wall, the assistant came over to me and said, 'I think we both know what has to happen…' So I was 'let go', but given two week's severance pay, which was really very decent of them. And then I promptly found a job where I was even more bored, and the location – an office building miles and miles from Hollywood – wasn't exciting either.'
>
> Source: Williams (2008).

To date, boredom at work is measured 'objectively' by referring to the repetitiveness of the job or by assessing the levels of employee boredom proneness or by a single item that refers to the emotion of feeling bored (for subjective and objective measurement, see also Chapter 5). Recently, a short multi-item questionnaire – the Dutch Boredom Scale (DUBS) – has been proposed that is based on the definition mentioned above (Reijseger et al., 2012). Example items are 'I feel bored at my job' and 'At work, time goes by very slowly'. Unfortunately, to date, no information is available about the prevalence of boredom at work.

Engagement

In contrast to burnout and boredom, everyday connotations of engagement are positive in nature. It is associated with involvement, commitment, passion, enthusiasm, focused effort and energy. In a similar vein, the Merriam-Webster dictionary describes engagement as 'emotional involvement or commitment' and 'the state of being in gear'. In the academic literature work engagement is either considered as the positive antithesis of burnout or as a distinct concept in its own right. According to the first perspective engagement is characterized by energy, involvement and perceived efficacy. In fact, they are the direct opposites of the three burnout dimensions (Maslach & Leiter, 1997). Put differently, burnout is seen as an erosion of engagement; energy turns into exhaustion, involvement turns into cynicism and perceived efficacy turns into ineffectiveness. By implication, engagement is assessed by the opposite pattern of scores on the three dimensions of the MBI: low scores on exhaustion and cynicism, and high scores on professional efficacy.

Alternatively, according to the second perspective work engagement is defined independently from burnout as '…a positive, fulfilling, work-related state of mind that is characterized by vigor, dedication and absorption' (Schaufeli, Salanova, González-Romá, & Bakker, 2002, p. 74). Vigor is characterized by high levels of energy and mental resilience while working, the willingness to invest effort in one's work and persistence even in the face of difficulties. Dedication refers to being strongly involved in one's work and experiencing a sense of significance, enthusiasm, inspiration, pride and challenge. Absorption, finally, is characterized by focused attention, being fully concentrated and happily engrossed in one's work, whereby time passes quickly and one has difficulties detaching oneself from work. Even though engagement is conceptualized as the 'opposite' of burnout, there is not the presumption that it is expressed by the opposite profile of MBI scores. For a description of engagement see the story of Mary – an engaged secretary (Work Psychology in Action box).

To assess work engagement in its own right a self-report questionnaire has been developed – the Utrecht Work Engagement Scale (UWES; Schaufeli, Bakker, & Salanova, 2006). It includes items such as 'I feel strong and vigorous in my job' (vigor), 'I'm enthusiastic about my job' (dedication) and 'I feel happy when I'm engrossed in my work' (absorption). Although no reliable scientific estimates exist about the prevalence of work engagement, various surveys of global consultancy firms suggest that roughly about 25% of the North American workforce can be considered 'engaged', against only 15% of European employees (Attridge, 2009). No systematic gender differences are found in levels of work engagement. Executives, managers, artists, farmers and teachers seem to be most engaged professional groups, whereas blue-collar workers, police officers, retail workers and homecare staff seem to be least engaged.

Replay

- Burnout includes exhaustion, mental distancing (cynicism or depersonalization) and lack of professional efficacy.
- Exhaustion and mental distancing constitute the core of burnout.
- Burnout can apply to people working in a wide range of occupations. It is *not* limited to professionals who work with other people.
- Boredom at work is characterized by low arousal and dissatisfaction, which result from under-stimulation.
- Work engagement includes vigor, dedication and absorption.
- Burnout, boredom and engagement can by assessed by short self-report questionnaires.
- Engagement is inversely related to burnout and boredom.

> ### Work Psychology in Action:
> ### Mary – an engaged secretary
>
> After finishing school Mary worked for a couple of years in several administrative jobs. She worked hard and liked her work a lot. After her first child was born she quit her job but remained active as a volunteer in the community (e.g. at school and in the local library). Currently she is still engaged in volunteer work: as a member of the board of the community centre, as treasurer of the parent–teacher–student association of her children's school and as a board member of a charity. Mary is a very energetic woman who likes to do something meaningful for other people. It is difficult for her not to be active and not participate in her community 'because there is always something to do'.
>
> In her current job she is very proactive and shows personal initiative. She took up her working career again after her second child started primary school. After caring for her children for about eight years it was difficult for her to find a new proper job. So she started with a temporary job to clean up and rearrange the archive of a homecare institution. After a short while she suggested that the manager set up a completely new archive that would suit the needs of professionals much better. He liked the idea, so Mary did the job and she did it very well. As a result she was offered a steady job as a secretary. Initially her job was rather simple but because Mary likes to take on new challenges her work became increasingly varied and responsible. She has learned a lot of new things, for instance to work with sophisticated software that is used for personnel planning and bookkeeping. She is acknowledged by the professionals for her efficiency, customer friendliness and cooperation, and her boss values her work greatly. Her commitment and helpfulness are illustrated by the fact that once she cleaned up the room of an elderly woman because the regular helper was unable to come. As a matter of fact, Mary is only responsible for the planning and financing of household help and not for the actual work itself. Many customers rely on Mary and share their ups and downs with her so she gets to know them quite well. Mary is a strong-minded, independent and assertive woman with a strong drive to make a difference for others.
>
> Source: Based on an interview reported in Schaufeli and Bakker (2007).

12.3 A Taxonomy of Employee Well-being

Various types of work-related well-being, including burnout, boredom and engagement, can be mapped using the so-called circumplex model of emotions (Russell, 1980). This model assumes that all human emotions may be plotted on

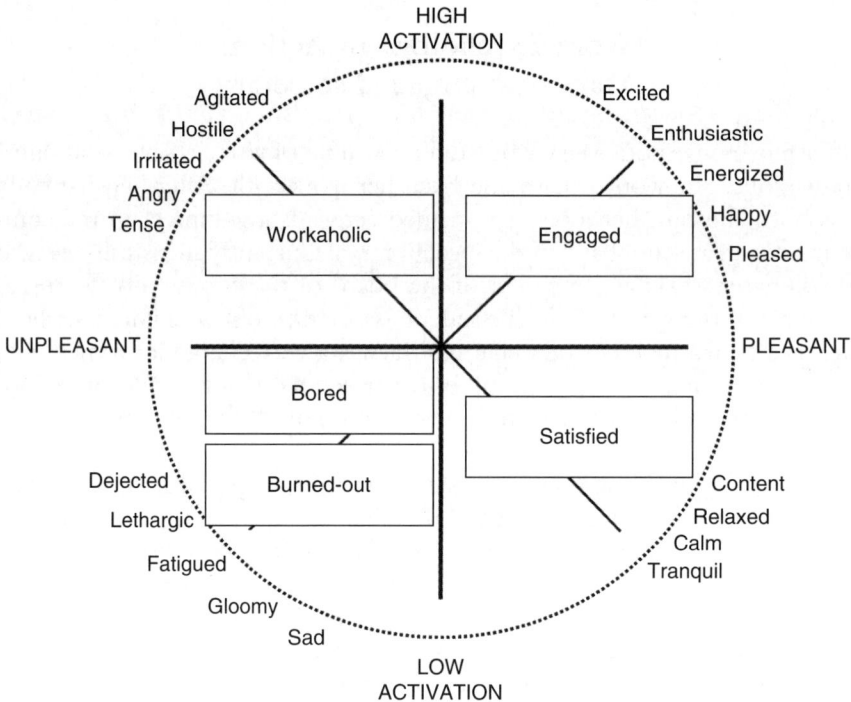

Figure 12.1 A taxonomy of work-related well-being (adapted from Russell, 1980).

the surface of a circle that is defined by two orthogonal dimensions that run from pleasure to displeasure and from activation to deactivation (see Figure 12.1). Put differently, each and every emotion is a combination of varying degrees of pleasure and activation. For instance, excitement is a pleasant and active emotion, whereas sadness is an unpleasant and inactive emotion. Additionally, calmness is pleasant and inactive, while hostility is unpleasant and active.

In a similar vein, these two fundamental dimensions may also constitute employee well-being, that is, employees who experience mainly negative emotions may suffer from burnout, boredom or workaholism, whereas employees who experience mainly positive emotions may feel satisfied or engaged. In addition, employees may either feel activated, as in workaholism and engagement, or deactivated, as in burn-out, boredom and satisfaction. This way, engaged employees are placed in the upper right quadrant of Figure 12.1, satisfied employees in the lower right quadrant, bored or burned-out employees in the lower left quadrant and finally workaholics in the upper left quadrant. Moreover, the intensity of the experience increases when moving from the centre to the surface of the circle along both diagonals. For instance, burned-out employees will feel more negative and less active than bored employees. Likewise, levels of engagement, satisfaction and workaholism may differ in intensity, depending on the distance from the centre of the circle.

This taxonomy allows us to discuss the differences between the various types of employee well-being more systematically. For instance, Figure 12.1 illustrates why studies consistently show that engagement and satisfaction, as well as burnout and workaholism, are positively associated with each other, whereas burnout and engagement are negatively related (Schaufeli & Bakker, 2010). The reason is that engagement and satisfaction are positive states, and burnout and workaholism are negative states. So far, only one study (Reijseger et al., 2012) has shown that boredom is positively related to burnout and negatively to engagement, which is also consistent with Figure 12.1. Using a similar circumplex model, Warr and Inceoglu (2012) showed that engagement is an energized motivational state with strong activating potential that is associated with *poor* person–job fit. This signifies that engaged employees want more from their job than they actually perceive; they are eager and look for new challenges. Satisfied employees, on the other hand, are satiated and lack that typical drive of their engaged colleagues; they are contented and experience a *good* fit with their job. Not surprisingly, engaged employees perform better than merely satisfied employees. A meta-analysis (Christian, Garza, & Slaughter, 2011) showed that work engagement was stronger related to performance than satisfaction and that the positive effect of work engagement on performance was still significant after controlling for satisfaction. In other words, engagement had an impact on performance over and beyond satisfaction. In essence, this illustrates the more 'active' nature of work engagement as compared to satisfaction.

Unlike work engagement and job satisfaction, workaholism is a negative state that is defined as a strong inner drive to work excessively hard (Taris, Schaufeli, & Shimazu, 2010). Workaholics have the compulsive drive to work incessantly and therefore tend to allocate an exceptional amount of time to work. By doing so they neglect other life domains, such as leisure and family. Their obsession with work motivates them to be very active, but at the same time workaholics do not enjoy their work, as illustrated by many studies (Ng, Sorensen, & Feldman, 2007). Like engaged employees, workaholics are active and work very hard but their underlying motivation differs fundamentally. A study by van Beek, Hu, Schaufeli, Taris and Schreurs (2012) among Chinese healthcare professionals showed that the former are positively and intrinsically motivated, for them work is inherently enjoyable and gratifying ('work is fun'). In contrast, workaholics are negatively motivated by the fear of not being able to meet their self-imposed, excessively high performance standards ('work is a must'). These standards result from internalization processes by which external standards of self-worth and social approval are adopted. In other words, workaholics do not work so hard because they like their work, but because they feel that they have to because otherwise they may fail and as a consequence feel very bad about themselves. Seen from this perspective, workaholism is a 'bad' type of working hard and engagement is a 'good' type of working hard. This is also illustrated by the fact that workaholism is positively and engagement is negatively related to burnout (van Beek, Taris, & Schaufeli, 2011).

Hence, it can be concluded that different psychological processes seem to underlie the different types of employee-related well-being that are included in Figure 12.1. Moreover, it is important to note that various psychometrical studies have shown that the questionnaires that are used to tap various forms of employee well-being, such as the MBI (burnout), DUBS (boredom) and UWES (engagement), can be discriminated from each other as well as from measures of workaholism and job satisfaction (e.g. Reijseger et al., 2012; Schaufeli, Taris, & van Rhenen, 2008).

Replay

- The nature of employee well-being varies along two dimensions: pleasure–displeasure and activation–deactivation.
- Engaged employees are willing to go the extra mile, whereas satisfied employees are satiated.
- Engagement and workaholism are both characterized by a strong drive, but the nature of that drive differs.
- Burnout (resulting from overstimulation) and boredom (resulting from understimulation) are the opposites of engagement.
- All five types of employee well-being can be assessed independently from each other.

12.4 Antecedents and Consequences of Burnout, Boredom and Work Engagement

As indicated previously, by the end of 2012 approximately 8,000 publications had appeared on burnout, boredom and engagement at work. It is beyond the scope of the current chapter to discuss this massive body of knowledge. Rather, we briefly summarize the main antecedents, consequences and correlates in a number of tables, which are based on reviews and meta-analyses. It is important to note that the vast majority of empirical studies are cross-sectional in nature, which means that all variables are measured at the same point in time (see also Chapter 2). Evidently, this does not allow us to draw any conclusions about causes and effects. For instance, a significant relation between work overload and burnout – measured at the same time – could mean that overload is an antecedent that causes burnout, but also that it is a consequence because employees who are exhausted are more likely to experience their job as highly demanding. Additionally, an increasing number of longitudinal studies, which include two or more measurement occasions, suggest that reciprocal relations exist. In other words and following our example, work overload may act as an antecedent as well as a consequence of burnout. This implies that in reality relations may be more complicated than assumed by the simple sequence: antecedents → employee well-being → consequences. For that reason we will refer to 'potential' antecedents and consequences.

Another complicating factor is that various antecedents may interact with each other. For instance, negative effects of job demands, such as work overload or role problems, may be buffered by job resources, such as job control and social support, which may 'neutralize' this effect and thus protect employees from burning out (see also Chapter 7). In a similar vein, these job resources might boost employee engagement, particularly when job demands are high and jobs are challenging.

Antecedents and consequences of burnout

Table 12.1 summarizes the most important possible antecedents of burnout and is based on various qualitative reviews (Halbesleben & Buckley, 2004; Schaufeli & Enzmann, 1998; Shirom, 2002) as well as two recent meta-analyses (Alarcon, 2011; Crawford, LePine, & Rich, 2010).

The most consistent finding is that quantitative demands (e.g. too much work to do, time pressure, long work hours and frequent contact with customers or clients; see Chapter 5) as well as qualitative job demands (e.g. conflicting work roles, inadequate information to fulfil the work role, emotionally charged situations, imbalance between work and home; see Chapter 6) may lead to burnout. The reason is that such job demands activate an energy depletion process whereby an employee's sustained increases in effort to meet these demands drain his or her energy backup (see Chapter 8). An illustrative study in more than 200 Pennsylvania hospitals showed that an unfavourable patient-to-nurse ratio, which caused nurses to use more effort to do their jobs, was positively related to burnout (Aiken, Clarke, Sloane, Sochalski, & Silber, 2002). It appeared that an increase of one patient per nurse in a hospital's staffing level increased nurse burnout by 23% and patient mortality by 7% (after controlling for patient and hospital characteristics, such as severity of the illness and size of the hospital). Moreover, burnout is also likely to occur when interpersonal resources (e.g. social support from colleagues and supervisors) or other resources (e.g. feedback, participation in decision making and job control) that are instrumental in achieving one's work goals are lacking. For instance, Neveux (2007) found among French prison guards that depletion of resources such as co-worker support, participation and skill utilization led to burnout and, in turn, to depression and sickness absence.

Table 12.2 summarizes the most important possible consequences of burnout and is largely based on the same sources as Table 12.1, as well as on a meta-analysis by Swider and Zimmerman (2010).

Burnout has negative consequences for the individual employee as well as for the organization he or she is working for. Individual consequences pertain

Table 12.1 Potential antecedents of burnout.

Job demands
- Work overload
- Time pressure
- Number of work hours
- Number of clients, recipients, etc.
- Role problems
- Work–home interference
- Emotional demands

Job resources
- Lack of social support from colleagues and supervisor
- Lack of feedback
- Poor participation in decision making
- Lack of job control

Table 12.2 Potential consequences of burnout.

Employee health
- Anxiety and depression
- Psychosomatic and cardiovascular complaints
- Sleep disturbances
- Common infections

Organizational outcomes
- Poor organizational commitment
- Turnover (intention)
- Sickness absence
- Job performance

particularly to the employee's mental health (i.e. anxiety, depression, poor sleep and psychosomatic symptoms such as headaches, nausea and hypertension) as well as physical health (i.e. cardiovascular disease and common infections like flu, cold and gastroenteritis). For instance, a recent longitudinal study among Finnish dentists spanning eight years found that burnout predicted depression, instead of the other way around (Hakanen & Schaufeli, 2012). Although burnout has been related to poor physical health, the underlying psychological mechanism is still unknown. This is illustrated by a recent meta-analysis that concluded that 'no potential biomarkers for burnout were found' (Danhof-Pont, van Veen, & Zitman, 2011; p. 505). Burnout therefore does not lead to poor health via physiological changes that are indicated by biological markers such as particular hormones or blood cells. Negative consequences of burnout for the organization typically reflect the employees' withdrawal, either mentally (e.g. poor commitment and loyalty) or physically (e.g. turnover and frequent sickness absence). A meta-analysis showed – not surprisingly – that burnout is more strongly related to work performance when this is self-assessed, as compared to supervisor ratings or objective measures (Taris, 2006). This is probably caused by common method bias (see Chapter 2), which inflates correlations.

Antecedents and consequences of boredom

As indicated above, research on boredom at work is still rather scarce compared to that on burnout and engagement. Table 12.3 is therefore based on the relatively few studies that have been reviewed by Loukidou et al. (2009), and van der Heijden, Schepers and Nijssen (2012).

Not surprisingly, the clearest and most straightforward antecedent of boredom is carrying out monotonous and short-cycle repetitive work tasks, as are often found in, for instance, mechanical assembly, inspection and monitoring jobs. In a somewhat similar vein, boredom at work has also been associated with mental underload (e.g. 'mindless' jobs) and when employee abilities exceed their task demands (i.e. skill under-utilization). Behavioural constraints that result from bureaucratization and standardization may also result in

Table 12.3 Potential antecedents and consequences of boredom at work.

Antecedents
- Monotonous and repetitive work
- Mental underload and poor skill utilization
- Behavioural constraints
- Absence of meaning

Consequences
- Distress (e.g. dissatisfaction, hostility)
- Alcohol and drug abuse
- Injuries and accidents
- Sickness absence
- Turnover (intention)
- Poor performance
- Counterproductive work behaviour

boredom. For instance, helping professionals might feel bored when, instead of helping clients, they find themselves filling out forms and writing reports most of their time: their professional helping skills are not properly utilized. In one way or another, all antecedents of boredom mentioned so far refer to a lack of stimulation or challenge at work. However, research findings are not always consistent because, for instance, it has also been found that some workers enjoy repetitiveness.

As can be seen from Table 12.3, the negative consequences of boredom are similar to those of burnout (e.g. distress, sickness absence, turnover, poor performance). In addition, occasional alcohol and drug abuse have been mentioned as well as work-related injuries and accidents. Probably the most typical consequence of boredom is the display of counterproductive work behaviours (see also Chapter 13). For instance, Bruursema, Kessler and Spector (2011) conducted a study in which they found that employees who were bored were are also more likely to misbehave, that is, bored employees exhibit harmful and nasty behaviours that affect other people (abuse), they purposely do the job incorrectly (production deviance), they destroy the physical environment (sabotage), they avoid work through being absent or late (withdrawal) and they steal. The authors assume that boredom at work leads to negative emotions, particularly anger, hostility and aggression, which provoke this damaging and destructive behaviour.

Antecedents and consequences of work engagement

Tables 12.4 and 12.5 display the antecedents and consequences of work engagement, respectively, and are based on three reviews (Schaufeli & Salanova, 2008; Simpson, 2009; Mauno, Kinnunen, Mäkikangas, & Feldt, 2010) as well as two meta-analyses (Christian, Garza, & Slaughter, 2011; Halbesleben, 2010).

Although engagement is most strongly and consistently associated with job resources, so-called challenge demands (i.e. workload, time urgency, mental demands and responsibility) may foster work engagement as well (see also Chapter 6). These

Table 12.4 Potential antecedents of work engagement.

Challenge demands
- Workload
- Time urgency
- Mental demands
- Responsibility

Job resources
- Job control
- Social support
- Performance feedback
- Task variety
- Opportunities to develop
- Transformational leadership

Table 12.5 Potential consequences of work engagement.

Attitudes and behaviours
- Organizational commitment
- Personal initiative
- Low turnover (intention)
- Low sickness absence

Performance
- Job/task performance
- Service quality
- Innovativeness
- Business unit performance

are demands that have the potential to promote mastery, growth or future gains. This is in contrast to hindrance demands (see Chapter 6), which thwart personal growth, learning and goal-attainment (e.g. interpersonal conflict, emotional demands, role problems). Like challenge demands, job resources have an inherent motivational potential and may therefore act as antecedents of engagement. Such resources may be located at the task level (i.e. job control, feedback and task variety), interpersonal level (i.e. social support from co-workers and supervisor, including recognition and rewards) and organizational level (opportunities for learning and development, and transformational leadership that focuses on coaching, inspiration and stimulation).

Work engagement (Table 12.5) might lead to positive attitudes and behaviours that point to high motivation such as commitment, initiative and presence (i.e. low turnover and sickness absence).

In addition, work engagement seems to lead to better performance, including extra-role performance that goes beyond the formal job requirements ('going the extra mile') and qualitative performance such as better service quality and innovativeness. Companies may also benefit from engaged workers. For instance, a meta-analysis across almost 8,000 business units of 36 companies showed that, compared to units with fewer engaged employees, the more engaged units had more loyal and satisfied customers, were more productive, had better safety records and were more profitable (Harter, Schmidt, & Hayes, 2002).

Replay

- The main antecedents of burnout are high quantitative and qualitative job demands as well as poor job resources.
- Burnout has a negative impact on the individual (health) and on the organization (performance, sickness absence).
- Monotonous, repetitive, unchallenging and meaningless jobs foster boredom at work.
- The negative effects of boredom are similar to those of burnout, except that counterproductive work behaviour is more salient.
- Challenging job demands and job resources boost work engagement.
- The personal and organizational effects of engagement are opposite to those of burnout.
- Burnout mainly affects employee health, whereas engagement mainly affects employee motivation.

12.5 Individual Differences in Employee Well-being

The role that individual differences play in employee well-being is complex, as is illustrated by Figure 12.2. Perhaps the most obvious role is that certain personality traits, such as emotional instability, may act as a vulnerability factor for developing burnout. On the contrary, emotional stability may act as a resistance factor that promotes work engagement. In both cases a causal relation is assumed between a particular individual difference factor and employee well-being (Figure 12.2a). However, employees may also select particular professions that match with their personality. For instance, 'feeling types' who are responsive to the needs of others, may choose a highly stressful job as a nurse and therefore burn out. In that case instead of a causal relationship an indirect relationship exists between personality and well-being. That means that people with a particular personality profile may choose a particular kind of job, which, in its turn, fosters unwell-being (Figure 12.2b). Individual differences may also act as a 'third variable' (Figure 12.2c). For instance, self-efficacious employees might perceive more job resources and challenges than their non-efficacious colleagues. At the same time, self-efficacy is positively related to work engagement. In this case, the positive relation between job resources and engagement (see above) is explained by an individual difference (self-efficacy) that is related to resources as well as engagement. Finally, individual differences might moderate the relation between job characteristics and well-being (Figure 12.2d). For instance, when exposed to high job demands employees with high levels of neuroticism (i.e. who are emotional instable) are more prone to burnout than those with lower levels. Alternatively,

(a) Direct effect of individual differences (D) on well-being (W)

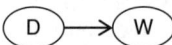

(b) Indirect effect of individual differences (D) on well-being (W) via choice of a particular job (J)

(c) Simultaneous effect of individual differences (D) as the third variable on both job characteristics (C) and well-being (W)

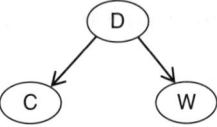

(d) Moderator effect of individual differences on the relationship between job characteristics (C) and well-being (W)

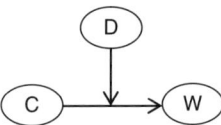

Figure 12.2 Various effects of individual differences on employee well-being.

extraverts are more engaged when they work in resourceful jobs than non-extraverts because they are quite energetic by nature. Hence, individual differences may also play a stress buffering or facilitating role.

Common individual differences

Table 12.6 presents an overview of the main individual differences that have been associated with burnout, boredom and work engagement. This table is based on the same sources as the previous tables as well as on two meta-analysis (Alcaron, Eschleman, & Bowling, 2009; Swider & Zimmerman, 2010).

It does not come as a surprise that burnout and engagement occur in employees with opposite personality profiles, as far as core individual differences are concerned. Burnout is associated with emotional instability, low levels of extraversion and negative dispositional affect, whereas work engagement is associated with emotional stability, extraversion and positive affect. This is illustrated by a study that mapped burned-out and engaged employees in a two-dimensional space that is defined by two orthogonal axes representing extraversion and emotional stability (Langelaan, Bakker, van Doornen, & Schaufeli, 2006). Burned-out employees clustered in the instability-low extraversion quadrant, whilst the engaged employees clustered in the opposite stability-high extraversion quadrant. There are also some indications that extraverts feel bored while doing monotonous and

Table 12.6 Individual differences and employee well-being.

Core individual differences
- Emotional stability
- Extraversion
- Positive/negative affect

Beliefs and core self-evaluations
- Self-efficacy
- Self-esteem
- Optimism

Inactivity (burnout)
- External locus of control
- Lack of hardiness
- Passive coping style

Need for stimulation (boredom)
- Sensation seeking
- Boredom proneness

Drive (work engagement)
- Need for achievement
- Conscientiousness

repetitive work tasks. This makes sense because, as noted before, feeling energetic is one of the hallmarks of extraversion.

In a similar vein, opposite patterns of basic beliefs and core self-evaluations are observed for burnout and work engagement. While burnout is associated with low levels of self-efficacy, self-esteem and optimism, the reverse is true for engagement. So far, research has not linked these beliefs and evaluations to boredom at work.

Specific individual differences

Earlier, common – albeit mirrored – relations of burnout and engagement with core individual differences, beliefs and self-evaluations were discussed. However, more typical relations are also observed of individual differences with each of the aspects of employee well-being. For instance, burnout is associated with dispositional indicators that reflect inactivity, such as external locus of control (i.e. the tendency to attribute outcomes of events to external circumstances, such as bad luck and powerful others rather than to one's own actions), lack of hardiness (i.e. the tendency not to interpret demanding situations in terms of commitment, control and challenge, but instead as stressful, uncontrollable and threatening) and a passive coping style (e.g. avoidance, denial). It is easy to see that such dispositions promote inactivity in employees, which undermines their attempts to deal successfully with high job demands and lacking job resources.

Boredom has been associated with dispositional factors that reflect the need for external or internal stimulation. The idea is that individuals differ in the amount of stimuli required to maintain an optimal level of arousal. Sensation seekers have a high need for varied, novel and complex experiences, and are willing to take considerable risks to experience such situations. They look for adventures and thrills, and are easily bored when their work is unchallenging, repetitive and lacks variety. In a similar vein, boredom-proneness has been associated with boredom at work. Boredom-proneness is a somewhat more comprehensive concept than boredom that also includes the need for internal stimulation, that is, the ability to keep oneself interested and entertained.

Finally, work engagement is linked with dispositional factors that underlie the employee's strong drive. More specifically, engaged employees are characterized by a high need for achievement. That means that engaged employees have a strong desire for significant accomplishment and mastering of skills, and pursue high performance standards. In fact, need for achievement is a facet of conscientiousness, which is a more comprehensive personality trait that also includes self-discipline, thoroughness, carefulness and self-organization. Since conscientiousness has consistently been shown to be related to job performance (Barrick & Mount; 1991), it might act as a so-called 'third variable' that explains the engagement–performance nexus.

Replay

- Relations between dispositions and employee well-being are complex. Dispositions may directly or indirectly influence well-being, or may act as third variables or moderators that explain relations with job characteristics or outcomes.
- Burnout, boredom and engagement are linked to similar common individual differences and fundamental beliefs and self-evaluations, albeit in different ways.
- Burnout, boredom and engagement are also linked with typical individual differences that refer to inactivity, the need for stimulation and drive, respectively.

12.6 Possible Explanations for Burnout, Boredom and Work Engagement

In this final section we briefly present the most important psychological explanations for the occurrence of burnout, boredom and work engagement.

Burnout

Most individual-level psychological explanations for burnout focus on employee expectations in relation to work. More specifically, it is assumed that the discrepancy between high ideals and aspirations on the one hand, and the harsh reality of everyday working life on the other constitutes the root cause of burnout. Seen from this perspective, burnout is the erosion of initial engagement (see Section 12.2), which is exemplified by the idealistically motivated human services professional. This is illustrated by the phase-model of disillusionment proposed by Edelwich and Brodsky (1980), which distinguishes between enthusiasm (1st phase), stagnation (2nd phase), frustration (3rd phase) and apathy (4th phase). Despite their popularity, such phase models have not been corroborated by empirical research.

In contrast, the interpersonal explanation of burnout received considerably more empirical support (Maslach, Schaufeli, & Leiter, 2001). The basic tenet of that approach is that burnout is considered to be a negative experience that results from emotional overload and is embedded in the context of interpersonal relationships at work. More specifically, it is assumed that exhaustion occurs first, leading to the development of cynicism and depersonalization, which leads subsequently to inefficacy (see also Section 12.2). For example, a study of hospital nurses yielded the following sequence: (i) stressful interactions with supervisors increase the nurses' feelings of exhaustion, (ii) high levels of exhaustion lead to cynicism, especially if nurses lack supportive contact with their co-workers, (iii) as cynicism persists, the nurses' feelings of efficacy diminish, although supportive contact with co-workers may help to decelerate this process (Leiter & Maslach, 1988).

But why are interactions with supervisors – or recipients, customers or co-workers, for that matter – so stressful in the first place? The answer is found in evolutionary psychology and has to do with lack of reciprocity (Buunk & Schaufeli, 1999). Humans are social animals who can only survive in groups and reciprocity is the 'psychological glue' that binds these social groups together. Evolutionarily speaking, people are predisposed to strive for balanced social relationships with others that are governed by the principle of reciprocity. But when this principle is violated and the investments in the relationship with others (e.g. time, energy and attention) are not proportional to the outcomes (e.g. recognition, information and support) energy is drained, which eventually may result in exhaustion. In an attempt to restore the balance between give and take, the employee starts to give less, which manifests itself in the withdrawal and mental distancing that are typical for burnout. However, this strategy is counterproductive and bound to be unsuccessful because it further diminishes positive outcomes. This is nicely illustrated by a study among doctors discussed earlier (Section 12.2) that showed that those who invest less in the relationships with their patients run a higher risk of future burnout (Bakker et al., 2000). Such social exchange relationships exist not only at the interpersonal level, but also at team and organizational level, that is, on these levels social exchange relationships exist that might lead to lack of reciprocity when the balance of give and take with the team or with the organization is disturbed (see Figure 12.3).

Following this reasoning and based on several studies, Schaufeli (2006) proposed a social exchange model that explains burnout as the result of an imbalance between investments and outcomes at the interpersonal, team and organizational level. This not only leads to burnout, but also to withdrawal from the team (e.g. isolation from other team members, lack of commitment) and from the organization (e.g. sickness absence, turnover).

Boredom

Only few psychological explanations exist on boredom that revolve around the role of arousal in monotonous tasks (Loukidou et al., 2009). In fact, two contradictory perspectives exist, each of which is supported by some limited empirical evidence. The first perspective assumes that low external stimulation might cause

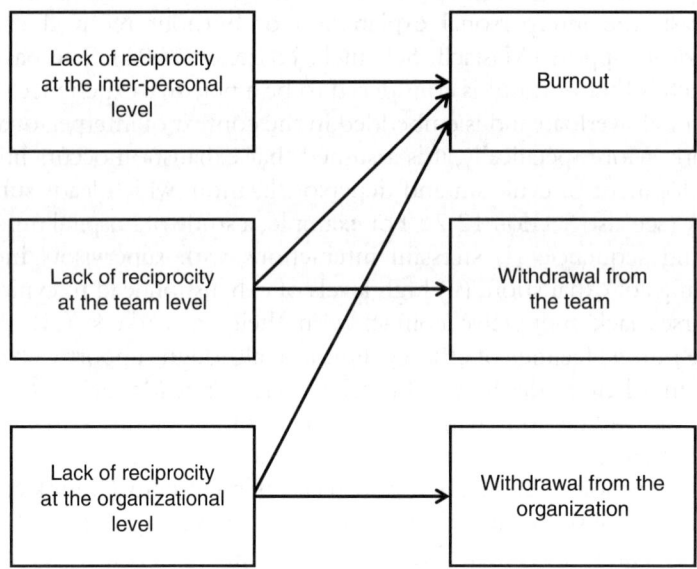

Figure 12.3 Burnout and withdrawal at different levels of social exchange (Schaufeli, 2006).

low internal arousal, which is expressed as inattention, distress, daydreaming and sleepiness, all typical indicators of boredom. In contrast, the rival view assumes that low external arousal has the exact opposite effect, namely a *high* level of internal arousal. This manifests itself by restlessness and the active struggle to remain active in order to compensate for the poorly stimulating work environment. Of course, as we have seen above, people may differ individually in their preferred need for stimulation. Both perspectives agree that monotony affects attention and that this, in its turn, will decrease performance. More specifically, when an uninteresting, unchallenging task has to be performed, attention will deteriorate because of either high or low internal arousal, and consequently performance will suffer.

Work engagement

Essentially, work engagement results from the inherently motivating nature of resources. By their very nature, job resources invigorate employees, encourage their persistence, and make them focus on their efforts, and that is exactly what work engagement is about. In a similar vein to job resources (see Chapter 4), personal resources are functional in accomplishing work goals, and they stimulate personal goals such as growth and development. They are defined as psychological characteristics or aspects of the self that are generally associated with resiliency and that refer to the ability to control and impact one's environment successfully.

Based on the motivating potential of job and personal resources, Bakker and Demerouti (2007) proposed a model of engagement that is displayed in Figure 12.4.

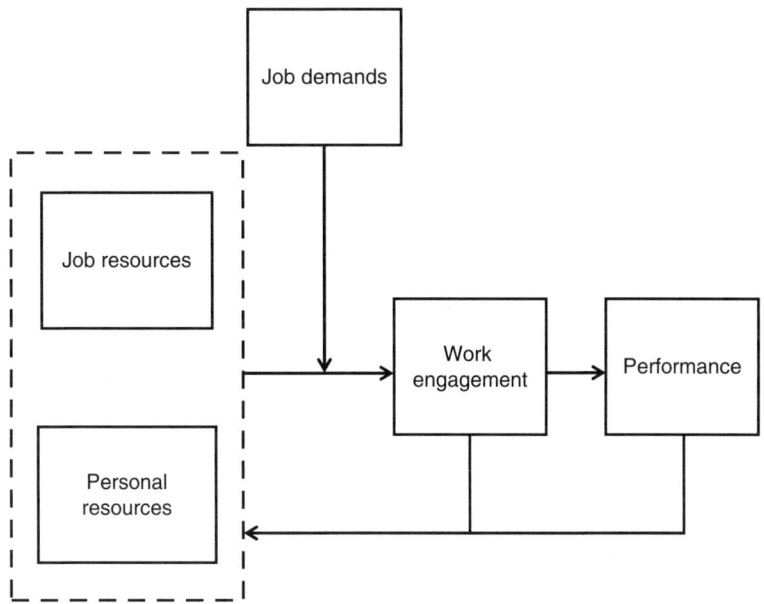

Figure 12.4 A model for work engagement (after Bakker & Demerouti, 2007).

This model, which is supported by a considerable amount of research, assumes that job and personal resources are particularly important when job demands are high. This means that resources become salient and gain their motivational potential when employees are confronted with high job demands. In that case job resources are especially effective in accomplishing work goals and will thus boost engagement. In its turn engagement increases performance, not only because it is associated with energy, persistence and focused effort, but also because it is associated with the appropriate attitudes and behaviours (e.g. organizational commitment, personal initiative and presence; see Table 12.5).

Most importantly, mounting empirical evidence suggests the existence of a feedback loop that runs back from performance and engagement to job and personal resources (Salanova, Schaufeli, Xanthopoulou, & Bakker, 2010). This feedback loop is consistent with notions of resource accumulation after successful performance. For instance, when an engaged employee accomplishes his or her work task, this not only increases his or her level of self-efficacy (a belief that acts as a personal resource), but also leads to positive feedback from one's supervisor (a job resource). Because of its dynamic nature, the model assumes an upward gain spiral that leads to more engagement, better performance and a progressive increase in performance. Indeed, some limited evidence for such a process has been found (see Salanova et al., 2010).

Replay

- The psychological explanation of burnout has to do with lacking reciprocity in social exchange relationships involving other persons, the team and the entire organization.

- The psychological explanation of boredom has to do with the role of internal arousal when carrying out monotonous work tasks. Arousal may be either too high or too low, but in any case performance is hampered.
- The psychological explanation of work engagement has to do with the inherent motivational quality of (job and personal) resources.

12.7 Conclusions

Employees feel different at work, and these feelings matter. In this chapter, three types of employee well-being have been discussed: burnout, boredom and work engagement. Burnout is a reaction to chronic job stress that is characterized particularly by exhaustion and mental distancing. These symptoms, which can be seen as psychological responses to *over*stimulation at work, represent the inability and the unwillingness to spend effort, respectively. Boredom is an unpleasant state of low arousal and dissatisfaction which, in contrast to burnout, results from *under*stimulation. Finally, and contrary to burnout and boredom, work engagement is a *pleasant* state that is characterized by energy and involvement – the direct opposites of exhaustion and mental distancing.

Employee well-being is related to the person characteristics as well as to the job characteristics. For instance, burnout, boredom and engagement are linked to typical individual differences that refer to inactivity, need for stimulation and drive, respectively. Furthermore, each of these three types of employee well-being is associated with a specific set of job characteristics. The most important causes of burnout are high job demands and poor job resources, whereas the opposite is true for work engagement. Boredom seems to be caused by monotony and lack of meaning.

The consequences of burnout and boredom are negative, whereas the consequences of work engagement are positive. Burnout and boredom lead to poor employee health and to increased costs for organizations, for instance in terms of sickness absence and deteriorated performance. Burnout and boredom should therefore be prevented. In contrast, work engagement is associated with positive individual and organizational outcomes, and should therefore be fostered. Research has identified various drivers and psychological mechanisms that may constitute the bases for preventing burnout and boredom, and for boosting work engagement. For instance, a mismatch between give and take has been uncovered as an explanation for burnout. This means that in order to decrease burnout the balance between give and take should be restored. Boredom results from unchallenging jobs and thus making jobs more meaningful and challenging would decrease boredom. In a similar vein the motivational potential of resources can be used to promote work engagement.

Discussion Points

1. Burnout and boredom are two negative patters of employee well-being at work. What (if possible) preventive strategies can organizations use?
2. How far can burnout and engagement be considered each other's opposite poles?

3. Engaged employees are positive and energetic at work, and they are more productive. But can employees also be 'too engaged'? Is there is an optimal level of engagement?
4. It has been maintained that in order to burn out, one first as to be on fire. Do you agree? Why (not)?
5. Do you think that burnout, engagement and boredom are 'contagious', that is that they spread from one employee to another? Why would this (not) be the case?

Learning by Doing

1. Read the stories of Peter, Geoff and Mary closely (Work Psychology in Action boxes). Write down the typical characteristics of burnout for Peter, the typical characteristics of boredom for Geoff and the typical characteristics of engagement for Mary. Do these characteristics overlap? Can you identify lack of reciprocity, under-stimulation and motivating resources in the stories of Peter, Geoff and Mary, respectively?
2. Interview a friend or a family member whom you consider to be 'engaged' at work and ask him or her what is energy draining (job demands) and what is energizing at work (job resources). Repeat the same with a friend or a family member whom you consider to be 'stressed'. Most likely in the former case the number of demands will outweigh the number of resources, whereas in the latter case the reverse will be true. Keep Tables 12.1 and 12.4 in mind while interviewing.
3. Download the short version of the Utrecht Work Engagement scale from www.wilmarschaufeli.nl> downloads> tests, as well as the test manual from downloads> test manuals. Ask some friends or family members to fill out the inventory and classify their levels of work engagement using Table 31 of the test manual.
4. Imagine you have to carry out an employee well-being survey for a hospital, for an IT company and for a chemical plant. Based on Tables 12.1–12.6, what aspects would you include and why? Try to design a short but powerful survey that fits the nature of the organization. Keep in mind that in hospitals employees work with people, in IT companies with information and in industrial plants with things.

Further Reading

On burnout

Maslach, C., Schaufeli, W. B., & Leiter, M. P. (2001). Job burnout. *Annual Review of Psychology, 52*, 397–422.

On boredom

Loukidou, L., Loan-Clarke, J., & Daniels, K. (2009). Boredom in the workplace: More than monotonous tasks. *International Journal of Management Reviews, 11*, 381–405.

On work engagement
Bakker, A. B., & Leiter, M. P. (Eds.) (2010). *Work engagement: A handbook of essential theory and research*. New York: Psychology Press.

References

Aiken, L. H., Clarke, S. P., Sloane, D. M., Sochalski, J., & Silber, J. H. (2002). Hospital nurse staffing and patient mortality, nurse burnout, and job satisfaction. *Journal of the American Medical Association, 288*, 1987–1993.

Alarcon, G. M. (2011). A meta-analysis of burnout with job demands, resources and attitudes. *Journal of Vocational Behavior, 79*, 549–562.

Alcaron, G. M., Eschleman, K. J., & Bowling, N. A. (2009). Relations between personality variables and burnout: A meta-analysis. *Work & Stress, 23*, 244–263.

Attridge, M. (2009). Measuring and managing employee work engagement: A review of the research and business literature. *Journal of Workplace Behavioral Health, 24*, 282–398.

Bakker, A. B., & Demerouti, E. (2007). Towards a model of work engagement. *Career Development International, 13*, 209–223.

Bakker, A. B., Schaufeli, W. B., Sixma, H. J., Bosveld, W., & van Dierendonck, D. (2000). Patient demands, lack of reciprocity, and burnout: A five-year longitudinal study among general practitioners. *Journal of Organizational Behavior, 21*, 425–441.

Barrick, M. R., & Mount, M. K. (1991). The Big Five personality dimension and job performance: A meta-analysis. *Personnel Psychology, 44*, 1–26.

Bruursema, K., Kessler, S. R., & Spector, P. E. (2011). Bored employees misbehaving: The relationship between boredom and counterproductive work behavior. *Work & Stress, 25*, 93–107.

Buunk, B. P., & Schaufeli, W. B. (1999). Reciprocity in Interpersonal Relationships: An evolutionary perspective on its importance for health and well-being. In W. Stroebe, & M. Hewstone (Eds.), *European Review of Social Psychology, Volume 10*, 260–291.

Christian, M. S., Garza, A. S., & Slaughter, J. E. (2011). Work engagement: A quantitative review and test of its relations with and contextual performance. *Personnel Psychology, 64*, 89–136.

Crawford, E. R., LePine, J. A., & Rich, B. L. (2010). Linking job demands and resources to employee engagement and burnout: A theoretical extension and meta-analytic test. *Journal of Applied Psychology, 95*, 834–848.

Danhof-Pont, M. B., van Veen, T., & Zitman, F. G. (2011). Biomarkers in burnout: A systematic review. *Journal of Psychosomatic Research, 70*, 505–524.

Edelwich, J., & Brodsky, A. (1980). *Burn-out: Stages of disillusionment in the helping professions*. New York: Human Services Press.

Farmer, F., & Sundberg, N. D. (1986). Boredom proneness: The development and correlates of a new scale. *Journal of Personality Assessment, 50*, 4–17.

Hakanen, J. J., & Schaufeli, W. B. (2012). Do burnout and work engagement predict depressive symptoms and life satisfaction? A three-wave seven-year prospective study. *Journal of Affective Disorders, 141*, 415–424.

Halbsleben, J. R. B (2010). A meta-analysis of work engagement: Relationships with burnout, demands, resources and consequences. In A. B. Bakker, & M. P. Leiter (Eds.), *Work engagement: A handbook of essential theory and research* (pp. 102–117). New York: Psychology Press.

Halbesleben, J. R. B., & Buckley, M. R. (2004). Burnout in organizational life. *Journal of Management, 30*, 859–879.

Harter, J. K., Schmidt, F. L., & Hayes, T. L. (2002). Business-unit-level relationships between employee satisfaction, employee engagement, and business outcomes: A meta-analysis. *Journal of Applied Psychology, 87*, 268–279.

Kant, I. J., Jansen, N. W. H., van Amelsfoort, L. G. P. M., Mohren, D. C. L., & Swaen, G. M. H. (2004). Burnout in de werkende bevolking. Resultaten van de Maastrichtse Cohort Studie [*Burnout in the working population: Results from the Maastricht Cohort Study*]. *Gedrag en Organisatie, 17*, 5–17.

Karasek, R. A., & Theorell, T. (1990). *Healthy work: Stress, productivity and the reconstruction of working life*. New York: Basic Books.

Kornhauser, A. (1965). *Mental health of the industrial worker: A Detroit study*. New York: John Wiley & Sons.

Langelaan, S., Bakker, A. B., van Doornen, L. J. P., & Schaufeli, W. B. (2006). Burnout and work engagement: Do individual differences make a difference? *Personality and Individual Differences, 40*, 521–532.

Lazarus, R. S., & Folkman, S. (1984). *Stress, appraisal and coping*. New York: Springer.

Leiter, M. P., & Maslach, C. (1988). The impact of interpersonal environment on burnout and organizational commitment. *Journal of Organizational Behavior, 9*, 297–308.

Loukidou, L., Loan-Clarke, J., & Daniels, K. (2009). Boredom in the workplace: More than monotonous tasks. *International Journal of Management Reviews, 11*, 381–405.

Maslach, C., Jackson, S. E., & Leiter, M. (1996). *Maslach Burnout Inventory manual* (3rd ed.). Palo Alto, CA: Consulting Psychologists Press.

Maslach C., & Leiter M. P. (1997). *The truth about burnout*. San Francisco: Jossey-Bass.

Maslach, C., Schaufeli, W. B., & Leiter, M. P. (2001). Job burnout. *Annual Review of Psychology, 52*, 397–422.

Mauno, S., Kinnunen, U., Mäkikangas, A., & Feldt, T. (2010). Job demands and resources as antecedents of work engagement: A qualitative review and directions for future research. In S. L. Albrecht (Ed.), *Handbook of employee engagement: Perspectives, issues, research and practice* (pp. 111–128). Northampton, MA: Edwin Elgar.

Mikulas, W., & Vodanovich, S. (1993). The essence of boredom. *The Psychological Record, 43*, 3–12.

Münsterberg, H. (1913). *Psychology and Industrial Efficiency*. Boston & New York: Houghton Mifflin (Reprinted Bristol:Thoemmes Press, 1999).

Neveux, J.-P. (2007). Jailed resources: Conservation of resources as applied to burnout among prison guards. *Journal of Organizational Psychology, 28*, 21–42.

Ng, T. W. H., Sorensen, K. L., & Feldman, D. C. (2007). Dimensions, antecedents, and consequences of workaholism: a conceptual integration and extension. *Journal of Organizational Behavior, 28*, 111–136.

O'Hanlon, J. F. (1981). Boredom: Practical consequences of a theory. *Acta Psychologica, 49*, 53–82.

Reijseger, G., Schaufeli, W. B., Peeters, M. C. W., Taris, T. W., van Beek I., & Ouweneel, E. (2012). Watching the paint dry: Initial validation of the Dutch Boredom Scale. *Anxiety, Stress & Coping: An International Journal*, doi:10.1080/10615806.2012.720676

Russell, J. A. (1980). A circumplex model of affect. *Journal of Personality and Social Psychology, 39*, 1161–1178.

Salanova, M., Schaufeli, W. B., Xanthopoulou, D., & Bakker, A. B. (2010). Gain spirals of resources and work engagement. In A. B. Bakker, & M. P. Leiter (Eds.), *Work engagement: A handbook of essential theory and research* (pp. 118–131). New York: Psychology Press.

Schaap, C., Schaufeli, W., & Hoogduin, K. (1995). Diagnostiek en behandeling van chronische werkstress en burnout [*Assessment and treatment of chronic job stress and burnout*]. *Directieve Therapie, 15*, 215–232.

Schaufeli, W. B. (2006). The balance of give and take: Toward a social exchange model of burnout. *International Review of Social Psychology, 19*, 87–131.

Schaufeli, W. B., & Bakker, A. B. (2007). Burnout en bevlogenheid [*Burnout and work engagement*]. In W. B. Schaufeli, & A. B. Bakker (Eds.). De psychologie van arbeid en gezondheid [*The psychology of work and health*] (pp. 341–358). Houten: Bohn Stafleu van Loghum.

Schaufeli, W. B., & Bakker, A. B. (2010). The conceptualization and measurement of work engagement. In A. B. Bakker, & M. P. Leiter (Eds.), *Work engagement: A handbook of essential theory and research* (pp. 10–24). New York: Psychology Press.

Schaufeli, W. B., Bakker, A. B., & Salanova, M. (2006). The measurement of work engagement with a short questionnaire: A cross-national study. *Educational and Psychological Measurement, 66*, 701–716.

Schaufeli, W. B., & Enzmann, D. (1998). *The burnout companion to research and practice: A critical analysis*. London: Taylor & Francis.

Schaufeli, W. B., Leiter, M. P., & Maslach, C. (2009). Burnout: 35 years of research and practice. *Career Development International, 14*, 204–220.

Schaufeli, W. B., & Salanova, M. (2008). Enhancing work engagement through the management of human resources. In K. Näswall, M. Sverke, & J. Hellgren (Eds.), *The individual in the changing working life* (pp. 380–404). Cambridge: Cambridge University Press.

Schaufeli, W. B., Salanova, M., González-Romá, V., & Bakker, A. B. (2002). The measurement of engagement and burnout: A two sample confirmatory factor analytic approach. *Journal of Happiness Studies, 3,* 71–92.

Schaufeli, W. B., & Taris, T. W. (2005). Commentary. The conceptualization and measurement of burnout: Common ground and worlds apart. *Work & Stress, 19,* 356–262.

Schaufeli, W. B., Taris, T. W., & van Rhenen, W. (2008). Workaholism, burnout and engagement: Three of a kind or three different kinds of employee well-being? *Applied Psychology: An International Review, 57,* 173–203.

Shirom, A. (2002). Job-related burnout: A review. In J. C. Quick, & L. R. Tetrick (Eds.), *Handbook of occupational health psychology* (pp. 245–264). Washington, DC: American Psychological Association.

Simpson, M. R. (2009). Engagement at work: A review of the literature. *International Journal of Nursing Studies, 46,* 1012–1024.

Stouffer, S. A., Suchman, E. A., de Vinney, L. C., Stra, S. A., & Williams, R. M. (1949). *The American soldier.* New York: John Wiley & Sons.

Swider, B. W., & Zimmerman, R. D. (2010). Born to burnout: A meta-analytic path model of personality, job burnout, and work outcomes. *Journal of Vocational Behavior, 76,* 847–506.

Taris, T. W. (2006). Is there a relationship between burnout and objective performance? A critical review of 16 studies. *Work & Stress, 20,* 316–334.

Taris, T. W., Schaufeli, W. B., & Shimazu, A. (2010). The push and pull of work: About the difference between workaholism and work engagement. In A. B. Bakker & M. P. Leiter (Eds.), *Work engagement: A handbook of essential theory and research* (pp. 39–53). New York: Psychology Press.

van Beek, I., Hu, Q., Schaufeli, W. B., Taris, T. W., & Schreurs, B. H. (2012). For fun, love or money. What drives workaholic, engaged and burned-out employees at work? *Applied Psychology: An International Review, 61,* 30–55.

van Beek, I., Taris. T. W., & Schaufeli, W. B. (2011). Workaholic and work engaged employees: Dead ringers or worlds apart? *Journal of Occupational Health Psychology, 16,* 468–482.

van der Heijden, G., Schepers, J., & Nijssen, E. (2012). Understanding workplace boredom among white collar employees: Temporal reactions and individual differences. *European Journal of Work & Organizational Psychology, 21,* 349–375.

Warr, P. B., & Inceoglu, I. (2012). Job engagement, job satisfaction and contrasting associations with person-job fit. *Journal of Occupational Health Psychology, 17,* 129–138.

Williams, G. (2008). *Daily Finance, May 18.* Retrieved from http://www.dailyfinance.com/2008/05/18/bored-of-work-you-may-have-a-case-of-boreout/.

13
Job Satisfaction, Motivation and Performance

NATHAN A. BOWLING

Chapter Objectives

After studying this chapter, you should be able to:

- define job satisfaction and job performance;
- discuss the causal nature of the relation between job satisfaction and job performance;
- discuss the factors (i.e. moderators) that influence the strength of the job satisfaction–job performance relation;
- discuss the role of motivation in the job satisfaction–job performance relation.

The relation between job satisfaction and job performance is among one of the most widely studied topics within work psychology. As evidence of its popularity as a research topic, several literature reviews (e.g. Iaffaldano & Muchinsky, 1985; Judge, Thoresen, Bono, & Patton, 2001) have been published that have examined the relation between job satisfaction and job performance. Although a widely held belief among managers and employees is simply that 'happy workers are productive workers' (Fisher, 2003, Study 1), researchers have identified several complexities regarding the job satisfaction–job performance relation. There is disagreement among work psychologists, for example, concerning whether

---

An Introduction to Contemporary Work Psychology, First Edition.
Edited by Maria C. W. Peeters, Jan de Jonge and Toon W. Taris.
© 2014 John Wiley & Sons, Ltd. Published 2014 by John Wiley & Sons, Ltd.

satisfaction causes performance, whether performance causes satisfaction or whether a causal relation even exists between the two.

The current chapter explores these and other complexities of the satisfaction–performance relation. After providing brief definitions of job satisfaction and job performance, the chapter reviews theory and empirical findings addressing the relation between satisfaction and performance. Attention is given to motivational processes as explanations of the satisfaction–performance relation. The chapter concludes with a discussion of the possibility that the strength of the satisfaction–performance relation depends on several factors, such as reward contingency, job complexity and job demands.

13.1 Defining Job Satisfaction and Job Performance

Because job satisfaction and job performance are both complex variables, it is important to provide clear definitions of each and to describe their various dimensions. The satisfaction and performance dimensions described in the following sub-sections will guide much of the discussion of the current chapter.

Job satisfaction

Job satisfaction is an attitude that represents the extent to which a person likes or dislikes his or her job (Brief, 1998). Like other attitudes, job satisfaction includes both an affective and a cognitive component (Schleicher, Watt, & Greguras, 2004). The affective component of job satisfaction reflects the emotions or feelings one has in response to one's job (e.g. feelings of excitement, contentment or joy), whereas the cognitive component refers to one's thoughts or beliefs about the job (e.g. beliefs that one's job offers autonomy, challenge or variety). As discussed below, the global satisfaction approach and the facet satisfaction approach represent the two primary ways of conceptualizing job satisfaction.

Global job satisfaction
Global job satisfaction focuses on workers' *overall* attitude toward their jobs and is illustrated by the following self-report items from the Michigan Organizational Assessment Questionnaire (Cammann, Fichman, Jenkins, & Klesh, 1979):

'All in all I am satisfied with my job.'
'In general, I like working here.'
'In general, I don't like my job.' (Note that this third item is reverse-scored.)

Facet job satisfaction
Facet job satisfaction, on the other hand, focuses on workers' attitudes toward specific aspects of their job. For example, the Job Descriptive Index (JDI; Smith, Kendall, & Hulin, 1969), the most commonly used measure of facet satisfaction, assesses satisfaction with five specific aspects of work: (i) work tasks, (ii) supervision, (iii) co-workers, (iv) pay and (v) promotional opportunities. The JDI, like other facet satisfaction measures, yields separate satisfaction scores for each job

satisfaction sub-dimension. Thus, the facet approach recognizes that a given worker can be satisfied with some aspects of work, but dissatisfied with others. The following example items from Beehr et al. (2006) are representative of the type of content typically assessed by facet satisfaction measures:

'All in all, I am very satisfied with the things I do at work.' (satisfaction with work tasks)
'Overall, I am very pleased with the way my manager supervises me.' (satisfaction with supervision)
'I am more pleased with my co-workers than with almost anyone I have ever worked with before.' (satisfaction with co-workers)
'All in all, I am very satisfied with my pay.' (satisfaction with pay)
'All in all, I am very satisfied with my chances for promotion.' (satisfaction with promotional opportunities)

Job performance

Job performance reflects the behaviours employees engage in, and from the standpoint of the organization are either productive or counterproductive (see LePine, Erez, & Johnson, 2002). Given this broad definition, it is not surprising that job satisfaction is generally regarded as a multi-faceted construct (see Campbell, 1990). Indeed, research supports the existence of three broad dimensions of job performance: (i) task performance, (ii) organizational citizenship behaviours and (iii) counterproductive work behaviours (for a discussion of this three-factor conceptualization of job performance see Rotundo & Sackett, 2002; for a slightly different taxonomy see Reijseger, Schaufeli, Peeters, & Taris, 2012). Each of these forms of job performance is defined below.

Task performance

Task performance, which is the form of performance with which managers and employees are generally most familiar, represents the extent to which workers effectively engage in the job duties formally identified in their job description (Borman & Motowidlo, 1993). As such, administrative decisions (e.g. promotions, pay increases, terminations) are typically determined by one's level of task performance. Although supervisor ratings of subordinates are most often used to assess task performance, it is possible in some jobs to collect objective indicators of task performance. The performance of a salesperson, for example, can be assessed by recording the total value of the products he or she has sold during a given amount of time.

Organizational citizenship behaviours

Organizational citizenship behaviours (OCBs) refer to behaviours not formally included in one's job description that are nonetheless helpful to the organization as a whole or to individual people at work, such as supervisors or co-workers (Organ & Ryan, 1995). Oftentimes, engaging in OCBs is described as 'going above and beyond the call of duty' (Podsakoff, MacKenzie, Paine, & Bachrach, 2000). Examples of OCBs include talking favourably to outsiders about one's employer, volunteering to work on unpleasant assignments and assisting an overextended co-worker with his or her job tasks. Although OCBs were initially seen by researchers as voluntary or discretionary behaviours that are not formally rewarded by one's organization, more recent research suggests that engaging in OCBs often does play a role in favourable administrative decisions (e.g. promotions; Hui, Lam, & Law, 2000).

Counterproductive work behaviours
Counterproductive work behaviours (CWBs) represent deviant behaviours that workers engage in for the purpose of harming their organization as a whole or harming individual people at work (Spector et al., 2006). Examples of CWBs include stealing from one's employer, bullying a co-worker and leaving work early without permission.

Employee withdrawal behaviour
Employee withdrawal, which includes any strategy one uses to avoid dissatisfying work (e.g. by being absent from work, being late or quitting one's job; Hanisch & Hulin, 1990), is included in the current chapter as a separate manifestation of job performance. Although withdrawal behaviour is sometimes included as a specific form of counterproductive work behaviour (Spector et al., 2006), it is treated as separate here because it has distinct underlying motives: whereas CWBs represent one's efforts to harm one's employer, withdrawal represents one's efforts to distance himself or herself from work.

Having provided definitions of different forms of job satisfaction and job performance, it is time to discuss the satisfaction-performance relation. The following sections review research examining job satisfaction's relation with task performance, OCBs and CWBs, and employee withdrawal behaviour (see Table 13.1 for

Table 13.1 Meta-analytic results examining the relation between global job satisfaction and different indices of job performance.

Performance index	Satisfaction–performance relation (average corrected correlation)	k	N	Relevant quantitative review
Task performance	0.30	312	54,471	Judge, Thoresen, Bono and Patton (2001)
Organizational citizenship behaviour	0.24	72	7,100	LePine, Erez and Johnson (2002)
Counterproductive work behaviour	−0.37	25	6,106	Dalal (2005)
Absenteeism	−0.24	12	3,732	Farrell and Stamm (1988)
Turnover	−0.19	67	24,566	Griffeth, Hom and Gaertner (2000)
Lateness	−0.11	15	3,767	Koslowsky, Sagie, Krausz and Singer (1997)

k = number of studies; N = total sample size.

a summary of quantitative reviews or meta-analyses linking global job satisfaction to different indices of job performance).

Replay

Job satisfaction and job performance are both complex variables. Different forms of job satisfaction have been studied, including global job satisfaction and facet job satisfaction. The various forms of job performance include task performance, OCBs, CWBs and employee withdrawal behaviour.

13.2 The Relation Between Job Satisfaction and Task Performance

Decades of research have found a positive relation between job satisfaction and task performance (Iaffaldano & Muchinsky, 1985; Judge, Thoresen, Bono, & Patton, 2001). Although researchers have disagreed on the precise strength of the satisfaction–task performance relation, the overwhelming consensus is that the relation is positive. In other words, workers who are satisfied are generally good performers and workers who are dissatisfied are generally poor performers. An influential meta-analysis by Iaffaldano and Muchinsky (1985), for example, found a modest positive relation between satisfaction and performance (average corrected correlation = 0.17). However, a more recent and comprehensive meta-analytic review of 312 studies (total sample size = 54,471) by Judge et al. (2001) found a relatively stronger positive satisfaction–performance relation (average corrected correlation = 0.30). Thus, based on the accumulated evidence, one can safely conclude that a positive relation exists between job satisfaction and task performance.

The meta-analyses cited above (Iaffaldano & Muchinsky, 1985; Judge et al. (2001) were primarily concerned with global job satisfaction. However, research has also examined the relations between job satisfaction facets and task performance. In a meta-analysis of the JDI facets, Kinicki, McKee-Ryan, Schriesheim and Carson (2002), for example, found that satisfaction with work itself (average corrected correlation = 0.18), supervision (average corrected correlation = 0.23), co-workers (average corrected correlation = 0.20), pay (average corrected correlation = 0.15), and promotional opportunities (average corrected correlation = 0.18) were each positively related to task performance. It is notable that these relations are consistently weaker than the global satisfaction–task performance relation reported by Judge et al. (2001). The relatively weaker correlations for facet satisfaction are consistent with the principle that relations are strongest when attitudes and behaviours are assessed at the same level of specificity (Fishbein & Ajzen, 1974), that is, broad attitudes are expected to be especially strong predictors of broadly defined behaviour, whereas narrow attitudes are expected to be especially strong predictors of narrowly defined behaviour. Because task performance is generally thought of as a broad or multi-faceted behaviour (see Campbell, 1990), one could expect that global job satisfaction will yield relatively stronger relations with it than would facet satisfaction.

Replay

Although researchers have disagreed about the precise strength of the job satisfaction–task performance relation, decades of research evidence have consistently found a positive relation between satisfaction and performance. Generally, this research has found stronger relations when global rather than facet measures are used to assess satisfaction.

13.3 Causal Nature of the Job Satisfaction– Task Performance Relation

Although it is a simple matter to show that job satisfaction and task performance are *related* to each another, it is much more difficult to show that a *causal* relation exists between the two. In other words, research suggesting a relation between satisfaction and performance does not necessarily demonstrate that satisfaction causes performance or that performance causes satisfaction. To complicate matters, opposing theoretical positions suggest that: (i) satisfaction causes performance, (ii) performance causes satisfaction, (iii) the satisfaction–performance relation is bidirectional (i.e. satisfaction and performance cause each other) or (iv) the satisfaction–performance relation is non-causal (i.e. spurious). The following sub-sections review each of these possibilities.

Satisfaction causes performance

Workers and managers generally believe that satisfaction causes performance (Fisher, 2003, Study 1). Indeed, this assumption is consistent with the classic notion in social psychology that attitudes predict behaviour (see Eagly & Chaiken, 1993). Surprisingly little attention, however, has directly addressed the mechanisms by which satisfaction might cause performance. Insights into such mechanisms might be gained from the work engagement literature (for discussions of the engagement-to-performance relation, see Demerouti & Cropanzano, 2010; Reijseger, Schaufeli, Peeters, & Taris, 2012). Although work engagement is not synonymous with job satisfaction – engagement is an affective/motivational response to one's job that consists of feelings of vigour, dedication and absorption, whereas job satisfaction has also a cognitive component and is thus not purely affective – the two share some similarities (e.g. both represent affective responses to one's job). As a result, the engagement literature could provide important insights into why job satisfaction might cause performance.

Borrowing from the work engagement literature (Demerouti & Cropanzano, 2010; Reijseger et al., 2012), Figure 13.1 highlights several variables that potentially mediate the satisfaction-to-performance relation. First, satisfaction may have beneficial effects on performance because it causes people to be more flexible, creative and open in their thinking (= cognitive flexibility). For this reason, satisfaction may have an especially strong positive effect on performance when job tasks require creativity and problem solving. Furthermore, this cognitive flexibil-

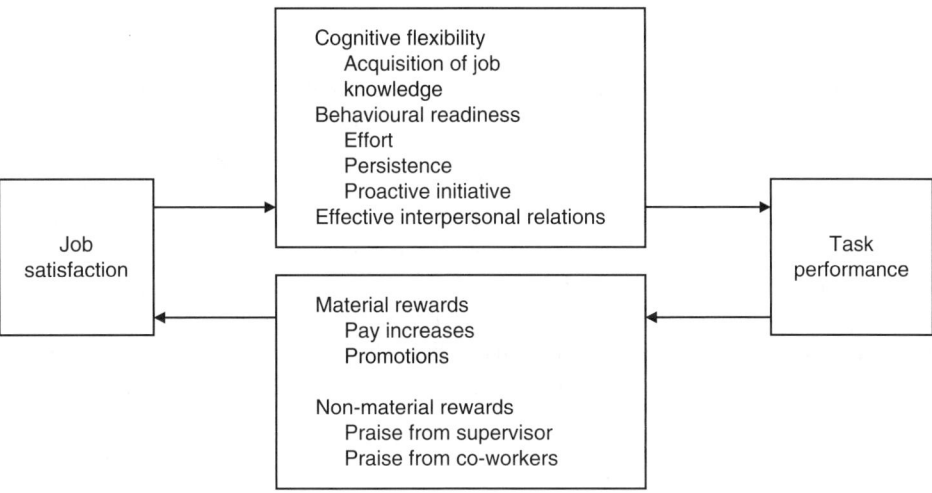

Figure 13.1 Summary of hypothesized mediators of the job satisfaction–task performance relation.

ity may motivate workers to acquire new job-specific knowledge, which in turn results in improved performance.

Furthermore, job satisfaction might impact task performance via effects on behavioural readiness. This possibility directly speaks to the motivational role of job satisfaction, that is, job satisfaction may influence performance by causing employees to display more effort, persistence and proactive initiative. This may occur because the positive emotions satisfied employees experience provide them with the energy and motivation needed to engage in effortful activity.

Finally, job satisfaction may cause task performance via effects on effective interpersonal relationships. That is, being highly satisfied may help workers get along well with their supervisors and co-workers. This may occur simply because people who display satisfaction and other positive emotions are more likeable and more pleasant to interact with than are those who do not display positive emotions. The presence of an effective interpersonal relationship, in turn, may support effective performance.

Similar motivation processes are also illustrated by the strong association that exists between job satisfaction and intrinsic motivation (i.e. motivation derived from the sheer enjoyment experienced when doing a task that one likes; see Eby, Freeman, Rush, & Lance, 1999), that is, the inherent satisfaction experienced when doing job tasks may provide an internal incentive that encourages one to display personal effort, to persist in the face of obstacles and to 'go above and beyond the call of duty' when performing one's job. Such a motivational process may cause one to perform at high levels even in the absence of external rewards (e.g. extra pay) or punishments (e.g. threats from one's supervisor).

If correct, a causal path from job satisfaction to task performance has important practical implications. Specifically, this perspective suggests that efforts to improve task performance should focus on increasing employee satisfaction.

Performance causes satisfaction

Other researchers have argued that task performance causes job satisfaction (Lawler & Porter, 1967). According to this perspective, good performance results in material rewards (e.g. pay raises, promotions) as well as non-material rewards (e.g. acknowledgment from supervisors and co-workers). These rewards, in turn, are expected to result in increased job satisfaction (see Figure 13.1). The practical implication of this perspective is that organizational efforts to improve job satisfaction are unlikely to have any impact on task performance because performance is thought to cause satisfaction and not vice versa. This would come as a surprise to many organizational leaders because often the motive for trying to improve worker satisfaction is that doing so is expected to ultimately result in increased performance.

The satisfaction–performance relation is bidirectional

Of course, it is possible that both of the above possibilities are correct: that satisfaction causes performance and that performance causes satisfaction (Wanous, 1974). Such a bidirectional relation may occur because satisfaction influences the motivational processes discussed above (thus producing a causal path from satisfaction to performance) while performance influences material and non-material rewards (thus producing a causal path from performance to satisfaction). A bidirectional relation between satisfaction and performance has important practical implications for organizations. Specifically, organizational efforts to improve job satisfaction may produce a virtuous cycle in which increased satisfaction results in increased performance and increased performance in turn results in increased satisfaction.

The satisfaction–performance relation is non-causal

A final possibility is that rather than being causal, the relation between satisfaction and performance is actually spurious (Bowling, 2007). A spurious relation exists when two variables are related not because one causes the other, but because the two share a common cause. The amount of ice cream sold in a given city, for example, is positively related to the amount of crime in that city (LeRoy, 2009). This relation, however, is not causal. That is, ice cream consumption does not cause crime and crime does not cause a hunger for ice cream. Instead, ice cream sales and crime rates are related because both are influenced by warm weather (i.e. crime rates and ice cream consumption both increase as the outdoor temperature increases). Similarly, satisfaction and performance may be related because they share similar causes. As will be discussed below, the work environment and employee personality are two categories of variables that may contribute to a spurious satisfaction–performance relation (Bowling, 2007). The practical implication of this possibility is that organizational efforts to improve employee satisfaction are unlikely to have any effects on performance because satisfaction and performance may not be causally related.

13.4 Empirical Tests of the Causal Relation Between Job Satisfaction and Task Performance

Although several studies have examined the relation between job satisfaction and task performance, very few have directly tested the causal nature of the relation. Generally speaking, the most rigorous means of testing causal relations involves the use of an experimental design in which participants are randomly assigned to different levels of an independent variable. However, because job satisfaction and task performance are not the types of variables that can easily be experimentally manipulated (i.e. a worker cannot be randomly assigned to be satisfied or dissatisfied or to be an effective-performing or ineffective-performing employee), it is very difficult to use an experimental design to examine the satisfaction–performance relation. Research, therefore, must *measure* rather than *manipulate* satisfaction and performance. The following sections provide a discussion of how longitudinal research and tests of spuriousness can be used to examine the causal nature of the satisfaction–performance relation.

Longitudinal research on the satisfaction–performance relation

Given that experimental designs are impractical, the most rigorous design available to test the causal nature of the satisfaction–performance relation involves the use of longitudinal data (see also Chapter 2). In these designs, satisfaction and performance are measured on two or more occasions. Job satisfaction, for example, could be measured at the beginning of the study and task performance could be measured 6 months later. Other longitudinal designs might measure performance prior to measuring satisfaction. If initial satisfaction is related to subsequent performance, then one may *tentatively* conclude that satisfaction caused performance. Likewise, if initial performance is related to subsequent satisfaction, then one may *tentatively* conclude that performance caused satisfaction. Note that these conclusions about causality are tentative because unlike experimental designs, non-experimental designs are unable to control for the effects of unmeasured variables.

Longitudinal designs provide the strongest tests of causal relations when they include measures of all study variables at every time point (Zapf, Dormann, & Frese, 1996). A researcher using a two-wave longitudinal design to examine the causal nature of the satisfaction–performance relation, for example, should therefore assess satisfaction *and* performance at *both* time points. Such an approach allows the researcher to examine whether Time 1 satisfaction is related to Time 2 performance controlling for the effects of Time 1 performance and whether Time 1 performance is related to Time 2 satisfaction controlling for the effects of Time 1 satisfaction. The strength of such designs rests in the fact that causes must come *before* their effects. Although longitudinal designs provide stronger tests of causal relations than do cross-sectional designs, it should be noted that they fall short of the rigor of experimental designs.

The findings of longitudinal studies have been inconsistent, with some suggesting that satisfaction causes performance, that performance causes satisfaction or that the relation between the two is bidirectional (see Riketta, 2008). Notably, a recent meta-analysis of 10 longitudinal studies (total sample size = 2,026) found that the path from Time 1 job satisfaction to Time 2 task performance controlling for Time 1 task performance (standardized regression coefficient = 0.03) as well as the path from Time 1 task performance to Time 2 job satisfaction controlling for Time 1 job satisfaction (standardized regression coefficient = 0.00) were both non-significant (Riketta, 2008). This suggests that satisfaction does not cause performance, nor does performance cause satisfaction.

Tests of the spuriousness hypothesis

Even longitudinal studies provide less-than-perfect tests of causal relations. One reason for this is that longitudinal research often fails to control for relevant third variables that might create a spurious relation between job satisfaction and job performance (see Bowling, 2007). For example, several variables, including employee personality traits (see Barrick, Mount, & Judge, 2001; Judge, Heller, & Mount, 2002) and situational variables (see Fried & Ferris, 1987), are related to both satisfaction and performance and are thus viable candidates for being third variables. Consistent with this perspective, meta-analytic evidence reported by Bowling (2007) found that controlling for employee personality (e.g. Five Factor Model characteristics, self-esteem and locus of control) caused an initially significant satisfaction–performance relation (taken directly from Judge et al., 2001) to become considerably weaker. Importantly, a significant (albeit weak) relation between satisfaction and performance remained after controlling for employee personality. Because situational variables, such as intrinsically motivating job characteristics (Fried & Ferris, 1987) and work stressors (Spector & Jex, 1998), are related to both satisfaction and performance, future research should examine whether the satisfaction–performance relation is further weakened if these factors are also controlled.

Replay

Different theoretical positions exist regarding the causal nature of the satisfaction–performance relation. Specifically, performance may cause satisfaction, satisfaction may cause performance, a bidirectional relation might exist between satisfaction and performance, or the satisfaction–performance relation may be spurious. The results of quantitative reviews, however, suggest that the relation between satisfaction and performance is unlikely to be causal (Bowling, 2007; Riketta, 2008), thus supporting the spuriousness hypothesis, that is, satisfaction and performance may be related because the two share a common set of causes.

13.5 The Relation Between Job Satisfaction, OCBs, CWBs and Employee Withdrawal

The previous section provided a review of research on the relation between job satisfaction and task performance. Job satisfaction is also potentially related to other indices of job performance, including OCBs, CWBs and employee withdrawal (see Table 13.1).

Job satisfaction and OCBs

Several theoretical perspectives suggest a positive relation between job satisfaction and OCBs. First, the principal of reciprocity suggests that satisfied workers will engage in OCBs as a means of rewarding their employers for providing a pleasant working environment (Dalal, 2005). A second theoretical perspective suggests that positive emotions are the immediate cause of OCBs (Spector & Fox, 2002). Thus, job satisfaction is expected to be positively related to OCBs because satisfaction largely represents a worker's positive emotional response to his or her job.

Consistent with the above theorizing, a considerable body of research has found a positive relation between global job satisfaction and OCBs. In the largest published quantitative review of the topic, LePine, Erez and Johnson (2002) found a mean global satisfaction–OCB corrected correlation of 0.24. Other quantitative reviews have yielded similar results (Dalal, 2005; Organ & Ryan, 1995).

Job satisfaction and CWBs

Much of the theory linking job satisfaction to CWBs parallels the theory linking job satisfaction to OCBs. First, the principle of reciprocity suggests that dissatisfied workers may engage in CWBs as a way of 'paying back' their organization for providing an unpleasant working environment (Dalal, 2005). Furthermore, negative work-related emotions, which may be symptomatic of high levels of job dissatisfaction, are expected to be the immediate cause of CWBs (Spector & Fox, 2002). Both of these theoretical perspectives predict a negative relation between job satisfaction and CWBs.

Consistent with the above theorizing, a meta-analysis shows a negative relation between global job satisfaction and CWBs (average corrected correlation = –0.37; Dalal, 2005). It is of note that this relation is somewhat stronger than the satisfaction–task performance relation reported by Judge et al. (2001). This pattern of findings is consistent with the idea that CWBs are more discretionary than is task performance, that is, workers may be able to vary the extent to which they engage in CWBs so that their level of CWBs matches their level of job satisfaction. Due to constraints created by the organization, there is little freedom to vary one's level of task performance to align with one's level of job satisfaction.

Although researchers have almost exclusively assumed causal paths from satisfaction to OCBs and from satisfaction to CWBs, cognitive dissonance processes (Festinger, 1957) allow for causal effects in the opposing direction. An employee who engages in high levels of OCBs and low levels of CWBs, for example, may subsequently develop increased job satisfaction as a way of justifying his or her behaviour. This suggests that the causal relation may go from OCBs/CWBs to job satisfaction rather than vice versa. Future longitudinal research is needed to test this possibility.

Job satisfaction and employee withdrawal

The conceptual link between job satisfaction and employee withdrawal behaviours is straightforward. Because it represents the various tactics that employees use to escape dissatisfying work, employee withdrawal is likely to be more common among dissatisfied than among satisfied workers (Hanisch & Hulin, 1990). In other words, theory suggests a negative relation between job satisfaction and employee withdrawal. This prediction has been supported by empirical evidence (see Table 13.1). Specifically, meta-analyses have found that global job satisfaction is negatively related to absenteeism (average corrected correlation = −0.24; Farrell & Stamm, 1988), lateness (average corrected correlation = −0.11; Koslowsky, Sagie, Krausz, & Singer, 1997) and turnover (average corrected correlation = −0.19; Griffeth, Hom, & Gaertner, 2000). Research has similarly found that global job satisfaction is negatively related to early departure from work (Iverson & Deery, 2001).

The above relations between job satisfaction and employee withdrawal may be described as being 'modest'. One explanation for why these effects are not stronger is that workers often engage in withdrawal behaviours for reasons other than a desire to escape unsatisfying work. For example, employees may be absent from work as a result of illness, they may be late due to unusually heavy traffic or they may be forced to quit their jobs because their spouse has been transferred to a faraway city. As a result, organizational interventions that improve employee satisfaction are likely to have little effect on withdrawal behaviours.

To this point the current chapter has discussed research examining whether job satisfaction and job performance are *generally* related. This overly simplifies the matter, however, as there are good reasons to expect that satisfaction and performance will be more strongly related to each other within some situations than within others. Thus, the following sections discuss the potential moderators of the job satisfaction–job performance relation.

Replay

Job satisfaction has been consistently linked to a number of indices of job performance besides task performance. Meta-analyses, for example, have found that global job satisfaction is positive related to OCBs and negatively related to CWBs. It is of particular note that satisfaction is more strongly related to CWBs than to task performance. Meta-analyses have also found negative relations between global job satisfaction and withdrawal behaviours, although these relations are generally modest.

> **Work Psychology in Action: When does dissatisfaction result in turnover?**
>
> Volumes of research have generally found that although job satisfaction and turnover are negatively related, the strength of this relation is typically modest (Griffeth et al., 2000). An interesting study by Carsten and Spector (1987), however, provides some fascinating insights into when satisfaction is most likely to be related to turnover. Specifically, they conducted a quantitative review (i.e. meta-analysis) to examine whether the strength of the satisfaction–turnover relation was influenced by the general health of the economy. As predicted, satisfaction yielded a relatively stronger relation with turnover during years when the national economy was healthy, but relatively weaker relations with turnover during years when the national economy was poor. In other words, dissatisfied workers seem willing to quit their jobs, but only when the economy is strong enough to provide alternative job opportunities.

13.6 When are Job Satisfaction and Job Performance Most Strongly Related?

In addition to examining the extent to which job satisfaction and job performance are generally related, it is also important to consider factors that potentially influence the strength of the satisfaction–performance relation. In other words, do moderator variables cause satisfaction and performance to be strongly related in some instances, but weakly related in others? Judge et al. (2001) reported several examples of such moderator effects. They found, for instance, that satisfaction and performance were more strongly related to each other within some occupations than within others. Specifically, the strongest satisfaction–performance relation was found for scientists/engineers (average corrected correlation = 0.45), whereas the weakest was found for nurses (average corrected correlation = 0.19). Satisfaction–performance relations of intermediate strength were found for managers/supervisors (average corrected correlation = 0.34), clerical workers/secretaries (average corrected correlation = 0.34) and teachers (average corrected correlation = 0.33). The current section considers a number of additional moderators of the satisfaction–performance relation, including reward contingency, job complexity, creative job demands and interpersonal job demands (see Figure 13.2).

Reward contingency

Reward contingency is among one of the most commonly examined moderators of the job satisfaction–job performance relation (Podsakoff & Williams, 1986). In a high-reward contingency situation, rewards (e.g. pay, promotions) are closely tied to the extent to which a worker effectively performs his or her job duties. On

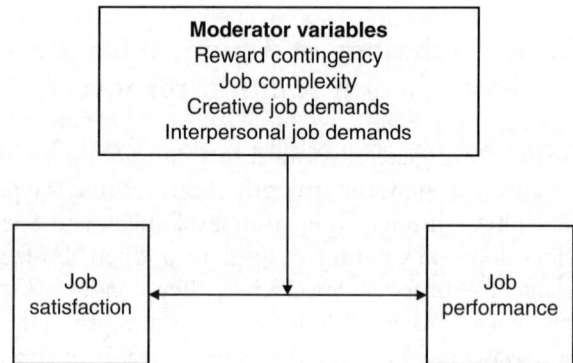

Figure 13.2 Summary of hypothesized moderators of the job satisfaction-job performance relation.

the other hand, in a low-reward contingency situation rewards are not dependent on how well one performs. Thus, effectively performing employees and ineffectively performing employees receive similar rewards. Satisfaction and performance are hypothesized to be most strongly related when reward contingency is high rather than low, that is, the hypothesis that rewards mediate the effects of performance on satisfaction (see Lawler & Porter, 1967) is likely to apply only to the extent that rewards are contingent upon one' performance. This causal chain, however, is compromised when reward contingency is low because performance has little effect on rewards. Consistent with this theorizing, the satisfaction–performance relation has been found to be stronger in high-reward contingency situations than in low-reward contingency situations (Podsakoff & Williams, 1986).

Job complexity

The satisfaction–performance relation is usually stronger among workers employed in high-complexity jobs than among those employed in low-complexity jobs. Within complex jobs, workers generally have a high degree of autonomy (Fried & Ferris, 1987; Hackman & Oldham, 1980). Because such jobs provide one with considerable latitude in how the job is done, satisfied workers are free to expend extra effort and dissatisfied workers are free to withhold effort. The high effort of satisfied workers is expected to translate into effective job performance, whereas the low effort of dissatisfied workers is expected to translate into ineffective job performance. Consistent with this prediction, the meta-analysis by Judge et al. (2001) found relatively stronger satisfaction-performance relations within high complexity jobs (average corrected correlation = 0.52) than within either medium complexity (average corrected correlation = 0.29) or low complexity jobs (average corrected correlation = 0.29). Additional research is needed to examine the extent to which autonomy underlies the moderating effects of job complexity.

Creative job demands

Jobs vary in the extent to which they require workers to engage in creative activities. For some occupations, such as artists, advertising executives and scientists, creativity is considered a prerequisite of effective job performance. In other jobs, such as tax accountant, assembly line worker and bus driver, however, creativity is considered less relevant and in some instances may even be incompatible with effective performance. High job satisfaction is more likely to be an asset in creative jobs than in non-creative jobs. This is because satisfaction, like other positive emotions, is expected to improve one's capacity for broad, flexible and creative thinking (Fredrickson, 1998). Such thinking is likely to contribute to effective performance within creative jobs. Meta-analytic evidence supports this prediction. Specifically, Bowling, Khazon, Meyer and Burrus (2012) found relatively stronger satisfaction–performance relations within jobs that had high creative demands (average corrected correlation = 0.38) than within jobs that had low creative demands (average corrected correlation = 0.19).

Interpersonal job demands

Some jobs require more frequent interpersonal interaction than others. Jobs such as nurses, social workers and teachers, for example, require considerable social contact, whereas jobs such as computer programmers, hotel maids and night watchmen require significantly less social contact. Satisfaction and performance may be more strongly related to each other within jobs requiring significant interpersonal interaction than within jobs that do not require significant interpersonal interaction. Among jobs that require high levels of social interaction, job satisfaction may influence job performance via effects on the extent to which other people (e.g. supervisors, co-workers, subordinates or customers) either facilitate or inhibit one's job performance. Indeed, other people encountered while at work can either enhance or interfere with the performance of one's job duties (Peters & O'Connor, 1980). To the extent that job satisfaction is 'contagious' (see Hatfield, Cacioppo, & Rapson, 1994), a satisfied target person may engender satisfaction in others who as a result facilitate rather than inhibit the job performance of the target person. Such contagious processes, however, are only likely to occur to the extent that one's job requires considerable interpersonal contact. Consistent with the above theorizing, recent meta-analytic evidence suggests a stronger job satisfaction–job performance relation for social jobs (average corrected correlation = 0.39) than for non-social jobs (average corrected correlation = 0.23; Bowling, Khazon, Meyer, & Burrus, 2012).

Replay

In addition to establishing whether or not job satisfaction and job performance are generally related to each other, it is important to also identify the variables that influence the strength of the satisfaction–performance relation. As reviewed here, several situational variables may produce such moderating effects. Specifically, the satisfaction–performance relation may be relatively strong when rewards are determined by one's performance levels, and when the job is complex requires one to be creative or requires a high degree of social interaction.

13.7 Conclusions

As the current chapter has illustrated, the considerable research attention given to the job satisfaction–job performance relation has uncovered many complexities. One such complexity is illustrated in the Work Psychology in Action box, which considers the long-term effects of organizational interventions on both satisfaction and performance.

> **Work Psychology in Action: Job design and job performance**
>
> Believing that 'happy workers are productive workers', organizational leaders often initiate interventions they assume will indirectly increase job performance via direct improvements on job satisfaction. One commonly used intervention is job redesign (see also Chapters 3 and 17), which involves changing employees' work tasks so that they are more interesting (and often more complex; see Hackman & Oldham, 1980). In one study of the effects of job redesign, Griffin (1991) compared the job satisfaction and job performance of bank tellers whose jobs had been redesigned with the job satisfaction and job performance of a control group of bank tellers whose jobs had not been redesigned (in this particular case, the aim of the job redesign intervention was to introduce more autonomy and variety into the tellers' jobs). A distinguishing feature of this study is that the researcher measured participants' job satisfaction and job performance on several occasions after the intervention was implemented. The results suggested that job redesign produced an initial increase in job satisfaction that disappeared over time. Job performance, on the other hand, was not initially affected by job redesign, but instead increased gradually across several months after the intervention was first introduced.

Although the job satisfaction–job performance relation has garnered extensive research attention, the causal nature of this relation has remained elusive. These complexities raise a number of issues addressed in the key discussion points found below.

Discussion Points

1. Despite the fact that many work psychologists believe that job satisfaction and job performance are weakly related (see Judge et al., 2001), the majority of laypeople believe that job satisfaction causes job performance (see Fisher, 2003, Study 1). Why might such disagreement exist between the opinions of work psychologists and the beliefs of laypeople?
2. The current chapter reviewed several potential moderators of the job satisfaction–job performance relation. These moderators include a number of situational factors. What other factors not discussed in the current chapter do you believe could potentially influence the relation between job satisfaction and job performance?

3. When selecting new employees, organizations are generally concerned with identifying which particular applicants possess the required knowledge, skills and abilities needed to perform the job effectively. When selecting new employees, should organizations use personality testing to screen-out those applicants who may be predisposed to be dissatisfied with work?
4. The current chapter implies that high levels of job satisfaction are good for both individual workers and their employers. Is high job satisfaction always desirable? Is dissatisfaction ever a good thing?

Learning by Doing

1. We all know someone who has a reputation of being exceptionally good at his or her job. Survey five or more outstanding workers whom you know personally. How satisfied are these people with their jobs? To answer this question, you should ask them to respond to the global job satisfaction scale from Cammann, Fichman, Jenkins and Klesh (1979) shown in Table 13.2.

    You can compute each person's job satisfaction score by calculating the average of the three numbers that they select. Normative data compiled by Bowling and Hammond (2008) found that the average worker had a score of 5.40 on this measure. How did the people whom you surveyed compare with the average worker? What do your findings suggest about the relation between job satisfaction and job performance?

2. As reviewed in the current chapter, considerable research attention has been given to whether satisfied workers perform better at their jobs than dissatisfied workers (see Judge et al. 2001). This research takes a *between-person* approach to the satisfaction–performance relation. A less researched question has adapted a *within-person* perspective: Does an individual worker perform better on days he or she is satisfied than on days he or she is dissatisfied (see Fisher, 2003)?

Table 13.2 Global job satisfaction scale from Cammann et al. (1979).

	Strongly disagree	Disagree	Slightly disagree	Neither agree nor disagree	Slightly agree	Agree	Strongly agree
1. All in all I am satisfied with my job.	1	2	3	4	5	6	7
2. In general, I like working here.	1	2	3	4	5	6	7
3. In general, I don't like my job.	7	6	5	4	3	2	1

Table 13.3 Daily job satisfaction and job performance record.

Day	Daily job satisfaction level 1 = Highly dissatisfied 2 = Slightly dissatisfied 3 = Neutral 4 = Slightly satisfied 5 = Highly satisfied	Daily job performance level 1 = Very poor performance 2 = Poor performance 3 = Average performance 4 = Good performance 5 = Excellent performance
1		
2		
3		
4		
5		
6		
7		
8		
9		
10		
11		
12		
13		
14		
15		
16		
17		
18		
19		
20		

Record your daily job satisfaction level and daily job performance level for 20 consecutive workdays using Table 13.3. Based on these data, does it appear that your daily satisfaction level is related to your daily performance level?

Acknowledgement

I would like to thank Caitlin Blackmore for providing helpful feedback on an earlier version of this chapter.

Further Reading

Bowling, N. A. (2007). Is the job satisfaction–job performance relationship spurious: A meta-analytic examination. *Journal of Vocational Behavior, 71,* 167–185.

Fisher, C. D. (2003). Why do lay people believe that satisfaction and performance are correlated? Possible sources of a commonsense theory. *Journal of Organizational Behavior, 24,* 753–777.

Harrison, D. A., Newman, D. A., & Roth, P. L. (2006). How important are job attitudes? Meta-analytic comparisons of integrative behavioral outcomes and time sequences. *Academy of Management Journal, 49*, 305–325.

Judge, T. A., Thoresen, C. J., Bono, J. E., & Patton, G. K. (2001). The job satisfaction–job performance relationship: A qualitative and quantitative review. *Psychological Bulletin, 127*, 376–407.

Riketta, M. (2008). The causal relation between job attitudes and performance: A meta-analysis of panel studies. *Journal of Applied Psychology, 93*, 471–481.

References

Barrick, M. R., Mount, M. K., & Judge, T. A. (2001). Personality and performance at the beginning of the new millennium: What do we know and where do we go next? *International Journal of Selection and Assessment, 9*, 9–30.

Beehr, T. A., Glaser, K. M., Beehr, M. J., Beehr, D. E., Wallwey, D. A., Erofeev, D., & Canali, K. G. (2006). The nature of satisfaction with subordinates: Its predictors and importance to supervisors. *Journal of Applied Social Psychology, 36*, 1523–1547.

Borman, W. C., & Motowidlo, S. J. (1993). Expanding the criterion domain to include elements of contextual performance. In N. Schmit, & W. C. Borman (Eds.), *Personnel selection in organizations* (pp. 71–98). San Francisco: Jossey-Bass.

Bowling, N.A. (2007). Is the job satisfaction–job performance relationship spurious: A meta-analytic examination. *Journal of Vocational Behavior, 71*, 167–185.

Bowling, N.A., & Hammond, G.D. (2008). A meta-analytic examination of the construct validity of the Michigan Organizational Assessment Questionnaire Job Satisfaction Subscale. *Journal of Vocational Behavior, 73*, 63–77.

Bowling, N. A., Khazon, S., Meyer, R. D., & Burrus, C. (2012). *Situational strength as a moderator of the relationship between job satisfaction and job performance: A meta-analytic examination*. Unpublished manuscript. Wright State University, Dayton, OH.

Brief, A. P. (1998). *Attitudes in and around organizations*. Thousand Oaks, CA: Sage Publications.

Cammann, C., Fichman, M., Jenkins, D., & Klesh, J. (1979). *The Michigan Organizational Assessment Questionnaire*. Unpublished manuscript. University of Michigan, Ann Arbor.

Campbell, J. P. (1990). Modeling the performance prediction problem in industrial and organizational psychology. In M. D. Dunnette, & L. M. Hough (Eds.), *Handbook of industrial and organizational psychology* (Vol. 1, 2nd ed., pp. 687–732). Palo Alto, CA: Consulting Psychologists Press.

Carsten, J. M., & Spector, P. E. (1987). Unemployment, job satisfaction, and employee turnover: A meta-analytic test of the Muchinsky Model. *Journal of Applied Psychology, 72*, 374–381.

Dalal, R. S. (2005). A meta-analysis of the relationship between organizational citizenship behavior and counterproductive work behavior. *Journal of Applied Psychology, 90*, 1241–1255.

Demerouti, E., & Cropanzano, R. (2010). From thought to action: Employee work engagement and job performance. In A. B. Bakker, & M. P. Leiter (Eds.), *Work engagement: A handbook of essential theory and research* (pp. 147–163). New York: Psychology Press.

Eagly, A. H., & Chaiken, S. (1993). *The psychology of attitudes*. Orlando, FL: Harcourt Brace Jovanovich.

Eby, L. T., Freeman, D. M., Rush, M. C., & Lance, C. E. (1999). Motivational basis of affective organizational commitment: A partial test of an integrative theoretical model. *Journal of Occupational and Organizational Psychology, 72*, 463–483.

Farrell, D., & Stamm, C. L. (1988). Meta-analysis of the correlates of employee absence. *Human Relations, 41*, 211–227.

Festinger, L. (1957). *A theory of cognitive dissonance*. Stanford, CA: Stanford University Press.

Fishbein, M., & Ajzen, I. (1974). Attitudes towards objects as predictors of single and multiple behavioral criteria. *Psychological Review, 81*, 59–74.

Fisher, C. D. (2003). Why do lay people believe that satisfaction and performance are correlated? Possible sources of a commonsense theory. *Journal of Organizational Behavior, 24*, 753–777.

Fredrickson, B. L. (1998). What good are positive emotions? *Review of General Psychology, 2*, 300–319.

Fried, Y., & Ferris, G. R. (1987). The validity of the Job Characteristics Model: A review and meta-analysis. *Personnel Psychology, 40*, 287–322.

Griffeth, R. W., Hom, P. W., & Gaertner, S. (2000). A meta-analysis of antecedents and correlates of employee turnover: Update, moderator tests, and research implications for the next millennium. *Journal of Management, 26*, 463–488.

Griffin, R. W. (1991). Effects of work redesign on employee perceptions, attitudes, and behaviors: A long-term investigation. *Academy of Management Journal, 34*, 425–435.

Hackman, J. R., & Oldham, G. R. (1980). *Work redesign*. Reading, MA: Addison-Wesley.

Hanisch, K. A., & Hulin, C. L. (1990). Job attitudes and organizational withdrawal: An examination of retirement and other voluntary withdrawal behaviors. *Journal of Vocational Behavior, 37*, 60–78.

Hatfield, E., Cacioppo, J. T., & Rapson, R. L. (1994). *Emotional contagion*. New York: Cambridge University Press.

Hui, C., Lam, S. K., & Law, K. S. (2000). Instrumental values of organizational citizenship behavior for promotion: A quasi-field experiment. *Journal of Applied Psychology, 85*, 822–828.

Iaffaldano, M. T., & Muchinsky, P. M. (1985). Job satisfaction and job performance: A meta-analysis. *Psychological Bulletin, 97*, 251–273.

Iverson, R. D., & Deery, S. J. (2001). Understanding the 'personological' basis of employee withdrawal: The influence of affective disposition on employee tardiness, early departure, and absenteeism. *Journal of Applied Psychology, 86*, 856–866.

Judge, T. A., Heller, D., & Mount, M. K. (2002). Five-factor model of personality and job satisfaction: A meta-analysis. *Organizational Behavior and Human Decision Process, 86*, 67–98.

Judge, T. A., Thoresen, C. J., Bono, J. E., & Patton, G. K. (2001). The job satisfaction–job performance relationship: A qualitative and quantitative review. *Psychological Bulletin, 127*, 376–407.

Kinicki, A. J., McKee-Ryan, F. M., Schriesheim, C. A., & Carson, K. P. (2002). Assessing the construct validity of the Job Descriptive Index: A review and meta-analysis. *Journal of Applied Psychology, 87*, 14–32.

Koslowsky, M., Sagie, A., Krausz, M., & Singer, A. D. (1997). Correlates of employee lateness: Some theoretical considerations. *Journal of Applied Psychology, 82*, 79–88.

Lawler, E. E., III, & Porter, L. W. (1967). The effects of performance on job satisfaction. *Industrial Relations, 7*, 20–28.

LePine, J. A., Erez, A., & Johnson, D. E. (2002). The nature and dimensionality of organizational citizenship behavior: A critical review and meta-analysis. *Journal of Applied Psychology, 87*, 52–65.

LeRoy, M. K. (2009). Research methods in political science: An introduction using MicroCase. Boston, MA: Thompson.

Organ, D. W., & Ryan, K. (1995). A meta-analytic review of attitudinal and dispositional predictors of organizational citizenship behavior. *Personnel Psychology, 48*, 775–802.

Peters, L. H., & O'Connor, E. J. (1980). Situational constraints and work outcomes: The influences of a frequently overlooked construct. *Academy of Management Review, 5*, 391–397.

Podsakoff, P. M., MacKenzie, S. B., Paine, J. B., & Bachrach, D. G. (2000). Organizational citizenship behaviors: A critical review of the theoretical and empirical literature and suggestions for future research. *Journal of Management, 26*, 513–563.

Podsakoff, P. M., & Williams, L. J. (1986). The relationship between job performance and job satisfaction. In E. A. Locke (Ed.), *Generalizing from laboratory to field settings* (pp. 207–253). Lexington, MA: Lexington Press.

Reijseger, G., Schaufeli, W. B., Peeters, M. C. W., & Taris, T. W. (2012). Ready, set, go! From engagement to performance. In J. Neves, & S. P. Gonçalves (Eds.), *Occupational health psychology: From burnout to well-being* (pp. 287–306). Lisbon: Edições Sílabo.

Riketta, M. (2008). The causal relation between job attitudes and performance: A meta-analysis of panel studies. *Journal of Applied Psychology, 93*, 471–481.

Rotundo, M., & Sackett, P. R. (2002). The relative importance of task, citizenship, and counterproductive performance to global ratings of job performance: A policy-capturing approach. *Journal of Applied Psychology, 87*, 66–80.

Schleicher, D. J., Watt, J. D., & Greguras, G. J. (2004). Reexamining the job satisfaction–performance relationship: The complexity of attitudes. *Journal of Applied Psychology, 89*, 165–177.

Smith, P. C., Kendall, L., & Hulin, C. L. (1969). *The measurement of satisfaction in work and retirement: A strategy for the study of attitudes*. Chicago, IL: Rand McNally.

Spector, P. E., & Fox, S. (2002). An emotion-centered model of voluntary work behavior: Some parallels between counterproductive work behavior and organizational citizenship behavior. *Human Resources Management Review, 12,* 269–292.

Spector, P. E., Fox, S., Penney, L. M., Bruursema, K., Goh, A., & Kessler, S. (2006). The dimensionality of counterproductivity: Are all counterproductive behaviors created equal? *Journal of Vocational Behavior, 68,* 446–460.

Spector, P. E., & Jex, S. M. (1998). Development of four self-report measures of job stressors and strain: Interpersonal Conflict at Work Scale, Organizational Constraints Scale, Quantitative Workload Inventory, and Physical Symptoms Inventory. *Journal of Occupational Health Psychology, 3,* 356–367.

Wanous, J. P. (1974). A causal-correlational analysis of the job satisfaction and performance relationship. *Journal of Applied Psychology, 59,* 139–144.

Zapf, D., Dormann, C., & Frese, M. (1996). Longitudinal studies in organizational stress research: A review of the literature with reference to methodological issues. *Journal of Occupational Health Psychology, 1,* 145–169.

14
Safety at Work

Nik Chmiel and Toon W. Taris

> ### Chapter Objectives
>
> After studying this chapter, you should be able to:
>
> - discuss the *responsibilities of employers and employees* vis-à-vis each other in preventing accidents at work;
> - discuss the concepts of *exposure and propensity* in the context of workplace safety;
> - distinguish among various types of *cognitive errors* that can be made at work;
> - distinguish among various types of *violations* that can be made at work;
> - describe *models that indicate how these errors can lead to accidents*;
> - discuss the *work-related factors that contribute to the occurrence of accidents and errors*;
> - explain how organizations can promote a *positive safety climate*.

25 March 1979 – In Harrisburg, Pennsylvania, Unit 2 of the Three Mile Island nuclear power plant was running at nearly full capacity when a minor disruption of the secondary, non-nuclear cooling circuit of the system occurred. The unit was automatically shut down within seconds, but the reactor continued to generate decay heat. As the pressure within the nuclear primary cooling system increased,

An Introduction to Contemporary Work Psychology, First Edition.
Edited by Maria C. W. Peeters, Jan de Jonge and Toon W. Taris.
© 2014 John Wiley & Sons, Ltd. Published 2014 by John Wiley & Sons, Ltd.

a safety valve opened automatically. However, when the pressure within the primary cooling system had returned to normal levels this valve was stuck open, resulting in a massive loss of radioactive coolant. Moreover, the reactor could now no longer be adequately cooled. The temperature within the reactor therefore continued to increase, ultimately resulting in nothing less than a partial meltdown of the nuclear core of Unit 2. The commission examining the causes of what is now known as the Three Mile Island nuclear accident concluded that, among other things, operators were unable to diagnose the source of the problems (the stuck valve) as they were not adequately trained to understand the meaning of a warning lamp in the control room. Moreover, additional controls that could have helped them understanding the problem were placed at the back of their desks, where they were out of the operators' sight (Kemeny, 1979). Checking these controls was not even part of the standard safety routines. Overall, human errors, inadequate safety procedures and bad workplace design allowed a minor technical failure to evolve into one of the largest nuclear accidents in history.

'Accidents will happen', 'Everybody makes mistakes': These sayings inevitably also hold true for the workplace. Sometimes the consequences of errors at work are minor, whereas in other instances they can be serious for the worker(s) involved, their colleagues, the organization they work for and even the general public, as the Three Mile Island nuclear accident demonstrated. In this chapter we discuss the inter-relation of organizational practices and provision with unsafe behaviours and the psychological precursors that are associated with accidents. We first briefly discuss facts and legal arrangements regarding the issues of errors, accidents and safety at work (Section 14.1). In Section 14.2 we consider two concepts in order to pinpoint the contribution of work psychologists to occupational safety: accident exposure and propensity. The concepts of active versus latent failures are discussed in Sections 14.3 and 14.4. Active failures refer to unsafe acts, such as various types of errors, whereas latent failures refer to the conditions under which active failures may evolve into accidents. In Section 14.5 the organizational and work-related practices associated with accidents are addressed. In Section 14.6 we discuss how organizations may promote workplace safety.

14.1 Accidents at Work

The death of someone at work is a catastrophic event for family, friends, colleagues and workplace, as is major injury such as fractures, amputation, dislocation of joints and blindness. At the very least, having a serious injury means that the injured person is away from work or unable to do their full range of normal duties for a particular period, and so is a considerable disruption for the individual and the organization. Hamalainen (2009) showed that the number of fatalities at work was 353,204 in 2001, whereas the number of occupational accidents leading to more than 3 days away from work amounted to some 268 million. The worldwide fatality rate per 100,000 workers was 15.2, with the rate being highest in Africa, 2.7 times the lowest rate, which was in Europe. Risk groups for accidents at work include male workers (who experienced accidents twice as often as female workers), younger workers and those working in agriculture, forestry, manufacturing and construction. As might be expected, accident rates are higher in manual (3.7% of the workers in this sector) than in non-manual jobs (1.8%) (Eurostat, 2010).

Historically, employers have not always been held liable for accidents that occurred to their employees during work time. For example, in the nineteenth century, US employers were legally obliged to provide their workers with a safe place to work and safe equipment to work with. However, when an employee asked for compensation due to a work-related accident, employers could often successfully defend themselves by claiming that they were not responsible for accidents. For example, they could argue that the employee's behaviour had contributed to the accident, that a fellow employee had been negligent or that the worker had been aware of the risks involved in doing the job and had knowingly assumed these risks. This also meant that there was little reason for employers to invest in safe working conditions (Wickens, Lee, Liu, & Becker, 2004).

> ### Work Psychology in Action: Safety law in the UK
>
> Laws around health and safety at work vary from country to country in their range and scope. Health and safety laws in the UK are some of the most comprehensive and place a duty on the employer to protect and keep employees informed about health and safety by:
>
> - making the workplace safe;
> - ensuring plant and machinery are safe;
> - ensuring that safe systems of work are set and followed;
> - ensuring articles and substances are moved, stored and used safely;
> - providing adequate welfare facilities;
> - providing information, instruction, training and supervision necessary for health and safety;
> - assessing the risks to health and safety.
>
> Further, the employee has a responsibility to look after themselves and others by:
>
> - taking 'reasonable' care;
> - co-operating with their employer;
> - correctly using work equipment;
> - not interfering with anything provided for employee health and safety.
>
> In short, employees must act to protect themselves and others, comply with safety procedures and regulations, and not sabotage health and safety provision.

Changing perspectives on workplace safety over roughly the last century have been reflected in three 'ages' to the scientific study of safety (Hale & Hovden, 1998). The first age was concerned with 'technical measures to guard machinery, stop explosions and prevent structures collapsing' (p. 129), and lasted from the nineteenth century until after 1945. The second age, initiated between the two world wars, witnessed research into prevention measures based on personnel selection, training and motivation, often referenced to as theories of 'accident proneness'. Hale and Hovden indicate that the technical and individual-based approaches merged in the 1960s and 1970s with developments in ergonomics and probabilistic risk analysis, and the study of human error as a field of inquiry. The third age of safety started in the 1990s, and is characterized by Hale and Hovden as being focused on management systems, and they typify the literature in this area (to at least the 1980s) as 'accumulated common sense and as general management principles applied to the specific field of safety' (p. 130), rather than science.

Replay

- Accidents at work occur frequently and may have serious consequences for the workers involved, their families, the organization and society as a whole.
- In the past, employers could often argue that they were not responsible for accidents happening at work. This meant that there was little reason for them to invest in safety measures.
- Perspectives on workplace safety have changed over the last century, from an emphasis on technical measures to increase safety (e.g. guard machinery and prevent structures collapsing), through individual-based prevention measures (e.g. personnel selection, training and motivation), to a focus on the application of general management principles applied to the field of safety.
- At present, laws around health and safety at work vary from country to country in their range and scope. However, usually employers and employees have a joint responsibility for safety at work; employers must make the workplace as safe as possible, while employees are expected to be careful and cooperative.

14.2 Accidents: Exposure and Propensity

It is important to differentiate between the general nature of an enterprise, system or endeavour and the particular circumstances involved in operating that system. Referring to road transport safety, Chapman (1973) defined 'exposure' as the number of opportunities for accidents of a certain type in a given time in a given area. For example, when driving there are more opportunities for accidents (i.e. greater exposure) if there are more intersections to negotiate than when driving along a straight empty road. Similarly, the more hazardous a working environment, the more opportunities there are for an accident. For instance, a building site is a far more dangerous working environment than an office. In short, exposure concerns the nature of the system under normal operating conditions.

'Propensity' refers to the probability that an accident occurs, given the opportunity for one (Chapman, 1973). For driving, Hodge and Richardson (1985) considered propensity to vary according to a number of vehicle, driver and environmental factors, suggesting these could include weather, the type of control at an intersection, light conditions (e.g. day or night), vehicle performance and driver performance. In the work environment, propensity could refer to a range of organizational and employee-related factors, including safety regulations, the degree to which workers are inclined to comply with these regulations, working times, work pressure, fatigue, skill level, etc. Thus, propensity concerns the *particular circumstances* involved in operating a particular system, independent from the nature of that system under normal operating conditions (exposure).

Chapman (1973) further described A (the expected number of accidents of a certain type over a specified time period) as $A = P \times E$, where $P =$ propensity and $E =$ exposure. In other words, the higher the number of opportunities for accidents (E) and the greater the presence of factors that could increase the likelihood of accidents to occur (P), the more accidents (A) will happen. In short, beyond the opportunity for accidents is the idea, pervasive in the safety literature, that accidents are the product of unsafe conditions and unsafe behaviours. Thus, jobs can well be inherently dangerous (exposure), but whether this potential for accidents actually materializes also depends on other factors, such as safety regulations and safety behaviour (propensity).

The distinction between exposure and propensity has practical implications as well. Because the number of accidents is a joint function of exposure and propensity, *both* should be taken into account when interpreting accident frequency data. For example, Smith, Huang, Ho and Chen (2006) found a significant association between company safety climate (a measure of the importance attached to safe behaviour in companies, incorporating aspects such as management commitment to safety and safety training; see Section 14.6) and injury rate based on data from 33 organizations from a variety of industrial sectors. However, this relation was reduced to non-significance once the hazardousness (or exposure) of the sectors was controlled for. Apparently, it was not propensity-related factors (safety climate) that accounted for the accident rates in these organizations, but rather exposure-related factors (the type of tasks and jobs done in these organizations). In organizational settings not all tasks or jobs are equally hazardous, so accident rates cannot meaningfully be compared across organizations without accounting for exposure.

What this discussion of exposure and propensity implies is that *organizations can, given a particular level of exposure, influence accident rates primarily through altering propensity*. They can affect how safely people behave *and/or* they can arrange the working environment to reduce unsafe working conditions. Organizational safety initiatives can thus be aimed at one or both of these. Note that in practice it may be difficult to detect the particular conditions that will contribute to an accident. Whereas these conditions are frequently implicated after an accident, unsafe behaviour is potentially more apparent, especially to job incumbents and co-workers (e.g. Wilson-Donnelly, Priest, Salas, & Burke, 2005). In preventing accidents at work, it is often more convenient to focus on propensity-related factors than on exposure-related factors such as the nature of the jobs or tasks involved.

As work psychologists, we are in the present chapter mainly concerned with unsafe behaviours and the psychological and organizational processes giving rise to them (i.e. propensity-related factors). The role of technical safeguards and defences designed to reduce the opportunity for accidents (exposure-related factors) will be discussed as needed. Further, although managerial decisions around safety and technology are themselves subject to psychological considerations, discussion of these is beyond the scope of this chapter. Below we first discuss the type of behaviours and organizational factors related to injuries to the people involved before considering models of how organizational and psychological factors relate to unsafe behaviours.

Replay

- *Exposure* refers to the number of opportunities for accidents of a certain type in a given time in a given area. In the work context, exposure refers to the inherent hazardousness of particular tasks or jobs.
- *Propensity* is the conditional probability that an accident occurs, given the opportunity for one. In the work context, one could think of factors that promote the likelihood that an accident occurs, given the inherent hazardousness of the task, for example safety behaviours.
- Accidents are more likely to occur when both exposure and propensity are high. The higher the number of opportunities for accidents (exposure, E) and the greater the presence of factors that could increase the likelihood of accidents to occur (propensity, P), the more accidents (A) will happen. Mathematically, this can be expressed as $A = P \times E$. Thus, *accident rates* reflect both exposure- and propensity-related factors. In analysing these rates, it is therefore important to distinguish between exposure and propensity.
- In preventing accidents, organizations can focus on exposure-related factors (by making the task itself safer), propensity-related factors (by making workers behave more safely) or both.

14.3 Safety-related Behaviours: Slips, Lapses, Mistakes and Violations

Many types of behaviour are involved in injuries, for example tripping over and falling, and many organizations have accident report forms with categories like this. However, such categories do not lend themselves to a ready understanding of the psychological aspects of accidents, as the behaviours concerned are too specific to particular situations and contexts (Sheehy & Chapman, 1987). A behavioural taxonomy is needed which aids insight into the generalizable psychological and organizational processes involved. The most influential and well-known of these has been provided by James Reason (1990) in his Generic Error-Modelling System (GEMS) Model.

A typology of errors: The GEMS Model

Reason proposed that all unsafe behaviours could be classified into two broad categories within the framework of purposeful activity related to safety: *unintended acts* in relation to planned actions and their goal, and *intended acts*. Unintended actions are further broken down into slips and lapses, and intended actions into mistakes and violations. The distinction among the five types of errors presented in Table 14.1 is based on three questions (Reason, 1990). The first of these is 'Did the action proceed according to plan?' If not, we are dealing with an unintended error (a slip, when a different action is executed than was initially planned, or a lapse, if some part of a planned action is not executed). If the action did proceed as planned, the second question is 'Did the action yield the desired results?', that is, whether or not the intended outcome is achieved. If not, either a knowledge-based (the situation at hand is understood wrongly) or rule-based (given a correct understanding of the situation, the wrong course of action is pursued) error could be the reason. If the action did yield the desired result, the final question is 'Was the action legitimate?', that is, did the person know that the action was against the rules (e.g. an unsafe action)? If so, the action was a violation, irrespective of its apparent success in achieving the specified goal. Table 14.1 also lists some examples that could fit in these five categories of errors.

Cognitive errors

Slips and lapses are defined as errors that result from some failure in the execution and/or storage of an action sequence, regardless of whether or not the plan that

Table 14.1 A typology of errors.

	Type of error	Example	Remedies
Unintended errors: action does not match intention	*Slip*: a simple action is not carried out as intended or planned	Make a spelling error, Freudian slips	Remove interruptions and distractions; install warnings and alarms to detect errors; provide sufficient time to complete the tasks
	Lapse: omit to perform a required action; short-term memory lapse	A mechanic forgets to tighten the wheel nuts after changing a tyre	
Intended errors: action matches intention, but does not achieve the desired outcome	*Rule-based error*: incorrect application of a rule	Ignore alarm in a real emergency situation, following a history of spurious alarms	Increase competence and knowledge (e.g. by training); regular drills and exercises for emergencies
	Knowledge-based error: the situation is wrongly understood	Rely on an out-of-date map while planning an unfamiliar route to a client	
Intended action, but not an error	*Violation*: deliberate deviation from rules, procedures, etc.; not really an error (achieves desired outcome); can be well-meaning	Neglect time-consuming safety regulations in order to get a job done in time; a van driver may have no option but to speed to complete the day's deliveries	Provide effective supervision; raise awareness of the why of safety regulations; eliminate reasons to cut corners

guided them was adequate to achieve its objective. On the other hand, *mistakes* are defined as deficiencies or failures in the judgmental and/or inferential processes involved in the selection of an objective, or in how to achieve this objective, irrespective of whether the actions necessary to realize this objective run according to plan.

Reason (1990) further related errors to a hierarchy of performance levels developed by Rasmussen (e.g. Rasmussen, 1986). Rasmussen studied workers engaged in fault-finding in electronic components using a verbal protocol technique, asking workers to explain what they were doing during their task. Rasmussen classified their work-related actions in terms of whether these were skill, rule or knowledge-based. *Skill-based actions* refer to routine actions in a highly familiar operating environment involving largely automatic cognitive (perceptual-motor) processing. At the other extreme, *knowledge-based actions* are required in novel situations and circumstances, and demand effortful problem-solving and reasoning to work out and decide on a course of action. *Rule-based actions* also involve problem-solving, but here a situation or set of circumstances has been encountered before, meaning that the action is governed by the selection and use of stored rules of the form *IF*<situation> *THEN*<action>, rather than a direct automatic response. In this sense, rule-based action is in the middle between skill- and knowledge-based action. According to Reason (1990), slips and lapses are errors at the skill-based level and are associated with attentional and memory failures. Mistakes are refined into two types: rule-based and knowledge-based. *Rule-based errors* are associated with problem-solving activities involving the misapplication of good rules, for example misclassifying a situation as one demanding a certain well-rehearsed action plan whereas actually demanding a different action plan, or the application of bad rules. *Knowledge-based errors* are associated with the limitations of human ability to solve problems and reason with new and unfamiliar circumstances. Oftentimes, the situation at hand is wrongly understood, meaning that no appropriate action was taken.

Reason (1990) documented examples of slips, lapses and mistakes from incidents in the nuclear power industry. For example, at the Davis-Besse nuclear power plant in the United States (which has a long history of safety issues), an operator, wanting to start the steam and feedwater rupture control system manually, inadvertently pressed the wrong two buttons on the control panel (a slip). At Three Mile Island a cooling system pressure relief valve had stuck open despite operators commanding it shut from the control panel. The belief that it was actually shut was a knowledge-based mistake. Wagenaar and Groeneweg (1987) analysed Dutch shipping reports of 100 accidents at sea. The accidents all resulted from several behavioural events, frequently involving two or more people, and had multiple causes. However, in 93% of the accidents failures of reasoning and cognitive rule following were involved. Similarly, Salminen and Tallberg (1996) found that human error could be implicated in a majority (more than 80%) of 99 serious accidents investigated in Finland. Clearly, human error is a major factor in many accidents.

Violations
Contrary to errors, violations are not seen as breakdowns in normal cognitive processing, but as deliberate flouting of safety procedures and rules. According to Reason (1990), 'While errors may be defined in relation to the cognitive

processes of the individual, violations can only be described with regard to a social context in which behaviour is governed by operating procedures, codes of practice, rules and the like ... violations can be defined as deliberate – but not necessarily reprehensible – deviations from those practices deemed necessary (by designers, managers and regulatory agencies)' (p. 195). Violations are therefore 'knowing' departures from specified safety rules and procedures, such as taking shortcuts rather than following procedures and non-compliance with self-protective precautions such as not wearing personal protective equipment like safety glasses or a hard hat. Reason (1990) identified as of greatest interest a category of 'deliberate but non-malevolent infringements'. Reason, Parker and Lawton (1998) subsequently suggested three major categories of violations: routine, optimizing and situational. Routine violations typically involved corner-cutting – taking a path of least effort. Optimizing violations involved optimizing non-functional goals ahead of safety, for example the enjoyment of speeding when driving. These two categories were linked to the attainment of personal goals and are unrelated to the attainment of work goals. However, situational violations occur when workers see violations as essential to 'get the job done', for example because strict adherence to all safety regulations makes it impossible to complete a task within the time allotted to that task, or because personal protective equipment is hard to access and use, that is, the latter type of violation is functional in achieving work goals.

Work Psychology in Action: Motives for non-compliance with safety regulations

Reason and colleagues (1998) distinguished among three types of violations: routine, optimizing and situational violations. Workers commit routine and optimizing violations primarily because they want to do things 'the easy way' or because they want to fulfil a personal need – the organization does not usually profit from such actions. However, situational violations occur because workers consider such violations as functional in doing their job – they feel that without such violations, it would be difficult to get the job done. Building on this idea, Lawton (1998) examined the views of 36 UK railway personnel as to their motives for non-compliance behind violations of risk-related rules in shunting operations. Out of 14 endorsed reasons, the most common referred to violations being seen as a quicker way of working, due to time pressure and due to high workload (i.e. situational violations). Least common were reasons connected to psychological gratification, that is, violations being seen as exciting or macho ways to work (i.e. optimizing violations). Lawton's findings thus provide some support for the classification of Reason et al. (1998). This suggests that workers may neglect safety regulations intended for their own good in order to achieve their work goals, a view supported by Hansez and Chmiel (2010), who showed that higher job demands were associated with more routine violations.

Replay

- There are three major classes of errors at work: *non-intended errors* (one's actions do not match one's intention), *intended errors* (one's action matches one's intention, but the desired result is not achieved) and *violations* (an action is performed as intended, but deliberately flouts safety rules and procedures).
- *Slips* refer to simple actions that are not carried out as intended or planned. *Lapses* refer to forgetting to perform required actions.
- *Knowledge-based errors* originate from a poor understanding of a situation. *Rule-based errors* involve the incorrect application of a rule – the rule does not fit a specific situation or cannot achieve the desired result.
- *Violations* are often frequently committed in the interest of the organization, that is, to achieve work goals.

14.4 Active and Latent Failures

Reason (1990) suggested that the human contributions to complex system breakdowns and accidents were a function of *active* and *latent* failures – an idea that has been extremely influential and which is essentially an expansion of the notion that accidents result from unsafe behaviours (propensity) and unsafe conditions (exposure, see Section 14.2). Active failures are unsafe acts of the sort discussed above, that is, cognitive errors or violations of safety rules. Latent failures fall into four categories: (i) fallible managerial decisions, (ii) line management deficiencies, (iii) psychological precursors to unsafe acts and (iv) inadequate defences against unsafe acts, such as alarms or automatic shutdowns. The key idea is that active and latent failures combine to contribute to major accidents.

Reason (1990) presented six case studies drawing out the characteristics of regulatory and managerial latent failures. These cases ranged across technological systems from chemical production (the Bhopal catastrophe in India), space exploration (the Challenger shuttle disaster in the USA) to transport (the King's Cross Fire and the sinking of the ferry *Herald of Free Enterprise* in Europe).

Swiss cheese: The Chernobyl disaster

Reason's (1990) analysis of the Chernobyl disaster in the Ukraine (then in the USSR) shows clearly how active and latent failures (in this case, regulatory and management deficiencies) combine to result in a major disaster. On 26 April 1986, at 01:24, two explosions blew off the 1,000-tonne concrete cap sealing the Chernobyl-4 nuclear reactor. There was widespread contamination 400 square miles around the Chernobyl plant, and more than 30 lives were lost. The plume of radioactive material spread through the atmosphere over Scandinavia and Western Europe, as far as the Hebridean islands off the north-west coast of Scotland.

The Chernobyl explosions occurred as a result of a test to see whether the electricity generated by the turbine generator of the Number 4 reactor unit could power the reactor's 'emergency core cooling system' for a few minutes when the turbine was no longer being driven by the reactor, but was still spinning inertially. Reason (1990) describes the core features of this disaster as follows:

- The quality of the test plan was afterwards assessed as poor, including the section on safety measures, and authority for the plan to proceed was given without formal approval of the Safety Technical Group.
- The person in charge had no knowledge of reactor physics, being an electrical engineer.
- The emergency core cooling system was disconnected as part of the test plan, but 5 minutes later the plant was asked by the local Kiev controller to continue supplying the grid with electricity, which it did at approximately 50% of full power. However, the emergency core cooling system was not reconnected, which meant that the reactor was running without this emergency system.
- The reactor was released from the grid 9 hours later. The idea was to idle the reactor to 2.5% of its capacity. Operating below 20% of the reactor's full power was known to be dangerous due to the design of the reactor – this could lead to a meltdown of its core. However, operators continued to reduce power and omitted to enter a 'hold power' order, eventually stabilizing power at 7%.

Reason concludes that the test should have been abandoned at this point, but it was not. Instead, the experimenters deliberately bypassed and disconnected other safety systems as well as all back-up systems, including diesel generators that would have allowed them to operate the reactor controls in the event of an emergency. They then shut down the turbine generator, resulting in serious cooling issues and, a few minutes later, in the explosions.

The Chernobyl case shows how active failures (violations of safety regulations and cognitive errors, e.g. due to lack of knowledge) and latent failures (including bad managerial decisions and inadequate defences) can lead to a major disaster. Note that each of these failures separately and on its own would not have led to this disaster. It is the *joint occurrence* of these failures that allowed the disaster to happen. This idea is formally represented in Reason's (1990) *Swiss Cheese model* – the sort of cheese with big holes in it. This model presents an organization's defences against disaster as a series of slices of Swiss cheese. Each slice symbolizes a separate barrier, and the holes in these slices represent the specific weaknesses in these barriers. They are assumed to vary continually in size and position, for example the solution to a particular safety issue may bring about another safety issue in a different part of the system, etc. Disaster occurs when all of the slices are aligned in such a way that a hazard – an active failure, i.e. an unsafe act – can pass through all the holes in all of the defences.

Psychological precursors of disaster: The Paddington train crash

A case study by Lawton and Ward (2005) illustrates not only how active and latent failures interact to contribute to an accident, but also how latent failures may be implicated in psychological precursors to unsafe acts. In 1999 two trains collided just outside Paddington Station, near Ladbroke Grove in London, United Kingdom.

Thirty-one people were killed and more than 500 injured. The immediate 'cause' was a signal passed at danger (SPAD), that is, the driver of one train went through a red light. A report on the accident, several hundred pages long, was compiled in 2000 by Lord Cullen. Lawton and Ward used the Cullen report as well as witness statements to analyse the factors contributing to the accident. The main features of the disaster identified by Lawton and Ward were as follows:

- Driver cognitive error, that is, information processing in human cognition is organized and shaped by our previous experiences and expectations. This is known as top-down processing (cf. Solso, 1998). In this case, it was likely that the driver who went through the red light had actually expected to see a green signal – a finding common to other investigations of SPADs.
- The driver had only recently trained and had no experience of the signal he went through. Evidence suggested that the driver was unaware of his error and could have mis-read the signal, thus misclassifying the situation (a knowledge-based error);
- There was a new track layout designed to allow more train throughput, leading to a very complex driving task – quite a challenge for a driver without previous experience with this track.
- The signal itself was poorly sited, creating viewing problems. The signal had a history of being passed at danger (eight SPADs had been reported between 1993 and 1998), leading Lord Cullen to include in his report the calculation that there was an 86% chance in each year of a SPAD at this signal.
- Drivers were not made aware of SPAD histories along their routes.
- Training methods were considered suspect, especially with regard to route handling.

An analysis of this and other train crashes led Lord Cullen to formulate 25 recommendations concerning safety, leadership and management and 41 recommendations directed at training, skills, competence and behaviour. Note that these recommendations were not directed at technological improvements, but rather aimed at reducing the opportunities for human error to occur.

Replay

- *Active failures* refer to unsafe acts, that is, cognitive errors or violations of safety rules.
- *Latent failures* include fallible managerial decisions, line management deficiencies, psychological precursors to unsafe acts and inadequate defences against unsafe acts.
- Accidents occur when active and latent failures combine, that is, when these occur simultaneously. This is formally represented in Reason's (1990) Swiss Cheese model.
- Latent failures may be mixed up with the *psychological precursors to unsafe acts*. For example, lack of experience or incorrect information processing may aggravate the adverse effects of latent failures.

14.5 Antecedents of Accidents at Work

Wagenaar, Hudson and Reason (1990) proposed a general accident causation scenario which 'describes how all accidents originate' (p. 274) – a bold claim that was built on Reason's (1990) analysis of active and latent failures, and with an emphasis on cognitive errors. Wagenaar et al. (1990) argued that an accident is the endpoint of a series of events that starts with *bad management decisions*. These decisions may create *latent failures*, which can be grouped into a limited number of classes or general failure types (GFTs; e.g. badly designed machines and work procedures). In turn, these latent failures are presumed to affect the *psychological*

> ### Work Psychology in Action: The general accident causation scenario
>
> Wagenaar and colleagues (1990) proposed that (i) bad management decisions result in (ii) latent failures. These latent failures result in (iii) psychological processes that are precursors of (iv) unsafe acts. When adequate defences are lacking, these unsafe acts will result in (v) accidents.
>
> Wagenaar, Hudson and Reason used this general accident causation scenario to analyse an example of a maintenance operator in a transformer station tragically killed by touching a wire carrying 10,000 volts. The man had returned early from a coffee break and mistaken which of two adjacent transformers (each in a separate block) he had been working on earlier in the day (the transformers were not clearly marked). He then violated the procedure for safely opening a locked door guarding the transformer. The correct procedure involved walking back some way to an electrical switch that would open the door only if the power to the transformer had been turned off. Rather than walk back, the operator opened the door by pushing his arm through a fence and opening the lock from the inside with a screwdriver, entering the block and touching the high voltage wire. Apparently operators regularly opened locked doors in this way.
>
> Thus, in terms of the general accident causation scenario defences were inadequate: no alarm was triggered when a fence was opened with the power still on and there was no automatic power shut-down. The unsafe acts were that the door was opened with a screwdriver and the wire touched without a power check. Psychological precursors were confusion between the transformer cells and the habitual response to violate procedures. Latent failures comprised: (i) labelling of cells that was ambiguous, (ii) a physical distance from cells to power switches that was too far, (iii) a wrongly designed alarm system, (iv) poor habits not corrected by supervisors and (v) insufficient time to finish the job. Management decisions allowed an out-of-date design not to be replaced and maintenance staff to be reduced.

processes determining the actual behaviour of workers at work. These processes (or psychological precursors) include lack of attention, inexperience, lack of skills, haste, misperceived risk and so forth. They 'invite' workers to commit *unsafe acts* (i.e. errors) that can potentially lead to accidents. Whether these accidents-waiting-to-happen actually materialize depends on the presence or absence of adequate defences. Wagenaar et al. (1990) argued that 'many unsafe acts are not simple slips, but intentional and reasoned actions that end in unforeseen results. Erroneous plans are not easily avoided on the shop floor, once they are invited by operational conditions replete with latent failures' (p. 273).

What is interesting in Wagenaar et al.'s (1990) accident causation scenario (and what distinguishes it from Reason's, 1990, similar Swiss Cheese model) is (i) their proposition that latent failures can be grouped in a limited number of groups of risk factors, (ii) the idea that these general failure types are due to bad management decisions, (iii) the model's emphasis on cognitive functioning and cognitive errors and (iv) their reasoning that these errors are *elicited* by the presence of particular sets of risk factors.

General failure types and the antecedents of accidents

With respect to managerial decision-making and other organizational failures, one may object that the accident case studies discussed above concern highly unusual circumstances entailing idiosyncratic elements and so may not generalize to other everyday accidents. However, similar characteristics are present in many other accident cases. This led Wagenaar et al. (1990) to define a limited number of GFTs describing sets of similar factors that increased the likelihood that accidents would happen. These were defined 'somewhat arbitrarily, but after reading and analysing hundreds of accident scenarios' (p. 287). The GFTs were initially grouped into three broad categories:

1. *Physical environment*: this category included design failures, missing defences, hardware defects, negligent housekeeping (e.g. a slippery wet floor) and error-enforcing conditions (i.e. tool design that takes no account of possible uses under extreme time pressure or by unqualified personnel);
2. *Human behaviour*: this category referred to poor procedures (bad planning, insufficient control) and defective training (e.g. lack of training in specific expertise so people act as novices, e.g. safety awareness training is usually insufficient); and
3. *Management*: these failure types included organizational failures (e.g. safety is not treated as an important goal), incompatible goals (e.g. production trade-offs with safety) and lack of communication (leading to absence of information).

A fourth category, *failures in maintenance*, was later added by Wagenaar, Groeneweg, Hudson and Reason (1994), yielding four major GFTs that are essentially independent. Based on this and other research (mainly retrospective analyses of accidents), we discuss here a number of factors associated with the occurrence of accidents. These factors are grouped for convenience into (i) management practices, (ii) job-related factors, (iii) physical environment, (iv) support from co-workers and supervisors, and (v) safety climate. In the present section the first four factors are discussed. Because of its overall importance for safety at work, the fifth factor (safety climate) deserves a separate discussion (Section 14.6).

Management practices and accident incidence
Empirical evidence suggests that management practices – i.e. how organizations are managed – affect accident rates in organizations. For example, Shannon, Mayr and Haines (1997) reviewed 10 studies examining the factors associated with injury rates. The organizational predictors of injury rates could be grouped under management style and culture (including empowerment of the workforce and good relations between management and workforce), and organizational philosophy on health and safety (including delegation of safety activities, training and an active role of the top management in health and safety matters). In a similar study, Vredenburgh (2002) reported that management practices (i.e. rewards for reporting safety hazards, safety training, selecting those with a good safety record, communication/feedback on incidents and unsafe behaviours, worker participation in safety decisions, and management commitment to safety) explained 16.5% of the differences among organizations in safety outcomes (a combination of injury frequency over 3 years weighted by the severity of outcome). Finally, focusing on the construction industry in the United States, Hoonakker et al. (2005) looked at the longitudinal effect of safety initiatives on safety performance (measured as the number of company claims for injuries). While larger companies generally had safety initiatives in place, less than 20% of small-size companies had any kind of safety initiatives. Moreover, companies reporting regularly scheduled safety meetings at the start of the study had better safety performance 4 years later, as compared to companies that did not schedule such meetings.

These and other findings suggest that organizations that actively promote safe working practices can substantially reduce their injury rates. However, other work characteristics may also affect injury rates. For example, Kaminski (2001) investigated whether work-related factors such as performance-based pay, the presence of temporary employees, hours worked per week, amount of formal training per year and the percentage of employees who worked on a production line were associated with injury rates in 86 US organizations. Moreover, she controlled for industry injury rate on the basis that some industries are more hazardous than others. Whereas hours per week, training and team-working were all negative predictors of injury rate, receiving performance-based pay was positively associated with injuries. This is consistent with the idea that workers may violate safety regulations in order to be more productive (cf. Section 14.3).

Job-related factors and accident incidence
It is possible to obtain some understanding of the job-related antecedents of occupational injury by interviewing injured workers, their foremen and co-workers.

> ### Work Psychology in Action: Characteristics of a high-performance work system
>
> Zacharatos, Barling and Iverson (2005) identified ten practices and defined them collectively as constituting a high-performance work system (HPWS). The practices were employment security, selective hiring, extensive training, self-managed teams and decentralized decision-making, reduced status distinctions, information sharing, compensation contingent on safe performance, transformational leadership, high-quality work and measurement of management practices. In their study, human resource directors in 138 manufacturing organizations completed questions about the extent to which they thought a practice existed in their organizations and estimated the percentage of employees to which a high commitment practice applied. Practices were combined into a single index measuring an HPWS. Human resources directors further reported the number of lost-time injuries and number of days lost due to eight specific types of injuries, ranging from fractures to superficial wounds. After controlling for the nature, size and age of the organizations, the HPWS index predicted an additional 8% of the variance in lost-time injuries, underlining the fact that the way organizations are managed influences safety at work.

Using this approach, Salminen, Saari, Saarela and Rasanen (1993) found that the risk of experiencing an accident at work increased with a higher need to save time and working to tight schedules, suggesting that high work pressure increases the risk that workers pay less attention to safety issues. In addition, accident risk was significantly greater for subcontractors, which could be due to the fact that these workers are less familiar with the conditions at the site than regular workers.

Barling, Kelloway and Iverson (2003) defined 'high-quality work' in terms of the extent of training received, task variety and job autonomy (see Chapter 3). Occupational injuries were measured by asking employees whether they had experienced an injury in the past year. They found that participants having high-quality work reported fewer occupational injuries.

Working times are also associated with injury rates. For example, Dembe, Erickson, Delbos and Banks (2005) showed that the chances of becoming injured were 37% higher for workers working 12 hours per day or more as compared to other workers, whereas working 60 hours per week resulted in a 23% higher risk of becoming injured. These figures were obtained after taking into account that working more hours *in itself* already results in higher exposure rates, since this means workers spend more time 'at risk'. They concluded that job schedules with long working hours are more risky than other jobs.

Summarizing, the available evidence suggests that the type of work conducted may entail risks for the safety and health of workers. As the studies discussed above show, risk factors include high work pressure, unfamiliarity with the work site, having a low-quality job (i.e. low-autonomy, low-variety and low-skills) and long working hours.

Physical work environment and accident incidence
Characteristics of the physical work environment and equipment-related factors may cause difficulties for workers. Some of these concern stressors such as lighting, noise, vibration and temperature. As regards lighting, good illumination improves vision and may make it easy for workers to perform their tasks in a safe manner. Noise and vibration are associated with the operation of heavy machinery and equipment that can be dangerous to workers. Furthermore, both low and high temperature may present a safety risk. Low temperatures may make it necessary for workers to wear protective clothing that may impair the proper (and safe) operation of tools, whereas high temperatures (e.g. exceeding 25 °C) may lead to lower reaction times, sleepiness and thermal discomfort. Indeed, most of these environmental conditions have the potential to reduce cognitive processing efficiency and, hence, increase the likelihood that errors occur (e.g. Hockey, 1986). Melamed, Yekutieli, Froom, Estela-Boneh and Ribak (1999) examined the safety impact of being exposed to these unfavourable job conditions. They found that being exposed to noise increased the odds of being injured at work by 15 to 36%, climate problems increased this likelihood by 28 to 30%, lighting problems led to a risk increment of 7% and excessive vibration increased the odds of being injured by 19%. Apparently, the characteristics of the physical work environment may substantially affect safety at work.

Support from colleagues or supervisors and accident incidence
The social environment is a major determinant of work behaviour. This also applies to safety at work. Previous research has shown that high levels of supervisory and co-worker support predicted whether a worker had been injured or not in the 12 months following the survey (Iverson & Erwin, 1997), with higher levels of support predicting fewer injuries. Similarly, Oliver, Cheyne, Tomas and Cox (2002) examined whether organizational involvement in safety (measured as indicators of safety management and policy, supervisor safety support and behaviour, and co-worker safety support and behaviour) was related to safety and accidents at work. As expected, greater involvement in safety predicted fewer accidents. These and other studies show that the presence of safety-supportive others in the workplace may reduce accident rates.

Replay

- Although many accidents occur due to highly unusual circumstances, it is possible to distinguish among several classes of characteristics that affect the chances that an accident will occur.

- Wagenaar and colleagues (1990) classified these circumstances and characteristics into a limited number of general failure types, referring to among others physical environment issues, human behaviour such as poor work procedures and defective training, management practices such as not treating safety as an important work goal, and bad maintenance of machinery and tools.
- Research has shown that such circumstances and characteristics are indeed related to the occurrence of accidents at work. By focusing on such circumstances and characteristics, organizations may be able to reduce the number of accidents happening in their organization.

14.6 Safety Climate, Safety Management and Safety Citizenship Behaviours

The preceding section showed that a variety of management practices and the consequences thereof (e.g. in terms of their effects on working conditions) may be associated with accidents. How these practices relate to different types of safety behaviour is an interesting question that may in part be addressed through the concept of *safety climate*. Dov Zohar, a leading researcher in this area, defined safety climate as 'the shared perceptions of employees about the task behaviours that are appropriate and adaptive in their work environments' (Zohar, 1980). These shared perceptions act as a frame of reference against which employees evaluate their own (intended) safety behaviours. For example, a metal worker may feel that it is fine to neglect a particular safety rule (e.g. wearing eye protection) simply because their colleagues do not use such protection either, signalling that neglecting this safety regulation is accepted in this organization. In other similar organizations not wearing eye protection may lead to being reprimanded by one's colleagues or supervisor. Zohar's seminal research on safety suggested that important dimensions for climate were (i) (workers' perceptions of) the importance of safety training programmes, (ii) management attitudes to safety, (iii) the effects of safe conduct on promotion opportunities, (iv) the level of risk in the workplace, (v) the pace of work demands related to safety, (vi) the status of the safety officer, (vii) the effects of safe conduct on social status and (viii) the status of the safety committee.

Although further research on the number and nature of the dimensions involved has not led to universal agreement, at present consensus has been reached that safety climate concerns *an organization's policies, procedures, and practices related to safety*. Subsequent empirical research has underlined the importance of (the dimensions of) safety climate for occupational safety. For example, Alper and Karsh's (2009) review showed that not checking safety procedures and management turning a blind eye when it comes to safety regulations are both factors that promote workers' non-compliance with safety precautions. Similarly, Beus, Payne, Bergman and Arthur (2010) found in their meta-analysis that a positive safety climate was associated with a lower rate of subsequent accidents and injuries. Moreover, Barling, Loughlin and Kelloway (2002) and Chmiel (2005) showed that a positive safety climate was associated with a lower self-reported frequency of injury involvement.

This evidence suggests that the presence of a positive safety climate is an antecedent of lower accident rates in organizations. However, the jury is still out as to whether the relations discussed above can be interpreted causally (cf. Chapter 2). For example, Beus et al. (2010) argued that high accident rates can also motivate organizations to take measures to reduce these accident rates, that is, accident rates come first and a positive safety climate follows. At this point it seems safe to conclude that safety climate and accident rates are closely related, and that both concepts can mutually affect each other.

Safety management
How can organizations establish a positive safety climate? In many respects, creating such a climate is a major organizational intervention, and much of the material discussed in Sections 16.2 and 16.3 of Chapter 16 (dealing with the design, implementation and evaluation of work stress interventions) is relevant here as well. However, it is possible to provide specific recommendations for improving safety at work. Table 14.2 presents five guidelines for creating a positive safety climate, based on the work of Wilson-Donnelly et al. (2005). These guidelines emphasize that the organization's management (especially those at the top) must be committed to safety, that this commitment must be communicated to those at the lower levels of organizations, that accidents must be freely discussed, that it should be acknowledged that the causes for these accidents may be located at all levels of the organization and that workers should be given the discretion, knowledge and skills to act safely, for example through training.

From the discussion above one might have inferred that errors and mistakes should always be evaluated negatively and, therefore, should be avoided at all costs. However, generally speaking this is not correct. From a systems perspective, errors and accidents inform organizations about the weak spots in their defences and thus help them in improving their safety structure. Basically, the idea behind *safety management* (i.e. an organization's system of procedures for the identification of workplace hazards and the reduction of accidents) is that organizations should use errors and accidents to their advantage, and the steps described in Table 14.2 will help organizations in establishing a climate that allows them to learn from such events. From this perspective, errors and accidents are important and useful signals that at least some of these procedures are open for improvement.

Moreover, it should be noted that safety violations – conscious deviations from an organization's safety regulations – are not inherently 'wrong' behaviours. Violations may occur when an individual realizes that a system is in jeopardy and that saving the system requires actions that are outside of normal operation. In such cases violations may not only improve safety, but can ultimately even become best practice in the situations that produced them. Stated differently, the system of safety regulations must not be static but should be amenable to new insights and methods. To some degree this idea goes against guideline 2 in Table 14.2; although deviations from safety practices should as a rule be penalized, organizations should consider the circumstances in which such behaviours occur and be willing to learn from these.

Table 14.2 Five guidelines for creating a positive safety climate.

1	*Make people believe in safety, and start at the top.* It is important that the upper-level management is committed to safety issues, in the form of both words and actions. Make sure that this is clear to employees at lower levels of the organization. Provide feedback to employees as regards their safety behaviours: this will motivate them to comply.
2	*Send appropriate signals that safety matters.* The safety policies and procedures of the organization should be clearly and precisely communicated to all involved. Unsafe behaviours should be penalized rather than tolerated or – worse still – normalized. To increase employee commitment to safety, employees may be involved in the development and implementation of a safety policy programme.
3	*Encourage discussion and documentation of errors.* Errors are basically free lessons: they show where the system's barriers are weak and organizations can use that knowledge to their advantage. Errors should therefore be openly discussed rather than covered up. It is advantageous to develop an error-reporting system that is overseen by an external organization (to help ensure anonymity and prevent non-punitive action from occurring). In this way employees will feel comfortable submitting reports of their errors. Of course, the organization must have access to the data so that it can be analysed.
4	*Examine all levels when searching for solutions.* There is a tendency for organizations to attribute accidents to errors of individual workers. However, problems may also be located at a higher level of the organization (e.g. bad management practices) and these should also be considered.
5	*Prepare people through training.* When unsafe practices have been identified, workers should be given the competencies to avoid these practices and behave more safely instead. This will often require some form of training. In many ways this is the most important step towards increasing the safety in an organization: whereas it is important to know what went wrong for what reason (steps 1–4), it is imperative that workers possess the knowledge and skills regarding the required behaviours to act safely.

Adapted from Wilson-Donnelly et al. (2005).

Safety citizenship behaviours
Until now we have discussed behaviours that have direct bearing on carrying out tasks safely. However, there is another class of behaviours relevant to accidents within organizations, and these can be called *safety citizenship behaviours* (SCBs). These behaviours are mostly discretionary and regarded as beyond an employee's usual job role. Hofmann, Morgeson and Gerras (2003) identified six dimensions of SCB based on organizational citizenship behaviours (e.g. Hofmann, Blair, Meriac, & Woehr, 2007; see also Chapter 13). These are (i) *helping*, largely related to aiding other crew members to work more safely, (ii) *voice*, largely concerned with speaking out on safety matters, (iii) *stewardship*, largely concerned with protecting others from risk, (iv) *whistleblowing*, largely concerned with reporting safety violations, (v) *civic virtue* or *keeping informed*, largely concerned with attending safety meetings, and (vi) *initiating safety-related change*, largely concerned with trying to improve safety procedures.

The central idea behind SCBs is that the person displaying them is essentially helping other people and their organization to become a safer place to work. However, it is possible that engaging in SCBs also has consequences for an employee's *own* approach to their safety-related job behaviour. For example, Chmiel and Hansez (2012) argued that some safety citizenship behaviours (such as initiating safety-related change and attending safety committees) would likely lead to enhanced appreciation and knowledge of the importance of safety practices and procedures. Consistent with this reasoning, engaging in SCBs has been shown to relate negatively to the number of accidents and injuries associated with rule violations (e.g. Clarke, 2006) and positively to compliance with safety rules and procedures (Chmiel & Hansez, 2012; Griffin & Neal, 2000). Apparently, engaging in discretionary SCBs is associated with workers defining these activities as more part of their job, with positive consequences for the safety of the workers involved.

Replay

- Safety climate concerns an organization's policies, procedures and practices related to safety. It is often measured in terms of the perceptions of employees about the task behaviours that are appropriate and adaptive in their work environments.
- Safety climate and accident rates are closely related. Whereas the presence of a positive safety climate is associated with lower accident rates, high accident rates may also motivate organizations to work on their safety climate, that is, safety climate and accident rates may mutually influence each other.
- A positive safety climate can be promoted through organizational intervention. Key features of such an intervention refer to involvement of the top management, clear and open communication about safety, and providing workers with the discretion, skills and knowledge required to work safely.
- Errors and accidents at work may serve a positive purpose by showing organizations the weak spots in their defences, that is, organizations can learn from accidents.
- SCBs (e.g. helping others to work more safely, initiating safer work procedures) are discretionary behaviours that go beyond an employee's usual job role and promote the safety in the organization.

14.7 Conclusions

We have focused in this chapter on the types of unsafe behaviours involved in accidents, considered how they might combine with unsafe conditions to contribute to accidents, and outlined how management practices and psychological precursors may combine to bring them about. In particular we have considered that management practices have some of their effect through the perceptions that employees have of those practices. Important psychological precursors appear to be both safety-specific and more general, for example involving safety knowledge and regarding safety as important. Further, we have discussed a number of organizational aspects that contribute to these psychological processes and states, including features of the working environment, and management and leadership.

The general picture that should emerge from our discussion of these topics in this chapter is that in many cases, fallible management decisions can bring about a work situation that is potentially hazardous and can lead workers to make mistakes – usually minor, but sometimes with serious consequences. Whether or not this potential for disaster materializes is dependent on an organization's defences; if these are appropriate, even major errors will not lead to accidents. However, in the absence of such defences, it is likely that organizations must deal with high accident rates. Note that the presence or absence of effective defences is usually a management decision as well, underlining management's responsibility in dealing with (and reducing) error and accident rates. Furthermore, we have discussed the steps to be taken in order to create a positive safety climate, and have shown that the presence of such a climate is usually associated with positive safety outcomes.

Discussion Points

1. In this chapter we have argued that errors and accidents are not necessarily bad for the organization, but rather that organizations could learn from these. In this sense, errors should not be avoided at all costs otherwise organizations distance themselves from the opportunity to learn. Are there also situations in which organizations should *encourage* workers to make errors? For instance, consider the case in which a product is being developed, or when workers attend training in order to acquire new skills, or when a new work routine or new machinery is implemented.
2. In this chapter, we argued that safety at work is strongly influenced by management decisions, for example in terms of safety climate, the instigation of safe working conditions and creating adequate defences that prevent errors from turning into accidents. Clearly, an organization's management bears a major responsibility for workplace safety. But where does this responsibility end? Can everything that might go wrong at work be foreseen by the management? Can it always be held responsible for errors and accidents at work? Where does an employer's responsibility for working safely end, and where does an employee's responsibility begin?
3. Since the introduction of computer networks, computer buffs have frequently been able to hack into the networks of large organizations, exposing the vulnerability of these organizations' defences against computer crime. In many countries these activities are punishable by law, even if the hacker had no other purpose than to show the organization that their defences against this type of crime were weak. What do you think – should these 'white hat' hackers be punished for committing a crime, or rather be thanked for pointing this organization to a weak spot in its defences?

Learning by Doing

1. Think of something that went wrong lately in your studies or job – your plans did not work out as expected and you had nobody but yourself to blame. Use Reason's (1990) generic error-modelling system theory to classify your error. Also think about the possible reasons why you made this error.
2. The main plot of disaster movies (which depict the antecedents, occurrence, consequences and – usually – solution of a catastrophe) such as *Jurassic Park, King Kong, Airport* and *The Towering Inferno* can be framed into Wagenaar et al.'s (1990) general accident causation scenario, with bad decisions leading to latent failures, latent failures to unsafe behaviours and failing defences resulting in disaster. The same applies to many crime movies (e.g. *Ocean's 11, Ocean's 12* and *Ocean's 13* are all about finding the weak spots in an organization's defences against theft). Spend an evening watching one of these (or a similar) movies with family or friends, and explain afterwards to them how the general accident causation scenario can be applied to it.
3. Consider your own workplace or university and find the weak spots in its defences against unsafe behaviour, that is, look around and search for potential safety issues. What sort of errors could you make here, potentially endangering your safety (exposure)? What additional circumstances are needed to increase the likelihood that these accidents will occur (propensity)? What sort of precautions (defences) are likely to have been taken to prevent these accidents from happening? And can these precautions be improved? Then go to a building site and compare your estimate of its accident exposure and accident propensity with that of your own organization. How can the possible differences in accident exposure and propensity be minimized?

Further Reading

Chmiel, N. (2008). Modern work and safety. In K. Naswall, J. Hellgren, & M. Sverke (Eds.), *The individual in the changing world of work* (pp. 169–192). Cambridge: Cambridge University Press.

Rasmussen, J. (1986). *Human information processing and human machine interaction*. Amsterdam: North Holland.

Reason, J. T. (1990). *Human error*. Cambridge: Cambridge University Press.

References

Alper, S. J., & Karsh, B. T. (2009). A systematic review of safety violations in industry. *Accident Analysis and Prevention, 41*, 739–754.

Barling, J., Kelloway, E. K., & Iverson, R. D. (2003). High-quality work, job satisfaction, and occupational injuries. *Journal of Applied Psychology, 88*, 276–283.

Barling, J., Loughlin, C., & Kelloway, E. K. (2002). Development and test of a model linking safety specific transformational leadership and occupational safety. *Journal of Applied Psychology, 87*, 488–496.

Beus, J. M., Payne, S. C., Bergman, M. E., & Arthur, W. (2010). Safety climate and injuries: An examination of theoretical and empirical relationships. *Journal of Applied Psychology, 93*, 713–727.

Chapman, R. (1973). The concept of exposure. *Accident Analysis & Prevention, 5*, 95–110.

Chmiel, N. (2005). Promoting healthy work: Self-reported minor injuries, work characteristics, and safety behaviour. In C. Korunka, & P. Hoffman (Eds.), *Change and quality in human service work* (pp. 277–288). Munich: Rainer Hampp Verlag.

Chmiel, N., & Hansez, I. (2012). *That's not my job! Job control, safety citizenship and safety violations.* Paper presented to the British Psychological Society, Division of Occupational Psychology, Chester, UK.

Clarke, S. (2006). The relationship between safety climate and safety performance: A meta-analytic review. *Journal of Occupational Health Psychology, 11*, 315–327.

Dembe, A. E., Erickson, J. B., Delbos, R. G., & Banks, S. M. (2005). The impact of overtime and long work hours on occupational injuries and illnesses: New evidence from the United States. *Occupational and Environmental Medicine, 62*, 588–597.

Eurostat (2010). *Health and safety at work in Europe (1999–2007): A statistical portrait.* Luxembourg: Publications Office of the European Union.

Griffin, M. A., & Neal, N. (2000). Perceptions of safety at work: A framework for linking safety climate to safety performance, knowledge, and motivation. *Journal of Occupational Health Psychology, 5*, 347–358.

Hale, A. R., & Hovden, J. (1998). Management and culture: the third age of safety. A review of approaches to organizational aspects of safety, health, and environment. In A. M. Feyer, & A. Williamson (Eds.), *Occupational injury, risk prevention and intervention: The third international conference on injury prevention and control* (pp. 129–165). London: Taylor & Francis.

Hamalainen, P. (2009). The effect of globalization on occupational accidents. *Safety Science, 47*, 733–742.

Hansez, I., & Chmiel, N. (2010). Safety behavior: job demands, job resources and perceived management commitment to safety. *Journal of Occupational Health Psychology, 15*, 267–278.

Hockey, G. R. J. (1986). Operator efficiency as a function of effects of environmental stress, fatigue and circadian rhythm. In K. Boff, L. Kaufman, & J. P. Thomas (Eds.), *Handbook of perception and human performance* (Vol. 2, pp. 44.43–44.44). New York: John Wiley & Sons.

Hodge, G. A., & Richardson, A. J. (1985). The role of accident exposure in transport system safety evaluations I: Intersection and link site exposure. *Journal of Advanced Transportation, 19*, 179–213.

Hofmann, B. J., Blair, C. A., Meriac, J. P., & Woehr, D. J. (2007). Expanding the criterion domain? A quantitative review of the OCB literature. *Journal of Applied Psychology, 92*, 555–566.

Hofmann, D. A., Morgeson, F. P., & Gerras, S. J. (2003). Climate as a moderator of the relationship between leader-member exchange and content specific citizenship: Safety climate as an exemplar. *Journal of Applied Psychology, 88*, 170–178.

Hoonakker, P., Loushine, T., Carayon, P., Kallman, J., Kapp, A., & Smith, M. J. (2005). The effect of safety initiatives on safety performance: A longitudinal study. *Applied Ergonomics, 36*, 461–469.

Iverson, R. D., & Erwin, P. J. (1997). Predicting occupational injury: The role of affectivity. *Journal of Occupational and Organizational Psychology, 70*, 113–128.

Kaminski, M. (2001). Unintended consequences: Organizational practices and their impact on workplace safety and productivity. *Journal of Occupational Health Psychology, 6*, 127–138.

Kemeny, J. G. (1979). *Report of the President's Commission on the accident at Three Mile Island: The need for change.* Washington, DC: The Commission.

Lawton, R. (1998). Not working to rule: Understanding procedural violations at work. *Safety Science, 28*, 77–95.

Lawton, R., & Ward, N. J. (2005). A systems analysis of the Ladbroke Grove rail crash. *Accident Analysis and Prevention, 37*, 235–244.

Melamed, S., Yekutieli, D., Froom, P., Kristal-Boneh, E., & Ribak, J. (1999). Adverse work and environmental conditions predict occupational injuries: The Israeli Cardiovascular Occupational Risk Factors Determination in Israel (CORDIS) Study. *American Journal of Epidemiology, 150*, 18–26.

Oliver, A., Cheyne, A., Tomas, J. M., & Cox, S. (2002). The effects of organizational and individual factors on occupational accidents. *Journal of Occupational and Organizational Psychology, 75*, 473–488.

Rasmussen, J. (1986). *Human information processing and human machine interaction*. Amsterdam: North Holland.

Reason, J. T. (1990). *Human error*. Cambridge: Cambridge University Press.

Reason, J. T., Parker, D., & Lawton, R. (1998). Organizational controls and safety: The varieties of rule-related behaviour. *Journal of Occupational and Organizational Psychology, 71*, 289–304.

Salminen, S., Saari, J., Saarela, K. L., & Rasanen, T. (1993). Organizational factors influencing occupational accidents. *Scandinavian Journal of Work, Environment & Health, 19*, 352–357.

Salminen, S., & Tallberg, T. (1996). Human errors in fatal and serious occupational accidents in Finland. *Ergonomics, 39*, 980–988.

Shannon, H. S., Mayr, J., & Haines, T. (1997). Overview of the relationship between organizational and workplace factors and injury rates. *Safety Science, 26*, 201–217.

Sheehy, N., & Chapman, A. (1987). Industrial accidents. In C. L. Cooper, & I. T. Robertson (Eds.), *International review of industrial and organizational psychology* (pp. 201–227). London: John Wiley & Sons.

Smith, G. S., Huang, Y-H., Ho, M., & Chen, P. (2006). The relationship between safety climate and injury rates across industries: The need to adjust for injury hazards. *Accident Analysis & Prevention, 38*, 556–562.

Solso, R. L. (1998). *Cognitive psychology* (5th ed.). Needham Heights, MA: Allyn and Bacon.

Vredenburgh, A. G. (2002). Organizational safety: Which management practices are most effective in reducing employee injury rates? *Journal of Safety Research, 33*, 259–276.

Wagenaar, W. A., & Groeneweg, J. (1987). Accidents at sea: Multiple causes and impossible consequences. *International Journal of Man-machine Studies, 27*, 587–598.

Wagenaar, W. A., Hudson, P. T. W., & Reason, J. T. (1990). Cognitive failures and accidents. *Applied Cognitive Psychology, 4*, 273–294.

Wagenaar, W. A., Groeneweg, J., Hudson, P. T. W., & Reason, J. T. (1994). Promoting safety in the oil industry. *Ergonomics, 37*, 1999–2013.

Wickens, C. D., Lee, J., Liu, Y., & Becker, S. G. (2004). *An introduction to human factors engineering* (2nd ed.). Upper Saddle River, NJ: Pearson.

Wilson-Donnelly, K. A., Priest, H. A., Salas, E., & Burke, C. S. (2005). The impact of organizational practices on safety in manufacturing: A review and reappraisal. *Human Factors and Ergonomics in Manufacturing, 15*, 135–176.

Zacharatos, A., Barling, J., & Iverson, R. D. (2005). High-performance work systems and occupational safety. *Journal of Applied Psychology, 90*, 77–93.

Zohar, D. (1980). Safety climate in industrial organisations: Theoretical and applied implications. *Journal of Applied Psychology, 65*, 96–102.

15
Sickness Absence and Sickness Presence

Rita Claes

> **Chapter Objectives**
>
> After studying this chapter, you should be able to:
>
> - define sickness absence and sickness presence;
> - discuss ways of measuring sickness absence and sickness presence;
> - compare the factors associated with sickness absence and sickness presence;
> - describe Aronsson and Gustafsson's (2005) model of sickness absence and sickness presence, and compare this model with other models;
> - discuss the societal context of sickness absence and sickness presence.

Work attendance refers to the degree to which workers are present or absent from work. *Presenteeism* refers to attendance at work despite feeling sick, that is, *sickness presence*. For example, a worker has a nasty fall at home on Sunday, aches all over, gets two days' sick leave prescribed, but still attends work on Monday. Conversely, *absenteeism* concerns non-attendance at work due to poor health and/or poor well-being (e.g. mental or physical complaints, or low work motivation), that is, *sickness absence*. In the latter example, the worker actually takes two prescribed days of sick leave.

An Introduction to Contemporary Work Psychology, First Edition.
Edited by Maria C. W. Peeters, Jan de Jonge and Toon W. Taris.
© 2014 John Wiley & Sons, Ltd. Published 2014 by John Wiley & Sons, Ltd.

Section 15.1 answers the question 'Why bother about sickness absence?' by summarizing its prevalence and costs. Section 15.2 considers various forms of sickness absence and Section 15.3 describes traditional models of sickness absence. This is followed by a discussion of the prevalence and costs of sickness presence in Section 15.4, which discusses the prevalence and costs of sickness presence. Section 15.5 introduces contemporary models that consider sickness absence vis-à-vis sickness presence. Finally, Section 15.6 presents an integrative, multi-level framework for research on and management of work attendance and sickness, and concludes with several practical implications.

15.1 Prevalence and Costs of Sickness Absence

Why bother about sickness absence? What is the prevalence of sickness absence? How dysfunctional is sickness absence for a worker, a work team, an organization or society as a whole?

Prevalence of sickness absence

In principle, there are three data sources that could provide insight into the prevalence of sickness absence: self-reported data, data recorded by organizations and international databases available from economic and statistical centres.

Self-reported data may refer to both self-certified and medically certified sickness absence. Since this type of data is provided by the workers themselves, it is a subjective way of data collection. It refers to sickness absence during a particular period, typically the past full year to cancel out seasonal fluctuations. Self-reported data on sickness absence are often collected by means of a single, retrospective question, for example 'How many days (spells, respectively) of sickness absence did you have in the last 12 months?'. Although the use of self-reported data has been criticized, there may be good reasons for collecting such data, for example maintenance of respondent anonymity or confidentiality, facilitation of particular research designs and research questions, and unavailability of records-based data. Moreover, self-reported data on absence appear to be reliable and valid to a large extent (Johns, 1994).

Contrary to self-reported sickness absence data, *records-based data* obtained by organizations are objective data, as they are collected independently from the workers themselves. This type of absence data is officially recorded and is usually medically certified. However, since there is considerable variety in registration criteria across studies (i.e. from which day on sickness absence is recorded and on which day it officially ends), these data are difficult to compare across studies.

International databases on sickness absence vary in terms of countries and years covered, and also in terms of indicators included. The major database providing sickness absence data for the European Union countries is the European Statistical System, abbreviated Eurostat (e.g. Eurostat, 2011). Worldwide data on sickness absence are provided by the Organisation for Economic Cooperation and Development (OECD; e.g. OECD, 2011). On the basis of these databases,

Table 15.1 Between-country differences in prevalence of sickness absence.

Indicator	Top three countries	Bottom three countries
Self-reported absence from work due to illness in number of days lost per person per year (OECD, 2011)	Spain 18.6% (2003) Switzerland 11.7% (2007) Finland 9.1% (2010)	Israel 3.9% (2009) USA 3.6% (2009) Korea 2.1% (2009)
Most serious work-related health problem resulted in sick leave in the past 12 months (Eurostat, 2011)	Czech Republic 97.7% (2007) The Netherlands 97.9% (2007) Slovenia 98.1% (2007)	Finland 43.0% (2007) Portugal 41.7% (2007) France 19.8% (2007)

Table 15.1 presents the three countries scoring highest and lowest on two indicators of sickness absence. This table illustrates the fact that self-reported sickness rates tend to be higher in European countries (Spain, Switzerland and Finland) than elsewhere (Israel, USA and Korea), at least in terms of the self-reported number of days lost per person due to illness. Furthermore, there are considerable differences among European countries in terms of sickness absence. Apparently, whether a serious health problem results in sick leave is at least partly contingent on contextual factors such as unemployment rates and employer's generosity of granting sick leave.

Moreover, although sometimes inconsistent findings arise in terms of demographic variables, the general agreement is that sickness absence is more prevalent among older or female workers. For example, in Belgium 78% of people aged 55–64 years reported that their most serious work-related health problem resulted in sick leave in the past 12 months, whereas in the younger age groups this was 68%. Also in Belgium, 72% of women reported that their most serious work-related health problem resulted in sick leave in the past 12 months, whereas for men this was 68%.

Costs of sickness absence

The dysfunctional effects of sickness absence mainly pertain to its costs, for example for the workers themselves, their colleagues/work group, the organization they work for or society as a whole.

Costs for the worker
For individual workers, sickness absence is associated with adverse outcomes for health and well-being (e.g. future sickness absence, disability and mortality), may lead to job dismissal up to exclusion from the labour market and could result in a weakened financial position up to social decline. Some countries have implemented

models of sick leave provision in which workers partially contribute financially to this provision (e.g. the costs of these arrangements are shared by some degree among workers, employers and the state), while other countries have implemented models in which workers are completely responsible for providing their own sick pay and rehabilitation costs, unless they are included in the benefits package in their employment contract. Note that sickness absence may also be *functional* for workers in that it provides them with opportunities to recover, allowing them to return to work in a better condition than before (see also Chapter 8). It may also stimulate workers to be proactive and to change their work environment by changing experienced antecedents of sickness absence (e.g. by quitting a highly demanding job or by job crafting; cf. Chapter 17).

Costs for colleagues
At the group level, colleagues of sick-absent group members may have to handle their assignments on top of their own jobs, thereby increasing their workload and eventually worsening their psychosocial work environment. Depending on group structure (e.g. size), group culture (e.g. absence norms) and organizational-level correlates (e.g. team organization), sickness absence of group members may negatively affect the group's performance, cohesion and job satisfaction.

Costs for the organization
The costs of sickness absence for the organization are predominantly financial. They refer to the organization's contribution (entirely or partially) to sick leave provision, for example organizations still have to pay a worker who is absent, at

Work Psychology in Action: Ill-health policy in a multinational energy provider

Over the years, a large multinational energy services provider has established a very favourable policy concerning the ill-health of its workforce. The current policy, which originated from the management of accidents at work, includes 30 granted sick leave days (which cannot be banked, and therefore cannot be considered as extra days off). Furthermore, there is one self-certified sick leave day per month, the use of which is followed up by the human resources department to discourage its unethical use. The company's ill-health policy also includes generous sickness insurance and a special social fund, so the organization is able to cover all costs related with ill-health and accidents at work (including high wage replacement rates). Finally, there are a number of social services to support long-term sick-absent workers in all their needs (e.g. medical, psychological, administrative), including a social assistant visiting sick-absent workers at home, access to a network of psychologists and the opportunity to contact external prevention consultants. The ill-health related benefits package the company offers is an important factor in the retention of its personnel.

least temporarily. Productivity loss in case of sickness absence is 100%, but costs may also include hiring replacement workers, paying for overtime work, a reduced quality of services, and costs for medical and disability services. Bearing in mind the costs of sickness absence, organizations have a strong incentive to keep these costs down by policies and practices.

Costs for society
Sickness absence imposes a substantial burden on society. It has implications for the public health situation (in terms of medical and social costs, such as the costs associated with insurance and assistance). Moreover, high levels of sickness absence reduce overall productivity in society, since this will lead to a lower proportion of the labour force that actively contributes to a country's economic performance.

Replay

- Sickness absence is non-attendance at work due to poor health and poor well-being; sickness presence is attendance at work despite feeling sick.
- Employee-reported data, records-based organizational data and international databases available from economic and statistical centres may all provide useful data on sickness absence.
- The prevalence of sickness absence varies across indicators, countries, age and gender (i.e. higher sickness absence rates are reported for older or female workers than for other people). Sickness absence can be dysfunctional for workers (e.g. job loss), for their work team (e.g. loss of productivity), for the organization they work for (e.g. due to sick leave provision) or for society as a whole (e.g. the costs of public health).

15.2 Forms of Sickness Absence

There are several ways to measure sickness absence. Below we discuss approaches that are based on their frequency, their duration or their volition.

Frequency-based approaches

A natural way of measuring sickness absence is to focus on how often an employee reports sick (regardless of duration and volition) during a particular time interval (typically a calendar year). The period between the start and the end of the time of absence due to sickness is called a *spell*. The number of spells of sickness absence during a particular interval is the *sickness absence frequency* for a particular employee.

Duration-based approaches

In these approaches, the duration of sickness absence is measured as the total sum of days absent (this may include multiple spells of sickness absence). Often a distinction is made between short-term and long-term sickness absence. Whether a particular sickness absence duration is classified as being short-term or long-term depends on the time frame chosen by researchers (cf. Dekkers-Sánchez, Hoving, Sluiter, & Frings-Dresen, 2008; Steel, Rentsch, & van Scotter, 2007). Short-term sickness absence may refer to durations ranging from 1 day up to 6 months, whereas long-term sickness absence may refer to durations of 3 or more days and can go beyond 12 months.

> **Work Psychology in Action: Sickness absence duration and employment contract in a city administration**
>
> The distinction between short-term and long-term sickness absence rates may have policy implications. Of the more than 1,000 employees of a large city administration, 37% have a tenured contract, whereas the other 63% hold a variety of temporary contracts. The tenured employees are predominantly male and older, while the temporary employees are mainly female and younger. Compared to other public and private organizations, sickness absence is high. An important cause of the high sickness absence rates in this organization is the long-term sickness absence among the tenured employees. Since the city administration aims to reduce sickness absence, a policy of 'pre-retirement due to medical reasons' for long-term sick-absent employees holding a tenured contract might help.
>
> Another factor stimulating sickness absence may be the lack of control and follow-up of employees who are absent. Recently, a policy concerning short-term sickness absence has been put into practice. It includes immediate control of sick-reported employees by an independent medical service, an obligation for employees to report sick immediately to their supervisor and a requirement for supervisors to deal with sick-absent employees (e.g. consult their job-related agenda, show interest in sick-absent employees and hold a return-to-work interview with employees in case of long-term sickness absence). The results of this intervention are unknown yet.

Volition-based approaches

In these approaches, a basic distinction is made between *voluntary and avoidable* absence on the one hand, and *involuntary and unavoidable* absence on the other, that is, workers often have a certain degree of freedom of choice whether to report sick or not. For example, having a cold or a headache does not necessarily imply that a worker is unable to go to work and perform adequately. Other factors than health may frequently influence a worker's decision to stay home or go to work.

Table 15.2 presents three different viewpoints on this issue. The bulk of the research discussed in this chapter adheres to the viewpoint of Schaufeli, Bakker

Table 15.2 Forms of sickness absence according to volition.

	Voluntary, avoidable absence	*Involuntary, unavoidable absence*
Wegge, Schmidt, Parkes, & van Dick (2007)	• This is not a form of sickness absence • It is not due to health and well-being, and is unexcused • It is within a worker's control; they decide for themselves whether they will report sick • It is typically short term • It can be measured by absence frequency	• This is 'true' sickness absence • It is due to health and well-being • It is beyond a worker's control; they are unable to work • It is typically long term • It can be measured by absence duration
Schaufeli, Bakker, & van Rhenen (2009)	• This is a form of 'true' sickness absence • Arises from psychological withdrawal from work, and reflects a motivational process • It is best measured as absence frequency	• This is a form of 'true' sickness absence • Arises from high levels of stress, and reflects … • a strain-related process • It is best measured as absence duration
Steel (2003)	The distinction between both forms of absence is oversold: both are forms of 'true' sickness absence Recommends using overall sickness absence metrics, that is, combinations of absence duration and absence frequency	

and van Rhenen (2009), who considered both voluntary and avoidable, and involuntary and unavoidable absence as 'true' sickness absence, although they differ in terms of underlying causes, that is, voluntary and avoidable absence often reflects lack of motivation and is best measured as absence frequency. In contrast, involuntary and unavoidable absence may result from high levels of job strain and is best measured in terms of absence duration.

Replay

- Several forms of sickness absence may be distinguished on the basis of their frequency, duration and volition.
- The frequency of sickness absence refers to the number of absence spells, regardless of their duration and volition.
- The lower and upper limits to denote sickness absence as short-term versus long-term largely overlap. Short-term sickness absence may range from 1 day

up to 6 months, whereas long-term sickness absence may range from 3 days up to more than 12 months.
- Regarding the volition of sickness absence, it is advised to combine voluntary and involuntary sickness absence in one overall metric.

15.3 Traditional Approaches of Examining Sickness Absence

Below, three approaches to study sickness absence are discussed. These approaches may be called 'traditional' in that they all consider employee health and well-being as the major determinant of sickness absence. However, from earlier research it is known that there are numerous other potential antecedents of sickness absence, which may be located at different levels of analysis (e.g. the individual worker, the work team or the organization; see Table 15.3). Individual-level studies are abundant, but with higher levels of abstraction

Table 15.3 Some potential antecedents of sickness absence.

Individual Person	Demographics (e.g. age, gender, education, race, socio-economic status, marital status, children, domestic work)
	Intellectual and physical abilities
	Personality (e.g. psychological hardiness, self-efficacy)
	Health and well-being (e.g. general health, burnout, stress)
Work	Tenure, union membership, occupation, hierarchical position
	Work values (e.g. meaning of work, absence norms)
	Work attitudes (e.g. satisfaction, involvement)
	Hours worked/week, contract type, net income, job security
	Psychosocial work environment (e.g. demands and resources, role clarity/conflicts, offensive behaviours)
	Sickness absence (e.g. history, perceived consequences)
Interface	Work–family and family–work interplay
Group	Properties (e.g. size, type, cohesion, composition)
	Psychosocial work environment (e.g. predictability, demands and resources, role clarity/conflicts, social support, trust, leadership)
	Group culture, absence culture
Organization	Properties (e.g. size, sector, industry, material setting)
	Structure, change
	Psychosocial work environment (e.g. perceived organizational support, trust, reward, justice)
	Organizational culture, absence culture
Society	Objective causes (e.g. general health situation)
	Behavioural reactions to macro-economic conditions (e.g. employment rate of older persons)
	Behavioural reactions to institutions (e.g. generosity of granting sick leave, strictness of employment protection)

(group, organization, society) relevant research becomes increasingly scarce. For example, Osterkamp and Röhn (2007) found three societal factors that were associated with high rates of sickness absence in a country: (i) generosity of granting sick leave, (ii) degree of employment protection and (iii) employment rate of older persons. Interesting as these findings are, the dearth of research on the higher-level determinants of sickness absence means that these results have yet to be confirmed.

The three approaches to examine sickness absence discussed below are not only similar in that they consider poor employee health and well-being as the major antecedent of sickness absence. They also construe the worker as a passive recipient of environmental circumstances, that is, workers are primarily assumed to *react* to their poor health and well-being at work. Finally, they consider sickness absence as the major outcome. Insight into these traditional approaches to examine sickness absence is necessary to fully understand the contemporary work attendance approaches that will be discussed later in this chapter.

First approach: General work stress models and sickness absence

One way to examine the antecedents of sickness absence is to use general job stress models for the theoretical basis of a study (see Chapters 3 and 4 for a discussion of such models). These models were designed to account for the occurrence of a variety of stress-related outcomes, including sickness absence. In an interesting study, Griep, Rotenberg, Choc, Toivanen and Landsbergis (2010) compared the explanatory power of two long-standing stress models – Karasek and Theorell's (1990) Demand–Control-Support (DCS) Model and Siegrist's (1996) Effort–Reward Imbalance (ERI) Model – with regard to sickness absence (see also Chapter 3). The DCS Model predicts stress at (and hence absence from) work from high job demands, low job control and low social support. The ERI Model predicts stress at work from an imbalance between work-related efforts and occupational rewards (i.e. work effort exceeds the rewards from work), and from high overcommitment to work as a personality characteristic.

Griep, Rotenberg, Choc, Toivanen and Landsbergis (2010) attempted to identify the best predictors of sickness absence and asked themselves whether the key characteristics of these stress models were the best predictors. Did one stress model account better for the data than another? Was a combination of the DCS Model and the ERI Model more powerful than each of these models separately? Looking at the effects obtained for the separate measures of these models, Griep et al. (2010) found that both high job demands and high effort predicted short-term (less than 10 days of absence) and long-term sickness absence. However, whereas job control and overcommitment were not associated with either type of sickness absence, low rewards and low social support predicted both types of absence. When both models were combined (i.e. all measures were analysed simultaneously), Griep et al. (2010) found that high demands, high control and high effort–reward imbalance, adjusted for social support and overcommitment, predicted short-term sickness absence. Apparently, these general job stress models can be used to study the antecedents of sickness absence.

> ### Work Psychology in Action: Replacement of short-term sick-absent teachers in a secondary school
>
> At a secondary school (about 900 pupils, aged 12–18 years), 63% of the teaching staff are female and most employees work part-time. Teachers' ages range from 25 to 60 years, and the ages of the majority lie between 30 and 40 years. The middle-aged and older teachers are usually permanently appointed – seniority being the sole criterion to attain this level in the school hierarchy – and they have career security. The younger teachers usually hold temporary appointments, implying career uncertainty. Sickness absence is both short-term and long-term, and its frequency varies strongly. The sickness absence policy of the school includes one self-certified sick leave day. Longer sick leave has to be medically certified. School management rarely requests external control of sick-absent teachers. Unpredictable short-term sickness absence (of usually just 1 day) is announced by school management each morning, with the replacements already assigned to the existing staff. For school management, the need for an appropriate substitute to cover for the sick-absent teacher is immediate. For the colleagues assigned to the replacements, the extra workload is sudden (i.e. an unpleasant surprise upon arrival at school) and causes frustration and job strain. The replacement policy is based on solidarity and engagement because teachers are only paid for teaching their own classes, not for any other extra tasks. For the pupils, replacements mean disruption (e.g. classes skipped, classes taught by another teacher, classes taught in larger groups of pupils). With predictable, long-term sickness absence (usually more than 2 weeks), school management can anticipate solutions for replacement of the sick-absent teacher (e.g. external teachers, temporarily extend part-time contracts to full-time contracts).

Second approach: Job strain and sickness absence

The second approach discussed here originated in the United States. On the basis of literature reviews, Darr and Johns (2008) proposed a *work strain-sickness absence model.* The model distinguishes two functions of sickness absence. First, sickness absence is a form of withdrawal behaviour. For this function, Darr and Johns (2008) hypothesized a positive relation between job strain and sickness absence: job strain may lead to sickness absence. Second, the restorative function of sickness absence provides employees with an opportunity to restore their resources and their ability to cope with job strain. Hence, a negative relation between prior sickness absence and job strain is hypothesized: sickness absence with coping potential may lead to less job strain after return to work. However, counter to the restorative function, adverse consequences that accompany being sick-absent (e.g. increased job responsibilities, job dissatisfaction, disrupted co-worker relationships and lower performance ratings) can exacerbate a worker's experience of job strain after return to work. Hence, Darr and Johns (2008) also hypothesized a weak positive relation between prior sickness absence and job strain: sickness absence with adverse consequences may lead to more job strain after return to work. They could confirm the withdrawal function of sickness absence, but found little support for its restorative function.

Third approach: Burnout and sickness absence

The third approach focuses on the relations between sickness absence on the one hand and burnout (cf. Chapter 12) on the other. The PUMA Model (PUMA is a Danish acronym for burnout, work motivation and job satisfaction) was developed in Denmark and is based on literature reviews as well as on discussions with focus groups, employers and employees' representatives (Borritz et al., 2006). The latter can be considered a specific asset of this approach compared to the other two. The PUMA Model proposes that antecedents such as psychosocial work environment, lifestyle and personality may influence the risk of burnout, which in turn may lead to sickness absence. Conversely, sickness absence might also influence burnout, that is, recovering from burnout during sickness absence could result in a decreasing level of burnout. Thus, burnout and sickness absence may mutually affect each other. Longitudinal and multilevel research confirmed that burnout could lead to sickness absence at the individual level (Borritz et al., 2006; Rugulies et al., 2007) and the work-unit level (Borritz et al., 2010), the latter being a specific asset of this approach compared to the other two approaches. However, the idea that sickness absence could also lead to lower levels of burnout was not supported.

Replay

- Potential antecedents of sickness absence may be located on four levels (worker, group, organization and society), and these antecedents may be intertwined within each level and across levels.
- The approaches of Griep et al. (2010), of Darr and Johns (2008), and of Borritz et al. (2006; PUMA) are traditional in considering employee health and well-being as the major antecedents of sickness absence, in their treatment of the worker as a passive recipient of environmental influences and in their focus on sickness absence as major outcome.
- Griep et al. (2010) used general job stress models (i.e. the DCS Model and the ERI Model) to identify potential antecedents of sickness absence. Darr and Johns (2008) developed the job strain-sickness absence model that combines withdrawal and restorative behaviour. Finally, the PUMA Model on burnout–sickness absence is partly based on discussions with employers and employees' representatives, and assumes that burnout and sickness absence will mutually influence each other.

15.4 Prevalence and Costs of Sickness Presence

In the preceding sections we primarily focused on sickness absence. Below we discuss its counterpart, sickness *presence*, in more detail.

Prevalence of sickness presence

As indicated earlier, sickness presence refers to a worker's attendance at work despite feeling sick. This means that the worker is often the most convenient (and perhaps the only) source to report sickness presence. Sickness presence is therefore virtually always measured with self-reports, with items like 'How often have you gone to work despite feeling that you really should have stayed away due to your state of health over the last 12 months' (with the response categories being 'never', 'once', '2–3 times', '4–5 times' and 'more than 5 times'; cf. Aronsson, Gustafsson, & Dallner, 2000). Unlike being sick-absent, a worker is under no obligation to attest formally when sick-present. Hence, for sickness presence, there exist neither organizational records-based data nor international databases.

From her review of self-report-based research on the prevalence of sickness presence, Claes (2011) concluded that 30–80% of the participants in these studies reported to have been working while actually being sick. These percentages were found despite differences among studies in terms of measures used, occupations studied, time of data collection and country in which the study was conducted. Sickness presence was especially high in occupations such as health care and education, which imply direct and frequent contact with relatively vulnerable others (patients, pupils). Workers in these contactual professions exhibited high professional identity, boundarylessness (i.e. finding it hard to say 'no' or to set limits with regard to demands and expectations of others) and loyalty, and considered themselves irreplaceable. Further, although research findings are sometimes inconsistent, it appears that sickness presence is more prevalent among female workers.

Costs of sickness presence

Parallel to sickness absence, the costs of sickness presence are multilevel and intertwined across levels. For the worker, sickness presence is mainly dysfunctional. It is linked with future ill-health (e.g. Bergström et al., 2009; Hansen & Andersen, 2009) and with productivity loss (e.g. Johns, 2011; Rantanen & Tuominen, 2011). It appears that employees who are present at work despite being sick tend to work inefficiently, sometimes actually work at reduced capacity, make more mistakes and provoke accidents at work (see also Chapter 14). Productivity loss due to sickness presence is usually measured by asking workers how much their work capacity has been reduced during sickness presence (Brooks, Hagen, Sathyanarayanan, Schultz, & Edington, 2010). Mattke, Balakrishnan, Bergamo and Newberry (2007) presented reviews of multi-item self-report questionnaires for measuring productivity loss during sickness presence. However, strategies to convert self-estimated productivity loss into financial terms have not yet been validated in organizations. Thus, the financial costs of self-reported productivity loss are not clear.

Note that in some circumstances it is undesirable to prevent sickness presence. First, sickness presence may be preferred to sickness absence when workers derive structure in their lives from their work. Second, it is also preferred where their work environment provides them with needed support from others (perhaps also regarding non-work issues). Third, sickness presence is recommended when their job performance helps them to get through (Sanderson, Tilse, Nicholson, Oldenburg, & Graves, 2007). Finally, in the short term sickness presence may be functional for the worker as a signal of high commitment and/or organizational citizenship behaviour.

At the group level, colleagues of sick-present group members may help them out because of their reduced working capacity and are at risk of becoming sick themselves by infectious illnesses. Depending on group structure, group culture and some organizational-level correlates (e.g. team organization), sick-present group members may negatively affect collective performance, cohesion and job satisfaction.

For the organization, the costs of sickness presence translate into reduced productivity and lower profits (especially in the long term, e.g. Böckerman & Laukkanen, 2010; Schultz, Chen, & Edington, 2009). This is not only due to the sick-present

---

Work Psychology in Action: Sickness presence in a market analysis consultancy

Sometimes sickness presence is the rule in an organization, regardless of the costs. The employees of a relatively small, private market analysis consultancy are, on average, 30 years old and highly educated (with most employees having at least one university degree). They have few domestic responsibilities. All are passionate about their jobs and deliver high-quality services. Their job demands are predominantly client-related. Client contacts are very frequent and occur 'multimedia', that is, both face-to-face and through all sorts of ICT-related media. Clients' ever-increasing demands are always met. Rewards from clients take the form of appreciation for a job well-done, followed by new assignments that ensure further business.

Sickness absence is exceptional in this organization, and sickness presence is more or less the rule. Even when provided with a medical certificate, some sick employees continue working on their projects to meet their clients' deadlines and their management's expectations. Sickness presence is fuelled by employees' individual boundarylessness, insufficient replaceability, pace at work, time pressure and a presenteeism culture – employees are simply expected not to become sick. Considerations about serious future ill-health due to sickness presence are put aside for the time being.

worker's wages that must be paid, but eventually also to lower-quality job output, loss of internal expertise and loss of knowledge on products/services and customers (Brooks et al., 2010). An organizational culture may become dysfunctional when it focuses on sickness presence at all costs, that is, a competitive presenteeism culture (Böckerman & Laukkanen).

Given its costs for individual workers, their work groups and their organizations, sickness presence will imply *costs for society* as well, that is, sickness presence is associated with overall productivity losses and may have long-term health effects that are even more critical with ageing workforces.

Researchers believe that the costs of sickness presence are higher than those of sickness absence. For example, Johns (2010) concluded that sickness presence accounts for more aggregate productivity loss than sickness absence. He referred to an iceberg effect where the costs of sickness absence form the small visible portion above the surface and the costs of sickness presence form the large invisible portion beneath the surface. Unfortunately, there are no estimates of the costs of sickness absence versus sickness presence available yet.

Replay

- Sickness presence refers to an employee's attendance at work despite feeling sick.
- Employee self-reports indicate that sickness presence ranges from 30% to 80%. It varies across countries, occupations, gender and time. It is especially high in contractual professions and for female workers.
- For sickness presence virtually all data are employee reports. There exist neither organizational records-based data nor international databases from economic and statistical centres.
- Sickness presence can be dysfunctional for workers (e.g. future ill-health), teams (e.g. productivity loss), organizations (e.g. competitive presenteeism culture) and society as a whole (e.g. long-term public health).

15.5 Decision Models of Sickness Absence versus Sickness Presence

Compared to the traditional approaches to study sickness absence discussed in Section 15.3, contemporary models of work attendance behaviours have a broader scope of antecedents (i.e. they start from health and well-being at work but also consider other aspects). Moreover, they treat the worker as an active agent, that is, workers decide how to behave when feeling sick. Finally, they incorporate sickness absence and sickness presence as separate and mutually exclusive behaviours. We refer to these contemporary models as *decision models of sickness absence versus sickness presence*. We describe three frameworks that – although they differ in terms of their terminology – build on each other and overlap to some extent (see Table 15.4).

Table 15.4 Decision models of sickness absence or sickness presence.

Illness Flexibility Model (after Johansson & Lundberg, 2004)

	Adjustment latitude ↓	Attendance requirements ↓		
Loss of function →	Work ability →	Sickness absence or presence	↗ ↘	Return to work Exclusion from labour market

Model of sickness presence and sickness absence (after Aronsson & Gustafsson, 2005)

		Negative person-related and work-related demands for presence ↓		
General health →	↗ ↘	Decision to sickness absence	↗ ↘	Return to work Exclusion from labour market
		Decision to sickness presence → ↑ Positive person-related and work-related demands for presence		Health

Dynamic model of presenteeism and absenteeism (after Johns, 2010)

		Context and person factors ↓		
Health event →	↗ ↘	Decision to sickness absence ↘		Individual consequences
		Decision to sickness presence ↗ ↑ Context and person factors		

The Illness Flexibility Model

The Illness Flexibility Model was developed by Johansson and Lundberg (2004), and assumes that although illness may result in loss of function this does not necessarily imply that workers are unable to work. Whether workers will report sick also depends on their opportunities to reduce or alter their work effort when feeling ill. If such opportunities are present, they may adjust their work efforts and their tasks depending on what sort of tasks they are still able to do (i.e. their work ability). In this sense, they are 'flexible' in what they do at work. Even when they are sick, they may still be able to work. Whether sickness presence or absence will occur further depends on the attendance requirements in the organization (i.e. whether being absent has negative consequences for the worker). Examples of attendance requirements are the organization of work (i.e. to which degree will team or organizational performance be affected when the worker is absent?) and financial position (e.g. do workers still receive some financial compensation when being sick?).

According to this model, the chances that sick workers will actually report sick are highest when they have little opportunity to reduce their work efforts (i.e. a worker is simply unable to achieve any work goals at all) and when attendance requirements are low (being sick-absent will have no negative consequences). Conversely, the chances of sickness presence are highest when sick workers have a high opportunity to reduce their work efforts (i.e. they will be able to adjust work goals to meet their current physical and/or psychological states) and when attendance requirements are high (being sick-absent has major negative consequences).

The Illness Flexibility Model emphasizes that workers decide for themselves whether they will report sick or not, and that their work tasks may not be fixed but could be flexible. Johansson and colleagues have found considerable support for their model in a range of studies (e.g. Johansson & Lundberg, 2004, 2009).

Aronsson and Gustafsson's model of sickness presence and sickness absence

According to Aronsson and Gustafsson's (2005) *model of sickness presence and sickness absence*, general health is an antecedent of sickness absence or presence. Whether sick workers decide to go to work or to stay home depends on person- and work-related demands for presence. 'Person-related demands for presence' include individual boundarylessness and own financial needs, while 'work-related demands for presence' refer to replaceability, having sufficient job resources, conflicting demands, control and pace at work, and time pressure.

These demands for presence are similar to the attendance requirements in the Illness Flexibility Model, but Aronsson and Gustafsson further distinguish between positive and negative demands for presence. The positive demands for presence are associated with higher levels of sickness presence (e.g. workers who feel they cannot be replaced at work or who need the money will work, even if their health seriously hinders their work performance). Conversely, negative demands for presence are associated with sickness absence (e.g. having an affluent sickness insurance could lead sick workers to decide to stay home). Thus, the main contribution of this model is that it proposes that sickness absence and presence have different antecedents. Empirical evidence for the Aronsson and Gustafsson model was found across countries and beyond Scandinavia (Claes, 2011; Johns, 2011).

Johns' dynamic model of presenteeism and absenteeism

The dynamic model of presenteeism and absenteeism was developed by Johns (2010, 2011). This model is similar to the Aronsson and Gustafsson model in that it links 'health events' to a worker's decision to report sick (sickness absence) or to go to work anyway (sickness presence). Furthermore, absence and presence are affected by context and person factors (neither necessarily 'demands for presence' nor 'attendance requirements'). For example, context factors include (i) job demands and job security, (ii) the organization's reward system, absence policy and absence/presence culture, and (iii) ease of replacement and adjustment latitude. Person factors include work attitudes, personality factors, stress, perceived absence legitimacy, proclivity for sick role, health locus of control and gender. Moreover,

Johns noted that the outcomes of sickness absence and presence are broader than just 'return to work' or 'exclusion from the labour market' or 'downstream health', that is, being absent or present may also have consequences for a worker's productivity, other-attributions, self-attributions, attendance and tenure.

Strengths and limitations

The most interesting feature of these three contemporary approaches to study sickness absence is that these models acknowledge that health issues *do not automatically* result in sickness absence, that is, reporting sick or going to work involves a worker's conscious decision to do so, and this decision may depend on a host of other factors than health alone (as was suggested by the traditional approaches discussed in Section 15.2). In this sense, each of these models extends the range of possible antecedents of sickness absence or sickness presence in its own way by emphasizing different sets of antecedents. By considering these antecedents, researchers and practitioners may extend their understanding of the effects of sickness on employees' behaviour. However, limitations of these contemporary approaches are that they tend to emphasize individual-level factors as antecedents of sickness absence or presence, and they are not suited for examining the antecedents of sickness absence/presence on higher levels (e.g. the work team or organization) since the antecedents included in these models are primarily located at the individual level.

Replay

- Contemporary models of work attendance are decision models of sickness absence versus sickness presence: the worker decides how to behave when being sick.
- The models described here (i.e. those of Johansson and Lundberg (2004), Aronsson and Gustafsson (2005), and Johns (2010)) share (i) the fact that they start from health and well-being at work, and then enter external aspects as additional antecedents of workers' decisions, (ii) a focus on sickness absence and sickness presence as mutually exclusive behaviours, (iii) their process orientation, in that they consider the consequences of the chosen work attendance behaviour, and (iv) shortcomings.
- Each model has its specific assets: (i) Johansson and Lundberg included 'work ability' as a separate step, (ii) Aronsson and Gustafsson are unique in referring to 'negative and positive person-related and work-related demands for presence' and (iii) Johns focused on personality and attribution, and included the largest variety of individual consequences.

15.6 A Multilevel Framework of Work Attendance and Sickness

The framework depicted in Figure 15.1 integrates many of the findings and viewpoints discussed in this chapter. It presents a multilevel framework for understanding work attendance behaviours and is in line with the decision-focused

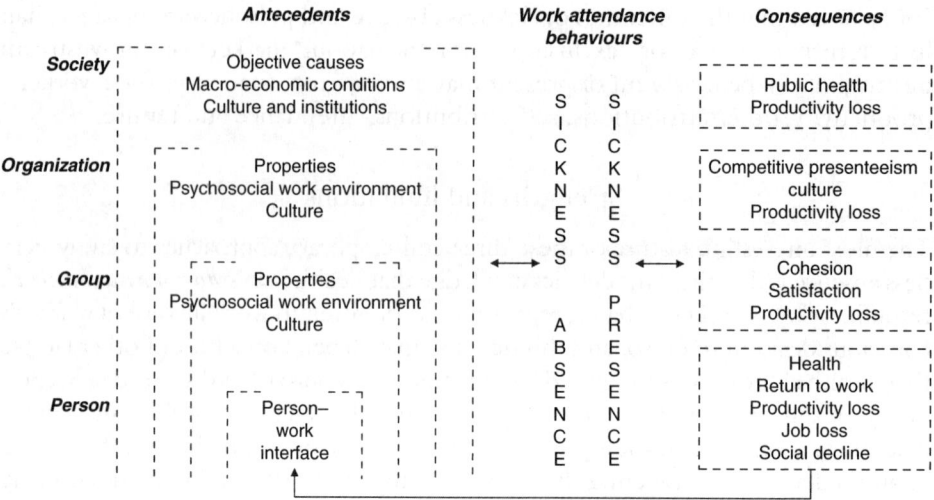

Figure 15.1 A multilevel framework for research on and management of work attendance and sickness.

models of Johansson and Lundberg (2004), Aronsson and Gustafsson (2005), and Johns (2010). In addition to these models, which were restricted to the worker level, the framework in Figure 15.1:

1. highlights antecedents on four levels embedded in each other (see multilevel antecedents of sickness absence and presence discussed earlier in this chapter);
2. includes consequences interacting within and across four levels (see multi-level costs of sickness absence and presence discussed earlier in this chapter);
3. foresees multiple feedback loops (see Darr and Johns' model and the PUMA Model).

The left side of Figure 15.1 features antecedents of sickness absence and sickness presence, located on four levels (the individual worker, the work group, the organization and society as a whole). It is noteworthy that the antecedents of sickness absence (cf. Table 15.3) overlap with those of sickness presence (Table 15.4). Also note that the psychosocial work environment as an antecedent of work attendance behaviour appears at several levels. It is therefore important to have instruments to measure these risk factors for sickness absence and sickness presence across levels, not just at the individual level. One useful instrument in this respect is the Copenhagen Psychosocial Questionnaire (COPSOQ; Bjorner, Albersten, & Rugulies, 2010), which covers eight clusters of risk factors located at various levels of analysis. Finally, although Table 15.3 provides an excellent impression of the possible higher-level antecedents of work attendance behaviour, it remains important to enlarge the set of possible societal antecedents when researching sickness absence and sickness presence cross-nationally, or when implementing practices for their prevention, mitigation and remediation in multinational organizations. For example, a country's gross domestic product and 'welfare regime' (i.e. how much social welfare provision there is and how that welfare is provided) reflect its opportunities and priorities for dealing with sickness absence and sickness presence. Note that it is likely that antecedents at different levels may be intertwined, for example national culture (i.e. values and practices), organizational culture, group culture and finally a worker's values are likely to be related.

At the core of Figure 15.1 are the two work attendance behaviours: sickness absence and sickness presence. These two behaviours are mutually exclusive. Essentially, it is the worker as an active agent who decides how to behave in case of ill-health or poor well-being: to be sick-absent or sick-present. This does not imply that these behaviours can only be studied at the individual level: employee-reported data on sickness absence and sickness presence can be aggregated to obtain group-level, organization-level and country-level rates. Thus, the two work attendance behaviours are multilevel phenomena in their own right.

The right side of Figure 15.1 presents possible consequences of sickness absence and sickness presence for each of the four levels of analysis. When comparing the earlier sections of this chapter on the costs of sickness absence and sickness presence with the consequences proposed in the decision models (see Table 15.4), one will notice a large overlap of consequences for both work attendance behaviours. Also note that health and productivity loss appear as outcomes of work attendance behaviours across levels. For example, productivity loss due to one sick-absent worker cumulates to productivity loss for his/her team and eventually for his/her company.

Finally, little research has addressed the issue whether the presumed antecedents of work attendance behaviours and their consequences might also be influenced by these behaviours and consequences. Figure 15.1 proposes three feedback loops: from work attendance behaviours to antecedents (e.g. high levels of sickness absence may lead to interventions that address adverse features of the psychosocial work environment), from consequences to work attendance behaviours (e.g. productivity loss at the group level may increase social pressure from one's work team to be sick present) and from consequences to antecedents (e.g. poor public health may be addressed by societal institutions). Although the evidence for these feedback loops is still scarce, it is important to keep in mind that it is at least possible that antecedents, work behaviours and outcomes mutually affect each other.

Practical implications

The framework presented in Figure 15.1 has several implications for research and practice. Three key recommendations will be presented here. First, since the antecedents and consequences of sickness absence and presence are located at different levels, research on work attendance should take a *multilevel approach*. For example, practical interventions to reduce sickness absence and sickness presence applied on the group level, organization level and society level (e.g. group incentives, organizational practices and governmental policies) might be more efficient and less resource-intensive in influencing individual-level attendance behaviours than worker-level interventions (e.g. close monitoring of workers who report being sick). Moreover, practices to reduce sickness absence and sickness presence (e.g. control of worker's attendance) at one level might be constrained, enabled or legitimized by policies and practices on another level (van Gestel & Nyberg, 2009).

Second, it is proposed that – whenever possible – sickness absence and sickness presence are *jointly addressed* for three reasons. First, the antecedents of both attendance behaviours overlap and may have contrasting effects on these behaviours. For instance, group pressure to reduce sickness absence may simultaneously lead to higher levels of sickness presence. Second, the consequences of sickness absence and sickness presence tend to co-vary. For example, work attendance behaviours may lead to both health and productivity loss. Third, sickness absence and sickness presence may affect each other. For example, organizational policies to reduce sickness absence may instil a fear of negative consequences of being sickness absent, thus indirectly increasing levels of sickness presence (Baker-McClearn, Greasley, Dale, & Griffith, 2010). Hence, practitioners should focus on interventions that favourably affect both types of work attendance behaviours. For instance, accommodating the psychosocial work environment, increasing the worker's work ability and encouraging workers to take sick leave when really necessary will reduce both sickness absence and sickness presence.

Third, considering the consequences of sickness absence and sickness presence, *prevention* is better than mitigation or remediation (see also Chapter 16). Early identification of workers at risk of sickness absence and sickness presence allows an early prevention of problems. For example, Duijts, Kant, van den Brandt and Swaen (2008) presented an instrument that could help to identify workers at risk for sickness absence. Their instrument includes 34 risk factors for sickness absence, including general and mental health, work-related factors and domestic circumstances. Unfortunately, there is no parallel screening instrument for sickness presence. As regards organizational-level interventions for preventing sickness absence and sickness presence, such measures include monitoring the health of the workforce, supporting healthy behaviour at work and providing adequate guidance/counselling for those workers who are sick-absent or sick-present. When prevention is insufficient, mitigating measures can be taken, such as increasing time for recovery, increasing social support and providing training. Remediation through work adjustment, rehabilitation and crisis support may be the ultimate solution to reduce sickness absence and sickness presence.

Replay

- An integrative framework for understanding sickness absence and sickness presence is based on the decision models, but adds antecedents and consequences at various levels of analysis, as well as possible feedback loops.
- Antecedents and consequences largely overlap for the two work attendance behaviours. Special attention should be given to the psychosocial work environment as an antecedent of both attendance behaviours, and to health and productivity loss as possible consequences of these behaviours.

- The multilevel framework guides research on and management of sickness absence and sickness presence. However, in practice it is impossible to always take into account all levels and possible interactions among levels, antecedents and outcomes. We advise researchers and practitioners to (i) take a multilevel approach, (ii) simultaneously study sickness absence and sickness presence, and (iii) focus on prevention rather than mitigation and remediation.

Discussion Points

1. Think of measures that could help organizations to reduce levels of sickness absence. Is it possible that these measures lead to higher levels of sickness presence? How can this 'sickness absence–sickness presence dilemma' be avoided?
2. How can sickness presence be handled within a virtual work mode, such as teleworking (i.e. work conducted from home using information technology)?
3. Which associations with sickness absence and presence might be predicted in each scenario shown in the table below? Team cohesiveness is the degree to which team members are attracted to each other and are motivated to reach the team objectives together. Team norms on work attendance are the shared standards of work attendance behaviour within the team.

Table 15.5

		Team cohesiveness	
		High	Low
Team norms on work attendance	Tight and clear		
	Loose and less explicit		

Learning by Doing

1. Schliwen and colleagues (2011) described three major models of sick leave provision. The *social insurance model* provides some income security for sick-absent currently employed. Social insurance can be bipartite (i.e. employees and employers) or tripartite (i.e. employees, employers and government), depending on who is paying for the costs of the system. The *employer liability model* refers to the country's labour legislation requiring all employers to provide their employees with sick leave of a specific duration and at a certain wage replacement rate. Financed by tax revenues, the *social assistance model* supports persons who are financially dependent due to circumstances, including illness or injury. What is the dominant model in your own country: what awaits you when being sick-absent?
2. Collaborate with two or three of your fellow students to find at least 10 employees (differing in age and gender) who are willing to be interviewed.

First, ask each employee 'How many days have you been sick-absent from work during the past 12 months' and 'How many days have you been sick-present at work during the past 12 months'. Second, try to get insight into the reasons for their sickness absence and sickness presence. Third, report your findings to the other students in your class by means of, for instance, a group presentation.

3. Write down five adjectives that come to mind when you think about sick-absent employees. Compare your list with those of a few fellow students. Which adjectives occur most across your lists? Is this how you (and your fellow students) perceive sick-absent employees?

Further Reading

Brooks, A., Hagen, S. E., Sathyanarayanan, S., Schultz, A. B., & Edington, D. W. (2010). Presenteeism: Critical issues. *Journal of Occupational and Environmental Medicine, 52*, 1055–1067.

Darr, W., & Johns, G. (2008). Work strain, health, and absenteeism: A meta-analysis. *Journal of Occupational Health Psychology, 13*, 293–318.

Johns, G. (2010). Presenteeism in the workplace: A review and research agenda. *Journal of Organizational Behavior, 31*, 519–564.

Web Sites

The European Union commissioned a joint inspection campaign on psychosocial risks at work (www.av.se/SLIC2012).

The International Labour Organization has put in action a programme on safety and health at work and the environment (SafeWork) (www.ilo.org).

References

Aronsson, G., & Gustafsson, K. (2005). Sickness presenteeism: Prevalence, attendance-pressure factors, and an outline of a model for research. *Journal of Occupational and Environmental Medicine, 47*, 958–966.

Aronsson, G., Gustafsson, K., & Dallner, M. (2000). Sick but yet at work: An empirical study of sickness presenteeism. *Journal of Epidemiology and Community Health, 54*, 502–509.

Baker-McClearn, D., Greasley, K., Dale, J., & Griffith, F. (2010). Absence management and presenteeism: The pressures on employees to attend work and the impact of attendance on performance. *Human Resource Management Journal, 20*, 311–328.

Bergström, G., Bodin, L., Hagberg, J., Lindh, T., Aronsson, G., & Josephson, M. (2009). Does sickness presenteeism have an impact on future general health? *International Archives of Occupational and Environmental Health, 82*, 1179–1190.

Bjorner, J. B., Albertsen, K., & Rugulies, R. (2010). Introduction to the supplement on the Copenhagen Psychosocial Questionnaire – in honour of Tage Søndergård Kristensen. *Scandinavian Journal of Public Health, 38 (Supplement 3)*, 4–7.

Böckerman, P., & Laukkanen, E. (2010). Predictors of sickness absence and presenteeism: Does the pattern differ by a respondent's health? *Journal of Occupational and Environmental Medicine, 52*, 332–335.

Borritz, M., Christensen, K. B., Bültmann, U., Rugulies, R., Lund, T., Andersen, I., Villadsen, E., Diderichsen, F., & Kristensen, T. S. (2010). Impact of burnout and psychosocial work characteristics on future long-term sickness absence. Prospective results of the Danish PUMA study among human service workers. *Journal of Occupational and Environmental Medicine, 52,* 964–970.

Borritz, M., Rugulies, R., Bjorner, J. B., Villadsen, E., Mikkelsen, O. A., & Kristensen, T. S. (2006). Burnout among employees in human service work: Design and baseline findings of the PUMA study. *Scandinavian Journal of Public Health, 34,* 49–58.

Brooks, A., Hagen, S. E., Sathyanarayanan, S., Schultz, A. B., & Edington, D. W. (2010). Presenteeism: Critical issues. *Journal of Occupational and Environmental Medicine, 52,* 1055–1067.

Claes, R. (2011). Employee correlates of sickness presence: A study across four European countries. *Work & Stress, 25,* 224–242.

Darr, W., & Johns, G. (2008). Work strain, health, and absenteeism: A meta-analysis. *Journal of Occupational Health Psychology, 13,* 293–318.

Dekkers-Sánchez, P. M., Hoving, J. L., Sluiter, J. K., & Frings-Dresen, M. H. W. (2008). Factors associated with long-term sick leave in sick-listed employees: A systematic review. *Occupational and Environmental Medicine, 65,* 153–157.

Duijts, S. F. A., Kant, I. J., van den Brandt, P. A., & Swaen, G. M. H. (2008). Psychometrics and validation of a screening instrument for sickness absence. *Occupational Medicine, 58,* 413–418.

Eurostat (2011). *Eurostat Statistics.* Retrieved December 21, 2011, from epp.eurostat.ec.europa.en.

Griep, R. H., Rotenberg, L., Choc, D., Toivanen, S., & Landsbergis, P. (2010). Beyond simple approaches to studying the association between work characteristics and absenteeism: Combining the DCS and ERI models. *Work & Stress, 24,* 179–195.

Hansen, C. D., & Andersen, J. H. (2009). Sick at work a risk factor for long-term sickness absence at a later date? *Journal of Epidemiology and Community Health, 63,* 397–402.

Johansson, G., & Lundberg, I. (2004). Adjustment latitude and attendance requirements as determinants of sickness absence or attendance: Empirical tests of the illness flexibility model. *Social Science & Medicine, 58,* 1857–1868.

Johansson, G., & Lundberg, I. (2009). Components of the illness flexibility model as explanations of socioeconomic differences in sickness absence. *International Journal of Health Services, 39,* 123–138.

Johns, G. (1994). Absenteeism estimates by employees and managers: Divergent perspectives and self-serving bias. *Journal of Applied Psychology, 79,* 229–239.

Johns, G. (2010). Presenteeism in the workplace: A review and research agenda. *Journal of Organizational Behavior, 31,* 519–564.

Johns, G. (2011). Attendance dynamics at work: The antecedents and correlates of presenteeism, absenteeism, and productivity loss. *Journal of Occupational Health Psychology, 16,* 483–500.

Karasek, R. A., & Theorell, T. (1990). *Healthy work: Stress, productivity and the reconstruction of working life.* New York: Basic Books.

Mattke, S., Balakrishnan, A., Bergamo, G., & Newberry, S. J. (2007). A review of methods to measure health-related productivity loss. *The American Journal of Managed Care, 13,* 211–217.

OECD (2011). *OECD Health Statistics (database).* Retrieved January 9, 2012, from www.OECD-ilibrary.org.

Osterkamp, R., & Röhn, O. (2007). Being on sick leave: Possible explanations for differences of sick-leave days across countries. *CESifo Economic Studies, 53,* 97–114.

Rantanen, I., & Tuominen, R. (2011). Relative magnitude of presenteeism and absenteeism and work-related factors affecting them among health care professionals. *International Archives of Occupational and Environmental Health, 84,* 225–230.

Rugulies, R., Christensen, K. B., Borritz, M., Villadsen, E., Bültmann, U., & Kristensen, T. S. (2007). The contribution of the psychosocial work environment to sickness absence in human service workers: Results of a 3-year follow-up study. *Work & Stress, 21,* 293–311.

Sanderson, K., Tilse, E., Nicholson, J., Oldenburg, B., & Graves, N. (2007). Which presenteeism measures are more sensitive to depression and anxiety? *Journal of Affective Disorders, 101,* 65–74.

Schaufeli, W. B., Bakker, A. B., & van Rhenen, W. (2009). How changes in job demands and resources predict burnout, work engagement, and sickness absenteeism. *Journal of Organizational Behavior, 30,* 893–917.

Schliwen, A., Earle, A., Hayes, J., & Heymann, S. J. (2011). The administration and financing of paid sick leave. *International Labour Review, 150,* 43–62.

Schultz, A. B., Chen, C. Y., & Edington, D. W. (2009). The cost and impact of health conditions on presenteeism to employers: A review of the literature. *Pharmacoecomomics, 27,* 365–378.

Siegrist, J. (1996). Adverse health effects of high-effort/low-reward conditions. *Journal of Occupational Health Psychology, 1*, 27–41.

Steel, R. P. (2003). Methodological and operational issues in the construction of absence variables. *Human Resource Management Review, 13*, 243–251.

Steel, R. P., Rentsch, J. R., & van Scotter, J. R. (2007). Timeframes and absence frameworks: A test of Steers and Rhodes' (1978) model of attendance. *Journal of Management, 13*, 180–195.

van Gestel, N., & Nyberg, D. (2009). Translating national policy changes into local HRM practices. *Personnel Review, 38*, 544–559.

Wegge, J., Schmidt, K.-H., Parkes, C., & van Dick, R. (2007). 'Taking a sickie': Job satisfaction and job involvement as interactive predictors of absenteeism in a public organization. *Journal of Occupational and Organizational Psychology, 80*, 77–89.

Part G

Interventions

16
Managing Psychosocial Risks in the Workplace
Prevention and Intervention

SILVIA PIGNATA, CAROLINE BIRON
AND MAUREEN F. DOLLARD

Chapter Objectives

After studying this chapter, you should be able to:

- discuss what an intervention is in relation to work psychology;
- develop an understanding of basic intervention concepts and approaches;
- explain how psychosocial risks can be prevented or managed;
- identify the classifications of interventions;
- understand the principles of participatory action research (PAR) and why it is used for work-stress interventions;
- understand why organizational interventions are more effective than individual approaches.

Given the dynamic environments in which people work and the adverse effects of work stressors on their well-being and morale (cf. Chapters 3–6), it is important for management to take steps to reduce psychosocial risk factors in the workplace. *Psychosocial risk factors* refer to organizational and/or work factors and interpersonal relationships in the work setting that may affect the health of workers. Steps can be taken by management to control these risk factors, including implementing stress management interventions. A *stress management intervention* is defined as 'any activity, program, or opportunity initiated by an organization, which focuses on reducing the presence of work-related stressors or on assisting individuals to minimize the negative outcomes of exposure to these stressors' (Ivancevich, Matteson, Freedman, & Phillips, 1990, p. 252).

In the following sections, we discuss the basic concepts and approaches relevant to these issues: (i) the two ways of classifying interventions, one focusing on the reduction or management of levels of work stress, and the other on the target of interventions (the individual, the organization or the interface between the two), (ii) the basic three-phase model for interventions (development, implementation and evaluation of its results) (iii) the critical factors in interventions, (iv) the principles of PAR, that is, how employees, line managers and directors can participate in the development and implementation of interventions, and finally (v) the psychosocial safety climate, which can be considered as the 'cause of the causes' of work stress.

16.1 Classes and Targets of Interventions

In this section we discuss two approaches to classifying interventions. The first of these focuses on the reduction or management of levels of work stress (i.e. primary, secondary and tertiary interventions). The second approach classifies interventions in terms of their target (i.e. the individual, the organization or the interface between them).

Primary, secondary and tertiary interventions

Interventions to reduce or manage work stress can be classified as primary, secondary or tertiary approaches (Cooper & Quick, 1999). According to Kompier and Cooper (1999), *primary interventions* are long-term approaches that aim to eliminate, reduce or alter stressors at work (e.g. reducing staff workloads). *Secondary interventions* aim to reduce or eliminate the effects of stress in employees who are showing signs of stress by modifying or changing their stress response to inevitable or unchangeable demands (e.g. relaxation training, time management, stress management programmes, programmes to increase employees' coping capacity and health-promotion activities; cf. Giga, Cooper, & Faragher, 2003). Finally, *tertiary interventions* focus on treating employees with serious stress-related health problems by providing professional medical treatment or psychological counselling to heal specific problems.

Richardson and Rothstein (2008) evaluated the effectiveness of various types of primary and secondary interventions. Their meta-analysis included 36 experimental studies, representing 55 interventions and a sample size of 2,847. They analysed the effectiveness of the following types of interventions: cognitive-behavioural, relaxation, organizational, multimodal and alternative. Note that these interventions may be classified as either primary or secondary interventions, depending on their target (i.e. staff members who do not show signs of stress versus staff members who are showing such signs). Their findings demonstrated that cognitive-behavioural programmes consistently produced larger effects than other types of interventions. Cognitive-behavioural interventions aim to teach workers about the role of their thoughts and emotions in managing stressful events and to educate them to change these thoughts in order to cope with stress in a more adaptive way (Bond & Bunce, 2000). Effects were mainly on psychological outcome variables and not on organizational outcomes such as performance or absenteeism. Regarding organizational interventions, their results found virtually no effect on any type of outcome variable. However, their meta-analysis only included five interventions at the primary level, so no conclusions could be drawn on the relative effectiveness of primary versus secondary interventions.

According to a review by LaMontagne, Keegel, Louie, Ostry and Landsbergis (2007), intervention programmes that are more comprehensive, in that they include primary, secondary and tertiary levels of interventions, are most effective in improving both individual (e.g. anxiety, depression) and organizational (e.g. absenteeism, job satisfaction) outcomes. They conclude that prevention programmes integrating all classes of interventions are more effective than other programmes because they address both the causes of stress and its consequences for workers.

Intervention targets

DeFrank and Cooper (1987) suggest a different prevention model based on the *targets* of interventions. Interventions to reduce stress in the workplace may target the individual, the organization or the interface between the individual and the organization. Generally, individual actions seek to increase the physical and psychological capacity of the individual to enable him/her to adapt to the stressful situation. In turn, organizational interventions aim to reduce stress on a macro level, for example by modifying certain aspects of the organizational structure, tackling leadership style, changing the culture or climate, or revising personnel selection processes and policies to adapt the working environment to employees' needs. Finally, actions which are taken on a more local level (i.e. within a team or a department) tend to emphasize the interface between the individual and the organization, for example by clarifying roles or by increasing staff involvement and autonomy. Below, we discuss each of these three types of intervention targets.

Individual interventions

Individual or person-directed interventions focus on individual employees or group of employees to improve their coping resources in order to deal more effectively with demanding situations (Giga et al., 2003) or to modify their appraisal of a stressor to reduce its threat (Geurts & Gründemann, 1999). These interventions include exercise, relaxation training, meditation, biofeedback, cognitive-behavioural therapy, exercise, time management, cognitive coping strategies, stress-management programmes and employee assistance programmes (DeFrank & Cooper, 1987; Giga, Noblet, Faragher, & Cooper, 2003; van der Hek & Plomp, 1997).

A comprehensive review of work-stress preventive interventions by Kompier and Kristensen (2001) showed that the majority of interventions to prevent mental health problems at work are individual and reactive strategies that focus primarily on changing the individual (through changing their cognitions), rather than changing the organization and reducing risk factors in the psychosocial work environment or the individual/organization interface.

Evidence suggests that psychosocial factors at work, such as high demands (e.g. heavy workload) and low resources (e.g. low levels of control or support), are important inhibitors of well-being and morale that cannot be changed by individual approaches. Primary prevention strategies that focus on causal factors should be the most effective intervention, and using comprehensive interventions that focus on all levels of the organization is crucial. Indeed, LaMontagne et al.'s (2007) review of the job-stress intervention evaluation literature concluded that interventions directed at the individual were '... an essential complement to organizationally-directed intervention, and the complementarity of primary, secondary, and tertiary intervention strategies' (p. 277).

Organizational interventions
Organizational (work-directed) interventions are often referred to as stressor reduction processes (Newman & Beehr, 1979) and include job redesign, restructuring jobs, selection and placement, training and education programmes, communication, clarifying employees' work roles and responsibilities, increasing employees' participation and decision-making authority, improving organizational structure, enhancing the physical environment, and addressing job demands and job resources (DeFrank & Cooper, 1987; Giga, Noblet et al., 2003; van der Hek & Plomp, 1997). These interventions focus on the work environment to improve the fit between each employee and the workplace (Geurts & Gründemann, 1999).

Empirical research suggests that organizational approaches can be effective in reducing exposure to psychosocial risks (Bond, Flaxman, & Loivette, 2006; Bourbonnais et al., 2006; Nielsen, Randall, & Albertsen, 2007) and are accompanied by significant and durable effects (Burke, 1993; Kompier & Kristensen, 2001). For example, in one of the largest intervention reviews to date, Taris et al. (2003) evaluated the effectiveness of a large-scale job-stress reduction programme implemented in 81 organizations within the Dutch domiciliary care sector. They found that a wide variety of measures were implemented, and that only work-directed interventions were linked to a reduction in levels of job stress, albeit the effects of those interventions were weak.

Note that organizational interventions are especially difficult to implement and to evaluate, mainly because they often entail multiple complex targets. Nevertheless, when interventions that aim to reduce or alter stressors are successfully implemented, they tend to be associated with positive outcomes. The past decade has seen the development of a small but promising body of literature showing improvements in employee health and well-being when interventions are (i) tailored to meet the needs of the participants, (ii) based on a systematic risk assessment, (iii) participative and (iv) properly implemented and evaluated (among others, Bond & Bunce, 2001; Bourbonnais et al., 2006; Holman, Axtell, Sprigg, Totterdell, & Wall, 2010).

Individual/organization interface-directed interventions
Individual/organization interface-directed interventions focus on the interplay between individual employees and the organization. For example, at the team or group level, this includes setting up co-worker support groups to improve relationships at work, improving person–environment fit, addressing role issues, and increasing workers' participation and autonomy (DeFrank & Cooper, 1987; Giga, Noblet et al., 2003; van der Hek & Plomp, 1997). Giga, Noblet et al. (2003) assert that combinations of organizational and individual intervention strategies are likely to be most effective in reducing stress, as together these address the organizational environment, the individual and the individual/organization interface.

The intervention targets versus the primary–secondary–tertiary prevention approach

Stress interventions have been traditionally categorized using one of the two abovementioned classification systems. However, the boundaries between these levels have been questioned as they are not mutually exclusive and may overlap (Giga et al., 2003). Consider the following example: if an organization had a training policy for managers where each manager would have to follow a course on how to cope with employees who are absent from work due to a mental health issue, this could be categorized as a *tertiary* prevention activity as it concerns employees who are already ill. Yet, it is also an *organizational* intervention, since it is part of the training policy. If this training was to result in managers being more supportive with their team in order to prevent conflicts (which are likely to arise when a person comes back to work after a long-term absence), the training could be considered as primary prevention, since it increased the level of support to the team and prevented potential conflicts.

As pointed out by Jordan et al. (2003), the preventive stress management theory focusing on levels, as proposed by Cooper and Quick (1999), is not directly transposable to the target approach presented by DeFrank and Cooper (1987), that is, primary level strategies do not necessarily entail a modification of the work and/or the organization, whereas secondary and tertiary level strategies are not always directed at individuals. For example, individual coaching for managers could potentially help them to develop better human resources practices, which in return are likely to have a positive effect on employees' well-being (Dellve, Skagert, & Vilhelmsson, 2007). If such a coaching initiative was integrated within a corporate policy and groups of managers were coached, it would be considered an *organizational* intervention. Because it aims to prevent employees becoming ill due to inappropriate management practices, this coaching initiative would also be considered as a primary level intervention. However, if this coaching initiative was intended for one or a few specific managers whose management practices were considered problematic, it could be considered to be an *individual* intervention. The underlying assumption is that coaching is a useful way of helping managers cope better with the demands of their managerial role, and this would be considered as a secondary prevention measure.

Table 16.1 Examples of interventions categorized by level and target.

Prevention level	Intervention target	
	Individual	Organizational
Primary	• Manage stress levels by having constructive internal discourse and promoting healthy lifestyles • Manage workload (avoid/communicate overload or need of resources, get support) • Preserve work–life balance	• Promote/support healthy work organization • Establish strong psychosocial safety climate • Enhance job design (autonomy, task significance, task feedback, skill variety, etc.) • Promote social support and collaboration • Flexible work schedule • Encourage participation • Establish clear roles and objectives • Build cohesive teams • Establish fair employment policies
Secondary	• Take relaxation courses • Exercise • Self-assertion strategies	• Offer self-assertion courses • Provide facilities for physical exercise • Stress-management training and time-management courses • Health-promotion activities
Tertiary	• Therapies, treatments • Training colleagues in dealing with a team member(s) with mental health/stress-related issues	• Progressive return to work after mental illness absences • Employee assistance programmes

For the purpose of coherence throughout this chapter, the terms 'organizational stress interventions' and 'work- and organizational-directed interventions' will be used to refer to interventions aimed at modifying aspects of the work environment, the organization of work processes and tasks, improving relationships or improving working conditions. Whether they are targeting individuals, groups or the whole organization, the term 'work- and organizational-level interventions' will refer to interventions that aim to reduce or eliminate sources of stress. Table 16.1 illustrates examples of each level of interventions (primary, secondary, tertiary) for individuals and for organizational targets.

Dominance of individual interventions

It seems intuitively plausible that organizations employing predominantly organization-directed, primary prevention strategies will show greater levels of employee well-being and morale relative to organizations employing predominantly individual-directed interventions alone. The dominant view is that work stress and its outcomes are more strongly related to work environment or job factors than to individual factors (Maslach & Schaufeli, 1993). Indeed, Burke (1993) pointed out that if the number and strength of occupational stressors were reduced, individuals at work would experience less stress. However, the intervention literature shows that work-stress programmes are predominantly reactive strategies (i.e. secondary or tertiary approaches) directed at individuals rather than proactive, organization-directed strategies (i.e. primary approaches; cf. Biron, Cooper, & Bond, 2009; Giga et al., 2003; Kompier, Cooper, & Geurts, 2000).

Kompier and Cooper (1999) assert that there are numerous reasons why stress interventions are predominantly individual and reactive. Among the reasons for this individual-directed approach is the lack of senior management involvement. For example, in the case of stress complaints, Kompier and Cooper argue that management are inclined to blame individual employees and their personalities, coping styles and lifestyles, and the potential role of stressful life events (i.e. divorce) or family situations instead of work environment factors. Secondly, because of their training, many professionals who specialize in interventions (e.g. occupational doctors and psychologists) are primarily interested in stress as a subjective experience, and as a result focus on individual differences and counselling, as they are more comfortable with changing individuals than changing organizations. Thirdly, stressors may be inherent in the job and there is limited empirical evidence that interventions in the psychosocial work environment may reduce mental health problems. In addition, there is a lack of prior risk evaluation, and the study of the costs and benefits (i.e. financial) of stress prevention has been largely neglected.

A fourth key reason noted by Kompier and Cooper (1999) is the absence of sound theoretical models of work stress as a basis for intervention. Although there are a number of debates, many would agree that psychosocial risks such as work overload or the lack of job control, social support and recognition of ones' efforts are, in the long term, strong predictors of poor physical and psychological health (Semmer, 2006; see also Chapters 3–7). Most would also agree that a healthy workforce is a competitive advantage for organizations. The costs associated with reduced performance due to sickness absenteeism and presenteeism (i.e. being present at work while ill; see Chapter 15) are substantial enough for employers to invest in keeping their workers present, healthy and well (Black, 2008; Foresight Mental Capital and Wellbeing Project, 2008). Nevertheless, as Karanika-Murray, Biron and Cooper (2012) argue, we still need sound theoretical models in order to understand how and why interventions bring change in employees' well-being and organizational performance. At the moment, we do not have a comprehensive understanding as to how change occurs during organizational interventions and therefore it is difficult to predict if the intervention will be successful, and for whom. In addition, there is the difficulty of conducting properly designed studies such as longitudinal studies with a randomized control group, and collecting and analysing both subjective and objective measures within the context of dynamic work environments.

These methodological difficulties are inherent in both conducting and evaluating the studies. It should also be noted that senior management often view work-stress research as a distraction from the primary processes and focus of the organization. There is also a tendency for stress researchers to collect 'soft' outcome variables in a questionnaire-oriented approach rather than collecting 'hard' objective data of stress such as productivity measures, sickness absenteeism rates and accident rates.

Finally, Kompier and Cooper (1999, p. 5) argue that stress research fails to use an interdisciplinary approach to relate psychosocial work characteristics to other

> **Work Psychology in Action: Organizational and individual/organizational interventions**
>
> Brun, Biron and Ivers (2008) conducted a study in a large Canadian university. In terms of organizational interventions, a permanent steering committee was created to take into account psychological health in managerial actions. For example, the committee implemented a 45-hour training programme on stress prevention for managers. Another initiative of the committee was the development of an organizational assistance programme (OAP) for psychological health in addition to the existing employee assistance programme. The OAP was especially intended to support managers facing difficulties with their team or specific employees.
>
> At the individual/organizational level, smaller departmental projects were developed and implemented. One of these was the student registry, responsible for all students' registration and graduation issues, and every aspect of their study. Using a PAR approach (see Section 16.2) with an external consultant, employees identified psychosocial risks which were considered more problematic. Several committees represented by workers and managers were created. Several interventions at both the organizational level and the individual/workplace interface were implemented. At the organizational level, the student registry processes were reviewed with an engineer in order to increase efficiency and reduce workload. Schedules and annual leave were also made more equitable following a recommendation by one of the committees.
>
> Also at the individual-organizational level, the roles of middle managers and some teams were clarified and redesigned. In order to support middle managers, an external consultant was appointed and managers could call him for a certain number of hours of individual coaching related to people management. Overall, Brun et al. (2008) showed that the interventions in the registry were associated with significant decreases in exposure to most psychosocial risks as well as in psychological distress. At the beginning of the project, 56% of employees reported high psychological distress, compared to 20% in a national sample of the population of Quebec. After 18 months, only 26% reported a high level of psychological distress.

policy areas such as '... productivity, labour market facets, company image, human resources management, [and] total quality management'.

Replay

- Two major approaches to classifying work-stress interventions have been proposed. The first one distinguishes among primary, secondary and tertiary interventions. The second one focuses on the target of these interventions: individual workers, the organization or the interface between both.
- These approaches are not mutually exclusive, but emphasize different aspects of these interventions that address the causes of stress and/or its consequences on workers and the organization.
- Organizational-level interventions particularly address the causes of stress. Furthermore, research shows that they can have positive effects in reducing exposure to psychosocial risks. However, there is still a tendency for organizations to select reactive, individual-level interventions.
- Individual interventions can have positive effects on employee psychological outcomes and on organizational outcomes. However, they should be complementary to a more integrated approach in which the causes of stress (such as work and organizational factors) are taken into account.

16.2 Designing, Implementing and Evaluating Interventions

To assess the effectiveness of interventions in changing employees' levels of well-being and positive attitudes, it is necessary to identify the key phases of an intervention. Goldenhar, LaMontagne, Katz, Heaney and Landsbergis (2001) proposed a three-phase model for occupational health and safety interventions which comprises the *development, implementation* and *evaluation* phases of an intervention. Each of these phases has integral research goals. The *development* phase aims to produce knowledge that can be used to develop appropriate interventions to reduce the prevalence of psychosocial stressors in the workplace. This phase aims to answer questions related to the changes needed and the best way to achieve them, the barriers preventing these changes, and the theories that might apply in that specific intervention context. There are several intervention models in occupational health and safety, and in occupational stress (Cox, Griffiths, & Rial-Gonzalez, 2000; Health & Safety Executive, 2003). All involve a risk assessment to identify who might be the workers at risk and what specific risks they are mainly exposed to. After identifying these risks and their consequences for workers, it is necessary to 'translate' the risks into action plans with concrete changes to address the problems.

The *implementation* phase evaluates the intervention implementation process by systematically documenting the strategies implemented in order to produce changes to the workplace. This phase describes what types of changes were implemented, the difficulties encountered and the target population.

Finally, the *evaluation* phase aims to demonstrate whether the intervention was successful in reducing the prevalence of adverse work factors and of illnesses. This is achieved by evaluating the effects of the intervention on the prevalence of psychosocial stressors in the workplace, on objective measures such as the prevalence of mental health problems and on the incidence of sickness absences. The benefit of this three-phase model in comparison to other models is that scientific knowledge is produced in each of the three phases.

Critical factors in interventions

There is a pressing call from industry and stress prevention practitioners for the content and the process of stress prevention to be reported and evaluated as part of any intervention strategy. Despite the wide variety of programmes to manage stress and improve employee well-being and morale, few evaluative studies of stress interventions have been documented in the literature (Caulfield, Chang, Dollard, & Elshaug, 2004; Cooper, 2001). This is primarily due to the methodological and conceptual difficulties inherent in stress-intervention research (Cox, Karanika, Griffiths, & Houdmont, 2007; Cox, Taris, & Nielsen, 2010; LaMontagne, Noblet, & Spector, 2012). As a result, there are calls for researchers to address the fundamental questions of what interventions work, when are they effective and 'why should and how could organizational level stress interventions work?' (Briner & Reynolds, 1999, p. 648).

Karanika-Murray, Biron and Cooper (2012) highlight the principles that should be taken into account when developing and implementing organizational interventions. These points are summarized in Table 16.2, along with the reasons as to why they are important.

Table 16.2 Critical process and contextual factors during interventions.

Critical factors	Why is it important?
1. Comprehensive interventions that combine individual and organizational-level actions	To address the causes and consequences of stress (preventing stress, helping people at risk and rehabilitating employees who have difficulties in dealing with stress)
2. Participative approaches	To ensure commitment from employees, middle managers and senior managers to have interventions tailored to the context and needs
3. Implementation framework	To ensure proper implementation, instead of planning only as far as the risk assessment
4. Assessment of risks, needs and context	To ensure that the right problems are targeted, that interventions are tailored and based on actual needs, and that interventions fit with the organizational context
5. Strong commitment and clearly defined roles	To ensure interventions will be implemented with adequate resources, to provide adequate support (especially to managers)

Adapted from Karanika-Murray et al. (2012).

Comprehensive interventions
As previously mentioned, programmes which encompass more than one level of prevention (e.g. primary, secondary, tertiary) are more likely than other programmes to yield positive results in terms of improving well-being and reducing stress (LaMontagne et al., 2007). Bond, Flaxman and Bunce (2008) give an interesting example of an intervention addressing more than one level. They trained people to increase their level of psychological flexibility, which refers to '... an ability to focus on the present moment and, depending upon what the situation affords, persist with or change one's (even inflexible, stereotypical) behaviour in the pursuit of goals and values' (p. 645). Their study was conducted with customer service centres in the financial sector. Bond et al. (2008) found that people who had higher levels of psychological flexibility benefited more from a participative action research intervention which aimed to increase job control. People with higher levels of psychological flexibility showed larger improvements in mental health and absenteeism. This study implies that delivery of an *individual-level intervention* (i.e. training on psychological flexibility) enabled an *organizational-level intervention* to improve job control to have greater effects.

Use of participative approaches
A second element that is crucial for the success of interventions is a participative approach. This is essential to ensure that people affected by the intervention are also involved in the development and implementation of the changes so that interventions are tailored to their needs (Giga et al., 2003; Jordan et al., 2003). Research shows that the more involved the stakeholders are in the process, the more effective the interventions are going to be (Nielsen & Randall, 2012). Before moving on to the other key points determining the success of interventions, we discuss below a type of research, PAR, which is often used for stress interventions. Indeed, research on the evaluation of interventions has found that the success of a stress-prevention programme depends on combining a *bottom-up* participative approach with a *top-down* approach that is supported by senior management (Kompier & Cooper, 1999).

The key principles of PAR, namely active participation, collaboration (perceived control and ownership) and empowerment of employees, seek to enhance the development of local knowledge and the likelihood of stronger consensus for change (Elden, 1986; Imada, 1991). PAR involves workers participating in all stages of the intervention and its evaluation in a cyclical learning process: (i) the definition of the problem, (ii) the development of techniques to gather evidence to inform the problem, (iii) making sense of the data, (iv) defining interventions, (v) implementing interventions and (vi) the evaluation of the results (Wadsworth, 1998). There are overlaps between the PAR methodology outlined and risk assessment approaches to work stress (Cox, Griffiths, & Rial-Gonzalez, 2000), but PAR promotes active learning and control through the direct participation of workers (Dollard, Le Blanc, & Cotton, 2008). PAR also provides a suitable method for dealing equitably with the power problems and political issues that occur in applied research (Dollard & Metzer, 1999; Landsbergis et al., 1993).

The difficulty in implementing successful organizational interventions is that they require cooperation and participation from employees, unions and management (Nytrø, Saksvik, Mikkelsen, Bohle, & Quinlan, 2000), who may be in conflict. In addition, factors such as organizational structure, size, resources, culture and values determine the appropriateness of interventions (Marshall & Cooper, 1981), and both the strategy and process of implementing an intervention may be as important as its content in achieving an effective outcome (Giga, Noblet et al., 2003; Nielsen, Randall & Albertsen, 2007). Indeed, organizational stress-reduction interventions often have little effect or may produce mixed effects, as their impact depends on various organizational characteristics that may be difficult to identify or control. In addition, Newman and Beehr (1979) assert that there is a particular need to consider 'the role that individual and situational differences (especially the passage of time) play in determining the effectiveness of stress management strategies' (p. 39).

Implementation framework
Another crucial element for successful interventions is a clear implementation framework. Several factors can be considered to understand how the intervention is going to be deployed (Nielsen & Randall, in press). These factors can relate to the initiation of the intervention, the development and implementation of intervention activities, the implementation strategy and the role of stakeholders (human resources, external consultants, managers, employees, senior management and so on). The success of the prevention approach depends as much on the implementation *process* as it does on the activity that is implemented, that is, both *what* is done and *how* it is done are important. Any solution or action plan is only as good as its implementation. All too often efforts are invested in the risk assessment phase without any planning regarding the subsequent phases of implementing and evaluating the interventions. Although the risk assessment phase is essential, measuring psychosocial risks without implementing any interventions is likely to raise expectations and generate cynicism for the employees (Biron, Gatrell, & Cooper, 2010). Ongoing monitoring of the implementation process, having specific, achievable and measurable goals, allocation of roles and responsibilities, and clear communication plans are all essential elements of well-implemented interventions. Monitoring what occurs during the implementation phase is also crucial in order to explain the results. The processes of interventions should be documented and evaluated as they have effects on what types of results can be expected (Nielsen & Randall, in press).

Assessing the risks, the needs and the context
A fourth important element for interventions is a strong evidence base and an assessment of the needs to ensure that the right problems are targeted by the intervention (Jordan et al., 2003). For example, Biron, et al. (2010) describe a study where a large private company developed a stress risk assessment that managers could use within their teams. However, several managers did not perceive the need for such a tool, and most were not comfortable having a discussion with their team to discuss the risk-assessment results. This

example shows that the intervention needs to meet the needs of those who will be using it. The risk assessment should also include measures of the symptoms, psychosocial risks, stakeholders' readiness to change and perceptions of the intervention process. Perceptions and motives that can act as barriers or facilitators to implementation should be monitored. Interventions should be based on a solid risk assessment and should be developed to address actual needs. As Semmer (2011) underlines, if interventions are not addressing needs, this equates to delivering smoking cessation sessions to non-smokers. Interventions also need to fit with the organizational context. Randall and Nielsen (2012) point out that 'Poor intervention fit is often linked to concurrent changes in the team or organizational context (e.g. restructuring, downsizing or re-organization) or to pre-intervention job design (e.g. a lack of opportunities for workers to participate in intervention activities as they cannot set aside other work demands)' (p. 124). Interventions need to be developed based on a solid diagnosis of psychosocial risks and employees' needs, and be tailored to the organizational context.

Strong commitment and clearly defined roles
A last element to consider is that the stakeholders identified have clearly defined roles, a coordinating group is established, there is wide participation in designing and implementing an intervention, and support is secured at both a local level (i.e. line managers, employees) and at organizational levels (especially senior management commitment) (Lewis, Yarker, & Donaldson-Feilder, 2012). Organizational interventions can sometimes imply major restructuring, which may affect work organization, processes, interpersonal

Work Psychology in Action: Defining the roles clearly

During a complex organizational intervention in a university, Brun et al. (2008) described how roles between human resources (HR) professionals, occupational health and safety (OHS) officers, and an external consultant got blurred and rather tense. The consultant was mandated to coach managers of a department undergoing an in-depth restructuring that was set in motion following a risk assessment and several meetings to develop an action plan. The budget to hire the consultant was provided by OHS. However, in coaching the managers, the consultant sometimes overlapped with the roles traditionally played by HR. The HR managers felt that their role was overtaken by the manager and that this should be their responsibility. Yet managers in the unit felt more comfortable discussing their issues with the consultant given his neutrality, since HR's role can conflict with coaching. Indeed, HR's role involves supporting managers, but can also involve disciplinary measures or ending a contract. It was made clear by the OHS officers that the consultant would be responsible for coaching managers only with issues relating to the implementation of the intervention.

relationships and working conditions. Having secured the commitment of the major stakeholders (i.e. senior management, line management, employees, human resource specialists, occupational health and safety staff) it is compulsory to ensure that these changes will be successfully implemented. Senior management, line managers and unions need to be aware that their commitment is not just to carry out a risk assessment and agree for a prevention approach to be initiated. Their commitment entails actual interventions and changes to the workplace. Often, the results of the risk assessment point out problems that involve management and this can be quite upsetting for managers. Thus, it is crucial to have proper support in place as managers are likely to be highly involved in the process.

Replay

- Successful interventions require development, implementation and evaluation phases. Compared to other approaches, attending to this three-phase model has the advantage that it produces scientific knowledge not only on the effects of the intervention, but also on process factors that are critical to successful implementation.
- Comprehensive interventions (e.g. encompassing both individual- and organizational-level measures) are usually more effective than other interventions.
- A participative approach in which all stakeholders participate in all phases of the intervention often helps to bring about the desired results.
- A clear implementation framework (describing what is done, as well as how, when and by whom it is done) is an essential element of a successful intervention.
- Be sure to target the right problems – the needs, risks and context of the intervention must be assessed.
- A strong commitment by management and clearly defined roles of the stakeholders promote successful interventions.

16.3 Work-stress Prevention as Business as Usual

Can you imagine that at any point in time an organization may be assessed for its performance in relation to the principles of stress management as outlined above? The expression of this performance is referred to as psychosocial safety climate (PSC). Table 16.3 presents an overview of the key characteristics of a good psychosocial safety climate, in the form of a short questionnaire tapping PSC. Based on the evidence regarding the principles of a successful work-stress intervention, Dollard and colleagues argue that if organizations held these principles as usual business practice and process, psychosocial risk factors would be prevented or better managed than is currently often the case. Workplaces that have high levels of PSC would be healthy places to work where production is not at the expense of health (Dollard & Karasek, 2010).

Table 16.3 A short measure of psychosocial safety climate.

Psychosocial safety climate
The following statements concern the psychological health and safety in your workplace. Please answer with the best option provided in relation to your organization. Answers are on a five-point scale: 1, *strongly disagree*; 2, *disagree*; 3, *neither disagree nor agree*; 4, *agree*; 5, *strongly agree*.

Management support and commitment
1. In my workplace senior management acts quickly to correct problems/issues that affect employees' psychological health.
2. Senior management acts decisively when a concern about an employees' psychological status is raised.
3. Senior management show support for stress prevention through involvement and commitment.

Management priority
4. Psychological well-being of staff is a priority for this organization.
5. Senior management clearly considers the psychological health of employees to be of great importance.
6. Senior management considers employee psychological health to be as important as productivity.

Organizational communication
7. There is good communication here about psychological safety issues which affect me.
8. Information about workplace psychological well-being is always brought to my attention by my manager/supervisor.
9. My contributions to resolving occupational health and safety concerns in the organization are listened to.

Organizational participation and involvement
10. Participation and consultation in psychological health and safety occurs with employees', unions, and health and safety representatives in my workplace.
11. Employees are encouraged to become involved in psychological safety and health matters.
12. In my organization, the prevention of stress involves all levels of the organization.

Adapted from Hall, Dollard and Coward (2010).

A basic assumption of PSC theory is that psychosocial safety climate is an antecedent to many work-stress risk factors (Dollard & Bakker, 2010). This is because in high PSC organizations, managers are concerned with the health and well-being of workers and will design jobs that have adequate demands and sufficient resources to ensure workers are both healthy and engaged. Conversely, in low PSC organizations there is a lack of regard for worker health and a lack of attention to the design of the job in relation to worker health. For example, without clear policies about disrespectful behaviour, hazardous behaviours such as bullying may flourish. PSC reflects the level of regard of managers for worker well-being and clearly precedes work conditions. Since PSC is a precursor to job design stress risk factors, PSC theory extends other well-known job-stress theories such as the Job Demands–Resources (JD–R) Model (Demerouti, Nachreiner, Bakker, & Schaufeli, 2001; see Chapter 4) and the Job Demand–Control Model (Karasek, 1979; see Chapter 3). Crucially, PSC theory answers the question 'Where do job demands and job resources come from?'.

Several studies on PSC have been conducted, providing support for the role of PSC as a predictor (or a leading indicator) of psychosocial risk factors, psychological health and engagement. For example, one study by Dollard and Bakker (2010) surveyed 18 schools in an Australian state education department. Since PSC is considered a climate construct, and a property of the organization, these researchers first aggregated survey scores from individuals to the school level. Using a longitudinal design, they found that PSC was related to a number of individual-level psychosocial risk factors (work pressure, emotional demands, skill discretion, psychological health, psychological distress, emotional exhaustion) and engagement, all assessed 10 months later, even after controlling for baseline levels in these measures.

Several other studies confirmed these findings, showing that PSC is related to demands (e.g. bullying and harassment, emotional demands, role conflict) that in turn are related to psychological health problems (Idris, Dollard, Coward, & Dormann, 2012; Law, Dollard, Tuckey, & Dormann, 2011). Furthermore, studies have shown that PSC is related to productivity related outcomes (e.g. engagement, performance; Idris, Dollard, & Winefield, 2011). Finally, in an Australian study of remote area nurses, Dollard and colleagues (2012) found that PSC predicted psychosocial risks (workload, control, supervisor support) and emotional exhaustion in *other* nurses in the same work unit 24 months later. Apparently, PSC predicts changes in both psychosocial risk factors and the presumed outcomes thereof (cf. Chapters 3–7). Insofar as PSC relates to continuous attention of an organization's management to health and safety issues, these findings show that considering work-stress prevention as 'business as usual' has positive consequences for both workers and the organization that they work for.

In the terminology introduced above, building PSC within an organization is a primary prevention strategy. PSC also has a secondary prevention function as it acts to moderate the relationship between work conditions, psychological health and engagement outcomes. In organizations with higher levels of PSC, employees would be supported to cope with job demands, for example by providing social support or flexibility in the workplace to meet demands or the opportunity to debrief after emotionally demanding experiences. This would help workers cope with demands and reduce the experience of distress. There is also evidence that PSC serves as a safety signal, indicating to employees that it is safe to utilize resources (e.g. control) that may already be available (see also Chapter 7). For example, in school teachers, high PSC may enable teachers to feel secure and supported to take a risk and utilize decision-making options such as classroom rescheduling to cope with demands (Dollard & Karasek, 2010).

Replay

- A theory that seeks to assess day-to-day management of work stress within an organization is PSC theory. The research findings provide evidence of PSC as a 'cause of the causes' and as a lead indicator of workplace psychosocial hazards (high job demands, low job resources), psychological health and employee engagement. Organizations that implement best practice stress-management principles should be good places to work.
- PSC measures (cf. Table 16.3) provide information about what to change in an organization at the primary level (to improve working conditions such as management priority, communication or participation systems) and at the secondary level (to reduce the impact of psychosocial hazards).

16.4 Conclusions

The stress-intervention literature highlights the conceptual and methodological issues in intervention research. This chapter has identified the guidelines and key factors that are crucial to effective stress interventions. Knowledge of the three distinct approaches (i.e. primary, secondary, tertiary) to stress interventions and the target population (i.e. individual, organization, individual/organization interface) is important in reducing psychosocial risk factors in the workplace. This chapter also highlights the complexity of interventions and the importance of how intervention strategies are developed, implemented and evaluated. PAR values those at the coalface and enables workers to participate in a learning cycle of stress prevention and management. Work stress is a serious workplace issue and efforts are continuously needed to identify, control risks, and improve interventions and the evaluation process. One approach to work-stress management is a 'business as usual' focus on building a healthy PSC in organizations. Despite the difficulties, there is a need for further research to identify what types of intervention strategies are effective in improving stressful work environments for both employees and organizations.

Discussion Points

1. You are newly appointed as the manager of a department with 80 employees in a company. You notice high absenteeism rates as well as a high turnover rate. Morale seems to be low, and after only a few weeks in the position three employees have already cried in your office because of conflicts with their co-workers. You decide to meet with the occupational health and safety officer of the company to discuss an intervention strategy. Based on the classes of interventions and their targets, develop a potential intervention which could be characterized as comprehensive (including all classes of interventions).
2. Propose ways in which you would evaluate an intervention, bearing in mind the various levels and targets.
3. Do you think that managers and employees would perceive the PSC of an organization similarly or differently? What implications would this have for stress in the organization?

Learning by Doing

1. Most of you will at some point in your lives have worked for an organization. Think of the organization you know best. Then assess the PSC for this organization, using the checklist given in Table 16.3. Scores should range from 12 to 60. A satisfactory level of PSC is a score of 41 or above. A lower score signifies higher risk for depression and job strain (Dollard et al., 2012).
2. Whatever the outcome of point 1, it is always possible to think of ways to improve the PSC of the organization. What would you like to improve in your organization? What sort of interventions would seem suitable for doing so: primary, secondary or tertiary? Would these interventions address individual workers, the organization or the interface between them?
3. Devise a plan for the implementation of one of the interventions that could reduce work stress in your organization. Pay special attention to the critical factors for successful intervention discussed in Table 16.2.

Further Reading

Biron, C., Karanika-Murray, M., & Cooper, C. L. (Eds.) (2012). *Improving organizational interventions for stress and well-being: Addressing process and context.* London: Routledge.

Bourbonnais, R., Brisson, C., Vinet, A., Vézina, M., Abdous, B., & Gaudet, B. (2006). Effectiveness of a participative intervention on psychosocial work factors to prevent mental health problems in a hospital setting. *Journal of Occupational and Environmental Medicine, 63,* 335–342.

Dollard, M. F., & Bakker, A. B. (2010). Psychosocial safety climate as a precursor to conducive work environments, psychological health problems, and employee engagement. *Journal of Occupational and Organizational Psychology, 83,* 579–599.

Dollard, M. F., & Gordon, J. A. (in press). Evaluation of a participatory risk management work stress intervention using an employee opinion survey. *International Journal of Stress Management.*

References

Biron, C., Cooper, C. L., & Bond, F. W. (2009). Mediators and moderators of organizational interventions to prevent occupational stress. In S. Cartwright, & C. L. Cooper (Eds.), *Oxford handbook of organizational well-being* (pp. 441–465). Oxford: Oxford University Press.

Biron, C., Gatrell, C., & Cooper, C. L. (2010). Autopsy of a failure: Evaluating process and contextual issues in an organizational-level work stress intervention. *International Journal of Stress Management, 17,* 135–158.

Black, C. (2008). *Working for a healthier tomorrow.* London: TSO.

Bond, F. W., & Bunce, D. (2000). Mediators of change in emotion-focused and problem-focused worksite stress management interventions. *Journal of Occupational Health Psychology, 5,* 156–163.

Bond, F. W., & Bunce, D. (2001). Job control mediates change in a work reorganization intervention for stress reduction. *Journal of Occupational Health Psychology, 6,* 290–302.

Bond, F. W., Flaxman, P. E., & Bunce, D. (2008). The influence of psychological flexibility on work redesign: Mediated moderation of a work reorganization intervention. *Journal of Applied Psychology, 93,* 645–654.

Bond, F. W., Flaxman, P. E., & Loivette, S. (2006). *A business case for the management standards for stress.* Norwich: Her Majesty's Stationery Office.

Bourbonnais, R., Brisson, C., Vinet, A., Vézina, M., Abdous, B., & Gaudet, B. (2006). Effectiveness of a participative intervention on psychosocial work factors to prevent mental health problems in a hospital setting. *Journal of Occupational and Environmental Medicine, 63,* 335–342.

Briner, R. B., & Reynolds, S. (1999). The costs, benefits, and limitations of organizational level stress interventions. *Journal of Organizational Behavior, 20,* 647–664.

Brun, J. P., Biron, C., & Ivers, H. (2008). *Strategic approach to preventing occupational stress* (R-577). Québec: Institut de recherche Robert-Sauvé en santé et en sécurité du travail.

Burke, R. J. (1993). Organizational-level interventions to reduce occupational stressors. *Work & Stress, 7,* 77–88.

Caulfield, N., Chang, D., Dollard, M. F., & Elshaug, C. (2004). A review of occupational stress interventions in Australia. *International Journal of Stress Management, 11,* 149–166.

Cooper, C. L. (2001). *Managerial, occupational and organizational stress research.* Aldershot: Ashgate.

Cooper, C. L., & Quick, J. C. (1999). *Stress and strain.* Oxford: Health Press Limited.

Cox, T., Griffiths, A., & Rial-Gonzalez, E. (2000). *Research on work-related stress.* Luxembourg: European Agency for Safety and Health at Work.

Cox, T., Karanika, M., Griffiths, A., & Houdmont, J. (2007). Evaluating organisational-level work stress interventions: Beyond traditional methods. *Work & Stress, 21,* 348–362.

Cox, T., Taris, T. W., & Nielsen, K. (2010). Organizational interventions: Issues and challenges. *Work & Stress, 24,* 217–218.

DeFrank, R. S., & Cooper, C. L. (1987). Worksite stress management interventions: Their effectiveness and conceptualisation. *Journal of Managerial Psychology, 2,* 4–10.

Dellve, L., Skagert, K., & Vilhelmsson, R. (2007). Leadership in workplace health promotion projects: 1- and 2-year effects on long-term work attendance. *European Journal of Public Health, 17,* 471–476.

Demerouti, E., Nachreiner, F., Bakker, A. B., & Schaufeli, W. B. (2001). The Job Demands-Resources model of burnout. *Journal of Applied Psychology, 86,* 499–512.

Dollard, M. F., Bailey, T., McLinton, S., Richards, P., McTernan, W., Taylor, A., & Bond, S. (2012). *The Australian Workplace Barometer: Report on psychosocial safety climate and worker health in Australia.* Canberra: Safe Work Australia.

Dollard, M. F., & Bakker, A. B. (2010). Psychosocial safety climate as a precursor to conducive work environments, psychological health problems, and employee engagement. *Journal of Occupational and Organizational Psychology, 83,* 579–599.

Dollard, M. F., & Karasek, R. A. (2010). Building psychosocial safety climate: Evaluation of a socially coordinated PAR risk management stress prevention study. In J. Houdmont, & S. Leka (Eds.), *Contemporary occupational health psychology: Global perspectives on research and practice* (pp. 208–234). Chichester: John Wiley & Sons.

Dollard, M. F., Le Blanc, P. M., & Cotton, S. J. (2008). Participatory action research as work stress intervention. In K. Näswall, J. Hellgren, & M. Sverke (Eds.), *Balancing work and well-being: The individual in the changing working life* (pp. 351–353). Cambridge: Cambridge University Press.

Dollard, M. F., & Metzer, J. C. (1999). Psychological research, practice and production: The occupational stress problem. *International Journal of Stress Management, 6,* 241–254.

Elden, M. (1986). Sharing the research work: Participative research and its role demands. In P. Reason, & J. Rowan (Eds.), *Human enquiry* (pp. 55–86). Chichester: John Wiley & Sons.

Foresight Mental Capital and Wellbeing Project. (2008). *Final project report.* London: The Government Office for Science.

Geurts, S., & Gründemann, R. (1999). Workplace stress and stress prevention in Europe. In M. Kompier, & C. Cooper (Eds.), *Preventing stress, improving productivity: European case studies in the workplace* (pp. 9–33). London: Routledge.

Giga, S. I., Cooper, C. L., & Faragher, B. (2003). The development of a framework for a comprehensive approach to stress management interventions at work. *International Journal of Stress Management, 10,* 280–296.

Giga, S. I., Noblet, A. J., Faragher, B., & Cooper, C. L. (2003). The UK perspective: A review of research on organisational stress management interventions. *Australian Psychologist, 38,* 158–164.

Goldenhar, L. M., LaMontagne, A. D., Katz, T., Heaney, C. A., & Landsbergis, P. (2001). The intervention research process in Occupational Safety and Health: An overview from the National Occupational Research Agenda Intervention Effectiveness Research Team. *Journal of Occupational and Environmental Medicine, 43*, 616–622.

Hall, G. B., Dollard, M. F., & Coward, J. (2010). Psychosocial Safety Climate: Development of the PSC-12. *International Journal of Stress Management, 4*, 353–383.

Health & Safety Executive. (2003). *Tackling stress in your organisation: A walkthrough*. Retrieved 2004, from http://www.hse.gov.uk/stress/walkthrough/index.htm.

Holman, D. J., Axtell, C. M., Sprigg, C. A., Totterdell, P., & Wall, T. D. (2010). The mediating role of job characteristics in job redesign interventions: A serendipitous quasi-experiment. *Journal of Organizational Behavior, 31*, 81–105.

Idris, M. A., Dollard, M. F., Coward, J., & Dormann, C. (2012). Psychosocial safety climate: Conceptual distinctiveness and effect on job demands and worker psychological well-being. *Safety Science, 50*, 19–28.

Idris, M. A., Dollard, M. F., & Winefield, A. H. (2011). Integrating psychosocial safety climate in the JD-R model: A study amongst Malaysian workers. *South African Journal of Industrial Psychology, 37*, 1–11.

Imada, A. S. (1991). The rationale and tools of participatory ergonomics. In K. Noro, & A. S. Imada (Eds.), *Participatory ergonomics* (pp. 30–51). London: Taylor & Francis.

Ivancevich, J. M., Matteson, M. T., Freedman, S. M., & Phillips, J. S. (1990). Worksite stress management interventions. *American Psychologist, 45*, 252–261.

Jordan, J., Gurr, E., Tinline, G., Giga, S. I., Faragher, B., & Cooper, C. L. (2003). *Beacons of excellence in stress prevention*. Manchester: Robertson Cooper Ltd & UMIST.

Karanika-Murray, M., Biron, C., & Cooper, C. L. (2012). Distilling the principles of successful organizational intervention implementation. In C. Biron, M. Karanika-Murray, & C. L. Cooper (Eds.), *Improving organizational interventions for stress and well-being: Addressing process and context* (pp. 353–361). London: Routledge.

Karasek, R. A. (1979). Job demands, job decision latitude, and mental strain: Implications for job redesign. *Administration Science Quarterly, 224*, 285–307.

Kompier, M. A. J., & Cooper, C. L. (Eds.) (1999). *Preventing stress, improving productivity: European case studies in the workplace*. London: Routledge.

Kompier, M. A. J., Cooper, C. L., & Geurts, S. A. E. (2000). A multiple case study approach to work stress prevention in Europe. *European Journal of Work and Organizational Psychology, 9*, 371–400.

Kompier, M. A. J., & Kristensen, T. S. (2001). Organizational work stress interventions in a theoretical, methodological and practical context. In J. Dunham (Ed.), *Stress in the workplace: Past, present and future* (pp. 164–190). London: Whurr Publishers.

LaMontagne, A. D., Keegel, T., Louie, A. M., Ostry, A., & Landsbergis, P. A. (2007). A systematic review of the job-stress intervention evaluation literature. *International Journal of Occupational and Environmental Health, 13*, 268–280.

LaMontagne, A. D., Noblet, A., & Spector, P. (2012). Intervention development and implementation: Understanding and addressing barriers to organizational-level interventions. In C. Biron, M. Karanika-Murray, & C. L. Cooper (Eds.), *Improving organizational interventions for stress and well-being: Addressing process and context* (pp. 21–38). London: Routledge.

Landsbergis, P. A., Schurman, S. J., Israel, B. A., Schnall, P. L., Hugentobler, M. K., Cahill, J., & Baker, D. (1993). Job stress and heart disease. *New Solutions, Summer*, 42–58.

Law, R., Dollard, M. F., Tuckey, M. R., & Dormann, C. (2011). Psychosocial safety climate as a lead indicator of workplace bullying and harassment, job resources, psychological health and employee engagement. *Accident Analysis and Prevention, 43*, 1782–1793.

Lewis, R., Yarker, J., & Donaldson-Feilder, E. (2012). The vital role of line managers in managing psychosocial risks. In C. Biron, M. Karanika-Murray, & C. L. Cooper (Eds.), *Improving organizational interventions for stress and well-being: Addressing process and context* (pp. 216–237). London: Routledge.

Marshall, J., & Cooper, C. L. (Eds.) (1981). *Coping with stress at work: Case studies from industry*. Aldershot: Gower.

Maslach, C., & Schaufeli, W. B. (1993). Historical and conceptual development of burnout. In W. B. Schaufeli, C. Maslach, & T. Marek (Eds.),

Professional burnout: Recent developments in theory and research (pp. 1–16). London: Taylor & Francis.

Newman, J. E., & Beehr, T. A. (1979). Personal and organizational strategies for handling job stress: A review of research and opinion. *Personnel Psychology, 32*, 1–43.

Nielsen, K., & Randall, R. (2012). The importance of employee participation and perceptions of changes in procedures in a teamworking intervention. *Work & Stress, 26*, 91–111.

Nielsen, K., & Randall, R. (in press). Opening the black box: Presenting a model for evaluating organizational-level interventions. *European Journal of Work and Organizational Psychology.*

Nielsen, K., Randall, R., & Albertsen, K. (2007). The impact of implementation and participants' appraisal on the outcomes of stress management interventions. *Journal of Organizational Behavior, 28*, 793–810.

Nytrø, K., Saksvik, P. Ø., Mikkelsen, A., Bohle, P., & Quinlan, M. (2000). The role and effects of process in occupational stress interventions. *Work & Stress, 14*, 213–225.

Randall, R., & Nielsen, K. (2012). Does the intervention fit? An explanatory model of intervention success and failure in complex organizational environments. In C. Biron, M. Karanika-Murray, & C. L. Cooper (Eds.), *Improving organizational interventions for stress and well-being: Addressing process and context* (pp. 120–134). London: Routledge.

Richardson, K. M., & Rothstein, H. R. (2008). Effects of occupational stress management intervention programs: A meta-analysis. *Journal of Occupational Health Psychology, 13*, 69–93.

Semmer, N. K. (2006). Job stress interventions and the organization of work. *Scandinavian Journal of Work, Environment & Health, 32*, 515–527.

Semmer, N. (2011). Job stress interventions and organization of work. In J. C. Quick, & L. E. Tetrick (Eds.), *Handbook of occupational health psychology* (2nd ed., pp. 299–318). Washington, DC: APA.

Taris, T. W., Kompier, M. A. J., Geurts, S. A. E., Schreurs, P. J. G., Schaufeli, W. B., de Boer, E., Sepmeijer, K. J., & Wattez, C. (2003). Stress management interventions in the Dutch domiciliary care sector: Findings from 81 organizations. *International Journal of Stress Management, 10*, 297–325.

van der Hek, H., & Plomp, H. N. (1997). Occupational stress management programmes: A practical overview of published effect studies. *Occupational Medicine, 47*, 133–141.

Wadsworth, Y. (1998). *What is participatory action research?* Retrieved January 20, 2013, from http://en.scientificcommons.org/35447541.

17
Job Crafting

EVANGELIA DEMEROUTI AND ARNOLD B. BAKKER

Chapter Objectives

After studying this chapter, you should be able to:

- understand the restrictions of top-down job redesign approaches;
- explain the gap that job crafting fills in top-down job redesign approaches;
- provide a thorough insight into what job crafting really is;
- describe some research evidence on the predictors and outcomes of job crafting;
- recognize unresolved and critical issues regarding job crafting;
- describe an intervention on how to stimulate job-crafting behaviour.

17.1 Introduction

The increasing popularity of self-managing teams, re-engineering and other organizational innovations, coupled with the increased flexibility in work arrangements made possible by advances in information technology, has considerably expanded the complexity of professional jobs. Consequently, each job position seems to be characterized by a unique constellation of working conditions that the organization can hardly be aware of. Not surprisingly, top-down organizational

---

An Introduction to Contemporary Work Psychology, First Edition.
Edited by Maria C. W. Peeters, Jan de Jonge and Toon W. Taris.
© 2014 John Wiley & Sons, Ltd. Published 2014 by John Wiley & Sons, Ltd.

interventions to improve motivation and organizational performance often seem partly ineffective (Biron, Karanika-Murray, & Cooper, 2012). Therefore organizations have started to recognize that redesign approaches initiated by individuals or job holders themselves (bottom-up) should be promoted and combined with approaches initiated by the organization.

The aim of this chapter is to zoom in on the process through which organizations can improve the working conditions for their employees by offering them the opportunity to do so themselves. This process is called *job crafting* and can be seen as a specific form of proactive behaviour in which the employee initiates changes in the level of job demands and job resources to make their own job more meaningful, engaging and satisfying. Our basic premise is that job crafting can be used next to top-down approaches to improve jobs in order to overcome the inadequacies of job redesign approaches. Job crafting can also be used to respond to the complexity of contemporary jobs and to deal with the needs of the current workforce. The chapter starts with a brief overview of the roots of job crafting, namely job redesign (Section 17.2). After presenting the inadequacies of classical job redesign approaches, we will continue with some attempts to individualize job redesign that can also be considered as precursors of job crafting. In the next section (Section 17.3), we provide an overview of job crafting as a job redesign approach and zoom in on its conceptualization and on its predictors and outcomes. In Section 17.4 we make the link between job crafting and the implementation of organizational change and innovation as these represent enduring requirements of modern organizations. As job crafting represents a relatively new construct in the literature, there are several issues that remain unresolved, as well as critical notes that can be made about it. These are presented in Section 17.5. In the following section (Section 17.6), we present some ideas on how to intervene and stimulate the job-crafting behaviour of employees. We end this chapter with some conclusions and suggestions for further reading (Section 17.7).

17.2 The Roots of Job Crafting

We first present a brief overview of the roots of job crafting, namely job redesign and the unresolved problems associated with it.

Job redesign and its unresolved problems

Job design describes 'how jobs, tasks, and roles are structured, enacted, and modified, as well as the impact of these structures, enactments, and modifications on individual, group, and organizational outcomes' (Grant & Parker, 2009, p. 319). Job design usually represents a top-down process in which organizations create jobs and form the conditions under which the job holders/incumbents execute their tasks (see also Chapter 3). In addition, job *redesign* is usually seen as the process through which the organization or supervisor changes something in the job, tasks or conditions of the individual (Tims & Bakker, 2010). We will focus particularly on job redesign in this chapter. An example of a traditional job redesign effort is the increase in individual and team autonomy in the production process. A more contemporary example concerns the introduction of project work where individuals within and outside an organization work interdependently on the development of a product, often under time pressure. In each case, the structure and content of the work can be redesigned by the organization, with as the ultimate goal the improvement of outcomes such as employee work engagement, performance and well-being.

Extensive reviews of the job redesign literature are available elsewhere and we do not aim to repeat them here (e.g. Morgeson & Humphrey, 2008; Parker & Ohly, 2008). A basic premise in the job redesign literature is that stimulating jobs foster motivating psychological states that contribute to favourable attitudinal and behavioural work outcomes (e.g. Fried, Grant, Levi, Hadani, & Slowik, 2007). During the past three decades, research on job redesign has played an important role in bringing theory into organizational practice. Prominent theories such as the Job Characteristics Model (Hackman & Oldham, 1980), Socio-Technical Systems Theory (Trist, 1981), Action Regulation Theory (Hacker, 2003) and the Interdisciplinary Work Design Framework (Campion & McClelland, 1993) have stimulated much of the research in the field. Researchers have accumulated extensive knowledge about the diverse task, knowledge and physical characteristics of jobs, the psychological and behavioural effects of job redesign, the mediating mechanisms that explain these effects, and the individual and contextual factors that moderate these effects (e.g. Grant & Parker, 2009; Humphrey, Nahrgang, & Morgeson, 2007). Moreover, existing research has helped organizational practice by providing guidelines for practitioners to design work to promote employee performance and well-being.

However, job redesign research has revealed mixed results. According to Fried (1991) this is probably due to the relative weak relation between stimulating job characteristics and work outcomes such as job performance, turnover and absenteeism (Fried, 1991). Namely, although research supports the hypothesized relations between stimulating job characteristics and attitudinal outcomes such as internal work motivation and job satisfaction, the magnitude of the association between the core job characteristics and these attitudinal outcomes appears to be moderate rather than high (Fried, 1991; Parker et al., 2001). Moreover, although the literature suggests a positive relation between employee motivation and job performance, this relation tends to be relatively weak (e.g. Demerouti & Bakker, 2006; Demerouti & Cropanzano, 2010; see also Chapter 13). These findings suggest that there are characteristics of the context or characteristics of employees that may play a role in moderating employee reactions (Johns, 2006). Some scholars have argued that there is a lack of systematic attention for the context – the situational opportunities and constraints that affect attitudes and behaviours (Fried et al., 2007; Johns, 2006).

Moreover, traditional job redesign approaches have been criticized for no longer reflecting and integrating the dramatic changes in the work contexts that have occurred during the past few decades (Grant & Parker, 2009; Humphrey et al., 2007). These changes include a shift from manufacturing to a service-oriented economy, an increase in the knowledge-based industry, growth in globalization and global operations across different countries, societies and cultures, and the growing use of innovative technologies and flexible work methods ranging from virtual teams to telework and new ways of working (ten Brummelhuis, Bakker, Hetland, & Keulemans, 2012) as a basis for operations. Simultaneously, the nature of the workforce itself is changing considerably, with more women involved, greater ethnic diversity, more educated employees, an aging population and altered psychological contracts between employers and employees. New approaches to job redesign have started to integrate these changes. The underlying factor in these new approaches is that they more actively involve the individual employee in the job redesign process.

Individualization of job redesign approaches

In response to the mixed findings regarding the effectiveness of job redesign approaches as well as to the changes in the job context and content along with changes in the workforce, job redesign approaches started to integrate more social aspects of the job (rather than only mechanistic aspects, such as tasks, structures and environmental conditions) which are inherent in many contemporary job functions (Grant & Parker, 2009).

Relational perspectives of job redesign focus on how jobs, roles and tasks are more socially embedded than ever before, based on increases in interdependence between and interactions with co-workers and service recipients. The emerging relational perspective on job redesign provides important insights into the social characteristics of work, which include interaction outside the organization, task interdependence, social support and interpersonal feedback (Morgeson & Humphrey, 2006). Moreover, Grant and Parker (2009) suggested that additional social characteristics of work include interpersonal display rules for emotions (Diefendorff & Richard, 2003) and opportunities to benefit others (task significance; Hackman & Oldham, 1980). Such characteristics connect employees' actions to the well-being of other people and are therefore important for job redesign.

According to Grant and Parker (2009), another contemporary approach to job redesign that reflects the move towards individualization of job redesign is *proactive perspectives*. Proactive perspectives capture the growing importance of employees taking the initiative to anticipate and create changes in how work is performed, based on increases in uncertainty and dynamism. Proactive perspectives focus particularly on anticipatory actions taken by employees to create changes in how jobs, roles and tasks are executed (Frese & Fay, 2001). Job redesign perspectives that apply the proactive approach aim at (i) *job redesign to stimulate proactivity*, which examines how organizations can structure jobs and tasks to encourage employees to take the initiative and actively shape their work tasks and contexts, and (ii) *job crafting, role adjustment, and idiosyncratic deals* that represent the proactive steps that employees take to modify the cognitive, physical and relational boundaries of their work and to propose personalized employment arrangements with managers and supervisors (Grant & Parker,

2009). Thus, the former focuses on how organizations can stimulate individuals (through job redesign approaches) to become proactive in their job, while the latter focuses on what individuals do themselves to change their jobs, which will be the issue of the next section.

Finally, before moving to job crafting we present a final way that illustrates how contemporary job redesign approaches can move towards more individualization of job redesign: the *time perspective*. Fried and colleagues (2007) suggested that leading job redesign theories have neglected to incorporate the temporal context in their premises which hinders their explanatory power and utility. They claim that time is a fundamental dimension of context, as it specifies when situational constraints and opportunities occur and how they are perceived (Johns, 2006). The failure to include time in job redesign theory limits the theory's ability to accurately predict individual attitudes and behaviours in organizations, as these may develop and change over time. In this way, most job redesign theories are static in nature (George & Jones, 2000). Fried et al. (2007) suggested that employees' reactions to stimulating jobs, and their efforts to craft more stimulating jobs, may depend on temporal aspects of their career aspirations and expectations. For instance, they suggested that employees may react more favourably to jobs that provide little stimulation early in their careers, if they perceive their current jobs as instrumental to career advancement, if they expect to advance in the near future and if their advancement occurs in line with occupational norms. However, in later career stages, employees are likely to develop preferences for more stimulating job characteristics (e.g. task significance) rather than other characteristics (e.g. task and skill variety, complexity). Taken together, this perspective on job redesign suggests that it may depend on the age and job tenure of the employee which job characteristics are important for the specific job. This emphasis on employee characteristics in job redesign literature signals the importance of the individualization of job redesign (or the reliance on bottom-up approaches next to top-down approaches).

Replay

Job redesign approaches have been influential in stimulating organizations to consider employee motivation and well-being as important organizational goals. Early job redesign approaches proved to be inadequate to serve the changing nature of the jobs that include more cognitive tasks, new technologies, relational aspects and employees with changing needs and competencies. As such, the job redesign literature has gradually recognized that the 'one-size-fits-all' approach is no longer sufficient (Grant & Parker, 2009). Moreover, the classical job redesign approach is generally top-down in nature (Oldham & Hackman, 2010). However, approaches that recognize the role of individuals as proactive agents that form their jobs and change their own job characteristics have come to complete the traditional job redesign literature (Fried et al., 2007; Grant & Parker, 2009). These approaches will be discussed in the next section.

17.3 Job Crafting as an Individual Job Redesign Approach

In this section we provide an overview of job crafting as a job redesign approach and particularly zoom in on its conceptualization, predictors and outcomes.

Conceptualization of job crafting

It is clear that the availability of well-designed jobs and optimal working conditions facilitate employee motivation and performance, but what if these favourable working conditions are not available? Employees may actively change the design of their jobs by choosing tasks, negotiating a different job content and assigning meaning to their tasks or jobs (Parker & Ohly, 2008). This process of employees shaping their jobs has been referred to as *job crafting* (Wrzesniewski & Dutton, 2001). Job crafting is defined as the physical and cognitive changes individuals make in their task or relational boundaries. Physical changes refer to changes in the form, scope or number of job tasks, whereas cognitive changes refer to changing how one sees the job. Wrzesniewski and Dutton (2001) noted that job crafting is not inherently 'good' or 'bad' for an organization. Its effect depends on the situation.

To explain what job crafting is we use the example of the maintenance technician who was interviewed by Berg, Wrzesniewski and Dutton (2010), and who told that he crafted his job in the form of taking on additional tasks. After having been in the organization for some time, he started to proactively help newcomers to learn the job. Because he turned out to be good at this, he became formally responsible for the training of new employees. As another example, consider this customer service representative, who reframed the perception of the job as a meaningful whole that positively impacts others rather than a collection of separate tasks (i.e. cognitive change as a form of job crafting): 'Technically, [my job is] putting in orders, entering orders, but really I see it as providing our customers with an enjoyable experience, a positive experience, which is a lot more meaningful to me than entering numbers' (Berg et al., 2010, p. 167).

According to Wrzesniewski and Dutton (2001), the motivation for job crafting arises from three individual needs. First, employees engage in job crafting because they have the need to take control over certain aspects of their work to avoid negative consequences such as alienation from work. Second, employees are motivated to change aspects of their work to enable a more positive sense of the self to be expressed and confirmed by others. Third, job crafting allows employees to fulfil the basic human need for connection to others. Additionally, Petrou, Demerouti, Peeters, Schaufeli and Hetland (2012) suggested that individuals craft their jobs in order to create conditions in which they can work more healthily and be more motivated.

The central characteristic of job crafting is that employees alter their tasks or other job characteristics on their own initiative (Tims, Bakker, & Derks, 2012). This distinguishes job crafting from other bottom-up redesign approaches such as *idiosyncratic deals* (i-deals), in which employees negotiate with their employers about their work conditions (Hornung, Rousseau, Glaser, Angerer, & Weigl, 2010; see also Chapter 5), or employee participation in job redesign (Nadin, Waterson, & Parker, 2001). Wrzesniewski and Dutton (2001) viewed job crafting as changes introduced by the individuals in the design and social environment of their jobs, which, in turn, alter work meanings and work identity. Lyons (2008) defined job crafting as spontaneous unsupervised changes in one's job scope. Moreover, job crafting is different from proactive work behaviours. Proactive work behaviours have in common that they are initiated by the person either by acting in advance of a future situation and/ or by taking control and causing change (Parker & Collins, 2010). An important benefit of proactive behaviour is that it is targeted to performance: employees who take the initiative to change certain things in their work environment are likely to contribute to organizational effectiveness (Tims et al., 2012). According to Tims and her colleagues, job crafting is different from previously studied proactive constructs because the changes that job crafters make are primarily aimed at improving their person–job fit and work motivation. This does not necessarily have to lead to an increase in organizational effectiveness.

> ### Work Psychology in Action: Two examples of job-crafting behaviours in a general hospital
>
> Female medical specialist:
>
> 'I organized a meeting for patients with a certain medical condition in the city where I work. During the time that I was busy with organizing the meeting, I kept asking myself: "Why am I doing this?" Then the day came and about 100 people showed up and I knew why I was doing this. We gave them information about their disease and it seemed to really help people. Although it took so much time and energy, it gave me much confidence seeing the positive effects of our work.'
>
> Male medical specialist:
>
> 'For me, I become bored seeing the same type of patients over and over again because it is too predictable and at times there is not enough variety. We've been discussing how to improve patient care and we've been trying to implement the idea of utilizing our team members' strengths. Using strengths may improve patient care while also helping us as individuals to enjoy our jobs and make the most out of it. For example, I like working with a specific population of patients within our department and I've expressed this to my colleagues. Now, when my colleagues have questions about this population, or if one checks in, we've worked out that I can handle most of the flow and activity with this population. At the same time, I give up a portion of my patient population that falls outside of this group to my colleagues. To achieve this, me and my team need to express what we like most about our work and talk about ways to help everyone in the team utilize their strengths. We are much more effective as doctors when we are able to do what we enjoy, which is usually also what we are best at.'

Job crafting from the perspective of the Job Demands–Resources Model

Although Wrzesniewski and Dutton (2001) defined job crafting as 'everyday' behaviour, most empirical conceptualizations do not tap this aspect. Lyons (2008) found that employees reported an average of 1.49 crafting episodes for the past year. In order to capture the 'everyday' changes in job characteristics that employees may pursue, some scholars (Petrou et al., 2012; Tims & Bakker, 2010) theoretically frame the definition of job crafting in the Job Demands–Resources (JD–R) Model (Bakker & Demerouti, 2007; Demerouti, Bakker, Nachreiner, & Schaufeli, 2001; see Chapter 4). As a result, job crafting is defined as the changes that employees may make to balance their job demands and job resources with their personal abilities and needs (cf. Tims & Bakker, 2010). Petrou et al. (2012) adopted a stance similar to Wrzesniewski and Dutton's (2001) social constructionist view (Gergen, 1994) of the workplace, and define job crafting as proactive employee behaviour consisting of resources seeking, challenges seeking and demands reducing. In doing so, job crafting can be conceived as unfolding on a daily basis and as being directed towards the work environment that surrounds the individual, namely specific job demands and job resources. Like Wrzesniewski and Dutton (2001), Petrou et al. (2012) suggested that even in the most stable environments with detailed job descriptions and clear work procedures, individuals can and do adjust the tasks they perform, and mobilize the resources they need to carry out their tasks successfully. In this way, individuals remain healthy and motivated.

As depicted in Chapter 4, the JD–R Model proposes two processes in the development of well-being and performance. In the health impairment process, job demands such as a heavy workload and emotionally demanding interactions with others relate primarily to impaired health, whereas in the motivational process, job resources such as autonomy and performance feedback are primarily related to work motivation and engagement. Note that work engagement represents the experience of vigour, dedication and absorption at work. Viewing the work environment from the JD–R perspective implies that individuals craft their jobs to make it 'fit'; they target their job demands and job resources.

As already indicated, Petrou and colleagues (2012) discriminated between three distinct job crafting behaviours: resources seeking, challenges seeking and demands reducing. Decreasing job resources has not been proposed and does not seem to be a purposeful behaviour of workers. Seeking job resources (e.g. feedback, advice from colleagues or the manager, maximizing job autonomy) can be a form of coping with job demands or achieving goals and completing tasks. Past research has examined positive outcomes of several resource-seeking behaviours, such as feedback seeking (Ashford, Blatt, & van de Walle, 2003) and social support seeking (Carver, Scheier, & Weintraub, 1989). Hobfoll (2001) also suggests that a basic human motivation is directed towards the accumulation of resources that are important for the protection of other valued resources.

Challenges seeking may include behaviours such as seeking new challenging tasks at work, keeping busy during one's working day or asking for more responsibilities once one has finished the assigned tasks (see also the examples in the Work Psychology in Action box). Csikszentmihalyi and Nakamura (1989) argued that when individuals engage in activities offering opportunities for growth, they seek challenges to maintain motivation and avoid boredom. This is consistent with the proposition that workers with active jobs (characterized by high job demands and high control) are likely to seek challenging situations that promote mastery (Karasek & Theorell, 1990).

The job-crafting strategy of reducing job demands can include behaviours targeted at minimizing the emotionally, mentally or physically demanding aspects of one's work, reducing one's workload or making sure one's work does not go at the cost of one's private life. From an organizational perspective, reducing job demands might be a health-protecting coping mechanism when demands are excessively high. Reducing job demands has not been systematically studied as organizational behaviour. However, in the literature 'task avoidance' has been described as a withdrawal-oriented coping mechanism (Parker & Endler, 1996), slow or sloppy work and poor attendance have been described as counterproductive behaviours (Gruys, 1999), and procrastination can be 'active behaviour' with positive outcomes (Chu & Choi, 2005). While reducing demands might be an instrumental strategy to deal with the threat of diminished health, it is possible that at the same time it can have detrimental effects on (specific aspects of) one's job performance.

Using this conceptualization, Petrou et al. (2012) conducted a study among 95 employees from several organizations who filled out a quantitative diary for five consecutive days. Findings not only confirmed the validity of the job-crafting conceptualization, including the three specific behaviours of resources seeking, challenges seeking and demands reducing, but also showed that job-crafting behaviours varied significantly from one day to another. Specifically, it was found that job crafting occurs on a daily basis as daily fluctuations of job crafting ranged between 31% (challenges seeking), 34% (resources seeking) and 78% (demands reducing).

Tims, Bakker and Derks (2012) developed and validated a scale to measure job-crafting behaviour in three separate studies conducted in The Netherlands ($N=1,181$). Job crafting was defined as the self-initiated changes that employees make in their own job demands and job resources to attain and/or optimize their personal (work) goals. They found four independent job-crafting dimensions, namely increasing social job resources, increasing structural job resources, increasing challenging job demands and decreasing hindering job demands. These dimensions could be reliably measured with 21 items. In terms of convergent validity (see also Chapter 2), job crafting was positively correlated with the 'active' constructs of proactive personality and personal initiative, and negatively with the 'inactive' construct cynicism. In support of criterion validity of the job-crafting conceptualization and measurement, results indicated that self-reports of job crafting correlated positively with colleague ratings of work engagement, employability and performance. Finally, self-rated job-crafting behaviours correlated positively with peer-rated job-crafting behaviours, which indicates that job crafting represents behaviours that others can also observe.

Replay

Job crafting can be conceived from the job characteristics perspective of the JD–R Model, discriminating between three distinct job-crafting behaviours: (i) resources seeking, (ii) challenges seeking and (iii) demands reducing. In this way, job crafting was found to occur on a daily basis. Moreover, this conceptualization resulted in reliable and valid measures of job crafting as self-reports on job crafting were related to peer ratings of one's job crafting and performance.

Predictors and outcomes of job crafting

In this section we provide an overview of the predictors and outcomes of job crafting.

Predictors of job crafting

As crafting represents discretionary behaviour on the part of the employee, decision latitude and job autonomy were already suggested by Wrzesniewski and Dutton (2001) to be important conditions that stimulate this behaviour. Several studies have indeed confirmed that decision latitude is positively related to job crafting (e.g. Leana, Appelbaum, & Shevchuk, 2009; Lyons, 2008). Other proposed predictors of job crafting include proactive personality (Bakker, Tims, & Derks, 2012), job control (Lyons, 2008), task interdependence and discretion to craft a job (Leana et al., 2009), job demands (Wrzesniewski & Dutton, 2001), task complexity (Ghitulescu, 2007) and job challenges (Berg, Wrzesniewski, & Dutton, 2010). Task complexity and job challenges were found to be positively related to job crafting, which indicates that demanding aspects of the job stimulate proactive behaviour (Berg et al., 2010; Ghitulescu, 2007). Note, however, that task interdependence was found to inhibit collective job crafting (the degree to which teams crafted jobs), but was unrelated to individual crafting (Leana et al., 2009).

Petrou et al. (2012) examined the situational conditions influencing job crafting on a daily basis, as well as the relationship between job crafting and state work engagement. Their diary study showed that on days that work pressure and autonomy were both high (i.e. 'active jobs'; cf. Karasek, 1979) individuals showed higher resource-seeking and lower demand-reducing behaviours.

Berg, Wrzesniewski and Dutton (2010) interviewed 33 employees in for-profit and non-profit organizations to examine how employees at different ranks describe the execution of their job-crafting behaviour. While employee rank was unrelated to the prevalence of job-crafting efforts, rank was related to how employees perceived the challenges to craft their job. Higher-rank employees tended to see the challenges they face in job crafting as located in their own expectations of how they and others should spend their time, while lower-rank employees tended to see their challenges as located in their prescribed jobs and others' expectations of them. Moreover, higher-rank employees adapted their own expectations and behaviours to get along with the perceived opportunities to job craft at work, while lower-rank employees adapted others' expectations and behaviours to create opportunities to job craft.

Outcomes of job crafting
Although research on the outcomes of job crafting is still in its infancy, there are some interesting empirical findings to be reported. Wrzesniewski and Dutton (2001) proposed that job crafters are satisfied workers, as job crafting represents a way to enhance one's experienced meaning at work. In support of this suggestion, Ghitulescu (2007) found a positive link between job crafting and organizational commitment. Positive significant correlations have also been found between episodes of work modification and the variables of self-image, perceived control and readiness to change (Lyons, 2008).

More research has been conducted on the relation between job crafting and work engagement. In their study among 95 dyads of employees ($N=190$) working in various organizations, Bakker, Tims and Derks (2012) found that employees who were characterized by a proactive personality were most likely to craft their jobs (increase their structural and social job resources, and increase their job challenges). Job crafting, in turn, was predictive of work engagement and colleague ratings of in-role performance. These findings suggest that to the extent that employees proactively adjust their work environment, they manage to stay engaged and perform well. In Tims et al.'s (2012) study, decreasing hindering job demands (e.g. role conflict, role ambiguity) was unrelated to work engagement. The reason for this is most probably that hindrance demands need to be taken care of in order to prevent exhaustion (Demerouti et al., 2001). However, hindrance demands do not seem to affect employee work engagement. Petrou et al. (2012) found that daily fluctuations in job crafting were related to daily fluctuations of work engagement. Specifically, it was shown that the more employees sought resources and challenges on a specific day, the more engaged they were in their job. In contrast, the more employees simplified their work on a specific day, the less engaged they were on that day. Note that reducing demands may have detrimental effects on the motivational process, for exmaple work engagement, but beneficial effects on the health impairment process, for example exhaustion (Petrou et al., 2012).

Furthermore, job crafting has been found to influence performance at work, which represents a very valuable outcome for organizations. Leana, Appelbaum and Shevchuk (2009) conducted performance assessments in 62 childcare centres and surveyed 232 teachers and aides to examine the extent to which workers crafted their jobs and how such crafting affected classroom quality. Results showed that collaborative crafting was positively related to performance, particularly for less experienced teachers. Note that in this study, collaborative crafting was also associated with higher levels of satisfaction and commitment.

Replay

There is evidence that people generally craft their jobs when they experience more autonomy and when the jobs are demanding. Moreover, job crafting occurs on days that employees experience high work pressure combined with high autonomy. However, the rank of a job seems to influence the degree to which one feels responsible for the crafting behaviours, with high-ranking employees feeling more responsible themselves for their job crafting than low-ranking employees. Moreover, the scarce empirical evidence up to now suggests that job crafting is beneficial for job satisfaction and organizational commitment. Preliminary findings also indicate that job crafting may have both beneficial (in case of resources and challenges seeking) and detrimental (in case of demands reducing) effects on work engagement. Also, job crafting has favourable effects on the performance of groups and individuals.

17.4 Linking Job Crafting with Organizational Change and Innovation

Job crafting falls under proactive employee behaviours enacted in the light of an increasingly uncertain and transformational work environment (Grant & Parker, 2009). Crafting a job not only requires but also triggers adaptive efforts. Job crafting can be the key to successfully dealing with today's workplace, where tasks and roles are already in flux. Because managers today do not simply require employees to change but also to proactively introduce changes (Grant & Parker, 2009), job crafting enhances employees' sustainable ability to adapt to the demands of the dynamic post-industrial workplace (Kira, van Eijnatten, & Balkin, 2010). Proactive actions that are useful during organizational change include (i) maximizing the pool of job resources that help employees deal or cope with change, (ii) keeping the work pressure associated with change at an optimal level and (iii) seeking challenges that will transform change to an engaging and efficacious experience (Avey, Wernsing, & Luthans, 2008). Those three behaviours are present in job crafting and thus form an ideal strategic advantage for employees in the context of change (Petrou et al., 2012).

Preliminary evidence indicates that job crafting can be useful during organizational change. For example, in a qualitative study during a merger, Kira, Balkin and San (2012) found that, among other activities, relational crafting (e.g. asking for supervisory support) and task crafting (e.g. prioritizing) were used as strategies to deal with the new situation at work. In a similar vein, job-crafting episodes have been associated with readiness to change (Lyons, 2008). However, the evidence on how different job-crafting behaviours and employee outcomes are inter-related is far from conclusive. As mentioned before, in a diary study among employees dealing with various changes, Petrou and colleagues (2012) found that seeking challenges was positively related to work engagement and demands reducing was negatively related to work engagement. Next to these daily effects, job crafting is found to have more enduring effects on work engagement and adaptation to change. In a longitudinal study conducted during the reorganization of a Dutch police department, Petrou, Demerouti and Schaufeli (2013) found that seeking resources was positively associated with work engagement, while reducing demands was negatively associated with work engagement one year later. Furthermore, within the same organization, seeking resources and seeking challenges were positively associated with adaptation to changes as reported by police officers, whereas reducing demands was negatively associated with adaptation (Petrou et al., 2013).

Replay

Taken together, research so far seems to suggest that job crafting can be a way through which individuals adapt change and innovations to themselves, which makes them more responsive and adaptive to the context of change and consequently facilitates successful implementation of organizational change and innovations. Preliminary findings further reveal a favourable implication of seeking resources and seeking challenges, and an unfavourable implication of reducing demands for motivation and performance within changing environments.

17.5 Unresolved Issues Regarding Job Crafting

Oldham and Hackman (2010) discussed several open issues regarding job crafting that remain to be answered. The first question that needs to be addressed is whether the benefits of job crafting derive from substantive changes in the work itself or mainly from involvement in the process of making those changes. It may be that employee-initiated changes in the redesign of jobs result in more complex, challenging and meaningful work, which is likely to foster positive work and personal outcomes. But it could also be the case that beneficial outcomes derive not from positive changes in job attributes but instead from simply being involved in job-crafting activities. Even when improvements in productivity and/or satisfaction are observed after individuals have crafted their jobs, the open question is why this is the case. Is it because the job now fits better with their own preferences and needs, or because the newly crafted jobs stretch their skills, or because crafting allowed them to eliminate inefficiencies and redundancies in work processes that had been frustrating them and impeded their productivity? Such explanations have been provided by Oldham and Hackman (2010), who further identified the danger of dysfunctional consequences of job crafting. Is it possible that job crafting will introduce inefficiencies in work processes? If employees adjust a product or service or characteristic of their work that is even slightly different from what existed before, disruptions in the work processes may develop that affect not only the crafter but also other employees, who may have to struggle to accommodate the newly modified product or service. How can job crafting be executed in a way that it lessens the likelihood of unanticipated problems that reduce the effectiveness of the work unit as a whole?

It should be noted that there is some discussion in the literature as to whether job crafting is a predictor or outcome of employee work engagement. Are enthusiastic and vigorous employees more likely to craft their jobs or does crafting one's job demands and resources facilitate work engagement? The preliminary answer is that both scenarios are possible. Bakker (2011) argued that employees who are engaged and perform well are able to create their own job and personal resources, which then foster engagement again over time. Engaged workers are active job crafters who change their job demands and resources if necessary. Consistent with this idea, Schaufeli, Bakker and van Rhenen (2009), in their study among Dutch managers of a telecom company, showed that changes in job resources predicted engagement over a one-year time period, and that engagement was predictive of increases in social support, autonomy, opportunities for development and performance feedback. In a similar vein, in their three-year panel study among 2,555 Finnish dentists, Hakanen, Perhoniemi and Toppinen-Tanner (2008) found that job resources predicted work engagement and were indirectly related to personal initiative. In addition, they found that personal initiative predicted work engagement and was indirectly related to future job resources. These findings are consistent with Bakker's (2011) model of work engagement, and suggest that job crafting and work engagement are reciprocally related.

17.6 Job Crafting as Redesign Tool: Ideas for Interventions

In 2012, van den Heuvel, Demerouti and Peeters developed a training programme to increase the awareness of employees within different layers of the organization regarding the ways in which they can adapt their job to their own needs so that they experience more pleasure, engagement and meaning in their work. The adjustments refer to the specific job demands and job resources, the two categories of job characteristics that are described in the JD–R Model. That process begins with awareness of the current working situation and the freedom that they have to make those adjustments. In this way, it becomes clear to employees what job demands and job resources they need to adjust or create.

The job-crafting training aims to increase participants' motivation and engagement through two different routes: (i) through promoting the self-directed behaviour of employees and (ii) through the strengthening of personal resources. With regard to the increase in self-directed behaviour at work, previous research has shown that it is possible to facilitate this through interventions (e.g. Demerouti, van Eeuwijk, Snelder, & Wild, 2011). The training combines learning about what job crafting is and what happens when employees craft their jobs, executing self-specified job-crafting assignments/actions for a period of several weeks and reflecting on the experiences of these job-crafting actions after they have been completed. In this way, individuals are encouraged to integrate job crafting in their daily work by learning to choose and to execute small job-crafting actions.

This training was tested (with pre and post measures) among 39 employees of a police district. These employees were assigned to three experimental groups, while the control group consisted of 47 employees. Each participant had to identify a colleague with a similar job, who was approached to fill in a questionnaire before and after the training in order to serve as the control group. The training had a positive effect on two job resources, namely contact with the supervisor and opportunities for developmental work. These were higher at Time 2 compared to Time 1, while for the control group no change was found. Next to job resources,

Work Psychology in Action: The job-crafting training

Job-crafting training is an intervention that consists of a number of phases:

1. *Organizing and communicating job crafting.* At this stage, all aspects of the training are organized and communicated in consultation with the organization that will apply the job-crafting training as a motivational intervention. The organization recruits a group of participants who will attend the training. The training starts with a job-crafting workshop that consists of a one-day session for small groups of employees. Through various explanations and exercises during the workshop, employees get to know the concept of job crafting. The workshop concludes with the development of a so-called Personal Crafting Plan (PCP). The PCP consists of specific crafting actions that the participants/employees have to undertake for a period of four weeks.
2. *Getting started with job crafting itself:* In this phase, the employees themselves keep a so-called 'crafting logbook'. This is a weekly logbook in which for a one-month period employees keep detailed reports of their crafting activities of that week as they have been specified in the PCP. Specifically, during the first week of van den Heuvel et al.'s (2012) job-crafting intervention, participants were asked to increase job resources (search for feedback and for social support), while during the second week they were instructed to decrease job demands. In the third week, participants were asked to seek job challenges, while during the fourth week they were again asked to increase three different job resources: autonomy, participation in decision-making and developmental possibilities. Moreover, participants were asked to make time to think about a number of reflection questions every week. Answering these questions each week was expected to increase personal effectiveness and meaning making.
3. *Exchange of experiences:* After the participants themselves had crafted their job for one month, they met again to exchange their experiences on the crafting actions. During this reflection meeting they discussed successes, problems and solutions. In this way, employees could learn from each other's best practices. Moreover, attention was paid to how employees in the future could overcome possible obstacles that hinder their job-crafting attempts.
4. *What is the effect?* In this phase, the effect of the job-crafting training on employee work engagement, motivation and well-being is investigated.

self-efficacy was also found to have increased in the training group but not in the control group. Finally, participants reported more positive emotions and fewer negative emotions after the training, which indicated that the job-crafting training not only influenced the working conditions but also employee well-being. Research has shown that people who often (vs. not) experience positive emotions are more open to new experiences as well as being more creative and cooperative (Avey, Wernsing, & Luthans, 2008).

17.7 Conclusions

In this chapter we suggests that job crafting is a job redesign approach that organizations can use (next to top-down approaches) to improve the jobs of their employees. The chapter began by presenting an overview of (top-down) job redesign approaches that organizations traditionally use. The job redesign literature has gradually recognized that the 'one-size-fits-all' approach to the implementation of improvements at work is no longer sufficient. Approaches that recognize the role of individuals as proactive agents who shape their own jobs and change their own job characteristics (bottom-up) have come to complete the traditional (top-down) job redesign literature. We discussed the phenomenon of job crafting – the physical and cognitive changes individuals make in their task or relational boundaries. We showed that job crafting (e.g. increasing challenging job demands and increasing job resources) can have important ramifications for employee work engagement and performance. Job-crafting interventions can be effectively used to encourage employees to modify their own work environment proactively in order to stay engaged.

Although job crafting is not a panacea for all organization problems, it is important for organizations to recognize its existence and to manage it such that it has beneficial effects on the employees and the organizations. We do not claim that job crafting should replace the (top-down) attempts of organizations to improve the work environment of their employees. However, we do suggest that organizations should allow, stimulate and train their employees to craft their jobs in a way that fits them and the organization better. It is important that organizations recognize that an individual employee is the person who knows his/her job best and who can recognize where there is room for improvement such that the job fits better with the person.

Discussion Points

1. Should job crafting refer only to adjustments of job demands and job resources?
2. How can a supervisor manage the job-crafting behaviours of his/her employees?
3. Why do you think that job crafting can make people more enthusiastic about their jobs?

Learning by Doing

1. Think back about your own study or working experience and try to recall situations in which you crafted your study or job. Try to answer the following questions:
   i. What did you craft?
   ii. When did you craft your study or job?
   iii. What was the result of your study or job crafting?
   iv. How did others react to your crafting actions?
2. Find an individual (e.g. a friend, family member or lecturer) who is performing paid work. Conduct an interview with him/her and try to find some information about his/her past job-crafting behaviour. Explain to the person what job crafting is and ask for specific examples indicating the person's past crafting behaviour. Ask further questions about the result of the crafting and the reactions of others to the crafting.
3. Find an individual with a supervisory role (e.g. lecturer, friend, family member). Have an interview with him/her and try to find some information about how this person deals with the job-crafting behaviours of his/her employees. Try to uncover what kind of employee job-crafting behaviours a supervisor can observe and how the supervisor reacts to such behaviours. Does he/she stimulate the employees or does he/she discourage them?
4. You have to convince the management of an organization that the organization should offer its employees the possibility of attending a job-crafting intervention. Try to come up with arguments that you can use based on the literature. Moreover, try to anticipate possible counter-arguments and questions from the organization.

Further Reading

Bakker, A. B., Tims, M., & Derks, D. (2012). Proactive personality and job performance: The role of job crafting and work engagement. *Human Relations*, 65, 1359–1378.

Berg, J. M., Wrzesniewski, A., & Dutton, J. E. (2010). Perceiving and responding to challenges in job crafting at different ranks: When proactivity requires adaptivity. *Journal of Organizational Behavior*, 31, 158–186.

Grant, A. M., & Parker, S. K. (2009). Redesigning work design theories: The rise of relational and proactive perspectives. *Academy of Management Annals*, 3, 273–331.

Petrou, P., Demerouti, E., Peeters, M. C. W., Schaufeli, W. B., & Hetland, J. (2012). Crafting a job on a daily basis: contextual antecedents and the effect of work engagement. *Journal of Organizational Behavior*, 33, 1120–1141.

Tims, M., & Bakker, A. B. (2010). Job crafting: Towards a new model of individual job redesign. *South African Journal of Industrial Psychology*, 36, 1–9.

References

Ashford, S. J., Blatt, R., & van de Walle, D. (2003). Reflections on the looking glass: A review of research on feedback-seeking behavior in organizations. *Journal of Management, 29*, 769–799.

Avey, J. B., Wernsing, T. S., & Luthans, F. (2008). Can positive employees help positive organization change? Impact of psychological capital and emotions on relevant attitudes and behaviors. *Journal of Applied Behavioral Science, 44*, 48–70.

Bakker, A. B. (2011). An evidence-based model of work engagement. *Current Directions in Psychological Science, 20*, 265–269.

Bakker, A. B., & Demerouti, E. (2007). The job demands–resources model: State of the art. *Journal of Managerial Psychology, 22*, 309–328.

Bakker, A. B., Tims, M., & Derks, D. (2012). Proactive personality and job performance: The role of job crafting and work engagement. *Human Relations, 65*, 1359–1378.

Berg, J. M., Wrzesniewski, A., & Dutton, J. E. (2010). Perceiving and responding to challenges in job crafting at different ranks: When proactivity requires adaptivity. *Journal of Organizational Behavior, 31*, 158–186.

Biron, C., Karanika-Murray, M., & Cooper, C. L. (Eds.) (2012). *Improving organizational interventions for stress and well-being: Addressing process and context*. London: Routledge.

Campion, M. A., & McClelland, C. L. (1993). Follow-up and extension of the interdisciplinary costs and benefits of enlarged jobs. *Journal of Applied Psychology, 78*, 339–351.

Carver, C. S., Scheier, M. F., & Weintraub, J. K. (1989). Assessing coping strategies: A theoretically based approach. *Journal of Personality and Social Psychology, 56*, 267–283.

Chu, A. H. C., & Choi, J. N. (2005). Rethinking procrastination: positive effects of 'active' procrastination behavior on attitudes and performance. *Journal of Social Psychology, 145*, 245–264.

Csikszentmihalyi, M., & Nakamura, J. (1989). The dynamics of intrinsic motivation: A study of adolescents. In C. Ames, & R. Ames (Eds.), *Research on motivation in education* (Vol. 3, pp. 45–71). New York: Academic Press.

Demerouti, E., & Bakker, A. B. (2006). Employee well-being and job performance: Where we stand and where we should go. In S. McIntyre, & J. Houdmont (Eds.), *Occupational health psychology: European perspectives on research, education and practice* (Vol. 1, pp. 83–111). Maia, Portugal: ISMAI Publications.

Demerouti, E., Bakker, A. B., Nachreiner, F., & Schaufeli, W. B. (2001). The job demands–resources model of burnout. *Journal of Applied Psychology, 86*, 499–512.

Demerouti, E., & Cropanzano, R. (2010). From thought to action: Employee work engagement and job performance. In A. B. Bakker, & M. P. Leiter (Eds.), *Work engagement: A handbook of essential theory and research* (pp. 147–163). Hove: Psychology Press.

Demerouti, E., van Eeuwijk, E., Snelder, M., & Wild, U. (2011). Assessing the effects of a 'personal effectiveness' training on psychological capital, assertiveness and self-awareness using self-other agreement. *Career Development International, 16*, 60–81.

Diefendorff, J. M., & Richard, E. M. (2003). Antecedents and consequences of emotional display rule perceptions. *Journal of Applied Psychology, 88*, 284–294.

Frese, M., & Fay, D. (2001). Personal initiative: An active performance concept for work in the 21st century. In B. M. Staw, & R. I. Sutton (Eds.), *Research in organizational behavior* (Vol. 23, pp. 133–187). San Diego: Elsevier Academic Press.

Fried, Y. (1991). Meta-analytic comparison of the job diagnostic survey and job characteristics inventory as correlates of work satisfaction and performance. *Journal of Applied Psychology, 76*, 690–697.

Fried, Y., Grant, A. M., Levi, A. S., Hadani, M., & Slowik, L. H. (2007). Job design in temporal context: A career dynamics perspective. *Journal of Organizational Behavior, 28*, 911–927.

George, J. M., & Jones, G. R. (2000). The role of time in theory and theory building. *Journal of Management, 26*, 657–684.

Gergen, K. J. (1994). *Realities and relationships: Soundings in social constructionism*. Cambridge, MA: Harvard University Press.

Ghitulescu, B. E. (2007). *Shaping tasks and relationships at work: Examining the antecedents and consequences of employee job crafting.* University of Pittsburgh.

Grant, A. M., & Parker, S. K. (2009). Redesigning work design theories: The rise of relational and proactive perspectives. *Academy of Management Annals, 3,* 273–331.

Gruys, M. L. (1999). *The dimensionality of deviant employee performance in the workplace.* Unpublished doctoral dissertation. University of Minnesota.

Hacker, W. (2003). Action regulation theory: A practical tool for the design of modern work. *European Journal of Work and Organizational Psychology, 12,* 105–130.

Hackman, J. R., & Oldham, G. R. (1980). *Work redesign.* Reading, MA: Addison-Wesley.

Hakanen, J. J., Perhoniemi, R., & Toppinen-Tanner, S. (2008). Positive gain spirals at work: From job resources to work engagement, personal initiative and work-unit innovativeness. *Journal of Vocational Behavior, 73,* 78–91.

Hobfoll, S. E. (2001). The influence of culture, community, and the nested-self in the stress process: Advancing conservation of resources theory. *Applied Psychology: An International Review, 50,* 337–370.

Hornung, S., Rousseau, D. M., Glaser, J., Angerer, P., & Weigel, M. (2010). Beyond top-down and bottom-up work redesign: Customizing job content through idiosyncratic deals. *Journal of Organizational Behavior, 31,* 187–215.

Humphrey, S. E., Nahrgang, J. D., & Morgeson, F. P. (2007). Integrating motivational, social, and contextual work design features: A meta-analytic summary and theoretical extension of the work design literature. *Journal of Applied Psychology, 92,* 1332–1356.

Johns, G. (2006). The essential impact of context on organizational behavior. *Academy of Management Review, 31,* 386–408.

Karasek, R. A. (1979). Job demands, job decision latitude, and mental strain: Implications for job redesign. *Administrative Science Quarterly, 24,* 285–306.

Karasek, R. A., & Theorell, T. (1990). *Healthy work: Stress, productivity and the reconstruction of working life.* New York: Basic Books.

Kira, M., Balkin, D. B., & San, E. (2012). Authentic work and organizational change: Longitudinal evidence from a merger. *Journal of Change Management, 12,* 31–51.

Kira, M., van Eijnatten, F. M., & Balkin, D. B. (2010). Crafting sustainable work: Development of personal resources. *Journal of Organizational Change Management, 27,* 713–721.

Leana, C., Appelbaum, E., & Shevchuk, I. (2009). Work process and quality of care in early childhood education: The role of job crafting. *Academy of Management Journal, 52,* 1169–1192.

Lyons, P. (2008). The crafting of jobs and individual differences. *Journal of Business Psychology, 23,* 25–36.

Morgeson, F. P., & Humphrey, S. E. (2006). The Work Design Questionnaire (WDQ): Developing and validating a comprehensive measure for assessing job design and the nature of work. *Journal of Applied Psychology, 91,* 1321–1339.

Morgeson, F. P., & Humphrey, S. E. (2008). Job and team design: Toward a more integrative conceptualization of work design. In J. Martocchio (Ed.), *Research in personnel and human resource management* (Vol. 27, pp. 39–92). Bingley, UK: Emerald Group.

Nadin, S. J., Waterson, P. E., & Parker, S. K. (2001). Participation in job redesign: An evaluation of the use of a sociotechnical tool and its impact. *Human Factors and Ergonomics in Manufacturing, 11,* 53–69.

Oldham, G. R., & Hackman, J. R. (2010). Not what it was and not what it will be: The future of job design research. *Journal of Organizational Behavior, 31,* 463–479.

Parker, S. K., & Collins, C. G. (2010). Taking stock: Integrating and differentiating multiple proactive behaviors. *Journal of Management, 36,* 633–662.

Parker, J. D., & Endler, N. S., (1996). Coping and defense: A historical overview. In M. Zeidner, & N. S. Endler (Eds.), *Handbook of coping: Theory, research, applications* (pp. 3–23). New York: John Wiley & Sons.

Parker, S. K., & Ohly, S. (2008). Designing motivating jobs: An expanded framework for linking work characteristics and motivation. In R. Kanfer, G. Chen, & R. D. Pritchard (Eds.), *Work motivation: Past, present and future* (pp. 233–284). New York: LEA/Psychology Press.

Parker, S. K., Wall, T. D., & Cordery, J. (2001). Future work design research and practice: Towards an elaborated model of work design. *Journal of Occupational and Organizational Psychology, 74,* 413–440.

Petrou, P., Demerouti, E., Peeters, M. C. W., Schaufeli, W. B., & Hetland, J. (2012). Crafting a job on a daily basis: contextual antecedents and the effect of work engagement. *Journal of Organizational Behavior, 33*, 1120–1141.

Petrou, P., Demerouti, E., & Schaufeli, W. B. (2013). Crafting the change: The role of employee job crafting behaviors for successful organizational change. Manuscript submitted for publication.

Schaufeli, W. B., Bakker, A. B., & van Rhenen, W. (2009). How changes in job demands and resources predict burnout, work engagement, and sickness absenteeism. *Journal of Organizational Behavior, 30*, 893–917.

ten Brummelhuis, L. L., Bakker, A. B., Hetland, J., & Keulemans, L. (2012). Do new ways of working foster work engagement? *Psicothema, 24*, 113–120.

Tims, M., & Bakker, A. B. (2010). Job crafting: Towards a new model of individual job redesign. *South African Journal of Industrial Psychology, 36*, 1–9.

Tims, M., Bakker, A. B., & Derks, D. (2012). Development and validation of the job crafting scale. *Journal of Vocational Behavior, 80*, 173–186.

Trist, E. L. (1981). The sociotechnical perspective. In A. H. van de Ven, & W. F. Joyce (Eds.), *Perspectives on organization design and behavior* (pp. 19–75). New York: John Wiley & Sons.

van den Heuvel, M., Demerouti, E., & Peeters, M. (2012). Succesvol job craften door middel van een groepstraining [*Succesful job crafting through group training*]. In J. de Jonge, M. Peeters, S. Sjollema, & H. de Zeeuw (Eds.), *Scherp in werk: 5 routes naar optimale inzetbaarheid* (pp. 27–49). Assen: Koninklijke van Gorcum BV.

Wrzesniewski, A., & Dutton, J. E. (2001). Crafting a job: Revisioning employees as active crafters of their work. *Academy of Management Review, 26*, 179–201.

18

Teams at Work

Amanda L. Thayer, Ramón Rico, Eduardo Salas
and Shannon L. Marlow

Chapter Objectives

After studying this chapter, you should be able to:

- understand the historical context of major team development and effectiveness models and teamwork competencies;
- define what a team is and describe the features of teams and team interventions;
- understand the key processes teams engage in and how they impact performance;
- describe the research evidence that supports the effectiveness of team training interventions;
- understand how models of teamwork and team effectiveness translate into practice in organizations;
- understand the limitations of models of team development and effectiveness, including how modern issues impact teamwork.

18.1 Teams at Work

While taking off from LaGuardia Airport in New York in 2009, the crew of Flight 1549 faced a rare but nevertheless life-threatening and disastrous situation when a flock of birds destroyed the airplane's engines (National Transportation Safety

An Introduction to Contemporary Work Psychology, First Edition.
Edited by Maria C. W. Peeters, Jan de Jonge and Toon W. Taris.
© 2014 John Wiley & Sons, Ltd. Published 2014 by John Wiley & Sons, Ltd.

Figure 18.1 US Airways Flight 1549 passengers wait for rescue assistance, having landed safely on the Hudson River in New York on January 15, 2009, after a flock of birds disabled both engines of the aircraft (Janis Krums, Rawporter).

Board, 2009). Although the odds were against a safe landing, Captain Sullenberger and his crew were able to strategically navigate the situation, safely landing the plane on the Hudson River and evacuating all 155 passengers (Figure 18.1). According to a subsequent National Transportation Safety Board report, the successful outcome was due to the crew's coordination in effectively responding to the emergency situation.

This incident serves as a prime example of effective teamwork. Team errors large and small result from teamwork failures across a wide variety of team contexts, including business, military units, research collaborations, medical institutions and more. These errors are typically not the fault of any one individual, but rather a failure to communicate and coordinate activities among team members. It is important that we consider why we use teams, the ways in which teamwork differs from individual task execution and how teamwork can be improved through training with considerations of modern issues faced by today's teams.

Historically, research on teams has ebbed and flowed according to changes within organizations and the environment in which they operate. However, team research has increased over the last 30 years and is anticipated to continue for the foreseeable future (Salas, Priest, Stagl, Sims, & Burke, 2007). Organizations are increasing their use of team-based structures to accomplish complex organizational objectives. This means abandoning traditional hierarchical structures and giving teams decision-making authority over day-to-day operations, rather than going through the formal chain of power. Furthermore, environmental factors such as technological advances, changing consumer needs, economic crises and political issues are changing the settings within which teams operate.

Team-based structures allow organizations to capitalize on the interaction of the diverse backgrounds and expertise of multiple individuals. Complex organizational objectives and problems often cannot be solved by one individual, and often require functionally diverse backgrounds among members. For instance, many of today's medical research questions require collaboration of scientists across varying disciplines (e.g. chemist, engineer, biologist), each of which fills a specified role within the team. This means they each contribute information about their area of expertise in order to accomplish goals that any one of the members could not accomplish alone. Each member brings a piece of the puzzle to the table. The field of biotechnology (a field of applied biology that synthesizes engineering, technology and medicine) is an example of how interdisciplinary teams of biologists, engineers, doctors and other professionals are able to achieve extraordinary outcomes through collaboration.

By adopting team-based structures to achieve goals, organizations are also shifting power within the organization. Traditionally, organizations have operated with a formal status or power hierarchy, where employees typically work alone under the direction of a manager (e.g. branch manager) who reports to a more senior manager (e.g. regional manager) all the way up to the chief executive officer of the organization. However, today's organizations are moving toward using empowered and self-managed teams. This fundamental change is altering team dynamics and has both theoretical and practical implications for ensuring team success, which we discuss in this chapter.

Finally, the settings in which teams operate are also changing. Globalization, technological advances and a shift towards a knowledge-based (rather than industrial) economy are having a profound impact on how teams function. Teams today are operating across geographic boundaries, utilizing the latest technologies to facilitate coordination and communication. To address problems such as the scientific endeavours mentioned previously, team members may be recruited from across the globe, promoting the use of virtual technologies to coordinate and communicate. This adjustment in how teams operate has both logistical and interpersonal implications, both in theory and practice. For instance, coordination in a multinational team may be a challenge given time zone differences and lack of face-to-face interaction, which has been cited as a major factor in reduction of mutual trust (Rico, Bachrach, Sánchez-Manzanares, & Collins, 2011; Tannenbaum, Mathieu, Salas, & Cohen, 2012).

In considering how and why teams have been utilized in the past, present and future, we now turn to defining teams and clarifying team task types and characteristics. We will then discuss teamwork and how team interventions can improve semi-autonomous team effectiveness. We conclude by considering the modern challenges faced by teams, including what we know about these challenges and what is still to be investigated.

Replay

Organizations are increasingly relying on teams to solve complex problems, often across multiple disciplines. In doing so, they are moving away from traditional hierarchies and toward team-based organizational structures. However, the nature of teamwork is also changing due to globalization, technological advances and the increasing complexity in the type of work being done by teams.

> **Work Psychology in Action: The context of teams in the workplace–the Hawthorne studies**
>
> Until the 1920s, organizations had failed to recognize the importance of social interactions on employee motivation and productivity. Between 1924 and 1932, Western Electric Company conducted a series of studies at its Hawthorne Works in Chicago, Illinois, United States, in order to examine the impact of physical working conditions (e.g. lighting and rest breaks), on employee productivity. In addition to evaluating the effect of changing working conditions, the researchers also conducted interviews about the working conditions, management and other aspects of their working environment. One notable study, the 'bank wiring observation room', focused on employee incentives. Researchers anticipated that employees would be more productive when they saw that their productivity was tied to rewards. However, individuals did not uniformly maximize their productivity, but rather seemed to conform to a group norm of what was an acceptable amount of work in order to protect the group from adverse effects such as layoffs.
>
> In these studies, Western Electric Company had planned to investigate the impact of changes in the physical working conditions within their factories on employee productivity. However, it became evident to the researchers that social interactions also seemed to play a role in how employees felt, thought, behaved and performed. Although the Hawthorne studies have been criticized heavily (e.g. Kompier, 2006), it cannot be denied that these studies set the stage for future research on work groups and work teams, including development of informal groups, formal and informal structures, group dynamics and the influence of norms.

18.2 Teams, Task Types and Team Characteristics

Much of the literature has treated work groups and teams as if they were the same, but they are not. *Work groups* are defined as a social entity, nested within a larger social and technical system, consisting of members who may work interdependently to complete shared tasks and whose outcomes affect others in the larger system as well as each other (Guzzo & Dickson, 1996). Although these definitional components are also descriptive of teams, teams are a more complex sociotechnical system than groups. *Teams* are defined as complex entities characterized by two or more individuals who interact socially, dynamically, recursively and adaptively. These individuals have shared goals, have held meaningful and high levels of tasks, have provided feedback and have goal interdependencies. Teams are often hierarchically structured with a limited life span; they have their expertise and roles distributed, and members are embedded within an organizational context that influences and is influenced by enacted teamwork behaviours, attitudes, performance outcomes and stakeholder judgments of team effectiveness (Salas,

Table 18.1 Integrated set of task types (Wildman et al., 2012a).

Task type	Description
Managing others	Directing, supervising or overseeing the work of others in an authoritative role
Advising others	Providing professional support, such as expert assistance or advice, in a consultative role where the advisor lacks authority over those whom he or she is advising
Human services	Social interaction where an individual or team is providing a good or service to another party
Negotiation	Social interaction in which two or more parties in conflict seek to resolve differences and reach agreement
Psychomotor action	Technical and/or motor functioning requiring psychological processing to perform calculated or elaborate movements, including the manipulation, operation or use of an already assembled product, machine or object, or a task that is achieved by engaging in psychomotor action of some sort
Defined problem solving	Problem-solving tasks with pre-determined or conclusive solutions or correct answers
Ill-defined problem solving	Problem-solving tasks lacking pre-determined or conclusive solutions or correct answers, such as idea, plan or knowledge generation

Stagl, Burke, & Goodwin, 2007). Thus, teams are a type of group whereby the nature of the task requires that members work together adaptively toward a common goal within specified roles and using agreed on processes.

However, all teams are not created equal. The degree to which certain factors impact performance depends on a variety of team characteristics (Horwitz, 2005). Researchers in the 1950s began distinguishing task type as an important characteristic of teams. In an attempt to synthesize the literature on task types and underlying team characteristics in a more simple yet comprehensive way, Wildman et al. (2012a) specified seven kinds of tasks teams engage in, noting that teams can work on more than one type of task (Table 18.1). These task types include *managing others* (i.e. directing, supervising or overseeing the work of others in an authoritative role), *advising others* (i.e. providing professional support, such as expert assistance or advice, in a consultative role where the advisor lacks authority over those whom he or she is advising), *human services* (i.e. social interaction where an individual or team is providing a good or service to another party), *negotiation* (i.e. social interaction in which two or more parties in conflict seek to resolve differences and reach agreement), *psychomotor action* (i.e. technical and/or motor functioning requiring psychological processing to perform calculated or elaborate movements, including the manipulation, operation or use of an already assembled product, machine or object, or a task that is achieved by engaging in psychomotor action of some sort), *defined problem solving* (i.e. problem-solving

Table 18.2 Integrated set of team-level characteristics (Wildman et al., 2012a).

Characteristic	Description	Discrete categories
Task interdependence	The extent to which outcomes of the team members are influenced by, or depend on, the actions of others	Pooled, sequential, reciprocal, team
Role structure	The extent to which roles are fundamentally different and therefore not interchangeable or each person is capable of performing every component	Functional, divisional
Leadership structure	The pattern, or distribution, of leadership functions such as setting direction and aligning goals among the members of the team	External manager, designated, temporary, distributed
Communication structure	The pattern, or flow, of communication and information sharing among the members of the team	Hub-and-wheel, star, chain
Physical distribution	The spatial location of the team members in reference to one another	Co-located, distributed
Team lifespan	The length of time for which the team exists as a functional, active unit	Ad hoc, long term

tasks with pre-determined or conclusive solutions or correct answers) and *ill-defined problem solving* (i.e. problem-solving tasks lacking pre-determined or conclusive solutions or correct answers, such as idea, plan or knowledge generation). These task types generalize across a variety of contexts, including military, government and civilian settings, and can be used to help inform organizations of the task-based training needs of the team. However, this tool describes *tasks* that individuals or teams can engage in and does little to describe the *team* itself.

Wildman and colleagues therefore also proposed six characteristics by which teams can be classified, which describe teams (not tasks or individuals) and allows for categorization of teams into discrete categories at any single snapshot in time (Table 18.2). *Task interdependence* is the extent to which outcomes of the team members are influenced by, or depend on, the actions of others. These interconnections among group members vary such that members can work independently (i.e. pooled interdependence), work on the task in a predetermined sequence much like an assembly line (i.e. sequential), work in pairs (i.e. reciprocal) or work together as a team to diagnose, problem-solve and collaborate on the task (i.e. team). The level of interdependence is critical to the definition of teams because it determines the degree to which members of a group must engage in teamwork. *Role structure* is the extent to which roles are fundamentally different and therefore not interchangeable. Role structure can be either functional or divisional. If members' roles are different and cannot be performed by the other members, the role structure is functional (i.e. each person has a specific function); if members can all perform each component of the task and the members are interchangeable, the role structure is divisional (i.e. the work can be divided among the members). *Leadership structure* refers to the pattern, or distribution, of leadership functions, such as setting direction and aligning goals, among the members of the team. Leadership can either be temporary (i.e. shared such that the leadership role rotates across time or tasks), distributed (i.e. shared such that leadership functions are divided among different members of the team so that there may be multiple leaders at any given time), designated (i.e. one member performs virtually all leadership functions) or led by an external manager (i.e. someone outside the team performs the leadership functions). *Communication structure* is the pattern, or flow, of communication and information shared among the members of the team. This flow of communication can be hub-and-wheel (i.e. communication passes through one central member, the hub, who disseminates the information), chain (i.e. information is passed up and down the line via some hierarchical structure such as rank or leadership position) or star (i.e. information is passed freely among members). *Physical distribution* references the spatial location of the team members in reference to one another such that members may be co-located (i.e. located in the same place) or distributed (i.e. located in different locations). Finally, *team lifespan* is the length of time for which the team exists as a functional, active unit. Teams can be either ad hoc (i.e. short term) or long term.

These team characteristics can be largely based on the type of task the team is engaged in. For instance, assembly of a product (a psychomotor action task) might not require that all members work together at the same time but rather that each person passes the product to the next (sequential interdependence). Thus, it is more effective for communication to flow through the chain as the product moves on to the next team member. Furthermore, this type of task would be best accomplished if all members were co-located. However, a new product development team (ill-defined problem solving) must engage in high levels of interdependent brainstorming, therefore communication should be open among all members (star), although members can be either co-located or distributed because they can use video conferencing to connect. Task types should be used to inform the team of its structure. Considering task type and team characteristics together helps to paint the picture of how teams interact to accomplish tasks and can help organizations better understand how to set the conditions for teams to be effective.

Replay

Not all teams are the same. They can differ by the type of task(s) they engage in as well as the characteristics of the team. Task type is useful for understanding what is required of individual members, which can be used to inform task-based training. Team characteristics are useful for describing the characteristics of the team, which allows for better understanding of how teams interact in order to accomplish work.

18.3 Teamwork and Team Competencies

Effective team performance depends on two primary sets of competencies: taskwork and teamwork. *Taskwork* describes the functions members perform in order to accomplish the team's task, whereas *teamwork* describes the interactions among members of the team (McIntyre & Salas, 1995). *Taskwork competencies* are the task-relevant knowledge, skills and abilities (KSAs) necessary for successful task completion, whereas *teamwork competencies* are those competencies that are necessary for members to work together effectively (Glickman et al., 1987). For instance, imagine a surgical team that is about to perform open heart surgery on a patient. This team consists of the surgeons, surgical nurses and an anaesthesiologist. Each member must have taskwork competencies to perform his/her role requirements: the surgical nurses must have the knowledge, skills and abilities to prepare the operating room and assist the surgeons, the anaesthesiologist must be able to safely put the patient under anaesthesia so the patient is not conscious during the surgery, and the surgeons must know where and how to make the incisions and perform the surgery. However, these team members must also be competent in teamwork: they need to interact in a way that helps each of them perform their individual duties and achieve the overall goal of keeping the patient safe and healthy.

Many taxonomies of teamwork and their competencies have been developed over the last two decades. Most notably, Marks, Mathieu and Zaccaro (2001) forwarded a framework of teamwork which argues that teams undergo performance cycles marked by recurring phases of transition and action. During *transition* phases, teams focus on strategizing or evaluating team actions toward goal accomplishment. *Action* phases are periods of time when teams are engaged in taskwork and working towards goal accomplishment.

Marks and colleagues also clarified the difference between *processes*, which reflect interactions among members toward accomplishment of task goals (i.e. what teams do), and *emergent states*, which represent what teams feel, believe and think. Some processes are more likely to occur during transition phases, during action phases or throughout both in order to maintain interpersonal relations. Specifically, teams engage in mission analysis and planning, specification of mission goals and strategy formulation during transition phases – this is the planning and evaluation phase. During action phases, members monitor progress toward goals, resources, environmental conditions and team members, provide assistance to team members as needed, and coordinate the timing and sequence of actions. Throughout transition and action phases, members also engage in interpersonal processes of managing conflict, building motivation and confidence, and managing affect (emotion). Imagine a military unit engaging in combat. Before they enter the battlefield, the members will first strategize about what they will do once they engage in combat (transition). They will then enact their plan by carrying out the decisions they made during the transition phase (action). Afterward, they might return to home base and discuss how they performed and what they need to do next (transition). Throughout all of these phases, the team is managing the interpersonal relationships among members, including maintaining motivation and managing conflict within the team.

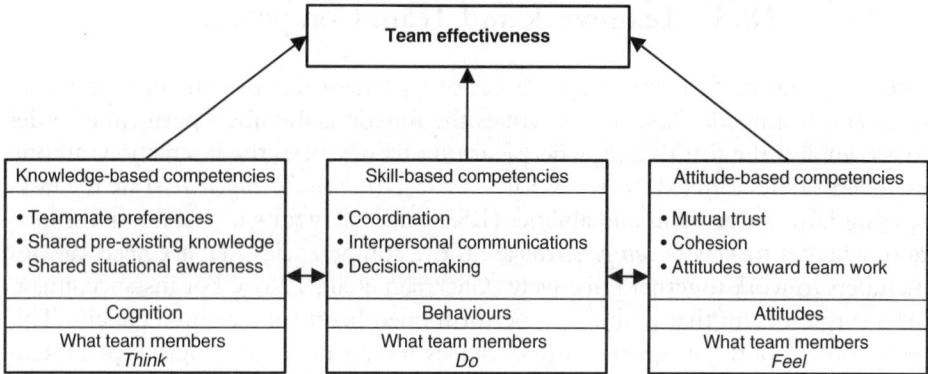

Figure 18.2 Competencies that impact team effectiveness (Cannon-Bowers & Salas, 2006).

Focusing on the teamwork competencies beyond these team processes, Cannon-Bowers and Salas (2006) specified three primary teamwork competencies necessary for team effectiveness (Figure 18.2): (i) knowledge-based, (ii) skill-based and (iii) attitude-based. Knowledge-based competencies include the cognition that members hold about their teammates, the task and the environment – these represent what teams *think*. Skill-based competencies are the behaviours that team members must be able to engage in, including coordination, communication and decision making as a team – these represent what teams *do*. Finally, attitude-based competencies represent what the team *feels*, including trust, cohesion and attitudes toward teamwork. Together, these are known as the ABCs of teamwork – attitudes, behaviours and cognitions that are important to teamwork and team effectiveness.

Replay

Team effectiveness depends on both taskwork (working on the task) and teamwork (interacting effectively with teammates). Teamwork processes revolve around planning (transition), task execution (action) and interpersonal processes. Teamwork competencies reflect what teams feel (attitudes), do (behaviours) and think (cognition): the ABCs of teamwork. Finally, some KSAs may be more important than others for team effectiveness, such as the big five of teamwork.

18.4 Models of Team Development and Team Effectiveness

Scholars and organizations have long been interested in (i) how teams develop and function, and (ii) the factors that make teams more or less effective in accomplishing their goals. We now describe some of the models of team development and team effectiveness that have been the most influential or the most encompassing of the existing research to date.

Team development

Research on the development and evolution of teams began in the mid-1960s and became a topic of focus in the 1980s and 1990s (Salas, Priest et al., 2007). Team development represents the path a team takes over its lifespan toward the accomplishment of its main tasks (Gersick, 1988). Tuckman's (1965, 1977) seminal Five Stage Model of Team Development delineated how teams develop over time and transition from one stage to the next. Specifically, this theory proposed that teams go through five distinct stages: (i) forming, (ii) storming, (iii) norming, (iv) performing and (v) adjourning. First, in the *forming* stage, members orient themselves to the team and determine how the team should function (e.g. roles, coordination patterns). The second stage, *storming*, is characterized by conflict and polarization around interpersonal issues. Here, members are resisting group influence to compete for acceptance of their own ideas for how the team operates. Third, the team goes through a *norming* process. Having come to consensus on how the team operates, members enact new roles and standards, and the team becomes more cohesive. In the fourth stage, the team is *performing*; issues of operational structure have been resolved and the team can focus on performance of the task. The fifth and final stage (which was added at a later date) is *adjourning*, in which the team completes the task and is terminated. Although this model is helpful in understanding the broad stages of development, it has received some criticism because teams often do not follow the process in the proposed order and different stages appear combined at a single moment in time.

In response, Gersick (1988) drew from the natural history literature, specifically Eldredge and Gould's (1972) 'punctuated equilibrium' paradigm, to develop the Punctuated Equilibrium Model of Team Development. After observing teams across a variety of contexts, Gersick noticed that several of the teams did not progress through stages suggested by Tuckman's model. Thus, Gersick proposed that teams alternate through long periods of regular work patterns and sudden periods of change, in which members adjust their approach in order to address shortcomings. These sudden periods of change are triggered by time and deadlines instead of an absolute amount of work. Gersick found that what was established in the teams' first meeting had lasting effects on the approach that the team would take for the first half of its lifespan, until its transition period.

Morgan, Salas and Glickman (1993) integrated and built on Tuckman and Gersick's models in developing the Team Evolution and Maturation (TEAM) Model. According to this model, teams begin with a *pre-forming* phase which accounts for the external forces that caused the team to form. For instance, the organization might decide that they need to pull together a task force to solve a problem. The team then goes through a *forming* phase, which consists of an initial meeting that sets the stage for the team. This is followed by *storming*, *norming* and an initial *performing-I* phase. After the initial performance phase, teams *transition* as needed and proceed to a second *performing-II* phase and *conforming*. Finally, after completion of the task, the team goes through *de-forming* and disbands.

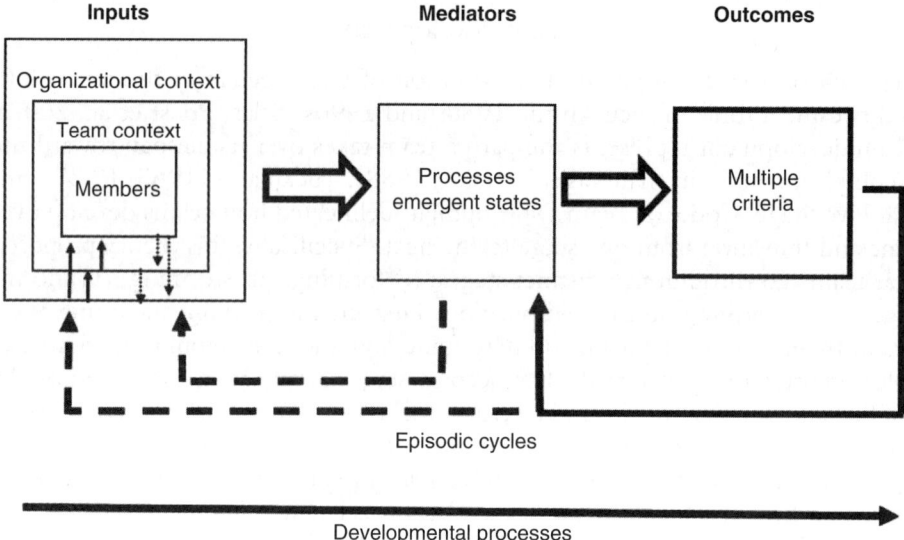

Figure 18.3 Team effectiveness framework (Mathieu et al., 2008).

Team effectiveness

Organizations ultimately utilize teams because they are typically more effective in completing highly complex tasks. However, there are many factors that can determine the effectiveness of teams, and researchers have spent a considerable amount of time learning how to make teams more effective. The majority of team effectiveness models focus on what causes team effectiveness. In a recent review of the team effectiveness literature, Mathieu, Maynard, Rapp and Gilson (2008; Figure 18.3) summarized the multitude of team effectiveness and synthesized them into a single, simple model. Specifically, *inputs* include the factors that enable or constrain member interactions, such as (i) characteristics of the members, (ii) team-level factors like task and team characteristics and (iii) organizational factors outside of the team, such as organizational degree of support. These inputs have an effect on the mediators (i.e. processes and emergent states) that occur within teams. As a reminder, processes are the things teams do as they engage in tasks (e.g. communicate, coordinate activities, monitor work load of other members) and emergent states represent how teams think and feel as a result of interacting with other members. In following the causal chain, *outcomes* are the results and the by-products of team activities, and can include multiple team criteria of effectiveness, such as team performance and satisfaction. Furthermore, this integrated model also accounts for the episodic cycles (transition, action) and developmental processes (stages of development) that occur in teams.

Replay

Team theories tend to focus on either team development or team effectiveness. Team development theories focus on how teams develop, mature and evolve over time. Team effectiveness theories focus on the causal nature of the factors that make teams more or less effective, including the characteristics of the individual, team and organization. Team effectiveness models generally focus on how relatively stable characteristics (antecedent factors) affect team attitudes, behaviours and cognitions (emergent states and processes), and eventually impact team effectiveness. In looking at these models together, organizations can better understand how to improve team effectiveness across time.

18.5 Team Cognition

The cognitive component of team competencies has received a great deal of attention over the last two decades. Team cognition is defined as the emergent cognitive activity taking place at the team level, based on the interaction of its members (Cooke, Goorman, & Winner, 2007). Although there are innumerable team cognition constructs discussed within the teams literature, we focus here on the two most commonly studied: team mental models (TMMs) and transactive memory systems (TMSs).

Extensive work has been done in examining TMMs. According to Cannon-Bowers and Salas (1990), team-level knowledge structures are organized around the team's *equipment* (knowledge about tools and technology), *tasks* (understanding of work procedures, strategies and contingency plans), *team interactions* (awareness of member responsibilities, role interdependencies and communication patterns) and *team members* (understanding teammate preferences, skills and habits). Thus, TMMs are defined as organized mental representations of the key elements within a team's environment that are shared across team members (Klimoski & Mohammed, 1994). There is extensive evidence that TMMs (i.e. teamwork and taskwork mental models) allow members to anticipate others' actions and coordinate more effectively (see Mohammed, Ferzandi, & Hamilton, 2010, for a summary of TMMs research). TMMs are emergent states that derive from the cognition of individuals but manifest as collective phenomena (Kozlowski & Klein, 2000).

Although TMMs have received the most attention within the teams literature, other team cognition constructs have also been studied. For instance, TMSs, or 'the team division of cognitive labor with respect to encoding, storage, retrieval, and communication of information' (Brandon & Hollingshead, 2004, p. 633), have also received attention (see Peltokorpi, 2008, for a review). TMSs represent the division of expertise and a shared awareness of who knows what within the group (Wegner, Giuliano, & Hertel, 1985). TMSs serve to allow for greater cognitive capacity and information processing. Consider biotechnology teams as an example of how a transactive system might help improve effectiveness. Biotechnology teams consist of members with expertise in diverse fields. As one can imagine, it would be nearly impossible for even the most intelligent of humans to be an expert in biology, engineering and medicine. However, if a team comprises individuals each having expertise in one of these areas, the team will be better able to accomplish its goals as long as members are aware of who knows what (i.e. the TMS). TMSs are therefore especially useful in promoting innovation within organizations. It has long been argued that diversity can be beneficial in creative or innovative tasks because it brings together a diverse set of perspectives and

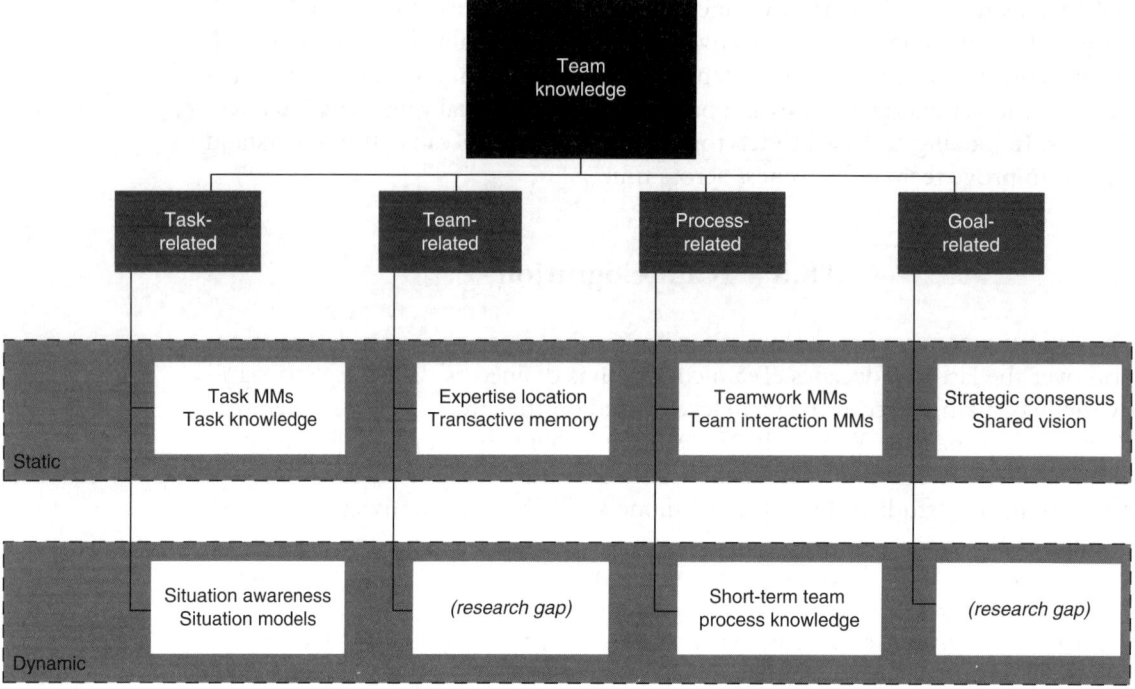

Figure 18.4 Organizing framework of team knowledge (Wildman et al., 2012b).

backgrounds. TMSs are therefore a tool through which teams can structure their knowledge of the functional diversity (i.e. expertise, roles) within the team.

Although these two constructs seem at odds with one another in that TMMs represent *overlap* of information about the task and team whereas TMSs represent *division* of information, several scholars have called for an examination of the overlap between these constructs (Peltokorpi, 2008). In fact, Wildman et al. (2012b) proposed a unified framework of team knowledge that synthesizes team knowledge constructs into a simplified heuristic (Figure 18.4). They argue that there are four primary types of team knowledge, including *task-related* (e.g. task mental models, situation awareness), *team-related* (e.g. transactive memory), *process related* (e.g. teamwork mental models, short-term process knowledge) and *goal-related* (e.g. strategic consensus). Furthermore, team knowledge structures can consist of *static* knowledge (i.e. relatively unchanging over time) or *dynamic* knowledge (i.e. moment-to-moment changes). This framework provides a method of synthesizing the multitude of team cognition constructs into manageable categories.

Replay

Team mental models (TMMs) are shared knowledge structures held by the team that serve to organize information regarding the team's equipment, task, interactions and teammates. Transactive memory systems (TMSs) represent a division of cognitive labour and a shared awareness of team member expertise, and are especially useful in diverse teams. Team cognition, or knowledge, has traditionally been studied as separate constructs but recent calls have resulted in initial attempts to synthesize and organize team knowledge constructs.

18.6 Team Development Interventions

Research on team interventions increased dramatically from the 1980s, focusing initially on team building and team training as methods of improving team effectiveness. Psychology and business began promoting both interventions as viable options for improving teamwork. However, until recently it has been relatively unclear as to exactly how effective these two interventions are for improving team processes and effectiveness. We now discuss the differences between team building and team training, and the effectiveness of each.

Team building

Team building is a class of formal and informal team-level interventions that focus on improving social relations and clarifying roles, as well as solving task and interpersonal problems that affect team functioning (Klein et al., 2009). Team building is a general intervention focused on interpersonal issues, goal setting and role clarification. For example, these exercises might include 'get to know you' exercises. Team building does not target specific skills or competencies and is often not systematic in nature. Although practitioners and managers within organizations often utilize team-building exercises to develop teams, research has been inconclusive as to the merit of these interventions, largely due to lack of consensus on what constitutes team building. However, team building is now assumed to have four primary components: (i) *goal setting* (i.e. setting objectives and developing individual and team goals; see Chapter 14), (ii) *interpersonal relations* (i.e. teamwork skills such as mutual supportiveness, communication and sharing of feelings), (iii) *role clarification* (i.e. communication regarding assigned roles within the team) and (iv) *problem solving* (i.e. identifying major task-related problems). A recent meta-analysis (see Chapter 2) found that team-building interventions were most effective in improving team processes and affective outcomes (emotions and attitudes). Furthermore, although all components of team building are effective in improving these outcomes, goal setting and role clarification have the most impact. When done properly through the use of science as a foundation, team building can have a positive influence on team processes and affective outcomes.

Team training

In contrast, team training has received wide empirical support with regard to its effectiveness in improving team outcomes. *Team training* is a set of strategies or instruction based on the science and practice of designing and delivering instruction that facilitates understanding and enactment of team competencies. It is used both to

Table 18.3 Team training interventions (Shuffler, DiazGranados, & Salas, 2011).

Training strategy	Purpose	Targeted knowledge, skills, and attitudes
Cross-training	Teaches each team member the duties and responsibilities of his/her teammates	Shared knowledge of tasks and responsibilities Mutual performance monitoring Back-up behaviours
Team self-correction training	Develops team's ability to diagnose teamwork breakdowns/issues within the team and reach effective solutions internally on a continual basis	Mutual performance monitoring Effective communication Leadership
Team coordination training	Targets the improvement of a team's shared mental-model framework or facilitates a common understanding of issues related to achieving team goals	Back-up behaviours Mutual performance monitoring Understanding of teamwork skills
Crew resource management	Provides instructional strategies designed to improve teamwork by applying well-tested training tools (e.g. simulators, role playing) targeted at a specific content	Communication Briefing Back-up behaviours Decision making Team adaptability Shared situation awareness

address real-time team breakdowns and to prepare teams prior to performing. Overall, the purpose of team training is to (i) understand the KSAs necessary for performance, (ii) practice using KSAs in a simulated environment that allows for transfer of the learned skill from the training environment to the performance environment and (iii) provide feedback to teams regarding their use of KSAs in practice.

There are many types of team training, including cross-training, team self-correction training, team-coordination training and crew resource management (CRM) training (Table 18.3), among others. *Cross-training* is a training technique in which each team member is taught about the duties and responsibilities of his/her teammates. Cross-training is intended to teach all members what each other member does, and allows members to share role responsibilities or take over for another member as needed. This particular type of training is useful in increasing shared knowledge of tasks and responsibilities, mutual performance monitoring and back-up behaviours (Volpe, Cannon-Bowers, Salas, & Spector, 1996). *Team self-correction training* is another type of team training that is designed to develop the team's ability to diagnose its own teamwork breakdowns, find solutions and correct behaviours internally. This type of training is particularly effective in improving communication, mutual performance monitoring and leadership (Smith-Jentsch, Cannon-Bowers, Tannenbaum, & Salas, 2008). *Team coordination training* targets accuracy and sharing of TMMs within the team, thus facilitating common understanding of team problems. Team coordination training is particularly useful in developing back-up behaviours, mutual performance monitoring and understanding of teamwork skills (Entin & Serfaty, 1999). Finally, CRM training provides strategies for improving teamwork by applying training tools such as simulators and role playing. CRM is one of the most widely cited training techniques and has been applied in a variety of contexts, namely aviation. CRM was designed to improve team communication, briefing, back-up behaviours, decision making, adaptability, pro-active error management and shared situation awareness (Salas, Burke, Bowers, & Wilson, 2001). Overall, team training has been found to be effective in improving teamwork in terms of cognition, affect, process and performance, although this depends on the training content, stability of team membership and team size (Salas et al., 2008). For a review of training, see Goldstein (1991).

Replay

Team building and team training are useful tools in developing teams as long as they are scientifically grounded. However, each type of team development intervention has its own place. Team building is useful in helping the team interact better among each other (i.e. process) and for affective outcomes such as team cohesion and mutual trust. On the other hand, team training is useful in developing specific taskwork and teamwork KSAs in order to improve team performance and cognitive outcomes.

18.7 Current Team Concerns

Today's teams are qualitatively different from the teams of yesterday due to the workplace becoming more globalized, organizations empowering teams and allowing for more autonomy, and technology opening up new avenues for collaboration. Thus, a variety of new concerns have become of increasing importance to organizations that utilize teams to solve problems. For instance, technological advances continue to facilitate a different version of teamwork than in the past, allowing for multicultural collaborations across geographic boundaries, a trend that is expected to continue over time. Thus, individual and cultural differences become a focal issue in considering teamwork practices. Additionally, as teams become the norm in many organizations, organizations must consider selection of individuals who are more apt to work well within team settings, and furthermore consider the compilation of the team beyond individuals.

Virtuality

Researchers and organizations began to realize the impending impact of technology and virtual communication on teamwork in the early 1990s. Since then, technological advances have allowed for collaboration that goes far beyond traditional teamwork practices. Traditionally, teams have been co-located, allowing for face-to-face interactions among members. However, technology has expanded means of communication from simple face-to-face communication to email, chat and video conferencing. Generally, these advances are regarded as beneficial to organizations because they allow for flexibility in composing teams who may be geographically distributed or conduct work at different times. However, it is unclear how virtual teams compare to traditional teams on many important factors. Research is beginning to evaluate the extent to which teams are able to develop cognitive knowledge structures without access to the traditional interpersonal cues afforded with face-to-face interaction. Furthermore, research is beginning to examine the affective component of teamwork in this context, given the development of trust, cohesion and collective efficacy may be largely contingent on the interactions among members (Rico et al., 2011).

Individual and cultural differences

In a similar vein, globalization and technological advances have expanded the capabilities of organizations to compose diverse teams from across the globe to accomplish advanced complex problems. Because of this, individual and cultural differences have become a focal issue in discussing teams. In particular, individualism–collectivism and collective orientation have received particular attention because they refer to whether individuals place greater value on the interests of the collective or themselves. This has particular implications for whether members will place the group needs and goals above their own. In fact, collectivism has a direct impact on attitudes toward teamwork, one of the important affective components of teamwork. Similarly, power distance has also been acknowledged as an important cultural indicator. It refers to the degree to which individuals prefer hierarchies compared to flattened (e.g. team) structures, such that low power distance individuals prefer team-based structures whereas high power distance individuals value status and authority. If some individuals place great value on formal status, this has implications for how semi-autonomous teams will handle shared leadership among team members (see also Chapter 3). Although not as widely considered in terms of implications for teams, other cultural variables such as tolerance for uncertain situations and time orientation may also be important considerations.

Although these differences can create conflict if not treated properly, researchers have offered some guidance on ways in which organizations can improve effectiveness in multicultural teams. Burke, Shuffler, Salas and Gelfand (2010) offered seven guidelines for creating a productive intercultural team environment: (i) engaging in leadership that creates and maintains cohesion, (ii) ensuring clear and meaningful communication, (iii) engaging in supportive behaviours to maximize team synergy, (iv) engaging in perspective taking (putting yourself in someone's shoes), (v) engaging in negotiation to find common ground, (vi) creating a sense of psychological safety to facilitate interaction and (vii) developing shared knowledge to aid coordination.

Team selection/composition

Researchers and practitioners have long acknowledged the importance of selecting individuals to work in teams. In line with the taskwork/teamwork distinction, it is not simply enough to hire an employee who can complete taskwork if he or she will be employed within a team context. It is also critical that the individual has the characteristics necessary to engage in effective teamwork, as acknowledged by a large majority of the team effectiveness models discussed previously. For instance, selecting individuals who are collectively oriented may help facilitate teamwork.

However, only recently has research begun to truly acknowledge the importance of team composition. In the case of team member composition, research is beginning to acknowledge that organizations should focus on the shared and unique characteristics of team members. For instance, it may not be good for all members on a team to be agreeable because they will likely fall prey to groupthink (i.e. conforming to the group consensus because of social influence) or fail to engage in effective decision-making processes due to an aversion of conflict. However, it may be useful to have one agreeable member in a team along with one extravert who will step forward as the leader. Stated differently, it is important to examine the differences among members as well as similarities, and how they interact to impact team process and performance.

Managing team diversity

Team diversity can fuel the needed positive organizational synergy, but it can also impair team members' communication, coordination and performance (van Knippenberg & Schippers, 2007). Extant diversity literature suggests that when team members simultaneously co-vary on several attributes (e.g. gender, educational background, nationality) and certain features of the team task or context make these differences salient, there is a high potential for the creation of subgroups (Lau & Murnighan, 2005). This phenomenon is known as team *faultlines*, which are 'hypothetical dividing lines that may split a group into subgroups based on one or more attributes' (Lau & Murnighan, 1998, p. 328). Faultlines have the potential to inhibit key team processes like elaboration of task-relevant information or communication (Homan, van Knippenberg, van Kleef, & de Dreu, 2007) and outcomes such as decision quality or social integration (Rico, Molleman, Sánchez-Manzanares, & van der Vegt, 2007).

Team faultlines research focuses on four main issues: (i) demonstrating a curvilinear relationship (inverted U) by showing that only moderate levels of team faultlines facilitate the achievement of higher levels of team performance (Gibson & Vermeulen, 2003), (ii) identifying task and other team member characteristics that mitigate the impact of faultlines on teamwork, such as openness to diversity or team autonomy(Rico et al., 2007), (iii) identifying those mediating mechanisms, such as conflict, group identification (Lau & Murnighan, 2005) or task-relevant information processing, that explain the effects of faultlines and (iv) determining how faultlines can be managed by using different managerial strategies, such as the combination of task role cross-cutting and superordinate goals assignment (Rico, Sánchez-Manzanares, Antino, &

Lau, 2012). As organizations are required to capitalize on the true potential of their diverse work teams, the study of diversity will continue to develop.

Multiple memberships

Teams today often do not abide by traditional norms of static membership. Decades ago, team members typically worked within one group to accomplish team tasks. However, an increasing emphasis on collaboration has also opened the door for membership in multiple teams at any given time. For instance, entrepreneurs, student project team members and scientists may collaborate with multiple teams on several projects at a given time. This new configuration and conceptualization of team membership has implications for a number of factors, including coordination and attention issues, burnout, team identity and cohesion, among others. To date, little or no research has focused on the effect of multiple team memberships in terms of individual, team and organizational outcomes. However, it is clearly the way in which many teams both today and in the future will operate.

Team coordination and adaptation

Finally, team coordination is amply acknowledged as a central process for team effectiveness, but lately there has been a growing interest in its role as a key mechanism enabling teams to adapt and cope with complex and/or changing circumstances or demands (Burke, Stagl, Salas, Pierce, & Kendall, 2006). Team coordination involves the use of strategies and behaviour patterns that integrate and align the actions, knowledge and objectives of interdependent members while pursuing common goals (Malone & Crowston, 1994). Extant team literature has identified two main coordination modes: explicit and implicit coordination (Rico, Sánchez-Manzanares, Gil, & Gibson, 2008). While explicit coordination relies on planning and communication as basic mechanisms, implicit coordination is based on shared knowledge (e.g. TMMs) that allows team members to anticipate and dynamically adapt to the actions of other team members in order to manage their multiple interdependences (Rico et al., 2008).

Recent studies with anaesthesia teams and cockpit crews indicate that coordination mechanisms are adapted to situational demands. Research results show that explicit coordination increases in unexpected or highly interdependent situations. However, in top-performing teams under unexpected situations there is a balance between implicit and explicit coordination processes. This suggests that a shared representation of the situation is crucial for successful coordination.

Replay

Teams today are rarely functioning in traditional homogenous, face-to-face, single-team contexts. Virtuality has opened doors for teams to cross geographic boundaries to collaborate, but these teams are particularly susceptible to process loss and problems with cohesion, trust and other affective components of teamwork. Furthermore, intercultural teams are becoming more common as globalization and virtuality open doors for collaborations with culturally different others. Although diversity can improve outcomes such as innovation and creativity, values and preferences may impact the way that individuals engage in teamwork.

Research has acknowledged that certain individuals may be more or less preferable for employment within a team context. However, less research has examined how whole teams should be composed, and which combination of characteristics among team members makes for the most effective team. Additionally, many individuals who work within team contexts do not work with a single team, but rather maintain multiple team memberships for various tasks or projects. The implications of multiple memberships have yet to be fully examined, but potential areas of concern include burnout, coordination issues and problems with team affect (e.g. cohesion, identity).

18.8 Are Teams Always the Answer?

Teams are useful for accomplishing complex tasks, but the use of teams is not always appropriate. In particular, team effectiveness is a function of process gains and process losses. Organizations can gain from increased expertise, collective motivation and coordination of resources. However, research indicates that the outputs of a team are not a direct sum of the individuals' efforts. Instead, process losses can occur. For instance, member conflict can be detrimental to the team's ability to work together, coordination issues can slow down task completion, groupthink (i.e. members conform to the ideas and actions of their team) can wash out individual contributions and members can engage in social loafing (i.e. decrease their effort when individual contributions are not noticeable or measurable). Thus,

$$\text{actual team effectiveness} = \text{potential effectiveness} + \text{process gain} - \text{process loss}$$

When organizations are considering using teams, they should consider whether the benefits (gains) outweigh the losses that might occur through team member interactions. If the task is not complex and could feasibly be completed by an individual, teams may not be appropriate because losses could outweigh gains.

Replay

Not all situations and tasks are appropriate for using teams. Team effectiveness is a function of process gains and process losses. When considering whether or not to use a team for task accomplishment, organizations should conduct a cost-benefit analysis.

18.9 Conclusions

Modern organizations are moving away from traditional hierarchies toward team-based structures. Teams differ by the type of task(s) they engage in as well as the characteristics of the team. The extent to which they are effective depends on both taskwork and teamwork, which is largely dependent on the characteristics of the team members, the team and the organization. Researchers are beginning to understand what characteristics make individuals better suited to work in teams, and what combination of characteristics makes a good team. Teamwork revolves around transition, action and interpersonal processes. Teamwork competencies reflect what teams feel (attitudes), do (behaviours) and think (cognition).

Team effectiveness can be improved through two types of team development interventions: team building and team training. Team building focuses on interpersonal issues, goal setting and role clarification, and is useful in improving team process and affective outcomes such as cohesion and mutual trust. Team training focuses on developing specific KSAs that translate into performance and cognitive outcomes.

The nature of teamwork is also changing due to globalization, technological advances and increasing complexity in the type of work being done by teams. Virtuality has opened doors for teams to cross geographic boundaries to collaborate, but these teams are particularly susceptible to process loss and problems with cohesion, trust and other affective components of teamwork. Additionally, many individuals maintain multiple team memberships for various tasks or projects. The implications of multiple memberships have yet to be fully examined, but potential areas of concern include burnout, coordination issues and problems with team affect (e.g. cohesion, identity).

Given all of this, teams should be used when it is appropriate. A cost–benefit analysis should be conducted whenever an organization is considering using teams to accomplish tasks.

Discussion Points

1. What should organizations pay attention to when designing teams? What factors might help or impede a team's effectiveness?
2. What problems do you think virtual teams might encounter and how do you think these issues may be addressed?
3. What are the differences between team building and team training? How can these strategies improve teamwork?
4. What other factors might change how teams function in the future?

Learning by Doing

1. Can you think of some effective team-building exercises that would especially benefit diverse teams? What about some exercises that would benefit virtual teams? Create and describe them.
2. Think of a time you have worked in a team. Using the expanded Tuckman and Gersick model proposed by Morgan, Salas and Glickman, describe how your team underwent the nine developmental stages.
3. Interview an individual (e.g. family member, friend, colleague) who has worked in a team. Identify the characteristics of the individuals that composed

the team, the characteristics of their team as a whole, and the characteristics of the organization or environment the team operated in. What were some of the characteristics that contributed to overall team effectiveness? How might you select such individuals when building a team? What kind of organizational policies or procedures should be in place to help the team be effective?
4. Describe how the three core teamwork competencies (the ABCs of teamwork) as described by the Cannon-Bowers and Salas (2006) may promote team effectiveness.

Acknowledgement

This work was supported by funding from the National Science Foundation grant to Dr. Matthew W. Ohland, Principal Investigator, Purdue University (0817403-DUE), subcontract to UCF (4101-25418). The views expressed in this work are those of the authors and do not necessarily reflect the organizations with which they are affiliated or their sponsoring institutions or agencies.

Further Reading

Salas, E., Goodwin, G. F., & Burke, C. S. (2008). *Team effectiveness in complex organizations: Cross-disciplinary perspectives and approaches* (SIOP Organizational Frontiers Series). New York: Taylor & Francis.

Salas, E., Priest, H. A., Stagl, K. C., Sims, D. E., & Burke, C. S. (2007). Work teams in organizations: A historical reflection and lessons learned. In L. Koppes (Ed.), *Historical perspectives in industrial and organizational psychology* (pp. 407–438). Mahwah, NJ: Lawrence Erlbaum Associates.

References

Brandon, D. P., & Hollingshead, A. B. (2004). Transactive memory systems in organizations: Matching tasks, expertise, and people. *Organization Science, 15*, 633–644.

Burke, C., Shuffler, M., Salas, E., & Gelfand, M. (2010). Multicultural teams: critical team processes and guidelines. In K. Lundby (Ed.), *Going global: Practical applications and recommendations for HR and OD professionals in the global workplace* (pp. 46–82). San Francisco: John Wiley & Sons.

Burke, C. S., Stagl, K. C., Salas, E., Pierce, L., & Kendall, D. L. (2006). Understanding team adaptation: A conceptual analysis and model. *Journal of Applied Psychology, 91*, 1189–1207.

Cannon-Bowers, J. A., & Salas, E. (1990). *Cognitive psychology and team training: Shared mental models in complex systems.* Paper presented at the Annual Meeting of the Society of Industrial and Organizational Psychology, Miami, FL.

Cannon-Bowers, J. A., & Salas, E. (2006). Team effectiveness and competencies. In W. Karwowski (Ed.), *International encyclopedia of ergonomics and human factors* (Vol. 2, pp. 2379–2383). London: Taylor & Francis.

Cooke, N. J., Gorman, J. C., & Winner, J. L. (2007). Team cognition. In F. Durso, R. Nickerson, S. Dumais, S. Lewandowsky, & T. Perfect (Eds.), *Handbook of applied cognition* (2nd ed., pp. 239–268). New York: John Wiley & Sons.

Eldredge, N., & Gould, S. J. (1972). Punctuated equilibria: An alternative to phyletic gradualism.

In T. J. Schopf (Ed.), *Models of paleobiology* (pp. 82–115). San Francisco: Freeman, Cooper and Co.

Entin, E., & Serfaty, D. (1999). Adaptive team coordination. *Human Factors, 41,* 312–325.

Gersick, C. J. G. (1988). Time and transition in work teams: Toward a new model of group development. *The Academy of Management Journal, 31,* 9–41.

Gibson, C., & Vermeulen, F. (2003). A healthy divide: Subgroups as a stimulus for team learning behavior. *Administrative Science Quarterly, 48,* 202–239.

Glickman, A. S., Zimmer, S., Montero, R. C., Guerette, P. J., Campbell, W. J., Morgan, B. B., Jr., & Salas, E. (1987). *The evolution of teamwork skills: An empirical assessment with implications for training* (Technical Report Number 87-016). Orlando: US Naval Training Systems Center Technical Reports.

Goldstein, H. I. (1991). Nonlinear multilevel models, with an application to discrete response data. *Biometrika, 78,* 45–51.

Guzzo, R. A., & Dickson, M. W. (1996). Teams in organizations: Recent research on performance and effectiveness. *Annual Review of Psychology, 47,* 307.

Homan, A. C., van Knippenberg, D., van Kleef, G. A., & de Dreu, C. W. (2007). Bridging faultlines by valuing diversity: Diversity beliefs, information elaboration, and performance in diverse work groups. *Journal of Applied Psychology, 92,* 1189–1199.

Horwitz, S. K. (2005). The compositional impact of team diversity on performance: Theoretical considerations. *Human Resource Development Review, 4,* 219–245.

Klein, C., DiazGranados, D., Salas, E., Le, H., Burke, C. S., Lyons, R., & Goodwin, G. F. (2009). Does team building work? *Small Group Research, 40,* 181–222.

Klimoski, R., & Mohammed, S. (1994). Team mental model: Construct or metaphor? *Journal of Management, 20,* 403.

Kompier, M. A. J. (2006). The Hawthorne effect is a myth, but what keeps the story going? *Scandinavian Journal of Work, Environment & Health, 32,* 402–412.

Kozlowski, S. J., & Klein, K. J. (2000). A multilevel approach to theory and research in organizations: Contextual, temporal, and emergent processes. In K. J. Klein, & S. J. Kozlowski (Eds.), *Multilevel theory, research, and methods in organizations: Foundations, extensions, and new directions* (pp. 3–90). San Francisco: Jossey-Bass.

Lau, D. C., & Murnighan, J. (1998). Demographic diversity and faultlines: The compositional dynamics of organizational groups. *Academy of Management Review, 23,* 325–340.

Lau, D. C., & Murnighann, J. (2005). Interactions within groups and subgroups: The effects of demographic faultlines. *Academy of Management Journal, 48,* 645–659.

Malone, T., & Crowston, K. (1994). The interdisciplinary study of coordination. *Acm Computing Surveys, 26,* 87–119.

Marks, M. A., Mathieu, J. E., & Zaccaro, S. J. (2001). A temporally based framework and taxonomy of team processes. *Academy of Management Review, 26,* 356–337.

Mathieu, J., Maynard, M., Rapp, T., & Gilson, L. (2008). Team effectiveness 1997–2007: A review of recent advancements and a glimpse into the future. *Journal of Management, 34,* 410–476.

McIntyre, R. M., & Salas, E. (1995). Measuring and managing for team performance: Lessons from complex environments. In R. A. Guzzo, & E. Salas (Eds.), *Team effectiveness and decision making in organizations* (pp. 9–45). San Francisco: Jossey-Bass.

Mohammed, S., Ferzandi, L., & Hamilton, K. (2010). Metaphor no more: A 15-year review of the team mental model construct. *Journal of Management, 36,* 876–910.

Morgan, B. B., Salas, E., & Glickman, A. S. (1993). An analysis of team evolution and maturation. *Journal of General Psychology, 120,* 277–291.

National Transportation Safety Board (2009). *Aircraft accident report: Loss of thrust in both engines after encountering a flock of birds and subsequent ditching on the Hudson River, US Airways Flight 1549, Airbus A320-214, N106US, Weehawken, New Jersey* (NTSB/AAR-10/13, PB2010-910403). Retrieved from http://www.ntsb.gov/doclib/reports/2010/aar1003.pdf.

Peltokorpi, V. (2008). Transactive memory systems. *Review of General Psychology, 12,* 378–394.

Rico, R., Bachrach, D. Sánchez-Manzanares, M., & Collins, B. (2011). The interactive effects of person-focused citizenship behavior, task interdependence and virtuality on team performance. *European Journal of Work and Organizational Psychology, 20,* 700–726.

Rico, R., Molleman, E., Sánchez-Manzanares, M., & van der Vegt, G. (2007). The effects of diversity faultlines and team task autonomy on decision quality and social integration. *Journal of Management, 33,* 111–132.

Rico, R., Sánchez-Manzanares, M., Antino, M., & Lau, D. (2012). Bridging team faultlines by combining task role assignment and goal structure strategies: Work teams (English). *Journal of Applied Psychology, 97,* 407–420.

Rico, R., Sánchez-Manzanares, M., Gil, F., & Gibson, C. (2008). Team implicit coordination processes: A team knowledge-based approach. *Academy of Management Review, 33,* 163–184.

Salas, E., Burke, C. S., Bowers, C. A., & Wilson, K. A. (2001). Team training in the skies: Does crew resource management (CRM) training work? *Human Factors, 43,* 641–674.

Salas, E., DiazGranados, D., Klein, C., Burke, C. S., Stagl, K. C., Goodwin, G. F., & Halpin, S. M. (2008). Does team training improve team performance? A meta-analysis. *Human Factors, 50,* 903–933.

Salas, E., Priest, H. A., Stagl, K. C., Sims, D. E., & Burke, C. S. (2007). Work teams in organizations: A historical reflection and lessons learned. In L. Koppes (Ed.), *Historical perspectives in industrial and organizational psychology* (pp. 407–438). Mahwah, NJ: Lawrence Erlbaum Associates.

Salas, E., Stagl, K. C., Burke, C. S., & Goodwin, G. F. (2007). Fostering team effectiveness in organizations: Toward an integrative theoretical framework of team performance. In J. W. Shuart, W. Spaulding, & J. Poland, (Eds.), *Modeling complex systems: Motivation, cognition and social processes, Nebraska Symposium on Motivation, 51,* (pp. 185–243). Lincoln, NE: University of Nebraska Press.

Shuffler, M. L., DiazGranados, D., & Salas, E. (2011). There's a science for that: Team development interventions in organizations. *Current Directions in Psychological Science, 20,* 365–372.

Smith-Jentsch, K., Cannon-Bowers, J., Tannenbaum, S., & Salas, E. (2008). Guided team self-correction: Impacts on team mental models, processes, and effectiveness. *Small Group Research, 39,* 303–327.

Tannenbaum, S., Mathieu, J., Salas, E., & Cohen, D. (2012). Teams are changing: Are research and practice evolving fast enough? *Industrial and Organizational Psychology-Perspectives On Science And Practice, 5,* 2–24.

Tuckman, B. W. (1965). Developmental sequence in small groups. *Psychological Bulletin, 63,* 384–399.

Tuckman, B. C. (1977). Stages of small-group development revisited. *Group & Organization Studies, 2,* 419–427.

van Knippenberg, D., & Schippers, M. (2007). Work group diversity. *Annual Review of Psychology, 58,* 515–541.

Volpe, C. E., Cannon-Bowers, J. A., Salas, E., & Spector, P. E. (1996). The impact of cross-training on team functioning: An empirical investigation. *Human Factors, 38,* 87–100.

Wegner, D. M., Giuliano, T., & Hertel, P. (1985). Cognitive interdependence in close relationships. In W. J. Ickes (Ed.), *Compatible and incompatible relationships* (pp. 253–276). New York: Springer-Verlag.

Wildman, J. L., Thayer, A. L., Rosen, M. A., Salas, E., Mathieu, J. E., & Rayne, S. R. (2012a). Task types and team-level attributes: Synthesis of team classification literature. *Human Resource Development Review, 11,* 97–129.

Wildman, J. L., Thayer, A. L., Pavlas, D., Salas, E., Stewart, J. E., & Howse, W. R. (2012b). Team knowledge research: Emerging trends and critical needs. *Human Factors, 54,* 84–111.

19

Positive Interventions
From Prevention to Amplification

CAROLYN M. YOUSSEF-MORGAN
AND DALE A. SUNDERMANN

Chapter Objectives

After studying this chapter, you should be able to:

- distinguish between various positive movements such as positive psychology, positive organizational behaviour and positive organizational scholarship;
- compare and contrast positivity and negativity;
- describe the distinct effects of positive emotions;
- explain the negativity bias;
- describe psychological capital (PsyCap) and its constituent resources;
- explain the criteria for effective interventions in general and effective positive interventions in particular;
- describe several successful positive work interventions.

19.1 Introduction

Interventions aiming at development, positive change and performance improvement are not new to the workplace. However, organizational scholars and practicing managers have recently begun to build upon these established practices to also explore the science of positive psychology in order to further improve

An Introduction to Contemporary Work Psychology, First Edition.
Edited by Maria C. W. Peeters, Jan de Jonge and Toon W. Taris.
© 2014 John Wiley & Sons, Ltd. Published 2014 by John Wiley & Sons, Ltd.

organizational performance and employee well-being. This is not to imply that established work interventions (see Chapter 16) are ineffective or have run their course, or to advocate positively oriented practices over all others. On the contrary, the established body of research and practice is critical to and foundational for the understanding and application of positive practices in the workplace.

This chapter is designed to apply perspectives from positive psychology to the workplace. These perspectives go beyond the traditional fixing, or preventing problems to amplification. A workplace free of problems and dysfunctions is not a success but simply without significant problems and dysfunctions. Amplification goes beyond simple problem elimination to also increasing personal productivity and fulfilment, as well as exceptional organizational performance and effectiveness. It is derived from a positive psychological perspective that rigorously investigates how to achieve the best possible work outcomes for individuals and organizations.

We start this chapter by introducing the origins of positive psychology and reviewing the positivity literature, which has grown exponentially over the last decade, some of which is also introduced in Chapter 10. We then discuss the differences between the relatively new disciplines of positive organizational scholarship (POS) and positive organizational behaviour (POB), and explore a wide range of positive interventions.

19.2 The Context of Positivity

The positive psychology movement may be considered a late response to humanistic psychologist Abraham Maslow's observation nearly 60 years ago that 'The science of Psychology has been far more successful on the negative than on the positive side. It has revealed to us much about man's shortcomings, his illness, his sins, but little about his potentialities, his virtues, his achievable, aspirations, or his full psychological height. It is as if Psychology has voluntarily restricted itself too only half its rightful jurisdiction, and that, the darker meaner half' (Maslow, 1954, p. 354).

Before World War II there were three distinct missions of psychological study: curing mental illness, identifying and nurturing human talent and productivity, and helping people achieve their potential and experience fulfilment. Following World War II, the field of psychology took a turn towards a medical model. This model emphasized the first mission of identifying and understanding dysfunctional conditions and treating them, at the expense of the other two more positively-oriented missions. Funding by the way of grants for mental health research drew scholars and practitioners toward providing therapy around the diagnoses and treatment of mental illness, and gave the field psychology recognition and acceptance as a subfield of the health profession (Seligman & Csikszentmihalyi, 2000).

However, in 1998, the mindset began to shift, primarily due to Martin Seligman's Presidential Address to the American Psychological Association. In his address, Seligman urged the psychological community to make a conscious decision to shift the dominant focus from mental illness (or what he referred to as the 'disease model') towards what had become a forgotten mission of psychology, i.e. to study the concepts of health, success, happiness and what makes life most worth living.

With the shared aspiration of bringing the science of positive psychology into the workplace, POB and POS have emerged over the past decade as the leading schools of thought in this area. POB refers to 'the study and application of positivity oriented human resource strengths and psychological capacities that can be measured, developed, and effectively managed for performance improvement in today's workplace' (Luthans, 2002a, p. 59). Thus, the focus of POB is on scientifically supported positive psychological resources such as self-efficacy, hope, optimism and resilience (Luthans, 2002b). These psychological resources are recognized to have valid and reliable measures, and demonstrated relations with quantifiable performance outcomes. As you learned in Chapter 10, these psychological resources are also malleable, or 'state-like', which makes them open to development and management through workplace interventions, and thus particularly relevant in this chapter.

POS emphasizes the organizational dynamics that can promote the development of human strength and resiliency, facilitate healing and restoration, and cultivate extraordinary individual and organizational performance (Cameron & Caza, 2004). Positive organizational scholars study a broad range of positive attributes that drive the processes and outcomes in organizations and their members. While similar in positive emphasis and overlapping in areas of research and practice, the primary emphasis of POS is on the positive features of the organization itself, such as positive relationships, processes and change, whereas POB is primarily concerned with specific qualities of the individual employee and the impact on individual performance. POB typically starts at the individual level and progresses to the group and organizational levels. POS typically begins at the organizational level and proceeds in the opposite direction (Luthans & Avolio, 2009). Moreover, a tangible performance impact is at the heart of POB, but is not required for POS.

Replay

The introduction of positive psychology into the workplace is a result of the psychological community's decision to make a shift in focus from the disease model towards the study of health, success and wellness. To date, the psychological resources that best meet POB's inclusion criteria are self-efficacy, hope, optimism and resilience. POS emphasizes the organizational dynamics that can promote the development of human strength and resiliency, facilitate healing and restoration, and cultivate extraordinary individual and organizational performance (Cameron & Caza, 2004).

19.3 Positive Psychology Challenges the Success Paradigm

A prevailing belief (the 'success paradigm') exists that people are positive as a result of being productive at work. Consistent with this notion, studies demonstrate that positive emotions (positivity) and productive performance are correlated, but can these correlations be interpreted causally? Lyubomirsky and colleagues (2005) explored in depth the notion of whether positive emotional states lead to success. These researchers investigated not only the association between positivity and success, but also the causal direction between those two important sets of phenomena: does happiness cause success or is it the other way around? Through a meta-analysis of 225 cross-sectional, longitudinal and experimental studies they were able to show that indeed positive affect leads to success in numerous life domains, including work, relationships, health and others.

In the workplace, research has revealed that positive workers have a higher likelihood of securing job interviews and positive evaluations by supervisors, as well as superior performance and productivity over their peers who are less happy. For example, Staw and colleagues (1994) found that employees high in positive affect received higher pay and more favourable supervisor evaluations 18 months later. Positive workers also reported lower levels of job burnout and counterproductive work behaviours such as supply theft, extended breaks and slow performance. Another study by Pelled and Xin (1999) found that the level of positivity measured at a moment in time could be used to predict absenteeism 5 months later. Avey, Reichard, Luthans and Hater (2011) conducted a meta-analysis of dozens of psychological capital studies and found significant support for the relationship between psychological capital and various dimensions of work performance, attitudes and behaviours. The results of the studies reflect the growing application of positivity and its unique impact on the workplace.

19.4 What is Unique about Positivity (and Negativity)?

The human tendency to overemphasize and amplify the negative over the positive by individuals has been widely recognized, both in theory and in practice (Baumeister, Bratslavsky, Finkenauer, & Vohs, 2001). From CEO to individual employee, the majority of attention, energy and resources appear to be expended on repairing the damage done by a negative event or engaging in behaviour to ensure a negative event does not occur. However, other research reveals that people tend to gravitate toward pleasant stimuli and experiences, which is reinforced through numerous biological, psychological and social mechanisms. This inclination resembles 'heliotropism', the tendency among all living system towards sources of life and positive energy, comparable to a plant leaning toward sunlight (Cameron, 2008).

Positive and negative stimuli: Unique functions

According to Cameron (2008), a negative bias can be explained through four distinctions between positivity and negativity: intensity, novelty, adaptation and singularity.

Intensity
Negative stimuli tend to be experienced more intensely because they are perceived to be more concentrated, specific and urgent. Ignoring positive stimuli is often inconsequential. On the other hand, negative stimuli tend to be perceived

as threatening and thus requiring immediate response. For example, an employee may perceive positive feedback from a supervisor to be a pleasant experience, but will likely dwell longer on and invest more time and energy in dealing with negative feedback. This is because of the perceived potential consequences of the negative feedback (e.g. job loss, reprimand or demotion).

Novelty
As a general rule, people experience more positive than negative events. As a result, negative events tend to be unusual, unexpected, surprising and sometimes even extreme, so they tend to stand out more. This applies to many facets of life, from the evening news to a bad customer service experience.

Adaptation
Positive experiences signal adequate functioning, which does not often trigger further action. On the other hand, negative experiences often signal maladaptation and a need for change and corrective action. For example, equipment breakdown, loss of market share to a new competitor, a highly visible lawsuit and other organizational crises will likely warrant more attention, energy and resources than extended periods of smooth operations and met goals.

Singularity
In a system, one negative or dysfunctional component can cause failure (see, for instance, Chapter 14 about safety), but one positive or functioning component rarely guarantees success. Thus, identifying, diagnosing and correcting single negative or dysfunctional factors in order to restore 'normal' system functioning tend to receive higher priority and a larger share of the resources in the workplace than recognizing, celebrating and rewarding what is right.

The objective of an exclusively happy life is unrealistic and would not likely lead to a fulfilled life. Both positivity and negativity are necessary for positive change. Moderate levels of negativity and dissatisfaction with the status quo can prevent complacency and motivate active goal pursuit. What is needed is more balance, as discussed next.

Positive and negative emotions: Unique mechanisms

According to Fredrickson's (2001) Broaden-and-Build Model, positive emotions have two distinct effects on thought-action repertoires that may influence work performance: a broadening effect and a building effect. The *broadening effect* enables and motivates the search for a wider range of alternatives, and the curiosity to explore unusual courses of action. This broadening effect has serious implications for creativity and innovation. For example, recent studies show that positivity is related to creative performance (Sweetman, Luthans, Avey, & Luthans, 2011). This broadening effect stands in sharp contrast to the narrowing effect of negativity, which tends to promote reactions that resemble a fight-or-flight survival mode and a limited range of tried-and-true options.

The *building effect* of positive emotions is where positive emotions can facilitate the development and replenishment of mental, physical, social and psychological resources, which may have been depleted in prior times of negativity or in preparation for future challenging times. For example, an employee who regularly receives positive feedback and recognition for accomplishments at work will likely handle a mistake, negative feedback from a supervisor or constructive criticism from a co-worker much better than an employee who is regularly criticized. The former may feel humbled but resilient and able to bounce back. The latter may become resentful and bitter, and lose confidence in his ability to do better in the future.

Replay

By nature, humans tend to gravitate toward positive, pleasant stimuli and experiences. The human tendency to overemphasize and amplify the negative over the positive has been widely recognized, both in theory and in practice. This negative bias can be explained through four distinctions between positivity and negativity: intensity, novelty, adaptation and singularity. Both positivity and negativity are necessary for positive change. However, positive and negative stimuli serve unique functions. Positive emotions have two distinct effects on thought-action repertoires: a broadening effect and a building effect.

19.5 Positive Workplace Interventions

In order for any intervention to be considered in this chapter it must be able to add value to the workplace and meet the following criteria:

1. It should yield recognized, desirable outcomes. These outcomes should be clearly caused by the changes (e.g. increased positivity) induced by the intervention.
2. It should attempt to change individual, group and/or organizational characteristics that are in fact malleable, and thus open to change, development and management.
3. It should to be qualitatively different from existing interventions and shown to yield desirable outcomes beyond these existing interventions.
4. The benefits of the intervention should exceed its costs, broadly defined to include direct, indirect and opportunity costs.

The remainder of this chapter will explore various positive interventions that meet the above four criteria.

Developing self-efficacy

Self-efficacy, or simply confidence, can be defined as 'one's belief about his or her ability to mobilize the motivation, cognitive resources, and courses of action necessary to execute a specific action within a given context' (Stajkovic & Luthans,

1998a, p. 66). There is now substantial support that self-efficacy is one of the strongest predictors of performance and success in numerous life domains, including the workplace (Stajkovic & Luthans, 1998b). Thus, developing employee self-efficacy is critical because it can lead to recognized desirable outcomes.

Unlike fixed personality traits, self-efficacy can be developed. There are four recognized approaches for developing self-efficacy: (i) mastery/success experiences, (ii) vicarious learning/modelling, (iii) social persuasion and (iv) physiological and psychological arousal.

Mastery/success experiences
This is the most effective approach to developing self-efficacy. Mastery experiences are created through repeated opportunities to experience success. In order to experience mastery, complex tasks can be broken down into easier-to-learn sub-skills so that an employee can experience small successes more frequently, which can help gradually develop self-efficacy. Mastery experiences can also be created by intentionally placing employees in situations where they have a good chance to experience success, that is, setting them up for success. Training interventions that utilize simulations, case-studies, what-if analyses and other experiential techniques can also enhance self-efficacy by providing mastery experiences.

Vicarious learning/modelling
In addition to learning from their own successes and failures, employees can also learn vicariously through observing and imitating others. When those who possess more experience model the desired skills and behaviours, they not only help employees learn these skills and behaviours, but they also help increase their confidence in their abilities to perform them. Vicarious learning/modelling is particularly relevant in situations where opportunities for mastery and successful experiences are impossible, prohibitively costly or too risky to provide, for example when initially training pilots or surgery residents who are not ready to handle real job situations.

Social persuasion
Self-efficacy can also be developed through the influence and support of others. When employees have supportive managers and co-workers cheering them on and instilling in them the belief that 'I can do this', they become more confident in their abilities. Positive feedback plays a critical role in social persuasion and confidence building, an idea that will be revisited later in this chapter.

Physiological and psychological arousal
While self-efficacy can be enhanced through mastery, modelling and social persuasion directed at specific actions within a specific context, a general emphasis on physical, mental and psychological well-being has also been found to contribute to self-efficacy. This is because general well-being can contribute to physiological and psychological arousal and stimulation, which can boost energy and motivation to take on and endure challenges.

Replay

Self-efficacy is 'one's belief about his or her ability to mobilize the motivation, cognitive resources, and courses of action necessary to execute a specific action within a given context'. There are four recognized approaches for developing self-efficacy: (i) mastery/success experiences, (ii) vicarious learning/modelling, (iii) social persuasion and (iv) physiological and psychological arousal.

Developing hope

Hope can be defined as 'a positive motivational state that is based on an interactively derived sense of successful (1) agency (goal-directed energy) and (2) pathways (planning to meet goals)' (Snyder, Irving, & Anderson, 1991, p. 287). Agency, also commonly referred to as 'willpower', is the *willful* determination to get what we want, as well as the energy investment to pursue realistic but challenging goals. Pathways, also referred to as 'waypower', is the ability to create multiple paths that can lead to goal achievement, so that when some paths are blocked, others can be pursued.

One's hope level reflects the cumulative levels of willpower and waypower, which result from the continuous iteration between one's perceptions and cognitive appraisals of agency and pathways. In other words, as long as willpower can be mobilized and waypower can be generated, hope can continue to thrive. Hopelessness sets in when agency or pathways are perceived to be exhausted.

Similar to self-efficacy, hope has been demonstrated to relate to success in many areas of life (Snyder, 2000). In the workplace, hope has been positively related to performance, job satisfaction, work happiness and organizational commitment (Youssef & Luthans, 2007), making its development a particularly relevant type of positive intervention. Also similar to efficacy, hope has a trait-like or 'hardwired' baseline, but it has also been found to be state-like and thus open to development and management (Snyder et al., 1996). Successful approaches to develop hope are discussed next.

Goal-setting

Setting effective goals has been demonstrated to be one of the most instrumental ways to boost motivation, productivity and satisfaction in the workplace (Locke & Latham, 2002). However, the role of goal setting in developing hope has also been supported. For example, goals that are specific, measurable, internalized, committed to, self-set and self-regulated are more conducive than vague, uncommitted or externally imposed goals to building hope and also to improve performance. 'Stretch goals' that challenge employees beyond their current abilities and comfort zones can promote hope agency and willpower. 'Stepping', or breaking down a goal into smaller sub-goals and milestones, can also help sustain determination to continue to pursue a challenging or large goal. Thus, many existing goal-setting interventions can be leveraged to build hope.

Contingency planning

Waypower can be developed through the regular practice of creating alternative plans. These plans can serve as alternative pathways when obstacles are confronted so that goal pursuit can be sustained. Interventions geared at training or coaching employees in creating realistic, viable contingency plans even before problems and crises render existing plans useless or obsolete is not only an effective approach to preventing hasty reactions to unexpected contingencies, but can also boost and amplify hope, even in the absence of actual crises and the need to switch plans.

Mental rehearsals
Waypower can also be developed through mentally rehearsing various potential scenarios, as well as the process of switching across paths when obstacles present themselves along a particular path. These mental rehearsals help instill a sense of preparedness that sustains hope and resists hopelessness when difficulties are actually experienced.

Replay

Hope is 'a positive motivational state that is based on an interactively derived sense of successful (1) agency (goal-directed energy) and (2) pathways (planning to meet goals)'. It can be developed through: goal setting, contingency planning and mental rehearsals.

Developing optimism

There are two recognized approaches to conceptualize optimism. The first approach defines optimism as general positive future expectancies (Carver & Scheier, 2002). Common notions such as viewing a glass as half full, expecting the best in people and situations, and believing that every cloud has a silver lining are all descriptors of optimism in this approach. The second approach is more specific, and defines optimism as an explanatory style that attributes positive events to personal, permanent and pervasive causes, and negative events to external, temporary and situation-specific ones. This explanatory style can help amplify the positive impact of success and prevent the destructive impact of failure (Seligman, 1998).

Extreme optimism can be delusional, and especially in the workplace can be irresponsible and risky. For example, extreme optimism in engineering, medicine, safety, quality control and other high-risk professions can threaten lives and lead to disasters. Instead, the emphasis in the positive literature is on balanced, realistic and flexible optimism that would accurately appraise situations to choose the proper balance of optimistic and pessimistic attributions (Peterson, 2000; Schneider, 2001).

Unrealistic optimism may promote irresponsible, unhealthy, or even dangerous uncalculated risk-taking (Weinstein, 1989). For example, extreme optimists may ignore sleep, exercise, healthy diet and regular physical check-ups as they perceive themselves to be less vulnerable to illness and more in control of their health than is objectively warranted. In business decisions, they may be subject to more perceptual biases and decision-making errors such as risky shifts and escalation of commitment. In safety situations, they may accept higher risk levels as they underestimate the potential dangers of their choices. On the other hand, realistic, flexible optimism can facilitate an iterative process of proactively seeking and acting on future opportunities based on an incrementally evolving understanding of one's capabilities and vulnerabilities, which can increase chances of success.

Optimism in general has been depicted as both trait-like and state-like. However, this type of realistic, flexible optimism has been shown to be a learned skill that can be taught and developed through interventions that focus on several positive mental processes: (i) leniency for the past, (ii) appreciation for the present and (iii) opportunity seeking for the future (Schneider, 2001).

Leniency for the past
Pessimists tend to judge themselves too harshly. They take too much responsibility and blame themselves for past failures, even when they were beyond their control. They also do not give themselves enough credit for past successes, or at least the good-faith efforts they invested in cases when failure resulted. Leniency for the past does not mean denial or an evasion of responsibility. Instead, positive interventions can help employees become more optimistic by teaching them to positively reframe setbacks, give themselves the benefit of the doubt and cast failures in the best possible light, especially when those failures and setbacks were uncontrollable or impossible to prevent (Carver & Scheier, 2002). Leniency for the past does not prevent employees from learning from past mistakes and reducing the probability of reoccurrence. In fact, being forgiving of oneself can help employees move past the bitterness and resentment of a bad situation to more effectively extract important lessons and move on.

Appreciation for the present
In the same way that past situations can be cast in a more positive light, appreciating the present implies finding the positive, even in negative situations, and attributing it to internal, permanent and pervasive causes. Optimism can be developed by learning to dwell on the negatives and focus more on the positives. A critical skill that helps in appreciating the present is positive self-talk, where managers and employees learn to mentally default to positive thought processes that help them make optimistic, rather than pessimistic, attributions.

Opportunity seeking for the future
Over time, leniency for the past, appreciation for the present and mastering the art of positive self-talk can result in a more positive mindset that is more conducive to growth and development based on a better understanding of one's strengths and weaknesses. Through this more positive mindset, future opportunities and challenges are more likely to be embraced and welcomed, rather than feared or avoided.

Replay

Optimism includes general positive future expectancies, as well as an explanatory style that attributes positive events to personal, permanent and pervasive causes, and negative events to external, temporary and situation-specific ones. It can be developed through: leniency for the past, appreciation for the present and opportunity seeking for the future.

Developing resilience

Even the most efficacious, hopeful and optimistic people are confronted with problems, failures and setbacks. Resilience can be defined as 'the capacity to rebound or bounce back from adversity, conflict, failure, or even positive events, progress, and increased responsibility' (Luthans, 2002b, p. 702). Similar to self-efficacy, hope and optimism, resilience has been shown to contribute to many desirable work outcomes (Youssef & Luthans, 2007).

Unlike the proactive nature of self-efficacy, hope and optimism, resilience tends to be more reactive in nature, in that it is often mobilized in response to negative situations to ensure effective coping and recovery. Without challenges, an individual may never realize how resilient he or she is. However, this 'bouncing back' capacity is not limited to coping and recovery back to a 'normal' or neutral state. Resilience allows employees to also learn and grow from challenges and setbacks so that these experiences can be leveraged as springboards for new levels of positivity. The resultant levels of positivity and success are thus expected to be higher than the original levels prior to facing the negative event, adversity or challenge.

Contrary to traditional psychological theories, which portrayed resilience as an exceptional, magical or mystical capacity that only a few possess, or a hard-wired super material that is fixed or trait-like, resilience has been shown to be state-like and open to development (Masten, 2001; Masten & Reed, 2002; Sutcliffe & Vogus, 2003). Masten and Reed (2002) describe three strategies for developing resilience: (i) asset- focused strategies, (ii) risk-focused strategies and (iii) process-focused strategies.

Asset-focused strategies

These strategies focus on enhancing the assets and resources that can increase the probability of success. These assets may include knowledge, skills, abilities, education and experience, which are recognized to enhance work outcomes. These assets and resources can be learned and enhanced through traditional training and development programmes. Asset-focused strategies may also include the development of social capital (relationships, networking). Interventions aiming at increasing open, transparent communication, social support, mentoring and leadership quality are examples of social capital development strategies that can enhance resilience. Assets can also include other positive psychological resources, such as self-efficacy, hope and optimism.

Risk-focused strategies

The purpose of this set of strategies is to mitigate risk factors that can lead to undesired outcomes. These risk-factors may include negative situations, asset deficiencies or even positive but overwhelming or challenging progress. For example, a promotion or an increase in responsibilities can be just as challenging or even more overwhelming than a frequently experienced setback in a familiar task at work. A resilient response is needed so that an employee is prepared to face, cope with, and grow and develop through both types of situations. Although risk-focused strategies in psychology are predominantly geared toward avoiding or preventing exposure to risky situations (e.g. drugs, alcohol, association with those who have negative influence), in work applications the emphasis is on risk management (see also Chapter 14). For example, in the above situation a risk-avoidance strategy would be to turn down the promotion or increase in responsibilities in favour of a safer route. On the other hand, a more effective strategy for work-related resilience would be to accurately assess one's assets and risk factors, take some calculated risks, develop an effective action plan that would leverage the available assets to mitigate the risk factors that the situation presents, and capitalize on the situation for learning, development and growth. Specific interventions to facilitate these risk-focused strategies can be offered through one-on-one coaching and mentoring, which can be initiated by the organization, the employee or both.

Process-focused strategies
The goal of process-focused strategies is to develop effective adaptational mechanisms that can facilitate the identification, development, utilization and maintenance of the proper mix of assets in managing pertinent risk factors. For example, interventions that aim to select the right employees for the roles they are expected to fulfil, increase organizational and job fit, or improve employees' coping skills, stress management skills or work–life balance can be considered process-focused strategies. They do not necessarily increase employees' assets or reduce their risks and challenges, but they help them better match their assets to their risk factors.

Work Psychology in Action: The US Army's comprehensive soldier fitness initiative

The army's comprehensive soldier fitness (CSF) initiative is a $125 million resilience training initiative designed to reduce the adverse psychological consequences for soldier and veterans. 'The key to psychological fitness is resilience', stated General George W. Casey, US Army Chief of Staff, 'and from here on, resilience will be taught and measured throughout the United States Army' (Casey, 2011). The US Army is attempting to empirically validate and assesses the CSF programme. The resilience development content is designed to be delivered in two ways. First, every member will complete web-based resilience modules. Second, master resilience trainers will receive in-depth training at the University of Pennsylvania and return to their assigned locations to train other soldiers, family members and army civilians. Assessing the impact of both delivery methods is currently underway (Lester, McBride, Bliese, & Adler, 2011). Master resilience training is one of the largest psychological interventions ever undertaken, involving thousands of non-commissioned officers as trainers and 1.1 million soldiers as participants (Reivich, Seligman, & McBride, 2011).

Replay

Resilience is 'the capacity to rebound or bounce back from adversity, conflict, failure, or even positive events, progress, and increased responsibility'. It can be developed through: asset-focused strategies, risk-focused strategies and process-focused strategies.

Developing psychological capital

Psychological capital (PsyCap) is a core construct that integrates self-efficacy, hope, optimism and resilience. It can be defined as 'an individual's positive psychological state of development that is characterized by (1) having confidence (self-efficacy) to take on and put in the necessary effort to succeed at challenging tasks; (2) making a positive attribution (optimism) about succeeding now and in the future; (3) persevering toward goals and, when necessary, redirecting paths to goals (hope) in order to succeed; and (4) when beset by problems and adversity, sustaining and bouncing back and even beyond (resiliency) to attain success' (Luthans, Youssef, & Avolio, 2007, p. 3).

> **Work Psychology in Action: PsyCap training interventions**
>
> Successful PsyCap training interventions have been implemented in 1–3 hours, face-to-face and online, with managers and employees from a wide range of industries, and with varying group sizes of trainees (Luthans, Avey, Avolio, & Peterson, 2010; Luthans, Avey, & Patera, 2008).
>
> In a typical PsyCap development intervention, participants develop hope as they are coached to set specific, measurable and personally meaningful 'stretch' goals and 'stepping' sub-goals. They then generate realistic pathways and learn to adopt approach (rather than avoidance) strategies to achieve their goals and overcome potential obstacles. They also develop an optimistic explanatory style as they take control, anticipate and plan for potential challenges and setbacks, and practice positive self-talk. Participants experience success and mastery in this simulated but realistic setting. They also experience vicarious learning and social persuasion from the facilitator and other participants, which help them develop self-efficacy. The setting also allows them to appraise their personal and social assets, risk management strategies and an adaptation process, which helps them develop their resiliency. The resulting increase in PsyCap capital can yield a 200% return on investment (Luthans et al., 2007).

These psychological resources are recognized to have valid and reliable measures, and demonstrated relationships with quantifiable performance outcomes. As you learned in Chapter 10, these psychological resources are also malleable, or 'state-like', which makes them open to development and management through workplace interventions, and thus particularly relevant in this chapter. The measurement, performance impact and developmental potential criteria are unique to POB, and to PsyCap as a higher-order core construct that integrates self-efficacy, hope, optimism and resilience.

Replay

Psychological capital is a core construct that integrates self-efficacy, hope, optimism and resilience. It can be defined as 'an individual's positive psychological state of development that is characterized by (1) having confidence (self-efficacy) to take on and put in the necessary effort to succeed at challenging tasks; (2) making a positive attribution (optimism) about succeeding now and in the future; (3) persevering toward goals and, when necessary, redirecting paths to goals (hope) in order to succeed; and (4) when beset by problems and adversity, sustaining and bouncing back and even beyond (resiliency) to attain success'.

Developing gratitude

Gratitude can be defined as 'a sense of thankfulness and joy in response to receiving a gift, whether the gift can be a tangible benefit from a specific other or a moment of peaceful bliss evoked by natural beauty' (Emmons, 2004, p. 554). Research supports the integral role of gratitude in increasing happiness and positivity. In a comparative study, Seligman, Steen, Park and Peterson (2005) compared five alternative happiness-enhancing interventions. Interestingly, the most effective interventions were directly related to gratitude.

Regularly identifying and appraising positive life situations
In this intervention, participants wrote down three things that went well every day, as well as causal explanations for each of these positive situations. They were asked to complete this exercise every night for one week. The outcomes for those participants were increased happiness and decreased depression for 6 months beyond the timeframe of the intervention. Interestingly, one of the outcomes of the intervention was that the participants voluntarily chose to continue to practice gratitude after the week had concluded, which is likely to have contributed to the sustained impact of the intervention.

The gratitude letter and visit
In this intervention, participants wrote and delivered a letter in which they expressed their gratitude to another person who they never had a chance to properly thank for an exceptional act of kindness toward them. Participants in this intervention showed the largest positive impact in terms of increased happiness and decreased depression

for at least a month. However, the outcomes were not as sustainable as the previous intervention, probably because of the one-time nature of the intervention. On the other hand, if individuals (and organizations) make outward expressions of gratitude a regular practice, the results of these interventions may be more sustainable.

Identifying and using one's strengths
Seligman and colleagues (2005) tested three different interventions in relation to personal strengths. Participants (i) wrote about a time when they were 'at their best', reflected on their strengths as reflected in their story and daily reflected on the story for a week, (ii) identified and received feedback about their top five 'signature strengths' using a valid and reliable personality assessment provided by the researchers or (iii) took the above personality assessment and were also instructed to use one of their top strengths every day in a new and unique way for a week.

While all three practices exhibit gratitude for one's strengths, only the first two produced transient boosts in happiness. Only the last practice yielded a sustainable impact of increased happiness and decreased depression for 6 months. Apparently, effective gratitude interventions need to be more action-oriented than simply identifying one's strengths. They should also include intentionally utilizing one's strengths in a meaningful way. Similar to identifying and appraising positive life situations, using one's strengths in new and unique ways was a practice that participants also chose to maintain beyond the duration of the intervention, which may have contributed to its positive outcomes.

Replay

Gratitude is 'a sense of thankfulness and joy in response to receiving a gift, whether the gift can be a tangible benefit from a specific other or a moment of peaceful bliss evoked by natural beauty'. It can be developed through (i) regularly identifying and appraising positive life situations, (ii) writing gratitude letters and making gratitude visits, and (iii) identifying and using one's strengths.

19.6 Creating a Positive Organizational Context

Selecting and developing positive individuals is only part of the equation. Just like most plants need fertile soil, proper climate and nutrition to grow and thrive, the success of positive interventions requires a positive organizational context in which positivity can be nurtured, sustained and multiplied.

Developing authentic leaders

Avolio and Luthans (2006, p. 2) define authentic leadership development as 'the process that draws upon a leader's life course, psychological capital, moral perspective, and a highly developed supporting organizational climate to produce greater self-awareness and self-regulated positive behaviours, which in turn foster continuous, positive self-development resulting in veritable, sustained performance.'

Authentic leadership development interventions capitalize on the prospective leader's talents and strengths, by enhancing the leader's self-awareness, which can facilitate accurate self-appraisals for stable traits and trait-like characteristics. Next is the leader's self-regulation, which can be addressed through motivation and behavioural management. The leader's psychological capital and moral perspective, which are more state-like, are then targeted through a combination of self-development and organizational interventions, within the context of a supportive organizational climate. Importantly, this supportive organizational climate is viewed to accelerate the processes necessary for authentic leadership development and amplify the impact of these processes and interventions.

Appreciative inquiry

Appreciative inquiry (AI) is defined as 'the cooperative search for the best in people, their organizations, and the world around them. It involves the systematic discovery of what gives a system "life" when it is most effective and capable in economic, ecological, and human terms' (Cooperrider & Whitney, 2005, pp. 247–248). AI recently emerged as a positive alternative to more the traditional organizational development interventions that emphasize problem-solving, gap analysis and other approaches that resemble the disease model in psychology. Instead, AI focuses on identifying, understanding and replicating what is going right at the organizational level.

In a typical AI intervention, an organization conducts a series of four one-day meetings, called an AI summit. Each day focuses on a distinct phase of what is referred to as the 4-D cycle: (i) the Discovery phase engages all stakeholders in identifying 'the best of what has been and what is', expressing and appreciating the organization's strengths and best practices, (ii) the Dream phase establishes a vision and higher purpose for the organization to achieve its full potential through sustaining its strengths and best practices, (iii) the Design phase builds a comprehensive action plan for prioritizing and replicating the organization's strengths and best practices, and (iv) the Destiny phase creates the implementation blueprint of the action plan developed in the design phase.

Work Psychology in Action: The case of Nutrimental Foods

In Brazil, government-sponsored Nutrimental Foods turned to AI after the Brazilian government decided to end its two-decade relationship as the company's partner in 1992. This decision created a new reality for Nutrimental and threatened the company's existence. All 750 employees that remained following massive layoffs engaged in the AI process, where they focused on discovering and developing the organization's positive core. As a result, Nutrimental experienced a notable turnaround in terms of productivity, profitability and employee retention (Barros & Cooperrider, 2000).

Promoting positive work behaviours

Developing an individual's psychological resources and attitudes does not always translate into positive behaviours at work, especially in the absence of rewards to motivate and sustain those behaviours. Research shows that when rewards are administered to employees contingent on behaving in productive ways, the desired behaviours are reinforced, which increases their frequency. This is also consistent with the long behaviourist traditions dating back to Pavlov, Watson and Skinner, who experimented with behavioural reinforcement in animals. The same techniques have been applied in the workplace with great success, and are now the foundations of many established reward systems.

Workplace behavioural management interventions attempt to modify existing behaviours or develop new, more positive ones through five steps: (i) identifying critical performance-related behaviours, (ii) measuring the current frequency of those behaviours, (iii) analysing the existing antecedents and consequences of the behaviours, (iv) intervening with positive reinforcers contingent on the desired behaviours and (v) evaluating the results. Three decades of research have consistently supported this approach (Stajkovic & Luthans, 1997, 2003).

Although people are unique in their needs and what they find motivating, three types of reinforcers are particularly powerful when administered contingently: money, feedback and recognition. On average, behavioural management interventions utilizing these three reinforcers can increase work performance by about 17% and have a success rate of about 63% (Stajkovic & Luthans, 1997, 2003). This effect has also been found to apply across industries and cultures (Welsh, Luthans, & Sommer, 1993).

Furthermore, contingent rewards tend to promote productive behaviours. This implies that managers should be trained in 'catching their employees doing something right' and providing them with positive feedback and recognition, rather than just focusing on detecting and punishing unacceptable behaviours. In line with this chapter, recent research shows that individuals and relationships thrive at a ratio of three positive interactions for every negative interaction in work settings. This ratio can be as high as five or six positive interactions for every negative interaction in personal contexts such as marriages (Fredrickson, 2009).

Replay

Positive work behaviours can be promoted through (i) identifying critical performance-related behaviours, (ii) measuring the current frequency of those behaviours, (iii) analysing the existing antecedents and consequences of the behaviours, (iv) intervening with positive reinforcers contingent on the desired behaviours and (v) evaluating the results. Three types of reinforcers are particularly powerful when administered contingently: money, feedback and recognition.

19.7 Selection-based Positive Interventions

Developmental interventions target malleable states and state-like characteristics that are open to development. On the other hand, stable traits and trait-like characteristics that are set through genetics or hardwiring should be addressed through effective selection and placement. For example, it is impractical to develop an introverted employee to become extroverted because extroversion is recognized to be one of the Big Five personality traits (Barrick & Mount, 1991), which exhibit high levels of stability over time. Instead, an organization should intentionally select employees who are predisposed toward extroversion where extroverted attitudes and behaviours can be conducive to superior performance, such as in sales positions. Several successful selection-based interventions are recognized in the literature. Below are two examples.

Selecting for optimism

Although optimism can be learned and developed, it also has a trait-like baseline that, if selected and properly matched with the right jobs, can have a direct impact on work performance. This notion was supported in a unique set of studies that Seligman conducted on the sales force of Metropolitan Life Insurance (Seligman, 1998).

> **Work Psychology in Action: Metropolitan Life Insurance**
>
> Initially, Metropolitan Life Insurance (MetLife) selected its sales force based on the results of an industry-recognized test, which focused on applicants' technical knowledge. However, Seligman's experiments showed that optimism may be even more critical for success in insurance sales positions. In his experiments, Seligman convinced MetLife to hire a 'special force' of applicants who failed the industry test but scored highly on a test that he had designed to measure optimism. Interestingly, optimists who failed the industry test outperformed pessimists who passed it.

Selecting for talent

According to the Gallup Organization, widely recognized for its polls, but also a leader in selection and placement, a strength can be defined as 'the ability to provide consistent, near-perfect performance in a given activity'. The key to building strengths is to identify employees' talents. Talents are naturally recurring patterns of thought, feeling or behaviour that can be productively applied. Employees should then be placed in roles where their talents are utilized on a daily basis, and developed along their dominant talent themes. Selection and placement based on talent, followed by development that is consistent with those talents, can yield strengths. Weakness should not be ignored. However, contrary to traditional methods of development where weak and problematic areas receive the most attention, in this approach deficiencies in certain areas may indicate poor selection and fit (Buckingham & Clifton, 2001).

> **Work Psychology in Action: A struggling hospital**
>
> St Lucie Medical Center, a struggling hospital in St Lucie County, Florida, with an annual personnel turnover rate of 35%, dissatisfied patients, low productivity, shrinking profits and poor morale adopted Gallup's strengths-based approach. A strengths-based survey identified pockets of highly engaged work units within the organization. St Lucie set out to replicate the dynamics of those work units by recognizing talent and nurturing strengths. Organizational action plans that included matching employee assignments with strengths resulted in a decrease in employee turnover rate of nearly 50% and improved morale. Subsequently, St Lucie Medical Center ranked number one on placement among 200 hospitals evaluated by Gallup within two years (Black, 2001).

Replay

Positive developmental interventions should target malleable states and state-like characteristics that are open to development and management. Stable traits and trait-like characteristics that are set through genetics or hardwiring should be addressed through effective selection and placement.

19.8 Conclusions

The goal of positive interventions is to go beyond fixing, or even preventing, problems and dysfunctions in the workplace. The purpose is to promote a physically, mentally and psychologically healthy workforce that provides a sustainable, human-based competitive advantage for organizations. Positive interventions promote an amplified environment where human strengths, capabilities and psychological resources are not simply managed to avoid problems but leveraged for a competitive advantage. Employers must recognize that despite humans' heliotropic tendencies towards the positive, employees are also hardwired to be biased toward negativity due to its intensity, novelty, singularity and adaptational implications. On the other hand, positivity is characterized by its broadening and building effects, making it qualitatively unique in its antecedents, processes and outcomes.

Positive interventions can add value in the workplace because they (i) yield recognized, desirable outcomes, (ii) target individual, group and/or organizational characteristics that are malleable and thus open to change, development and management, (iii) are qualitatively different from or cause desirable outcomes that go beyond existing interventions and (iv) yield benefits that exceed their costs.

In this chapter several successful interventions are discussed and shown to meet the above criteria. These interventions include the development of PsyCap and its constituent resources of self-efficacy, hope, optimism and resilience, the development of gratitude, and the promotion of positive behaviours through behavioural modification. Successful positive interventions also include selecting for talents and optimism, and creating a positive organizational context through authentic leadership development and appreciative inquiry.

Positivity in organizations and other life domains has attracted many scholars and practitioners due to its intuitive appeal and tangible results in terms of individual and organizational performance and well-being. It is now apparent that a more balanced perspective is necessary when designing work interventions. Both positivity and negativity are needed and serve unique, complementary purposes that are indispensable for organizational success and effectiveness.

Discussion Points

1. Does positivity have a place in the workplace? Explain.
2. Should an organization be responsible for the development of an individual's psychological capital or is that up to the individual? Explain.
3. To what extent can an organization develop its employees' positivity? Explain.
4. If humans are naturally attracted to what is positive and life giving, why are they so biased towards negativity?
5. In what ways are positive interventions unique and different from the majority of existing work interventions?

Learning by Doing

Do not be concerned if positivity does not come naturally. You are not alone. Research by Lyubomirsky (2007) shows that as much as 50% of the capacity for positivity is determined by genetics or is 'hardwired' in the brain at a very early age. However, 40% of positivity is open to development. The good news is that only 10% of positivity is based on life circumstances such as income, marital status, physical attractiveness, job conditions or even health and success. Below are some tips to help you increase your positivity. Imagine you supervise or manage 100 employees. How might you take advantage of the information in this chapter and the methods listed below to improve your productivity and the productivity of the work team you are responsible for?

Meditate
Mediation does not have to be elaborate. Just 5–7 minutes a day can be sufficient. Simply take a few deep breaths and focus only on breathing. If your mind wanders bring it back to your deep breathing. Studies demonstrate that a person can

decrease stress, improve immune function and increase positivity with regular meditation (Shapiro, Schwartz, & Santere, 2005).

Journal strengths
Identify a time when you were at your best and then reflect on the personal strengths you presented in that event/situation. Review this story every day for a week and reflect on the identified strength. Then identify another time when you were at your best and repeat (Seligman, Steen, Park, & Peterson, 2005).

Journal three positive events
Each evening for 30 days identify and write down three things that went well during the day and explain what caused them to go well (Seligman et al. 2005).

Exercise
Increase your heart rate by engaging in cardiovascular activities such as jogging, biking and elliptical training. Research shows that regular cardio activity alone, 45 minutes a day, three days a week, is as effective in elevating mild to moderate levels of depression as antidepressant medication. Exercise is also known to improve mood, motivate and enhance work performance (Babyak et al., 2000).

Further Reading

Diener, E., & Biswas-Diener, R. (2008). *Happiness: Unlocking the mysteries of psychological wealth*. Malden, MA: Blackwell.

Donaldson, S. I., Csikszentmihalyi, M., & Nakamura, J. (2011). *Applied positive psychology: Improving everyday life, health, schools, work and society*. New York: Routledge.

Fredrickson, B. L. (2009). *Positivity*. New York: Crown/Random House.

Luthans, F., Youssef, C. M., & Avolio, B. J. (2007). *Psychological capital: Developing the human competitive edge*. Oxford: Oxford University Press.

Lyubomirsky, S. (2007). *The how of happiness: A new approach to getting the life you want*. New York: Penguin.

References

Avey, J. B., Reichard, R., Luthans, F., & Mhatre, K. H. (2011). Meta-analysis of the impact of positive psychological capital on employee attitudes, behaviors, and performance. *Human Resource Development Quarterly, 22*, 127–152.

Avolio, B. J., & Luthans, F. (2006). *The high impact leader: Moments matter in accelerating authentic leadership*. New York: McGraw-Hill.

Babyak, M., Blumenthal, J., Herman, S., Khatri, P., Poraiswamy, P., Moore, K., & Krishnan, K. (2000). Exercise treatment for major depression: Maintenance of therapeutic benefit at ten months. *Psychosomatic Medicine, 62*, 633–638.

Barrick, M. R., & Mount, M. K. (1991). The big five personality dimensions and job performance: A meta-analysis. *Personnel Psychology, 44*, 1–26.

Barros, I., & Cooperrider, D. L. (2000). A story of nutrimental in Brazil: How wholeness, appreciation, and inquiry bring out the best in human organization. *Organization Development Journal, 18*, 22–28.

Baumeister, R. F., Bratslavsky, E., Finkenaur, C., & Vohs, K. D. (2001). Bad is stronger than good. *Review of General Psychology, 5*, 323–370.

Black, B. (2001). The road to recovery. *Gallup Management Journal*. Retrieved from http://gmj.gallup.com/content/772/road-recovery.aspx.

Buckingham, M., & Clifton, D. O. (2001). *Now, discover your strengths.* New York: Free Press.

Cameron, K. S. (2008). Paradox in positive organizational change. *Journal of Applied Behavioral Science, 44*, 7–24.

Cameron, K. S., & Caza, A. (2004). Contributions to the discipline of positive organizational scholarship. *American Behavioral Scientist, 47*, 731–739.

Casey, G. W. (2011). Comprehensive solider fitness: A vision for psychological resilience in the U.S. army. *American Psychologist, 66*, 1–3.

Carver, C., & Scheier, M. (2002). Optimism. In C. R. Snyder, & S. Lopez (Eds.), *Handbook of positive psychology* (pp. 231–243). Oxford: Oxford University Press.

Cooperrider, D. L., & Whitney, D. (2005). *Appreciative inquiry: A positive revolution in change.* San Francisco: Berrett-Koehler.

Emmons, R. A. (2004). Gratitude. In C. Peterson, & M. Seligman (Eds.), *Character strengths and virtues: A handbook and classification* (pp. 553–568). Oxford: Oxford University Press.

Fredrickson, B. L. (2001). The role of positive emotions in positive psychology: The broaden-and-build theory of positive emotions. *American Psychologist, 56*, 218–226.

Fredrickson, B. L. (2009). *Positivity.* New York: Crown/Random House.

Lester, P. B., McBride, S., Bliese, P. D., & Adler, A. B. (2011). Bringing science to bear: An empirical assessment of the comprehensive solider fitness program. *American Psychologist, 66*, 77–81.

Locke, E. A., & Latham, G. P. (2002). Building a practically useful theory of goal setting and task motivation: A 35-year odyssey. *American Psychologist, 57*, 705–717.

Luthans, F. (2002a). Positive organizational behavior: Developing and managing psychological strengths. *Academy of Management Executive, 16*, 57–72.

Luthans, F. (2002b). The need for and meaning of positive organizational behavior. *Journal of Organizational Behavior, 23*, 695–106.

Luthans, F., Avey, J. B., Avolio, B. J., & Peterson, S. J. (2010). The development and resulting performance impact of positive psychological capital. *Human Resource Development Quarterly, 21*, 41–67.

Luthans, F., Avey, J. B., & Patera, J. L. (2008). Experimental analysis of a web-based training intervention to develop positive psychological capital. *Academy of Management Learning and Education, 7*, 209–221.

Luthans, F., & Avolio, B. J. (2009). The 'point' of positive organizational behavior. *Journal of Organizational Behavior, 30*, 291–307.

Luthans, F., Youssef, C. M., & Avolio, B. J. (2007). *Psychological capital: Developing the human competitive edge.* New York: Oxford University Press.

Lyubomirsky, S. (2007). *The how of happiness: A new approach to getting the life you want.* New York: Penguin.

Lyubomirsky, S., King, L., & Diener, E. (2005). The benefits of frequent positive affect: Does happiness lead to success? *Psychological Bulletin, 131*, 803–855.

Maslow, A. H. (1954). *Motivation and personality.* New York: Harper.

Masten, A. S. (2001). Ordinary magic: Resilience process in development. *American Psychologist, 56*, 227–239.

Masten, A. S., & Reed, M. J. (2002). Resilience in development. In C. R. Snyder, & S. Lopez (Eds.), *Handbook of positive psychology* (pp. 74–88). Oxford: Oxford University Press.

Pelled, L. H., & Xin, K. R. (1999). Down and out: An investigation of the relationship between mood and employee withdrawal behavior. *Journal of Management, 6*, 875–895.

Peterson, C. (2000). The future of optimism. *American Psychologist, 55*, 44–55.

Reivich, K., Seligman, M. E. P., & McBride, S. (2011). Master resilience training in the U.S. Army. *American Psychologist, 66*, 25–34.

Schneider, S. L. (2001). In search of realistic optimism. *American Psychologist, 56*, 250–263.

Seligman, M. E. P. (1998). *Learned optimism.* New York: Pocket Books.

Seligman, M. E. P., & Csikszentmihalyi, M. (2000). Positive psychology. *American Psychologist, 55*, 5–14.

Seligman, M. E. P., Steen, T. A., Park, N., & Peterson, C. (2005). Positive psychology progress: Empirical validation of interventions. *American Psychologist, 60*, 410–421.

Shapiro, S. L., Schwartz, G. E., & Santere, C. (2005). Meditation and positive psychology. In C. R. Snyder, & S. J. Lopez (Eds.), *Handbook of positive psychology* (pp. 632–645). New York: Oxford University Press.

Snyder, C. R. (2000). *Handbook of hope: Theory, measures and applications*. San Diego: Academic Press.

Snyder, C. R., Irving, L., & Anderson, J. (1991). Hope and health: Measuring the will and the ways. In C. R. Snyder, & D. R. Forsyth (Eds.), *Handbook of social and clinical psychology* (pp. 285–305). Elmsford, NY: Pergamon.

Snyder, C. R., Sympson, S. C., Ybasco, F. C., Borders, T. F., Babyak, M. A., & Higgins, R. L. (1996). Development and validation of the state hope scale. *Journal of Personality and Social Psychology, 70*, 321–335.

Stajkovic, A. D., & Luthans, F. (1997). A meta-analysis of the effects of organizational behavior modification on task performance: 1975–95. *Academy of Management Journal, 40*, 1122–1149.

Stajkovic, A., & Luthans, F. (1998a). Social cognitive theory and self-efficacy: Going beyond traditional motivational and behavioral approaches. *Organizational Dynamics, 26*, 62–74.

Stajkovic, A. D., & Luthans, F. (1998b). Self-efficacy and work-related performance: A meta-analysis. *Psychological Bulletin, 124*, 240–261.

Stajkovic, A., & Luthans F. (2003). Behavioral management and task performance in organizations: Conceptual background, meta-analysis, and test of alternative models. *Personnel Psychology, 56*, 155–194.

Staw, B. M., Sutton, R. I., & Pelled, L. H. (1994). Employee positive emotion and favorable outcomes at the workplace. *Organization Science, 5*, 51–71.

Sutcliffe, K. M., & Vogus, T. (2003). Organizing for resilience. In K. S. Cameron, J. E. Dutton, & R. E. Quinn (Eds.), *Positive organizational scholarship* (pp. 94–110). San Francisco: Berrett-Koehler.

Sweetman, D., Luthans, F., Avey, J. B., & Luthans, B. C. (2011). Relationship between possible positive psychological capital and creative perfromance. *Canadian Journal of Administrative Sciences, 28*, 4–13.

Weinstein, N. D. (1989). Optimistic biases about personal risks. *Science, 8*, 1232–1233.

Welsh, D. H. B., Luthans, F., & Sommer, S. M. (1993). Managing Russian factory workers: The impact of U.S.-based behavioral and participative techniques. *Academy of Management Journal, 36*, 58–79.

Youssef, C. M., & Luthans, F. (2007). Positive organizational behavior in the workplace: The impact of hope, optimism, and resilience. *Journal of Management, 33*, 774–800.

Index

ability 22, 128, 139, 140
ability requirements approach 22, 23
abnormal work hours 197, 200, 206–10, 214
   and distress 209
   and family life 208
   and fatigue 208
   and health 207–10
   and well-being 208
   definition 206–7
   empirical evidence 208–10
   prevalence 207
   risks 207–8
absence policy 382
absence/presence culture 382
absenteeism 367
   and job demands 126
   and job design 84
   and job satisfaction 332
   and psychological flexibility 403
   and salaries 50
   and stress-management interventions 395
   and work design 82
   see also sickness absence
absorption 300, 301
abusive supervision 179
accident proneness 345
accidents 342–66
   and failures in maintenance 356, 359
   and human behaviour 355
   and lack of communication 355
   and management practices 354, 355, 356, 359
   and physical work environment 358, 359
   and safety climate 362
   and social support 358
   and subjective demands 134
   and the physical environment 355
   antecedents of 354–9
   discussion of 360
   exposure 345–7
   incidence 357–8
   liability for 344, 345
   of miners 12–13
   prevention 345
   propensity for 346–7
   risk groups for 343–4
accomplishments 146, 296, 298
actigraphs 206
action phases 441
action programs 148
action regulation theory 145, 147–52, 155, 163, 416
activation 125, 127
activation–deactivation 304
activation-enhancing mechanism 103, 109
active failures 351–3
active learning 71–2, 403
active learning hypothesis 71–2
active recovery mechanism 213, 215
activities 4–5
activity–rest cycle 206, 207, 214
adaptation 426, 462
adaptive structuration theory (AST) 221, 232–5

An Introduction to Contemporary Work Psychology, First Edition.
Edited by Maria C. W. Peeters, Jan de Jonge and Toon W. Taris.
© 2014 John Wiley & Sons, Ltd. Published 2014 by John Wiley & Sons, Ltd.

adaptive testing 42
additional decrement (AD) 74–5
adrenal glands 197, 198
advising 438
affect 203, 252, 259, 310
affective path of enrichment 274
age 244–7, 261, 417
agency 78, 465
aggression 102, 179, 245
agreeableness 278
agriculture 7, 8
airline cockpits 229
air traffic control 138, 261
alcohol 244, 250
allostatic load 199, 200, 214
allostatic load theory 199
allostatic systems 200
alpha coefficients 38
alternative forms reliability 35, 36–7
ambiguous behaviour 180
ambulance call-out scheduling 229
anaesthesia teams 452
antecedent–outcome models 272, 274
anxiety 10, 306, 395
applied psychology 13
appreciation 163, 186, 467
appreciative inquiry (AI) 473
arousal 154, 464
asset-focused strategies 468
attention 154
attitude 126, 135, 172, 235, 308, 359
automatic emotion regulation 160–1
automatic mode 151
automatic processes 150
automatic regulation 162
automation 223
automatization 149, 150, 152
autonomy (AU)
  and end-user engagement 80
  and high-quality work 357
  and job control 172
  and job demands 97
  and job discretion 95
  and motivation 92
  and NWW 19

and recovery from work 215
and resources 95
and social support 95
and the Vitamin Model 75
and work–family conflict 285
and work–family enrichment 281
and work-time control 212
as a job resource 102
avoidance-focused coping 283

balance mechanism 103
bank wiring observation room 437
behaviour 323–4
  and accidents 355
  and engagement 308
  and gender 270
  and group cohesiveness 181
  and job demands 126
  and job simplification 172
  challenges-seeking 421, 422
  counterproductive 307
  demands-reducing 421, 422, 423
  feedback-seeking 421
  proactive 420
  resources-seeking 421, 422, 423
  restrictions on 148
  risky 10
  safety-related 347
  social support-seeking 421
  unhealthy 203
  see also positive organizational behaviour
behavioural description approach 22, 23
behavioural lifestyle mechanism 203, 204, 205
behavioural modification 477
behavioural readiness 327
behaviour-based work–family conflict 270
behaviourism 474
behaviour requirements approach 22, 23
Bhopal disaster 351
biofeedback 395
biotechnology teams 436, 445
body clock 207, 208, 210

body mass index (BMI) 282
body positions 153
body temperature 207
bonuses 81
boredom 293–320
  and arousal 316
  and counterproductive work behaviour 309
  and dispositional factors 311–12
  and distress 307
  and engagement 299–300
  and extraversion 310
  and health 316
  and job demands 73
  and performance 307, 316
  and sickness absence 307, 316
  and turnover 307
  and underload 154, 306
  and under-stimulation 125, 298, 301, 304, 316
  and well-being 302, 316
  avoidance 422
  causes 306–7
  consequences 306–7
  definition 298
  explanations for 313–14, 316
  in popular culture 9
  measurement 299
  research 295
bottom-up participative approach 403
boundarylessness 378, 380
boundaryless work 213, 214, 215
breaks 208, 211, 212, 215, 437
Broaden-and-Build Model 462
broadening effect 462
buffering effect 95, 173, 175
building effect 463
bullying 5, 179, 408
bureaucratization 306
burnout 293–320
  and accomplishment 296, 298
  and cardiovascular symptoms 306
  and CSEs 253
  and cynicism 297, 298, 301
  and depersonalization 296
  and emotional instability 309, 310

and engagement 303
and health 306, 309, 316
and interpersonal
  resources 305
and job demands 92, 97,
  305, 309
and job resources 92, 95, 309
and locus of control 311
and mental distancing 297,
  298, 301
and neuroticism 309
and optimism 311
and overload 304, 313
and overstimulation 316
and performance 316
and psychosomatic
  symptoms 306
and reciprocity 315
and self-efficacy 311
and self-esteem 296, 311
and sickness absence 309,
  316, 377
and stress 316
and subjective demands 134
and the ERI Model 78
and the JD-R Model 93
and uncertainty 157
and well-being 302, 316
and withdrawal from team 313
and women 248, 250, 298
and workaholism 303
and work–family conflict 279
and work obstacles 157
antecedents 91
as a multidimensional
  construct 297
biomarkers 306
causes 305–6
consequences 305–6
definition 296, 297
explanations for 312–13
history of 294–5
incidence 298
interpersonal explanation 313

carcinogenous substances 5
cardiovascular reactivity 94
cardiovascular symptoms 77, 78,
  127, 157, 209, 306
career development 255

career opportunities 75, 77, 78
career outlook 5
caring 183, 189, 190
catecholamines 197
challenge demands 146, 147,
  161, 307, 308
challenge–hindrance
  stressors 146
Challenger disaster 351
challenge seeking 421, 422, 425
Chemnitz 12
Chernobyl disaster 351–2
chronological approach 246
chunks 151
circadian rhythms 207–210, 215
circumplex model of
  emotions 301
civic virtue 361
Civility, Respect and Engagement
  at Work (CREW) 46
classical psychometric theory 42
classical test theory
  (CTT) 34–43, 41
coaching 397, 406
  see also training
coal industry 79
cockpit crews 452
coefficient of precision 38
coefficient of stability 36
cognitive activation theory of
  stress (CATS) 197
cognitive appraisals 259
cognitive-behavioural
  programmes 394, 395
cognitive-behavioural
  therapy 395
cognitive coping strategies 395
cognitive demands 102, 105,
  107, 145, 149, 154, 163
cognitive detachment 105, 107
cognitive development 91
cognitive errors 348–9, 353
cognitive image 148
cognitive load 18, 154
cognitive resources 102, 105,
  107
collaboration 452
collectivism 450
combat stress see war stress
commitment 16, 97, 126, 425

common method variance
  (CMV) 40, 42, 43, 49,
  132, 135
communication
  and accidents 355
  and multicultural teams 450
  and stress management 396
  and training 449
  new means of 19
  structure 440
  virtual 449–50, 452, 454
competence
  and action regulation theory 163
  and feedback 95
  and resources 95
compensation mechanism 103
competition 268, 271
complexity 102, 151, 418
components approach 275–6
comprehensive soldier fitness
  (CSF) 469
comprehensive stress-management
  interventions 403
computer-adaptive testing 42
computer crime 363
computer-supported cooperative
  work (CSCW) 229
computer technology 138
  see also information and
  communications technology
concentration 125
concurrent validation 40
conflict 141, 179, 180, 441,
  451, 453
conscientiousness 251, 278, 312
Conservation of Resources
  (COR) theory 93
constant effect (CE) 74–5
constellations 162
construct contamination 40, 42, 43
construct deficiency 40, 43
construct validation strategies
  39, 40
consultation 83
consumer needs 435
content validation strategies 39, 40
contingency planning 465–6
control 187, 255, 260, 424
  see also job control
control beliefs 173, 174, 175

controlled processes 150
convenience sampling 49, 51
co-ordinated activities 4–5
co-ordination meeting 233
Copenhagen Psychosocial Questionnaire (COPSOQ) 384
coping 72, 73, 95–6, 184, 282–3, 286, 311, 395
coping hypothesis 95
core self-evaluation (CSE) 252, 253
correlation 50
cortisol 198, 206
cost-benefit analysis 454
counselling 181, 394
counterproductive work behaviour (CWB) 126, 253, 309, 323, 324, 331–3, 422
covariation *see* correlation
co-worker support groups 397
creative job demands 334–5
creativity
   and conflict 180
   and detachment 106–7
   and job resources 103, 105
crew resource management (CRM) 448, 449
crisis support 386
criterion contamination 41
criterion deficiency 41
criterion-referenced validation strategies 40
Cronbach's alpha 36, 38
cross-domain principle 279, 280
cross-training 448
Cullen Report 353
culture 9, 11, 189, 283–4
curvilinear effects 75, 76
customer satisfaction 309
cynicism 95, 248, 297, 298, 301, 313

data collection techniques 22, 23
Davis-Besse nuclear power plant 349
deadlines 123
decision latitude 69, 70
decision making 85, 124, 396
decision models 380–4

dedication 300, 301
deep acting 160, 162
degradation 94
Demand–Control–Support (DCS) Model 24, 63, 69–73, 118, 120, 176
   and ancilliary interventions 84
   and job demands 95
   and job design 85
   and policy 82–4
   and sickness absence 375, 377
   and stress 294
   evaluation 72–73
   nature of demands 146
Demand-Induced Strain Compensation (DISC) Model 24, 89, 99–109
   see also extended DISC Model (DISC-R)
demand reduction 425, 426
demands
   and job control 175
   and resources 162–3
   and role stress 179
   nature of 145–62
   qualitative 146
   relating to internal processes 145
   see also challenge demands; cognitive demands; emotional demands; environmental demands; hindrance demands; interpersonal demands; job demands; motivational demands; qualitative demands; quantitative demands; physical demands; role demands; volitional demands
demands-reducing behaviour 421, 422, 423
demographic changes 19, 223
depersonalization 296, 313
depression 10, 72, 78, 175, 306
De Re Metallica 12
De Re Militari 12
Design phase 473
design studies 21
Destiny phase 473

detachment 103–7, 110, 212
developmental interventions 475
diagnostic profile 107–8
diaries 54, 258, 259, 425
diet 250
direct spillover 273
Discovery phase 473
DISC questionnaire (DISQ) 102, 107
discretionary behaviour 423
disease model 473
display rules 158, 162, 417
distress 146, 209, 307
distributed cognition 228, 229
Docklands Light Railway 230
doctors 11
domain specificity principle 273
Dream phase 473
dual-earner couples 267, 271
Dutch Boredom Scale (DUBS) 299, 303
dynamic model of presenteeism and absenteeism 381, 382–3

economic crises 435
education 16, 20, 417
effort 77–9
effort–recovery balance 212
effort–recovery theory 197, 199, 200, 214
Effort–Reward Imbalance (ERI) Model 24, 63, 77–9, 84, 85, 95, 163, 186, 375, 377
eldercare responsibilities 267
electronic books 223
electronic patient record (EPR) system 234–5
email 223
emergent states 441
emotional demands 93, 102, 107, 145, 158–62, 408
emotional detachment 107, 108
emotional deviance 161, 162
emotional dissonance 97, 160
emotional exhaustion 296
emotional instability 309, 310
emotional labour 145, 158–62, 180
emotional resources 102, 107, 108

emotional stability 102, 252, 309, 310
emotional support 102, 182, 184, 187, 190
emotion-focused coping 283
emotions 162, 462–3
emotion work 18, 145, 158–62, 180
employability 20, 21
employee assistance programmes 395
employee attitude surveys 54
employee retention 473
employment
  and health 11, 77
  and status 10
  and well-being 11
  protection 375
  social benefits 10
  see also unemployment
empowerment 172, 403, 449
enactive mastery 256
end-user engagement 80
energetic process 93, 97
engagement 293–320
  and attitude 308
  and boredom 299–300
  and burnout 303
  and challenge demands 307, 308
  and challenge seeking 425
  and conscientiousness 312
  and customer satisfaction 309
  and demand reduction 425
  and dispositional factors 312
  and emotional stability 309, 310
  and extraversion 310
  and job crafting 424, 425, 429
  and job resources 95, 97, 98, 304, 307, 308, 309, 427
  and motivation 308, 309
  and performance 312
  and positive affect 310
  and project work 416
  and PSC 408
  and resources 95
  and responsibility 307
  and sickness absence 308
  and supervisory coaching 98
  and the JD-R Model 95
  and turnover 308
  and well-being 302, 316
  assessment 301, 303
  causes 307–9
  definition 299, 300
  distinguished from satisfaction 304
  explanations for 307–9, 314–16
engineering 21
entrepreneurs 268, 452
environment 152, 396
environmental demands 152
equity 75
ergonomics 15, 21, 138, 139, 152, 226, 345
errors
  and accidents 362, 363
  and subjective demands 134
  and working memory 154
  cognitive 348–9, 353
  discussion of 361
  documentation of 361
  knowledge based 348, 349, 351, 353
  non-intended 350
  of teams 435
  rule based 348, 349
  see also generic error-modelling system
esteem 77, 78, 79, 189, 190
ethnic diversity 417
ethnicity 244, 248–9, 250
ethnography 228
European Foundation for the Improvement of Living and Working Conditions (EFILW) 200
European Statistical System (Eurostat) 368
European Survey on Working Conditions 207
European Working Time Directive (EWTD) 201
evaluation 132
exercise 395
exhaustion 146, 296, 297, 300, 301, 313, 316, 424
existential realism 44–7, 50–5
expansion approach 270, 271
expansionist theory of multiple roles 270
expectations 179, 312
experience sampling 52, 53, 258
expert ratings 132
extended DISC Model (DISC-R) 104–5, 106–10
external organizational factors 122
external recovery 210, 211, 212, 215
extraversion 278, 281, 285, 310, 475
eye protection 359

facet job satisfaction 322–2
factories 13
family
  and social support 184
  definition 268–9
  resources 281, 285
family–work conflict (FWC) 272, 279, 280, 282, 284, 285
family–work enrichment (FEW) 272, 281–2, 284, 285
fatigue
  and abnormal work hours 208
  and arousal 154
  and burnout 297
  and cognitive demands 154
  and computer technology 138
  and degradation 94
  and focusing 154
  and job demands 138, 139
  and performance 94, 138
  and reduced capacity 154
  and rest 125, 128
  and shift rotation 209, 210
  and subjective demands 134
  and work hours 203, 205, 223
  in ammunition factories 294
  see also fatigue-like states
fatigue-like states 125, 128
  see also fatigue

feedback (FB) 66, 68, 69
  and competence 95
  and job demands 97, 123
  and learning 95
  and motivation 92
  and self-efficacy 256
  and social persuasion 464
  and social support 181
  and uncertainty 157
  as a reinforcer 474
  positive and negative 462
  use of 151
feedback loops 385
feedback-seeking
    behaviour 421
field experiments 45–7
five-stage model of team
    development 443
flexibility
  and automatization 150
  and competition 268
  and mobile working 224
  and PSC 408
  and work–family policies 283
  and work-time control 212
  in human action 149
  of work 19, 81, 414
  organizational 124
  psychological 403
  requirement for 20, 21
  spatial 20
  temporal 19, 20
flight attendants 158
flow 54
focus groups 52, 53
focusing 154
formative evaluation 228
free periods 211
friendships 16, 184
full mediation 94
functional approach 246
functional units 149

Gallup Organization 475
gap analysis 473
gender 244, 247–8, 270, 382
general accident causation
    scenario 355
general failure types (GFTs) 354,
    355–9

generalizability 44, 45, 47–51,
    54–6
Generic Error-Modelling System
    (GEMS) 347, 348–51
globalization 19, 21, 417, 436,
    449, 450, 452
global job satisfaction 322
goal attainment 156, 244, 308
goal-directed activities 4
goal setting 151, 447, 465
goals, operators, methods and
    selection rules (GOMS) 228
grand theories 90
grand-tour questions 52
gratitude 471–2
Groening, Matt 10
group cohesiveness 181
group discussion 47
group identification 451
groupthink 451, 453
guessing parameter 42

hackers 363
halo effect 136
happy–productive worker
    thesis 31
harassment 179, 180, 190, 408
hardiness 311
Hawthorne studies 16, 64,
    65, 437
health
  and boredom 316
  and burnout 306, 309, 316
  and emotional demands 93
  and emotion work 161–2
  and employment 11
  and job control 72, 73,
    191, 399
  and job demands 71–3, 92,
    93, 100, 125, 129, 140,
    163, 421, 424
  and job motivation 92
  and job resources 92, 100
  and lean production 124
  and locus of control 174
  and managerial support 285
  and motivation 109
  and multiple roles 270
  and off-the-job events 104
  and overload 399

  and overtime 204, 205, 214
  and presenteeism 399
  and PSC 407, 408
  and qualitative demands 163
  and recovery from work 105,
    197
  and satisfaction 40
  and shift work 99, 209, 210
  and sickness absence 385,
    386, 399
  and sickness presence 385, 386
  and social support 72, 73
  and stress 190, 197, 198, 394
  and the DCSM 69
  and the ERI Model 77
  and the human relations
    movement 17
  and the JD–R Model 421
  and unemployment 10, 77
  and work hours 202–5,
    207–10, 214
  and work psychology 5, 17
  and work–family
    enrichment 282
  and workload 93, 421
  mental 74–7, 306, 396, 403
  of miners 12, 17
Health and Safety Executive 83
health-impairment process 93,
    97, 424
health information theory
    (HIT) 221
heart disease 72
heliotropism 461, 476
Herald of Free Enterprise
    disaster 351
hierarchies 163, 435, 436, 453
hierarchy of functional units 149
high-performance work systems
    (HPWS) 124, 125, 357
high-quality work 357
high-strain jobs 70, 104, 105
hindrance demands 146, 147,
    308, 424
hindrance stressors 179
Hippocratic Collection 11
hope 128, 260, 465–6,
    468, 477
hopelessness 465
hostility 180, 189

human computer interaction
    (HCI) 221, 227, 228
human factors 15, 225
    see also ergonomics
human relations
    movement 16–17
human resource management
    (HRM) 123, 124, 125,
    137, 140
humour 286
hypothalamic–pituitary–adrenal
    (HPA) system 197, 198, 200

ideal processes 151
'i deals' *see* idiosyncratic deals
idiosyncratic deals ('i-deals') 20,
    135, 417, 419
illegitimate tasks 20
ill-health policy 370
Illness Flexibility Model 381–2
immune system 127, 200
inactivity 250
incentives 124, 437
incivility 46
income 10, 248
independent variables 44–5
indicator tool 83
indirect spillover 273
individual characteristics 75,
    243–66
    see also worker characteristics
individual/organizational
    interface-directed
    interventions 397
individual stress-management
    interventions 395–400
individualism 450
Industrial Fatigue Research
    Board 294
Industrial Revolution 10, 13, 17,
    64, 268
inefficacy 313
information and communications
    technology (ICT) 10, 20,
    21, 123
information overload 223
information revolution 18
information systems 232
information technology
    (IT) 222, 223, 233

injuries 343, 346, 357
innovation 100, 123–5, 139,
    425–6
Institute of Social Research
    (University of Michigan) 294
instrumental path of
    enrichment 274
instrumental support 182, 184,
    187, 188, 190
integration 269
intellectual mode 151
intended acts 348
intended errors 350
intensification of work 20
interaction (effect) 95, 100, 128,
    162, 176,
interdisciplinary work design
    framework 416
interfaces 227
internal organizational
    factors 122
internal recovery 210, 211, 212,
    215
internal reliability 35–8
internal validity 46
International Labour Office 200–1
International Labour
    Organization (ILO) 7
International Organization for
    Standardization (ISO) 120
internet-based surveys 54
interpersonal contact 75
interpersonal demands 296
interpersonal relations 447
inter-rater reliability 35, 36, 37
inter-role conflict 284
interruptions 157
inter-sender conflict 155
interviews 52, 53, 132, 372
intra-sender conflict 155
introversion 475
investment, in employee skills 124
involuntary absence 372–3
iso-strain jobs 70
item difficulty parameter 41
item discrimination parameter 42
item response theory (IRT) 41, 42

job analysis 96–7
job characteristics

    and attitudinal outcomes 416
    and individual
        characteristics 75
    and job features 76
    and mental health 75
    and overcommitment 79
    and performance 190
    and satisfaction–performance
        relation 330
    and the Vitamin Model 73–6
    and well-being 76, 190
    everyday changes 421
    interactions between 100
    see also job characteristics
        approach; Job Characteristics
        Model
job characteristics approach 22
    see also job characteristics; Job
        Characteristics Model
Job Characteristics Model
    (JCM) 24, 63, 65–9, 416
    and ancilliary interventions 84
    and job design 85
    and motivation 92
    and policy 82–4
    evaluation 67
    see also job characteristics; job
        characteristics approach
job complexity 334–5
Job Content Questionnaire
    (JCQ) 71
job control 172–95
    and health 191
    and autonomy 172
    and decision authority 172
    and demands 175
    and empowerment 172
    and health 72, 73, 399
    and job decision latitude 172
    and job demands 304
    and leadership 187–8
    and learning 72, 173, 175
    and locus of control 176
    and mobile working 224
    and motivation 172, 173,
        175, 190
    and overload 120
    and participation 172
    and performance 175, 178, 191
    and pressure 120

job control (*cont'd*)
    and PSC 408
    and resources 176
    and satisfaction 172, 175
    and self-efficacy 173, 176
    and self-reports 175
    and social meaning 190
    and stress 172, 173, 175, 176
    and the DCSM 71–2
    and the Vitamin Model 75
    and well-being 175, 178
    assessment 83
    definition 69
    functions 173–4
    guidance 83
    in the working
        environment 190
    interventions for
        improving 176–7
    objective ratings 175
    outcomes 172–95
    research 174–6
job crafting 414–33
    and commitment 425
    and control 424
    and employee rank 423, 424
    and engagement 424, 425,
        426, 429
    and innovation 425–6
    and job demands 421, 422, 423
    and job resources 421
    and motivation 420, 426
    and organizational
        change 425–6
    and performance 424, 426
    and pressure 424
    and satisfaction 424, 425
    and self-efficacy 429
    and self-image 424
    and the JD–R model 421–3
    and well-being 429
    as an individual job redesign
        approach 419–29
    conceptualization 419–20
    definition 415, 419, 420, 421
    dysfunctional
        consequences 426
    outcomes 424, 425
    predictors 423
    roots 415–18

training 427–9
unresolved issues 426–7
job decision latitude 172
Job Demand–Control
    Model 162, 173, 175, 408
job demands
    and ability 128, 140
    and attitudes 126
    and autonomy 97
    and behaviour 126
    and boredom 73, 144
    and burnout 92, 97, 305, 309
    and coping 73
    and depression 72
    and emotional dissonance 97
    and exhaustion 424
    and fatigue 138, 139
    and feedback 97, 123
    and health 71, 72, 73, 92, 93,
        100, 125, 129, 140, 163,
        421, 424
    and heart disease 72
    and high-performance work
        systems 125
    and human resource
        management 140
    and job control 304
    and job crafting 421, 422, 423
    and job performance 125
    and job resources 103, 105,
        108, 109, 110
    and learning 126
    and morale 396
    and motivation 73, 92, 100,
        424
    and negative affect 144
    and organizational
        citizenship 126
    and overload 304
    and performance 126
    and performance appraisal 123
    and private life constraints 128,
        140
    and productivity 100
    and PSC 408
    and psychological capital 128,
        140
    and recovery 106
    and recruitment 123
    and rewards 163

    and role ambiguity 156
    and role problems 304
    and satisfaction 126
    and self-regulation 101
    and sickness absence 126, 375
    and skill development 126
    and social support 72, 97, 304
    and strain 95, 97
    and stress 109, 135, 375
    and stressors 145
    and the DCSM 69–73
    and the Vitamin Model 75
    and training 123
    and turnover 126
    and under-stimulation 73
    and well-being 97, 125, 129,
        140, 396
    and worker characteristics 140
    and work–family conflict 285
    and work–home
        interference 128
    as effort 77
    assessment 83, 132–5
    creative 334–5
    definition 102
    guidance 83
    interpersonal 335
    qualitative *see* qualitative job
        demands
    quantitative *see* quantitative
        job demands
    safety related 359
    self-rated measures 132–7
    types 102
    unclear 156
Job Demands–Resources
    Model (JD–R Model) 24,
    89, 91–9, 108, 109, 118,
    173
    and health 421
    and job analysis 96–7
    and job crafting 421–3
    and PSC 408
    and well-being 421
    and work–family
        enrichment 281
    empirical test of 98
    evaluation 98–9
    evidence for 97
    key assumptions 92–7

Job Descriptive Index
    (JDI) 322–3
job design 63–88, 415
    and absenteeism 84
    and motivation 419
    and performance 419
    and recovery from work 211
    and working conditions 419
    guidance on 84
    involvement of employees
        in 80
    political regulation 64
    research 223
    socio-technical approach 172
    see also job redesign
Job Diagnostic Survey (JDS) 68,
    69
job discretion 95
job performance *see* performance
job prospects 163
job redesign 137, 138, 139, 396,
    415–17, 420
    and diagnostic profile 107–8
    and motivation 418
    and Taylorism 16
    and technology 417
    and the DCSM 71
    and well-being 418
    bottom-up approaches 419
    continuous 231
    individualization of 417–18
    relational perspectives 417
    research 416
    time perspective 418
    top-down
        interventions 414–15
    to stimulate
        proactivity 417–18
job redesign *see also* job design
job resources
    and burnout 92, 95, 309
    and commitment 97
    and creativity 103, 105
    and engagement 95, 97, 98,
        304, 307, 308, 309, 427
    and health 92, 100
    and job crafting 421
    and job demands 103, 105,
        108, 109, 110
    and learning 105

and morale 396
and motivation 92, 95, 97, 100
and PSC 408
and self-efficacy 309
and stress 109
and well-being 396
and work–family conflict 285
definition 102
stress-buffering effects 101,
    103, 106
job restructuring 396
job satisfaction
    see satisfaction
job security 163, 382
job simplification 232
joint optimization 80
justice 180, 189
just-in-time management 123

King's Cross disaster 351
knowledge-based action 349
knowledge-based errors 348,
    349, 351, 353
knowledge-based industry 417
knowledge-based mode 151
knowledge, skills and abilities
    (KSAs) 441, 442, 448, 454
knowledge work 18, 20

laboratory experiments 44–5,
    47, 56
labour market 122–4, 139
labour statistics 7
lack of recovery
    mechanism 202–5
Landauer, Thomas 235
lapses 348, 351
laptops 224
lateness 332
latent failures 351–5
layoffs 52
laziness 14, 15
leaders 472–4
leadership 12, 16, 42, 181,
    186–8, 440, 449, 450
lean manufacturing 123
lean production 124
learning
    opportunities 281
    orientation 255, 260

active 403
    and detachment 106–7
    and feedback 95
    and job control 72, 173, 175
    and job demands 126
    and job resources 105
    vicarious 464
leave 283
legal institutions 122, 124, 139
leniency 467
lifelong learning 20
lifespan approach 247
lifestyle 244, 249–50
lifting 102, 153
lighting 16, 358, 437
load effects 199
locus of control (LoC)
    and burnout 311
    and dynamic model of
        presenteeism and
        absenteeism 382
    and health 174
    and job control 176
    and stress 176
    and work–family conflict 278,
        279
    definition 252
London Underground 226,
    229–30
low-strain jobs 70
Lyons Electronic Office
    (LEO) system 235–6

maladaptation 462
management
    and accidents 354, 355, 356,
        359, 362, 363
    attitudes to safety 359
    implementation of layoffs 52
    just-in-time 123
    of conflict 441
    of performance 137, 139, 213
    scientific 14–15
    style 123, 125
    systems 345
management standards for
    work-related stress 138–9
management standards
    process 84
managerial support 284, 285

manufacturing 18, 20, 69, 123, 416
Marienthal 10
marital dissatisfaction 273
Maslach Burnout Inventory (MBI) 297, 298, 300, 303
mass production 13
mastery experiences 464
matching hypothesis 100–2
meaningfulness of work 66
measurement 32–4
media 228
mediation 94
medical care 138
medical model 459
medical research teams 436
meditation 395
memory biases 53
mental distancing 297, 298, 301
mental effort 154
mental health 74–7, 396, 403
mental models 148
mental rehearsals 466
meta-analysis 55
metabolic disorders 209
meta-paradigm 90
Metropolitan Life Insurance 475
Michigan Organizational Assessment Questionnaire 322
micro-breaks 211
microcomputers 223
middle-range theories 90–1
military manuals 12, 17
mills 13
miners
  accidents 12–13
  diseases 12, 17
mini-breaks 211
minimal specification 80, 231
mission analysis 441
mistakes 347–50
  see also errors
mobbing 179
mobile working 224–5
model development 90–1
model of sickness presence and sickness absence 381, 382
modelling 464

moderation (effect) 75, 94, 162, 333, 713
modern psychometric theory 41–2
money 474
mood 135
Moore's law 223
morale
  and job demands 396
  and job resources 396
  and scientific management 16
  and stress 402
  survey of 41
  see also motivation
mortality 10
motivating potential score (MPS) 68, 85
motivation
  and autonomy 92
  and complexity 151
  and control beliefs 174
  and CSEs 253
  and engagement 308, 309
  and feedback 92
  and health 109
  and human resource management 124
  and JCM 92
  and job characteristics 65–9, 416
  and job control 172, 173, 175, 190
  and job crafting 420, 426
  and job demands 73, 100, 424
  and job design 419
  and job redesign 418
  and job resources 92, 95, 97, 100
  and job simplification 172
  and performance 416
  and positive psychology 98
  and productivity 64
  and resources 93
  and satisfaction 151, 327
  and self-evaluation 244
  and STST 81
  and task significance 92–3
  and teamwork 441
  and variety 151
  antecedents 16

in action regulation theory 148
  maintenance 422
  measures 42
  of soldiers 12
motivational demands 145, 149
motivational enhancement process 97
multicultural teams 450, 452
multidimensionality of constructs 102
multi-functional roles *see* multi-skilled roles
multinational teams 436
multi-skilled roles 81
musculoskeletal discomfort 211

National Programme for Information Technology (NPfIT) 221
needs assessment 404
negative affect 135, 144, 180, 203, 252,
negative bias 461
negative stimuli 461–3
negativity 477
negotiation 438, 450
neuroticism 278, 279, 281, 285, 309
new media technologies 19
new ways of working (NWW) 19
night shifts 213
night work 207, 213, 214
Nine to Five 9
nomological networks 40, 43
non-intended errors 350
non-probability sampling 49, 51
non-response bias 49, 51
non-zero probability 51
nuclear electricity plant control 138
nurses 158
Nutrimental Foods 473

objective employee characteristics 244, 245–50
objective measurement 129–32, 136–7
objective ratings, and job control 175
observational studies 52, 53

observation method 52
observed ratio 35
occupational health and safety (OHS) 405, 406
occupational medicine 12–13, 17, 152
off-the-job events 103–4
older persons 375
open-ended questions 52
openness to experiences 278
operant conditioning 91
operational definition 32
opportunity seeking 467
optimism 42, 96, 97, 111, 255, 466–70, 475, 477
optimizing violations 350
Organisation for Economic Cooperation and Development (OECD) 368
organizational approach 246
organizational change and job crafting 425–6
organizational citizenship behaviour (OCB) 126, 245, 253, 323–4, 331, 333, 361
organizational climate 472, 473
organizational constraints scale 157
organizational culture 379
organizational flexibility 124
organizational performance 124
organizational psychology 227, 229
  distinguished from work psychology 6
organizational renewal 124
organizational restructuring 52
organizational stress-management interventions 397, 398
organizational structure 225, 396
organizational time demands 284
overcommitment 78, 79, 375
overlapping schedules 270
overload 120–1, 154, 156, 179, 223, 277, 285, 304, 313, 399
overstimulation 298, 304, 316
overtaxing regulation 157, 158
overtime 119–21, 197, 200–1, 214
  and health 204, 205, 214

and well-being 204, 214
excessive 205, 206
mandatory 205
quality of 204–5

Paddington train crash 352–3
PAR approach 401, 403, 409
parallel design 231
parental leave 268
partial mediation 94
participant observation 53, 228
participation 172, 396, 403–4, 406
participative approach (stress management) 403–4, 406
passive jobs 70, 119
passive recovery mechanism 211, 213, 215
patient-to-nurse ratio 305
pay-for-performance systems 17
pay inequity 247
pensions 16
performance
  and activation 125
  and boredom 307, 316
  and burnout 316
  and challenge demands 146, 161
  and conscientiousness 312
  and CSEs 253
  and degradation 94
  and emotion work 161
  and engagement 312
  and ethnicity 248
  and fatigue 94, 138
  and gender 248
  and human resource management 137
  and job characteristics 67, 190
  and job control 175, 191
  and job crafting 424, 426, 429
  and job demands 126
  and job design 419
  and leadership 12, 16
  and motivation 416
  and positive psychology 458–9
  and positivity 477
  and pressure 117
  and project work 416
  and PSC 408

and role demands 156
and satisfaction 32, 55, 321–36
and self-efficacy 261
and self-evaluation 244
and states 244
and stress 294
and subjective demands 134
and subjective employee characteristics 261
and task analysis 21
and the DCSM 69
and the DISC Model 103
and the JD-R Model 94
and well-being 5
and work psychology 5, 11
appraisal 123
cues 135
definition 323–5
management 137, 139, 213
of teachers 258
of tasks 323, 325–30
sustainable 5, 6, 11
performance-based approach 246
performance-protection strategies 93
performance-related incentives 124
permanent employment 20
personal crafting plan (PCP) 428
personal digital assistants (PDAs) 53–4
personal growth 146
personality 135, 250, 270, 277, 278, 281, 383, 423, 424
personal resources 96–8, 110, 111, 259–61
person-directed interventions 395–6
person–environment fit 137, 163
person–job fit 303
personnel psychology 6
person–role conflict 155
phase model of disillusionment 312
physical demands 102, 107, 145, 152–3
  and ergonomics 152
  and hindrance demands 147
  and stressors 152

physical detachment 107
physical distribution 440
physical resources 102, 107
physiological arousal 464
placement 396
planning 14, 148, 151
political institutions 122, 124, 139
political issues 403, 435
popular culture 9, 11
positive affect 252
positive intervention 458–80
positive life situations 471
positive organizational behaviour (POB) 459, 460
positive organizational context 472
positive organizational scholarship (POS) 459, 460
positive psychology
   and motivation 98
   and performance 458–9
   and the success paradigm 460–1
   and well-being 458–9
positive stimuli 461–2, 463
positive work behaviours 474
positivity 57, 460, 461, 476, 477
power distance 450
power problems 403
power relationships 225
practical support 184
precision 44–6, 50, 56
predictive validation 40
pre-retirement 372
presenteeism 35, 367, 379, 380, 399
   see also sickness presence
pressure 117, 120, 121, 424
preventive stress management theory 397
primary prevention strategies 408
primary stress-management interventions 394, 396–8, 400
proactive actions 425
proactive personality 417, 423, 424
proactive perspectives 417
proactive work behaviours 420

probabilistic principles 103
probability sampling 47, 48, 49, 51
problem-focused coping 282
problem solving 85, 151, 438–9, 473, 447
process analysis 94
process-focused strategies 469
procrastination 422
production deviance 307
productivity
   active learning hypothesis 72
   and AI 473
   and coping 72, 73
   and friendships 16
   and happiness 31
   and job demands 100
   and motivation 64
   and positivity 460
   and PSC 408
   and qualitative demands 163
   and satisfaction 31, 35, 43
   and sickness absence 370, 386
   and sickness presence 378, 379, 380, 385, 386
   and STST 81
   and Taylorism 16
   and teams 16
   and technology 235
   and working conditions 437
   and work psychology 11
   antecedents 16
professional efficiency 297, 301
profit 11, 16, 473
project work 416
promotion opportunities 247
propensity 351
protective clothing 13
psychological arousal 464
psychological capital (PsyCap) 128, 140, 255, 260, 470–3, 477
psychological contract 20, 21, 417
psychological effort 69
psychological flexibility 403
psychological resources 474
psychological safety 180, 450
psychological saturation 154
psychological vitamins 74, 76
psychometric theory 42

psychomotor action 438, 440
psychosocial hazards 409
psychosocial risks 393–413
psychosocial safety climate (PSC) 406–9
psychosocial work environment 384, 386
psychosomatic complaints 157, 175
psychosomatic disorders 253
psychosomatic symptoms 146, 306
psychotechnics 13, 17
PUMA Model 377
punctuated equilibrium paradigm 443

qualitative job demands 118–19, 144–68
qualitative overload 154
qualitative research 51
qualitative underload 154
quality of life 10
quantitative job demands 117–43
quantitative overload 154
quantitative techniques 53
quantitative underload 154
quasi-experiments 46–7

random sampling 48, 51
rating 135, 136
reactivity 53, 198
reciprocity 77, 79, 313, 315
recognition 474
records 55
records-based data 368
recovery from work 104–106, 109, 196–219
recovery theory 104
recreational programmes 16
recruitment 12, 123, 137
re-engineering 414
regulation obstacles 156, 157, 158
regulation problems 145, 156–8
regulation requirements 151–2
regulation uncertainty 156, 157, 158
   see also uncertainty
regulatory resources 152
rehabilitation 386

reinforcement 474
relatedness 95
relational crafting 425
Relative Deprivation Model 10, 11
relaxation training 395
reliability 34–8, 39, 55, 56
remuneration 78
repetitive strain injuries 211
replaceability 380
representational states 228
research design 43–55
research design requirements 44
resilience 96, 128, 255, 260, 468–470, 477
resistance to degradation 94
resource depletion 202
resource-increasing coping strategies 283
resources
   and autonomy 95
   and competence 95
   and cynicism 95
   and demands 162–3
   and engagement 95
   and job control 176
   and motivation 93
   and relatedness 95
   family 281, 285
   personal 96, 98, 110, 111, 259, 260, 261
   regulatory 152
resources-seeking behaviour 421, 422, 423
response rate 49, 51
responsibility 66, 307
rest periods 16
return-to-work interviews 372
reward contingency 333–4
rewards 77–9, 163, 186, 474
risk analysis 345
risk assessment 405, 406
risk-focused strategies 468–9
risky behaviour 10
role accumulation theory 270, 271
role adjustment 417
role ambiguity 147, 155, 156, 179
role clarification 447
role conflict 147, 155–7, 179, 277, 285, 408
role demands 155, 156

role expectations 156
role overload 155, 179, 277, 279
role requirements 75
role–role conflict 155
roles 81, 83, 105, 270, 405–6
role strain 269
role stress 155–6, 179, 269
role stress theory 269
role stressors 277, 278, 279
role structure 439
role theory 155
role uncertainty 156
Romans 12, 17
routine violations 350
routinization 149, 150, 152
rule-based actions 349
rule-based errors 351, 348, 349

sabotage 307
safety 21, 342–66
   climate 346, 359, 360–3
   committee 359
   historical perspectives 345
   laws (UK) 344–5
   officers 359
   performance 245
   regulations 350
   training 355, 359, 361, 363
safety citizenship behaviours (SCBs) 361–2
safety-related change 361
salaries 50, 75, 77, 79
sampling 51
sandwiched generation 285–6
satisfaction
   and absenteeism 332
   and affect 252
   and behavioural readiness 327
   and challenge demands 161
   and complexity 151, 418
   and counterproductive work behaviour 331–3
   and creative job demands 334–5
   and emotional stability 252
   and emotion work 161
   and employee withdrawal 332, 333
   and family–work conflict 281
   and genetic predisposition 252

   and health 40
   and job characteristics 67, 416
   and job control 172, 175
   and job crafting 424, 425
   and job demands 126
   and lateness 332
   and leadership 181
   and mandatory overtime 205
   and motivation 327
   and optimism/pessimism 42
   and organizational citizenship behaviour 331, 333
   and performance 32, 55, 321–36
   and productivity 31, 35, 43
   and qualitative demands 163
   and role demands 156
   and sickness presence 35
   and stress-management interventions 395
   and task performance 325–30
   and turnover 40, 332–3
   and variety 151
   and women 248, 250
   and work–family conflict 279
   and work–family enrichment 282
   antecedents 16
   definition 322–3
   distinguished from engagement 304
   evaluation 132
   facet 322–3
   global 322
   in relationships 285
   measurement 41, 42
scarcity approach 269
scientific management 14–15, 17, 28, 64, 172
secondary data 54
secondary research 54–5
secondary stress-management interventions 394, 397–8, 400
selection 137, 475–6
   bias 7–8
   of workers 14
   and job demands 139
   and stress management 396
   for teams 451

selection-based positive
    interventions 475–6
self-awareness 473
self-directed behaviour 427
self-efficacy 111, 174, 256, 260
    and assets 468
    and burnout 311
    and challenges 309
    and job control 173, 176
    and job crafting training 429
    and job resources 309
    and performance 261
    and personal resources 96
    and psychological capital 128, 470, 471
    and the ERI Model 77
    definition 252, 254
    development 463–5, 477
    micro-intervention to increase 256–7
    moderating role 97
self-employment 268
self-esteem
    and burnout 296, 311
    and personal resources 96
    and the ERI Model 77
    definition 252
    moderating role 97
self-evaluation 244, 252
self-integration 77
self-management 81, 414
self-rated measures 132–7
self-regulation 20, 77, 101, 473
self-reports 42, 43, 49, 134, 175
self-rostering 213
self-scheduling 213, 215
self-talk 470
semi-autonomous work groups (SAWGs) 81, 82
sensitivity requirements 147
sequential interdependence 440
service organizations 158
service sector 7, 8, 18, 20, 416
shell shock 294
shift work 99, 197, 207–10, 215
sick leave 369, 375
sick pay 16
sickness absence
    and boredom 307, 316
    and burnout 309, 316, 377
    and engagement 308
    and health 385, 386, 399
    and job demands 375
    and job strain 376–7
    and productivity 370, 386
    and psychological flexibility 403
    and social support 375
    and stress 375
    antecedents 374, 375, 377, 384, 386
    approaches to studying 374–7
    costs 5, 369–70, 384
    databases 368
    decision models 380–3
    definition 367
    duration-based approaches 371–2, 37
    forms 371–4
    frequency-based approaches 371, 373
    functional 370
    practices to reduce 386
    prevalence 368–9, 375
    prevention 386
    screening instrument 386
    volition-based approaches 372, 373, 374
    see also absenteeism
sickness presence
    and gender 378
    and health 379, 380, 385, 386
    and productivity 378, 379, 380, 385, 386
    and professional identity 378
    and profitability 379
    and satisfaction 35
    antecedents 386
    costs 378, 384
    decision models 380–3
    definition 378, 380
    in a market analysis consultancy 379–80
    practices to reduce 386
    prevalence 378
    prevention 386
    see also presenteeism
signal passed at danger (SPAD) 253
similarity-attraction theory 248
simplification 14, 17, 154, 172
single parents 267
situational violations 350
skill-based actions 349
skills
    acquisition 228
    development 126
skill variety (SV) 65, 68, 69, 418
sleep difficulties 203, 209, 215, 225, 306
slips 348, 351
smartphones 19, 224
smoking 10, 244
snapshot approach 50
social capital development strategies 468
social constructionism 421
social debt 185
social exchange model 313–14
social information 135
social interactions 172–95
social loafing 453
social marginality 248
social meaning 186–8
social networking 223
social persuasion 256, 464
social stressors 173, 178–80, 186, 190
social support 180–6
    and autonomy 95
    and caring 183
    and coping 184
    and feedback 181
    and health 72, 73, 185
    and job demands 72, 97, 304
    and PSC 408
    and sickness absence 375
    and stress 181, 184
    and the DCSM 70–2
    and work–family conflict 277, 278, 279, 285
    effects on employees 184
    meaning of 187–8
    negative effects 184–5
    networks 285
    seeking 421
    sources 183–4
socio-technical systems theory (STST) 63, 79–84, 172, 221, 230–2, 234–5, 416

soft systems analysis 231
software development 229
soldiers 12
spatial flexibility 20, 213, 215
spells 371
spillover models 272–5
split-half reliability 37
spousal support 281
spuriousness hypothesis 330
St Lucie Medical Center 476
stability 20
standardization 15, 306
standing 153
state approach 250
state-like characteristics 244, 251, 254–6, 260, 261, 475
states 250, 251, 257, 259–61, 475
status 10, 75, 359
stepping 465
stewardship 361
stock-investment simulations 259
stock purchase plans 16
strain
   and challenge demands 146
   and CSEs 253
   and emotion work 161
   and gender 248
   and job demands 95, 97,
   and role demands 156
   and sickness absence 376–7
   and social stressors 186
   and stressors 173, 184
   hypothesis 71–2
strain-based work–family conflict 270
stratified sampling 48, 51
strengths 472
stress
   and burnout 316
   and control beliefs 174, 175
   and coping theory 294
   and CSEs 253
   and Demand–Control–Support Model 294
   and emotion work 159–60
   and gender 247
   and goal attainment 156
   and health 197, 198
   and job control 172, 173, 175, 176
   and Job Demand–Control Model 175
   and job demands 109, 135, 375
   and job resources 109
   and locus of control 176
   and mobile working 225
   and morale 402
   and optimism/pessimism 42
   and performance 294
   and qualitative demands 146
   and recovery from work 104, 109
   and shift work 209
   and sickness absence 375
   and social interactions 178
   and social support 181, 184
   and the ERI Model 77
   and uncertainty 156, 157
   and vacations 211
   and well-being 402
   and work–family conflict 279
   definition 197
   environmental factors 152, 399
   in World War II 196
   interventions 360
   management 394–401
   manifestations of 197
   measurement 42, 133
   person-environment fit approach 137
   prevention 406–9
   reduction 394
   research 294, 400
   responses to 200
   risk factors 408
   symptoms 146
   work related 138–9
   see also cognitive activation theory of stress; stress management interventions
stress appraisal theory 146
stress buffering (mechanism) 101, 103, 106, 109
stress management intervention 393–406
stressors
   and challenge demands 146, 147
   and exhaustion 297
   and health 198
   and hindrance demands 146, 147
   and job control 173, 175
   and job demands 145
   and physical demands 152
   and satisfaction–performance relation 330
   and social support 184
   and strain 173, 184
   and stress-management interventions 394, 395
   and work–family conflict 277, 285
   and work–home interference 203
   exposure to 200
   prevalence 401
   reduction processes 396
   social 178–80, 186, 190
stretch goals 465, 470
strikes 16
structured interviews 52
students 45
stupidity 14
subcontractors 357
sub-goals 470
subject attrition 45
subjective demands 134
subjective employee characteristics 244, 250–60
subjective measures 129, 132–7
substance use 245
success 460–1, 465
summative evaluation 228
superordinate goals assignment 451
supervision 17, 75, 98, 132, 184, 408
support 80–1, 83, 185–6, 188
surface acting 160, 162
surveys 43, 47–51, 54, 56, 132, 135
sustainable performance 5, 6, 11
Swiss Cheese model 352, 353, 355
sympathetic activation 94
sympathetic–adrenal–medullary (SAM) system 197, 198, 200
system design 85

systems approach 225–7
Systems Engineering Initiative for Patient Safety (SEIPS) 226

tailored testing 42
talent 250, 475–6, 477
tardiness 245
target approach (stress management) 397, 400
tasks
  analysis 21–3
  avoidance 422
  complexity 423
  crafting 425
  design 151
  elements 126
  interdependence 423, 439
  planning 14
  redesign 23
  simplification 14, 17
  social meaning of 188–9
  role cross-cutting 451
  training for 14
  types 437–40
  variety 281, 357, 418
task–action grammar (TAG) 228
task characteristics approach 22, 23
task identity (TI) 65–6
task-representation techniques 22, 23
task significance (TS) 66, 68, 69, 92–3, 417, 418
task-simulation techniques 22, 23
taskwork 441, 454
Taylorism 14, 15, 16, 28, 172
teachers 258, 375
team-based structures 435, 436
team building 447, 454
team competencies 441–2
team coordination training 449
team development interventions 447–9
team errors 435
Team Evolution and Maturation (TEAM) model 443
team knowledge 446
team mental models (TMMs) 445, 446, 449, 452
teams 16, 229, 434–57

faultlines 451
training 447–9, 454
virtual 19, 233, 417
team self-correction training 448–9
teamwork 441–2, 449–50, 454
technical equipment 102
technological innovations 123, 124, 139
technology 220–38
  and demographic changes 223
  and experience sampling 53
  and job redesign 417
  and job roles 81
  and manufacturing jobs 18
  and organizational psychology 229
  and organizational structure 225
  and power relationships 225
  and productivity 235
  and scientific management 15
  and teams 229, 435, 449–50
  and work–family interaction 268, 271
  changing nature of 223–5
  effects on work tasks 10
  failure 221, 222, 236
  future 223
  interfaces with 227
  media 19
  rejection of 221
  research on 223
  social context 229
  systems approach 225–7
telework 417
temperature 358
temporal flexibility 20
tenure 246–7
tertiary stress-management interventions 394, 397–8, 400
test content strategies 39
test–retest reliability 35, 36
test theory 34–43
texting 223
theory of work–family enrichment 274
threat avoidance vigilance 157
Three Mile Island 342–3

time and motion studies 15, 28
time balance 275
time-based work–family conflict 270
time demands 270
time management 395
time orientations 450
time perspective 418
time pressure 102, 146, 147
tobacco 250
top-down participative approach 403
top-down processing 353
training
  and asset-focused strategies 468
  and communication 449
  and high-quality work 357
  and job demands 123, 139
  and leadership 449
  as stress management intervention 396
  defective 359
  for managers 397
  in decision making 85
  in job crafting 427–9
  in problem solving 85
  in quasi-experiments 47
  in relaxation 395
  methods 353
  of teams 447–9, 454
  PsyCap interventions 470–1
  safety 355, 359, 361, 363
  throughout career 20
  to conduct tasks 14
trait-like characteristics 244, 251, 252–4, 257, 260, 261, 475
traits 250
transactional stress and coping theory 91
transactive memory systems (TMSs) 445, 446
transition phases 441
triple-match principle (TMP) 102–3, 106, 108, 109
true score 35
turnover
  and boredom 307
  and CSEs 253
  and engagement 308

and job demands 126
and organizational action plans 476
and satisfaction 40, 332–3
and the ERI Model 78
and the human relations movement 16
and work–family conflict 279
two-wave panel design 50

uncertainty 122, 124, 139, 147, 156, 157
underload 154, 306
undermining 179
understaffing 124
under-stimulation 73, 125, 298, 301, 304
unemployment 7, 8, 10, 73, 77, 369
  see also employment
unhealthy behaviours 203
unintended acts 348
unionization 16
unstructured interviews 52
usability 228
user-centred design 236
Utrecht Work Engagement Scale (UWES) 301, 303

vacations 211, 212, 213
valence 268
validation strategies 39, 40
validity 38–41, 55, 56, 65
variable relationship strategies 39
variance analysis 231
variance at source 80, 81
variety 151
VBBA 133
Vegetius 12
verbal protocol technique 349
vicarious learning 464
videoconferencing 19
vigilance 125, 157
vigour 300, 301
violations 347–51, 360
  see also errors
virtual communication 449–50, 452, 454
virtual meetings 19
virtual teams 19, 233, 417

Vitamin Model (VM) 24, 63, 73–6, 84, 85
vocational psychology 14
volitional demands 149
voluntary absence 372–3
volunteer work 27, 28, 268
Volvo 82

wages 16
war stress 196
waypower 465, 466
Wealth of Nations 41
weekend work 197
well-being
  affective 74
  and abnormal work hours 208
  and boredom 302, 316
  and burnout 302, 316
  and employment 11
  and engagement 302, 316
  and group cohesiveness 181
  and human resource management 137
  and job characteristics 76, 190
  and job control 175, 178
  and job crafting training 429
  and job demands 97, 125, 129, 140, 396
  and job redesign 418
  and job resources 396
  and justice 180
  and managerial support 285
  and meaning at work 186
  and mobile working 224
  and multiple roles 270
  and off-the-job events
  and organizational performance 124
  and overtime 204, 214
  and performance 5
  and positive psychology 458–9
  and positivity 477
  and pressure 117
  and project work 416
  and PSC 407
  and social activities 286
  and stress 402
  and STST 81
  and subjective employee characteristics 261

and the human relations movement 16, 17
and the JD–R Model 421
and uncertainty 156
and work 5, 11
and workaholism 302
and work psychology 5, 17
and work–family conflict 286
individual differences in 309–12
of miners 12, 17
taxonomy of 301–4
Western Electric Company 16, 64, 65, 437
whistleblowing 361
willpower 465
withdrawal behaviour 307, 313, 324–5, 332, 333
within-person fluctuations 257
women
  and burnout 248, 250, 298
  and developmental assignments 247
  and domestic tasks 285
  and job satisfaction 248, 250
  and job strain 248
  and multiple roles 270
  and promotion opportunities 247, 250
  and sickness presence 378
  and stress 247
  and work–family enrichment 282
  and work–family interaction 268
  career orientations 247
  increasing participation in workforce 267, 417
  pay inequity 247
  working conditions 250
work ability 383
work adjustment 386
workaholism 294, 302, 303
workarounds 221
work attendance 367–90
work-directed interventions 398
worker characteristics 13, 118–19, 140
  see also individual characteristics
work–family balance 268, 275–6

work–family conflict 270, 277–80, 282–3, 285
work–family culture 283–4
work–family enrichment 271, 274, 279, 280–2, 284, 285
work–family interaction 267–89
work–family policies 283–4
work–family spillover 270
workforce
  changes in 18–19
  diversity of 19–20
work groups 81, 437
work–home interference 128, 203, 205, 212
work hours
  abnormal 197, 200, 206–10, 214
  and fatigue 203, 205, 223
  and health 203, 205, 214
  and mobile working 225
  and sleep 203
  demanding 200
  limits 201, 205
  long 197, 200–6, 214
working conditions 89, 137–9, 186–9
  and job design 419
  and productivity 437
  for women 250
  psychosocial 137, 138–9
working memory 150, 154
working time 122
work intensification 124
work–life balance 215, 223, 224
workload 120, 146, 408, 421
work–non-work balance 212
work obstacles 156–8
work organization 157
work pressure 20
work psychology
  aim 5
  and demographic changes 19
  and health 5, 8, 17
  and performance 5, 11
  and productivity 11
  and profit 11
  and technology 226
  and well-being 5, 8, 17
  definition 6
  distinguished from organization and personnel psychology 6
  from 1850 to 1930 13–15
  from 1930–present 15–17
  research methods in 31–57
  selection bias in 7–8
work–rest cycles 215
work schedules 210
work space 81
work strain-sickness absence model 376
work-time control (WTC) 212–13, 215
work-time flexibility 215
work-to-family conflict (WFC) 272
work-to-family enrichment (WFE) 272
work to rule 80
workplace design 18
workplace redesign 137, 138, 139

Yerkes–Dodson law 125